THE BRITISH EMPIRE, 1815–1939

The BRITISH EMPIRE 1815-1939

PAUL KNAPLUND

New York · HOWARD FERTIG · 1969

HOWARD FERTIG, INC. EDITION 1969
Published by arrangement with Mrs. Dorothy Knaplund

Library of Congress Catalog Card Number: 68-9617

PRINTED IN THE UNITED STATES OF AMERICA
BY NOBLE OFFSET PRINTERS, INC.

To

Dorothy King Knaplund

CONTENTS

Part III. Commonwealth and Empire, 1870–1901; India, 1858–1905

Part IV. Storm and Stress, 1901–1939

LIST OF MAPS

LIST OF MAPS

PREFACE

As a boy in Norway the author had his first lessons in British imperial history. His parents recounted how their grandparents had suffered during the British blockade, 1807–1814, and the disgraceful affair at the home town of Bodo in 1821, in which Norway was compelled to pay damages for having arrested British smugglers. During the Anglo-Boer war his sympathies were strongly on the side of the Boers, and the famous guerrilla leader, General de Wet, was his great hero. Filled with curiosity, he watched English tourists who came to view the world-renowned tide current near his island home. They wore heavy boots, queer hats, and odd-looking clothes, and they picked periwinkles – they were indeed a strange and fascinating people.

His first systematic study of the history of the British empire began in the autumn of 1913 when as a graduate student in the University of Wisconsin he investigated the political unification of British South Africa. The late Professor A. L. P. Dennis directed this early research, and the author will always remember with the deepest gratitude Professor Dennis and the late Professor Dana C. Munro, as well as the other fine scholars who then composed the history department of the University of Wisconsin. They encouraged and made it possible for a young immigrant to find his life work. He has been inspired by successive generations of students at the University – the thousands of undergraduates whom he has sought to guide in a survey of British history, and the graduate students who have worked with him in lecture courses and seminars.

On four occasions the author spent from three to ten months working with British public and private archives. Results of these investigations have appeared in articles and books published over a period of seventeen years, and a goodly share of them are incorporated in the present volume.

In the long period during which material was gathered and this book written the author has been aided by institutions as well as by private individuals, and has incurred obligations that can be only imperfectly discharged by expressions of thanks. The University of Wisconsin has provided working conditions conducive to research and writing; the Wisconsin State Historical Society has supplied a wealth of printed material; and the great British repositories, the British Museum and the Public Record Office, have furnished the manuscript sources used. Everywhere he has received aid, kindly and cheerfully given. He feels particularly indebted to the trustees of the Gladstone Papers, the late Right Hon. the Viscount Gladstone, and the late Lord Gladstone of Hawarden, who permitted him to use without restriction that magnificent collection. He also wishes to record his indebtedness to a courteous and gallant gentleman, the late Colonel Dudley Mills, R.E., whose father, Arthur Mills, M.P., about a century ago took an active interest in British immigration and colonial reform. Colonel Mills entered British colonial service at Hongkong in 1881; for thirty years he served in various parts of the empire; he was an excellent observer and a discriminating critic. The results of his extensive service, observations, and reading were given without stint to the author in informal discussions.

Friends and colleagues in the historical profession have read the manuscript in whole or in part. Professor C. W. de Kiewiet of the University of Iowa has read the chapters dealing with South Africa, Professor Herbert Heaton of the University of Minnesota those relating to Australasia, Professor Morley Scott of the University of Michigan the sections pertaining to British North America, Professor Philo M. Buck of the University of Wisconsin two of the India chapters, and Professor H. D. Jordan of Clark University has given advice on the entire manuscript. These scholars as well as the editor of Harper's Historical Series, Dr. Guy Stanton Ford, have corrected errors and made helpful suggestions for which the author wishes to express heartfelt thanks. Throughout the long years of writing his wife, Dorothy King Knaplund, has been his faithful assistant and friendly critic. Not all suggestions received have been followed; for the organization, interpretation, and point of view the author alone is responsible. He has sought to present within the limited scope of this book what to him seemed most essential to know and understand in the history of the British empire, 1815–1939.

GENERAL INTRODUCTION

Although the American Revolution shattered the first British empire, by 1815 a new one had been erected, one with potentialities undreamed of at that time. A century later this empire embraced one-fourth of the land and of the population of the globe; it included a greater variety of races, cultures, and natural resources than has ever been gathered within one political unit; it had evolved a unique political organization, being an empire in the accepted meaning of that word as well as a commonwealth of nations. The growth and development of this curiosity among world states formed one of the phenomena of the period between the close of the Napoleonic epoch and the outbreak of the Nazi War.

In the course of the nineteenth century the British empire came to represent not so much a political system as a way of life. As such it owed much to the temper, customs, and traditions of the English people and even more to economic, social, and political conditions peculiar to the Victorian era. In previous centuries Englishmen, safe in their island home, had developed a system of government which protected the rights of the individual, established the supremacy of a special type of law, and laid the basis for democratic institutions. This governmental system was not derived from abstract thinking; a result of human action, it could not be attributed to human design. No Hammurabi, Moses, or Solon drafted the English common law or invented the English political institutions. They matured through the use of empirical methods in efforts to solve political and economic problems; Englishmen applied to each new device the simple yet searching test: "Does it work?" Like Topsy, both the English constitution and the British empire "just growed."

The political and constitutional framework of this empire followed English models. Before the opening of the nineteenth century English colonies, whether founded by English settlers or, as in the case of Lower Canada, by immigrants from a foreign land, had been given self-governing institutions. When at later dates colonists demanded more complete control over local affairs, the requests were granted; thus by degrees Canada, Australia, New Zealand, South Africa, and Newfoundland acquired autonomy. Moreover, self-government was not limited to communities wholly or in the main of British or European origin, for representative institutions were granted to Ceylon, Cyprus, India, and Malta. Departing from the accepted methods of empire-building, British statesmen erected a structure whose cornerstone was freedom.

In the creation of this edifice, though English experience and the English genius for political improvisation counted for much, they were not the only elements of significance. Time and circumstances too were important factors. For about sixty years after Waterloo the peoples of continental Europe were occupied with efforts to secure democratic institutions and build nation states. During that time Britain felt secure and strong. Viewing with a certain condescension the struggles of Frenchmen, Germans, Italians, and other politically immature races, she offered asylum to their refugees – rulers, statesmen, reactionaries, and radicals. Only the English type of government seemed capable of safeguarding peace, security, and the pursuit of happiness for human beings. British statesmen therefore recommended its adoption in Europe, and quite naturally favored its establishment in the settlements beyond the sea. Furthermore, the middle years of the nineteenth century, the years when self-governing institutions were founded in British North America and Australasia, was a period of idealism and hope. It was then believed that political liberty and free trade would usher in an era of universal peace and prosperity. Men expected that "the nations of the world should grow great in common."

But in the seventies the European climate of opinion changed; generous thinking gave way to cynical materialism; and as the nineteenth century closed, men were disregarding the religious, political, and economic evangels of their fathers. Ruthlessly the nations of Europe appropriated land in Africa, Asia, and Oceania. Because of the growth of a system of alliances and the launching of a race in armaments the idea of a community of interest among them lost vitality. In the hapless twentieth century matters grew worse. Increased international tension culminated in the great Four Years' War. Again a ray of hope appeared; it was expected that the senseless blood-letting and unspeakable misery of the war period would compel people to appreciate the need for world unity and universal cooperation. This vision found expression in the organization of a League of Nations. Again the vision faded; an age darker, more brutal than that which followed the fall of the Roman empire descended upon the European continent; the spirit of man was enslaved as never before; law, human rights, human decency were scoffed at, trodden under foot. Great nations submitted to the leadership of men whose motto seemed to be: "Evil, be thou my good," and by September, 1939, indiscriminate slaughter and wanton destruction began sweeping over large areas of Europe.

In the last quarter of the nineteenth century when the temper of the people hardened and land-grabbing became the favorite sport of statesmen, the imperial policy of Britain was modified. She was not behindhand in seizing non-European lands. Indeed with all barriers down she had great initial advantages — control of the seas, enormous wealth, and claims previously staked by her explorers, traders, and missionaries. Millions of square miles came under her direct or indirect control. But during this era of European expansion the ideals of an earlier age were not wholly abandoned. Trusteeship for backward peoples was not always just an empty phrase on the lips of sentimental English humanitarians, but was applied both in Africa and in Oceania. Beyond the sea British nations arose, and, advancing in true English fashion from precedent, they acquired more and more of the attributes of independent states. Finally conditions existing *de facto* were recognized *de jure.* It was proclaimed that Britain, Canada, Australia, New Zealand, South Africa, the Irish Free State, and Newfoundland were equal in status; officially the British Commonwealth, a league of free nations, came into being. Overseas Britain supported the mother country in the Four Years' War; and the British nations, excepting Eire, hastened to her aid when Nazi Germany vowed destruction of her and all she stood for. From the far corners of the earth sons of Britain and men who had accepted her principles of government and her way of life joined in the great battle for the preservation of freedom and human rights.

PART I

From War to Peace, 1815–1837;
India, 1813–1858

INTRODUCTION

THE British empire of the mid-eighteenth century virtually fulfilled the requirements of a self-sufficient economic unit. It was based on the theory that if the economic interests of any part clashed with those of England, the former must be sacrificed. Moreover, English statesmen acted on the principle that all portions of the empire were political dependencies of England. The attempts to enforce this political and economic supremacy over the old colonies in America precipitated the American Revolution; and the successful revolt of the thirteen colonies seriously impaired the self-sufficiency of the empire, for the British West Indies needed to import foodstuffs, a need which could not be satisfied by the remaining British colonies in North America. Before the empire had adjusted itself to the new conditions Britain became involved in the war with France and Napoleon which lasted with only a brief intermission from 1793 until 1815. During this period of storm and stress it was, of course, impossible to effect a reorganization of the British empire on a mercantilistic basis; and when peace was restored, powerful economic interests opposed a return to the old order.

Among the political effects of the successful outcome of the American Revolution, the most important was perhaps the establishment among British statesmen of a belief that English settlement colonies were bound to become independent. During the greater part of the nineteenth century this belief deeply affected the attitude of England toward colonization and colonial problems. The other lesson which might have been deduced, namely, that Burke had uttered words containing profound political wisdom when he advocated a conciliatory attitude toward the colonists in America and faith in the strength of love and affection as bonds of empire, was not appreciated until after Queen Victoria had ascended the throne, and then by but a few. Several changes had, however, taken place in the political structure of the empire between the outbreak of the American Revolution and the beginning of the French wars, of which some were attributable to the American conflict and its outcome. Among these may be noted the Declaratory Act of 1778, whereby Great Britain formally abandoned her claims to tax the colonies; the Canadian Constitutional Act, 1791, which established representative government in Lower and Upper Canada; Pitt's East India Act, 1784, which created a system of dual control for British India; the founding of a penal colony in Australia; and, near home, the repeal of restrictions upon the commerce of Ireland and the restoration to her parliament of a considerable amount of political independence.

Apart from these changes, as well as external events, two new forces came into existence in the latter half of the eighteenth century which greatly influenced the history of the British empire. These were the industrial revolution and a strong Christian humanitarian movement. The former created unemployment and other social and economic conditions which stimulated emigration and strengthened the demand for relaxing or abandoning the old laws governing trade and navigation. While the immediate effects of the industrial changes were discouraging to imperial expansion, their ultimate results, partly through the accumulation of surplus capital, helped to stimulate British enterprise overseas. Among the manifestations of Christian humanitarianism were the demand for the abolition first of the slave trade and then of slavery, and the widespread interest in foreign missions. The anti-slavery movement shaped the course of empire history in the West Indies and Africa, and the influence of the missionary societies was felt in these regions as well as in India and the South Seas. Nor were the results of the missionary efforts limited to religious, social, and economic problems. Missionaries frequently meddled with "high politics," now promoting, now retarding imperial expansion. Particularly in the years 1815–1837 the friends of the slaves and the enthusiasts for converting the heathen helped to mold imperial policies both at home and abroad.

Although in 1814 Britain was comparatively moderate in her territorial demands upon defeated enemies, her new acquisitions in the West Indies and South Africa added materially to the complications of colonial issues. The need for safeguarding what she had and protecting her trade routes had been the determining factor in deciding what to keep or give up after the war; and this same factor shaped the attitude of her statesmen toward expansion, 1815–1837. France was the only possible rival in the colonial field, but her rivalry was not considered serious although in 1829 it caused Britain to make sure her claim to all of Australia. In India large areas were added to the territory under British control; these annexations resulted from conditions that existed within India rather than, as at a later date, threats of Russian aggression. In Africa the anti-slavery forces favored British exploration of and activities in the basin of the Niger, but in South Africa the missionaries resisted demands by the colonists for annexation. The commerce of Britain expanded in Europe and South America, and independent traders battered down the barriers which the East India Company had erected against them in India and China. The defeat of the company eventually paved the way for interference by the British government in the affairs of China.

In the early years of peace British statesmen were under the influence of the psychology engendered by the French Revolution and the long war. They dreaded change. After 1822, however, a reforming group among the Tories gained control of the government. Prominent among them were George Canning, foreign secretary, 1822–1827, and prime minister for a short time before his death in the latter year; Sir Robert Peel, who though conservative in politics was anxious for administrative reforms; and William Huskisson, who as president of the board of trade and secretary of state for war and the colonies made far-reaching changes particularly in the commercial policy of Britain. But more significant for the imperial policy than the reforms accomplished was the new spirit which now animated British statesmen. No longer were old institutions regarded as sacrosanct. This became true especially after the Whigs had replaced the Tories in 1830 and the Great Reform Bill had been placed on the statute book.

Meanwhile the administrative machinery of the empire had been improved. The secretaryship for war and the colonies was established in 1801; in 1812 the colonial office was organized as a separate unit; and thirteen years later its first permanent undersecretary, R. W. Hay, was appointed. In 1836 he was succeeded by James (later Sir James) Stephen, who since 1813 had been connected with that office as legal counselor and for two years had served as assistant undersecretary. This able, liberal, and enlightened public servant had already secured great influence in the administration of the colonies, and as permanent head of the office he strove with considerable success to make the government of the colonies more efficient and more responsive to the needs and wishes of the peoples concerned.

In the years after 1815 much unemployment resulted from the demobilization of the army and navy, the change from war to peace, general trade depression, and the introduction of machines in the textile industry. The population of the United Kingdom seemed redundant, and the authorities responsible for poor relief began urging emigration of the paupers. The government then not only abandoned its former opposition but began to aid emigration. By the middle of the twenties parliament voted considerable sums for the purpose of sending Irish paupers to Canada, and at the close of the decade the energetic and resourceful Edward Gibbon Wakefield commenced his work as champion of systematic colonization. Wakefield helped to revolutionize the attitude of England toward the colonial empire, and as this period closes South Australia was founded ostensibly on the basis of the principles he advocated.

While Britain was engaged in effecting the transition from war to peace, in attempting to catch up with arrears in the fields of social and political reforms, and in preventing Europe from being embroiled in a new series of wars, the British settlements in North America, South Africa, and Australia were expanding, growing conscious of their special needs and their future possibilities, and with each year becoming more and more dissatisfied with the restrictions imposed upon them by the imperial government. Concessions were granted to all the colonies, especially to the Canadas. But the concessions fell short of the demands of the colonists, and in 1837 uprisings in the Canadas directed the attention of British statesmen to the need for overhauling the entire colonial system.

Although the problems of the overseas empire were not studied carefully by any of the statesmen who held front-rank positions in the government, 1815–1837, Britain aided materially in fostering growth in wealth, in population, and in self-governing institutions beyond the seas. British North America, South Africa, and Australia made relatively rapid progress. On the contrary the older colonies in the West Indies faced decay. The abolition of the slave trade and of slavery and the weakening of the privileged position which their sugar had held in the English market impaired an economic system which rested on unsound foundations. In India the opening of the trade to free competition proved a doubtful blessing to the natives since the machine-made cotton goods from Lancashire ruined their chief industry.

The history of the British empire of the late Hanoverian period is unintelligible without an appreciation of the problems which then faced the British Isles. For an understanding of the empire it is necessary to understand Britain. British statesmen, administrators, industrialists, traders, missionaries, anti-slavery agitators, and emigrants shaped the destiny of the empire. Sometimes the results of their efforts are obvious. It is easy to see the influence of Wilberforce and his anti-slavery crusade upon the West Indies and South Africa, of the missionaries on the frontier policy at the Cape, of promoters of land settlement in Canada, of E. G. Wakefield upon emigration and colonization, and of William Huskisson upon the economic policy of the empire. Other influences emanating from or connected with the internal development in Britain may be less evident, as for instance the connections between canal building in the mother country in the late eighteenth and that in Canada in the early part of the nineteenth century, between the scientific cattle-breeding in England and the successful efforts to produce sheep suitable for Australia. Nor should the student of the history of this epoch be unmindful of the fact that steam and electricity had not then annihilated the distances which separated Britain from her colonies. It might take from four to twelve weeks to reach Quebec from London, and from four to seven months to reach Sydney or Calcutta. Traveling was slow and the wave-path dangerous. Though the component parts were widely separated, the British empire was a unit; the history of its overseas portions cannot be understood without a knowledge of Britain.

CHAPTER 1

BRITAIN, 1815–1837

IN 1815 Britain emerged triumphant from an ordeal by battle which had lasted nearly a quarter of a century. Though the strain had been severe, the United Kingdom had not only survived but actually gathered strength during the test; and when peace came, Britain ranked as the first power in the world. She had been the organizer and the paymistress of the coalitions which ultimately broke the overwhelming power of France and Napoleon. Her foreign secretary, Lord Castlereagh, had shown great skill in building up and keeping together the victorious alliance, and at the peace conferences he held a commanding position. A British general, the Duke of Wellington, had administered body blows to the towering Napoleonic empire in the famous campaign in the Spanish peninsula and delivered the final knockout by defeating Napoleon at Waterloo. But great as was the skill of her diplomatists and her soldiers, the victories at sea had been the really decisive ones in determining the outcome of the contest. Since that glorious October 21, 1805, when Nelson at Trafalgar defeated the combined fleets of France and Spain, the world had been at Britain's feet. For a decade the colonies of Spain, France, Holland, and Denmark had either voluntarily or involuntarily opened their harbors to British traders, and European marts had been dependent upon British merchants for tropical and semi-tropical products. Despite Napoleon's efforts to paralyze the trade of Britain by closing the ports of the Continent to her shipping, she had continued to sell to Europe not only products from overseas but also the output of her own looms and foundries. As the war closed, Britain's sea power was supreme and she held a dominant position in the fields of industry and finance. The latter, which had been important in the defeat of Napoleon, was no less significant in building up the British empire of the nineteenth century.

Though scattered, the British empire of the period 1815–1837 was more of an economic and political unit than that of our own day. Consequently, events in the British Isles, political, social, and economic conditions and problems, deeply affected the course of empire history. In 1815 Britain was war-weary. Lord Castlereagh had the support of a large majority of his countrymen when by means of a grand alliance and a system of international congresses he sought to safeguard the peace settlements and prevent the outbreak of future conflicts. Although conspicuous for his lack of understanding of the great issues in home politics, he showed deep insight and a remarkable breadth of view in arranging peace with France. Peace, not revenge, was his chief object. Hence, he insisted that France should not be shorn of her old provinces, even such comparatively recent acquisitions as Alsace and Lorraine; she was not called upon to pay an unreasonably large war indemnity; and she was left with colonies. France remained a balanced empire. At this time Lord Castlereagh was far and away Britain's greatest statesman, but until his death in 1822 his talents and energies were devoted to foreign affairs. The same was almost equally true of George Canning, Castlereagh's successor as foreign secretary and strong man of the British government. And the international issues of those days centered in Europe and the Near East. Africa south of the Sahara, the Americas, Asia, and Oceania then offered no really vexing problems for the statesmen of Britain. They were therefore not compelled to think imperially in the more modern sense.

After international relations, internal political reforms most often forced themselves upon the attention of British statesmen. The work of repairing the outworn political machinery of Britain begun after the American revolt was checked by the French Revolution and the ensuing wars. The excesses of the French Jacobins discredited even moderate reform in England; and at the close of the eighteenth century the prime minister, William Pitt the younger, had so completely abandoned the reform program of his youth as to sponsor severe repressive measures against those who advocated change. Until the twenties the governing classes of England feared reform; to them any change presaged a revolution and a reign of terror as in the France of 1793. Meanwhile the number of anomalies in the British government had increased; industrial centers such as Leeds and Birmingham lacked any spokesman in parliament while decayed boroughs like Grampound had several. The political system, if such it might be called, was an offense to reason, common sense, and powerful economic interests. The last, represented by the industrial and commercial classes, were anxious to curb the political power of the landed aristocracy; hence the assaults against the unreformed house of commons partook of the character of a class struggle.

The years which followed the conclusion of peace were years of economic depression and much suffering. Men pinned their faith in political reform as the remedy for the problems of the time. Agitators like William Cobbett and "Orator" Hunt taught the English laboring classes to regard an extension of the franchise and a more equitable representation in the house of commons as a cure-all for social and economic ills. A young scion of a noble house, Lord John Russell, destined twice later to become prime minister, lent his support to the demand for parliamentary reform; and both in and outside the house of commons this cause was championed by one of the greatest orators of that day, Henry Brougham. Gradually the dread of change vanished. After 1822 the young Tories, George Canning, William Huskisson, and Sir Robert Peel, sponsored a more liberal foreign policy, humanization of England's criminal law, and far-reaching modifications of her tariff and trade laws. In 1828 the Test and Corporation Acts which had prevented dissenters from holding civil and military offices were repealed, and in the following year Catholics were admitted to the house of commons. In 1830 a Whig, Earl Grey, replaced the Tory Duke of Wellington as prime minister. After an intense and prolonged conflict Grey secured the passage of the Great Reform Bill which modestly enlarged the electorate by about 250,000 voters, established the principle that representation in the house of commons should be based upon population, and strengthened the political power of the middle classes.

While the struggle for political reform lasted it absorbed the attention of the politically minded, and its successful outcome brought to the front men less shackled by tradition. The eighteenth century and the long war had left a veritable Augean stable for the English statesmen of the nineteenth century. The Tory reformers of the 1820's began the cleaning-up process in law and administration, a process which when started could not be limited to home affairs. Huskisson, while tidying trade and navigation laws, made significant changes in Britain's commercial system; and as colonial secretary, 1827–1828, he infused a new spirit into the administration of the colonies — a spirit of reasonableness and efficiency. This new spirit was even more evident when the Whigs came in. Their first colonial secretary, Lord Goderich, was a man with few ideas, but his parliamentary undersecretary, Lord Howick, was an able and resolute administrator. Beginning in 1831 important questions concerning the colonial empire, such as emigration, the colonial land policy, the appointments in the colonial service, and colonial self-government, attracted much attention; thus the defeat of standpat Toryism at home paved the way for the adoption of a more liberal colonial policy.

Social and economic movements and problems within the British Isles have been more potent than the political issues in shaping the attitude of Britain toward the empire. Within the period two forces — Christian humanitarianism and the industrial revolution — were especially active. Late in the eighteenth century groups of earnest men began to ponder their duties to the Negroes held in bondage and to the millions of human beings who had not heard the Gospel of the Man from Galilee. In 1772, Chief Justice Mansfield decided in the famous case of James Somerset, a Negro slave brought by his master from Jamaica to England, that upon setting foot on English soil the slave became free and that slavery "is so odious that nothing can be suffered to support it but positive law." Shortly afterward Granville Sharp, Thomas Clarkson, and William Wilberforce started the great fight, first against the slave trade and then against slavery, which in 1833 resulted in its abolition within the British empire. Contemporaneously with this struggle the great missionary societies were organized. The Baptist Society for Propagating the Gospel was founded in 1792, the London Missionary Society in 1795, the Church Missionary Society in 1799, and the Wesleyan Methodist Missionary Society in 1814. These organizations sent their representatives to the West Indies, Africa, India, China, and Oceania. In the British slave colonies the missionaries became a thorn in the flesh of planters, planter-controlled legislatures, and royal governors. To the missionaries the slave was a human being with a soul to be saved. They supplied the anti-slavery agitators at home with facts showing the evils of slavery, the failure of efforts to better the conditions of the slaves, and the need for destroying slavery as an institution. The Anti-Slavery Society was organized in 1823 under the leadership of Thomas (later Sir Thomas) Fowell Buxton, a wealthy brewer and philanthropist. During the early 1820's Francis Place, the famous ex-tailor, developed a technique for political agitation which became so effective that it was commonly said, "Give me *Place* for a fulcrum and I shall move the earth" — a technique the efficiency of which was demonstrated in the conflict against the laws that prohibited organizations of workingmen as well as in the struggle for the passage of the Great Reform Bill. George Stephen, whose father had married a sister of Wilberforce and whose brother was the famous colonial undersecretary Sir James Stephen, borrowed Place's methods and even improved upon them, with the result that the Anti-Slavery Society became such an effective pressure group that the opposition to slave emancipation was routed. In 1834 the slaves were freed — an event of the greatest significance for the British colonies in the West Indies and South Africa.

Widespread and durable as was the influence of the British anti-slavery sentiment upon the history of the British empire, that of the British missionaries was even more far reaching. In South Africa the London Missionary Society shaped the policy of the government toward the natives and toward colonial expansion. In India a Baptist missionary, William Carey, exercised much influence; the missionaries, Samuel Marsden and John Williams, were pioneers of the British empire in the south Seas. Closely related to the personal influence which the missionaries exerted in the colonies or on the frontiers was the power wielded by their organizations at home. Mission literature spread knowledge of distant lands; the missionary point of view was represented in parliament by Buxton and in the government by Charles Grant, better known as Lord Glenelg, president of the board of control, 1830–1834, and colonial secretary, 1835–1839, and by James Stephen whose connections with the colonial office extended from 1813 until 1847. This unusually efficient civil servant was sincerely interested in the welfare of slaves and backward races, and his administration of the colonies was deeply tinged with Christian humanitarianism. As the period ends, Buxton was organizing the Aborigines Protection Society; and the meetings and demonstrations by the friends of the native races held from time to time at Exeter Hall in London vitally affected empire history.

The "Saints" had a large share in building up the British empire, but that of the worshipers of mammon was even larger. Economic and social changes in the period of the industrial revolution were responsible for conditions in England which made it desirable and even necessary that a considerable part of her laboring population should seek new homes overseas. Improved sanitary conditions resulted in a rapid growth in the population after 1750. Between 1750 and 1821 the population of England and Wales increased from about six to more than twelve millions. Draining of swamps, new methods of crop rotation, better cultivation of the soil, the use of cultivated grasses and the turnip, and scientific breeding of farm animals increased the amount of foodstuffs produced in the country; but the need for food increased even faster. Moreover, the progress in agriculture was often at the expense of the poorer classes, the agricultural laborers and small farmers. Scientific agriculture required larger farms and the enclosure of the commons. Between 1700 and 1760, 208 acts authorized the enclosure of 312,263 acres, but during the next forty years the number of such acts was 2000 and the area 3,180,871 acres; from 1802 to 1844 the figures were respectively 1883 and 2,549,345. This meant that the poor man's goose and cow could no longer feed on the common, he had lost his stake in the land of England, he had become a proletarian who must move out or starve. The agricultural progress coincided with a series of inventions which transformed the textile and hosiery industries. By 1815 the power loom made life difficult for the hand loom weavers and the introduction of knitting frames threw a large number of knitters out of work. Resentment against the use of labor-saving machines found vent in widespread disorders, 1811–1813; the smashing of stocking frames in the so-called Luddite riots in 1812 necessitated the mobilization of more than 12,000 soldiers. To the unemployment resulting from the new machinery was added that caused by the demobilization of about a quarter of a million soldiers and sailors in 1815. The labor market was glutted, and bad harvests increased the seriousness of the economic depression.

With easy-going Lord Liverpool as prime minister, the Tory government of 1815 showed concern only for the interests of those who were politically powerful. Faced with a decline in the prices of agricultural products, parliament passed a corn law which forbade importation of wheat until the domestic price had reached about $2.50 a bushel. Thus prices on foodstuffs were kept unreasonably high in a period of general unemployment and falling wages. It has been estimated that the weekly earnings of hand-loom weavers in England were 26*s.* 8*d.* in 1797–1804, 14*s.* 7*d.* in 1804–1818, 8*s.* 9*d.* in 1818–1825, 6*s.* 4*d.* in 1825–1832, and 5*s.* 6*d.* in 1832–1834. Although this class was harder hit than most others, the wage and employment situation for adult males was often desperate at this time. Until 1824 combinations among workmen were illegal; and while labor unions were permitted after that date their activities were hedged about by so many restrictions as to make them virtually ineffective.

The textile industries of England, especially the cotton industry, grew at an extraordinarily rapid rate in the early part of the nineteenth century. The importation of raw cotton rose from 56 million pounds in 1801 to 247 million pounds in 1830. The work in the new mills was done mainly by women and children. In 1816 it was found that only 17.7 per cent of the persons employed in Scottish textile mills were adult males; the employment figures for six mills in Nottinghamshire disclosed but 18.54 per cent adult males. Neither law nor custom fixed a standard for wages and conditions of work in these mills. True, beginning in 1802 ineffectual acts attempted to safeguard the unfortunate pauper children apprentices indentured for work in the new factories, but the economic doctrine of *laissez faire* seemed satisfactory to the governing classes of England. Consequently, in the early thirties government investigations of factory conditions disclosed the most awful exploitation of children; ten years later a similar study of the employment of women and children in the mines revealed conditions so shocking that the bill which prohibited them from working underground passed without opposition.

Life was hard for the workingmen of England; the country appeared crowded; and the government was generally unsympathetic toward them. Demonstrations against the corn laws, against unemployment, and against the existing political system were put down with a heavy hand. Though England was the richest country in the world life was far from being "merrie" for her toiling masses. Nor did the theories of the political economists hold any hope of better times ahead. On the contrary, Malthus' gloomy prognostication that the growth of the population tended to outstrip that of the food supply, and dogmatic assertions that manual workers must always hover on the brink of destitution were then venerated as immutable laws — theories which deservedly earned for economics the label "the dismal science." Under these conditions English laborers were willing to face the dangers and hardships of the long ocean voyage to America or Australia in foul, stinking holds of ships that now would be deemed unfit for cattle boats. In the years 1815–1837 about 400,000 emigrants left the British Isles for British colonies. While some of these were men of means, younger sons, or adventurers, the majority belonged to the laboring classes who gambled on a chance that on the frontier life would offer for themselves and their children economic opportunities not found at home. The human material for empire-building was abundant largely because the conditions for labor were bad in England, worse in Scotland, and worst of all in Ireland.

North of the Tweed the political, social, and economic conditions were even less favorable to the workingmen than those in England. Scotland was poor in natural resources and the Scottish laboring classes had less protection from law and tradition than had the English. No organized system of poor relief provided help for the destitute of Scotland. In some places the parish aided the needy among its own members, but dissenters were left out; and the well-to-do Scotsmen seem to have been content to let their less prosperous neighbors depend upon the uncertainties of charity. In the Lowlands of Scotland the industrial revolution had made headway before 1815. Coal mines were opened, and men, women, and children worked the customary long hours at low wages and with little or no safeguards against accidents. Mothers deposited their babies with neighbors and carried daily on their backs up mine shafts from 35 hundredweight to 2 tons of the coal hewed by their sons and husbands. In the Glasgow district cotton mills sprang up in which women and children were exploited. The men on the Clyde rioted and fought; the demonstrations only made matters worse. As in England, the law and the power and machinery of the government were on the side of the employers. And occasionally provocative agents were hired by officials to entrap workingmen. In the Highlands the situation was desperate. With the break-up of the clans in the last half of the eighteenth century the clansmen were no longer needed as fighters. The chiefs claimed and asserted their rights as proprietors of the land. Wool-growing became profitable. Estates were cleared — "Bonnie Scotland," it was said, "ceased to be the home for men, it had become the home for sheep." The descendants of those who had followed Montrose and Prince Charlie were compelled to leave moor and glen to become starving crofters and cottars by the sea. They were told it was all in the interest of progress (scant solace) and scolded because they were loth to go. Some would not emigrate; but many bade goodbye to crags, moors, and glens where their fathers had toiled, fought, and died, to build homes in far-off Canada, Australia, and New Zealand.

Across the Irish Sea the people were as usual in a worse plight than those of Great Britain. The legislative union of 1801 failed to bring peace, prosperity, and contentment to the Irish. Memories of ancient wrongs, an alien church, absentee landlordism, and racial and religious animosities kept the island in turmoil. Crime and disorder were rampant. Secret societies flourished. Orangemen fought "Whitefeet" and "Blackfeet." The arrogance of the conqueror was matched by the defiance of the conquered. The land was overpopulated, and on the greater portion of the Emerald Isle lay the awful pall of dire poverty and frequent famine. Industries were developing in Ulster, but efforts to attract capital to and encourage enterprise in the other provinces proved unavailing. The population rose from about 4,200,000 in 1791 to nearly 7,000,000 in 1821. Wilmot Horton, parliamentary undersecretary of state for the colonies, told a select committee of the house of commons in 1825 that he knew of places in Ireland where 100 families tried to eke out subsistence from 270 acres of rented land. Daniel O'Connell related to the same committee that in some districts only one in twenty could get steady employment and that the wages of those employed often were as low as twopence a day "without victuals." Seven years later the O'Connor Don, M.P., testified before a similar committee that in Roscommon County only one out of every four adult males could get work, that a laborer in steady employment might make nine pounds in a year, and that the average rent per acre for potato land was often eight pounds or eight guineas a year. Millions lived in mud cabins covered with thatch or sod which failed to keep out the rain, cabins which frequently had no chimneys and no furniture, not even a bedstead. To own a box or a "dresser" on which to lay a plate was reckoned a luxury. A cast iron pot and a milk tub were often the only utensils. The whole family lived in this single room, sharing it with the pig. The children were generally dressed in rags if not absolutely naked. The food consisted, except on the coast, of potatoes with milk or water. Before the new crop matured, the people suffered want; and if it were deficient or failed, as it usually did every five or six years, "the scourge of famine and distress is felt in every corner of the country."

Congestion and misery were recognized as important causes of the disorders which infected Ireland like a chronic disease. The surplus labor of the island sought employment in England

and Scotland, thereby threatening to force still lower the depressed status of their own labor. The Irish were not wanted in Great Britain, while at the same time the Irish landlords regarded the redundant population a hindrance to their own plans for an improved system of agriculture. Emigration to the British colonies and the United States seemed the only possible solution of the economic problems of Ireland and the sole avenue of escape from misery and degradation by all Irishmen whose energy had not vanished and whose senses were not benumbed. And even those who had sunk very low were shipped off like so much human wreckage to Quebec and other places, either to perish or to rise in new lands under hard but more equitable conditions.

Unemployment, the burden of the cost of poor relief, and the conviction that her population was "redundant" caused Britain to look to the colonies for a solution of pressing social problems. Since 1787 delinquents had been shipped to Australia; perhaps the crown lands overseas might take care of those who were socially dependent. Emigration as a means for relieving distress in the Highlands of Scotland had been tried early in the century and it was revived in 1815–1816. In 1817 a select committee on the poor law recommended "that all obstacles to seeking employment wherever it can be found, even out of the realm, should be removed; and every facility that is reasonable afforded to those who may wish to resort to some of our colonies." Two years later the committee repeated this advice and called special attention to the unoccupied land in the colonies where "the labour of man, assisted by a genial and healthy climate, would produce an early and abundant return." Although trade revived somewhat in the early twenties, the problem of poor relief remained – the replies to an inquiry sent in 1825 to all the parishes of England showed that a majority of the married laborers usually received aid from the poor rates. In that year Ireland was swept by a famine which called for heroic remedies.

The government had meanwhile removed all obstacles to emigration and began subsidizing the removal of people from Britain to the colonies. The first experiment in aided emigration on an extensive scale was made in 1819 when parliament voted £50,000 for sending 5000 settlers to the eastern section of Cape Colony. The distress in Ireland led to a series of parliamentary grants for removing paupers to British North America. For this purpose £15,000 was voted in 1823, £30,000 in 1825, and £20,480 in 1827. The sums were considerable in view of the fact that for eleven out of the seventeen years, 1815–1832, the national budget failed to balance. Nevertheless, neither the direct government aid to emigration nor the practice adopted by many parishes of paying the passage money of paupers willing to leave the country provided much relief. Finally large tracts of colonial land were granted to companies on condition that they should bring out settlers; and at the close of the twenties the able and energetic although somewhat unscrupulous Wakefield produced a scheme for emigration on a large scale, the expense of which was to be borne by a fund created by the sale of land in the colonies. He planned to build up well-balanced overseas communities. In 1831 this method of aided emigration was adopted by the government, but the practice of shipping out those who were socially undesirable still continued. New South Wales complained bitterly of the type of immigrants sent to Sydney. Wakefield's influence was perhaps the greatest single factor in transforming Britain's attitude toward colonization and colonial policy; a more extended treatment of his work is reserved for a later chapter.

The industrial revolution created on the one hand unemployment and an industrial proletariat and on the other increased wealth for a few. The new plutocracy, merchant princes and captains of industry, was enterprising and hard-headed. To the newly rich old methods and policies were far from sacred; their goal was more business and higher profit at any cost. This might be obtained by relaxing ancient restrictions on trade and navigation, an object achieved in part while William Huskisson was president of the board of trade, 1823–1827. The new commercial policy ultimately affected the relations between Britain and her leading colonies, but its first and principal aim was to facilitate an expansion of Britain's trade with the independent nations of Europe and America. The importance of the intra-imperial trade tended to decline in comparison with the foreign trade of Britain, and heavy attacks were directed against the timber and sugar preferences accorded in the British market to the produce of North American and West Indian colonies. The colonial empire had been created to serve the economic interests of Britain, but new conditions in trade and industry reduced the importance of overseas possessions. The United States supplied cotton, the raw material most necessary for the British textile industry; and the United States and Germany were gradually becoming the best customers for the output of mills and foundries. Doubts arose whether colonies were necessary for industrial and commercial prosperity. The middle class whose political power increased after the passage of the Great Reform Bill was willing to remove political and economic restrictions fettering the colonies and their trade; and the new capitalists frowned upon ventures in colonial expansion which might increase the cost of the imperial government. They felt that the tax burden was already too heavy.

Surveying Britain, 1815–1837, in the setting of her imperial history we find that the following topics are of the greatest significance: the absorption of British statesmen and the public generally with problems connected with foreign affairs and domestic reform; the growth of Christian humanitarianism as exemplified in a deep and widespread interest in slavery, the treatment of backward races, and missions to the heathen; the economic changes and the effects of the transition from war to peace which increased unemployment and poverty and made migration of laborers necessary. Although the colonies began to be looked upon as means for relieving distress at home, the new moneyed classes were not deeply interested in the colonial empire. They were inclined to oppose imperial expansion and to favor what has since been labeled a more liberal colonial policy. The capitalistic middle class endorsed *laissez faire* as a guiding principle for solving both domestic and imperial problems. Against this background we must view the empire and the imperial policy of the late Hanoverian period.

CHAPTER 2

THE GEOGRAPHY OF THE EMPIRE, 1815–1837

THE British overseas empire of 1815 was, like that empire today, a scattered, diversified, heterogeneous, rather haphazard sort of thing. Bound together by the sea and held by sea power, created in part by private and in part by public enterprise, it was largely a by-product of trade, of the mercantile system, and of naval supremacy. Only small portions of this empire had been colonized originally by British emigrants. Much of it had been wrested from European rivals — Dutch, French, and Spanish — and retained many traces of the foreign occupation. The most valued of the British possessions, those in India, were administered, subject to the supervision of the home government, by the East India Company, the last and greatest of the trading and exploring joint-stock companies of the Elizabethan era. Except for India, the majority of the colonies were islands, naval or trading stations, and ports of call. Many of them were keys to or jumping-off places for territorial expansion. Britain occupied the fringe of three continents. Great opportunities for acquiring and settling new lands existed in America, Africa, and Australia; but in 1815 these opportunities were not appreciated by the people of the British Isles.

In Europe Heligoland, Gilbraltar, Malta, and the Ionian Islands gave Britain firm control of the North Sea and the

Mediterranean. None of these colonies brought gain to the British capitalists or offered homes and opportunities for economic and social betterment for the poor. They were symbols and instruments of naval power, nothing else.

In North America, on the other hand, Britain held the remnants of one great empire, remnants that formed the nucleus for another. Newfoundland, the Maritime Provinces, and the Canadas were poor both in resources and in population compared with the United States, but Britain had claims to other lands between the Atlantic and Pacific that were destined to supply homes for hundreds of thousands of British emigrants, and economic opportunities for both rich and poor. In 1815 most of the British North American settlements were of the tidewater type — they had fairly direct access to the sea either immediately or by river routes., Lower Canada boasted the largest population, then as now predominantly French in race, language, and culture. Loyalists who had left the United States after the Revolution, other American immigrants, and recent arrivals from the British Isles had founded along the upper St. Lawrence and its tributaries straggling settlements stretching toward Lake Huron. Since 1791 these settlements had formed the province of Upper Canada. North of the Great Lakes and between them and the Rocky Mountains lay a vast territory, an inland empire whose character and resources were little known and whose boundaries were undefined. Over the great western plains and in the forest land north of the prairies roamed large herds of buffalo, some Indians, and a handful of white and halfbreed trappers and fur traders. Since 1670 the land had been claimed and of late more or less controlled by the Hudson's Bay Company. In 1815 this company had a rival for its fur trade in the North West Company, but before long the two combined. The traders hated the settlers, as those whom Lord Selkirk had recently brought to the banks of the Red River found to their grief. Three-quarters of a century were to pass before the plowman began really to displace the Indian and the trapper. Seamen, explorers, and fur traders had also furnished Britain with claims to the westward slope of the Rockies and to islands along the shore of the Pacific. But no settlements had been established and none knew the extent of the area to which Britain might assert title.

Fish and fur gave value to the older possessions, Newfoundland and the Hudson's Bay Company's territory then called Rupert's Land. The other North American possessions were esteemed but little, though their stock had risen somewhat during the recent war by virtue of the grain, timber, and naval stores supplied by them to the mother country. The crown land of Upper Canada and New Brunswick had provided means for rewarding the exiled Loyalists from the United States, and this land seemed also to offer a solution for poverty and unemployment at home.

To the south and in the region of the Caribbean, Britain held numerous islands and two possessions on the mainland. Bermuda, the Bahamas, Barbados, and the Leeward Islands had been settled early by voluntary immigrants from the British Isles. Other possessions had been conquered from Spain, France, and the Netherlands, the most recent acquisitions being St. Lucia, Tobago, Trinidad, and Guiana. Logwood-cutters of an earlier age had helped to secure for Britain a part of Honduras in Central America. Both Honduras and Guiana seemed to offer opportunities for further expansion on the American continent.

The West Indies had long been counted among the most valued jewels in the British crown. Producing sugar in large quantities, they fitted admirably into the order of things under the mercantilist dispensation. Their products supplemented those of the mother country, and were the source of a profitable three-cornered trade with England and the west coast of Africa – sugar for England, trinkets for Africa, slaves for the West Indies. But although the islands still offered a chance of profits for the capitalists, they no longer attracted British emigrants. Fortunes had been made in sugar and slaves, and slave traders and absentee plantation owners of Bristol and Liverpool were maintaining a powerful lobby at Westminster. In 1807 the West Indies suffered a crushing blow with the abolition of the slave trade, and their economic prosperity was further endangered by the successful attack on the monopoly which sugar from these islands enjoyed in the British market. This attack came mainly from the sugar interests of India and Mauritius, encouraged by the growing animosity toward monopolies of any sort. Though the cloud in the east was as yet but the size of a man's hand, it aroused apprehension because the economic foundation of the West Indies had many fissures. To the hazards which generally attend a lopsided economic system was added that of soil exhaustion. The sugar crop was uncertain and new areas had to be cleared. Cheap labor was a necessity. Its supply had been curtailed by the abolition of the slave trade; and an even more serious blow, the abolition of slavery itself, was impending. The planters scented danger; but with an obtuseness rather common in such circles they bent their strength to the stemming of the flood rather than to the building of an ark. Time was against them. The West Indies were doomed to become before long relatively unimportant in the economy of the British empire.

Gold, slaves, and the traffic with India had early drawn Englishmen to the African shore of the Atlantic. But by 1815 African gold had become a legend kept alive only by the term "guinea" in the English monetary system and by the name Gold Coast applied to a portion of Africa. With the abolition of the trade in "black ivory" the Gold Coast and the Slave Coast of the Bay of Guinea became practically valueless. The Company of Merchants Trading to Africa had withdrawn from the Gambia and was soon to be disbanded. The colony at Sierra Leone, founded by Granville Sharp and his associates as a home for former Negro slaves who had aided Britain during the American Revolution, languished. It possessed, however, the best harbor on the west coast of Africa; and with other places which Britain held or soon acquired on the Gambia and the Guinea coast it furnished contacts when the products of this section of the African continent began to find a ready market in Europe and America. Off the African coast the island of St. Helena had since 1656 been a welcome haven for returning East Indiamen, and it now gained prominence as the prison for Napoleon; because he had to be closely guarded, Britain seized the island groups of the Ascension and Tristan da Cunha. Though barren of resources, their occupation eased the British mind in regard to the possibility that the illustrious prisoner might escape, and it also strengthened the British naval supremacy in the South Atlantic. Concern for the trade with India led Britain in 1814 to retain the Cape of Good Hope taken from the Dutch, and the former French possessions of Mauritius and the Seychelles. The value of the Cape consisted largely in its harbor, Table Bay. The land itself with its Boer farmers counted for little; none then knew of the fabulous mineral wealth hidden in the subcontinent. Mauritius in French hands had been a nest for privateers in the wars of the eighteenth century. By annexing the island Britain further safeguarded the trade routes to the east, and her power in the eastern waters became really paramount.

On the mainland of India, "John Company" (colloquial for the East India Company) had rapidly extended its sway since the defeat of the French and the acquisition in 1765 of the right to collect territorial revenue and exercise political power. The company had gradually lost its commercial character, and with the renewal of its charter in 1813 it was deprived of the monopoly of the India trade. Though still nominally independent, the chartered company had become the agency and instrument for British control of and expansion in India. Britain was there to stay. The need for safeguarding what it had of both trade and territory, the anarchical conditions existing in many of the Indian states, and the apprehension aroused by

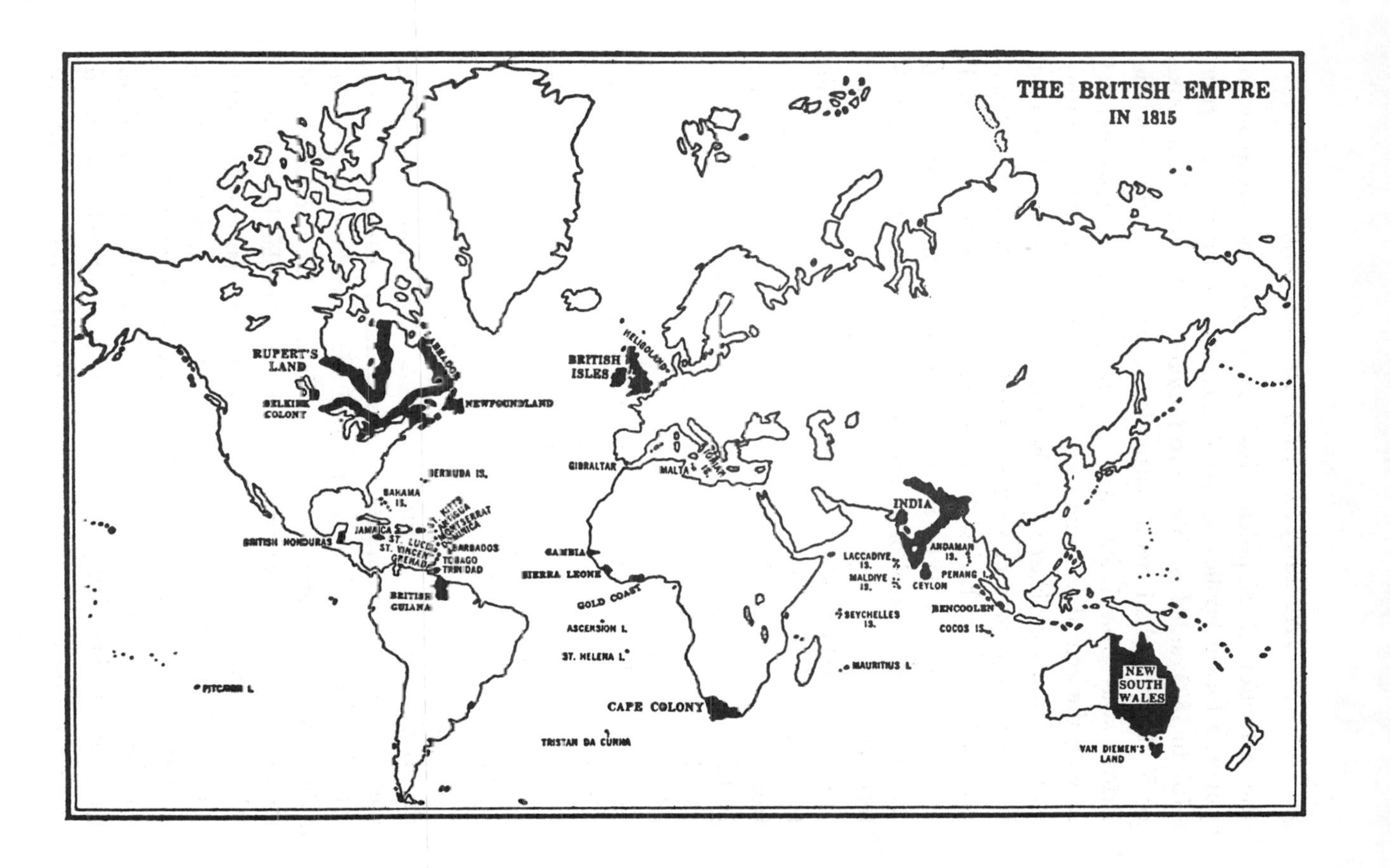
THE BRITISH EMPIRE
IN 1815
RUPERT'S LAND
SELKIRK COLONY
LABRADOR
NEWFOUNDLAND
BERMUDA IS.
BAHAMA IS.
JAMAICA
ST. KITTS
ANTIGUA
MONTSERRAT
DOMINICA
ST. LUCIA
ST. VINCENT
GRENADA
BARBADOS
TOBAGO
TRINIDAD
BRITISH HONDURAS
BRITISH GUIANA
PITCAIRN I.
BRITISH ISLES
HELIGOLAND
GIBRALTAR
MALTA
IONIAN IS.
GAMBIA
SIERRA LEONE
GOLD COAST
ASCENSION I.
ST. HELENA I.
CAPE COLONY
TRISTAN DA CUNHA
INDIA
LACCADIVE IS.
MALDIVE IS.
CEYLON
ANDAMAN IS.
PENANG I.
BENCOOLEN
COCOS IS.
SEYCHELLES IS.
MAURITIUS I.
NEW SOUTH WALES
VAN DIEMEN'S LAND

the activities of Napoleon had compelled the company to pursue a forward policy. Lord Wellesley, governor general from 1797 to 1805, aided by his more famous brother the later Duke of Wellington, had been particularly active in extending the British sway over India. And a new period of expansion set in with the arrival in India in 1813 of the Earl of Moira, afterward Marquis of Hastings. By war and diplomacy the East India Company was making itself supreme south of the Himalayas. While wars had still to be fought, states to be annexed, and native princes to be mollified, the issue was no longer in doubt. British control of India had become a matter of "manifest destiny."

The troubled period that preceded 1815 had compelled Britain to establish connections with many of the states which controlled the gates to India. Fear of Napoleon led to British activity in the Arabian and Persian Gulfs, in Mesopotamia, in Persia, and in Afghanistan—activity that supplied contacts and precedents for further economic, political, and diplomatic interference in these regions. The British government, says Sir Alfred Lyall, had been "launched . . . upon that much larger expanse of Asiatic war and diplomacy in which it has ever since been, with intervals, engaged." The hand was on the plow, there could be no turning back.

On the eastern shore of the Bay of Bengal stakes had been driven that forecast future expansion. The island of Penang and the small strip on the mainland, the Province Wellesley, introduced the British to the tangled affairs of the Malay Peninsula. The East India Company still held the wretched but strategically important post, Bencoolen, on the island of Sumatra. While Malacca was given up temporarily and Java permanently after 1815, the British occupation of the latter had at least one important result: it brought thither as governor the energetic and resourceful Sir Stamford Raffles. His stay in the island gave him the knowledge of that region and fostered in his mind the conviction of its importance for Britain which in 1819 led him to secure for his country the island of Singapore, one of the most strategically located naval and commercial bases in the world.

Beating France by a narrow margin, Britain had earmarked the continent of Australia, then called New Holland, as her possession, the future home for a British nation. As yet the outlook for the latter was not very promising. Successive ship-loads of convicts had given the two Australian colonies, New South Wales and Tasmania, then known as Van Diemen's Land, an unsavory reputation. But many of the transported convicts were not so bad as their punishment and enforced associations implied. The harsh criminal code caused men to be convicted who proved a real asset to a colony. Moreover, free immigrants were arriving in growing numbers; by 1815 the great southland was looked upon as a place that offered opportunities to both those with and those without capital. The humble sheep was being enthroned king; and the recent discovery of paths along the ridges of the Blue Mountains of New South Wales had opened grassy plains and fertile valleys for exploitation by farmer and pastoralist. Australia, the Cinderella of Britain's offspring, soon made the fable a reality.

Prior to 1815, Britain had established connections and bases for territorial claims where no formal annexation had taken place. Explorers of the eighteenth century such as Byron, Wallis, Carteret, and Cook had hoisted the British flag, scattered lead plates, and carved names on trees in the Falkland Islands, Tahiti, New Zealand, and sundry other places where these acts later counted when the appearance of rival powers made neglected lands valuable. Traders and adventurers, sealers and whalers, had forced the South Sea to yield its secrets and provide openings to British enterprise. And missionaries now being sent to out-of-the-way places began to enlighten their supporters at home about immortal souls that might be saved and economic resources that might be tapped if *Pax Britannica* were extended to the remotest corners of the globe.

During the twenty-two years of almost continuous warfare that preceded the Congress of Vienna the flags of France, Holland, and Denmark were lowered everywhere outside of Europe, and many of the Spanish and Portuguese colonies were at the mercy of Britain. But in 1815 John Bull was not a land-grabber. When peace came, although he kept Heligoland, Malta, the Ionian Islands, Trinidad, Tobago, St. Lucia, parts of Guiana, the Cape of Good Hope, Mauritius, the Seychelles, Ceylon, and some less valuable islands, the Ionian Islands were not annexed, and Danish, Dutch, and French colonies in both the east and west were restored to their former owners. Prominent among these retrocessions were Java, the Isle of Bourbon, Guadaloupe, and the French factories in India. France regained even her fishery rights off Newfoundland, an act of generosity criticized in parliament and destined to cause trouble later. In the debates in parliament over the treaties of peace some critics of the government maintained that too little rather than too much had been given up. To the few who wanted Britain to retain more of her conquests, Lord Castlereagh replied loftily that the chief object of a peace treaty was peace. France shorn of colonies, irritated, and smarting under humiliating punishments would be restless, ever plotting revenge. Treated gently, with her colonies restored, she might settle down to the work of peace, develop trade, become prosperous and contented. But behind this grand sentiment which also contained much practical wisdom one will discern that Lord Castlereagh and his colleagues doubted the value of colonial possessions. To him and to them colonies were important only as trading stations and producers of goods that Britain herself could not supply. Colonization proper they viewed rather as an evil than as a blessing.

For more than a generation after Waterloo preoccupation with affairs at home, the burden of a heavy public debt, the growth of liberal economic doctrines, and the absence of rivals in fields for overseas expansion made Britain indifferent or hostile toward policies and schemes that entailed a widening of imperial boundaries. In parliament Joseph Hume and other advocates of retrenchment in government expenditures urged the abandonment of useless and costly colonies. One of them, Sir J. Coffin, went so far as to wish even Canada sunk to the bottom of the sea. The great utilitarians — Jeremy Bentham, James Mill, and their followers — regarded colonies as a burden and an encumbrance; and the growing free trade sentiment among the middle class enfranchised in 1832 lent strength to the anti-colonial views. Furthermore, political, social, and economic changes and reforms at home absorbed the major part of the interests of the general public, of parliament, and of successive governments. A discussion of a colonial question generally served as a signal for honorable members to leave the house of commons; the secretaryship for war and the colonies was classed among the less important posts in a ministry.

But British imperialism was not dead. The empire continued to grow despite governmental indifference and the theories of political and economic philosophers. Indeed the statesmen responsible for the destinies of Britain seem to have felt rather than seen that stagnation or retrogression meant decay, and none of them entertained seriously any thought of cutting colonies adrift. Henry Goulburn and Wilmot Horton as parliamentary undersecretaries for the colonies, 1812–1827, and by virtue of this post official spokesmen for the government on colonial questions, repeatedly referred to the colonies as a source of glory, political power, and economic strength for Britain. And later William Huskisson and Sir George Murray, who succeeded each other as colonial secretaries, 1827–1830, discouraged all talk of abandoning any colony. Leading statesmen of the period — Earl Grey, Sir Robert Peel, and the Duke of Wellington — were not little Englanders though, excepting the duke, they at times looked upon colonies as an honorable obligation rather than an asset.

Outside of parliament it is not until the 1830's with the appearance of Wakefield and his group of colonial reformers that we find a concerted effort made to arouse public and official opinion in favor of colonies and colonization. Of course there had always been individuals who approved of both. In 1816 a writer who signed himself "A British Traveller" published a book in which he strongly condemned the prevailing laxity in the administration of the Trade and Navigation Acts and argued that colonies were necessary for the greatness of England. And it is not without significance that the *Edinburgh Review* of January, 1828, urged emigration to South America for the purpose of making it British. Despite the economists' emphasis upon the importance of the European as against the colonial markets, British traders continued to seek new outlets and to develop their old traffic with distant lands. They demanded aid and protection by the government which necessitated enlargements of imperial obligations. And in India and elsewhere the usual frontier conditions as well as other factors created a necessity for going forward. New stones were continually being added to the imperial edifice.

The most important of these territorial acquisitions were made in India. Though both the court of directors of the East India Company and the British government had decided to limit severely Britain's responsibilities in India, the logic of events forced them to sanction a forward policy. As Sir Alfred Lyall has pointed out, the British could not enjoy an imperial position without assuming imperial obligations in India, and by throwing a cordon around their own possessions the anarchy became more intolerable in the territories still open to the predatory raids of the Pindaris and other robber bands. Furthermore, the chiefs of the Maratha confederacy in central India, still smarting under former defeats inflicted by the British, hoped to retrieve their old position of paramountcy. Lord Hastings, governor general from 1813 to 1823, was compelled to take steps for the extermination of the Pindaris, who mustered more than 40,000 well-equipped horsemen bent on plunder. The war against them merged into the third Maratha war, concluded in 1818. The results of these wars were annexation by the British of large tracts of territory formerly belonging to the Maratha states and the establishment of a British protectorate over the remnants of these states as well as over other Indian states, notably those of Rajputana in western India. The external relations of these states now came into British hands and internal affairs were subject to British supervision. Peace and order replaced the former anarchy from Cape Comorin in the south to the mouths of the Indus, the Great Desert, and the Sutlej River in the northwest. Meanwhile Britain's power expanded also in the north, where the Gurkha state of Nepal had controlled the southern slopes of the Himalayas overlooking Bengal; the Gurkhas often made raids into the rich British territory of the plain. The sharply contested Gurkha war, 1814–1816, led to the annexation of extensive areas along the southern slopes of the Himalayas formerly claimed by Nepal, brought British India into contact with the Chinese empire, and converted Nepal into a friend and ally of Britain.

East of the Bay of Bengal, Burma had grown into a formidable power while the British were making themselves masters of India. In the early part of the nineteenth century the Burmese seized Assam and threatened Bengal from the northeast. The aggressive and overbearing attitude of the Burmese made war between them and the British inevitable. The first Burmese war, 1824–1826, secured for Britain the provinces of Aracan and Tenasserim on the eastern shore of the Bay of Bengal and the protectorate over Assam and other territories northeast of the province of Bengal, with control of the great river Brahmaputra.

By a treaty of March, 1824, the Dutch surrendered their establishments in India and the city of Malacca on the Malay Peninsula and abandoned their opposition to the British occupation of Singapore in exchange for the British settlements in Sumatra and the relinquishment of British claims to territory and commercial privileges in the islands south of the Straits of

Singapore. Shortly afterward the British acquired Naning, adjacent to Malacca, from the native rulers. Penang with the Province Wellesley, Malacca, Naning, and Singapore insured British control of the main sea route between India and China. These posts also offered obvious advantages for later economic and political expansion in the Malay Peninsula where the presence of rich tin mines supplied inducements and the piratical propensities of its inhabitants, the cruelties perpetrated by the Siamese and others, and the activities of Chinese British subjects created need for intervention by Britain. Singapore under the benevolent and efficient administration of Sir Stamford Raffles and his successors was transformed from a pirates' nest with about 150 wretched inhabitants to a prosperous city which in 1836 had a population of 29,984, with exports and imports valued at fourteen million Spanish dollars. As a free city, Singapore enjoyed great advantages, soon outstripped its competitors, and became the chief base for the British trade in that part of the world.

Though George Canning, the great British foreign secretary, foresaw the rapid growth in the importance of Singapore, the British government had little to do with either the acquisition or the development of the place. The supineness of British statesmen in regard to the opportunities in the Far East is revealed not only in the readiness with which Britain in 1824 acquiesced in a Dutch monopoly in wide areas but also by their failure, ten years later, to support Lord Napier in his efforts to obtain better conditions for trading with China.

British influence, although not British political domination, expanded rapidly in the Pacific during the years 1815–1837. British whalers, traders, and missionaries left deep marks among the inhabitants of Pacific islands – the two former groups mainly by creating their particular brands of a hell on earth while the last-named scored considerable success in directing attention to a heaven to be gained hereafter. Indeed in Tahiti, British missionaries maintained a theocracy for several years. But the British government spurned the chances to build an empire of Pacific islands. Overtures for cession from Hawaii in 1822 and from Tahiti three years later were turned down by Britain. Though a British resident was appointed to New Zealand, this future dominion might have been lost if Wakefield and his friends had not been so insistent in demanding the annexation which took place in 1840. Only in the case of the Falklands was Britain willing to act decisively. In spite of the protests of Argentina, these islands were proclaimed British territory in January, 1833. Evidently the whalers with their oil and spermaceti found it easier to gain the ear of the foreign office than did the missionaries.

The general attitude of indifference or hostility toward territorial expansion which had largely determined the British policy in Asia and the Pacific was also noticeable in the treatment of the various African problems. True, some of the explorers of Western Africa received support from the government, but extensions of the British colonies in this region were sanctioned only with great reluctance. Had it not been for the efforts of the anti-slavery people the British flag would have been lowered on the Gold Coast and perhaps also in Sierra Leone. What actually happened was that the government in 1821 took over the control of the Gold Coast from the Company of Merchants Trading to Africa, and for a few years the three principal British possessions — the Gambia, Sierra Leone, and the Gold Coast — were administered as a unit. In 1827 the last-named was again turned over to the merchants with an annual subsidy of about £3500. This arrangement lasted until 1843. The population of Sierra Leone was swelled by Maroons from Jamaica and by the thousands whom British cruisers saved from the clutches of slavers. Treaties with neighboring chiefs brought a few new additions to the area of the West African colonies. In 1816 Bathurst on the Gambia was founded as a trading post; later acquisitions placed the control of the mouth of this great river in British hands. But the opportunities thus offered for territorial expansion were neglected, and the French ultimately gained ascendancy in Western Africa.

Kaffir wars forced the governors at the Cape to extend the eastern boundary of that colony from the Great Fish River, which formed the limit in 1814, to the Keiskamma and then to the Kei River. But these annexations did not please the home government. In 1835, to the disgust of both the governor and the colonists, Lord Glenelg, the colonial secretary, ordered the annexations given up and the boundary fixed where it had been in 1819.

Generally speaking, Britain showed a determination to hold what she held and accept the windfalls. In 1829 when French occupation of Western Australia loomed as a possibility, the British flag immediately went up in this region; and in the boundary disputes between North American colonies and the United States British statesmen showed no inclination to surrender soil to which Britain might have a title.

Though lands were annexed in Asia, in Africa, and in the Pacific, the most striking feature of imperial growth within the period under discussion is found in the development of the colonies where Britain's immigrants could find new homes. By 1837 the number of Australian colonies had risen to four with a population of about 150,000, and the British trade with these dependencies had reached an annual value of two million pounds. In North America, Upper Canada experienced the most rapid growth. The population of this province rose from about 77,000 in 1811 to 358,187, a considerable proportion of this increase being due to immigration from the British Isles. Whereas the government in 1815 had discouraged emigration, it now sought to stimulate the exodus to British colonies by means of land grants, free passage, and bounties. In ten years, 1828–1837, nearly 360,000, exclusive of convicts, left the United Kingdom for British possessions overseas. In Australia and North America sturdy frontiersmen were conquering the wilderness, developing the resources, and increasing the strength of the empire.

The missionary societies greatly increased their activities between 1815 and 1837. Stations were established in Africa, in India, in China, and in the South Sea Islands. At home the work enjoyed the powerful support of William Wilberforce and his friends; and in the field men like William Carey, Samuel Marsden, Robert Moffat, John Philip, and John Williams in various ways influenced the course and character of imperial expansion and imperial policy.

As the Victorian era opened, the steamship had passed the experimental stage. Soon great steamship lines connected Britain with distant lands. Steam vessels made the extirpation of piracy possible, facilitated overseas trade, and stimulated colonization and empire-building. A new weapon had been forged, agencies created for the spread of British power and influence over the globe.

CHAPTER 3

THE DECLINE OF THE OLD IMPERIAL SYSTEM

WHEN the dispute between Britain and her American colonies was nearing its fateful climax, Burke advised his countrymen to govern the dependencies "on the principles of freedom" and to pin their faith in affection as the most durable imperial tie. His advice and warning went unheeded. The empire was wrecked, and half a century passed before his countrymen appreciated the lessons which could be deduced from the American Revolution.

In most respects, the British colonial policy of 1815 was identical with that of 1775. The colonies were governed from Downing Street for the benefit of the mother country. The imperial parliament recognized only a few self-imposed limits on its power to legislate for all portions of the empire; the crown denied the existence of the right of colonists to control or to supervise executive action; and colonial trade and shipping continued to be regulated in the interest of the United Kingdom. All colonies were dependencies, though their degree of dependence varied as did their legal and administrative systems. The Australian colonies, New South Wales and Van Diemen's Land, were penal settlements. The inhabitants – convicts, ex-convicts, and free settlers – possessed none of the political rights and privileges ordinarily enjoyed by Englishmen. The governor was supreme, and practically every detail in government, administration, and business was dependent on his will or whim. At the Cape the governor ruled and reigned, but unlike his colleague at Sydney, he could not regulate the minutiae of social and economic life. Gibraltar was a military station. Subject to the supervision of a department of the imperial government, the board of control, "John Company" governed British India. Excepting those recently acquired, the West Indian colonies as well as those of North America had elective assemblies with considerable power over local affairs. But neither in the election of these bodies nor in the authority exercised by them do we find uniformity of system.

In the colonies founded as English settlements, English law had been established as far as it was deemed suitable to local needs — a point generally left to be determined by the king in council, that is to say, the imperial government of the day. A British emigrant supposedly carried the English common law with him, unless he went to Australia or to a colony acquired by cession or by conquest, in which case he might be subject to the legal system of the former owner of that colony. Thus Lower Canada and St. Lucia kept French law antedating the Code Napoléon; Mauritius had the old French criminal law and in other fields the Code Napoléon; British Guiana, the Cape, and Ceylon retained their Roman Dutch Law and various laws of the Batavian Republic; Trinidad had the law of Spain; Malta preserved the Maltese code; and in British India no general legal system existed. In all these possessions except Malta and India the laws of the old homelands had been modified to suit local conditions before Britain assumed control; after that date they might be altered by the king in council unless specific laws or rights had been guaranteed by treaty.

Both crown and parliament claimed supreme power over all the colonies, but no well-defined line of demarcation separated their respective spheres of authority. Generally speaking, ceded and conquered colonies were controlled by the crown as to both administration and legislation. The power of the crown to legislate directly ceased with the creation of a legislature in a colony, though indirectly the lawmaking power might still be exercised either negatively by using the veto or positively by having the representatives of the crown initiate legislation. Parliament claimed the right to pass laws for all the colonies, subject only to the limitation fixed by the Declaratory Act of 1778 not to levy internal taxes for imperial purposes. If the legislative power of parliament clashed with that of the crown, the latter gave way. Failure of parliament to legislate for ceded and conquered colonies did not imply a surrender of this power; nor did parliament ever admit that its legislative authority lapsed with the establishment of a colonial legislature. On various occasions between 1815 and 1833 the imperial parliament affirmed its right to supervise and regulate slave-holding in the West Indies, despite vehement protests from Jamaica and some of the other colonies; by virtue of this supreme power parliament in 1833 abolished slavery everywhere in the British empire.

The practical functioning of the coexisting lawmaking authority of parliament and crown in the colonies may be seen by comparing the early changes in the government and institutions of New South Wales with similar changes at the Cape. In the former, a settlement colony, the supreme court and the legislative council were created by acts of parliament, while the Cape, a ceded colony, secured these grants by orders in council. But it is significant that in 1836 a separate government for the eastern district of the Cape was set up by an act of parliament. In fact, the constitutional development of the empire tended more and more toward the exercise of parliamentary supremacy over the crown in matters colonial. Formerly the founding of colonies and the granting of their constitutions had been reckoned among the prerogatives of the crown. But South Australia owes her existence as a separate colony to an act of parliament; and the departure from earlier practice marked by the passing of the Canadian Constitutional Act of 1791 which established legislatures for the Canadas was treated as a precedent when parliament in 1832 provided Newfoundland with a constitution.

However, except in the fields of commerce, navigation, the slave trade, and slavery, parliament seldom interfered either directly or indirectly in the government and administration of the colonies or with colonial policy. The task of governing the overseas possessions remained in the hands of the executive departments; only on rare occasions did parliament look into and debate colonial questions. The colonial office, the board of trade, the treasury, and now and then the home office, singly or combined, regulated the affairs of the dependencies. The orders in council supplying laws and constitutions for ceded and conquered colonies emanated from one or more of these departments. They supervised the enforcement of the laws applicable to all the colonies and scrutinized all colonial legislation, appointments, and appropriations. Sentences passed by colonial courts might be reviewed and altered by the home government, and the governor, whose powers were extensive even in colonies with elective assemblies, acted as an agent of the crown.

In the days before steam and electricity had annihilated distance, a governor in Australia or at the Cape had of necessity to decide many questions before instructions could arrive from London. And if, as was the case with Governor Macquarie of New South Wales, 1810–1821, he possessed energy, ambition, executive ability, and the confidence of the secretary of state for the colonies, he might rule as monarch of all he surveyed. The power of a governor, however, depended not only upon the distance of the colony from England, his constitutional position, and his own ability and personality, but also upon the character, ability, and personality of the colonial secretary, the state of organization — or lack of it — at the colonial office, and the relations that existed between this department and its head and several other departments and commissions and their heads. Colonial grievances might be redressed by means of the right of petition enjoyed by all the colonists. Such petitions were often presented to both king and parliament and were used in attacks upon unpopular ministers.

Lack of coordination was a fundamental weakness of the old imperial system. Until 1854 the colonial office and the war office had the same head. In war time, the war functions quite naturally absorbed the major part of the attention of the holder of this secretaryship, and when the Napoleonic war was over the post ceased to be regarded as important. Between 1815 and 1837 only one of its occupants, William Huskisson, combined executive ability of the highest order with liberality of outlook, political sagacity, and interest in colonial problems. His brief tenure at the colonial office, 1827–1828, was marked by an earnest attempt to grapple with vital issues in colonial relations and colonial policy, but it was too short to be fruitful. The office suffered also from lack of system in handling its work. Not until James Stephen in 1836 became permanent undersecretary of state for the colonies was a definite routine adopted in reading, commenting upon, and forwarding incoming dispatches and laws, and in drafting replies to colonial governors and reports on colonial bills and acts. The slackness that had prevailed may be gauged to some extent by the fact that the governor of St. Kitts at one time allowed nearly four years to slip by before he forwarded the measures passed by his council, and that even in the case of an important colony such as Lower Canada more than twelve months elapsed before the laws of 1833 were sent home. Indeed, by enacting annual laws some of the West Indian governors and councils nullified the efforts of the home government to control their legislation.

But the most serious defect of the old administration of the colonies was divided authority at home. The colonial office performed most of the work and was, of course, blamed if things went wrong overseas. Colonial reformers accused this office of having a "sighing room" where hopes and aspirations of the colonists languished and expired. All delays in deciding on colonial laws and petitions, all bad appointments, all refusals to give up imperial patronage in the colonies, and all mischievous rules and restrictions were attributed to the colonial office. Hostile critics, notably Charles Buller and Edward Gibbon Wakefield, failed to appreciate that most of the grievances of which they complained had their root in the absence of a single source of authority to decide colonial questions. Other departments of the government exercised powers equal to or exceeding those of the colonial office in passing on the validity of colonial laws, the expenditure of money, and the appointment of many officials overseas. And these departments, particularly the board of trade and the treasury, while jealous in guarding their prerogatives in matters colonial, often showed a deplorable lack of zeal in performing the work connected therewith. Colonial bills and acts were forwarded to and reported upon by the colonial office and the board of trade. But in many cases the law officers of the crown, the home office, the treasury, the commissioners of customs, and other boards and commissions might have to be consulted before a report on a colonial law could be submitted to the king in council for final approval or rejection. Occasionally this necessitated a circular correspondence with colonial governors and their advisers which in the days of slow communication invariably meant delays of months or years, even though everyone concerned acted with all possible dispatch which they usually did not. All decisions and regulations dealing with trade, commerce, and navigation required the sanction of the board of trade. And after 1831 all expenditure of money needed the approval of the lords of the treasury. This latter arrangement was, of course, designed to check extravagance and systematize the finances of the empire. It may have saved money for the British taxpayer, but inasmuch as the treasury almost invariably waited from two months to a year before deciding questions referred to it from the colonial office, the arrangement bore hard on the colonies. Questions concerning religion and public worship in the colonies wherever the Anglican church was established or represented were referred to the home office or the bishop of London or the archbishop of Canterbury; those relating to police, enforcement of laws, punishment and pardons of criminals often went to the home office and to the law officers of the crown. This lack of coordination between the departments concerned and the almost criminal negligence of several of them when colonial issues called for settlement were a heritage from the past which James Stephen strove hard, and vainly, to destroy — it was, indeed, a *heriditas damnosa* which caused much suffering and dissatisfaction beyond the seas.

Appointments in the colonial service were made either by one of the executive departments at home or by the representative of the crown in the colony, subject to confirmation by the imperial government. With numerous acts regulating trade and navigation for the whole empire still in force, a goodly share of the colonial patronage fell to the board of trade and the treasury. Church appointments necessitated reference to the home office and English ecclesiastical authorities. Thus in patronage too, divided authority and counsel and departmental jealousies interfered with good government. Besides, lax standards and indifference to the welfare of the colonies often prevailed in the choice of their officials. Though conditions had improved since 1775, many unworthy men occupied offices of trust in the colonial service. In 1815 absenteeism was common. Lord Cochrane disclosed in the house of commons, February 28, 1816, that Lord Castlereagh's secretary drew a salary of £7000 per annum as vendue master of Malta, and that the harbor and quarantine masters for that island filled their places with deputies. Sir Francis Burton spent in the province about one of the twenty-three years he held the office as lieutenant-governor of Lower Canada. Similar instances were common in the West Indies. A glaring, though perhaps not wholly typical, example of what the old colonial system might produce is that of John Caldwell, receiver-general of Lower Canada, who in 1823 was found guilty of defalcations totaling £96,000 but went scot free. Pluralism in the public service was complained of in Lower Canada, and well-founded charges of unfitness formed a legitimate source for dissatisfaction in the North American as well as in other colonies. The first chief justice appointed for South Australia played hide and seek with the officers of the law in England to avoid imprisonment for debt and finally succeeded in embarking for his distant post under the cover of night. Little wonder that in 1836 G. Cornewall Lewis told his friend Edmund Head: "To a man who has an English career open to him, Colonial Office is a miserable *pis aller*. This would not be the case if the colonial appointments were not so scandalously bad as they have been, and, as I fear, they are likely still to be." And shortly afterward Lewis, who was a distinguished student of colonial government, again wrote to Head: "The scum of England is poured into the colonies: briefless barristers, broken-down merchants, ruined debauchees, the offal of every calling and profession are crammed into colonial places." Lewis may have exaggerated, but even James Stephen described the early years of the nineteenth century as "replete with abuse" in the colonial administration. When unfit men were given appointments overseas, the colonists suffered, and the evils resulting therefrom were painted in glaring colors by men on the spot who perhaps had had their own eyes fixed on the loaves and fishes that went to strangers.

Politically and socially England was oligarchical and aristocratic. But the forces of democracy were actively driving in outposts and even battering at the walls. On the frontiers men were born or became by force of circumstances democrats, restive under restraint, clamorous for their real or fancied rights and privileges. They felt fettered by their system of government and irked by restrictions imposed by the mother country.

Established and loaded with favors at home, it was but natural that the Church of England should seek to obtain a privileged position in the colonies, and that attempts of that sort should receive support from the imperial government. But no uniform policy in regard to the church and religion had been adopted for the overseas empire. In the older West Indian colonies the

Church of England was established by law, supported by local taxes and, after 1826, by grants from home. In the colonies more recently acquired, such as St. Lucia, the Roman Catholic Church was considered established since its revenues were guaranteed by the secular authorities. In Canada confusion reigned. The Constitutional Act of 1791 endowed the "protestant" church with land equivalent to one-seventh of the land alienated by the crown. But the term "protestant" remained to be defined, since, contrary to its usual custom, the Anglican church in Canada not only claimed to be protestant but asserted it was *the* protestant church under the terms of the act of 1791. At times the colonial office was inclined to accept this interpretation of the act, an interpretation objected to by Presbyterians, Methodists, and other dissenters. Legal opinion sometimes favored the view that Canada had three established churches, namely, the Roman Catholic, by the terms of the Treaty of Paris in 1763 and the Quebec Act of 1774, the Church of England, and the Church of Scotland. In the Maritime Provinces of British North America, the high dignitaries of the Church of England enjoyed special favors such as the use of naval vessels, and occasionally this church was granted crown land. At the Cape all clergymen were paid salaries by the government. Anglican, Presbyterian, and Roman Catholic chaplains served at the convict establishments in Australia; but when land was set aside in New South Wales for the support of education and the clergy, the colonial office instructions of 1825 show that the Anglicans were intended to be the only beneficiaries.

Except for a fairly vigorous attempt in the eighteenth century to have Anglican bishops appointed in the American colonies and the work done for the church by an affiliated organization, the Society for the Propagation of the Gospel, the Church of England had neglected the colonial field. By an old custom the bishop of London exercised jurisdiction "over all English clergymen, wheresoever officiating, who had no bishop of their own." And most of the overseas clergymen had no local bishop. In 1815 bishoprics existed for only Nova Scotia and Quebec. Thirteen years later, when Charles Blomfield became bishop of London, there were five colonial bishoprics; by 1840 the number had risen to ten. But in view of the extent of the empire, the number was still insufficient, and the tasks confronting the bishop of London were too heavy for any human being however great his ability, his strength, and his zeal.

Although the Anglican church had long failed to perform its duties overseas, when dissenters began to threaten its position it showed an inclination to employ the weapons of Caesar instead of those of Christ. Belatedly the Anglicans tried to repair past mistakes and to secure a privileged position, but they had the misfortune, first, of running counter to the spirit of the time — even at home the church was beginning to lose many special favors — and, secondly, of representing if not a type of religion at least a state of mind that failed to appeal to the frontiersmen. The result was that nearly everywhere in the empire religious issues added fuel to the flame of political discontent. The colonists were averse to the founding of church establishments in their midst and to spiritual dictation from the protestant churches in the British Isles.

In the seventeenth century the Church of England had been established in Jamaica and in some of the other West Indian islands. It was the church of the planter oligarchy; it made no serious effort to convert the slaves. When Moravian, Baptist, and other missionaries began work among the Negroes, they encountered the hostility of both church and lay authorities. Imprisonment and other penalties were inflicted upon dissenting clergymen and missionaries, and it was only after the anti-slavery movement had gained much headway in England that the authorities in Jamaica began to concede religious toleration; even then many attempts were made to obstruct missionary work by branding the missionaries as fomenters of discontent among the Negroes and colored. In the West Indies, however, the success of the dissenting church bodies was so great that Stephen believed they might someday establish a theocracy in the islands.

In Canada, instead of pouring oil on troubled waters, religion simply intensified the fury of the elements. The Anglicans formed a minority among the protestants of Upper Canada; but led by the redoubtable Dr. Strachan, first Anglican bishop of Toronto, they claimed all the land known as Clergy Reserves set aside by the act of 1791. Dr. Strachan's connections with the political clique at Toronto known as the "family compact," the objections of settlers to the reservation of land for church purposes, the opposition of other protestant church bodies to the claims of the Anglicans made the question of the Clergy Reserves a major political issue in the province, one that affected the attitude of the colonists toward the question of imperial control. Writing in January, 1840, C. Poulett Thomson, then governor general of Canada, said: "The Clergy Reserves have been, and are, the great overwhelming grievance—the root of all the troubles of the province, the cause of the rebellion—the never-failing watchword at the hustings—the perpetual source of discord, strife, and hatred." And it is significant that a staunch Anglican judge in Nova Scotia admitted: "Every attempt on the part of the Government to give preeminence to the Church creates ten enemies for one friend."

Until the thirties the imperial government supported the efforts of the Church of England to secure a dominant position overseas. Writing to Governor Macquarie of New South Wales, May 13, 1820, the colonial secretary, Lord Bathurst, stressed the need for implanting in the minds of the younger generation in the colony "the Principles of the Established Church." And in the draft of a charter for a corporation to manage the church and school estates of New South Wales dated January 1, 1825, it was expressly stated that the money from "*the Clergy and school account*" should "be applied and expended in and toward the maintenance and support of the Clergy of the Established Church of England in the said Colony . . . and toward the maintenance and support of Schools and School Masters in any

Parish in the said Colony, in connection with the Established Church." The decision to supplement from imperial funds the revenues of the Church of England in the West Indies pointed in the same direction.

But ten years later this policy had been abandoned. In 1835 Lord Glenelg admitted the futility of attempting "to select any one Church as the exclusive object of Public Endowment" in Australia. Such efforts would not be tolerated in the colonies. For this reason the colonial office frowned on the action of Sir John Colborne, lieutenant-governor of Upper Canada, in establishing endowments for Anglican rectories in January, 1936, and later turned a deaf ear to pleas of the bishop of Nova Scotia for land grants in support of his clergy. It was recognized that public opinion in the colonies ran strongly counter to the bestowal of favors upon one particular church. Indeed, the relations between a Presbyterian divine, Dr. John Dunmore Lang, of Australia and the Presbyterians of Scotland and between the Methodist leader, Dr. Egerton Ryerson, in Upper Canada and the Methodist conference of England show that colonial objections to ecclesiastical control from home were not confined to opposition to the Church of England. In religion and the church the colonists desired self-government.

The British empire had been founded on trade, and its governmental system had been devised with the object of benefiting the economic interests of the mother country. But times had changed since the passage of the navigation acts of the seventeenth and the sundry colonial trade laws of the eighteenth century. What may then have been a logical and beneficent economic organization of the empire, judged by English standards, had by 1815 become a mere patchwork, demonstrably illogical, unnecessary, and injurious even to the homeland. British shipping no longer stood in need of protection against Dutch and other rivals. The American Revolution, the annexations following the wars with France and Napoleon, and the revolutions in Spanish America gave rise to new conditions and necessitated alterations in the old system. And as the nineteenth century advanced and the effects of the industrial revolution were felt and better appreciated by British statesmen, the economic foundation of the colonial system was steadily undermined. There was no rational need to discourage by governmental action the rise of colonial manufactures — they had no chance in competition with the new English machines. Cotton was now more important than sugar for the trade and industry of Britain, and cotton could be bought most cheaply in the United States, a foreign country. Moreover, the foreign markets were growing more important than the colonial. British business men and manufacturers wanted to buy cheap and sell dear, but they were blocked by various preferences granted to colonial produce. Self-interest had been the guiding motive in the shaping of the old imperial system, and now self-interest urged its abandonment.

Few English laws have aroused more controversy than those that attempted to reserve the carrying trade of the empire to British and colonial ships manned mainly by British subjects. Though often severely criticized, the great Navigation Act of 1661 remained unaltered in its main features until its repeal in 1849. But the system it had helped to create had long been tottering. In the years of peace that followed Waterloo the conviction prevailed that the British merchant marine had no need for special protection; that the Navigation Acts were unnecessary for supplying the royal navy with trained seamen; that they hampered commerce, increased freight rates, and mulcted consumers both in Britain and in the colonies for the benefit of a small number of shipowners. Theoretical economists such as David Ricardo and James M'Cullock never wearied of exposing the fallacies of restricting trade and navigation, and practical statesmen ultimately realized that mercantilism must be destroyed — root and branch.

The work of demolishing the old economic system began in the eighteenth century. The Navigation Acts stipulated that goods from Asia, Africa, and America should be brought into

England (later Great Britain and the United Kingdom) only in English (British) or colonial ships. But when trade was resumed with the former colonies in North America their goods could be brought to Britain in their own ships, now those of a foreign state. A similar change had to be made when Spanish and Portuguese colonies in South America succeeded in shaking off the yoke of the Old World. Hence, in 1825, Huskisson, then president of the board of trade, secured the passage of regulations whereby American goods might be imported "in British ships or in ships of country of origin and from which they are imported." At the same time fear of retaliation caused Britain to remove the discriminatory duties on goods brought in foreign bottoms.

The course of events compelled her to alter other essential features of the system governing colonial trade. Before the American Revolution, British colonies could not as a rule import goods directly from a foreign country. In their attempts to enforce this regulation, British statesmen fostered close economic connections between the West Indian sugar islands and the North American colonies; the former became dependent upon the latter for foodstuffs and other primary necessities of life. When the revolution stopped this trade the West Indies suffered, and not in silence. The sugar planters could be heard at Westminster. Their profits were threatened if the old prohibition against direct trade between the sugar islands and a foreign state remained in force. Need prevailed over logic, and the West Indies were permitted to import from the United States, though at first only in British ships. In 1793 Britain became involved in the war with France and shipping grew scarce. Hence, when in the following year she concluded the Jay Treaty with the United States, American vessels not above 70 tons burden were granted permission to bring goods from their country to the West Indies. This need to carry American goods in American bottoms was so great that though the article of the Jay Treaty dealing with the West Indian trade failed to be ratified by the

American senate, Britain by orders in council put into effect the concession to American shipping. Further inroads on the system of trade and navigation were made by the Free Port Act of 1805 and by orders in council of 1806. Subject to certain restrictions, foreign vessels might now trade with a limited number of colonial ports in the West Indies and in British North America. These concessions were carried still further by a warehousing act of 1824. During the reforming period of his career William Pitt the younger made an attempt to rationalize the regulations of shipping and commerce. He failed; but benefiting by the fact that the Navigation Acts had not been applied to India, American vessels received from Pitt permission to trade there, with the result that the Yankees could supply the West Indies with eastern wares more cheaply than could the British. This constituted smuggling, but the New England conscience had never been particularly sensitive on that point. In 1815 when peace came, the Navigation Acts were not fully applied to the Cape of Good Hope and to British possessions east thereof; Dutch planters of British Guiana were allowed to import from and export to the Netherlands; the economic bonds between Trinidad and Spanish America were not completely severed; and the United States regained the right to trade with India, but not that of trading directly with the British West Indies in American ships. Thus the old garment covering imperial trade and navigation became badly rent.

The twenties brought to the front in Britain the reforming Tories, Canning, Peel, Robinson, and Huskisson. They shocked the die-hards on many points, and not least with their "heresies" on commerce and navigation. Robinson, the later Lord Goderich, when known by the sobriquet "Prosperity," won a niche side by side with his abler and more famous colleague, Huskisson, among the enlightened British statesmen. As president of the board of trade Robinson denounced the restrictions on trade and navigation that handicapped the West Indies in competing with Brazil and Cuba. He and Huskisson, his successor in this office, secured the passage of acts which permitted export of certain colonial articles in foreign or British ships directly to European ports. Huskisson actually strove to promote direct trade "between foreign countries and our colonies generally." By a commercial treaty with Prussia, Prussian ships obtained permission to trade with British colonies in return for extending to British commerce and shipping the most-favored-nation treatment. Similar reciprocity treaties were later concluded with other European states, and in 1830 a dispute of long standing with the United States was settled by permitting American ships to trade with the British West Indies. The carrying trade within the empire remained, however, a monopoly for British shipping until 1849.

Preferences and bounties had held an important place in the British imperial system of the seventeenth and eighteenth centuries. Several articles of colonial produce, notably sugar and tobacco, had a monopoly of the home market. Preferences had also been granted to colonial timber, but not until 1809 was the preference on Canadian timber made so high as to exclude that from the Baltic; and when Huskisson revised the system of imperial trade in the twenties Canadian grain secured such preferential treatment as to evoke protest from English agriculturists. The fish from Newfoundland and the Maritime Provinces of North America was safeguarded against foreign competition in the British and West Indian markets; preferences ranging from 5 to 30 per cent were intended to preserve the colonial market for British goods.

But the economic organization of the empire was as haphazard as was its political and administrative system. The West Indian sugar preferences did not extend to the produce of India and Mauritius, and when merchants and sugar planters of the East demanded equal treatment with the West Indies they met fierce opposition. Likewise when Huskisson established a substantial preference for Canadian grain, that of Australia was left out of the reckoning. Furthermore, the preferential system had many loopholes and sometimes defeated its own purpose. Thus, during the thirties colonial coffee paid a duty of 6*d.* per pound while foreign coffee paid 1*s.* 3*d.* But Brazilian coffee coming by way of the Cape paid only 9*d.* per pound. Consequently much coffee came into Britain by that route. The colonial preference made the article dear to the consumers without benefiting the coffee growers in the British colonies. At this time, it was asserted, the colonial timber preference of 45*s.* per load caused enterprising merchants to ship Norwegian and Baltic timber to British North America and send it thence to Britain to be entered as a product of those colonies. In 1840 John M'Gregor, an official at the board of trade, testified that the imperial prohibition of sugar refining in the colonies had had the interesting and unforeseen result of making the British West Indies consumers of the products of their Brazilian and Cuban rivals whose sugar was refined in bond in Britain and reshipped to the West Indies.

The lack of logic in their commercial system bothered Englishmen little compared with the irritation aroused by the undeniable fact that it made dear articles of common consumption. Colonies were costly anyway; why, it was asked, should the users of timber be asked to pay exorbitant prices for that article just because it was a staple of British colonies in North America? To a hard-headed generation it seemed unreasonable to subsidize the owners of sugar plantations in Jamaica. And after 1833, sentimental cries against the foreign slave-grown sugar failed to check the demand for repeal of prohibitory sugar duties. Moreover, it was pointed out that the restrictions on shipping added materially to the cost of goods by compelling ships to go in ballast one way, and that the imperial preferences tended to limit the foreign market for British manufacturers.

Under the old dispensation the imperial tariff system was extremely complicated. Duties were imposed by acts of parliament or by orders in council or by colonial acts. The variations were numerous and the machinery for enforcing the tariff regulations was cumbersome and expensive. With the adoption of the distinction that colonial legislatures could levy customs duties for revenue only, whereas those imposed by imperial authorities existed solely for the regulation of commerce, there had grown up dual customs establishments in nearly all the more important colonies. Often the imperial duties were so low as to be unremunerative, hardly paying for the cost of collecting them. At the same time the presence of imperial customs officers was resented by the colonists, partly because these officials came from the outside. Colonists objected to paying taxes for the purpose of providing jobs for strangers.

Changed and changing views on imperial issues were nowhere more in evidence than on the topic of emigration. In 1815 the government opposed emigration on the ground that it sapped the strength of the mother country. Ten years later public funds were used to move part of the surplus population of the mother country to the colonies because, it was argued, getting rid of paupers and delinquents would improve conditions at home. In 1825 this argument weighed heavily in Wilmot Horton's favor when he sought and obtained money from the house of commons to be used for the purpose of removing Irish paupers to Upper Canada. But the Horton scheme of emigration embraced more than merely ridding the country of paupers; it included plans for giving the emigrants aid in making them useful and productive members of the colonial society. Consequently, he argued that the aided emigration conferred both negative and positive benefits on the United Kingdom. From being a burden on the community in Ireland, the emigrants became producers adding strength to the empire as tillers of the soil in British North America. Wilmot Horton had glimpses of a wider horizon than that bounded by the shores of the British Isles.

No single individual did more to broaden the vista on the subject of emigration, as well as on other imperial questions, than Edward Gibbon Wakefield. While serving three years in Newgate Prison for abducting an heiress, this gifted and remarkable man had apparently ample time to reflect on and gather information concerning the colonies and colonial policy. The result was his celebrated *Letter from Sydney* published in 1829, and other works and broadsides dealing with various phases of colonial relations and colonial policy. His famous doctrine of systematic colonization touched many topics: colonial land should not be given away even to *bona fide* settlers but sold at a "sufficient price" (in practice this price proved difficult to fix). He asserted that by this method capital would be attracted to the new settlements, they would be assured of a labor supply, and they could be kept more compact. Funds obtained from the sale of land should be used to bring carefully selected immigrants. Wakefield wished to found socially well-balanced communities beyond the sea, "Little Englands" which should be granted a large amount of self-government. An examination of his theories will reveal that his views on emigration differed radically from those held by the imperial government in the twenties. He was opposed to shoveling out paupers and other undesirables, and he advocated the migration of people representing a cross section of society in England, with the lowest stratum omitted. His attention was fixed on what was to be built up — created. He was the colonizer *par excellence*. His colonies were to be replicas of the mother country, remaining — just how he never tried to explain — united with England. He had an imperial vision. And when, largely as a result of Wakefield's influence, the colonial office under the leadership of Lords Goderich and Howick in 1831 adopted a definite scheme of selling Australian lands and applying some of the money thus realized to aid emigration, it became evident that the government had reversed completely its former stand on emigration and had decided to use the lands on the frontiers for truly imperial purposes.

Weariness and distrust of the old system, hope and aspiration for the new, found expression in speeches in the house of commons. Agents of the West Indian colonies such as Joseph Hume and James Marryatt denounced the misrule of the dependencies and pleaded that they should be treated not as foreign possessions but as integral parts of the empire. And to give effect to this point of view Hume proposed on August 16, 1831, an amendment to the Reform Bill giving the colonies nineteen representatives in the house of commons. This was, however, negatived without a division. From 1816 until 1835 the most clear-sighted exponent of a new imperial policy was probably Sir James Mackintosh. Speaking in the debate on the army estimates, February 28, 1816, he pointed out that Britain must look to the Canadians' attachment to the mother country as the only sure and worth-while bond of union. Twelve years later he described the union between Britain and the colonies as an alliance, and gave as maxims of a sound colonial policy: "A full and efficient protection from all foreign influence; full permission to conduct the whole of their own internal affairs; compelling them to pay all the reasonable expenses of their own government, and giving them, at the same time, a perfect control over the expenditure of the money; and imposing no restrictions of any kind upon the industry or traffic of the people." Similar views were held at one time by E. G. (later Lord) Stanley, who in 1828 advised the government to enter into a noble competition with the United States in making the people of North America happy and contented. Two years later Lord Althorp, chancellor of the exchequer in the reform ministry of Lord Grey, averred that Canada could be kept only by a policy of conciliation and that the people there should be given a free and independent constitution. These views were expressed even more forcefully in the house of commons on February 18, 1831, by Lord Howick, the undersecretary of state for the colonies. The imperial government, he said, should avoid vexatious interference in the internal affairs of the colonies. They should be protected against foreign attacks, their prosperity should be promoted, and they should be taught to combine with the mother country for common welfare in peace and common defense in war. If treated in a conciliatory spirit friendship would result; and the colonies, he asserted, would prove more useful as willing allies than as reluctant subjects.

That these statements were not empty words is shown by the

surrender to Lower Canada in 1831 of the crown revenues under the Quebec Act and the relinquishment in 1835 of the colonial office patronage in the Canadas. But by then events had moved far and rapidly, and the concessions, significant though they were, failed to satisfy the demands of the radical element in Lower Canada. In the year Victoria ascended the throne rebellions broke out in the Canadas; the situation in other colonies may be gauged by the outburst of Lord Aberdeen in December, 1834, when he assumed charge of the colonial office, "Thank God, Heligoland is quiet."

Faced with the possibility of a second disruption of the empire, British statesmen began to examine the imperial system. It was found to be outworn and inefficient. The conditions which brought it into being had disappeared or were disappearing, and the system itself could be called one only by courtesy. Reason and self-interest pointed toward the shedding of the worn garment. The reforms of the preceding decade had habituated both rulers and ruled to changes. The means and methods used in governing colonies were undergoing basic changes; a few more might bring beneficial results. British statesmen were growing weary of colonial contests, doubting the value of the overseas possessions; and by reason of their weariness and pessimism they were willing to give up old convictions. Only a small band of colonial reformers led by Wakefield had real faith in the future of the overseas empire. They favored colonization and imperial expansion; they dreamed of making Britain a mother of nations. Though unrelenting in their assaults upon government from Downing Street, they lacked a clear vision of the future relationship between Britain and the settlements overseas except that it should be based on freedom. If the imperial relationship were placed on this foundation the reformers felt certain that the colonies of their own free choice would glory in the name of Britain, cluster around her in peace and war. Thus in an atmosphere of mingled pessimism and optimism the old order vanished.

CHAPTER 4

BRITISH NORTH AMERICA, *1815–1837*

ATHWART the main highway to British North America lies the island of Newfoundland. More than three centuries had passed since English seamen made landfall there and began to fish in its waters. Wealth had been garnered on the Grand Banks as well as along the shores of Newfoundland and Labrador; the fisheries were important too as a training school for seamen in an age when Britain strove for maritime supremacy. The riches of the sea made Newfoundland valuable; but though it was labeled "England's oldest colony," the interior was unexplored and permanent settlements were discouraged until the nineteenth century. Fishing fleets from England's west country left for the island in the spring and returned in the autumn. To the average Englishman, Newfoundland was a land "of codfish and dogs, of fogs and bogs."

In the early days of exploitation of the fisheries of Newfoundland merchants in towns of southwestern England secured control of this industry; they opposed colonization of the island and harried the colonists. Nevertheless, by the end of the eighteenth century the resident population outnumbered the seasonal. The Napoleonic war brought prosperity to the island and stimulated emigration thither. The older colonists had come chiefly from Dorset, Devon, and Cornwall, but most of the later arrivals were

Irish. In 1814 about 7000 new settlers are said to have landed in Newfoundland; the population, estimated at 20,000 in 1804, had passed the 50,000 mark twenty years later. By 1815 St. John's, then as now the chief urban center, was no longer a mere fishing village.

In 1809 Labrador was transferred to Newfoundland for governmental purposes, but here too only the coast was known, no real settlement existed, and the boundaries were not defined until 1927. Off Newfoundland fishing was carried on both inshore and on the banks. The cod was the main object of pursuit, although by the beginning of the period seal and salmon added materially to the total value of the catch. War prices boosted the value of the export of Newfoundland above two million pounds in 1814. But with peace the market collapsed, and in succeeding years famine stalked the land. The fishermen had not made provision during the fat years for the lean that followed, a failure due in part perhaps to the proverbial improvidence of their class, but also explainable by the fact that the Newfoundland fishermen whether resident or seasonal were kept in a state of peonage by the merchants who furnished all the supplies and took the catch.

When France ceded her claims to Newfoundland by the Treaty of Utrecht in 1713, she retained two small islands and the right to fish and utilize land along sections of the coast later known as the "treaty shore." This right plagued Newfoundland, Britain, and France until 1904. During the period of the old empire, Newfoundland had been an outpost of New England, and American claims to fish there were recognized after 1783 and confirmed by an agreement of 1818. Thus arose another set of rights of foreigners in the waters of the island that was the seed of later irritating disputes.

Visiting governors provided Newfoundland with the framework of a government, and now and then the English parliament passed laws and regulations for the island, but they were inadequate for the needs of the heterogeneous population, which contained a large lawless element. English statesmen as a rule gave little thought to its problems; the west country merchants had things pretty much their own way especially since no governor spent a winter in the island until 1817. Neglect is written large on the pages of the early history of "England's oldest colony."

Crossing Cabot Strait one sights the Maritime Provinces. In

1815 these comprised four separate colonies: Nova Scotia, New Brunswick, Cape Breton, and Prince Edward Island. Outwardly the Maritimes except Prince Edward Island bear much resemblance to Newfoundland – a rockbound, deeply indented coast behind which forests abound. As in Newfoundland, a large percentage of the population was dependent on the sea for its livelihood, but unlike the island, the Maritimes were early considered suitable for permanent colonization. In this region James I had sold baronetcies; the old French settlements in Acadia have been immortalized in poetry and legend. To Halifax in 1749 were sent discharged veterans of the British army. Expatriated Scottish Highlanders founded homes and

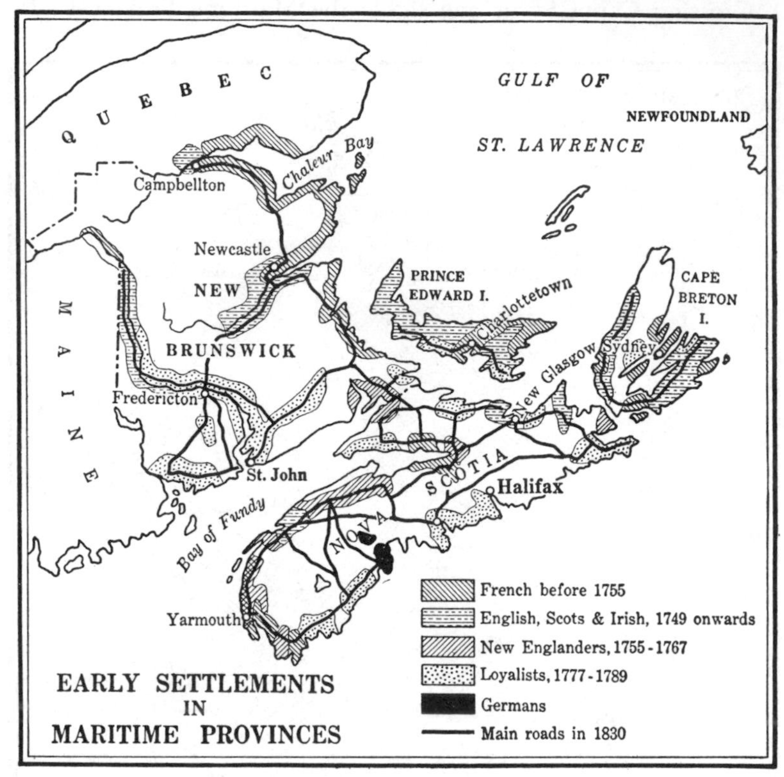

gave a meaning to the name Nova Scotia. Some Germans and a considerable number of immigrants from New England had established themselves in the Maritimes before the American Revolution, and the backwash of this upheaval brought about 30,000 United Empire Loyalists into Nova Scotia. A few of these later went to Upper Canada, but the bulk remained and left permanent marks on the social, economic, and political life of Nova Scotia and New Brunswick.

The wars with France and the United States enhanced the prosperity and importance of the Maritimes. The products of the sea, the fields, and the forests commanded fabulous prices. The sea dogs of Nova Scotia were employed profitably both in the fisheries and aboard privateers, and the export of timber and local shipbuilding offered work to many and profit for not a few. Halifax was an important base for the British navy in American waters. And at the turn of the century Prince Edward, Duke of Kent, the father of Queen Victoria, lent distinction to the social life of this port.

Though the population of the Maritime Provinces was small (in 1815 it fell short of 150,000) these colonies formed in many respects a striking contrast to Newfoundland. The early immigrants in Nova Scotia, the Loyalists in particular, represented a better class of people than those who had first settled in Newfoundland. Except for Cape Breton the Maritimes had elective assemblies and other institutions characteristic of a permanent and advanced state of society. Their resources were more varied and they had attained a degree of economic self-sufficiency unknown on the eastern shore of Cabot Strait.

Forests and mountains formed a barrier between New Brunswick and Lower Canada. Here the French settlements of the seventeenth century had spread from the cities of Quebec and Montreal first along the north and then along the south bank of the St. Lawrence. Though held by Britain for half a century, the province in its basic character in 1815 differed but slightly from the French regime. True, the urban centers contained a considerable trading and commercial element almost exclusively British, and English-speaking farmers had taken possession of the soil in the Eastern Townships of the province; nevertheless Lower Canada as a whole was French in speech and race, and the population already revealed many of the traits that have set it apart as a French-Canadian nationality. The British government had made no consistent attempt to Anglicize the colony. The civil law, the church, and the system of landholding remained, broadly speaking, as of old. However, in the sphere of politics an important innovation had been made with the establishment of representative institutions in Lower Canada by the Constitutional Act of 1791. The act erected

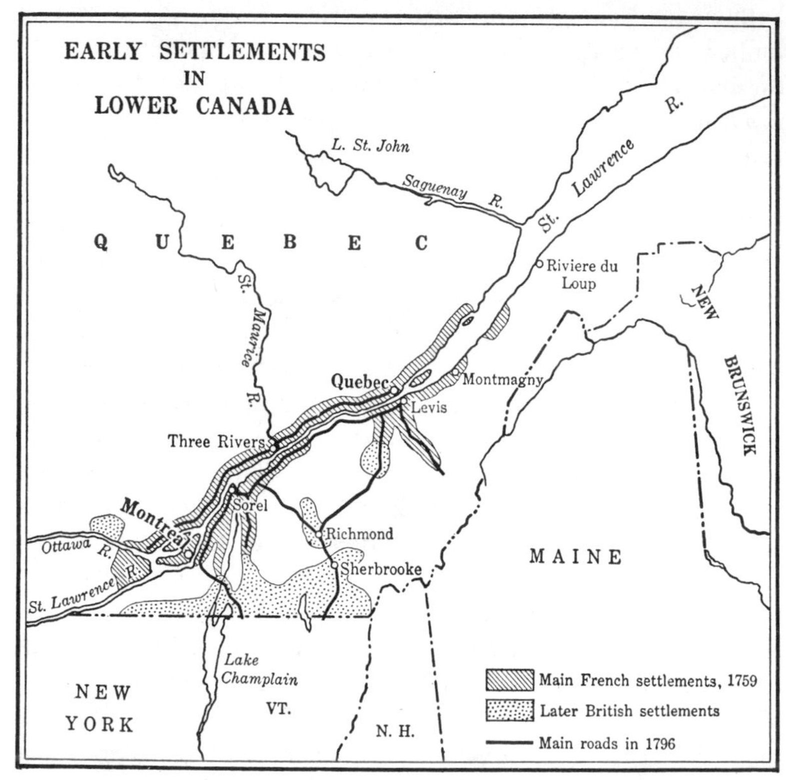

a bicameral legislature, with the upper house, the legislative council, nominated by the governor, while the lower, the assembly, was elected. The franchise was liberal. Though this political system was new to them, the French-Canadians proved apt pupils, and by 1815 they used English political weapons expertly in defending their rights and interests and in attempting to obtain complete control over the local government.

Lower Canada had few attractions for immigrants from the United States or Europe. The church, the language, and the semi-feudal system of landholding singly or combined acted as deterrents on prospective settlers from the British Isles. But the remarkable fecundity of the French-Canadians, which challenged the alleged record of the children of Israel in the land of Goshen, had produced a great increase from natural sources. Largely for this reason a population estimated at between sixty and seventy thousand when Britain captured the province had grown to about 335,000 in 1814.

The recent wars with France had proved a boon to Lower Canada. Interrupting but slightly the illicit trade with the United States, the conflict produced a brisk demand for Canadian produce for the British troops in the Canadas as well as for Britain; but the large amount of money that flowed to Lower Canada in the years immediately preceding 1815 had not materially disturbed the habits and mode of life of the country folk. The French-Canadians continued to live the simple life, giving not affluence but stability to the province. Quebec was the center of a large lumber trade, and Montreal, at the head of the ocean navigation of the St. Lawrence and at the point where that river is joined by the Ottawa, was the distributing center for Upper Canada and for the fur trade of the far west.

Upper Canada, which in 1791 became a separate colony, had been founded by Loyalists from the United States who would rather desert their old colonial homesteads than change their political allegiance. The imperial government had striven as effectively as possible under the circumstances to aid the Loyalists during the early years of the settlement and had provided generous land grants for them and their children; for a score of years this generosity attracted Scottish Highlanders and non-Loyalist Americans as well. But the War of 1812 checked the growth of Upper Canada, drove out many of the lately arrived Americans, and for a second time tested the devotion and endurance of the Loyalists. Excepting an old French settlement along the Detroit River, Upper Canada in 1815 was thoroughly British and undivided in its attachment to the empire. It was a frontier rural community. At the lower end of Lake Ontario, Kingston, its largest city, had a population of about 3500; its capital, York, later Toronto, near the upper end

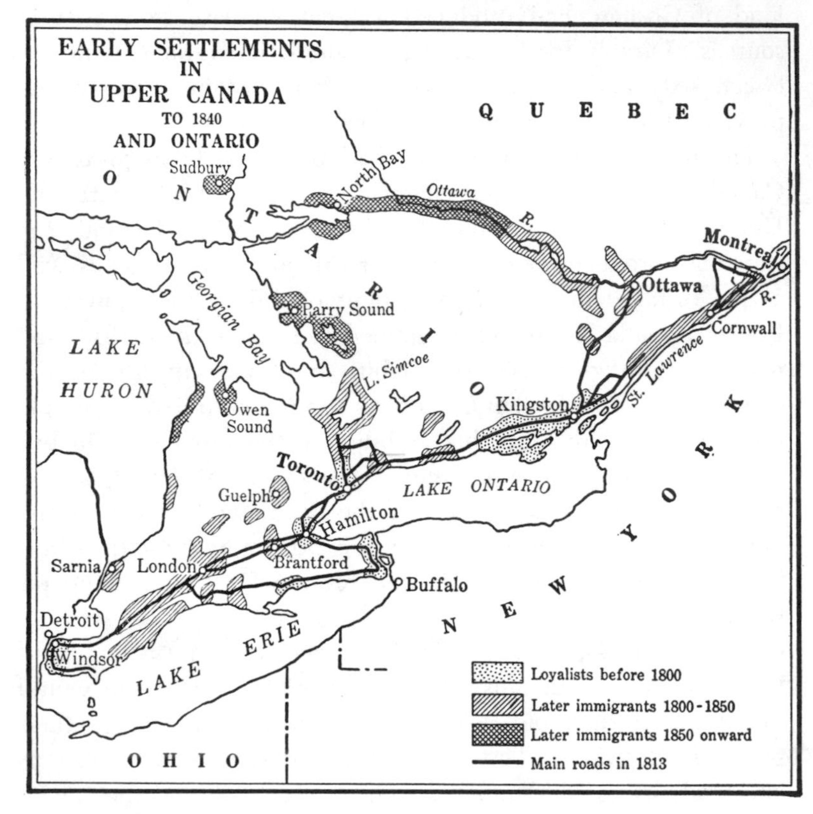

was hardly more than a village in the woods. The province lacked capital and manufacturing industries, while rapids and falls cut off the main portion of it from direct contact with the sea. But the population, though hardly 100,000 strong, was energetic, resourceful, and inured to the hardships of the frontier; the province had a vast amount of unoccupied land, and it soon attracted the greater share of the British emigrants who wished to stay within the empire.

North and west of Lake Superior lay the extensive tract to which the Hudson's Bay Company claimed title by virtue of the charter of 1670. Officers and employees of this company and of its Canadian rival, the North West Company, had explored the region northward to the Arctic Ocean and westward to the Pacific, but most of the knowledge of the land thus obtained was purposely kept from the outside world lest interlopers destroy the fur trade. The natural outlet of the greater part of this region was by way of Hudson Bay, although the North West Company, with headquarters at Montreal, used the Ottawa River and the upper lakes. Late in the eighteenth century the discovery of the Columbia River revealed the possibility of a western outlet for the fur trade. The Hudson's Bay Company strove to gain control of this channel and soon found itself faced with a formidable opposition from the United States.

A treaty of 1818 between Great Britain and the United States fixed the boundary of British North America from the Lake of the Woods to the Rocky Mountains at the 49th parallel. West of the mountains the northern limits of the British claims were determined by the Anglo-Russian convention of 1825 at 54° 40′, but the southern remained a bone of contention between Britain and the United States until 1846. At the eastern extremity of British North America a much smaller region along the New Brunswick-Maine boundary caused disputes between the two powers, finally ended by the Webster-Ashburton Treaty of 1842. Another question fraught with dangerous possibilities – that of armaments on the Great Lakes – was happily solved by a convention of 1817, whereby Britain and the United States agreed not to maintain more than four vessels each on the lakes, including Lake Champlain; these vessels were limited to 100 tons burden each, with an armament of one 18-pound cannon.

The easternmost and the westernmost of the British possessions in North America represented a more imperfectly developed economic organization and progressed more slowly than did the middle colonies. Newfoundland depended on fish, and Rupert's Land on fur. In both regions many of the necessities of life were brought in from the outside; they lagged behind the Canadas and the Maritimes, and neither attracted emigrants from the British Isles. In Newfoundland the economic depression of the post-war era reached its lowest depth in the winter 1817–1818. "Famine, frost, and fire combined, like three avenging furies to scourge the unfortunate island." Outbreaks on the part of the lawless elements in the population further endangered the existence of the settlement. The storm was weathered, however; Newfoundland gradually became adjusted to peace conditions, and slowly steps were taken to reduce the dependence of the inhabitants upon the fisheries. The imperial government had earlier conceded to the settlers the right to acquire land titles; to Dr. William Carson belongs the honor of being a pioneer in farming, and agriculture received strong support from Sir Thomas Cochrane, governor, 1825–1834. Roads were built, country houses sprang up, and by degrees the colony assumed the aspect of a well-ordered society. The establishment of the Bank of North America at St. John's in 1836 may, indeed, be taken as proof that the oldest colony of England had at last outgrown its swaddling clothes.

In 1815 the Hudson's Bay Company was engaged in cutthroat competition with its rival, the North West Company. The system of the Nor'Westers, whereby the servants of the company shared in the profit, encouraged enterprise and for a while the older concern had its back to the wall. But the advantage possessed by the Hudson's Bay Company in controlling the natural outlet for the fur trade of the northwest, Hudson Bay, told heavily in its favor, and in 1821 the ruinous competition ended with the fusion of the two companies. Rejuvenated, the Hudson's Bay Company now entered a period of great activity. In 1820 George (later Sir George) Simpson became governor of the company in America, and under his guidance it challenged Russian and American competitors.

The imperial government gave the company lease to the territory claimed by Britain west of the Rockies; and agreements with the Russians, then masters of Alaska, provided new outlets for trade in the north, while in the south, the region of the Columbia River, the activities of its energetic servants, James Douglas and Dr. MacLoughlin, made the Hudson's Bay Company the real contender with the United States for the control of Oregon.

A settlement at Red River founded in 1812 by Lord Selkirk, then majority stockholder in the Hudson's Bay Company, experienced more than the usual share of hardships meted out to frontier communities. Twice, in 1814 and again in 1816, the Nor'Westers compelled the settlers to flee. With the cessation of attacks from human enemies, nature began a series of onslaughts in the form of locusts, frosts, and floods. Seed grain and breed animals had to be brought in either from Europe or from the nearest settlements in the United States, which in the early days meant the Illinois country and later Prairie du Chien in the present state of Wisconsin. Scores of settlers became discouraged, drifted across the border, or joined the ranks of servants of the Hudson's Bay Company. No manufactures could thrive in the infant community; and as a source of supplies for the Hudson's Bay Company the colony competed with the buffalo, still plentiful, which furnished pemmican, a food product admirably suited for the needs of roving trappers and traders. Nevertheless, the dour Scotsmen who formed the backbone of the Selkirk colony clung to the farms wrested from the wilderness, and by 1837 the settlement had become firmly and permanently established.

Though the Maritimes and the Canadas were far ahead of Newfoundland and Rupert's Land in social, economic, and political development, they were in 1815 still frontier communities. All had an abundance of untilled land and unexploited forest and mineral resources. They lacked capital and had few industries other than those of the household. Neither want nor wealth could be said to exist. Judged by English standards social life was crude, but on the whole the society was healthy and vigorous. And though the progress of the British North American colonies in the period 1815–1837 failed to keep abreast of that of adjoining sections of the United States, the advance when compared with that of other British colonies or Europe was rapid. In the first two decades after the peace the total population of the Maritimes and the Canadas rose from about 600,000 to nearly 1,500,000. The rate of increase was smallest in Prince Edward Island and largest in Upper Canada. The reasons for this become clear when it is remembered that a considerable share of the growth in the population is attributable to immigration and that a majority of the newcomers settled on the land. Absentee landlordism kept people from settling in Prince Edward Island, whereas Upper Canada had millions of acres of fertile soil that might be secured in free and common socage.

In the Maritime Provinces the settlements spread slowly inland from the shores of bays and inlets and along the rivers such as the St. John and St. Croix in New Brunswick. But, except in Prince Edward Island, the soil in the Maritimes could not compare in fertility with that of Upper Canada. Consequently Nova Scotia and New Brunswick offered poor prospects for British immigrants and the increase in the population was due largely to the growth of towns.

Immigrants flocked to Upper Canada where the population practically quadrupled between 1815 and 1837. The progress of land settlement and improvement in the means of communication were the outstanding events in the economic history of the colony. The alienation of the public domain went on so rapidly that at the time of Lord Durham's Report, 1839, out of 17,653,544 acres only 1,147,019 remained in the hands of the crown. Most of the land granted by the crown to the church, to land companies, and to private individuals had not yet been occupied. By the Constitutional Act of 1791 the protestant church in the Canadas was to have an amount of land equal to one-seventh of the land alienated by the crown. This grant, known as the Clergy Reserves, became a source of conflict between the protestant churches in Upper Canada. Official practice, especially in the years 1830–1836 while Sir John Colborne was lieutenant-governor of the province, generally favored the claims of the Anglican church to the Clergy Reserves. The progress of this church was aided thereby, but since the land usually was held for higher prices the grant retarded settlement and the building of schools and roads.

Different both in intent and in results were the grants made to the land companies. The oldest of these, the Canada Land Company organized in 1824, purchased about 2,480,000 acres in Upper Canada from the government at a low price on condition that the company should build roads and otherwise improve the land and bring in settlers. In Lower Canada the British American Land Company secured about 800,000 acres on similar terms. Among the largest individual grantees was Colonel Thomas Talbot, who is said to have had 518,000 acres placed at his disposal on condition that settlers were brought out. The most ambitious colonizing venture undertaken directly by the imperial government was that of 1823–1825 when about 2500 Irish were settled in the Peterborough district of Upper Canada. Millions of acres were distributed in large and small blocks to settlers and speculators and as a reward for military or political services. The largest gift in the aggregate made without restriction or condition was that of 3,200,000 acres to the United Empire Loyalists and their children. The early years of the nineteenth century, in particular, witnessed many generous land grants. But as time passed, the haphazard and unrestricted alienation of land had to be abandoned; and in 1831, under the influence of the agitation set afoot by Wakefield, the imperial government decided to adopt a uniform system of land sales applicable to all of British North America.

The methods used in alienating crown lands, especially in Upper Canada, were sharply criticized by the colonial reformers.

These methods formed part and parcel of the old colonial system, tainted as it was with favoritism and privilege. On the other hand, it may be well to bear in mind that companies like the Canada Land Company and individuals of the type of Colonel Talbot devoted organizing talents, money, and time to and achieved a fair amount of success in settling Upper Canada; and that neither they nor most of the other companies and individuals who secured Canadian land reaped pecuniary profits worthy of mention.

Of industries other than farming and fishing the British North American colonies could boast but few. The abundance of timber stimulated shipbuilding in the Maritime Provinces and Lower Canada. Quebec, Saint John, Yarmouth, Pictou, and Lunenburg were important centers for this industry. But the timber used could apparently not compare in quality with that of England and the Baltic, and the colonial shipbuilders and owners found to their chagrin that Lloyds persisted in giving their vessels a lower insurance rating than that accorded ships of European origin. Still, Canadians point with pride to the fact that the *Royal William*, one of the first vessels to cross the Atlantic under steam (1833), was built in Quebec, and that Samuel Cunard, founder of the famous steamship line that bears his name, was a native of Halifax, where he began his shipping career.

Sawmills and flour and grist mills were found in all the colonies. Coal was mined in Cape Breton and Nova Scotia. There were iron works at Three Rivers in Lower Canada, and small foundries had been established in sundry other places. But generally speaking, the colonies were still undeveloped; the principal exports were the produce of the farms, the forests, and the fisheries. Particularly in the Canadas, the farms as a rule formed self-sufficient economic units. A rude plenty characterized the economic life in most of the settlements. Furthermore, lack of population, of capital, and of means of communication hampered them all, especially Upper Canada. Fortunately ignorance of frontier conditions caused Englishmen who desired to become squires or who expected to reap profit from a rise in land values to pour money into the colony. Similar in effect were the expenditures made by the imperial government on colonial garrisons and public works. But though considerable sums of money were thus brought in, the shortage of currency and financial insecurity greatly hindered the progress of Upper Canada.

This province also suffered by being isolated from the rest of the world for nearly half the year. The War of 1812 had aroused the imperial government to a realization of the need for roads and canals for military defense. Reinforced by the ever-present economic demand for better means of communication, the military arguments for their improvement became unanswerable. Aided in part by the home government, the colonial authorities and private local enterprise soon after 1815 took up the task of linking the Lower St. Lawrence with the Great Lakes. The Lachine and Cornwall Canals made navigation possible on the Upper St. Lawrence; the Rideau Canal provided a safe water route from Lake Ontario to Montreal; and the Welland Canal connected Lakes Ontario and Erie. By the end of the thirties a navigable route had been provided from the sea to the interior of British North America.

Judged by present-day standards of social and economic well-being, British North America was new, young, and perhaps a bit raw. The seigneurs of Lower Canada had failed to supply that province with an aristocracy, and eighteenth-century efforts to build up a stratified society in Upper Canada had proved futile. Travelers from England complained loudly of the uppishness of Canadian laborers and servants, a characteristic which was attributed to American influence. The struggle for existence overshadowed all other interests. Economically the frontiers offered new opportunities for the settlers; culturally a leveling-down process probably caused loss of spiritual values.

Still, the pioneers of British North America appreciated that man "liveth not by bread alone." It was a part of the equalitarian philosophy prevalent on the frontier that educational opportunities should be the same for all. The application of this principle was especially noticeable in the origin of the common school system in Upper Canada, although there as well as in the other colonies religious influence and more particularly religious animosities played an important role in the early development of education. At the opening of the nineteenth century King's College, Nova Scotia, and the College of New Brunswick bore testimony to the colonists' zeal for higher education. By acts of 1811 and 1816, Nova Scotia and New Brunswick founded a free school system, and in 1825 Prince Edward Island followed their example. In Lower Canada the old educational system suffered a decline following the British occupation and especially after the dissolution of the Society of Jesus and the sequestration of its estates. The Anglican church tried with small success to build up its own educational machinery for the whole province, and the Royal Institution founded under its aegis in 1818 materially aided the cause of education. In 1824 steps were taken for the founding of schools in each parish of Lower Canada under the control of the Catholic clergy, and in the Eastern Townships elementary schools were supplemented by secondary institutions at Stonstead and Charleston. The rivalry between Anglicans and Methodists in Upper Canada aided the establishment of higher institutions of learning. Dr. Strachan, leader of the Anglicans, founded schools at Kingston, Cornwall, and York; and Dr. Egerton Ryerson, head of the Methodists, established an academy at Coburg. The Presbyterians were not far behind. In 1832 they initiated the movement which resulted in the founding of Queen's University, Kingston. The Upper Canada's common school act of 1816 paved the way for the establishment of free and secular schools. Thus from Cabot Strait to the shores of Lake Huron the foundation had been laid for state-aided, democratic educational systems. Moreover, in the years of turmoil and strife from 1815 to 1837 the struggling communities of British North America not only tried to provide educational opportunities for its youth in the lower branches of learning and spent thereupon more money annually than the government of Britain did for this purpose, but they also took steps to establish such renowned institutions of higher learning as Dalhousie, McGill, Queens, and the University of Toronto.

Few political ties except their common dependence on the mother country bound the North American colonies to each other. True, the governor of Lower Canada held the title governor general of British North America, but this title gave him no authority in another colony when not actually present there. Nevertheless, these colonies had much in common. They were all nurtured by English political ideas and traditions; their institutions, except those of the French in Lower Canada, were modeled after British patterns; and in the early nineteenth century they all showed the same symptoms of restiveness under the paternalistic control of the imperial government. But the reins were held tightly while the old Tories kept control at home and Lord Bathurst was at the colonial office. Upon his retirement in 1827, more heed was paid to complaints from overseas. The short administration of William Huskisson augured well; Lord Goderich, 1830–1833, made important changes; and the well-meaning but singularly ineffective Lord Glenelg, 1835–1839, granted sweeping concessions. All this failed to satisfy the Canadians. Rebellions broke out, and the sins of predecessors and colleagues were heaped on the head of Glenelg. Driven from office, he has fared badly at the hands of historians.

In this period political issues were hotly debated in all the colonies of British North America. Excepting Cape Breton, which was reunited with Nova Scotia in 1820, Newfoundland was the only dependency under direct control of the imperial government in North America that in 1815 had no elective assembly. This was remedied by an act of 1832. However, the new legislature, with an elected but practically impotent second chamber, was fashioned on a model then deemed out of date east of Cabot Strait. The assemblies of the other colonies could claim a respectable age. The oldest, that of Nova Scotia, dated from 1758; and the youngest, those in the Canadas, from 1792. They were all elected on a liberal franchise, and each aspired to be a replica of the British house of commons. Hence all chafed under the checks imposed by legislative and executive councils, by governors who both ruled and reigned, and by the all-powerful home government. After 1815 the North American assemblies began to clamor for the substance of power. Following English precedent, they demanded control over the purse, limitation of the authority of the executive and the judiciary, and a diminution of the power exercised by the imperial government over local affairs in the colonies. Economic, racial, and religious differences and grievances gave vitality to the demands for colonial autonomy. As the century advanced the issues involved became more clearly defined; and by 1837 a constructive program, namely, that of responsible government, was assuming definite shape in the minds of colonial reformers on both sides of the Atlantic. This program aimed at making the executive branch of the government responsible to the elective assembly. It was sufficiently concrete to be understood in its broad outlines and sufficiently in harmony with English practice to gain support in the colonies.

In the Maritime Provinces no distinction existed in 1815 between the executive and the legislative councils. To separate the two became one of the first objects of the reform parties in the assemblies. After a stubborn fight, the imperial government granted this concession to Nova Scotia and New Brunswick in 1832 and to Prince Edward Island seven years later. But the results proved disappointing. As in the Canadas, the leading officials continued to be members of both councils; and since the unofficial legislative councilors were appointed for life and chosen because of their wealth, social position, and conservative views they were usually unresponsive to the sentiments that decided elections to the assemblies. Among the Maritime colonies, Prince Edward Island, the smallest, was also the least advanced politically and economically. Here Lieutenant-governor Charles Douglas Smith went so far in emulating Charles I as to call only four assemblies from 1813 to 1824; he dismissed each discourteously, and governed without any for four years, 1820–1824. Vainly the assembly of Prince Edward Island tried to force the absentee proprietors to pay a fair share of the cost of the government. Attempts to make it possible for the tenants to secure title to the land also failed. The popular party won no substantial victory in the period under discussion. Nor was much gained even in Nova Scotia until 1836 when Joseph Howe was elected to the assembly. Under his leadership the reform party ultimately secured control of the government. In New Brunswick a strong oligarchy, composed mainly of United Empire Loyalists, their descendants, and members of the Church of England, opposed the politically more radical and the dissenting groups. Nevertheless, led by L. A. Wilmot the reformers made progress. Religious equality was granted; the crown revenues were handed over to the legislature in return for a civil list; and the executive council was enlarged to include representatives of various interests in the colony.

Though the constitutional conflicts in the Maritimes, 1815–1837, were not without significance, they paled in comparison with the contests raging in the Canadas. The French of Lower Canada had kept their church, their language, and many of their old laws and institutions. Still they had grievances. The British minority, represented chiefly by officials and the commercial interests in Quebec and Montreal, was loath to concede equality to the French. A strong desire existed to treat them as a conquered and therefore inferior people. And though the position of the Roman Catholic Church was strong, privileges such as the control over education were lost when Britain conquered Canada. Attempts were made to entrench the Anglican church in both ecclesiastical and educational affairs, with the result that the Roman Catholic Church in Lower Canada became closely identified with the struggle for preserving the French-Canadian character of the colony.

In 1839 Lord Durham reported that in Canada "two nations were warring in the bosom of a single state." This was on the whole a fairly accurate summing up of the political situation in Lower Canada, 1815–1837. A few English-speaking reformers such as John Neilson of Quebec and some of the more recently arrived immigrants from the British Isles joined the French Canadians in opposition to the ruling clique, but their number was small. By and large the English element in the province was satisfied with the existing system while the French demanded its overthrow. The Constitutional Act of 1791 provided for an elective lower house, the assembly, and a nominated first chamber, the legislative council. Soon the French secured absolute control over the former while the English continued to dominate the latter. Moreover, the governor's executive council as well as the judiciary remained English, and behind them loomed the even more formidable power of the imperial government. Thus arose the interesting situation that French-Canadians battled against the English for political rights won by Englishmen in the great conflicts of the seventeenth century, and English governors were attacked by French-Canadians for violating English political principles.

In the conflicts which disturbed Lower Canada and caused the imperial government much embarrassment the object of the French-Canadian leaders was control of the government of the province by means of the supremacy of the assembly. Among the grievances were pluralism and absenteeism in the holding of offices, the presence of judges in the legislative council, and the unrepresentative character of that body; but the greatest conflict centered around the control of the purse. Following English precedent, the assembly demanded complete power over expenditures, an issue complicated by the fact that in Lower Canada the crown had revenues from land and other sources independently of legislative appropriations. While insufficient to meet all the expenses of government, these revenues yielded about one-third of the necessary amount; and since the imperial government defrayed the cost of defense the governor might in a pinch draw upon the military chest. The fixed crown revenues, however, were raised in the province and the assembly could therefore justifiably claim the right to decide how this money should be spent. Such a demand was made by the assembly in 1810. The governor refused to listen; but scolding speeches, prorogations, and dissolutions failed to shake the determination of the lower house. Suspended during the war, 1812–1815, the contest flared up afterward and the radical party now found a bold and intrepid if not always wise leader in Louis Joseph Papineau. Elected to the assembly in 1812, he was chosen speaker in 1815 and soon acquired complete mastery over that body as well as over a strong majority of the voters of Lower Canada.

For some years the struggle was kept well within the flexible boundaries of political propriety. Governors Prevost and Sherbrooke, 1812–1818, were conciliatory and enjoyed personal popularity. Animosities softened, but the conflict over who controlled the purse proved irrepressible. In 1818 Sherbrooke placed before the assembly a complete statement of the financial situation, and the money needed above the fixed revenue was voted for one year. In 1819 the assembly examined all income from whatever source derived and proceeded to specify in detail how the money should be spent. The refusal of the legislative council to concur in the appropriations widened the issue of who controlled the purse; it now embraced the question of the relative position and power of the two houses of the legislature. The upper house was identified with the ruling English clique which in the political conflict invoked the magic formula of patriotism, loyalty to king and country; the assembly became the rampart behind which French-Canadians fought for the protection of church, language, and ancient institutions.

During the governorship of Lord Dalhousie, 1820–1828, the strife grew intense. Influenced by Canadian commercial interests, the imperial government in 1822 produced a bill for the union of the Canadas, the elimination of French as a parliamentary language, and the establishment of secular control over the Roman Catholic Church in Canada. Great was the outcry in Lower Canada against this bill; it was withdrawn, but the mischief wrought could not be eradicated. Defense of church and language united the French-Canadians into a solid political phalanx. In vain Dalhousie sought an agreement with the assembly whereby appropriations covering the salaries of permanent officials could be guaranteed for more than one year; this sum was known as the civil list. For years the civil list was a principal issue in the strife. Some ground was lost by the governor in 1825 when during his absence in England the lieutenant-governor, Sir Francis Burton, permitted the assembly to examine all sources of provincial revenue. Thus a precedent was established. As in 1819 the assembly itemized expenditures, and again the legislative council withheld assent. The assembly then proceeded to direct by means of resolutions the way in which the provincial revenue should be spent; it expected the governor to obey its order. He refused, and continued to defray the cost of civil administration and the judiciary from crown revenues, denying the assembly any control over these. Personal animosity further embittered relations between Dalhousie and Papineau.

The year 1828 brought hope of a solution of the Canadian question. Dalhousie was transferred to India and Huskisson had replaced Bathurst at the colonial office. In England Lower Canadian problems were studied by a committee of the house of commons which recommended that judges except the chief justice should not serve on the legislative council and that this body should have a majority of non-officials. The committee also expressed the opinion "that the real interests of the province would be best promoted by placing the receipt and expenditure of the whole public revenue under the superintendence and control of the house of assembly." The report heartened Papineau and his followers, but Huskisson left the colonial office and nothing was done to conciliate the Canadians.

In the early thirties their hope rose anew. The French revolution of 1830 and the fall of the Tories in England presaged reforms. The judges were excluded from the legislative council, and the imperial government offered to turn crown revenues over to the assembly in return for a fixed appropriation of about £19,500 to cover the cost of the judiciary. Papineau accepted the concessions but not the conditions attached to them. Instead of meeting the imperial government halfway, the French-Canadians outlined new demands including an elective legislative council and heaped unmeasured abuse upon the governor, Lord Aylmer. John Neilson and the handful of other reformers with British antecedents now parted company with Papineau. Freed from their restraining influence, he became more violent. The program of his party was outlined in the ninety-two resolutions of 1834, which bestowed praise upon the government of the United States, and restated legitimate grievances such as pluralism in officeholding. Their constructive program included demands for an elective legislative council and control over the executive.

The opponents of Papineau had, however, not remained inactive; and a new colonial secretary, Lord Stanley, was more willing to listen to them than to Papineau. A house of commons committee in 1834 offered no acceptable plan. The recall of Aylmer and the sending out of a special commission to study the Canadian question failed to mend matters. Lord Glenelg, who became colonial secretary in 1835, was anxious to placate but irresolute in his handling of the colonists; moreover, he lacked influence in the cabinet. The chief issues were now the fixed civil list, which Papineau refused to grant, and the demand for an elective legislative council. In England the temper hardened. Canadian proposals to cut off supplies were met by ten resolutions introduced in the house of commons by Lord John Russell on March 6, 1837, which aimed at strengthening the hands of the governor of Lower Canada and contained a flat refusal of the request for an elective legislative council and other Canadian demands, although offering to the assembly control of the revenues in return for a guarantee of the salaries of judges and a fixed civil list. The house of commons concurred. Papineau and his party regarded the resolutions as a challenge. When the assembly, convened in August, 1837, refused to vote supplies, prorogation followed. Excitement grew. Agitators urged the people to rise. The Roman Catholic Church counseled peace and Papineau quailed before the storm. When fighting broke out late in 1837, he took no part in it and fled to the United States. The rebellion was a small affair confined in the main to isolated outbreaks in the neighborhood of Montreal, the bulk of the French-Canadians refused to rise, and British troops under the command of Sir John Colborne, a veteran of the Napoleonic wars, experienced little difficulty in quelling the disturbances. Constitutionally, the immediate effect was the suspension of the Constitutional Act of 1791 and the placing of the government of Lower Canada in the hands of the governor and a small council nominated by him.

While these events were occurring in Lower Canada, the political situation in Upper Canada yearly grew more tense, so that simultaneously with the uprising in the lower province disturbances broke out near Toronto. The seeds for these had been sown during many years of political conflict — a conflict which reveals both differences from and similarities to the struggle that went on below. No two nationalities joined issue in Upper Canada. The population remained overwhelmingly British. But there was a tendency to form political alliances between the recent arrivals from the British Isles and those from the United States in opposition to the United Empire Loyalists who claimed a monopoly of political, economic, and social influence and power. The leading members of the loyalist group, residing at or near Toronto (York until 1834), were dubbed "the family compact." They looked upon themselves as the bulwark of the British empire in America, the true defenders of everything English in church and state. During the greater part of this period this party was led by Dr. John Strachan, later appointed first Anglican bishop of Toronto, and Chief Justice John Beverly Robinson.

Attacks on the "extortion and oppression" by the ruling clique started early in the century, but the War of 1812 ended the political agitation. The war over, trouble broke out anew in 1818 when a Scotsman, Robert Gourlay, lately arrived in the colony, began to inquire into the general conditions in the province and the reasons for its slow progress. The authorities took alarm, had Gourlay arrested and deported, and some who had attended a convention called by him lost their land grants. These high-handed methods aroused opposition, and by 1821 the lines began to be clearly drawn between Tories and reformers. On the political side, the interest centered around efforts by the assembly to control the introduction of money bills and to check the power of the executive. Parliamentary leaders like Marshall Bidwell and the Baldwins, W. W. and Robert, had studied the constitutional development of England. In 1828 W. W. Baldwin suggested impeachment as a means for controlling executive action; and eight years later his son Robert asked for a cabinet "whose opinions and policy would be in harmony with the opinions and policies of the representatives of the people." The Baldwins hoped to effect the necessary changes by constitutional methods – through evolution. But the Tories nailed their flag to the mast and cried no surrender. And in Upper Canada the unyielding attitude of the "family compact" brought a popular leader, William Lyon Mackenzie, to the front. Expelled five times from the assembly he became a Canadian John Wilkes to the extent of being elected mayor of York; and he led the extremists that flew to arms in 1837.

In Upper Canada the reformers did not enjoy such a long

period with full control over the assembly as did Papineau and his followers in Lower Canada. At times the "family compact" had a majority in the Upper Canadian assembly, and the fact that the parties were so nearly balanced tempted the lieutenant-governors to take an active part in the politics of the province. The most hardy among the perennial political issues of Upper Canada was that of the Clergy Reserves. As already noted, the Constitutional Act of 1791 provided an endowment for the protestant church of the province equal to one-seventh of the land alienated by the crown; this land was claimed exclusively by the Anglicans. Herein they received support from the "family compact." On the other hand, the Presbyterians argued that since Canada was acquired after the union between England and Scotland and their church was established in Great Britain and indubitably protestant, they were entitled to a share in the Clergy Reserves. Moreover, in the thirties the Methodists had a strong following in Upper Canada; they too had a strong claim to be classed among protestants, and in Dr. Egerton Ryerson they had an astute and farsighted leader. From these religious groups, called dissenters by the Anglicans, the reform party drew much strength. Their demand for responsible government (the assembly should control the executive branch of the government) was therefore bracketed with plans for secularizing the Clergy Reserves. The "family compact," intrenched in the executive and legislative councils and actively aided by successive lieutenant-governors, rallied their supporters around the Anglican church and the existing institutions. Like many good men before him, Dr. Strachan had an elastic conscience in choosing means when defending the privileges of his church; his famous ecclesiastical chart of 1827 revealed gross carelessness in the handling of religious statistics. The figures were obviously padded; the Anglicans were not nearly so strong in Upper Canada as Strachan claimed. His falsifications were used with effect on the hustings, and when Lieutenant-governor Colborne proceeded in January, 1836, to endow Anglican rectories the temper of the opposition rose dangerously. Colborne's act was disapproved in Downing Street, but his successor, Sir Francis Bond Head, committed an even grosser blunder later in the year by throwing himself heart and soul into a campaign for securing a conservative majority in the assembly. He won a Pyrrhic victory. The radicals grew desperate and began to plot concerted action with their confreres in Lower Canada. Mackenzie appealed to arms, but men of weight like Robert Baldwin and Dr. Egerton Ryerson counseled peace. As a result the extremists formed a small minority and few heeded Mackenzie's summons in December, 1837. The rebellion in Upper Canada was only a skirmish. It collapsed immediately and Mackenzie fled across the border.

Judged by the actual fighting which took place, the Canadian rebellions of 1837 were trifling affairs. But the effects of a movement or action are not always proportionate to the amount of force employed. The ripples from the Canadas became waves that washed the shores of distant colonies. Indeed they assumed tidal proportions, and before they subsided they had swept away England's old imperial system.

CHAPTER 5

THE WEST INDIES

THE British colonies in the West Indies presented in 1815 strongly marked contrasts to those of North America. The climatic, geographical, and physiographical differences are, of course, obvious. But the social and economic differences were not less striking. The colonies of the north had been and were being peopled from Europe; the inhabitants of the West Indies were mainly Africans. Freemen fished, cleared the forests, and tilled the soil in the north; bondsmen toiled on the tropical plantations of the south. Attempts had been made to perpetuate European class distinctions on the banks of the St. Lawrence. They had failed. A semi-feudal society could not thrive there, and the economic and political development of Newfoundland, the Maritime Provinces, and the Canadas went steadily in the direction of greater freedom and larger opportunities for the poor and the oppressed. English freemen had originally settled on the islands in the Caribbean, but the economic system founded by them had long since been replaced by one based on large plantations and slave gangs. North America promised independence and an honest livelihood for the many; the West Indies had provided wealth for a few, misery and degradation for multitudes. Both regions were subject to English laws. In the north they were supplemented by custom and local legislation so as to offer chances for improvement — social, economic, and political — for those who lived by the sweat of their brow; in the south they were altered and interpreted for the purpose of perpetuating bondage and legalizing man's inhumanity to man. Growth in the north; in the south decay.

Passing from British North America to the West Indies one may call at the Bermudas, equidistant from Halifax and Nassau in the Bahamas. On the highway between England and her earliest colonies on the mainland of America, the Bermudas were settled about the same time as Virginia. Small in area and with limited resources, the islands have been, and are, chiefly important as a naval station.

Far different has been the history of the British West Indies. Considered valuable from the time of their discovery, Caribbean islands were long a bone of contention among the maritime nations of Europe. It was here that Elizabethan sailors won title to immortal fame. From the days of Hawkins and Drake to those of Rodney and Nelson, the West Indies loom large in the annals of the British navy. And not in those of the navy alone; for though little military glory was won there, more British soldiers were sacrificed in efforts to gain and keep these tropical islands than in the conquest and defense of what Britain holds and has held north of Florida. In the period of the old empire, the West Indies ranked first in importance among the overseas possessions. At the opening of the nineteenth century they accounted for about one-third of England's export and import trade; even in 1830 the West Indies took £2,800,000 worth of British exports as against £1,900,000 for British North America; and as late as 1840, Britain collected £4,500,000 in duty on West Indian sugar.

Using the term West Indies a bit loosely, we shall make it include all the British dependencies south of the Bermudas. Barbados, farthest east, boasts of having been under the British flag continuously since 1627. The history of the northernmost group, the Bahamas, is somewhat similar. Though occupied since 1646, the Bahamas were not really settled till after the American Revolution, when some two thousand Loyalists from the United States found homes there. Jamaica, captured from Spain in 1655, was abandoned by the majority of her Spanish settlers and colonized anew from Britain. Hence the island is often classed among her settlement colonies. St. Kitts, Nevis, Montserrat, Antigua, and

others of the smaller islands were settled by British immigrants in the seventeenth century, but changed masters several times before they became permanently British. These islands, with Dominica, are called the Leeward Islands. Britain's title to the Windward Islands of Grenada and St. Vincent dates from 1783. St. Lucia, included in the Windward group, Tobago, Trinidad, and the three colonies on the mainland of South America — Essequibo, Demerara, and Berbice, later united as British Guiana

— were part of the spoils of the war with France and Napoleon. British Honduras, though not formally annexed until 1862, had been considered British territory since the seventeenth century.

All these colonies, except some of the Bahamas, lie within the tropics, and in the days before the advent of modern medical knowledge the climate was reputed very unhealthy for Europeans. Save Barbados, the islands are mountainous, summits of a submerged mountain range. The majority of them are small in area; Jamaica, the largest, measures only 4207 square miles. Many are of volcanic origin, and the soil is generally fertile. Guiana is in the main a low-lying, swampy region along the rivers that give names to its principal divisions. The present area is 90,000 square miles. But in 1815 little more than the coastal fringe was occupied, and the boundaries were not defined until late in the nineteenth century.

The chief produce of the British West Indian colonies had been cacao, coffee, cotton, indigo, rum, sugar, and tobacco. Of these coffee, sugar, and its by-product, rum, continued to hold their own, with sugar the most important. The production of these articles had been stimulated by bounties and monopolies. The islands had become dependent on the mother country and the mainland colonies for timber, grain, fish, and manufactured goods, and upon Africa for cheap labor. The plantation method of farming has been aptly described as "soil mining." Where the amount of land was limited, as in most of the West Indian islands, exhaustion of the soil was one of the many factors which in 1815 threatened to destroy the economic foundation and importance of the British West Indies.

No reliable census figures exist for this period, but one million is probably a fairly accurate estimate for the total population of these colonies in 1815, with some loss between this date and 1838. Since the middle of the eighteenth century the whites had steadily declined in number, and with the cessation of the slave trade in 1808, the number of Negroes had decreased despite smuggling from neighboring French and Spanish colonies.

Deaths always exceeded births among the slaves. The population was strangely mixed. Except in Guiana, Honduras, and Trinidad, the aborigines had disappeared. The whites, forming less than 10 per cent of the total, were mainly British in origin, though Dutch, French, and Spanish dominated in the colonies most recently acquired. The mixed bloods, or colored, outnumbered the whites, and they in turn were heavily outnumbered by the blacks, of whom all but an insignificant percentage were slaves.

In the seventeenth century small landed proprietors dominated in the British West Indies. But the growth of sugar plantations and their concomitant, African slavery, drove out the small landowners. The islands ceased to attract British emigrants, and efforts by so-called "deficiency laws" to compel the planters to keep the number of whites at a certain ratio to the blacks failed. In the eighteenth century it became customary for planters to establish their permanent homes in England. Their children were educated there, and each succeeding generation increased the evils of absentee landlordism. In England the West Indian planters strove to equal the East Indian nabobs in display of wealth. Their plantations were looked upon as mere sources of revenue to be managed by attorneys and overseers, and thus the islands were drained of wealth and of the people who might have at least postponed economic ruin and political collapse. West Indian society became boorish and degraded. Concubinage was common among the whites; the blacks, being mere chattel, were discouraged from marrying. The majority of the colored were free, but had neither social nor political status. Occasionally a planter educated his illegitimate offspring, but most of them were turned adrift; the highest ambition of a colored girl was to be "kept" by a white man. Small as was the number of whites, it included in some of the islands several that had become mere "trash," even to the extent of doing menial labor for blacks.

The established church had failed to serve as a Christianizing and civilizing influence. In the early days it made few attempts to instruct the blacks in the tenets of Christianity; and when Moravian, Baptist, and Wesleyan missionaries began to work among the Africans, Anglican clergymen aided the planters in persecuting the newcomers and denying them religious toleration. In this field, however, the changes were for the better in the period under discussion. In 1824, two bishoprics, Barbados and Jamaica, were established, both endowed by the imperial government. The number of Anglican rectors and vicars was increased, and they began to realize that the gospel of Christ embraced other than the whites. Rather grudgingly religious toleration had to be conceded, though the Baptist missionaries continued to be suspected and occasionally mistreated. Education, most shamefully neglected during the two centuries of British rule in West Indian islands, received an impetus in 1830 with the completion of the buildings of Codrington College, Barbados, and the beginnings of the educational work of the Mico Charity in the West Indies. Through the efforts of Thomas Fowell Buxton, the abolitionist, the Mico Legacy, established to free Christian slaves in Algiers but now no longer needed for this purpose, was used to educate West Indian children irrespective of creed and color. The British government added £17,000 to the legacy of £120,000, and in 1835 the Mico training school opened in Kingston, Jamaica.

Honduras, St. Lucia, Trinidad, and Guiana were governed as crown colonies; the other dependencies had elective assemblies, some dating from the early part of the seventeenth century. The franchise was narrow, confined to the whites and not embracing even all of them. For instance, Jamaica with a white population of between twenty and thirty thousand does not seem to have had more than two thousand electors. The nominated legislative councils resembled those found in British North America at this time, and each of the dozen colonies had a governor appointed by the crown. The assemblies had striven, with a measure of success, to become replicas of the house of commons. Indeed, in some respects they had greater powers than that venerable body had. In the West Indies, private members could introduce money bills, and, except for small permanent grants to the crown from some of the colonies, the West Indian assemblies had complete control over revenues and expenditures. Supplies were voted for a year or even less – in Jamaica at times for but three months. Minute directions were given concerning the use of the appropriations, and to be doubly sure of controlling the expenditures the assemblies at times constituted themselves commissions for spending the money and auditing the accounts.

Being virtually closed corporations, the West Indian assemblies proved difficult to handle for the birds of passage who occupied the governors' chairs. The governors' veto power was more than matched by the assemblies' control over the purse. Like their counterpart in the old American colonies, the legislatures in the West Indies frequently browbeat the governors into yielding to local demands. Even the power of the imperial government to veto or disallow colonial laws might be nullified by the simple device of either not sending the laws home or by passing annual laws. Shifts to circumvent the assemblies were, of course, resorted to by the often sorely tried governors. Among these shifts that of paying officials by fees instead of fixed salaries was perhaps the most invidious. Therefrom arose gross abuses in the form of excessive remunerations and sinecures. Several of the most important positions in the West Indies were held by absentees who left the work to be done by poorly trained deputies.

West Indian legislatures had at an early date taken a firm stand against imperial interference in local affairs. In 1651 the Barbadian assembly defied the Commonwealth government; since that time claims to complete local autonomy had been voiced frequently. As against the crown, the assemblies could quote the decision of Judge Mansfield, 1774, in Chapman vs. Hall, which affirmed that the establishment of an elected legislature ended the power of the crown to interfere in colonial legislation. But the position of the imperial parliament was different. At no time had Parliament surrendered its claims to supremacy over all portions of the empire.

During the eighteenth century the exposed position of the British West Indies made the assemblies wary. Trafalgar and the defeat of Napoleon removed the foreign danger. These events coincided with the growth of the anti-slavery agitation in England. The abolition of the slave trade had been a serious blow to the West Indian planters, but from a constitutional point of view the act could be defended as a use of the imperial government's power to regulate commerce. The efforts to define the position and ameliorate the treatment of the slaves fell into a different category. From 1815 until the abolition of slavery in 1833 the West Indian legislatures, led by that of Jamaica, fought tenaciously for their right to control slavery as a purely local institution. In England this point of view was urged by the agents of the West Indian colonies, by West Indian planters and merchants, and by the West India Committee. But in parliament the Tories, although unwilling to interfere with the vested interests of the slave owners, could not agree to any curtailment of the legislative supremacy of the imperial parliament. And radicals such as Henry Brougham and Sir Samuel Romilly, who might in the abstract have sympathized with the colonial claims for local self-government, were bitterly hostile to the use which West Indian assemblies might make of this power. Thus it was that the humanitarians who advocated imperial supervision of the treatment of the slaves gained support from interests otherwise antagonistic.

Nor did the abolition of slavery put an end to the debate on the constitutional position of the West Indian colonies; on the contrary, it grew more intense. In impotent rage some of the West Indian assemblies, especially that of Jamaica, sought to nullify the effects of the Emancipation Act and to perpetuate the bondage of the blacks. But now they fell afoul not only of the anti-slavery forces in and outside of parliament, but of powerful permanent officials in the colonial office, notably Henry Taylor and James Stephen. Because of their positions, neither of these men had taken any part in the agitation for the abolition of slavery, but both had become thoroughly conversant with all moves and tricks used by the West Indian legislatures in thwarting the imperial government. Taylor had had general supervision of West Indian affairs since 1823, and Stephen, who became permanent undersecretary in 1836, read and reported on all colonial laws. Bills and acts intended to oppress the former slaves were promptly recommended for disallowance. In clear and pungent phrases, Taylor and Stephen called the attention of secretaries of state and of parliamentary undersecretaries to the contumacy of the West Indian assemblies, to their bad faith, and to their unfitness as legislative bodies. At a time when the British colonies in North America gained more and more local autonomy, those of the West Indies, partly on account of their own folly and intransigeance, lost ground rapidly. And in 1839, the year of Lord Durham's Report, the Melbourne government made a serious effort to terminate for five years the elected assembly of Jamaica. The debates on the suspension of the Jamaica constitution are interesting, not the least because among the opponents of the measure were men like Sir Robert Peel and Lord Stanley who usually resisted concessions to colonial demands for more freedom. Because of the exigencies of party warfare they now talked loftily about colonial rights. On the other hand, in favor of suspending the constitution were Lord John Russell, who had aided in drafting the Great Reform Bill, and Charles Buller, fresh from Canada and from drafting Lord Durham's Report. And Buller, the champion of responsible government for the colonies, demanded the termination of an elective assembly for Jamaica because the existing form of government "has been contrived and worked for no purpose but that of enabling a petty handful of tyrants to inflict the greatest possible amount of suffering and degradation on the many."

The crown colonies of Trinidad and St. Lucia had nominated legislative councils but no assemblies. Remodeling took place in 1831–1832, when separate executive and legislative councils were set up. English law gradually replaced that of Spain in Trinidad, but the French law in St. Lucia had greater power of resistance and continued till our own day as the civil law of the island. In Guiana, Essequibo and Demarara formed one governmental unit and Berbice the other. Both had "courts of policy" to which planters elected members by a system of indirect elections. Guaranteed by the treaty of cession, 1803, the legislatures continued to function with slight changes. In 1831 the two provinces were united but the old institutions were retained.

Significant as are some of the constitutional issues raised in the West Indies, they were of slight importance in comparison with the economic and social ones. Indeed there was but one dominant issue — that of slavery. Economic conditions made this paramount. But the economic problems were tied up with other questions than slavery. Local, imperial, and world conditions and policies acted and reacted upon the West Indian situation. The decline of the British West Indies had set in before the slave trade had ended and long before the slaves were freed. West Indian prosperity was too much linked with outside factors, too artificial, to endure. Absentee landlordism, changes in the imperial structure as well as in imperial policies, shifting economic conditions outside the empire: these factors singly or combined were more instrumental in undermining the economic foundation of the West Indies than were the abolitionists led by William Wilberforce and his friends.

When the West Indian planters left their properties to the care of agents and chose to waste their substance in England, the descent began. Matthew Lewis, one of these planters who in 1816–1817 visited the islands, discovered that attorneys and overseers made poor substitutes for proprietors. Others would have found the same, but few came out. Too many estates were often grouped under one management. Little was done to refertilize the soil or to bring new land under cultivation, where as in Jamaica it was available. In an age of inventions, the machinery of the sugar mills remained as of yore. The estate managers mortgaged the future by exhausting the plantations and overworking the slaves; the owners in England squandered current profits and borrowed on those to come. Meanwhile competitors forged ahead. Aided by Whitney's cotton gin, large areas of fertile soil, and a plentiful supply of labor, the planters of the southern states of the American union drove West Indian cotton out of the English market. The sugar growers of Cuba and Brazil flooded the European market with their product. They had advantages as to both soil and labor. Between 1808 and 1815 slaves were smuggled into the British West Indies, but the peace released war vessels for patrol duty and the punishments for engaging in the slave trade made this business too hazardous for British subjects. The creole Negroes could not keep up the supply of slaves from natural sources. Matthew Lewis tried his best to make slave babies survive. He failed. Most of the planters never so much as tried.

But had the British sugar islands still a monopoly of the home market? Yes and no. There had been rejoicing when Tobago, St. Lucia, Trinidad, and Guiana were annexed, but Jamaica and Barbados found that these colonies were more dangerous as rivals within than outside the British empire. The products of the new possessions enjoyed the same treatment in the British market as did those of the old, and they had rich unexploited soil in abundance. Taking a twenty-year average, Britain's import of West Indian sugar increased after 1815, but a large share of this import came from the colonies recently acquired. From 20 to 30 per cent of the cacao and cotton imported by Britain from the West Indies in the twenties came from the new colonies. In despair, planters of Jamaica asked for the retrocession of the recent annexations.

But not from these alone were the old West Indian interests threatened. In 1813 the India trade was thrown open and in the following year Mauritius became a British colony. The east imperiled the west. Shortly afterward John Gladstone of Liverpool, father of the famous W. E. Gladstone, began agitating for equality of treatment for cotton from the east. But this proved of little importance since neither the East nor the West Indies could compete with American cotton. Sugar was different. The West India interest succeeded in getting a preference of 10*s.* per cwt. over East Indian sugar. But in 1825 the duties on sugar from Mauritius were equalized with those on the West Indian product, and the sugar from Mauritius sold from 6*s.* to 18*s.* a cwt. below that from Jamaica. The import of the Mauritian sugar rose from 234,577 cwts. in 1821 to 434,276 cwts. seven years later. In the twenties the decline in cotton shipments from India caused a drop in the freight rate on sugar of 17*s.* to 18*s.* per cwt. Thus the West Indian preference was more than wiped out. But worse was to follow. In 1830 the duty on East Indian sugar was lowered from 37*s.* to 32*s.* and that on the West Indian from 27*s.* to 24*s.*, thus reducing the preference by 2*s.* a cwt. In 1836 the duties were equalized.

In other fields too time was against the British West Indies. The American Revolution and the Trade and Navigation Acts deprived the sugar colonies of a market and of a source of such supplies as timber, grain, and fish. The remaining British colonies in North America could not make up for these losses. To buy in England all necessities formerly bought in the old colonies added to their cost. The relaxation of restrictions on American-West Indian trade, especially after 1794, proved short-lived. The peace failed to restore the old direct trade. The lifting of the ban in 1822 on direct trade between the British West Indies and the outside world brought few benefits. Europe could buy sugar cheaper from Brazil and Cuba, and in 1823 new quarrels over trade and shipping between the British colonies and the United States led to the renewal of restrictions on this traffic. When the restrictions were repealed in 1830, the West Indian planters were beyond redemption.

During these years the conflict over slavery raged with increasing fury. The English humanitarians won a resounding victory when the slave trade was abolished in 1807. But little success crowned their efforts to make the prohibition effective by means of an efficient system of registering the slaves. The crown colony of Trinidad had such a system set up by order in council in 1812, but the attempt by Wilberforce in 1815 to make it general by an imperial act failed. The West India interest was too strong and the imperial government resorted to mere admonitions. Local registry acts proved to be but sham affairs; moreover, the registration controversy drove cautious reformers of Wilberforce's type into the camp of the advocates of destroying slavery root and branch, among whom the elder James Stephen, a brother-in-law of Wilberforce, was outstanding in ability and zeal.

In 1823 a ten-year war for the abolition of slavery in the British empire began in parliament. Wilberforce, T. F. Buxton, Henry Brougham, and Dr. Lushington were the shock troop of the abolitionists. On behalf of the government Canning expressed sympathy for their ultimate aim but warned against hasty action. Vested interests must not be hurt; the slaves ought to be trained for freedom. This supplied a clue for Charles Ellis and James Marryatt, leading spokesmen in the house of commons for the West India interest. Paying lip service to the cause of the slaves, they advocated "melioration" as most likely to bring benefit to all parties. But the measures of amelioration had to be passed and applied by the local governments. Ellis, Marryatt, and their allies carefully pointed out that the economic and social institutions in the West Indies had grown up as a result of an imperial policy. To destroy them ruthlessly would bring hardship and injury to colonies that had always cooperated loyally in building up and maintaining the strength of the British empire.

The period that followed has been succinctly described by Sir Henry Taylor. "In 1824," he writes, "the government of Lord Liverpool had taken up a position of mediator between the saints and the planters. . . . The slaves were not to be enfranchised [i.e., freed], but their condition was to be meliorated as the word went. A model code was devised, according to which the lash was to be taken out of the hands of the driver, punishments were to be inflicted only under the authority of stipendiary magistrates, the hours of labor were to be limited, the allowances of food were to be regulated, husbands and wives and children were not to be sold apart, and protectors were to be appointed who were to watch over the enforcement of the code and make half-yearly reports on all matters affecting the welfare of the slaves."

The planter-controlled assemblies remained obdurate. Small concessions were made — none on vital points. With a courage worthy of a better cause, they defied both the abolitionists and the imperial government, thereby hastening the ruin of their cause. In England, humanitarians, irrespective of creed and party, dissenters incensed by tales of wrongs inflicted upon co-religionists by the West Indian oligarchies, and reformers in politics and economics rallied to the banner of Wilberforce and Buxton. Powerful assistance came from the East India interests, who fought those of the West Indies on the issue of tariff preferences. God and mammon joined hands. The reports of the official slave protectors supplied the abolitionists with campaign material. Dispatches were transferred from parliamentary papers to Zachary Macaulay's *Monthly Anti-Slavery Reporter*. In the words of Sir Henry Taylor: "'The howlings and wailings of the saints were seen to be supported by the unquestionable facts, officially authenticated; the cry of the country for the abolition of slavery waxed louder every year; strange rumors reached the ears of the Negroes; they became excited and disturbed, imagining that the king had given them their freedom and that the fact and the freedom were kept from them by their owners; there was plotting and conspiracy; and at length came the insurrection of 1831 in Jamaica, in which of Negroes some hundreds lost their lives, of the whites not one." The last statement is inaccurate. A dozen whites and about four hundred blacks were killed in the uprising. Nearly two hundred Negroes were shot, hanged, or flogged to death in the orgy of reprisal that followed the suppression of the disturbances. Charged with a series of judicial murders, the Jamaica government lost whatever confidence moderate humanitarians might still have had in the island authorities. Practically all the West Indian governments had evaded or neglected advice and recommendations from home. In England the Tories had fallen, and the reformed parliament proved ready to remove abuses both at home and overseas. Inflamed by fresh tales of the blood guiltiness of the West Indian planters, the advocates of emancipation redoubled their efforts, and on August 29, 1833, the great bill which abolished slavery in the British empire became law. Wilberforce was then dying, and James Stephen had been dead one year. It was his son, the future permanent undersecretary, who drafted the Emancipation Act.

Viewed in retrospect, the Emancipation Act was a cautious, conservative measure. Slave children of six and under became free on August 1, 1834. The older children and adult slaves on that day were emancipated but not freed. An ingenious and complicated system of apprenticeship was set up to last six years for field slaves and four for those in other occupations. During this period, optimistically labeled one of training for and adjustment to freedom, the apprentices might be released by their masters or by the colonial governments or they might purchase their freedom. If not freed, they were compelled to work 45 hours weekly for their old masters or for others who might purchase their services. The allowances required by law for the slaves were to be given to the apprentices; and if they grew their own food, time for work on the provision grounds should be included in the 45-hour week. In addition to the services from the apprentices, the slave owners received a compensation of £20,000,000 from the imperial treasury. Of this sum, £16,589,373 for 670,000 slaves went to the West Indies. The money was distributed by imperial commissioners. Many details connected with the establishment of the new order were left in the hands of the local authorities. But a body of special magistrates, appointed and paid by the crown, was intrusted with extensive powers to enforce the act and protect the apprentices. The payment of compensation for the slaves was made contingent upon the passing of local laws to make the imperial statute effective. The bribe produced results. All the West Indian legislatures passed abolition acts, but not all of these conformed to the spirit of the emancipation measure. Antigua went the abolition act one better by dispensing with the apprenticeship, providing full freedom for its slaves August 1, 1834. But the Jamaica abolition law was so defective that approval was given to it only on condition that a slave aid bill should be passed.

There was rejoicing among the abolitionists in England and rejoicing among the Negroes in the West Indies when the long-awaited August 1 dawned. But reality fell far short of what had been anticipated in both circles. As a class the planters accepted emancipation under duress. They complained that the proffered compensation was but a fraction of what the slaves were worth. The intricate scheme of fixing the value of slaves, basing it in part upon the number of slaves and the value of the export of any given colony, put the older colonies at a disadvantage. The compensation per slave varied from £13 in the Bahamas to £53 in Honduras. The planters decided to extract all possible profit from the apprenticeship arrangement. While it lasted, their power over the former slaves was practically as great as of old. But the protection which law and custom had provided for the slaves had been swept away. The Negroes, whose expectations had been keyed to a high pitch, found that they got stones for bread. Planters refused to assume responsibility for old or sick slaves; pregnant women were compelled to work in the field; the apprentices were denied water and other refreshments while they toiled; the guards were removed from their provision grounds, and access to these was often made difficult. The Negroes in turn were perhaps even less willing workers than before; they believed themselves cheated out of full freedom, and nourished exaggerated hopes concerning the aid and protection to be had from the special magistrates. The lot of these officials appears to have been a hard one. Too few in numbers, they had to cover great distances and to be exposed to all sorts of abuse and contumely. Often they were denied the simplest hospitality. Indeed to accept it from a planter made them suspect in the eyes of the Negroes and their friends, the missionaries. The latter could and did report magistrates deemed negligent to the Anti-Slavery Society in England, and these complaints seldom failed to reach the imperial government. Planters, on the other hand, had troublesome magistrates arrested, often on trumped-up charges, tried, and sentenced to fines and imprisonment by juries and judges belonging to their own class. Governors, such as Lord Sligo and Sir Lionel Smith in Jamaica, found their position unendurable. It was impossible to please both the saints and the planters, and either party was powerful enough to cause trouble.

An abolutionist delegation, which included Joseph Sturge, a Birmingham merchant filled with zeal for the cause of the Negroes, went out to study the condition of the apprentices. Perhaps they were taken in by their wards, but even so, plenty of abuses could be found to shock the sensibilities of such emissaries. The story of the ill treatment suffered by one young apprentice, James Williams, was printed and widely circulated in England. Humanitarian speakers at Exeter Hall lashed both the colonial governments and the government at home for their failure to protect the Negroes. The colonial office, guided in the West Indian affairs by a trinity of humanitarians – Glenelg, Stephen, and Taylor – decided that the apprenticeship system must go. Parliament agreed. And under this double or treble pressure the West Indian legislatures consented to end all apprenticeships on August 1, 1838.

CHAPTER 6

BRITISH AFRICA

NONE of Britain's African possessions attracted as much attention in the early part of the nineteenth century as did St. Helena while Napoleon was confined there. But when the illustrious prisoner died in 1821, the island sank back into obscurity. Occasionally the old posts along the Guinea coast and the newer ones on the coast of Western Africa were discussed in the press and in parliament. The fight against slavery and the slave trade brought them into prominence; but the West African empire of Britain had not yet begun to take form — in fact, none dreamed of its coming. Now and then the *Anti-Slavery Reporter* would turn the searchlight on Mauritius and reveal shocking conditions on its plantations, the owners of which frequently raised the question of equalizing the duties on their sugar with those on the West Indian product, only to provoke a sharp retort from the West Indian lobby. But even in this quarter nothing significant happened. Not so with the Cape of Good Hope. Little noticed in 1815, this remote station gradually rose in prominence so that by 1837 Cape questions were hotly debated both in and outside of parliament.

To the searchers for a sea route to India, the subcontinent of Africa remained a barrier for generations after Bartholomew Diaz had rounded the Cape of Good Hope. The early explorers and merchants traveling to India found nothing to attract them along the coast of the present Union of South Africa. Arid on the west and practically harborless on the east, the land repelled the mariners. Even the famous harbor of Table Bay offered but an indifferent shelter to which the records of numerous wrecks testify. However ships did occasionally call at Table Bay, usually to replenish diminishing water supplies. Its location was strategic, and the tales of the soil and climate of the Cape peninsula brought to Holland by shipwrecked sailors finally induced the Dutch East India Company to establish there a halfway station on the road to the east. Jan van Riebeeck led the little band of servants of the company that founded Capetown in 1652. Created to serve the needs of passing ships, the new port was not intended to develop into a colony. At no time did the Dutch seek to create in South Africa a New Netherlands such as they dreamed of founding on the banks of the Hudson in North America. For the most part migration to the Cape was frowned upon. Yet the needs of ships for vegetables, meat, and other provisions could not be supplied without farmers. A small number of the company's servants were made free burghers and settled on land in the neighborhood of Capetown. The majority of these were Dutch; but Germans, French Huguenots, and others made up nearly half of the number of pioneers. Among the minority groups the Huguenots, though early denationalized, proved in South Africa, as elsewhere, a powerful leaven for the whole community. To these South African colonists the name Boer seems to have been given rather early; they themselves have shown a preference for the term Afrikaner or Afrikander.

The colony at the Cape was first occupied by the British from 1795 till 1802. Surrendered by the Treaty of Amiens, it was recaptured following the renewal of the war against France and her satellites, among which Holland was one. In 1814 Britain secured title to the Cape. The white population then numbered about 25,000 souls. Fairly dense in the western district around

Capetown and in the Berg Valley beyond the first range of mountains, it was widely scattered farther north and east over the 120,000 square miles then included within the colonial boundaries.

South Africa has presented Britain with what Gladstone called a "great unsolved and perhaps unsolvable problem." This problem has been made difficult because of the existence there of an old white settlement alien in race and origin, because of the geographical features of the country and the presence of a large non-European population, and because of the colonial policy and the forces both in and outside of government circles which shaped and formulated that policy when the Cape of Good Hope was annexed and during the first generation following the annexation. South Africa became part and parcel of the British empire and the course of South African history has been affected by both local and imperial forces and factors.

As already noted, South Africa turns its worst side to those who merely skirt its coast. The Europeans who made landfall did not suspect the existence of fertile land, of a healthful climate, and of fabulous mineral wealth. Nor did the early settlers find it easy to move inland. No natural highway aided the spread of settlements. On the other hand, when the pioneers finally pushed beyond the districts of Cape and Stellenbosch, the scant and irregular rainfall and the type of farming then feasible and profitable – cattle-raising – scattered the settlers as thinly as in the semi-arid regions of the United States in the day of the cattleman. The typical Boer farmer became a rancher who needed wide spaces to move with his herd in search of new pastures. He had to roam, to trek. The craving for solitude which has been described as one of his outstanding traits of character grew out of economic needs. The trek-Boer disliked village life and may at times have felt a genuine aversion for the society of his fellows, not unlike the "desert rat" of Wyoming and the "sourdough" of Alaska. Otherwise the Boer rather resembled the patriarchs of early Hebrew history. Like them he moved with family, slaves, servants, and herds. The covered ox-wagon served as home, means of transport, and barricade as the need arose. On the veld, under sunny skies, far from Capetown, that cosmopolitan tavern of the seas, the Boers developed as a hardy and virile folk, men and women whose wants were few and easily satisfied, who feared God, not man. Impatient of restraint, not tied to the homestead as tillers of the soil, they moved freely and were ready to pull up stakes when irked by the presence of neighbors or the actions of government.

When white men came to South Africa, they found Hottentots and Bushmen. The latter were aboriginal; a yellowish-brown race of small, shy hunters, they could be neither enslaved nor trained in European ways. Bothersome to the settlers, these sons of South Africa were hunted by whites and blacks alike and well-nigh exterminated until they found refuge in the Kalahari Desert far to the north of Capetown. The Hottentots were larger than the Bushmen but resembled them in skin color. They had herds of cattle and fat-tailed sheep. Though unsuited for slavery, the Hottentots, despite their shiftless and thieving habits, were used as servants, and their daughters sometimes became the wives and often the concubines of the early white men at the Cape. Their racial purity and social organization had disappeared when the British became masters of the Cape of Good Hope. But the blood of the Hottentots, mingled with European, Malayan, and black, flows in the veins of the Cape colored folk and in those of the Griquas. From the beginning the British enrolled Hottentots as soldiers or mounted police. Like other dark-skinned people, they loved to wear a uniform, and in common with most primitive races they possessed an almost uncanny ability to follow the tracks of man and beast.

To remedy labor shortage, the Dutch East India Company in an evil hour for South Africa decided to bring in slaves from West Africa and Malaya. Most kinds of menial labor then became degrading, the badge of inferior social status and race. The door of opportunity was shut to the laboring classes of

Europe. The subcontinent could not really become a white man's country. The color bar was there to stay.

Late in the eighteenth century bands of descendants of Europeans and Hottentots migrated northward and established themselves along the middle portion of the Orange River. Under the leadership of men of their own blood or of missionaries they founded villages, fought the Bantu, shed their old name of "Bastaards"; as Griquas they flit across the stage of South African history.

Hottentots, colored, and slaves formed perhaps two-thirds of the total population of the Cape Colony in 1814, thus creating a slave and colored problem; and in the last quarter of the eighteenth century the native problem became more complex with the advent of the Kaffirs. In 1815 a black cloud hovered over the eastern border of the colony. Already it had broken several times in storms of Kaffir wars, the accounts of which fill so many pages in the histories of South Africa. Kaffir was the name applied to the outpost tribes of the great Bantu race which had moved slowly southward from the region of the great African lakes till they met and clashed with the other latecomers in South Africa, the whites, in the valley of the Great Fish River some six hundred miles east of Capetown. Strong and warlike, the Kaffirs were both pastoralists and tillers of the soil. They needed space to move in and land for their fields. Like the Europeans they came to settle; fearless of danger they matched themselves with assegais and ox-hide shields against white men mounted on horses and armed with elephant guns; and recklessly they charged laagers of ox wagons from behind which spoke the white man's thunder. In 1779 the first Kaffir war was fought and, despite the advantages of firearms and horses, the colonists barely held their own. The Fish River was recognized as the boundary between the colony and the land of the Kaffirs, but the colonial frontier was weakly held. The Xosas, one of the Kaffir tribes, crossed the river and settled in the rectangle about sixty miles long between the Fish River where it flows eastward, and the sea, a region then called Zuurveld, later renamed Albany. Thence they were driven by the British in 1812. But the Fish River made a poor military frontier; treaty obligations sat lightly on the Kaffir; and the white man's cattle tempted him. Cattle-stealing by Kaffirs and counter raids by settlers or border patrols or military forces called commandos, with burning of farmsteads and native kraals and murder by both blacks and whites, became

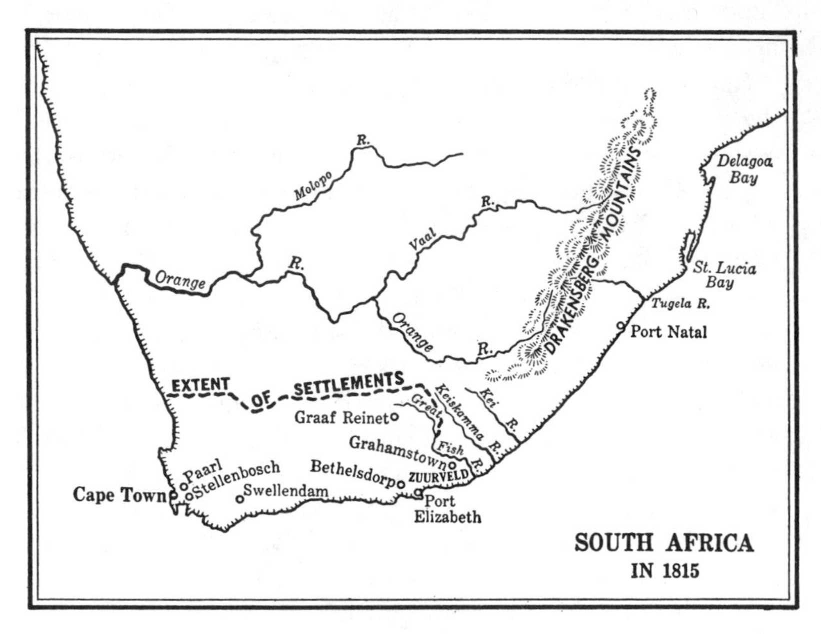

common occurrences. Britain here inherited a frontier problem which became *the* great native problem.

On this scene had appeared Christian missionaries from Europe during the period of the Dutch occupation. They introduced a new and, for the colonial authorities and farmers whether Dutch or British, most disturbing element. Although messengers of the Prince of Peace, the missionaries brought strife. They trusted in God, but did not disdain using worldly weapons. Attention has been called in an earlier chapter to the fact that the late eighteenth and early nineteenth century witnessed the rise of the humanitarian, the missionary, and the anti-slavery movements in England; and that proponents of these movements, like Wilberforce and Buxton, exerted a strong influence in government circles. Besides, the eighteenth century's romantic notion of the noble savage continued to be held by many in high places — South Africa had both free "noble" savages and slaves and lowly colored. Unlike the West Indian planter, the Boer farmer had no powerful lobby to present his case at Westminster, no shipping and mercantile interest that could plead his cause.

The Moravians had been the first missionaries at the Cape. Though expelled at first by the Dutch authorities, they came back and on the whole seem to have worked for their Master without greatly antagonizing the white settlers. Representatives of the Glasgow, the Wesleyan, the London, the Church, and other missionary societies followed. Several of these were at work before Britain took permanent possession of the colony. Individuals among the missionaries were often unpopular with farmers and magistrates, but no single group stirred up so much excitement both in South Africa and in London as did the men of the London Missionary Society. One of its earliest representatives, Vanderkemp, an eccentric Dutchman, founded in 1803 the station of Bethelsdorp in the eastern province, and the place soon acquired the reputation of being a haven for lazy, thieving Hottentots. In 1811 a missionary, Mr. Read, called the attention of Wilberforce to the plight of the South African natives and slaves. Wilberforce's long association with the agitation against the slave trade had caused him to become strongly biased in favor of the blacks. A result of his early association with the South African native question was the Black Circuit and its aftermath, the Slachter's Nek rebellion, of which more will be said later. At this point we simply wish to call to mind that Britain acquired with the Cape Colony questions of far-reaching importance and with many complex ramifications.

It was at an unpropitious time that the Cape of Good Hope became a British colony. The fight to overthrow slavery had begun in England; the Boers were slaveholders. The imperial government had abandoned the liberal attitude that had prompted the passage of the Quebec Act of 1774 and the Canadian Constitutional Act of 1791. In the West Indies the presence of elective assemblies greatly complicated the work of improving the lot of the Negroes; common sense seemed to argue against the establishment of similar bodies in South Africa at least until the slavery and native questions had been settled. Protected by law the French element in Canada was defying efforts at Anglicization. Even liberal-minded Englishmen like Lord Durham felt that a mistake had been committed on this point. The French-Canadians should have been denationalized. Warned by the experience in Canada, the English authorities now sought to Anglicize the Boers. But the Dutch farmer of the veld clung as obstinately to his language and nationality as did the *habitant* of Lower Canada. Indeed, much of what had happened in the world between the passage of the Quebec Act and the formal British annexation of the Cape had tended to create, stimulate, and strengthen the spirit of nationalism. Though living in a remote spot the Dutch at the Cape had not been untouched by events in America and France. This, too, must be kept in mind if we are to understand the whys and wherefores of South African history between 1814 and the issuance in 1837 of Piet Retief's proclamation justifying the migration of Boers.

The British government valued the Cape as a halfway station on the road to India. The six million pounds involved in the treaty of cession was not, as so often asserted, Britain's compensation to Holland for the loss of the Cape of Good Hope and Guiana but an inducement offered by Castlereagh to get Dutch acquiescence to a union with Belgium. Now that both St. Helena and Mauritius were held by Britain, Table Bay was not indispensable for the English trade with the east. As for the colony at the Cape, in 1814 and for a long time afterward it was looked upon as a liability. At this time the home government discouraged enterprises which might lead to further annexations in South

Africa. Acts of individual Englishmen at Port Natal and Delagoa Bay were disavowed. Britain had enough land.

This did not mean, however, that the boundaries of the Cape of Good Hope were or could be restricted. Travelers, explorers, traders, and missionaries went beyond the rather uncertain line which in the north and northeast marked the limits of the colony. The trek-Boers, as was the habit of frontiersmen everywhere, pushed slowly but steadily onward. One or perhaps two or more farms of about six thousand acres each had been the customary holding of these cattle farmers. The herds grew; families multiplied; the sight of smoke from a neighbor's home disturbed the trek-Boer; on he moved and with him almost imperceptibly moved the colonial boundary. Missionaries, aided by Barend Barends, Adam and Cornelis Kok, and Andries Waterboer, chiefs of migratory mixed bloods, the Griquas, built villages and endeavored to found states in the valley of the Orange, which was perhaps 100 to 200 miles in advance of the colonial frontier of 1814. In these early days, that is to say in the eighteen-twenties and thirties, the missionaries generally opposed further annexations by Britain in South Africa; later, as will be seen, they became so much the advocates of imperial expansion there that no less an authority than Herman Merivale, permanent undersecretary of state for the colonies, 1847–1859, wrote in the latter year that the missionaries were responsible for all the British annexations in South Africa. The change of heart came with the Great Trek. Before that event missionaries seem to have dreamed of founding theocratically governed Griqua states that would form a screen between the white settlements and the Bantu. But this never had any chance of realization. The pasture land of the South African plateau beckoned, and the trek-Boer heeded the call. The boundaries on the north and northeast delimited in 1819 by the governor at the Cape, Lord Charles Somerset, were considerably in advance of what had been claimed five years earlier. In those directions the farmers met no serious opposition, and they were relatively free to follow their migrating needs and impulses.

Not so to the east. A fairly dense Kaffir population formed a barrier to expansion and a danger to the frontier settlements. In 1819 the imperial government appropriated £50,000 to aid British emigrants to South Africa. The main purpose of this assisted emigration seems to have been to relieve the pressure of the redundant population at home, but it was also used to fill the waste spaces in the Zuurveld and to check Kaffir inroads. In the same year Lord Charles Somerset pushed the Kaffirs back from the Fish River to the left bank of the Keiskamma and endeavored to keep the ten to twenty-five-mile wide area between the two rivers unoccupied as a buffer between whites and blacks. This, however, proved impossible of realization. Both Kaffirs and whites settled in the ceded territory. The old border difficulties continued; and in December, 1834, a horde of Kaffirs fifteen to twenty thousand strong crossed the Great Fish River, killed, burned, plundered, and sent the settlers flying for safety to Grahamstown and other places with military garrisons. After a severe struggle the Kaffirs were compelled to withdraw, but the war had cost the settlers in the neighborhood of £300,000 and the imperial government about £160,000 over and above the annual military charge for the Cape of £96,000. The governor, Sir Benjamin D'Urban, now decided upon a drastic departure from the old frontier policy. All the land between the Keiskamma and the Kei rivers was declared British territory. At first he intended to clear the district (now called Adelaide in honor of the queen of William IV) of Xosas, but later he allowed members of the tribe to stay provided they renounced their tribal allegiance and became British subjects. In addition, remnants of a friendly Kaffir tribe, the Fingoes, were planted on land evacuated by Xosas.

But D'Urban had reckoned without the missionaries. The most famous and militant of the anti-colonial group, Dr. John Philip, superintendent of the London Missionary Society in South Africa, went to England. Lord Glenelg, an evangelical, had succeeded Lord Aberdeen at the colonial office in April, 1835, and Glenelg lent a willing ear to Dr. Philip, who seldom missed an opportunity to revile the colonists and praise the natives. Residing in England at this time was Captain (later Sir) Andries Stockenström, a Cape colonist of Swedish origin, an able but crotchety man who had served as landdrost and commissioner-general in the eastern district of Cape Colony. Dr. Philip, Stockenström, and other missionaries and ex-Cape officials with a grievance united in denouncing the conduct of the colonial farmers and authorities toward the natives and in opposing the frontier policy of Sir Benjamin D'Urban. As a result, Lord Glenelg in a dispatch of December 26, 1835, severely rebuked the governor and decreed: "The claim of sovereignty over the new province bounded by the Keiskamma and the Kei must be renounced. It rests upon a conquest resulting from a war in which, as far as I am at present enabled to judge, the original justice is on the side of the conquered, not of the victorious party." Stockenström, who had given very damaging testimony against the Cape government and settlers before the house of commons' committee on the aborigines, was sent out as lieutenant-governor of the eastern province and made virtually independent of the governor at Capetown. As the representative of King William IV, Stockenström on December 5, 1836, concluded solemn treaties with Kaffir chiefs whereby the territory annexed by D'Urban was restored to them and the boundary fixed as of 1819. These treaties formed a part of a series of formal engagements between representatives of the British government and Bantu and Griqua chiefs. The chiefs were treated as sovereigns and Dr. Philip assured the aborigines committee that the Kaffirs "are quite capable of understanding a system of international law, and of appreciating it." Needless to say, this statement as well as the treaty policy filled the colonists with despair — a feeling intensified when Sir Benjamin D'Urban, whose frontier policy had won approval in the exposed districts, was dismissed by Lord Glenelg.

When the missionaries resisted encroachment upon the territory of the Kaffirs, they could generally expect aid from a powerful faction in England that opposed any widening of the imperial boundaries; similarly when they strove to improve the lot of the colored people within the Cape Colony they were certain of support from the humanitarian and anti-slavery forces. Indeed the colored, slavery, and native questions at the Cape were closely intertwined. To the original Dutch settlers the Hottentots and Bushmen were "black, stinking dogs." Offense they doubtless gave to the white man's olfactory nerves; in other respects they proved equally troublesome. Boer farmers read the Bible, and the good book said that the sons of Ham should serve. The doctrine suited the farmers. But though Bushmen were hunted like vermin, the treatment of the Hottentots compares favorably with contemporary actions by Europeans toward natives in other quarters of the globe. Still Mr. Read, the missionary, undoubtedly had some good reasons for his appeal to Wilberforce to come to the aid of the oppressed at the Cape. As a result a judicial inquiry known as the Black Circuit took place in the eastern districts in 1812. Only a small percentage of Read's charges were substantiated, and the inquiry shocked and humiliated the Boer farmers. No longer could they do as they pleased with their servants. The English appeared bent on introducing the novel doctrine of equality between races.

In after years the grievances arising from the Black Circuit were kept fresh in the memories of Boers on account of the episode known as the Slachter's Nek rebellion. Frederick Bezuidenhout, a farmer living in a wild, remote spot on the northeast frontier of the colony, failed to obey repeated summons to reply to charges of mistreating a Hottentot servant. The matter dragged for three years. The local officials bungled, and finally in 1815 an officer accompanied by Hottentot soldiers went to arrest the farmer. He resisted and was shot by a Hottentot. At the funeral a brother of the dead man, Johannes Bezuidenhout, vowed vengeance. A few hot-heads joined him willingly, others joined under duress, all took an oath to resist the British; and messengers were sent to enlist the support of Kaffirs. Boer commandos put down the uprising, but Johannes Bezuidenhout died fighting Hottentot soldiers. Five other leaders were hung at Slachter's Nek. Though Boer officials figured largely in bringing this episode to a head as well as in the closing scene of the drama, upon the English fell the blame for it. The trouble grew out of the Black Circuit and the use made of Hottentots in arresting a white man. Trek-Boers told and retold the story as illustrating British preference for natives over Boers. The Bezuidenhout brothers became national heroes, and the execution at Slachter's Nek served as a prologue to the Great Trek.

Lord Charles Somerset, governor at the Cape from 1814 to 1827, was a soldier and a high Tory. Restrictions on the freedom of the colored people in the form of pass laws, their liability to forced labor and to occasional whippings seem not to have disturbed him greatly — indeed, soldiers in the British army at that time probably received more barbarous floggings than did Hottentot servants at the Cape. But the influence and activities of the missionaries and their friends grew both in the colony and at home. Wilberforce and Buxton brought the affairs at the Cape to the attention of the house of commons. In 1823 a government commission went out to study and report on conditions in the colony. However, the results of these efforts failed to please the friends of the African natives. Dr. Philip, who had arrived in South Africa in February, 1819, returned to England seven years later and presented a report dealing with the Cape colored question to the directors of the London Missionary Society. They in turn forwarded it to the colonial secretary, Lord Bathurst. Meeting with scant encouragement in this quarter Philip set to work compiling a book on South Africa. His famous *Researches in South Africa Illustrating the Civil, Moral, and Religious Condition of the Native Tribes* appeared in the spring of 1828. Herein he criticized severely the treatment accorded the colored people by the colonists and the colonial authorities. He recommended full civil equality for his protégés. Buxton then went into action and secured in the following July the passage by the house of commons of a resolution directing the government to send such instructions "as should most effectually secure to all the natives of South Africa the same freedom and protection as are enjoyed by other people, whether English or Dutch." The new colonial secretary, Sir George Murray, favored the resolution and lost no time in transmitting it to South Africa; it crossed a Cape ordinance which had achieved the object of Buxton's resolution.

This, the famous fiftieth ordinance, repealed all pass, apprenticeship, and vagrancy laws and regulations especially applicable to non-Europeans, and in other respects gave them civil and political rights equal to those of Europeans. The ordinance had been suggested by Captain Stockenström, drafted by the chief justice of the Cape supreme court, and approved by the acting governor, General Bourke, and his council. Missionaries and other philanthropically-minded individuals supported it, but the majority of the colonists received it with consternation. They repudiated the doctrine of racial equality and viewed with alarm its social and economic effects. Though a large number of Hottentot servants paid little heed to the boon conferred upon them, others seized the opportunity afforded by the new freedom to take to the road. Vagrant and squatting Hottentots soon became a veritable pest, and the local authorities were powerless. In the opinion of the judges of the supreme court of the Cape of 1834, "no law . . . for the suppression of vagrancy in the Colony can be carried into effective operation in respect to the Hottentots, so long as the Second Section of the 50th Ordinance stands unrepealed." And this section, which conferred equality of status, could not be repealed without the assent of the imperial government — an assent impossible to secure, partly because the question of the colored and the natives at the Cape had now become linked with that of the newly emancipated slaves.

South Africa had no plantations and slave gangs comparable to those in the West Indies. Most of the bondsmen served in households; and writers on South African history seldom fail to point out the comparative humanity of the slavery at the Cape. Furthermore, the Cape of Good Hope as a crown colony came under the direct supervision of the imperial government. Consequently registration of the slaves was adopted in 1816 and the ameliorating measures which the imperial authorities had vainly recommended to West Indian legislatures were put into operation in South Africa. After 1823 regulations regarding Sunday labor, the length of the working day, pay for overtime, education of slave children, respect for the family ties of the slaves, and proper food and clothing were adopted for the Cape. The Trinidad slave code was extended to South Africa in 1826, and soon protectors of the slaves began to send in reports to the colonial secretary.

These reports and rebukes administered to the Cape authorities by Secretaries Murray and Goderich revealed that though the South African slave might be better treated than his fellow in Mauritius or in most of the West Indian colonies his position was on the whole worse than South African historians care to admit. And there was probably much truth in the statement made by a Cape correspondent in the *Anti-Slavery Monthly Reporter,* January 31, 1827, that "with all its boasted alleviations, and in spite of every sweetening ingredient, slavery at the Cape is assuredly still a bitter and baneful draught."

It seems certain, however, that public opinion at the Cape never appeared so implacably hostile to the emancipation of slaves as was that of the West Indies. Slavery never formed the groundwork for South Africa's economic system. Plans for a gradual abolition of slavery were suggested in 1828 by a Society for Redeeming Slaves at Capetown, and two years later by slaveholders in the district of Graaff-Reinet. But neither effort found a sympathetic reception in England. The abolitionists distrusted all remedies but their own. And the *Anti-Slavery Reporter* described the address of the Cape society as partaking "more of the peculiarity of colonial logic" and as revealing more sympathy "with the feelings and prejudices of slave-holders than suits our taste or judgment." He who was not with the abolitionists was against them.

On September 1, 1834, the slaves in the Cape Colony were emancipated. The regulations concerning apprenticeship and the appointment of special magistrates were practically the same as for the West Indies, with the exception that at the Cape the apprenticeship period became in practice a four-year period since most slaves were employed at household work. The appointment of special magistrates was resented as an evidence of partiality for dark-skinned folk, but otherwise the colonists showed at first little ill will toward the emancipation measure. However, this changed when the slave-owners found that they would receive only £1,247,401 for the 35,745 slaves above six years of age who had been valued at £3,041,290; that the claims for compensation had to be proved before a commission in London; that expenses connected therewith and a stamp duty on the necessary documents would be deducted; and that the owners of slaves would not receive cash but government bonds. Needing cash, farmers sold their claims at a discount to agents who soon scoured the countryside; some slave-owners trekked without bothering about collecting the compensation due them; it has been computed that the abolition of slavery cost South African Boers more than £2,000,000. The colony was small and poor; and this loss, coming as it did when large sections of the eastern province had been devastated by the Kaffirs, might well seem staggering. Moreover, colonial ordinances aimed at preventing the manumitted from becoming vagrants were promptly disallowed by the imperial government.

This sharp reminder of their political impotence stimulated the desire of colonists to gain control over their own affairs. The autocratic government which Britain found at the Cape continued with little change until 1825 when an advisory council was appointed to assist the governor. But the councilors were all officials, and the governor might ignore their recommendations provided he could satisfy the secretary of state. Two years later fundamental changes were made in the judiciary and the district government of the colony. The supreme court was made independent of the governor; and the district boards, composed of local officials known by the Dutch names of landdrosts and heemraden, gave way to resident magistrates and civil commissioners, a change which increased the power of the governor. The unsalaried heemraden had been chosen from the burghers of the district, which meant that they had usually been Boers, while the new paid officials might be men unconnected with the local community. To compensate the burghers for the loss of the representative element found in the old district boards and in the burgher senate at Capetown, two of the officials on the governor's council were replaced by two burghers. But the change in nowise increased the power of that body.

By the time these reforms went into effect, 1828, the British immigrants in the eastern districts had begun to grumble audibly against the undemocratic character of their government. The burghers of Capetown and surrounding territory joined them in demanding local autonomy. But the reformers split on the slavery issue. In 1828 John Fairbairn, son-in-law of Dr. Philip and editor of the *Capetown Commercial Advertiser*, was an ardent advocate of political reform, but he belonged to the anti slavery party and soon parted company with Christoffel Brand of the *Zuid Afrikaan*, who opposed the new slavery regulations. A similar cleavage appeared in the debates in the house of commons when Cape petitions for representative institutions were presented. James Marryatt and other spokesmen for the West India interests supported the demands of South Africa, while the anti-slavery leader, Dr. Lushington, opposed them. With the aid of the secretary of state, Sir George Murray, the anti-slavery forces for several years successfully blocked concessions to the colonists at the Cape. A change came with the abolition of slavery. In 1833 two councils, an executive and a legislative, replaced the advisory council of 1825. The new legislative council of ten to twelve members was composed of five officials and five to seven burghers nominated by the governor. This small beginning of representative government was carried a step further in 1836 when provisions were made for the creation of elective boards, presided over by resident magistrates, for the towns and the villages of the colony.

South Africa moved more slowly in the direction of local autonomy than did British North America. Slavery retarded the growth of self-government at the Cape, and a further obstacle was supplied by the foreign origin of the majority of the colonists. Lord Charles Somerset brought to South Africa Scottish preachers and schoolmasters for the Dutch Reformed Church and the state schools; and in July, 1822, he decreed that between January 1, 1823, and January 1, 1827, the English language should be introduced and used exclusively in all "Judicial and Official Acts and Proceedings." Although the operation of this ordinance had to be postponed, a commission sent from home to inquire into the problems of the Cape in 1823 recommended replacing Roman Dutch law and Dutch institutions with English law and English institutions. Reforms in the local government and the judiciary, 1827–1828, pointed in this direction, and attempts were made to require a knowledge of English from all men serving on juries. In 1830 the cleavage between Dutch and English settlers in South Africa provided Sir George Murray with an argument against granting the request for representative institutions; it appears that British statesmen wished to avoid duplicating the Lower Canada problems in South Africa. However, the discrimination against the use of their language acted as a powerful irritant to the trek-Boers.

From the beginning, the Cape of Good Hope held a position betwixt and between the East Indian and other colonial possessions of Britain. By an imperial act the Cape after April, 1814, was for certain purposes placed within the limits of the jurisdiction of the East India Company and made a depot for Indian goods, except tea. The Cape wine had already been given a substantial preference over wine from Spain and Portugal, and government bounties had been paid to the South African wine farmers. During the twenties restrictions on trade with the Cape were removed, but at the same time a reduction in the wine duties proved disadvantageous to the Cape growers. In October, 1831, the British duty on Cape wines was fixed at 2*s.* 9*d.* and on foreign wines at 5*s.* 6*d.* a gallon. But this preference proved insufficient to counterbalance the handicaps of quality and distance, and the Cape export of wine fell off rapidly. Merinos, Southdowns, and Saxon sheep were brought to South Africa in an effort to stimulate wool-growing, and Lord Charles Somerset, whose interest in horses was so great that Lady Holland called him a jockey, tried to improve the breed of horses at the Cape. Between 1815 and 1835 the value of the export and import trade grew but slowly, despite improvements resulting from the stabilization of the currency in 1826, and the establishment of new banks.

Excepting the British wine duties, none of the regulations affecting industry and commerce had such interest for the average Boer farmer as those dealing with land and landholding. The Dutch East India Company during the later period of its existence had allowed a good deal of latitude in this respect. The frontier farmer who found a good tract of land would set up a beacon, commissioners would investigate and report, and if the claim was validated the farmer would get land the extent of which was determined by half an hour's walk in every direction from the central beacon. This amount, usually reckoned as about six thousand acres, could be held for a year upon payment of 24 rix dollars. In practice the land was held in perpetuity, and none bothered much about inequalities as regards type of land, about boundaries or the legal position of the lessee. In 1813 a British governor, Sir John Cradock, attempted to establish a real land system by requiring fixed boundaries for the holdings and proper deeds, limiting the size of farms to six thousand acres, and establishing security of tenure with an annual quit rent graduated in accordance with the quality of the land. The rent might now run as high as 250 rix dollars per year and mineral rights were reserved for the government. The farmers considered the new arrangement an interference with time-honored practices, and they objected to the imposition of higher rents. In 1820 when nearly five thousand British immigrants settled in the Zuurveld, the government followed North American precedent in offering one hundred acres, subject to quit rent, to each adult male. The amount seemed generous to the immigrants while in England, but upon arrival in South Africa they found it inadequate for the prevailing system of farming. They were then granted more land. The Boers, however, continued to fret under the British land ordinances, especially after 1832 when a new imperial scheme for handling colonial land, whereby all should be sold at public auction at a fairly high price, went into effect. This was in harmony with the new imperial policy governing colonial land grants. The trek-Boer felt that he had received a mortal blow. On all sides he was hemmed in by distasteful regulations. Soon scouts were sent to investigate the land northeast of the colonial boundary; preparations were made for extensive treks.

In the twenty-odd years which had passed between the cession of the Cape to Britain and the departure of the Voortrekkers great improvements had been made in many fields. Schools, hospitals, banks, and roads had been built or established; new towns had been founded especially in the eastern districts; religious equality and freedom of the press had been granted; and in the case of municipalities representative institutions had been conceded. However, most of these improvements but little affected the farmers, especially those on the frontiers. They saw themselves hedged about by Griquas and Kaffirs whose defenders seemingly had the ear and enjoyed the confidence of the authorities at home. The slaves had been liberated with inadequate compensation for the owners; non-Europeans had been put on a basis of equality with the whites. The Boer farmers found that land could no longer be acquired as easily as before; their old institutions were threatened with destruction. As their sense of grievance increased, they heard about rich pasture lands to be had beyond the colonial boundaries. The wilderness had no terror for the trek-Boer. Homestead ties sat but lightly upon him; freedom was dear to him — freedom from meddlesome officials and prating missionaries. In 1834 the advance guard of the Boer migration, the Voortrekkers, began to move. At first a bit spasmodic, the movement soon grew and eventually became a great outward rush. It was no mere jumping off to a nearby station; it was the migration of fairly large, compact bodies of people in search of homes where they could be free from molestation. In the words of their great leader, Piet Retief, they went in search of a country "in which we shall permanently reside." A manifesto of the emigrant farmers led by Retief justifying their action and appealing for support appeared in the *Grahamstown Journal* of February 2, 1837. Thus in the year of the accession of Queen Victoria, in the year of the rebellions in the Canadas, the migration of Boers, known as the Great Trek, reached its greatest proportion. White South Africa was being torn asunder.

CHAPTER 7

AUSTRALIA

LATE discovered by Europeans, the continent of Australia at first received the least promising of immigrants. Portuguese, Spanish, French, and Dutch explorers visited the great southland in the sixteenth and seventeenth centuries. They saw and even set foot on the northern, western, and southern coasts which offered little to tempt trader or settler. The English arrived late, but fate steered them to the eastern coast where a plentiful rainfall and splendid harbors promised success for a European settlement. In 1770 Captain Cook accompanied by Joseph Banks, the naturalist, discovered Botany Bay and sailed along the shores of New South Wales and Queensland for hundreds of miles. Cook reported favorably though temperately on what he saw, but Banks waxed so enthusiastic over the land that his description induced the British government to choose Botany Bay as the site for a penal colony. A small fleet with about 750 convicts left England in 1787 and reached Botany Bay the following January. But the commander, Captain Phillip, judged the place ill suited for a settlement. A few miles farther north, however, he found a spot that seemed to possess the necessary qualifications. And the British flag went up at Port Jackson on January 26, 1788, marking the beginning of British occupation of Australia.

With convicts and their guards Phillip founded New South

Wales. An able man of a sanguine temperament, he predicted success for the colony from the first. Others were not so sure. And, indeed, it required an unusual amount of optimism to prophesy a future for the new settlement. The human material used was about the worst England could produce. The quality of the soil and the natural products of the land proved disappointing. In the early years supplies had to be brought from India or the Cape, America or Europe. At times famine threatened to wipe out the colony, and not infrequently the perverseness and wickedness of man led it to the brink of ruin. Sordid tales of vice, greed, corruption, and insubordination fill the early annals of Australia. They fall outside the scope of our study, but can be read in many books.

Every European settlement founded overseas has gone through an era of hardship and suffering, and Governor Phillip's penal colony had a long and difficult period of apprenticeship. But he and his successors as governors of New South Wales were of the bulldog breed. Despite failures and disappointments they struggled on and by 1815 the worst storms had been weathered. Fertile lands had been found in the valleys of the Hawkesbury and the Hunter. The discovery of coal near the mouth of the latter river heartened those who had faith in the future of Australia, and, reminiscently, they named the coal district Newcastle. In 1813 Gregory Blaxland with a few companions found paths along the ridges of the Blue Mountains leading to good grass land in valleys and plateaus farther west. Men now knew that the settlement had room for expansion. Captain John MacArthur of Camden, often a troublemaker in Australian politics, made amends for much mischief by demonstrating that the flocks of New South Wales could produce fleece acceptable in the wool marts of England. And since January 1, 1810, the unruly population of the colony had been forced into submission and discipline under the stern but beneficent rule of Governor Macquarie.

In addition to the original settlement at Port Jackson, Norfolk

Island had been occupied as a secondary penal station. In 1803 Van Diemen's Land, later named Tasmania, was chosen for the same purpose. By 1815 perhaps the most hectic days in Australian history had passed, but for the greater part of the continent the historic period had scarcely begun. Large stretches of the coast

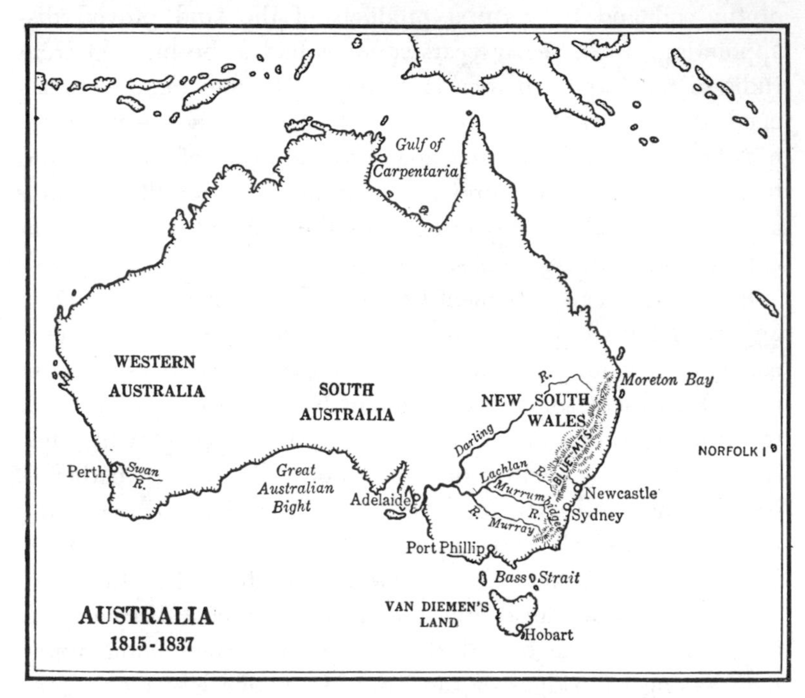

and nearly all the interior were as yet unexplored. Life in Australia was rough and crude; a free English settler in the Australian bush possessed fewer civil rights than did the trek-Boer on the veld of South Africa. More isolated than any other of the settlement colonies of England and bearing the stamp of convictism, New South Wales and Van Diemen's Land could not compete with North America in bidding for British emigrants. Special inducements had to be held out to free settlers for Australia.

Largely because of the efforts of George Bass and Matthew Flinders the exploration and survey of the coast of Australia went on rapidly in the early years of the nineteenth century. Their work was continued though not finished by Captain King, son of a former governor of New South Wales, from 1817 to 1822. Blaxland's discovery of pasture lands beyond the coastal mountains gave a tremendous stimulus to the exploration of the interior. The river systems of the Darling, the Lachlan, the Murrumbidgee, and the Murray were traced; the hypothesis of a great lake in the interior of Australia was advanced and exploded; and before the close of the thirties large sections of the arid regions of the continent had been traversed.

Activities of American whalers and French explorers caused Governor Darling of New South Wales to claim Western Australia for Britain in 1829. At this time Captain Sterling and Thomas Peel, wealthy cousin of Sir Robert Peel, founded the ill-starred Swan River settlement which ultimately grew into the colony and state of Western Australia. Not long afterward squatters, prominent among whom were Edward Henty and John Batman, laid the foundations for Victoria. And in 1836 Wakefield's colony, South Australia, came into existence. Meanwhile the frontiers of the mother colony, New South Wales, moved westward to the plains of Bathurst and Liverpool and northward to Port Macquarie and Moreton Bay.

South Australia alone among the states of Australia has never had, as part of its population, transported criminals serving a sentence. Wakefield and his friends opposed it; at the time they founded South Australia the transportation of criminals to New South Wales was about to be discontinued. When it ceased, the mother colony entered a new era of political progress which soon raised it to a plane equal to that of the older settlements of British North America.

The first four governors of New South Wales – Phillip, Hunter, King, and Bligh – were naval officers. The discipline aboard the ships of the royal navy in those days bore a strong resemblance to that in a penal institution – perhaps for that reason they were chosen as governors of Britain's largest prison. But prison discipline was not easy to enforce in Australia. The illimitable space of the new land tempted convicts to seek freedom in the bush. Most of those who did so perished, but this failed to deter others from taking a risk with the unknown. The treatment accorded convicts, particularly in Van Diemen's Land, was such that even death might be a welcome escape. Occasionally they got away in boats or as stowaways. However, the great majority remained, and the governors were expected to make them tillers of the soil, since reform of the criminals had been one of the objects of those who sponsored transportation. But to convert jailbirds into farmers often proved a superhuman task; in the beginning the guards caused almost as much trouble for successive governors as did the criminals under sentence. The marines who had gone out with the first fleet were shortly afterward replaced by the New South Wales Corps recruited in England for that purpose. The quality of the corps was poor as to both officers and men. The difficulties with the often mutinous troops reached a climax in 1808 when the officers deposed and imprisoned Governor Bligh.

Great changes were wrought in New South Wales by Governor Lachlan Macquarie, 1810–1821. He brought with him his own regiment, the 73rd Highland. The New South Wales Corps ceased to exist. With the authority conferred by his military rank, Macquarie combined the autocratic powers then wielded by the governor of New South Wales and a disposition to use his power to the full. John MacArthur, leader in the uprising against Governor Bligh, went to England and was detained there for several years. Other turbulent spirits either left the country or submitted. Subject to scant supervision from home, Governor Macquarie acted as supreme judge, administrator, and legislator. He could sentence a man to death and there was no appeal; he granted land titles, decided what should be grown on the land and the price thereof; he regulated the industries, the currency, the rate of exchange — in short, practically every detail in the economic and social life of New South Wales came under his supervision. Before 1815 the government and public opinion at home had other and more pressing topics to consider than the state of the prison colony in the antipodes. And even after the close of the war, colonial questions generally seemed of little importance. Macquarie governed arbitrarily, but a master was needed. Peace and order replaced disturbances and chaos. More land was brought under cultivation, the flocks of sheep grew, and special efforts were made to rehabilitate the ex-convicts and restore them to an honored place in society. On the latter point Macquarie met with much opposition from officers of the garrison and the free settlers. Indeed, his good work both hastened his recall and helped to end the political system which he represented.

After 1816 restrictions upon emigation of free settlers to New South Wales were removed. The colony gained a reputation as a place where fortunes might be made. Newcomers with capital arrived, but the colonial autocracy proved irksome to both free and freed settlers. W. C. Wentworth, a son of a deportee, became the first native Australian champion of civil and political rights. A graduate of Cambridge University, in 1819 he published in England a book on Australia. Herein he described the opportunities afforded by the colony and attacked its form of government. Five years later he started the *Australian,* the first privately owned newspaper in Australia, which soon become the organ for those who advocated a change of the governmental system. Even before the youthful Wentworth began his career as a reformer, the redoubtable John MacArthur had launched attacks on the existing political despotism. A long sojourn in England supplied him with opportunity to establish connections with members of parliament. Soon questions about Macquarie and New South Wales were asked with an embarrassing frequency in parliament. The government had to take notice.

In 1819 Lord Bathurst, the colonial secretary, sent Mr. J. T. Bigge, a London barrister, to New South Wales to report upon the colony and its institutions. He made thorough inquiries and submitted lengthy reports which were presented to parliament. About this time it was also discovered that New South Wales as a settlement colony should be governed under regulations approved by parliament; consequently the New South Wales Judicature Act was passed in 1823. The act provided for trial by jury in civil cases and created a supreme court and a legislative council of from five to seven members. At first this body was only a feeble imitation of a lawmaking assembly. Its members were officials, appointed by the governor, who had the power to initiate and veto legislation and to put into effect bills rejected by the council – pending approval by the secretary of state. Feeble though it was, the council did limit the power of the governor. His authority was also challenged from another quarter. Chief Justice Forbes of the new supreme court followed old traditions of the English judiciary in assuming an independent attitude toward the governor in his interpretation of bills submitted to the council and in his decisions from the bench. The separation of the executive from the legislative council came in 1825. The chief justice then ceased to be a member of the lawmaking body, which now included three non-official members.

In the twenties agitation for representative institutions grew stronger. Sir Thomas Brisbane, Macquarie's successor, expressed sympathy with the demands for a more liberal form of government, but Governor Darling, 1826–1833, held different views. He tried to check political agitation and to curb the press. He recommended, however, that the legislative council should include elected members; this the colonial secretary, William Huskisson, refused to sanction. A temporary act of 1828 made trial by jury possible in criminal cases, enlarged the legislative council to include from ten to fifteen members with a bare majority of officials, took away the authority of the governor to enact laws without the approval of the council, and limited the power exerted by the chief justice over legislation.

Both on the question of jury trial in criminal cases and on

that of representative government, colonial opinion was sharply divided. By 1830 the population of New South Wales numbered approximately 50,000, about equally divided between free settlers and convicts. Free immigrants were arriving in increasing numbers, but many of these showed no eagerness for the establishment of juries and a legislative assembly which might include ex-felons. Although trial by jury in criminal cases was conceded in 1830, the grant of representative government became tied up with the question of transportation. In New South Wales the so-called "exclusionists," headed by John MacArthur and his son James, favored discontinuance of transportation and had little enthusiasm for a popularly elected legislature. Yet Australian petitions favoring the latter arrived in England, especially after the passage of the Reform Bill, only to be coldly received by the government of Lord Grey. Lord Howick, parliamentary under-secretary of state for the colonies, cited the cleavage in colonial opinion as one of the reasons for postponing the grant of a legislative assembly.

Among the leading advocates of a representative government for New South Wales were Sir John Jamison, Dr. John Dunmore Lang, and W. C. Wentworth. In 1835 these men organized the Australian Patriotic Association which maintained a parliamentary agent at Westminster. The first so chosen was Sir Henry Lytton Bulwer. His successor, Charles Buller, frankly told the Australians that the transportation system and free institutions were incompatible. They must make a choice between the two. Meanwhile, in 1837–1838, a committee on transportation, headed by another colonial reformer, Sir William Molesworth, made a careful study of its character and effects upon Australia. The committee advised the abandonment of the system for New South Wales. This recommendation synchronized with the rebellions in the Canadas which brought the colonial question prominently before the British public. The government adopted the report of the transportation committee and agreed to make the legislature for New South Wales two-thirds elective.

Australia had no serious native problem. Unlike the Kaffirs of South Africa, the Australian aborigines could offer little opposition to colonization by Europeans. At first friendly, the blackfellows soon became the victims of outrages at the hands of white derelicts. Retaliation followed in the form of thefts and murder of white men. The natives were too backward, being still in the stone age, to resist invaders. Convicts, individual settlers, and occasionally government officials treated the aborigines of Australia as intruders or as vermin to be exterminated. In Van Diemen's Land, Lieutenant-governor Arthur in 1835 organized a systematic hunt for natives. Although he failed to capture all of them, the aboriginal inhabitants before long shared the fate of the Beothucks of Newfoundland – joining the ranks of vanished races. The blackfellows on the mainland of Australia were more fortunate. The continent provided them refuge until the missionary and humanitarian sentiments in England had become sufficiently interested and powerful to intercede effectively in behalf of the Australian natives.

When Captain Phillip set sail for Australia with his shiploads of convicts, the government expected that they would settle on the land upon the expiration of their sentence. But little thought had been given to the problems of a new community. Seed grain and cattle were sent out with the first fleet, but not until 1796 did the settlement get its first plow. Since the settlement was a prison farm, all agricultural operations had at first to be conducted by the government, and for nearly a generation after independent farmers had established themselves the government continued to operate farms and to purchase farm products.

James Ruse, an expiree, received a grant of one acre of land at Parramatta in 1789 and became the first independent farmer in Australia. His success with wheat-growing stimulated others of his class to take up farming, and before the close of the century a few free settlers had arrived. But in agriculture as in other pursuits both the government and the settlers suffered many setbacks. Drought and floods often ruined the crops. Yet by 1802 it had become evident that, barring special misfortunes, New South Wales could grow its own breadcorn. With the development of farming, the question of landholding arose. At first it seemed that the colony would be confined to the relatively narrow strip between the mountains and the sea, which contained only a small amount of fertile land. The discovery of grassy plains and fine natural sheep pastures beyond the mountains changed the outlook. Now the supply of land seemed inexhaustible. The altered perspective is revealed in the size of the land grants. In the early days an ex-convict received 30 acres if single, 50 acres if married, and 10 acres for each child. Discharged soldiers who took up farming were granted 80 and free settlers 100 acres each. Extra allotments were offered as rewards for meritorious service, and officers of the garrison usually secured extensive areas. Captain Phillip dreamed of establishing a semi-feudal land system; this of course could not thrive any better in Australia than in North America. In New South Wales the problems of land and labor supply became closely associated. Land was cleared by convicts working in gangs under government overseers, and the cleared areas were sold at 5*s.* per acre. Another method was to lend convicts, fed and clothed by the government, to private employers for the purpose of bringing land into cultivation. Finally it became customary to supply a landowner with a convict for each one hundred acres. Indeed shortly after the opening of the nineteenth century all convicts belonging to the better class were either employed by the government or assigned to settlers as laborers or servants.

At the same time it became customary to offer land grants in proportion to the amount of capital spent in the colony or on bringing out settlers. Among the beneficiaries of this arrangement were the Blaxland brothers who in 1805 received from the government 8000 acres and the service of one convict for each one hundred acres on condition that they spend £6000 on cultivating new land and bringing colonists to Australia. John MacArthur was granted 5000 acres as a reward for his experiments in sheep-raising. By 1817 the rule had been established that no crown land should be alienated except in proportion to capital owned by the grantee and spent by him for settling the land. But exceptions to the rule were numerous, especially after wool-growing proved a success. The estate of the MacArthurs of Camden continued to increase so that in 1836 the family owned about 50,000 acres. As in British North America, private land companies secured large tracts. Two of these, the Australian Agricultural Association and the Tasmanian Land Company, obtained 500,000 acres each. The promoters of the Swan River settlement sought 4,000,000 and obtained about 1,000,000 acres.

In 1831 the colonial office adopted for the entire empire Wakefield's principle not to give land away to settlers but to sell it at auction with a fixed upset price (in New South Wales 5*s.* per acre) and to use part of the revenue thus obtained to aid selected emigrants. Soon considerable funds had accumulated, or had been anticipated to accumulate, for this purpose. The amount of money advanced by the imperial treasury to aid Australian immigrants increased from £10,000 in 1831 to £136,000 in 1836, and the number of free immigrants rose from 457 in the former year to 10,189 in 1838. By this time plans were maturing for the creation of the Colonial Land and Emigration Commission which later rendered valuable service in settling the waste lands of Australia.

The growing of grain and the raising of livestock naturally were among the first concerns of the authorities in New South Wales. Before long, however, need arose for exportable commodities to be sold or bartered for the various articles needed even in a frontier settlement. In the early days efforts to foster trade were hampered by the monopoly which the East India Company enjoyed east of the Cape of Good Hope. However, interlopers, especially from America, paid little heed to the legal restrictions on trade, though neither they nor the colonial authorities could at first overcome the obstacles presented by the failure of New South Wales to produce exportable goods. For somewhat more than a quarter of a century whaling in Australian waters brought material benefits — the social and moral were extremely dubious — to the new colony. Whalers from Sydney plied their trade off New Zealand and in the waters of Antarctica. But the rapid extermination of the animals reduced the revenue from whaling. Gold was not discovered in Australia until the middle of the nineteenth century. Manufacturing industries developed slowly, and decades passed before even the moderate needs of the small settlement could be supplied on the spot. But the settlers came from England where wool had been a staple commodity for centuries and where now the domestic supply fell far short of the need. That Australian pioneers should think of wool-growing was perhaps natural. Wool could be kept, easily transported, and it usually fetched a good price in the English market. John MacArthur, whose actions in many other matters were anything but blameless, deserves well of Australia as the founder of her sheep industry. By importing merinos from the Cape and other breeds from England, by watchful care and scientific experimentation, MacArthur had by 1815 demonstrated that Australia could produce fleece capable of satisfying even the exacting standards of the woolen manufacturers of England.

In the early years, Australian wool had the benefit of an English preferential tariff, paying a duty of only 1*d.* per pound as against 6*d.* for foreign wool. But the tariff changes of the twenties wiped out the preferences on wool so that the growers of Australia had to meet the full force of German and Spanish competition. Yet they more than held their own. Exports of wool from New South Wales alone rose from 60,000 pounds in 1814 to 1,134,000 pounds in 1831, and by that year Van Diemen's Land had passed the mother colony in wool export. In 1838 the sheep runs of New South Wales contained 2,750,000 animals.

Lack of ready money or of a serviceable medium of exchange in the early years proved as much of a handicap for the economic development of Australia as did the absence of exportable goods.

The home government evidently believed that a prison farm had no need for money and therefore sent none. Forced to fall back on their own devices, the colonists tried various substitutes for money and finally decided to adopt rum for this purpose. As the early American settlers had employed wampum and beaver skins, so those of New South Wales utilized rum. In vain the government tried to restrict its use. The article was in universal demand. Apart from its serviceability as a medium of exchange, employers of convicts found that rum was a prize which nearly all of them coveted. One governor after another strove fruitlessly to limit its consumption. Drunkenness became a common and appalling vice. Finally Macquarie erected government distilleries as an outlet for the surplus stores of grain, and at the same time brought in more currency. The latter helped to lower the consumption of rum, although years passed before the motley population of Australia could be called temperate in its use of intoxicating liquors.

English and foreign coins, especially Spanish dollars, circulated at first rather indiscriminately in New South Wales. Various types of paper money were also tried. Finally in 1817, Macquarie brought order into the monetary situation by granting a charter to the Bank of New South Wales without consulting the home authorities. Though reprimanded for the act, the governor left the bank as founded, and Commissioner Bigge, who reported adversely on many of Macquarie's measures, in 1823 bore testimony to the utility of Macquarie's bank. Governor Brisbane renewed its charter and soon other banks appeared. Banking in Australia as elsewhere suffered many vicissitudes in the period of settlement, but experience proved that Macquarie conferred a lasting benefit upon the colony by "providing and regulating the colonial currency."

Even when compared with the not too exacting standards of the American frontiers, life in New South Wales in the early days must be judged extremely crude and brutal. True, some of the deportees were political prisoners who ranked high in character and culture, but the majority of the transported convicts were hardened felons whose treatment both on the voyage out and in the colony tended to lower them to greater depths of depravity. For many years Australia was used as "a mere dump for human rubbish." This seems to have been especially the case with the women. Upon landing in New South Wales many of the prisoners in 1815 were "assigned" to farmers, shopkeepers, and officials. Often little care was shown in the selection of the new employers — an instance occurred of a male convict being assigned to his own wife. Witnesses before Molesworth's committee on transportation revealed that assigned servants and laborers were often worse treated than the West Indian slaves. With luck and good conduct, however, a deportee might earn a conditional pardon upon or shortly after his arrival in the colony. Only the hardened offenders were kept in chain gangs; "repeaters" might be sent to Norfolk Island or Van Diemen's Land, which acquired reputations as veritable hells on earth where prisoners welcomed death as a means of escape.

But the problems arising from the transportation system were not confined to those of punishment. Rehabilitation for the expiree presented difficulties of no mean proportion. The free settlers and especially the officers of the garrison usually refused to associate with ex-convicts even though they had reformed. Some of them were educated and had held responsible positions before they collided with the authorities at home. In the early days New South Wales lacked men qualified to serve as magistrates and in other offices of trust. Governors were forced to use ex-convicts; Macquarie was particularly insistent that a man's past should not be a barrier to employment under the government. He appointed ex-convicts to the bench and invited some of them to the government house, much to the disgust of the social élite of Sydney. Macquarie erred perhaps in being overly friendly to emancipists and unduly suspicious of free settlers, but his policy gave hope to men and women who carried the stigma of transportation.

The guiltless children of the convicts often had to pay for the sins of their fathers; and in common with those born of free settlers they had the disadvantage of growing up in a society where vice often flourished and social standards were low. That young Australia so soon shook off the evil effects of early associations is indeed a convincing argument against the doctrine of innate depravity.

In addition to the conditions existing in Sydney and other places where convicts gathered in large numbers, the life on the sheep ranches and wheat farms early helped to distinguish the Australian colonies and colonists from those of British North America. The lonely soul-devouring life of the shepherd made him greedy for the company offered by the public houses of the towns. Except in the valleys of the Hawkesbury and the Hunter, small farmers were rare in New South Wales. The husking and threshing bees that are mentioned so often in contemporary accounts from the Canadian frontier seem to have been nonexistent in Australia. Socially and economically the frontier life differed from that of other English colonies. Although middle-class settlers came to Australia as they did to Canada, and the pioneers on the Bathurst and Liverpool plains represented a purer English stock than did those of the Huron Tract of Upper Canada, the new environment in America proved more favorable for the preservation of the amenities of English life.

Picked from jails and deprived of social and political rights, the early settlers of New South Wales quite naturally did not compare with those of the Massachusetts Bay Colony or Nova Scotia in their attitude toward religion and education. And it took time before the churches and missionary societies of Great Britain began to be actively interested in the spiritual welfare of the Australian colonists. This work had to be undertaken by the government. In the early days army chaplains looked after the care of souls; of schools there were none. But in 1802 the farmers in the valley of the Hawkesbury raised the salary of a schoolmaster by voluntary subscription, the schoolhouse being erected by the government. Three years later the imperial government ordered Governor Bligh to allot in each township four hundred acres for the support of a clergyman and two hundred acres for a schoolmaster. In 1810 certain customs dues were set aside to provide schools for orphans. From 1813 till 1826 the home government paid the salaries of clergymen, but after that date only the salaries of the chaplains for the convicts were paid from home.

That the colonial office was alive to the need for supplying churches and schools for New South Wales was clearly shown in Lord Bathurst's instructions to Commissioner Bigge, January 6, 1819. "You will," Bathurst wrote, "also turn your attention to the possibility of diffusing throughout the colony, adequate means of education and religious instruction; bearing always in mind in your suggestions, that these two branches ought in all cases to be inseparably connected." The close union of church and school was further emphasized in the instructions to Governor Brisbane in 1825, for the creation of a church and school corporation to be endowed with one-seventh, in extent and value, of the government land in the colony. The first land grant of this sort was made in February, 1829, and the last in May of the following year. The corporation itself never exerted much influence and was dissolved in 1833. The reason for its lack of influence as well as its short span of life was mainly that it formed part of a plan, soon abandoned, to set up an established church in Australia.

Governor Macquarie discouraged clergymen other than those of the established church from coming to Australia, and despite the presence of numerous Roman Catholics among the convicts no chaplain of that faith was supplied between 1808 and 1819. On the other hand, the archdeacon of the Anglicans in New South Wales was a member of the legislative council, 1825–1837. After 1820 the Catholics increased their activities among both the convicts and the free settlers, and when in 1833 the later Bishop Ullathorne came out as vicar-general the Catholic mission was well established. The need for Church of Scotland clergymen had been recognized somewhat earlier than that for the Roman Catholics, but active work on behalf of the Presbyterians did not begin until 1823 when John Dunmore Lang arrived in New South Wales. Although it was clearly the intention of the home government in the twenties to establish the Church of England in Australia, small contributions were made both to Presbyterians and to Roman Catholics. In the thirties, Governor Bourke noticed that the endowed Church of England school in Sydney languished while the non-sectarian school founded by Dr. Lang flourished. Bourke read the signs of the time correctly and in 1833 recommended that the government establish secular schools and cease to favor any particular creed. Two years later a dispatch from Lord Glenelg established religious equality in Australia. The Anglican bishopric of Sydney was created in 1837. Marsden, the Anglican, Lang, the Presbyterian, and Ullathorne, the Catholic, were the outstanding religious leaders of Australia in the first half of the nineteenth century.

As already indicated, the history of Australia before 1837 is largely that of New South Wales. To be sure, Van Diemen's Land became a separate colony in 1825 and received all the government institutions granted to New South Wales. But the island continued to be in the main only a convict station for many years after. Western Australia, or the Swan River settlement, experienced a tremendous boom at the time of its founding in 1829. The colony was, however, literally and metaphorically built on sand. Bitter disappointment and financial ruin became the common lot of both promoters and settlers, and many weary years passed before the colony emerged from the slough of despond. Adelaide was founded in South Australia, just as the time limit set for this chapter approaches. E. G. Wakefield and his friends planted this settlement and kept it before the public mind in England. Large tracts of land were disposed of and a considerable number of settlers went out. But South Australia like Western Australia had to pass through a period of severe depression before the colony could be said to be securely established. Both owe their founding in large measure to the fact that Britain possessed sufficient private capital and dreamers of colonial Utopias and the government had the requisite financial strength to risk new ventures and to shoulder the burden of the cost of founding new colonies in the antipodes. On the other hand, the Port Phillip settlement, which became Victoria, was established by pioneers of the American type. The initial cost for Britain was slight, and this colony in its early days experienced neither the great boom nor the disastrous slump that befell Western and South Australia.

In 1837 the colonies of Australia were either in their swaddling clothes or still labeled convict stations. Their white population had increased tenfold since 1815 but had hardly reached 150,000. In political and economic progress they lagged behind the British colonies in North America. But they were on the threshold of a period of rapid expansion. The work of the transportation committee soon rid New South Wales of convictism. In part as a corollary to this change and in part as a result of the Canadian rebellions and Lord Durham's Report, true representative institutions were before long granted to the mother colony of Australia. The sheep industry had begun to flourish, and government authorities at home and in the antipodes were cooperating in bringing in selected free immigrants. Religious equality had been conceded, and energetic leaders in religion and education were joining hands with those in politics and business to make the infant communities of Australia worthy of the loins whence they sprang.

CHAPTER 8

INDIA, 1813–1858

INDIA formed a part of the British empire even in the days of "John Company." From the beginning the conditions under which the company operated had been fixed by royal charters, and with the assumption of territorial powers in 1765 its freedom of action became further restricted by parliamentary statutes. As the nineteenth century advanced, the ebb and flow of policies in India were more and more affected by the fears or tendencies or movements that were shaping the ideas of British political, industrial, and commercial leaders. The rise of the middle class and the growth of the missionary societies at home left their impress upon India, and the industrial revolution brought ruin to the hand-loom weavers of both countries, since the trade of India was regulated in the interest of the paramount power. India moved in the orbit of Britain and Britain's overseas empire.

In an earlier chapter we sketched the spread of British power in India up to the close of the Hanoverian period. By then the domain controlled by Britain was bounded by the Himalayas and the sea, except in the west and northwest where the amirs of Sind and the Sikh confederacy in the Punjab held extensive areas of Indian territory. The rest of the subcontinent either had been annexed outright or had acknowledged by treaties its dependence upon British rule. In addition to possessions in India proper, provinces of Burma had been acquired by the company; and portions of the Malay Peninsula, including the island of Singapore, had been placed under its jurisdiction. Portuguese, Dutch, and French had either been expelled or rendered harmless. But no sooner had the old gateways to India been secured to Britain by annexations and her control of the sea than the specter of "the bear that walks like a man" began to haunt her statesmen. It rose with Tilsit. Napoleon and Tsar Alexander I of Russia were plotting to divide the earth, the east to fall to the latter. The subsequent quarrel and war between them, 1812–1814, allayed that fear for a moment; but by the 1820's Englishmen heard with alarm rumors of Russian activity in the Middle East. Lord Palmerston, who guided Britain's foreign policy in the thirties, regarded the Russo-Turkish treaty of friendship of 1833 as a challenge to Britain. Stories of Russian plots to seize northern Norway as a base for attacks upon the British Isles and of efforts to gain control over Persia stirred him deeply. The danger seemed greatest in the lands bordering India. Here, he felt, Russia must be forestalled. Lord Auckland, who in 1836 succeeded Lord William Bentinck as governor general of India, shared Palmerston's apprehensions.

Afghanistan held the key position on the land route to India. Vainly its ruler, Dost Mohammed, professed friendship for the English. Protests by the court of directors of the East India Company were ignored. The government at home and Lord Auckland in India agreed that in order to safeguard the northwest approaches to India, Shah Shujah, a descendant of former rulers of Afghanistan and for many years a pensioner of the British, must be placed on the throne of his fathers. In 1838 British armies moved northward through Sind, Kandahar and Kabul were occupied, Dost Mohammed fled, and Shah Shujah was proclaimed his successor. But the warlike tribes of Afghanistan refused to accept the new ruler. Akbar Khan, a son of Dost Mohammed, appeared on the scene. The Afghans flocked to his standard. Indecision paralyzed the British; their political agent at Kabul was murdered; and in the dead of winter, 1841–1842, their army, consisting of 4000 fighting men and 12,000 camp followers, evacuated Kabul and retreated toward India. Harassed by day and night, the retreat became a rout – only one man reached safety at Jelalabad. Though the tragedy was avenged in a measure later in 1842 and Kabul reoccupied, complete withdrawal soon followed and Dost Mohammed returned. Russophobe ministers in Downing Street had scorned the advice of Indian experts, and humiliating disasters had resulted therefrom. Britain mourned and India paid.

The first Afghan war had further results. The amirs of Sind, through whose territories the British marched and had their lines of communication, proved less accommodating than had been expected. Quarrels arose. British claims were pressed ruthlessly by the commander-in-chief, Sir Charles Napier. War broke out in 1843 and Sind was added to British India. To the north of Sind lay the Sikh state. The founder of this state, Ranjit Singh, had been a friend of the English, although he had refused them permission to march through his kingdom in the attack upon Afghanistan. When he died in 1839, he left a well-trained and splendidly equipped army but no heir capable of controlling effectively the power he had built up. Disorders followed; the Sikh army, encouraged by the reverses suffered by the British in Afghanistan, was anxious to test its strength. In 1845 the Sikhs threw down the gauntlet by crossing the Sutlej into a demilitarized tract on the British side of the river. The challenge was accepted and after severe fighting the Sikhs were driven back. Their capital, Lahore, was seized; and shorn of some of its territory the Punjab became a protected state but retained its army. Two years of uneasy peace followed. Toward the close of 1848 the second Sikh war broke out. At first the great military machine of Ranjit Singh fought the British to a standstill — on the fatal field of Chilianwala, January 13, 1849, the British lost 2400 officers and men, four guns, and the colors of three regiments. But shortly afterward the aged British commander-in-chief, Sir Hugh Gough, crushed the Sikhs, and the Punjab was annexed. This completed the conquest of India proper.

In the lands bordering India on the east, British power continued to grow. The court at Ava forgot the lessons of the first Burmese war. When British merchants suffered indignities at Rangoon, Lord Dalhousie, governor general of India, declared war. Better managed than the first, the second Burmese war, 1852, lasted but two months. Pegu was ceded, and all of Lower Burma thus passed into the hands of the British. Theoretically the conquest came under the control of the East India Company, although a member of its court of directors declared before a select committee of the house of commons, "The Court of Directors have no knowledge whatever of the origin, progress, or present state of war in Burmah." "John Company" and India were mere tools of Britain.

Under the masterful rule of Lord Dalhousie, 1848–1856, the territory in India governed directly by the British was further augmented by the application of "the doctrine of lapse." This meant that Dalhousie refused to recognize adopted sons as heirs to dependent Indian states. In the absence of an heir of his body, the territories of a ruler of such a state escheated to the British. About 150,000 square miles were thus secured. The most important among the states absorbed were Nagpur, Saxtara, and Jhansi. In each case "the good of the people" was given as a principal reason for the annexation. This principle applied with a great deal of justice in the case of Oudh. Under British protection since the beginning of the century, Oudh had suffered from chronic misrule. Warnings by successive governors general went unheeded. Dalhousie then acted with characteristic vigor; the kingdom was annexed in February, 1856. Not since the days of Lord Wellesley fifty years earlier had there been such large additions to British India. That Dalhousie aimed thereby to benefit the people concerned cannot be doubted; but the annexations aroused apprehension and hostility. Vested interests suffered. To avenge a wrong, the disinherited Rani or Princess of Jhansi rallied her people to a desperate fight against the British during the mutiny of 1857 and died on the field of battle. Nana Sahib, adopted son of the last Peshwa or chief of the Maratha confederacy, was refused the pension bestowed upon his father and so became an implacable enemy of the British. The annexation of Oudh, the leading Mohammedan kingdom of northern India, was one of the immediate causes of the Indian Mutiny.

But before we tell the story of the explosion which put an end to the venerable East India Company, it will be necessary to consider the nature and character of its rule, its relations with the government of Britain, and the economic and social condition of British India during the first half of the nineteenth century.

The territories governed directly by the British were at first grouped in the presidencies of Bombay, Madras, and Bengal. As the last-named grew unwieldy, plans for divisions were discussed and ultimately the North-Western Provinces were put under a lieutenant-governor. The area not annexed by the British was in the company's day, as in our own, divided among several hundred native states. The relations between them and the company were usually defined by treaties. Lord Wellesley, 1797–1805, founded the system of surrounding the company's territories with a ring fence of protected or allied states, a policy continued by his successors. Lord Hastings, 1813–1823, did much in defining and clarifying the respective positions of the paramount power and the dependent states. In each case control over foreign relations and external defense rested with the British. Some of the states were bound to maintain military forces of a certain strength, and the more important of them accepted British officials called residents. The position of the Indian states has since been described as one of "subordinate cooperation." Generally speaking, the company concerned itself less with the internal administration of the native states than has been the case since India passed under the direct control of the crown.

Lord North's act of 1773 began the work of placing the territorial administration of the great joint-stock company that controlled India under the supervision of the home government. Ten years later the activities of Warren Hastings, the most illustrious of the rulers of India in the days of the company, and the rumors concerning them assiduously spread in England led to the passage of Pitt's East India Act in 1784. This famous statute wrought many changes in the government of India, particularly in the judiciary and in the position and powers of the governor general. The two bodies representing the stockholders, the court of directors and the court of proprietors, especially the latter, lost much of their power. A new department, the board of control, was created; its president was always a member of the British government, often with a seat in the cabinet. The board of control had authority to supervise the territorial administration of the East India Company and early assumed charge of India's relations with foreign powers. The crown could recall the governor general and any other official in India accused or suspected of misconduct, and provisions were made for a tribunal to hear charges and to try accused officials. A secret committee of the court of directors served as intermediary between that body and the board of control.

In the nineteenth century a trading company which enjoyed sovereign territorial powers became more and more of an anomaly; its commercial monopoly had long been watched by jealous eyes. Consequently with each renewal of its charter, the East India Company lost powers and privileges. The trade east of the Cape of Good Hope was opened to private enterprise, and the substance of power in the government of India passed into the hands of the British government years before 1858. Concurrently with these changes the governor general received additional authority both in his relations with his council and in his relations with the governors of Madras and Bombay.

The vigorous policy of Lord Wellesley created financial embarrassments for the company and led to commitments of various kinds of which the home government had to take cognizance. Moreover, after 1806 Napoleon's closing of the ports of continental Europe against English trade created a situation in England which increased the pressure for permission to trade freely with India. The company fought hard against the demands of traders, planters, and missionaries for an open door. In 1812–1813 former governors and governors general, including the venerable Warren Hastings, appeared before the bar of the house of commons in support of the company's trade monopoly. The result was a compromise. The Charter Act of 1813 deprived the company of its trading monopoly in India, though retaining it for China; missionaries and others engaged in lawful pursuits might enter India under license from the court of directors or the board of control; rules were laid down for the expenditure of the territorial revenues of the company and its system of bookkeeping; and although the patronage remained with the court of directors, the appointments of higher officials were subject to the approval of the crown.

With the renewal of the company's charter in 1833 its commercial privileges were swept away. European settlers in India were freed from some of the restrictions imposed upon them, and provisions were made for safeguarding the rights of the natives and for the extinction of slavery. The act of 1833 declared that the East India Company held territorial possessions "in trust for His Majesty, his heirs and successors" and that parliament had the right "in all respects to legislate for the said Territories, and all the Inhabitants thereof." Article 87 deserves special mention. It reads: "No Native of the said Territories, nor any natural-born Subject of His Majesty resident therein, shall, by reason only of his religion, place of birth, descent, colour, or any of them be disabled from holding any Place, Office, or Employment under the said Company." Anticipating the end of the company, the act stipulated that its stockholders might be bought out at a fixed rate, and that for this purpose the company was to deposit with the National Debt Commission two million pounds annually. After 1833 the governor general of Bengal was styled governor general of India, and to his council of three was added a fourth, a law member, who served whenever the council met for legislative purposes. The first so appointed was T. B. Macaulay, the historian, who rendered valuable aid in the consolidation and codification of Indian laws.

Twenty years later, in 1853, after thorough inquiries and voluminous reports by committees of both houses of parliament, the charter of the East India Company was renewed for the last time, without a fixed term of its duration. The Indian territories were to remain "under the government of the Company, in trust for the Crown, until Parliament should otherwise direct." The court of directors was reduced in number from twenty-four to sixteen, six of whom were to be appointed by the crown. The court lost its control over Indian patronage, and steps were taken to open the civil service of India to general competition.

The position of the governor general grew steadily in importance from the time of Warren Hastings to that of Lord Dalhousie. Too far distant to be controlled effectively by any body residing in England, he was unaffected by the decline of the company. He became virtually independent of his council, and his authority over the governors of Bombay and Madras was greatly increased. Lord Dalhousie wielded such power as falls to few among mortals.

Though modified in details, Pitt's act of 1784 supplied the framework for the government of India until 1858. Its "elaborate system of checks and counterchecks" was adversely criticized by Sir Courtenay Ilbert, the modern authority on the government of India. Upon retirement from office, Lord William Bentinck, governor general from 1828 to 1834, pointed out defects in the machinery of government which he had managed. Lord Curzon, famous both as viceroy of India from 1898 to 1905 and as an authority on Indian history and administration, speaks of the handiwork of the younger Pitt in terms of unmeasured contempt. "Had a Committee," he writes, "been assembled from the padded chambers of Bedlam, they could hardly have devised anything more extravagant in its madness, or more mischievous in its operation." Against this may be quoted John Stuart Mill. After a long period in the service of the India government in London, Mill told a committee of the house of lords on June 21, 1852, "The present constitution of the India Government, considering the great difficulties of the case, seems to me to have worked very satisfactorily." If to Mill's "considering the great difficulties of the case" we add "and of the time," we may judge less harshly of Pitt and "John Company."

Historians have often lashed the East India Company, and indeed there were blots aplenty on its escutcheon. India had a pagoda tree to shake, and volunteers for picking the fruit were not wanting. However, the Indian nabobs, servants of the company enriched by private trade and other illegal methods, whose vulgar display of wealth displeased the English aristocrats, belong to the eighteenth century; the stockholders usually had to be content with the relatively modest return of 10 per cent. But India was, and is, a poor country, so that any return upon money invested there might prove a serious drain. Judged by the English standards of the time, the governor general's salary of £25,000 per year could hardly be called excessive — a governor of a small West Indian island often received £5000. But allowances of various kinds increased the cost of the office, and most of its occupants were granted pensions of about

£5000 upon retirement. Generous salaries were paid the higher officials and the members of the council (Macaulay saved £7000 annually out of his salary). The employees of the company were entitled to handsome pensions. India alone among Britain's overseas possessions carried the cost of her government, including the home charges, and paid for her external defense. Whether some of the wars for which India paid, such as that with Afghanistan in 1839–1842, were fought in her interest is debatable; the cost of these wars added to that of her government constitute the "drain" so often lamented by Indian nationalist writers.

Land supplied the main source of income for the government of India. From an early date the company tried to stabilize and increase the land revenue. In Bengal the old tax farmers, the *Zemindars*, were by "the permanent settlement" of 1793 recognized as landlords and made responsible for fixed payments to the government. The tenants' rights were not defined, and the increase in population and in the number of intermediate holders of leases led to a decline in the position of the tenants. In the presidencies of Madras and Bombay the old Hindu system of village communities with corporate right of ownership and corporate responsibility for taxes had survived the rule of the Moguls, though in some districts a feudal system of landholding had taken its place. Here the government generally dealt directly with the ryots, or peasants, sweeping away the old landlords. Hailed as a great step forward, this reform like so many others brought a not unmixed blessing. The tax or rent which the peasants had to pay amounted to about one-third of the produce grown. Assessed every year, it tended to discourage improvements since a greater yield meant a higher tax. Complaints of over-assessment were frequent. A host of minor officials swooped down upon the peasants and, in the words of an ex-Indian official, Sir Charles Trevelyan, fixed "from the recesses of [their] own breast what each individual shall pay." Installments were to be paid in cash at fixed times. Sometimes the peasant could not get remission in case of cattle plague or crop failure. His position became nearly identical with that of the Irish cottars of the middle of the nineteenth century. The old arrangements for the Indian peasants had offered opportunities for payment in kind, and the feudal lords had acted as buffers between the peasants and the government. Now the ryot faced the government alone; officials could report increases in the land revenues, but spokesmen for the peasants asserted that the new system compelled them to borrow money at usurious rates, that they had to sell their crop at low price, and that in some cases failure to pay had resulted in torture of villagers. Speaking in the house of commons on July 11, 1854, John Bright said: "The fact was quite clear that the taxation was so unjust and onerous that it was impossible to pay it; and then cruelties were resorted to unknown to civilized countries, and scarcely fit for the barbarous Governments which the British Government in India had supplanted." The company, however, was not unmindful of the need for aiding the peasants. During the five years preceding the parliamentary inquiries of 1852, £100,000 was spent annually for irrigation and £42,000 for roads in the Madras presidency alone.

The Indian artisan suffered even more than the peasant from the impact of the West upon the East; and the weakening of the company had the effect of removing a shock absorber. Aided by the latest inventions and government regulations, Lancashire crushed the village cotton manufactures in India. Sir William Hunter, the eminent authority on the history of British India, admits that when the Europeans came to India her people were unsurpassed "in fabrics of cotton and silk, in goldsmith's work and jewelry." Shortly afterward she became an exporter of raw cotton, although the East India Company fostered cotton-weaving and gathered weavers around its forts. The disappearance of native courts and the impoverishment of large sections of the Indian aristocracy deprived the skilled Indian workman of his most important home market, "while, on the other hand," says Sir William Hunter, "the English capitalist has enlisted in his service forces of nature against which the village artisans in vain try to compete." The truth of this statement stands clearly revealed in the evidence presented before the select committee on East Indian produce in 1840. In 1814, Great Britain imported 1,266,608 pieces of cotton goods from India, but by 1835 this import had fallen to 306,086 pieces; at the same time the Indian import of British cotton goods rose from 818,208 to 51,777,270 yards. No wonder that Dacca, an Indian manufacturing center, declined in population from 300,000 to about 36,000. This disparity between the Indian export and import was made good only in part by her export of raw cotton, which rose from 9,368,000 pounds in 1813 to 48,329,660 pounds in 1838, by which time India supplied one-eighth of Britain's import of cotton. A preferential tariff in favor of Indian cotton could not offset the advantages in soil, climate, and lower freight rates enjoyed by the cotton growers of the United States, and the tariff preference soon went by the board.

Other articles exported from India were silk, raw and manufactured, sugar, grain, linseed, spices, and drugs. The British duty on Indian raw silk, 1*d.* per pound, was equal to that on silk from other countries. In 1826–1840 silk goods from India paid an ad valorem duty of 20 per cent. This was strongly objected to by the silk manufacturers of England as being too low. In 1836 the duty on East Indian sugar was equalized with that on sugar from the British West Indies, and the export of sugar from Bengal soon trebled; but sugar could be carried profitably only as deadweight for lighter and costlier wares. When the limit on the demand for sugar for this purpose had been met, the freight rates were prohibitory.

In addition to the obstacles which distance imposed on Indian exporters, the tariff and navigation laws were against them. As an aid to British shipping, Indian customs duties were doubled on goods brought in non-British bottoms. The Indian duties on English manufactures in 1840 were 2 per cent on woolens and 3 per cent on silks and cottons, whereas the British tariffs on Indian produce were 10 per cent on cottons, 20 per cent on silks, and 30 per cent on woolens. This discrimination against the wares of India also extended to the colonies of Britain. Thus in Ceylon cotton goods from England paid a duty of 5 per cent, while 10 to 20 per cent was levied on Indian cottons; in Australia goods of British origin, except spirits, were admitted duty free, but on articles from India the duty was 5 per cent; by order in council of February 22, 1832, goods, wares, and merchandise of British or British colonial origin paid at the Cape a duty of 3 per cent, whereas similar goods from India paid 10 per cent. Furthermore, Britain imposed high revenue duties on Indian spices and drugs. In 1840 the customs duty on cardamom was 42 per cent; on ginger, 63 per cent; on *coculus indicus,* 3500 per cent; and on *nux vomica,* 4000 per cent.

That the interests of the natives of India had on the whole suffered less while the company enjoyed a monopoly of trade and controlled the administration than since the removal of trade barriers and the curbing of the company was the consensus of the witnesses who appeared before the select committee of 1840. The charge of the representatives of the English silk weavers that the company was more concerned over Indian than English laborers was a tribute to the court of directors. In 1840 R. M. Martin, a careful student of intra-imperial trade, produced elaborate figures showing that with the company in control, the balance favoring India ranged from one to two million pounds annually, but after 1813 it had fallen to less than a half a million.

Between 1827 and 1836 India took yearly from 8 to 10 per cent of Britain's export; as a consumer of British goods she was exceeded only by Germany and the United States. The effects of the Anglo-Indian trade relations were tersely summarized by Sir Charles Trevelyan before the committee on Indian produce when he said: "We have swept away their manufactures, they have nothing to depend upon but the produce of their land,

and I think it would be extremely unjust not to give equal privileges in the market of the mother country to that." Indeed, with the produce of the soil India was expected to pay both for the manufactured goods that she bought and the charges in England for the cost of her government. Between May 1, 1838, and May 1, 1839, these totaled £3,643,980, divided as follows: civil charges, £1,643,980; military charges, £2,000,000. The total equaled the cost of the import of British manufactures. The economic interests of India suffered by being exposed to the competition of the new machine industries of Britain and by being discriminated against by imperial and colonial tariffs. It is also clear that a good deal of the injury was due to a deliberate policy. India's interests were made subservient to those of Britain. Mercantilistic principles governed Anglo-Indian trade after they had been abandoned at home.

Not in material affairs alone did India pay for an unsought union. In the field of education the harm done was due to lack of understanding. Before the arrival of Europeans and surviving into the nineteenth century, village schools existed in both Hindu and Mohammedan states. The schools were concerned chiefly with religious instruction; they cannot be called either democratic or efficient. Nevertheless, elementary and secondary education in early eighteenth-century India can stand comparison with that which even northwestern Europe could then offer. Catholic and protestant missionaries came to India in the wake of explorers and traders, and the Catholics soon had flourishing missions. But the attitude of the English toward education in India seems to have been shaped more by that of the Danes than by any other rival. By 1730 Danish missionaries at Tranquebar had founded schools in which the vernacular was used; they encouraged native literature, and experimented with a purely secular education. After 1801 the Danish schools passed under the control of the Society for the Promotion of Christian Knowledge and the Church Missionary Society. Their administration was at first less liberal than that of the Danes, but they soon changed. Respect for the native tongue, though not for their religion, characterized the missionary schools. Although they were derided as inefficient by educational experts and despised by the high-caste Hindus as havens for children of the depressed classes, these schools survived and left deep marks on India.

Not long after the East India Company had gained control over Bengal the question of education was considered by governors general. Warren Hastings founded the Calcutta Madrasa for Mohammedans, and Lord Wellesley established a civilian college at Fort William. In 1793 Wilberforce, whose interests ranged far beyond slave emancipation, vainly urged that the company should provide educational facilities for the people of India. Twenty years later success crowned his efforts. The Charter Act of 1813 stipulated that £10,000 should "be set apart and applied to revival and improvement of literature, and the encouragement of the learned natives of India, and for the introduction and promotion of the sciences among the inhabitants of India." But no effective step was taken for carrying this order into effect until 1823, when a committee of public instruction was appointed. Soon afterward a few schools were opened and in 1833 the yearly grant for education was increased to £100,000. Then a bitter conflict developed as to whether English or oriental education should be provided for the youth of India. In a famous minute of February 2, 1835, Macaulay settled the issue. As might be expected, he favored the English system. Though biased and vehement in his denunciation of what Arabic and Sanskrit had to offer as compared to English, his conclusion that it was neither just nor expedient to train the Indians in oriental lore to the exclusion of a knowledge of western art, science, literature, and philosophy can hardly be challenged. The acceptance of Macaulay's point of view did not mean that the government of India ceased to assist oriental education. Reports of 1842–1843 from fifty-one colleges show that 5132 students studied English, 1819 Hindi, 1504 Urdu, 2718

Bengali, 426 Sanskrit, 572 Arabic, and 706 Persian. In 1844 Lord Hardinge founded 101 vernacular schools in Bengal. Realizing its inability to provide education for the masses of India, the government accepted the "filtering-down" theory. That is to say, by creating a highly educated upper class it was hoped that the light would spread to the less fortunate – predicating an altruism rarely found.

Education was among the many subjects considered by the parliamentary committees on India in 1852 and 1853, a result of which was the dispatch of July 19, 1854, from Sir Charles Wood, president of the board of control, to Lord Dalhousie. This dispatch presented a plan for preparatory schools using the vernacular, government colleges of a higher grade, and a university for each of the three presidencies, with grants-in-aid on a large scale to the various educational institutions. In 1857 universities were founded at Calcutta, Madras, and Bombay. But the educational program outlined in Wood's dispatch was too ambitious. India and the company lacked the necessary resources for putting it into operation. It was not, however, out of harmony with the practical efforts made by the company during the preceding twenty years. Serious thought had been given to the gigantic task of providing education for India's millions. Where the authorities in India and at home erred was in viewing Indian education too much through English spectacles and failing to utilize the possibilities offered by the old village schools.

The probable effects of the introduction of European education upon Anglo Indian relations received some attention; as might be expected, the forecasts differed widely. In 1852 Lord Ellenborough, ex-governor general and former president of the board of control, declared that European education would destroy England's power in India. Sir Charles Trevelyan, who had served for twelve years in India, affirmed in 1838 and reiterated fifteen years later his belief "that the ultimate result of the policy of improving and educating India will be to postpone the separation [from England] for a long indefinite time."

In India as in other places a century ago religion and education were closely interlocked. The company strove with a fair amount of success to hold the balance between rival religions and competing sects. Fear of offending non-Christians caused the government to withhold assistance from schools in which the Bible was used as text. Before 1813 Christian missionaries were excluded from the company's territories, but after that date both English and foreign missionary societies took up active work in British India. Soon the pressure for company aid grew increasingly strong, especially from the Church of England. Financial assistance to the Christian churches usually took the form of providing chaplains for the British soldiers; it is worthy of notice that in 1852 the establishment of the Church of England, supported by the company, numbered 128 in holy orders, including three bishops, and far exceeded that of the other denominations. In religious matters too the company sought to even the scales by small contributions to Mohammedans and Hindus, including one to the notorious temple of Juggernaut in Orissa.

By the middle of the nineteenth century the pressure of western ideas and western civilization on India became increasingly ruthless and insistent. This pressure seemed especially severe under Lord Dalhousie. Trained under Peel and Gladstone, Dalhousie holds an honored place in the galaxy of illustrious men included in the Peel ministry of 1841–1846. In range of interests, versatility of intellect, fertility of imagination, grasp on the theoretical as well as the practical aspects of the problem at hand, quickness of decision, and tenacity in putting a plan into execution, Lord Dalhousie probably ranks first among all the proconsuls of Britain. But he too was earthborn. Failure to appreciate the human side of governmental problems was his one great weakness. Wars in the Punjab, in Burma, and in the Crimea filled the greater part of Dalhousie's eight years of service in India. Preparations for and prosecution of wars and the organization of conquered and "lapsed" territories called for tremendous exertion on the part of the governor general. Dalhousie did everything well, but in common with all disciples of Sir Robert Peel, his chief concern seems to have been administration. Finance and public accounts were given careful attention. A unified postal service was organized within India and with Europe; the importance of both technical and literary education was fully recognized; and he did much to inspire the policy formulated by the famous education dispatch of 1854. Time and energy were devoted to problems of internal improvements. Lord Dalhousie created a public works department and inaugurated the policy of borrowing for works of public utility instead of depending solely on the small and uncertain cash balances. More than 4000 miles of road were built during his term of office; surveys and detailed plans for the building, financing, and administration of railroads were either opened or under construction when he left; the Ganges irrigation canal was completed, and further works were planned under his direction. Other topics of economic importance such as tea-growing and forest conservation did not escape his watchful eye. In the great survey of his administration dated February 28, 1856, Dalhousie points with pardonable pride to the doubling of the annual tonnage at the port of Calcutta since he took over the government of India. Lord Curzon, no mean judge of rulers and administrators, says of Lord Dalhousie: "Whether we regard his policy in respect of public works or railways . . . or telegraphs or roads or irrigation or posts or education or industries or jails, or the institution of the first Indian Legislative Council or the creation of a separate government for Bengal, or the reduction of interest on the public debt, or the reform of the medical and commissariat services of the army, we are equally astounded at the range of his activities and the extent of his accomplishment. In all these respects modern India has been built upon the foundations which Dalhousie laid."

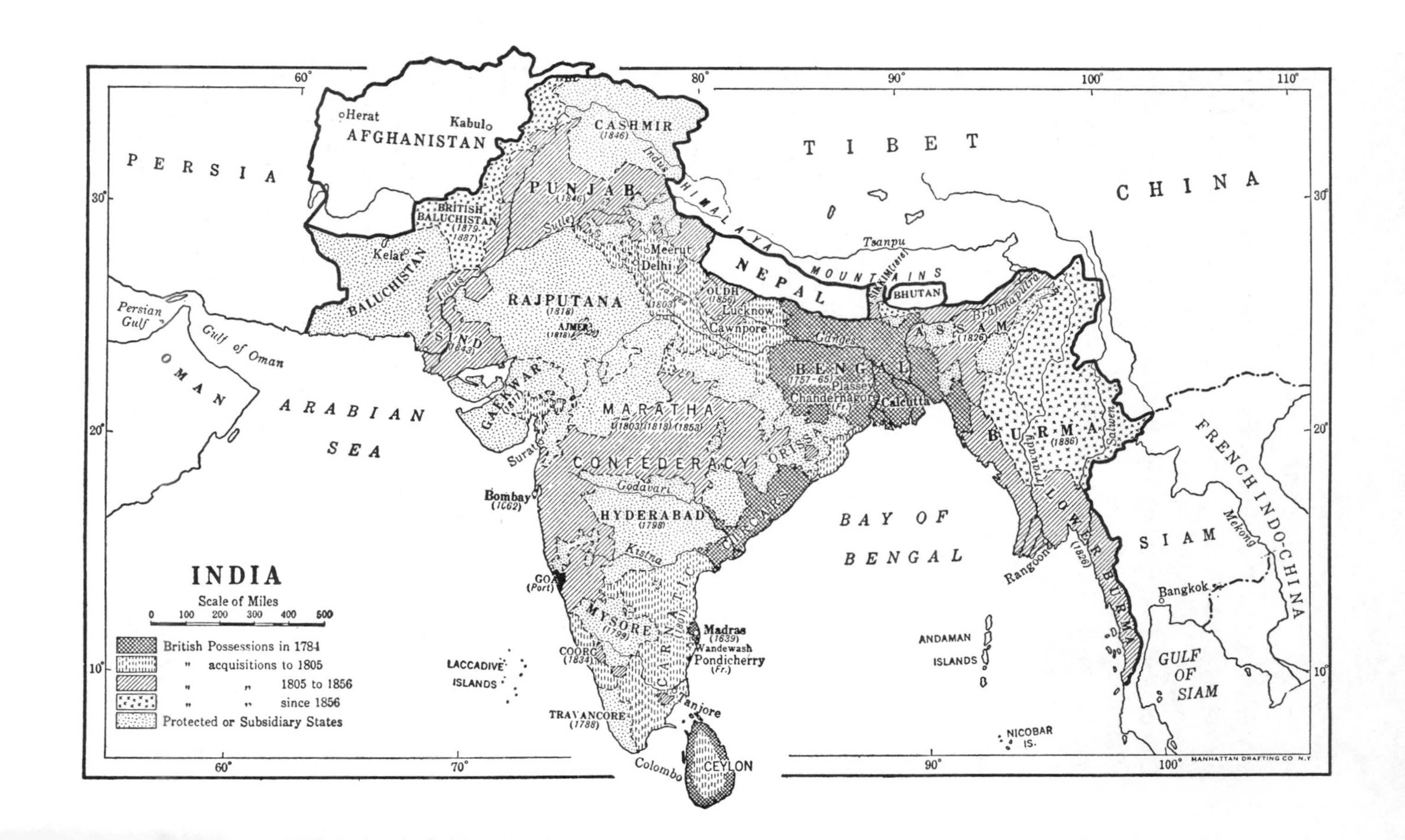
INDIA
Scale of Miles
0 100 200 300 400 500
British Possessions in 1784
" acquisitions to 1805
" " 1805 to 1856
" " since 1856
Protected or Subsidiary States
PERSIA
AFGHANISTAN
Herat
Kabul
Kelat
BALUCHISTAN
BRITISH BALUCHISTAN (1879-1887)
CASHMIR (1846)
PUNJAB (1846)
Indus
Sutlej
SIND (1843)
RAJPUTANA (1818)
AJMER (1818)
Meerut
Delhi
OUDH (1856)
Lucknow
Cawnpore
Ganges
NEPAL
HIMALAYA MOUNTAINS
SIKKIM (1816)
BHUTAN
TIBET
Tsanpu
CHINA
ASSAM (1826)
Brahmaputra
BENGAL (1757-65)
Plassey
Chandernagore (Fr.)
Calcutta
BURMA (1886)
Irrawaddy
Salwen
LOWER BURMA (1826)
Rangoon
SIAM
Bangkok
Mekong
FRENCH INDO-CHINA
GULF OF SIAM
MARATHA (1803)(1818)(1853)
CONFEDERACY
ORISSA
CIRCARS
GAEKWAR (1817)
Surat
Bombay (1662)
GOA (Port)
HYDERABAD (1798)
Godavari
Kistna
MYSORE (1799)
CARNATIC (1801)
COORG (1834)
TRAVANCORE (1788)
Madras (1639)
Wandewash
Pondicherry (Fr.)
Tanjore
CEYLON
Colombo
Persian Gulf
Gulf of Oman
OMAN
ARABIAN SEA
BAY OF BENGAL
LACCADIVE ISLANDS
ANDAMAN ISLANDS
NICOBAR IS.
MANHATTAN DRAFTING CO. N.Y.

The last sentence sums up both Dalhousie's service to India and his responsibility for the Mutiny of 1857. For more than a century India had experienced a succession of stunning blows to her old order. Her political system crumbled; the social and economic bases of her society were undermined; her religion, her education, her culture seemed doomed. That India was governed for the benefit of England was, considering the period, less a cause for reproach than that she was governed in accordance with English ideas. The failure to understand India and the Indians embodies the gravamen of the charge against Dalhousie, his predecessors, and his contemporaries. The greased cartridges were a symbol of this lack of understanding. To supply the Sepoys with cartridges covered with paper glazed with the fat of the cow and the pig, thereby exposing Hindus to sacrilege and Mohammedans to defilement, was a crime and a blunder of the first magnitude. Still this was but a spark. The mine had been laid earlier.

The vague feeling that danger threatened the foundations of Indian life may be reckoned a root cause of the Mutiny. Personal grievances, in addition to those connected with the greased cartridges, furnished an abundance of proximate causes. Dispossessed princes and landowners, young and ambitious Indians to whom neither the army nor the civil service offered chances for a career, native soldiers alarmed by a general service order requiring them to serve across dark and mysterious seas – all were ready to join in a desperate struggle against the foreign masters. Moreover, rumors of English defeats in the Crimea, 1854–1856, had shaken the faith in their invincibility, and the army in India had been weakened by recall of European troops. Quickness of decision cannot be included among the virtues of Dalhousie's successor, Lord Canning. And this virtue was also sadly lacking among the officers in command at Meerut on May 10, 1857, when mutinous soldiers were allowed to escape, reach Delhi, and arouse the garrison and populace of that great city. The last of the Mogul emperors was dragged from obscurity and vested with emblems of authority. The power of Britain in India shook to its foundations.

But luck did not desert the British. Only in Oudh did the rising become national in character. The Sikhs of the Punjab and the native armies of Madras and Bombay remained loyal. The Gurkhas of Nepal sent aid to the British and neither Afghans nor Burmese tried to profit by Britain's plight. But Oudh, the North-Western Provinces, Lower Bengal, and sections of central India were sufficiently permeated with the spirit of revolt to constitute a most serious danger to the British rule. The details of the history of the Mutiny must not detain us. The historic associations and strategic value of Delhi, the old capital of the Mogul empire; the importance of Lucknow, capital of Oudh, and its magnificent defense by a handful of British and loyal Indian soldiers; the atrocities of Nana Sahib, the heroism of the Rani of Jhansi — these and many other topics have aroused the interest of historians and students of the Mutiny. Apart from the broader implications of the struggle, the rising of the Sepoys supplied plenty of tales of horrible barbarities, of courage and resourcefulness, of loyalty and devotion. By December, 1857, the greatest danger was over, but the end did not come till a year later. Lord Canning, who does not seem great in the early days of the Mutiny, looms gigantic in that most trying of periods when the fighting is over and there remains the task of healing the wounds. Braving storms in press and parliament at home, he declared boldly: "We are not going, either in anger or from indolence, to punish wholesale, whether by wholesale hangings or burnings, or by the less violent but not one jot less offensive course of refusing trust and countenance and favour and honour to any man because he is of a class or creed." Out of the tumult and carnage of the Indian Mutiny emerged "Clemency" Canning.

The Mutiny ended the career of the East India Company. After considerable maneuvering parliament passed the Government of India Act in 1858. On November first of that year a proclamation by Queen Victoria announced to the peoples of India that they had passed under the direct control of the British crown.

Cheap wisdom gained by hindsight makes it easy to find fault with the work of the East India Company. Selfish and grasping it doubtless was. But its record in administration compares favorably with that of chartered companies and European colonial governments, both contemporary and of later times. That an earlier assumption of direct government by the crown would have meant happier conditions for India is open to doubt. Only the most fervent sentimentalists can believe that the peoples of India would have enjoyed better conditions under native rulers. The company rescued India from chaos and anarchy. The West was bound to impose its will and its civilization upon the East, and the English were not the least fit among Europeans to act as the agents of the occident. The humanitarians and missionaries of England may at times have shown an inadequate appreciation of the old Indian culture and bigoted zeal in propagating their own ideas. But considered from the point of view of the teeming millions the Indian civilizations, whether Hindu or Mohammedan, as they existed in the middle of the eighteenth century when the company began to secure territories, offered poor prospects. The suppression, under the aegis of the company, of human sacrifice, widow burning, religious bodies with murderous rites, and human slavery offended native religious and social groups and vested economic interests; but who now will denounce these acts? Against the economic decline of India may be balanced first the probability that it would have come without the presence of the company and, secondly, the fact that the company brought peace to India. As we have seen, the ruthless exposure of Indian manufactures to the rival machine industries of England came in part because the company's power had been curbed.

Servants of the company time and again announced to their masters and to the world the ideals for the rulers of India. Lord

William Bentinck, later governor general of India, declared in 1804 that "British greatness should be founded upon Indian happiness." This view was endorsed by other illustrious Indian administrators. Sir Thomas Munro, the great governor of Madras, advocated that the natives of India should be accorded liberal treatment. This, he said, had "always been found the most effectual way of elevating the character of any people." In 1837 another famous governor of India, Sir Charles Metcalfe, said: "Our dominion can only endure by the affections of the people; by their feeling that, under British rule, they are more prosperous, and happy, and free, than they could be under any other Government; and that their welfare and our rule are linked together." "I think," John Stuart Mill told the house of lords committee of 1852, "that the permanence of the connection between India and England depends upon our being able to give good government to India, and to persuade the people of India that we do so." To govern India for the Indians would, in the judgment of Sir Charles Trevelyan, postpone the separation of India from England; and when it came, "Trained by us to happiness and independence, and endowed with our learning and political institutions, India will remain the proudest monument of British benevolence."

To the strong Indian governors and liberal English thinkers of the first half of the nineteenth century there was nothing terrifying in using native Indians in the service of the company. In 1852 it was estimated that in Bengal alone 40,000 Indians were employed in the lower grades of this service, exclusive of that of watchmen. At that time the highest post within the reach of a native paid an annual salary of £1560. Sir Thomas Munro advocated their employment because he foresaw the time when it would be best for both countries that Britain withdraw from India. Montstuart Elphinstone urged that the people of India be educated for and given a share in the government of their country so that when the time for separation came "we should resign our power into the hands of the people for whose benefit it is entrusted." And Macaulay declared in the house of commons on July 10, 1833, that the day when the Indians as a result of good government had outgrown the existing institutions and demanded freedom "will be the proudest day in English history."

Practice may and often did fall short of these ideals. But it is significant that in the first half of the nineteenth century such ideals were entertained by rulers of India and by leaders of public opinion in England. Let him who will scoff; but the program for the government of India proclaimed in 1812 by a select committee of the house of commons — that they should aim "to protect the weak from oppression, and to secure to every individual the fruits of his industry" — remains a noble one.

PART II

The New Course and *Laissez Faire*, 1837–1870

INTRODUCTION

IN the first half of the reign of Queen Victoria British social and economic conditions were greatly altered and the old imperial system was demolished. Freedom replaced dependence as the chief characteristic of the relations between Britain and her principal settlement colonies beyond the sea. The foundation was laid for the British Commonwealth of Nations.

The British economic revolutions which began in the eighteenth century had made rapid progress by the middle of the nineteenth. The country became literally the workshop of the world. British industrialists pioneered in utilizing machinery in textile manufactures, and benefited greatly by inventions and discoveries relating to the production of iron and steel, the growth of railroads, the use of iron in shipbuilding, and the modern system of credit and banking. The industrial development fostered trade; and the large profits accruing from industry, trade, and shipping helped to make Britain the world's banking center. In the second quarter of the nineteenth century the British agricultural interests suffered a relative decline in economic importance and an actual loss in political influence, with the result that the greatest bulwark of the protective tariff system, the protection for the grain growers, was abolished in 1846, and a few years later Britain became a free trade country. This change in the tariff policy made obsolete the trade and navigation laws which regulated the economic life of the colonies and the connection between them and the mother country. With their repeal the basic reasons for governing the colonies from Downing Street had lost validity.

As in both earlier and later periods, consideration for the real or supposed needs of Britain (principally England) determined domestic and imperial policies of British statesmen. Nevertheless, the economic interpretation of history does not suffice to explain the development of the British empire. Within the period 1837–1870 high standards were set up in the administrative system at home, and a spirit of idealism prevailed in the western world. Judged by the new tests of governmental efficiency, the then existing machinery for governing colonies was ready for the scrap heap, and no new one could be devised in this pre-telegraph era, when the steamship was still in the experimental stage and the democratic movements in the Old World stimulated the desire of the frontiersmen for self-determination. Since Britain was then practically without a rival in the field of colonization, fear of foreign foes, the most formidable obstacle to political experiments and the greatest aid to promotion of the usual methods of imperial consolidation, was non-existent. Historians of Greece pointed to the strength and durability of "the silken ties of love and affection" in keeping the colonies of ancient Hellas united with their mother cities, and statesmen quoted Burke in defending the adoption of a colonial policy based upon freedom and "voluntaryism." In the middle years of the nineteenth century there prevailed a strong faith in political democracy as a cure for the ills of nations and empires, a faith that aided the establishment of self-government in British colonies in North America and Australia. Indeed the British Commonwealth of Nations represents one of the great results of the political idealism which in 1848 produced political revolutions and experiments in Europe. However, students of the history of the British empire must beware of over-simplification. Numerous and complex forces have influenced its development.

From the standpoint of constitutional history, the outstanding events in the British empire between 1837 and 1870 were the grant of self-government to the Australasian and North American colonies, the inauguration of the Canadian federation, the gradual loss of autonomy in the British West Indies, and the assumption by the home government of direct control over British India. But remarkable progress in many other fields merits attention. In North America the boundaries of the empire were more clearly defined; and despite British lukewarmness and even open hostility to imperial expansion, the frontiers moved forward in Africa and Asia. Heavy emigration from the British Isles helped swell the population of the colonies, and the rapid accumulation of wealth at home facilitated experiments in colonization, the financing of new enterprises in British North America and Australasia, and improvements in imperial communication. As they grew in wealth and population the colonies became more assertive toward the mother country. State-supported schools and universities provided new opportunities for the rising generation, and the frontier settlements rapidly lost their "newness," assuming the character of well-established and well-ordered communities.

CHAPTER 9

THE BRITISH ISLES, 1837–1870

WHEN in June, 1837, Queen Victoria ascended the throne, Britain had been at peace for more than twenty years. Although war clouds had gathered ominously in the Low Countries and broken in the Near East, British statesmen had managed to steer clear. Wars in India and on the South African frontiers seemed so remote that only faint echoes reached Britain. The threatening situation in the Canadas failed to arouse apprehension; the wounds inflicted by the French wars were healing; the reform wave of the early part of the decade had subsided; and, apart from the perennial Irish question, only economic problems seemed worthy of cognizance. In the late thirties Britain was in the trough of a severe depression, but even economic problems secured only perfunctory attention from the moribund government headed by Lord Melbourne.

Despite governmental lethargy, Britain was already far advanced in an age of profound changes. Utilitarianism, humanitarianism, industrialism, and a host of other isms aided by scientific discoveries and inventions were altering at a steadily mounting pace the framework of English society. In politics and government sober, earnest men such as Sir Robert Peel, Richard Cobden, John Bright, Lord Ashley, Lord John Russell, W. E. Gladstone, John Stuart Mill, and a brilliant Jew, Benjamin

Disraeli, shaped the character of the new reign. Under the leadership of Peel, Toryism gave way to a cautiously progressive conservatism; and under pressure from philosophical radicals and middle-class leaders, Whiggism surrendered to liberalism. Growth in national wealth, absorption with commercial and industrial problems, absence of serious political disturbances, and satisfaction with everything English were outstanding characteristics of the first half of the new reign.

In the year of Queen Victoria's accession, however, the forces had begun to gather for the only political movement that shook Victorian complacency. Dissatisfaction with the results of the Reform Act, grievances resulting from the enforcement of the new poor law, and general economic distress caused the laboring classes to rally to the banner of the Chartists. The program of the Peoples' Charter, drawn up in 1838, was political; it now seems very moderate. But a hundred years ago proposals like universal manhood suffrage, annual parliaments, and vote by ballot appeared revolutionary. From 1838 until 1842 aristocrats and middle-class capitalists were alarmed by evidences of class consciousness among workingmen. But inept leadership soon caused a break in the ranks of the Chartists, and the workers transferred their support to the Anti-Corn Law League. Nearly a generation later, John Bright, a founder of this league, led British labor in a successful fight for the extension of the franchise; it gave the vote to householders in the towns by the Reform Act of 1867.

Apart from the act of 1867, the working classes scored no political gain between 1837 and 1870, but the spirit of the age was in their favor. By degrees the privileges of caste and religion were whittled down. Jews were admitted to the house of commons; the property qualifications for a seat in this house were removed; the prerogatives of the state church to marry and bury people were cancelled; the annual state grant of £20,000 authorized in 1833 for elementary education had risen to £842,119 by 1860; and in 1853 the appointment of a civil service commission heralded the day when talent, training, and character, rather than birth and connections, would determine admission to the civil administration of the country. Of more immediate benefit to the "lower order" were the Factory and Mines Acts of the forties and fifties. Some of the worst horrors of child labor were eliminated, and a shorter working day for children, women, and young persons was secured. At the same time improved education and more intelligent leadership of trade unions enabled the adult male laborers to organize fairly effectively for the protection of their interests. The cooperative movement, started by the Rochdale Pioneers in 1844, also benefited labor in various ways.

The Anti-Corn Law League promised cheap bread and increased employment if the tariff on grain were lifted. With effective slogans, efficient leaders like Richard Cobden and John Bright, and financial aid from the long purses of the industrialists, the league naturally obtained a large following. Indeed, great show of strength was required to drive the serried ranks of the landed aristocracy of England off the field. Time too fought on the side of Cobden and Bright. In the thirties and forties powerful agricultural interests defended protective tariffs. From 1842 to 1845 Sir Robert Peel destroyed the outworks of the protective tariff system by lowering or removing the duties on several hundred articles. Only the citadel, the heavy import duties on grain, remained. Like Joshua before Jericho, Cobden led his host, chanting shock-producing anthems around this stronghold. As the years went by, its walls were undermined by proof that the soil of England could not produce enough food for the increasing population — nearly 25 per cent of the grain needed had to be imported — and in 1845 the Irish famine set off the charge which sent them crumbling. In June, 1846, the corn laws were repealed. A comparatively small duty on grain remained until 1849, and a registration fee of 1*s.* per quarter lasted a few years longer, but the advocates of free trade had won.

The repeal of the corn laws did not materially reduce the price of grain until the seventies, but while the average day's work of a laborer was worth 16 pounds of wheat in the forties, its value had risen thirty years later to 23 pounds; an index figure of 100 for wages in 1850 had become 154 in 1874. Thus the position of the wage earners improved materially in the generation that followed the adoption of free trade in grain. Among the causes of this improvement, free trade, the development of the transportation system, and the industrial growth doubtless were most important. Protection, pronounced not only dead but damned by Disraeli in 1852, was buried by Gladstone in 1860. The British industrialists could now as never before buy in the cheapest market and sell in the dearest. That this arrangement for the time being benefited them and in part those whom they employed may be taken for granted.

There were setbacks following the economic recovery of 1842–1845, such as the panic of 1857 and the cotton famine caused by the Civil War in the United States; nevertheless industrially, commercially, and financially Britain progressed rapidly within the period under consideration. The value of exported goods produced or manufactured in the United Kingdom rose from £42,069,245 in 1837 to £199,586,322 in 1870. The key industries – textiles, iron and steel manufactures, and coal mining – showed healthy and even abnormal growth. The Continent might develop shoe and boot and toy industries, and the United States might exhibit a McCormick reaper and a Singer sewing machine, but nothing worried Britain. Her textile industries grew steadily, though not at such an abnormal rate as iron and steel manufacturing. The building of railroads, begun in the twenties, went forward feverishly in the forties; by 1870 Britain had 13,563 miles in operation. The European continent, India, and especially America eagerly adopted the new means of communication and bought a large amount of needed supplies from England. As late as 1870 the United States purchased her iron rails from the United Kingdom. Within the same period iron began to replace wood as the material for shipbuilding; at its close steamships were driving the sailing vessels off the main highways of the ocean. In the middle years of the nineteenth century British shipowners often bought American-built vessels; but by the end of the sixties the shipyards of the Tyne, the Clyde, and the Mersey were receiving orders from foreign countries. Discoveries by Henry Bessemer and others made mass production of steel possible; and Britain, with age-long experience in handling iron and with the ore and the coal in close proximity, profited by the new methods.

The domestic consumption of coal in Britain more than doubled between 1851 and 1871, reaching the enormous total of 117,000,000 tons in the latter year. In addition, the foreign demand rose rapidly; it has been computed that in 1871 Britain supplied more than 53 per cent of the world's production of coal. In the late sixties her steam tonnage passed the million mark and in 1875 it had become 1,900,000. The Cunard, the Peninsular and Oriental, and other famous British steamship lines were well established before 1870. All helped to build up British overseas trade.

Almost paralleling the growth of England as an industrial country was her rise to the position of the world's banker. Manufacturers and shipowners amassed large fortunes. But not content with the capital accumulated by the captains of industry and shipping magnates, the government provided opportunities for the mite of the wage earner to become fruitful. Thrift was encouraged by institutions such as Postal Savings Banks, and both small and large savings were safeguarded by a stable system of banking and currency. Retrenchment in expenditures was preached and practiced by successive governments; apart from the Crimean War, 1854–1856, Britain engaged in no costly foreign ventures. As a result, despite rapid economic expansion and rising prices, the tax revenues were increased by only about 25 per cent between 1841–1846 and 1871–1876.

Few restrictions hampered British enterprise and taxes were light. Furthermore, business was aided by new company laws, the establishment of joint-stock banks, the clearing house system, the increased use of checks, and the vast augmentation of the world's supply of gold by rich finds in California and Australia. Clever and cautious yet enterprising statesmen, bankers, and business men laid a deep and solid financial foundation for the economic structure of Britain. Sufficient capital was stored up to warrant even risky undertakings in overseas investment and exploitation. Colonial and foreign governments borrowed in London. To the profits of industry, commerce, and shipping were added revenues from banking services. Professor Clapham has estimated that Britain in 1870 had £800,000,000 invested abroad and that in one year, 1873, the export of capital amounted to £83,500,000.

While Britain grew financially better equipped for empire-building and developed commercial agencies to aid in this process, the human material for the same purpose continued to increase. Despite the exodus of about six and one-half million persons, the population of Britain increased from 26,730,929 in 1841 to 31,484,661 in 1871. Ireland suffered a loss of two and three-quarter million; but the surplus in Great Britain, only partially accounted for by Irish immigration, more than offset that deficit. The Irish emigration will be dealt with later; but the outward flow of millions of Englishmen during 1837–1870, when, as we have seen, conditions were growing better, requires some explanation.

Among the more obvious reasons for the large emigration we may note: the gold discoveries in California and Australia, special efforts on the part of British colonies and the United States to attract immigrants by liberal land grants, the work of the Colonial Land and Emigration Commission and of the proponents and agencies for systematic colonization, improvements in ocean transportation, propaganda by steamship companies, and the increased number of newly established settlements beyond the seas where both the communities and individual settlers acted as magnets for relatives and friends. The report of the Children's Employment Commission in 1842 disclosed shocking conditions in the mines. The worst abuses were removed by the Mines Act of the same year, but the investigations conducted by a similar commission twenty years later showed that tens of thousands of children employed in the lace-making, straw-plaiting, pottery, and other unregulated industries were exploited to the limit of human endurance. The conditions among the English working classes in 1844, described by Friedrich Engels, had changed greatly for the better by 1870; but British labor still had legitimate grievances. Wages had improved, though not in the same ratio as the accumulation of wealth; the gulf between wealth and poverty was wider in 1870 than in 1840. The number and effectiveness of labor unions had increased materially, but they still struggled under legal disabilities that hampered their work. Education does not make for contentment with hardship and lack of opportunity, and the more widespread book learning among workers doubtless stimulated discontent.

It should also be kept in mind that the period which showed such large growth of the total population of England was characterized by a relative decline in the rural population. The country folk had to move. To many who had always lived on the land the choice lay between joining the ranks of the proletariat in mining and industrial centers or continuing beyond the seas their old occupation where limitless areas of fertile land beckoned and held out promises of economic independence, even wealth. No wonder rural workers chose to go where they had easy access to land. The heavier emigration in years of relative plenty which has puzzled economic historians is easily explained by the fact that in prosperous times passage money could be saved and that the even greater prosperity then found in North America and Australia increased the pull of those regions and made it easier for immigrants to send for relatives left behind. Thus in the quinquennium 1866–1870, the British emigration figures stood at 1,112,127, while in the depression period, 1837–1841, they had been only 376,798. With strong hope of bettering themselves and providing opportunities for their children, hundreds of thousands of Englishmen decided to turn from their fathers' graves "to houseless wilds, where nameless rivers flow."

Though Scots are reluctant to admit it, Scotland had become politically and economically tied to the chariot of England. Social development may have followed somewhat different lines in Scotland, but otherwise her history was pretty much that of the sister kingdom. A more liberal franchise was also granted north of the Tweed, and the changes made in the Scottish poor law and poor relief put the indigent in a better position than formerly. In the forties the split in the Kirk caused by disputes over church patronage affected Scotland more deeply than did the contemporary Oxford Movement in England. The seceding Free Church people undertook to found a settlement in New Zealand, but it is doubtful if religion played an important role in Scottish emigration. Here as elsewhere the mainspring in emigration was economic.

In the Glasgow district the textile industries which had flourished in 1830 declined rapidly during the next forty years, a loss which was more than made good by the growth in the iron industry, shipbuilding, and coal mining. Between 1843 and 1863 the south of Scotland produced 25 per cent or more of the United Kingdom's annual output of pig iron. In the Glasgow area alone the 31 blast furnaces with an output of 44,000 tons in 1833 had become 122 furnaces producing 1,040,000 tons in 1861. These changes and the dislocation of industries caused hardship in many quarters.

The depopulation of the Highlands continued. At the opening of the century the sheep drove out the people; fifty years later the sheep runs in many places gave way to hunting preserves, requiring even fewer caretakers than the sheep. Thus a patriotic Scot lamented:

"The auld life is gone, root and branch

. . . .

And the dun herds of deer, and the few forest rangers
On the Gael's noblest mountains are all
That remain."

Distress was the common lot of the crofters of the north. Aided emigration on a considerable scale caused the transfer of several thousand Scots from the Highlands and the islands to America and Australia.

To the sons of Erin it seemed that a triple curse rested on their island — landlordism, an alien church, and foreign political dominance. Sir Robert Peel appreciated the need for reforms in Ireland, but his most promising measure, a new land bill, was blocked by the house of lords. Political unrest tore the country, and famine and disease laid their blight upon it. The only remedy sure of instant approbation by both houses of parliament in England was the quack nostrum — coercive legislation. Not until Peel's great disciple, Gladstone, came to power in 1868 did an English prime minister seriously grapple with the root causes of the Irish discontent. Meanwhile the population of Ireland had sunk from 8,300,000 in 1845 to 5,174,836 in 1871. Irishmen had fled or been driven overseas, crossed to England and Scotland, or fallen victims to starvation and the diseases which follow in its train.

In the thirties the governments of Grey and Melbourne tried in vain to reduce the privileges of the established church — the church of a small minority — in Ireland, and to correct the abuses of the tithe system. Time and again bills to that effect passed the house of commons only to be thrown out or mutilated by the lords, where Anglican bishops and their allies acted on the principle that neither justice nor charity should be practiced in dealing with Ireland. Finally in 1839, a Tithe Commutation Act was passed which changed contributions to the state church into a rent charge, reducing it on paper but leaving the main burden on the backs of the Catholic peasantry as before. A Municipal Reform Act gave to three or four of the largest cities of Ireland a limited amount of self-government, and a new poor law extended to the island the doubtful blessing of prohibition of outdoor relief.

Daniel O'Connell, the great leader of Catholic Ireland, became convinced that nothing effective could be done until the Act of Union was repealed. Though often violent in speech, he was moderate in action. During the thirties he stayed his hand, hoping against hope that remedial legislation would be passed. By 1840 it became clear that nothing could be achieved by the Melbourne government and that it would soon be supplanted by a Conservative ministry under Sir Robert Peel. From the latter O'Connell expected nothing. He then launched a great repeal campaign and fixed on 1843 as the repeal year. He admonished his followers not to use force; he hoped that a monster repeal demonstration to take place at Clontarf would force England to yield. But he dealt with foes as hard of heart as the Pharaoh whom Moses tried to persuade. Peel outlawed the proposed meeting and concentrated military forces in Ireland and naval forces on the coasts. O'Connell, firm in his resolve to avoid bloodshed, canceled the meeting. Four years later he died, a broken man.

Even before the fiasco of 1843 younger men, impatient with O'Connell's tactics, had started the Young Ireland movement. Among its leaders were Charles Gavan Duffy, William Smith O'Brien, John Mitchell, Thomas Francis Meagher, and Thomas D'Arcy McGee. They founded two newspapers, *The Nation* and *The United Irishman;* the titles were significant. This group hoped to bring together all Irishmen, irrespective of creed and social status, in one great effort to secure political autonomy. They had no scruples against fighting and drew inspiration from contemporary revolutionary movements on the Continent. The February revolution, 1848, in France encouraged them greatly. They expected aid from republican France, but were disappointed; the new republic needed the good will of England. When a few among the extremists tried to arouse Ireland to revolt they suffered a further disillusionment. The movement collapsed. Some of the leaders were arrested; others saved themselves by flight.

In the fifties Ireland was too paralyzed by the effects of the famine and the heavy emigration to cause much trouble. But unforeseen results of the emigration now became apparent. In 1858 expatriated Irishmen founded in New York the Fenian Republican Brotherhood in the hope of rallying Irish-Americans and American foes of England to the cause of Irish freedom. After the close of the Civil War in the United States some of the thousands of Irish ex-soldiers were ready for extreme measures, using their American citizenship as a protecting cloak. But the British government was forewarned. Scattered outbreaks in Ireland were promptly suppressed. Fenians then conceived a harebrained scheme of seizing Canada and demanding the freedom of Ireland as ransom. Slackness on the part of American authorities enabled the Fenians to make a raid into Canada in 1866, but they were promptly dealt with by the Canadians. The following year the scene for Fenian activities was England. Plots to capture the castle and arsenal at Chester, an attack upon a prison van at Manchester, and an explosion at Clerkenwell Prison in London stirred England. The Fenian activities aroused in Gladstone a realization of the magnitude and ramifications of the Irish question.

Sir Robert Peel tried to deal with religious, educational, and economic aspects of the problems of Ireland. A substantial state grant was made to the Jesuit seminary for training priests at Maynooth; and since Roman Catholics were excluded from Trinity College, Dublin, he took steps to establish non-sectarian Queen's Colleges at Cork, Belfast, and Galway. These, however, were denounced as godless by the Catholics, who preferred to build a university of their own. A commission headed by Lord Devon was appointed to study the land problem; some of its far-seeing recommendations were incorporated in 1845 in a bill sponsored by Peel but ruined in the house of lords.

Then came the great famine. Failure of the potato crop in 1845 and 1846 caused millions of Irishmen to face death by starvation. The government brought in large quantities of Indian corn, started extensive public works, suspended the poor law prohibition of outdoor relief, and proposed the repeal of the corn laws. Private organizations in England raised substantial sums for relief in Ireland. Aided, and in some cases compulsory, emigration was resorted to. But the task of famine relief exceeded the capacity and skill of both private and public relief agencies. Tens, perhaps hundreds, of thousands died from starvation or from diseases brought on by their weakened physical condition. Heartless landlords utilized the non-payment of rent as a means for clearing their estates. To the vast number of Irishmen who went to British colonies and the United States during and shortly after the famine, the English efforts at relief counted as naught. The sufferings of Ireland were laid at the door of England. Filled with a burning hatred for the oppressor, these immigrants inculcated that same sentiment into their children. The dispersion of the Irish made the Irish problem truly imperial.

Famine and emigration relieved somewhat the population pressure, yet in the agricultural south and west rents continued high and there was neither fixity of tenure nor compensation to the outgoing tenant for improvements made by him. The Encumbered Estates Act of 1851 was intended to aid the peasantry by facilitating the sale of land. But whatever benefits it brought seem to have been withheld from the tenants. A flare-up on a small scale of ancient anti-popery feeling in England, caused in part by the secession of leading Oxford reformers to the Church of Rome, worked to the disadvantage of Ireland. It was felt that the Irish Catholics must be kept in check.

In December, 1868, Gladstone assumed office as prime minister, determined to lop off the obnoxious branches from the Irish upas tree. The established church, which to him seemed the most iniquitous, was disestablished and partly disendowed in 1869. He then took up the land question and passed an act which bettered the position of Irish tenants. But an effort to settle the problem of Irish education foundered on the rock of religious animosity. Although he worked mightily for Ireland, he failed. Each time the flame of Irish discontent seemed about to flicker out, it was fanned anew from across the sea. There was now not one but many Irelands. Consequently the first British prime minister who had earnestly endeavored to heal the wounds of Ireland was taunted with having "legalized confiscation, consecrated sacrilege, and condoned treason" in Ireland; he had to invoke repressive legislation to keep the island quiet. Ireland had become the great unsolved and apparently unsolvable problem.

CHAPTER 10

THE IMPERIAL FRONTIERS, 1837–1870

OPPOSITION to expansion was a fixed policy of the British government in the first half of the Victorian era. Britain then had opportunity to acquire territory as never before or since, and she had the population surplus and the financial strength to meet the needs of widening frontiers; but her statesmen doubted the value of overseas colonies and often begrudged the cost of keeping what she had, to say nothing of sacrificing blood and treasure for new acquisitions. In spite of this governmental policy, frontiers were pushed forward and new footholds secured in various parts of the globe. Traders and missionaries continued to act as the advance guard of empire; humanitarian and anti-slavery interests frequently brought effective pressure to bear upon statesmen for annexations; and notwithstanding assertions to the contrary, few British statesmen dared surrender territories to which the empire had claims, though some of them, notably Lord Aberdeen, were willing to compromise with competitors and often refused support to official and unofficial agents of British imperialism. The foreign rivals for overseas possessions were few, yet their real or suspected designs now and again stirred Britain to action that led to further annexation; in India and elsewhere the usual frontier forces not infrequently compelled statesmen in Downing Street to sanction the occupation of new lands.

As has been noted earlier, England was busy with her industrial and commercial development in the second and third quarters of the nineteenth century. Foodstuffs and raw material were being imported in increasing quantities from foreign countries; and foreign countries, particularly Germany and the United States, became the principal buyers of British manufactured goods. Among the British possessions, India and the West Indies continued to be good customers; the settlement colonies of North America and Australia lagged far behind. Though a poor market for British goods, these offered opportunities for the surplus population of the British Isles. The vast continent of Africa had no attractions comparable to those of the more densely populated regions of Europe and America, either as a source of raw materials or as a market, and the islands of the Pacific were no more promising. Commercial motives and a zeal for retrenchment in government expenditures were dominant in shaping Britain's imperial policy in this period; the shopkeepers' profit-and-loss point of view often put a wet blanket on demands for expansion.

The British statesmen of the period had, of course, to pay special heed to the demands of the major economic interests of the United Kingdom. To convert European nations to the adoption of free trade seemed vastly more important than to annex new lands. But commerce was a word with magic qualities, and assertions that certain annexations would increase trade received respectful attention. Missionaries perceived this; God and mammon joined forces in urging the British public to consider the value of distant lands. John Williams, the renowned missionary to the South Seas, asked in his *Narrative of Missionary Enterprises*, 1840, for support of missions because they promoted trade; and David Livingstone told a select committee on West Africa in 1865: "The missionaries always promote trade. . . . Wherever I have seen a mission established the mission promotes civilization and commerce." Before the end of the thirties the Anti-Slavery Society discovered that the traffic in African slaves could not be destroyed until the continent had been opened to legitimate trade – heartening news for the British traders operating in Western Africa. Missionaries, humanitarians, and traders cooperated in demanding government aid for explorations of the Niger and the Zambezi, explorations which provided bases for later annexations. This unofficial triple alliance was responsible for the acquisition of Lagos on the Gulf of Guinea, for the purchase of the Danish ports on the Gold Coast, for the hoisting of the British flag in other portions of Western Africa, and for the blocking of efforts to have it lowered in the Gambia. It is significant that Manchester, the city that gave its name to the so-called Little England school of economists, listened eagerly to what Livingstone had to tell about commercial opportunities in Africa and that its chamber of commerce protested against the ceding of the Gambia to France. Though Britain by the famous conventions of 1852 and 1854 surrendered to the emigrant Boers the large areas which she had claimed beyond the Vaal and between the Orange and the Vaal respectively, her territorial responsibilities in South Africa were much greater in 1870 than they had been in 1837. Natal, Kaffraria, Basutoland, and sundry other stretches of territory to the north and east of the old boundary of the Cape Colony had been annexed or had come under British control. So active had the missionaries been in bringing this about that Herman Merivale, permanent undersecretary of state for the colonies, 1848–1859, attributed to missionary influence all current British annexations in South Africa.

The rivalry of foreign powers, later so potent in arousing British interest in African lands, was hardly felt in the period we are considering. British and French traders met without serious conflict in Western Africa. Occasionally zealous British efforts to end the African slave trade evoked protests from the French, and reports of the activities of French and German explorers in Africa mildly stirred the acquisitive instinct of some Englishmen, but nothing serious happened. It was otherwise in Asia. With watchful care Britain observed moves that might imperil the safety of India. The French relations with Egypt in 1839 caused Britain to occupy Aden and Perim, thereby controlling the southern exit from the Red Sea. With Russia in mind, Britain in the sixties obtained control of the Bahrein Islands in the Persian Gulf. Anxiety for her Indian empire led to the Afghan war, 1839–1842, and later to the Crimean war. The former served as a prelude for the absorption of Sind and the Punjab into British India; and the Anglo-Russian rivalry in the Middle East resulted in a war with Persia, 1856–1857. Farther east where annexations did not seem to threaten India, the activities of Russia caused little concern. The Russian seizure of Vladivostock in 1858 and other attempts to consolidate her influence in the North Pacific failed to arouse Britain, though by the sixties Australia showed symptoms of alarm over Russian expansion.

The interests of British traders were served in the second Burmese war in 1852, and in the annexation of Lower Burma which resulted therefrom. Farther south, British economic penetration, to be followed by occupation and political control, proceeded slowly but steadily in the Malay Peninsula. East of the Strait of Malacca trade had long suffered because of the depredations of pirates. With the surrender of the East India Company's monopoly of the China trade in 1833, it became more directly a duty of the British government to protect trade in the eastern waters. The use of steam war vessels facilitated the stamping out of piracy, and government money was freely spent for this purpose. British trade increased; a by-product of the hunting down of the pirates was the British seizure of the island of Labuan, off the coast of North Borneo. British influence in this region was further extended by James (later Rajah Sir James) Brooke, who in the forties established himself as virtual ruler of Sarawak in northern Borneo. But British commercial interests scored their greatest gains in the Far East as results of England's wars with China, 1840–1842 and 1857–1860. New ports were opened for British trade; the important island and port of Hong-

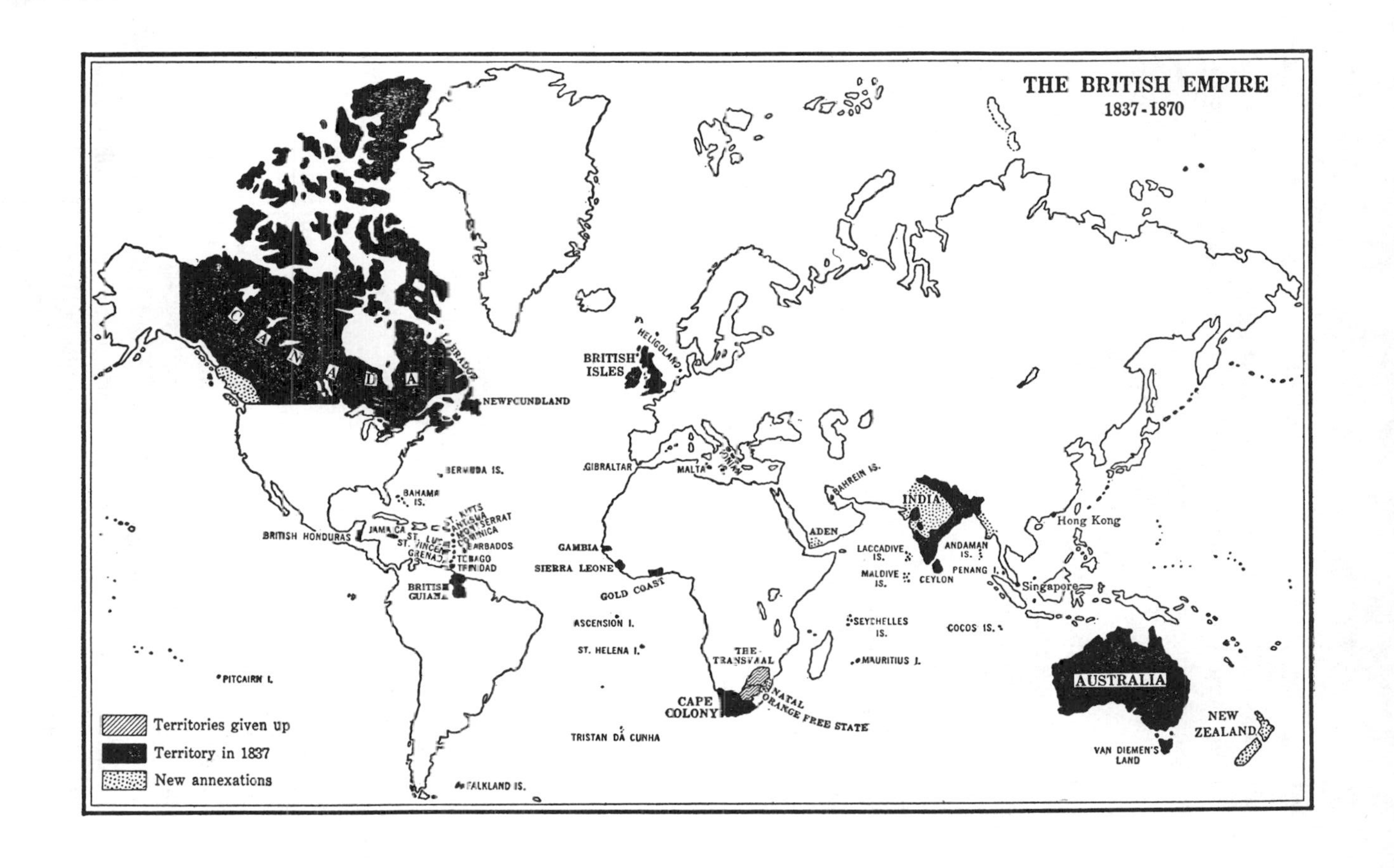

THE BRITISH EMPIRE
1837-1870
CANADA
LABRADOR
NEWFOUNDLAND
BERMUDA IS.
BAHAMA IS.
BRITISH HONDURAS
JAMAICA
BARBADOS
TOBAGO
TRINIDAD
BRITISH GUIANA
FALKLAND IS.
PITCAIRN I.
BRITISH ISLES
HELIGOLAND
GIBRALTAR
MALTA
GAMBIA
SIERRA LEONE
GOLD COAST
ASCENSION I.
ST. HELENA I.
TRISTAN DA CUNHA
THE TRANSVAAL
CAPE COLONY
NATAL
ORANGE FREE STATE
ADEN
BAHREIN IS.
INDIA
LACCADIVE IS.
MALDIVE IS.
CEYLON
ANDAMAN IS.
PENANG I.
SEYCHELLES IS.
MAURITIUS I.
COCOS IS.
Hong Kong
Singapore
AUSTRALIA
VAN DIEMEN'S LAND
NEW ZEALAND
Territories given up
Territory in 1837
New annexations

kong was ceded to Britain; and opportunities were secured for British capital and enterprise which ultimately led to British commercial hegemony over southern China.

In the Pacific British missionaries and adventurers continued active, especially in Tahiti, Fiji, and the Sandwich Islands. An ambitious British naval officer proclaimed the last-named British territory in 1843, but his act was disavowed by the home government. British missionaries aided by the British consul, George Pritchard, controlled Tahiti for several years; but their high-handed treatment of French Roman Catholic missionaries resulted in armed interference by the government of France, and Lord Aberdeen and Sir Robert Peel allowed the French to annex the island. In 1862, the chieftains of Fiji, doubtless prompted by missionaries, asked for the protection of Queen Victoria, but the Palmerston government refused the request. However, in 1840 Britain secured a splendid possession in the South Pacific by annexing New Zealand. In this case the missionaries, fearful of losing their influence over the natives, opposed annexation. Acts of British and American sailors, whalers, sealers, and adventurers created such conditions that intervention by a foreign government became inevitable. The annexation of New Zealand was hastened by the propaganda engineered by Wakefield and his systematic colonizers, who alleged that France was ready to take possession of the islands.

The British empire in North America was coterminous with the United States for more than three thousand miles. In the thirties and early forties New Brunswick-Maine border squabbles brought much bad blood to the surface on both sides, but a compromise boundary agreed upon in 1842 proved satisfactory. The rebellions in the Canadas in 1837, the asylum which rebel leaders found in the United States, acts of irresponsible adventurers both British and American, disputes arising from attempts to recover fugitive slaves, the Civil War in the United States, and the activities of Irish-Americans shortly afterward supplied material for misunderstanding and disputes between London and

Washington; fortunately, none had serious consequences. In the forties, however, the undefined state of the boundary west of the Rocky Mountains threatened a serious rupture. Both Britain and the United States claimed the larger portion of the Oregon country; anti-British feeling ran high in America in the election of 1844 – "Fifty-four forty or fight" was the then popular slogan. If the United States had adhered to this extreme demand British North America would have been without an outlet to the Pacific and war would doubtless have followed. Fortunately, calmer counsel prevailed. The British foreign secretary, Lord Aberdeen, was, as usual, conciliatory, and both sides receded. The Oregon Treaty of 1846, which fixed the boundary at the 49th parallel from the Rockies to the sea and left all of Vancouver Island in British hands, represented a sane solution of the problem. The non-expansionistic policy of the British government and Lord Aberdeen's own pacifistic views prevented Anglo-American friction over California and Texas when British commercial interests wished to check the advance of the republic in both regions. They received no encouragement from the prime minister or foreign secretary.

Britain and the United States clashed in Central America, a region whose importance was enhanced with the discovery of gold in California and the growing need for an isthmian canal. British contact with Central America dated back to the days of Queen Elizabeth. Britain had had a foothold in Honduras since the seventeenth century, and treaties with the Indians on the Mosquito Coast had strengthened her influence there. The United States felt or feigned apprehension. To check alleged spread of British influence it was suggested that the proposed isthmian waterway should be in American hands, and the American government invoked the Monroe Doctrine. But here Britain refused to surrender, and the treaty of 1850, known in America as the Clayton-Bulwer Treaty, recognized the common interests of the two powers in the projected canal. Later Britain agreed to withdraw from the Mosquito Coast, but the claims established by the buccaneers and logwood-cutters of an earlier age received international recognition when the British government in 1862 formally proclaimed Belize, now British Honduras, a British colony.

In South America the boundaries of British Guiana were undetermined to the west and northwest when Britain obtained this territory from the Dutch. In the years 1841–1843, Robert (later Sir Robert) Schomburgk traced a boundary and erected boundary posts. When the republic of Venezuela protested, Lord Aberdeen agreed to remove these boundary posts and to cede territory along the Orinoco River, a concession not accepted by Venezuela. The whole question was left for final settlement until the closing years of the century.

Several actions by the British government during 1837–1870 disprove the oft-made assertion that Britain has always been grasping. Most significant of these were the surrenders effected in South Africa by the Sand River and Bloemfontein conventions, 1852 and 1854, and the transfer of the Ionian Islands to Greece in 1864. The Boer trek of the thirties created a perplexing problem for British statesmen. On the one hand they were disinclined to extend their territorial responsibilities in South Africa since only the port and naval base at Capetown were deemed of any value; but on the other hand roving groups of uncontrolled armed white farmers were apt to stir up trouble with warlike natives — they might continue to keep slaves and even establish connections with foreign countries. The powerful missionary societies were hostile to the trekking farmers, and in part because of their insistence, the home government claimed that the emigrants were British subjects and that the land they occupied was British territory. To forestall future complications Natal was annexed in 1843, the Orange River Sovereignty was established a few years later, and when the recalcitrant Boers continued to trek, Britain followed them across the Vaal River. By 1850 it seemed as if the British empire might have to be extended northward almost indefinitely for the sole purpose of keeping under control a handful of farmers who wished to free themselves from their British allegiance. The native wars at the Cape had proved expensive and kept troops there which might be needed at home. The efforts to reduce government expenditures and at the same time provide adequate protection for the British Isles, the feeling that neither land nor people in South Africa were worth the money spent to govern and defend them, and a belief that no foreign rival could effect a successful junction with the emigrant Boers to the detriment of British interests in Africa led to the surrender, by the Sand River Convention of 1852 and the Bloemfontein Convention of 1854, of the trans-Vaal territory and the Orange River Sovereignty respectively. Thus were founded two Boer states, the South African Republic and the Orange Free State.

The Ionian Islands had proved of little value as a naval base and the islanders fretted under British rule, which, incidentally, was an annual expense to the taxpayers of Britain. In 1864 desire to relieve the exchequer of profitless expenditures, combined with friendship for Greece, resulted in a transfer of the islands, in accordance with the wishes of the inhabitants, to the Hellenic kingdom.

As the century wore on, the influence of the missionaries on the course of British expansion waned, while gold seekers and concession hunters became more aggressive. At the close of the sixties British prospectors for gold in the valley of the Limpopo urged Britain onward; diamond diggers in the land of the Griquas pleaded for British protection. On September 1, 1870, "a tall, lanky, anaemic fair-haired boy," Cecil Rhodes, later famous as an empire-builder, landed in South Africa. At this time the international stage was being set, politically and economically, for the last and greatest act in the drama of the Europeanization of the world; in it Britain was destined to play a leading rôle.

The term *laissez faire* may properly be applied to the frontier policy of the British empire, 1837–1870. British statesmen neither planned nor desired further annexations, but in many instances they could only retard, not check, the growth of the empire. Dynamic forces often operated on the periphery rather than at the center, and improved means of communications proved mighty auxiliaries for the empire-builders. Meanwhile, undisturbed by the theories of economic philosophers and the plans of imperial statesmen, vast areas within the ring fence of the imperial boundaries were being occupied. The home government itself lent much aid. The proceeds from the sale of waste lands in the colonies, especially in Australia, helped to defray the cost of transporting more than three hundred thousand British emigrants overseas, and favorable concessions were granted to men and corporations who undertook to find homes in the colonies for thousands more. Liberal land policies, favorable reports, and cash sent home by early settlers proved powerful magnets attracting immigrants to British North America and Australasia. As usual in frontier communities, large increases in the population from births further swelled the millions of British subjects beyond the sea. As the leading colonies grew in wealth and population their status changed; foundations were laid for new British nations.

CHAPTER 11

A NEW IMPERIAL SYSTEM

IN 1837 the British imperial system was crumbling. At home economic changes were destroying basic reasons for controlling the colonies from Downing Street, and overseas the clamor for self-government was waxing more insistent. Rebellions in the Canadas compelled statesmen to examine the relations between Britain and her dependencies. Clearly they were unsatisfactory – unsuited for the needs of the time. Within the next thirty years the British colonies of North America and Australasia received responsible government, which meant that in all internal affairs the executive branch of the government was controlled by the elected chamber of the legislature. Attempts were made to enumerate colonial subjects, topics over which the mother country could exercise no supervision, but these failed. The intra-imperial relations were handled on the principle that in colonies with a large European population the imperial government should keep hands off; consequently these colonies obtained control over crown lands and the natives within their borders and the right to regulate their customs tariffs. By 1870 they had become almost independent, except in their relations with foreign powers. The old concept of empire – control of all units within this political entity from one center – had become obsolete. Freedom, partnership, and cooperation had replaced dependence as chief characteristics of the British imperial system. The cornerstone had been laid for an absolutely new political structure, the British Commonwealth of Nations.

In recording the history and development of Britain's new imperial system, 1837–1870, it will be necessary to explain why the old was discarded, to analyze the views of reformers and statesmen responsible for the changes, and to discuss their extent and character.

Imperial tariff preferences had been an essential element of the British imperial system that existed in 1837. However, with the adoption of free trade the preferential tariffs were swept away. Only one of them, that on colonial-grown sugar, caused any controversy. West Indian planters argued to no avail that their sugar, the product of free labor, should be protected against the slave-grown sugar of Cuba and Porto Rico. Their opponents insisted that under proper management free labor was more efficient than slave labor and that British consumers should not be compelled to subsidize broken-down plantations in the West Indies. In 1854 British colonial sugar ceased to receive preferential treatment from the tariff of the United Kingdom. Meanwhile the colonies were no longer required to grant preferences to British goods. The repeal of the Navigation Acts in 1849 was expected to benefit colonial trade by lowering freight rates; and imperial aid in providing the West Indies with cheap coolie labor from India was intended to compensate these islands for the losses they suffered from changes in the imperial economic policy.

Hard-headed business sense dictated that the protective tariff, imperial preferences, and Navigation Acts should be scrapped and that colonies should be considered from a strictly profit-and-loss point of view. In the middle decades of the nineteenth century Englishmen were acutely tax-conscious. Successive governments preached and practiced economy, and chancellors of the exchequer were embarrassed by the colonial expenditures — for military defense alone they amounted to about three million pounds per year. Even Disraeli, later a high priest of British imperialism, was so inconvenienced in 1852 by the drain imposed by colonies on the imperial treasury that he called them millstones around the neck of Britain. The feeling that colonies were no longer a source of profit — that on the contrary they were a burden and an encumbrance — engendered an anti-colonial sentiment in Britain. Among those who doubted the value of colonies were the great champions of free trade, Richard Cobden and John Bright. They looked upon the overseas empire as the legacy of an age that had applied a wrong fiscal policy and been guilty of imperialistic wars. Both believed optimistically that all Europe would follow the example of Britain — adopt free trade and thereby inaugurate an era of universal peace. They saw no place for colonies in the British national economy. Bright in particular was more than a utilitarian economist; he was a strong believer in political democracy, an intrepid defender of the weak and oppressed. To him it was perfectly clear that the colonies should be given freedom, independence if they wanted it. Separation of Australasia from Britain would confer benefit on both. Around Cobden and Bright were clustered political and economic theorists known collectively as the Manchester school. They were advocates of *laissez faire,* enemies of imperial expansion, supporters of colonial autonomy. Although not strong numerically, the Manchester school included many persons of weight and influence; among them was Goldwin Smith, regius professor of modern history at Oxford, who in 1862–1863 contributed a series of articles to a liberal London newspaper, the *Daily News,* in which he argued in favor of colonial independence.

The separatists helped to destroy the old imperial system but contributed little to the development of the ideal embodied in the present British Commonwealth. In this work the services of Wakefield, Durham, Buller, and Molesworth were preeminent. Wakefield, a restless schemer, a fruitful originator of ideas, and a great promoter, did splendid spade work by arousing interest in colonial problems. His plans for systematic colonization were visionary and at times resembled grandiose real estate speculations, but he helped to create a new conception of empire. South Australia and New Zealand owe much to him; it was largely due to his suggestion that the British government created the Colonial Land and Emigration Commission which from 1840 to 1872 aided in transferring more than 300,000 emigrants from the United Kingdom to new homes in British colonies. Wakefield was much interested in the "art of colonization." He urged colonial self-government and quarreled violently with the colonial office. An autocrat by disposition, he fell out with the assembly of New Zealand whither he emigrated in 1853. He was as much distrusted there as he had been at home, and his last years were an anticlimax to his great career as colonial reformer. A lonely and broken man, Wakefield died in New Zealand in 1862.

Wakefield knew little about the science of government; Durham on the other hand had both knowledge and experience in this field. He had assisted in drafting the Great Reform Bill, had been lord privy seal in the government of his father-in-law, Earl Grey, and had represented Britain in Russia. A man of outstanding ability, his five months' sojourn in Canada in 1838 as high commissioner and governor general was epoch-making in the history of the British empire. With great insight he diagnosed the ills of the Canadas and exposed the weakness of the colonial system in a report justly famous. By endorsing the demand for responsible government sponsored by Robert Baldwin in Upper Canada and Joseph Howe in Nova Scotia, Durham lent weight and influence to the agitation for this reform, an agitation well within reach of success at the time of his death in 1840.

Charles Buller was not handicapped by the outbursts of violent temper which often marred Durham's efforts or by the shady past and the "inequalities of character" which impeded Wakefield. Clever and witty, Buller knew how to win friends and conciliate enemies; a pupil of Carlyle and disciple of Bentham, he belonged to the philosophical radicals. Elected to parliament in 1830, he voted for the extinction of the pocket borough which he represented and criticized the Reform Bill for not being sufficiently thoroughgoing. He came under the influence of Wakefield rather early and served as parliamentary agent or lobbyist for the Australian Patriotic Association and as Durham's secretary on the mission to Canada. In 1840 Buller aided materially in the passage of the Canadian Union Act and championed the cause of responsible government for the colonies in vigorous, though in spots grossly unfair, articles contributed to the *Colonial Gazette.* Later he was in close touch with Lord Grey, colonial secretary from 1846 to 1852, who described his death in 1848 as "in every way a very great loss indeed."

Sir William Molesworth, a solid, somewhat pedestrian country squire, placed his wealth and capacity for hard work at the disposal of the colonial reform movement. He carried weight in the house of commons; his newspaper, the *Morning Chronicle,* was of great value to the reformers. Molesworth held office as secretary of state for the colonies for a few months prior to his death in 1855.

The agitation at home for reform of the British imperial system was complemented by similar efforts in the colonies. The first really workable reform program, responsible government, was prepared by Robert Baldwin and Joseph Howe independently of each other; the latter argued his case ably and forcefully in *Letters to Lord John Russell,* 1839; and both helped to launch self-government in British North America. In Australia W. C. Wentworth pioneered in the struggle to obtain for New South Wales rights and privileges generally accorded settlement colonies; and John Dunmore Lang fought strenuously for Australian self-determination in secular as well as ecclesiastical affairs, although when he advocated "freedom and independence for the golden lands of Australia" he went beyond what his fellow colonists desired and the mother country would give. In the late forties and early fifties a sojourner in Australia, Robert Lowe, later famous as opponent of parliamentary reform in England, gave valuable support to the efforts of the colonists to gain control over their own affairs.

The advocates of a new imperial system were aided by the fact that the existing one was outmoded, by the belief that the colonies were destined to become independent, and by the spirit of freedom and tolerance so strong in the England of the mid-nineteenth century. That the administration of the overseas empire existing in 1837 was inefficient and injurious to the real interest of the dependencies was admitted by all who were familiar with the situation. Indeed, James Stephen was most vehement in his denunciation of the delays in decisions on colonial problems caused by circulatory correspondence between the half dozen departments, boards, or commissions that had to be consulted beforehand. He vainly sought to break the habit of the lords of the treasury never to answer in less than two months a letter dealing with expenditure of money in a colony; sometimes they waited two years. That the charter of a bank in New Brunswick was annulled nearly three years after it had opened for business caused Stephen and his colleagues at the colonial office much grief. To them it was clear that the colonists must be left much latitude in handling their economic and social problems; otherwise they would suffer hardship and grow discontented. Therefore on points dealing with colonial administration the reformers had powerful allies at the colonial office, and they found sympathy among the statesmen who under the direction of Sir Robert Peel sought to abolish sinecures, pluralism, and absenteeism in the holding of offices whether secular or spiritual.

When reports of unrest in the Canadas reached Britain, the thoughts of men turned quite naturally to the former experience with American colonies, and this experience colored much of the thinking on colonial problems. It was generally believed that the overseas settlements were destined for independence; like ripe fruit they would fall from the parent stem – or, to use a metaphor heard frequently at that time, the colonies were children who in due time would establish households independent of parental control. Considering this outcome inevitable, friends of the colonies urged that they should be trained for their future status while yet united with Britain. The idea found sympathetic hearing from a generation which applauded the struggle of Greeks, Germans, and Italians for democratic nation states. Students of Greek history like George Grote thought that Britain should imitate the colonial policy of the city-states of ancient Hellas who left their offspring free; and the lessons deduced from their experience reinforced Burke's argument that freedom and voluntaryism were the strongest imperial ties. This type of historical argument greatly influenced Gladstone, who in the middle years of the nineteenth century urged his countrymen to heed Burke when he said that by granting freedom to the colonies their separation from Britain would be postponed perhaps indefinitely. Thus ran the most constructive arguments for the introduction of a new imperial system.

Statesmen frame policies, officials administer them; in so doing they may build up precedents that alter old and inaugurate new principles of government. The permanent officials are experts, instructing and educating the birds of passage who under the English democratic system occupy ministerial posts. So it is now and so it was a century ago. In the first half of the Victorian age only one secretary of state for the colonies, Earl Grey, held that office for more than five years; three permanent undersecretaries averaged more than eleven. Besides they had served in the office or studied colonial problems before they reached the highest rank in the service. Before his appointment Herman Merivale, 1847–1859, had delivered a series of lectures on the colonies which form an important source for the history of British imperial policy. James Stephen, 1836–1847, and Sir Frederic Rogers, 1860–1871, were promoted from subordinate posts. All three were able men with liberal views who furthered the cause of colonial self-government without striving to break up the empire. Of the three, Rogers was least alarmed over the prospect of separation; Stephen topped the others in administrative ability and zeal. His term as permanent undersecretary coincided with the period when the reformers exposed the evils of the existing system of colonial government and demanded change. They knew that Stephen was thoroughly acquainted with colonial problems, that he was a man of untiring energy and strong convictions; hence they concluded that he was responsible for all defects and mistakes in the administration of the colonies. Nicknaming him "King Stephen," "Mr. Oversecretary," and "Mr. Mother-country," they abused the hapless official. The picture of Stephen drawn by Buller in his famous *Responsible Government for Colonies* is a caricature and a libel. Far from being one who pigeonholed colonial documents and caused demands from overseas to expire in the "sighing room" at the colonial office, Stephen persistently urged his superiors to pay heed to what colonists wanted and to remove their grievances. Working in the seclusion of office, he served the cause of colonial reform more effectively than did most of his critics in parliament and the press.

Few of the leading statesmen of the period 1837–1870 gave sustained attention to overseas Britain. Most of them were pessimists, believing that the colonies would become independent; however, they were not separatists. On this point the Conservative leaders, Wellington, Peel, and Derby, agreed with the Liberal, Melbourne, Russell, Grey, and Palmerston. Wellington, the Iron Duke, the greatest national figure in England from the middle thirties till his death in 1852, looked upon the colonies as "sources of great influence, power, and prosperity to this country." And when his relative, Sir Charles Bagot, governor general of Canada, pursued policies that in the duke's judgment might endanger her connection with Britain, he wrote in disgust, "What a fool the man must be." Sir Robert Peel, the most constructive of the British statesmen in the 1840's, viewed the colonies as an honorable obligation to be kept as long as they wished to remain united with Britain. And Lord Derby, twice colonial secretary and thrice prime minister, discouraged a Cape judge from publishing a book which might strengthen the separatist argument. In 1852 when Disraeli was so impatient with the colonies, Derby, then prime minister, showed great solicitude for the defense of those in North America. Lord Melbourne, prime minister from 1835 to 1841 and political mentor of Queen Victoria, believed that the independence of Canada would be a grievous loss and "a heavy blow to the character and reputation" of Britain. Lord John Russell, sponsor of the Great Reform Bill, colonial secretary, foreign secretary, and prime minister, 1846–1852, 1865–1866, considered it the duty of the British government "to keep together and maintain together the various parts of this splendid empire." When Canadians talked of annexation to the United States, Lord Grey, the colonial secretary, wrote to the governor general of Canada, Lord Elgin, January 9, 1850: "Your Lordship will therefore understand that you are commanded by Her Majesty to resist to the utmost of your power, any attempt which may be made to bring about the separation of Canada from the British Dominions, and to mark in the strongest manner Her Majesty's displeasure with all those who may directly or indirectly encourage such a change." Lord Palmerston, who dominated British politics, 1855–1865, showed both in 1856 and in 1861 that he had not the slightest intention of allowing British North America to be seized by the United States. Of the statesmen who held key positions in British governments between 1837 and 1870, only Lord Granville, colonial secretary, 1868–1870, was rightfully suspected of sympathizing with colonial separatists.

By the close of the forties the colonial reform movement had gained momentum. Both in parliament and outside men of influence aided colonization projects. Bishops and other dignitaries in the Church of England supported the Canterbury settlement in New Zealand; the colonial office was keenly interested in emigration; and leading British statesmen had become converted to the idea of giving the colonies responsible government. Among the newspapers the *Spectator,* the *Colonial Gazette,* and the

Morning Chronicle were the chief organs of the colonial reformers, and in the early sixties the *Daily News* and *The Times* gave them support.

Responsible government was secured first by the colonies of North America. Durham recommended it for Canada; but in September, 1839, when Lord John Russell sent out and instructed C. Poulett Thomson (afterward Lord Sydenham), the new governor general of Canada, he vetoed the grant of responsible government. However, on October 16, 1839, Russell sent a dispatch to Thomson which altered the tenure of office of the members of the executive council in the North American colonies from good behavior, which usually meant life, to the term of Her Majesty's pleasure. This dispatch was drafted by James Stephen for the purpose of making it possible for a new governor to dismiss old councilors who might be in disagreement with his views. But there was need also for harmony between the executive council and the legislature, and in the end that need was considered more important than the need for harmony between the councilors and the governor. In 1841 Lord Sydenham found it convenient to appoint to the first executive council of United Canada men who could defend and secure the passage of the government's bills in the assembly. He was his own prime minister. His immediate successors strove to maintain his system, but they failed. Lord Elgin, 1847–1854, adopted the position of a constitutional ruler; that is to say, he stood aloof from party strife. Simple expediency caused him to select the executive council from the group that controlled the assembly and to sign measures recommended by his ministers and agreed to by the parliament of Canada. The crucial test came in 1849 when Elgin approved a bill which provided compensation for losses sustained in the rebellion. This measure was bitterly opposed by the British minority on the ground that it provided compensation for rebels. The "Loyalists" rioted, burned the parliament building at Montreal, insulted the governor general, and appealed to the home government. The prime minister, Lord John Russell, the colonial secretary, Lord Grey, and other leaders in the British parliament sustained Elgin. Responsible government was then definitely established. A year earlier it had been recognized as a guiding principle in the government of Nova Scotia.

What had been granted to Canada could not be withheld from the Australian colonies. In the debates in the British parliament on a new government bill for these colonies, 1849–1850, the cry was raised, "Consult the wishes of the people." The bill conceded to the Australians the right to draw up their own constitutions. These were prepared separately by New South Wales, Victoria, and South Australia. Details were eliminated at home, but in all essentials the colonists had their way. No mention was made of responsible government in these acts. In practice it was tacitly applied. The same thing happened in New Zealand, which in 1852 received a liberal constitution; and when Queensland separated from New South Wales in 1859 responsible government was established without debate. Responsible government was not, however, introduced indiscriminately. The Cape of Good Hope secured representative government in 1853; not until nineteen years later was responsible government granted. Special local conditions in the West Indies caused the home government to deprive these colonies of autonomy. On the eve of the creation of the Dominion of Canada, which secured more freedom than had been conceded to any other colony of Britain, Jamaica lost her elected assembly and was reduced to the status of a crown colony.

In 1839 when Lord Durham and his associates spoke of responsible government they had in mind colonial control over purely local affairs. The dominion status of today was not envisaged. They believed, moreover, in the feasibility of drawing a line of demarcation between local and imperial subjects. Among the latter Durham placed "the constitution and the form of government — the regulation of foreign relations, and of trade with the mother country, the other British colonies, and foreign nations — and the disposal of public lands." Lord John Russell, on the other hand, considered such a division of power impracticable. The matter was dropped for the moment, to be taken up in the house of commons toward the end of the forties by J. A. Roebuck, Molesworth, and Gladstone, and debated later in connection with the Australian constitutions.

The advocates of the separation of powers called attention to the constitution of the United States which distinguishes between the powers to be exercised by the state and the federal governments. The constitution of the Roman empire providing self-government in the municipalities supplied another precedent. In 1849 Gladstone cited the Canadian Rebellion Losses Bill as proof of the need for separating colonial and imperial subjects. He felt that the Canadian act stultified the imperial government in granting compensation to rebels for losses sustained when in arms against the government.

The colonists too discussed the separation of powers. In 1839 Joseph Howe approved the suggestion made by Lord Durham; and Robert Lowe, speaking at Sydney College, New South Wales, on January 26, 1846, said: "A line of demarcation should be drawn between Imperial and Colonial legislation, and all meddling interference in matters of domestic nature should be utterly and forever renounced." The legislative council of New South Wales took up the cry. In a solemn "Declaration and Remonstrance," it protested against withholding from the local legislature control over the crown lands and the revenues derived therefrom, customs tariff, and local patronage, and denounced the reservation of bills "for the signification of Her Majesty's Pleasure, unless they affect the Prerogatives of the Crown, or the general interests of the Empire." Lord Grey opposed the idea; but his Conservative successor at the colonial office, Sir John Pakington, in dismissing the demand stated that if a practicable plan could be suggested the government was not indisposed "to meet the views" of the colonists.

This answer was treated in Australia as an encouragement. In drafting their constitutions, 1853–1854, South Australia embodied in her bill an affirmation of the principle of a division of powers, and the bills from New South Wales and Victoria contained lists of imperial subjects. The three colonies agreed, however, that the judicial committee of the privy council should have the final power to decide on disputed points concerning the reservation and disallowance of their laws. When the bills arrived in England they were examined and reported upon by Sir Frederic Rogers of the colonial office. The portions dealing with the separation of powers were subjected to the closest scrutiny and commented upon adversely. Sir Frederic denied that the imperial veto power had been abused; though it had been used very rarely, to abandon it might have serious consequences. He was especially loth to surrender all supervision of the treatment of foreigners. If the Australian request were granted, he feared that the imperial government "will be bound to protect from foreign aggression a community of persons whom it cannot restrain from giving just cause of offense."

The topic of the separation of the powers caused much discussion in the cabinet. Sir George Grey, who was then colonial secretary, Lord John Russell, W. E. Gladstone, and Sir William Molesworth prepared lengthy memoranda on it. Grey and Russell shared the views of Rogers, whereas Gladstone and Molesworth supported the colonies. Grey denied that Pakington had made explicit or implied promises. The colonies had, in Grey's judgment, exceeded their authority in the attempts to limit the veto power; these parts of the bills should be omitted. He felt, however, that the government must proceed cautiously so as not to arouse the anger of the colonists. The views of Lord John Russell expressed in 1839 remained unchanged. No satisfactory dividing line, he thought, could be drawn between imperial and colonial subjects. "Either you would limit the Crown too strictly, or you would include subjects, which in nine cases out of ten, ought to be left to the Colonial Legislature." And even if agreement were reached on the particular line of separation, quarrels might arise over definitions. Russell's final verdict was that the imperial government should agree to the Australian bills, "but that every provision circumscribing the Prerogative, in respect to allowing or disallowing Bills, should be carefully struck out." Gladstone contended that neither imperial interests nor imperial honor would be sacrificed by limiting the veto power of the home government. A line could be drawn, it had been done in the case of the American constitution. By abandoning the veto power over colonial laws the government would go back to the sound practices of the seventeenth century and avoid the danger and possible dishonor connected with interference in local conflicts. Reference to the judicial committee of the privy council would remove the risk of clashes between the colonial and the imperial governments. Molesworth followed Gladstone's line of reasoning. He felt that to conform with the wishes of the colonies would be politic and that successive colonial secretaries had made implied promises by asking the colonies to submit plans for a division of power; but he agreed with Grey that the question was one to be decided solely by the imperial government; and for this purpose he presented to the cabinet in December, 1854, the draft of a bill.

The bill never reached parliament; but in the light of later developments it is interesting to note what an advanced colonial reformer of 1854 wished to withhold from a colony with responsible government. In the category of "Imperial" matters, Molesworth placed foreign affairs, defense, "regulation of commerce and navigation with Great Britain, with any Colony or dependency of Great Britain, and with any foreign nation," transmission of letters by sea, coinage, "appointment, removal, and salary of the Governor"; the power of the governor to convene, prorogue, or dissolve the legislature; laws relating to bankruptcy, slavery, and the slave trade, treason and naturalization, patents and copyrights, tenure of office and salaries of judges, the appellate jurisdiction of the crown, and courts necessary to try matters involving imperial interests. The majority of the cabinet agreed with Grey and Russell; the Australian bills were amended as desired by them; and the constitution of the empire was allowed to grow in the approved English fashion until the passage of the Statute of Westminster in 1931.

Time soon whittled away at the powers that Durham and Molesworth wished to reserve for the imperial government. The control over the customs tariff was too intimately connected with taxation and local economic interests to be left to an outside power when colonial self-government had been conceded; furthermore, the colonies as debtor communities lacked cash, and the frontiersmen disliked direct taxes. Customs tariffs have seemed particularly helpful in new countries as a comparatively painless method of extracting taxes. When the Canadians protested against the repeal of the colonial preferences in 1846, Gladstone, who was then at the colonial office, lectured them on the blessings of free trade, but admitted that henceforth the colonies were free to levy tariffs in accordance with their own needs and wishes. The sermon made no impression, though the hint was taken. The Canadians began to increase their import duties, and in 1859 their tariff established a limited amount of protection. English free traders were alarmed at the failure of the colonies to follow the example set by the mother country; and English manufacturers protested against having their wares treated in the same fashion as foreign goods in a colony for whose defense they were taxed. It was alleged that the Canadians even levied duties on the supplies for the imperial troops in Canada. The colonial secretary, the Duke of Newcastle, forwarded to Canada complaints of English manufacturers and added remonstrances of his own. But he was worsted in the contest with the Canadian minister of finance, Alexander Galt. When the Dominion of Canada came into existence it obtained the right to grant (as a means of inducement) tariff favors to the British North American colonies that remained outside the federation. In the late sixties the Australasian colonies attempted to secure the power to levy differential duties on goods of Australasian origin. The home government opposed this because it seemed to conflict with commercial treaties. But the concession to Canada concerning the tariff made it impossible to resist further the Australasian request, and the right to levy differential duties was granted by an imperial act of 1873. This grant was inevitable; Disraeli, who in June of the preceding year had spoken eloquently about the need for restricting the tariff autonomy of the colonies, was absent from the house of commons when the Australian Differential Tariff Bill was up for discussion. Moreover, a precedent for direct negotiations of commercial treaties between colonies and foreign powers had been set by the Elgin Reciprocity Treaty of 1854, which regulated commercial relations between the United States and British North America. The main work in bringing this about was done by Lord Elgin, governor general of Canada, who went to Washington and secured the ratification of the treaty by the United States senate.

The control of the crown lands in the self-governing colonies went the same way as the control over their tariffs. The colonists asserted with much truth, as did the legislature of New South Wales in 1851, that the value of the public lands was "imparted to them by the labour and capital of the people of this Colony," and that the revenue derived from the sale of such lands "is as much their property as the ordinary Revenue." The colonists had their way as usual.

The regulation of native affairs was in a different category from that of tariff and crown lands. In Australia the rights of the blackfellows had been ignored; in North America arrangements had been made with the Indians whereby they received annual presents from the imperial government. In New Zealand and South Africa strong native tribes held land desired by the settlers; encroachment by the colonists might, and not infrequently did, lead to wars, the cost of which devolved largely upon the home government. Vainly humanitarians and missionaries tried to protect natives against the white settlers. The latter usually won; by the middle of the sixties Britain had divested herself of the responsibility for native policy in the self-governing colonies of

British North America and Australasia. Only in South Africa did she continue, even after self-government had been conceded, to invest the governor at the Cape with special power for the protection of the natives.

Between 1840 and 1870 the Church of England, as well as the dissenting church bodies, was very active overseas. Thirty-five Anglican bishoprics, including two coadjutors, were established in British colonies and at military stations during this period. Many of these were missionary bishoprics; and much of the work done in connection with them was taken care of by the Society for Propagating the Gospel and kindred organizations. The connection between the colonial churches and the established church of England formed a topic for negotiations between the colonial office and the archbishop of Canterbury, for debates in parliament, and for imperial legislation. On March 27, 1846, Gladstone wrote to Sir Frederic Rogers that he had discussed the matter of the Australian church with the archbishop: "I said to the Archbishop and he concurred in it, that the nearer the internal law of the Church for those Colonies could be brought to the footing of voluntary compact, . . . the better." This principle was adopted generally. In Canada the question of the Clergy Reserves was settled in 1854; the church in the West Indies was disestablished in the early seventies. In ecclesiastical affairs, too, the colonists must be free.

The grant of self-government to colonies coincided with a movement to strengthen the defenses of the United Kingdom. For thirty years after Waterloo Britain felt so secure that defense was neglected; Wellington had welcomed opportunities of saving regiments from disbandment by sending them overseas as garrisons. But by 1845 he had become alarmed at the defenseless state of Britain. Fear of war with France, the Crimean War, and changes in naval construction – "steam has bridged the Channel" – produced preparedness agitation. To grant increases in military and naval appropriations, when Britain was not actually at war as in 1854–1856, ran counter to the financial policy then generally followed. India provided her own defense; for the colonies on the other hand Britain paid practically the whole bill. Wakefield and Molesworth urged removal of the colonial garrisons; military authorities pointed out that most of them were practically useless in case of a war and that a goodly portion of the forty to fifty thousand men in these garrisons ought to be brought home and would be much more effective there; and treasury officials explained the savings that might be effected thereby. Lord Grey strove, 1848–1851, for recognition of the principle that self-government begets self-defense. Gladstone, taking up this argument, urged further that to adopt the policy of colonial self-defense meant a return to the sound policy followed in the seventeenth and eighteenth centuries. It was believed that protected by Britain, the settlers were reckless in encroaching upon native rights. Indeed, Gladstone and Lord Grey seem to have suspected that colonial "war profiteers" had a hand in bringing about wars both in South Africa and in New Zealand.

New South Wales, Victoria, and Ceylon agreed to pay the greater portion of the cost of their garrisons; nevertheless, a committee in 1859 found that the colonial garrisons cost nearly four million pounds, of which the colonies contributed less than one-tenth. Two years later a house of commons committee reported in favor of withdrawing the garrisons from colonies with responsible government. The house of commons concurred, but effective steps in this direction were postponed till about 1867. In the next four years the imperial garrisons were withdrawn from Canada and Australasia. Troops were kept to protect imperial naval stations like Halifax and Esquimalt in North America; the native situation precluded their withdrawal from South Africa; and the imperial government gave solemn pledges to protect every portion of the empire against foreign foes. By 1873 the colonial defense question had been settled along the following lines: the maintenance of law and order in and local defense for self-governing colonies devolved upon them; naval defense was an imperial duty. Nevertheless, an act passed in 1865 empowered the colonies to build local navies. Victoria, at that time most self-reliant among the colonies, took the hint and began to build a small navy.

By the close of the sixties the imperial ties seemed to have reached the vanishing point with reference to the principal colonies in North America and Australasia. In the former region a federation had been created which men seriously considered calling a kingdom. Local affairs in these colonies, including control over crown lands, native affairs, and customs tariffs, had been handed over to the colonists. True, they were not to legislate contrary to the laws of England and they were bound by imperial commercial treaties; but old-style imperialists considered these means of control illusory. At home voices were heard advocating separation; in Victoria demands arose for a recognition of a purely personal union between that colony and Britain; New Zealand felt aggrieved because the garrison was recalled before the Maori war had ended; and in North America a movement for annexation to the United States raised its head.

Gladstone then spoke eloquently about having faith in freedom and voluntaryism as the strongest imperial ties. Others were not so idealistic. However, new links were forged and efforts were made to stem what seemed to be a tide of imperial disintegration. Steampship lines and the telegraph began to bring North America, South Africa, and Australasia closer to Britain. About two million British emigrants had gone to the colonies since 1837. Many of these were Irish who hated England, but others kept alive a friendly feeling for the old home; connections were now greatly facilitated by better postal communications, for each year it became easier to get English books and newspapers. Colonists who returned to the homeland were, however, amazed at the ignorance and indifference toward the colonies shown by the average Englishman. In 1869 they and Englishmen who felt apprehensive about the course of events organized the Colonial Society, later called the Royal Colonial Institute, to combat the forces of disintegration. Earlier Joseph Howe had advocated imperial federation, and some in England shared his views. In 1870 an imperial federation movement was being launched, and soon afterward the most powerful of centripetal forces, fear of foreign aggression, loomed on the horizon. A new era was dawning.

CHAPTER 12

NORTH AMERICA: FROM THE REBELLIONS TO THE FEDERATION

SETTLEMENT of boundary disputes with the United States, establishment of colonial self-government, large growth in wealth and population, formation of a federation, and acquisition of the great northwest for the Dominion of Canada form the high spots in the history of British North America during the first half of the Victorian age.

The relations with the United States were occasionally vexatious, once threatening, but never really alarming in the period under discussion. At its opening, New Brunswick and the state of Maine disputed violently over the possession of territory along their border. But neither London nor Washington wanted to fight, and the dispute was settled amicably in 1842. At the other end of the long international boundary the situation looked serious a few years later. The boundary between the Rockies and the ocean had not been determined in 1818; the Oregon country was being settled; and in the election of 1844 the American electorate twisted the Lion's tail by shouting "Fifty-four forty or fight." By pushing the boundary so far to the north the United States would have adjoined Alaska, then owned by Russia, and the British northwest would have been deprived of an outlet to the Pacific. Compliant though Britain was in matters affecting colonial boundaries, war might have resulted if the American government had insisted on 54°40′. However, reason prevailed; and a treaty of 1846 continued the 49th parallel as the boundary west of the Rockies. The whole of Vancouver Island was recognized as British, but San Juan Island, to the south of Vancouver Island, was awarded to the United States in 1872 by the German emperor as arbitrator in the boundary dispute.

Sundry other issues stirred up momentary irritation on both sides. Border ruffians, Canadian rebels, and rebel sympathizers caused trouble in 1838. The destruction by British armed forces of the *Caroline* in American waters in December, 1837, and the arrest and trial for murder of one of the participants in the raid, Alexander McLeod, in the courts of New York supplied occasions for exchange of acrimonious diplomatic dispatches. Complaints over Canadian aid lent to fugitive slaves and over crimping in Canada during the Civil War aroused ill feeling at times. After the Civil War the activities of the Irish Fenians living in the United States and the expense caused by their actual and threatened raids on Canada formed a basis for legitimate Canadian grievances. Disputes concerning fisheries were more or less perennial. Canadian irritation with the mother country over the repeal of tariff preferences led to a movement in favor of union with the United States in 1849. But Lord Elgin took prompt action and the Reciprocity Treaty of 1854 eased the tension. Another annexation movement raised its head in 1870 but soon collapsed. Strong bodies of opinion north of the boundary such as the French-Canadian, the old Loyalist, and the official British blocked any move for secession from the British empire. Nor did American plans in the sixties to secure British territory west of the Great Lakes meet with any encouragement. The finger of manifest destiny for the United States pointed west, not north; though the possibility that the direction might be changed was a factor in causing Britain to accede to Canadian demands for self-government and to insist upon a British North American federation.

Though the protracted disputes with the assembly of Lower Canada and the investigations and reports by committees of the house of commons should have forewarned them, British statesmen seem to have been taken by surprise when the rebellions broke out in 1837. Britain denied that the Canadians had any substantial grievance, and the program of responsible government formulated by reformers seemed incompatible with a colonial status. Nevertheless, the fact of the rebellion could not be denied; Lower Canada was placed under military control, and means had to be found for solving the Canadian problem. For this purpose Lord Durham was sent out in 1838 as governor general and high commissioner for British North America. He took with him an able staff, including Charles Buller, Edward Gibbon Wakefield, and Thomas Turton. Wakefield and Turton had been in the clutches of the law and could therefore receive no official appointment; their presence on Durham's staff supplied material for criticism, but Durham paid no heed. He arrived in Canada in May, 1838, appointed a new council for Lower Canada, and selected commissions to study the various phases of the Canadian problem. He established friendly relations with the United States, decreed the banishment of rebels then in exile and the deportation of eight rebel leaders without trial, and granted amnesty to others. He studied intensively the Canadian questions as well as basic principles of a sound colonial policy. Lord Durham, however, had powerful political enemies at home where Lord Melbourne led a weak government. Some of Durham's actions, especially that of deporting rebels without due process of law, were severely criticized, and the prime minister failed to support him. He was "let down" by his superiors. When the news of this reached Durham, he defended himself before the people of Canada, resigned his commission, returned home in November, 1838, reported on his mission in January, 1839, and died the following year.

Lord Durham's Report on Canada is the most important constitutional document connected with the evolution of the British

Commonwealth of Nations. It is valuable for its information and remarkable for its analysis of the Canadian situation and its recommendation of policies to be adopted. Durham favored the union of the Canadas, with a government based on colonial autonomy and the responsibility of ministers to the popularly elected branch of the legislature, the scope of British interference being limited to purely imperial questions. He advocated the denationalization of the French-Canadians; he considered a federation of all British North American colonies desirable though not practicable at the moment. Lord John Russell, who became colonial secretary in the autumn of 1839, prepared a bill for the union of the Canadas based on Lord Durham's Report; the principle of responsible government neither he, nor the permanent undersecretary, James Stephen, nor parliament, nor C. Poulett Thomson, the new governor general appointed by Russell, was ready to concede. But it had been demanded by Upper Canadian reformers, and Joseph Howe of Nova Scotia presented well-reasoned arguments in its favor in a series of letters to Lord John Russell.

Within ten years the reform had been conceded to Canada and Nova Scotia. Thomson arrived in Canada on October 19, 1839. He had been instructed not to grant responsible government but was later authorized to change the membership of his executive council if necessary for an efficient administration. Thomson was an experienced house of commons man, a man of affairs, an excellent administrator, but no theorist. There was much work to do in Canada, and he meant to do it. He lectured, wheedled, threatened; he represented the crown, and all Canadians were monarchists; his was the hand of a master and this was needed for Canada.

By an imperial act of 1840 the two Canadas were united and given a two-chambered legislature, a nominated legislative council, and an elective assembly in which the two provinces had equal representation. Thomson (who became Lord Sydenham in August, 1840) secured the assent of the people of Upper

Canada to the act of union, met the first parliament of the United Canada, formulated its legislative program, and carried this through in record time. He was governor, prime minister, and political boss. The ministers were his puppets, but of necessity they must have a following in the assembly. At first Robert Baldwin was one of them, holding the office of solicitor-general; however, he soon resigned and introduced resolutions favoring responsible government in the assembly. These were amended at the instigation of the governor general so as to becloud the issue. Responsible government was shelved for the time being. It soon reappeared. Sir Charles Bagot, a diplomatist but not a house of commons man, succeeded Lord Sydenham. As a diplomatist, Bagot had learned the value of compromise and the desirability of getting things done without much regard for abstract theory. Instead of fighting to the last ditch against reformers and French-Canadians he intrusted to their leaders, Robert Baldwin and Louis Hippolyte Lafontaine, the formation of a government. At home Wellington growled and called Bagot a fool; Stanley, the colonial secretary, remonstrated — Bagot could not be disavowed nor was it practicable to recall him. Shortly afterward ill health forced him to resign. His successor, Sir Charles Metcalfe, had behind him a long and honorable record in the Indian service and had been fairly successful as governor of Jamaica, but he had never faced a situation like that in Canada. He tried to reign and govern. The Baldwin-Lafontaine ministry was dismissed, and the influence of the crown was used to elect "loyalists"; Metcalfe secured a majority of six in the assembly of eighty-four members — a hollow victory.

Meanwhile at the colonial office something akin to a tradition had developed to the effect that the governor general of Canada must be left unhampered. Syndenham had lectured to instead of being lectured by his chief. Bagot's tenure was short and circumstances compelled him to act contrary to the wishes of Downing Street. When a successor had to be found for Metcalfe,

James Stephen wrote: "A man fit to govern Canada must and will act, as Lord Metcalfe had always done, on his own judgment and responsibility." And Stephen observed further: "Canada appears to me to have shaken off or laid aside the Colonial relations to this Country and to have become, in everything but the name, a distinct State . . . self-governed so completely and so inevitably, as to render almost superfluous and unmeaning any attempt to prescribe to the Governor any line of policy on any internal question whatever." So wrote the powerful permanent undersecretary on January 12, 1846. A year later Lord Elgin, a nobleman of ancient lineage and Durham's son-in-law, went to Canada as governor general. Elgin had had experience as governor of Jamaica; he combined liberal views with a clear understanding of governmental problems; and he enjoyed the confidence of leading men belonging to both parties and all factions in the imperial parliament. By this time the British cabinet had decided to abandon resistance to colonial demands. Elgin adopted the party form of government, chose his ministers from the majority group or groups in the Canadian assembly, intrusted them with patronage and other powers vested by the Union Act in the governor and his executive council, and ultimately withdrew from the deliberations of this body. He assumed the position of a constitutional sovereign, refused to depart from it when urged to do so by the opponents of the Rebellion Losses Bill in 1849, and was sustained by the government and parliament at home.

Thus the system of responsible government in Canada triumphed in a severe test. A year earlier it had been adopted in Nova Scotia, and shortly afterward New Brunswick, Prince Edward Island, and Newfoundland likewise became self-governing.

Imperial interference in the affairs of British North America disappeared rapidly between 1846 and 1870. Control of crown revenues, patronage, crown lands, native affairs, and tariffs was handed over to the colonial authorities. By settling the question of the Clergy Reserves (a settlement long blocked by English ecclesiastical influence) in 1854, Canada removed a source of conflict with the church and parliament of England. French treaty rights in Newfoundland and American fishery rights in the coastal waters of British North America necessitated, however, a supervision and guidance by home authorities in fields which the colonists would have liked to control.

In the vast area north and west of the Great Lakes as far west as the Rockies the Hudson's Bay Company remained in control until the end of the period. With the delimitation of the Oregon boundary in 1846, the question of the disposal of the British portion of the Oregon country had to be decided. The Hudson's Bay Company requested control of Vancouver Island. Opposition came from two quarters: Sir James Stephen objected to the transfer of the island on the ground that it meant a return to the old and unfit method of colonization by chartered companies; and colonial reformers opposed the request because, they asserted, the company had always been an enemy of colonization. One of this group, J. E. Fitzgerald, supplied material for bitter attacks on the Hudson's Bay Company in the house of commons. However, the company had powerful connections and the home government did not wish to be saddled with Vancouver Island. Hence the company secured control of this island in 1849 on the promise, not fulfilled, to further settlements. Later, when reports of gold discoveries brought settlers to Vancouver Island it was organized as a crown colony. In the late fifties a gold rush to the Fraser River district on the mainland led to the establishment of another crown colony, New Caledonia. Meanwhile, the Hudson's Bay Company had lost its trade monopoly west of the Rockies and surrendered its territorial rights on Vancouver Island. In 1866 the two crown colonies were united as British Columbia.

The charter of 1670 made the Hudson's Bay Company virtually sovereign in Rupert's Land, but outside its vaguely defined boundaries the company operated on the basis of a license secured in 1838 from the imperial government for a period of twenty-one years. The independent position of the great fur-trading corporation is strikingly illustrated by the fact that its arrangement with the Russians for the use of Alaskan ports was not disturbed by the Crimean War — while Britain and Russia fought in Europe, Britons and Russians were trading amicably in North America. The middle decades of the nineteenth century were on the whole peaceful and prosperous for the Hudson's Bay Company. However, its territorial rights and trading monopoly conflicted with the tendencies prevailing at that time in Britain. Charges that the company obstructed settlements and oppressed settlers were aired before a committee of the British parliament in 1857. Its monopoly of trade outside of Rupert's Land was lost in 1859 and ten years later its territory was sold to the Dominion of Canada.

The onward march of democracy was noted everywhere in British North America. In the east, a bitter struggle between the nominated legislative council and the elected assembly of Newfoundland ended in a victory for the latter; in the west even the settlers of the Selkirk colony at the Red River achieved a nominal share in the government with the creation of a council. In the sixties Canadians appeared in the valley of the Red River and started clamoring for self-government. Self-governing institutions for municipalities and counties were created in Canada by Lord Sydenham. Even conservative Prince Edward Island secured practically universal manhood suffrage in 1853 and an elective legislative council in 1863. The legislative council for Canada was made elective in 1856. And as we have seen, the greatest of all political issues — those connected with responsible government, the control of the purse, patronage, and the civil list — were settled in accordance with the popular demand.

Now and again religion and race embittered political strife in the British North American colonies. Catholics fought protestants in Newfoundland until a threefold division of the patronage was agreed upon — one-third to Catholics, one-third to Anglicans, and one-third to Methodists. In Canada the extreme radicals of Canada West (formerly Upper Canada), led by George Brown, were anti-Catholic, while *le parti rouge,* their counterpart in Canada East (Lower Canada), "professed themselves hostile, not only to a State religion, but to any religion at all." It was indeed hard to keep religion out of politics as long as the question of the Clergy Reserves remained unsettled. Sydenham wrestled with it and by threats and cajolery persuaded the legislature of Upper Canada, where the issue was especially important, to pass a bill providing for a distribution of the reserves, one-half to be divided between the Anglican and Presbyterian churches and the other half to go to the other religious denominations. But Sydenham's arch-enemy, the Anglican Bishop Strachan of Toronto, working through his powerful ecclesiastical friends in England, secured the disallowance of the bill by the home government. The imperial parliament then passed an act which provided for the distribution of the proceeds of previous sales in the ratio of two to one to the Anglican and Presbyterian churches respectively, and specified that of future proceeds one-third should go to the Church of England and one-sixth to the Presbyterians, and the remainder should be applied "for purposes of public worship and religious instruction in Canda." This solution did not please Canada; and the Clergy Reserves remained a favorite topic of discussion on the hustings, especially by the radicals. Following much political maneuvering, the question was finally settled in 1854, after the passage of an imperial act empowering Canada to dispose of the issue. Old beneficiaries could continue to receive payments from, or might commute their life interest in, the funds of the Clergy Reserves; the balance of past and future proceeds was divided among the local units of secular government in proportion to population.

Simultaneously with the disposal of this question, another issue of long standing, that of the seignioral tenures in Canada East, was settled. Feudal rights and dues were abolished; and after exhaustive inquiries the seigniors were compensated from provincial funds except in the case of a small annual rental which the farmers might continue to pay or redeem after arrangements with whoever held the seignioral rights. Proportional grants were made from the provincial treasury to the local units in Canada East and Canada West that did not benefit by the abolition of the seignioral tenures.

In Prince Edward Island the problem of absentee proprietors and their extensive holdings continued to trouble. The local legislature tried various devices to force the absentee owners to relax their grip on the colony. Bills were passed imposing heavy taxes on land, but despite support for these measures by James Stephen, they were disallowed. The colony then proceeded to buy out the proprietors. It was a slow process and more than 400,000 acres remained in the latter's hands when Prince Edward Island joined the Dominion in 1873. In the other two Maritime Provinces the railroad question overshadowed all others during the fifties. It was generally agreed that a railroad should be built linking these colonies with Canada; but the questions of the eastern terminal, the distribution of its cost, whether military or economic interests should dominate in the choice of route, and whether the road should be linked with the railroads of northeastern United States aroused sharp dissension — and practically nothing was done.

The two Canadas had been united in 1840 on the basis of equal representation in the new parliament for the two old provinces. This had been part of the price demanded by Upper Canada for its consent to the union and a means for preventing the French-Canadians from controlling the assembly. This arrangement meant under-representation for Lower Canada; hence it was distasteful to that province. Soon the situation was reversed. A steady flow of immigrants caused Canada West to exceed Canada East in population. When Canada West became under-represented, the politicians, especially the group of radicals known as "Clear Grits," complained loudly. Representation by population — in common parlance, "rep. by pop." — became the rallying cry. An increase in the size of the assembly from 84 to 130 failed to satisfy because the representation continued on the fifty-fifty basis. The capital was first at Kingston in Canada West, then at Montreal in Canada East. When the burning of the parliament building in the riots of 1849 necessitated a new move, arrangements were made for a movable capital — the legislature would meet for a certain number of sessions at Toronto and for an equal number of sessions at Quebec. Naturally this proved inconvenient. The final solution was the establishment of the capital at Bytown, now Ottawa, a lumbering village on the border between Canada East and Canada West; however, this did not end all friction. The French-Canadians continued to dominate in the older section, and the numerous ministries with hyphenated labels — Baldwin-Lafontaine, Hincks-Morin, MacNab-Morin, MacNab-Taché — testify to the need for satisfying racial as well as provincial demands. Nor did the rise of a conservative party which cut across the old provincial borders solve the problem. The new party lead by John A. Macdonald and G. E. Cartier was no more successful than the old grouping of parties had been. A suggestion that the government should have a double majority in the assembly, which meant the support of the majority among the sixty-five members from each province, was clearly impractical. Frequent legislative deadlocks and short-lived ministries made progress impossible. Year by year the need for a new constitutional arrangement became more pressing. At the same time the Civil War in the United States and speculations as to what would happen when that war was over turned minds of men in both British North America and Britain to thoughts of a federation or union of the British colonies. The political and constitutional exigencies of Canada, the economic and financial needs of all the colonies, a sense of the weakness inherent in disunion, and the strong desire for the union of all of British North America on the part of British statesmen made that solution a reality.

The theoretical discussion of a union or federation dates from the eighteenth century. Lord Durham had considered such an arrangement desirable though not practicable. Ten years later the topic was discussed again, this time in Canada, as a means for checking an annexation movement, but nothing was achieved. In the late fifties, however, the question was discussed widely in the Canadian press and parliament. The governor general, Sir Edmund Head, was then requested by Henry Labouchere, the colonial secretary, to take it in hand. Consequently, when proroguing the Canadian parliament on August 16, 1858, Head said, "I propose in the course of the recess to communicate with Her Majesty's Government and with the Governments of our sister Colonies. . . . I am desirous of inviting them to discuss with us the principles on which a bond of federal character uniting the Provinces of British North America may hereafter be practicable." But a change of government at home altered the situation. The new colonial secretary, Sir Edward Bulwer Lytton, viewed Head's speech with displeasure, and on September 10, 1858, he informed the governor general of Canada and the lieutenant-governors of New Brunswick, Nova Scotia, Newfoundland, and Prince Edward Island that the question of the federation of the British North American colonies was of an imperial character and "therefore one which it properly belongs to the Executive authority of the Empire, and not that of any separate province, to initiate."

The rebuke failed to check the ardor of colonial advocates of a British North American federation. It appeared impossible to govern Canada under the arrangements effected by the Union Act, nor could the act be amended. The representation by population requested by Canada West was not acceptable to the representatives from Canada East. At that time voices favoring a union were heard in the Maritimes, but here the need seemed to be rather for a union limited to the three Maritime Provinces than for their inclusion in a larger union with Canada. However, the old leader of the Conservatives in Nova Scotia, James W. Johnstone, suggested the desirability of a British North American union, and the leader of the Liberals, Joseph Howe, fell in with the suggestion. The advocates of an intercolonial railroad linking Quebec with Halifax strongly supported the larger union; so did the London banking firms, Baring Bros. and Glyn, Mills & Co., which had considerable financial interest in Canada; Edward W. Watkin, the representative of the English stockholders in the Grand Trunk Railroad, became one of the most active proponents of a British North American union. Difficulties with the United States arising from the Civil War greatly aided the advocates of union, and the strong probability that the United States would denounce the Reciprocity Treaty of 1854 when its term of ten years had expired aroused both commercial interests and those who feared that the great neighbor desired to keep the colonies weak and separated in order to annex them.

The question of uniting or federating the colonies reached the stage of practical politics in the spring of 1864, when the political leaders of Canada formed a coalition government "for the purpose of removing existing difficulties by introducing the federal principle into Canada, coupled with such provisions as will permit the Maritime Provinces and the North-West Territory to be incorporated into the same system of government." George Brown, Alexander Galt, John A. Macdonald, George Etienne Cartier, and other influential men in Canada then decided to work for a united British North America. Meanwhile the Maritime Provinces had arranged for a conference to discuss a local union. Delegates from Canada were admitted to this conference; it met in September, 1864, first at Charlottetown, Prince Edward Island, then at Halifax, Nova Scotia, and St. John, New Brunswick. The Canadians presented well-reasoned proposals for a large British North American union, and it was finally decided to accept the invitation of the government of Canada to meet at Quebec for the purpose of considering plans to this end.

On October 10, 1864, the historic conference which settled the future of British North America met at the old capital of Canada. Since the opening of the Charlottetown conference six weeks earlier a powerful educational propaganda had prepared the people for the change that was to come. The preliminary work had been done so well that the conference at Quebec completed its task in three weeks. The result was embodied in seventy-two resolutions which formed the basis for the constitution of the Dominion of Canada. Before the delegates convened, the repeal of the Union Act of 1840 had been decided upon. Canada East and Canada West were rebaptized Quebec and Ontario. The character of the new political arrangement for British North America was settled after a brief debate. Ontario preferred a legislative union while Quebec and the Maritimes stood firm in demanding a federation. With the American Civil War as a warning example of the result of a weak central government, the fathers of the Canadian federation planned to make theirs strong. It was agreed at Quebec that the power not delegated to the provinces or withheld from the federal government should be in the hands of the latter. Moreover, the name province affixed to the units in the Canadian federal state and the title lieutenant-governor adopted for the head of its executive testify to the supremacy of the central power. The plan for the federation of Canada prepared at Quebec embodied a series of compromises. In the new parliament the senate was to represent the federal principle; but instead of providing equal representation from each unit as is the case in the United States, the Canadian system established three regions, Ontario, Quebec, and the Maritimes, each with twenty-four senators appointed for life by the federal executive. On the other hand, the advocates of representation by population had their wish recognized in the arrangement proposed for the house of commons. Quebec was made the pivotal province; the ratio of representation for all the provinces was fixed by that established in Quebec when its population was divided by 65, the number of its representatives in the lower house. This system was applied in the first election and after each decennial census.

The financial problem presented considerable difficulty since united Canada had incurred a proportionately larger public debt than the Maritimes and her system of taxation had also differed from theirs. It was finally agreed that the federation should assume the provincial debts up to certain fixed limits and be given control over the most important sources of revenue in return for an annual per capita grant to the provinces. The Maritimes were deeply interested in the projected railroad from Halifax to Quebec, and the new federal government was to assume responsibility for its completion at an early date as well as for improved means of communication with the northwest.

Early in November, 1864, the federation scheme was placed before the British North American colonies and the authorities at home. It was given a mixed reception. The people of Canada accepted it without much difficulty, but the Maritimes demurred — they had wanted a sectional union. Prince Edward Island rejected it and so did the people of New Brunswick. In Nova Scotia the prime minister, Charles (later Sir Charles) Tupper, staved off defeat by not submitting the federation proposal to a vote of the people. His powerful political opponent, Joseph Howe, at first seemed to approve the project for a united British North America but after the Quebec conference he was definitely hostile to it, as were also the lieutenant-governors of Nova Scotia and New Brunswick, Sir Richard Graves Macdonnell and Sir Arthur Gordon.

For a while it looked as if sectional interests would wreck the federation plan; then the imperial government came to its rescue. In 1858 Lytton, a Conservative colonial secretary, had put a wet blanket on Head's effort to foster a North American union. His Liberal successor, the Duke of Newcastle, had been a colonial reformer in the late forties and still retained some of his old views. In 1862 he informed the North American colonies that the question of federation was one to be decided by them. Ill health compelled him to retire from office in April, 1864, but his successor, Edward Cardwell, shared his views. The most active supporter of a British North American federation in the imperial government was the chancellor of the exchequer, W. E. Gladstone. An ardent advocate of the doctrine that "self-government begets self-defense," he had urged recall of the imperial garrisons from the North American colonies; this, however, could not be done while the Civil War raged in the United States. In Britain a general fear prevailed that whatever the outcome of this war might be, British North America would be in serious danger of attack from her neighbor. Gladstone showed a special interest in this question, and on July 12, 1864, he submitted to the cabinet a lengthy memorandum on the defense of Canada. Therein he urged "that efforts should be made, without delay, to ascertain whether it is practicable to establish a Federation or Political Union of these Colonies; and that, if it is practicable, we should encourage and assist it by every means in our power, and upon such terms as may be most agreeable to the people themselves." On the same day he wrote to Sir Arthur Gordon, who was then in England, inviting him to a breakfast for the purpose of discussing the North American situation. Gordon presented a strong case against the larger federation. In his judgment, the desire for it was dictated by the necessity for disuniting Canada rather than by a wish to bring the other colonies together, and he believed that a federal union would do more harm than good. However, he failed to convince his host. Edward Cardwell, the colonial secretary, supported Gladstone. Writing to him on October 27, 1864, Cardwell expressed fear that the selfishness of the smaller colonies might destroy the plan for a real union of British North America and thereby run the new state on the rock on which the United States had gone to pieces. He believed that the imperial government "should be justified in exerting a good deal of firmness in supporting the sound policy of Upper Canada against the unsound policy of the Lower Provinces." Pressure was applied. Macdonnell was replaced as lieutenant-governor of Nova Scotia by Sir William Fenwick Williams, a native of the province and a supporter of the proposed federation. Gordon denounced the constitution proposed by the Quebec conference as one framed by arch-jobbers and "so devised as to provide for the very maximum of jobbing and corruption"; but he bowed to the wishes of the home government, dissolved the legislature of New Brunswick, and secured in the following election a majority for the plan which he detested. In December, 1866, delegates from the colonies met in London with representatives of the imperial government and framed the British North America Act.

The act followed in all essentials the resolutions adopted at Quebec two years earlier. The federal subsidy to the Maritime Provinces was increased slightly; the existence of the separate religious schools in Canada was assured; and the new state was baptized the Dominion of Canada. Lord Carnarvon, who in 1858 as parliamentary undersecretary had felt uneasiness about Head's proposal for a union, was now colonial secretary, and he piloted the bill successfully through parliament. Protests from the Maritimes led by Joseph Howe, and by John Bright in the house of commons, were to no avail. The bill became law on March 28 and the federation was proclaimed officially July 1, 1867.

For more than a decade an aggressive element in western Canada had cast longing eyes on the imperial domain of the Hudson's Bay Company. Exploring expeditions in 1857–1858 had studied the possibilities of improved communications with this western realm; plans had been discussed for a water route to Lake Superior by way of the Ottawa, Lake Nipissing, and Georgian Bay, and for a railroad north of the lakes. A handful of Canadians had migrated to the Red River settlement and made themselves conspicuous and unpopular by their open advocacy of a union with Canada. Such union could, however, not be achieved before the founding of the Dominion. Now a state had been created which might acquire and govern this vast territory. Agitation in the United States for annexation of the western portion of British North America stimulated the movement for its cession to Canada. The imperial government exerted pressure on both the Dominion and the Hudson's Bay Company, with the result that the latter sold its territorial rights and its monopoly of trade in Rupert's Land for £300,000, but retained extensive tracts of land and the right to continue as a trading corporation. When a large number of the settlers on the Red River, fearing for the safety of their land titles and generally hostile to Canada, refused to be transferred, a republic was proclaimed under the leadership of Louis Riel. A combined imperial and Canadian force, commanded by Colonel Garnet Wolseley, was sent to the Red River in the summer of 1870. Riel fled, and Fort Garry was occupied without a blow. The transfer of territory became effective on July 15, 1870. The same year Manitoba was organized and admitted as a province of the Dominion.

On the Pacific coast the governor and legislative council of the small colony of British Columbia proved unwilling to aid in the completion of the Dominion from sea to sea. But here also the imperial government made its will known. A new governor, Anthony Musgrave, was appointed and instructed to effect union with Canada, and the legislative council was given an elective majority. The Dominion government offered large inducements. In 1871, on being promised responsible government, annual subsidies from the federal treasury, and a transcontinental railroad, British Columbia joined Canada.

Prince Edward Island had participated in the discussions looking toward a federation. But the people of the island favored a union of the Maritime Provinces rather than one which included Canada; they feared that the tariff policy of the new federation might prove harmful to their economic interests. Canada, on the other hand, was anxious to secure the adherence of Prince Edward Island—it would round off the Dominion and make both fishery and customs patrol easier. The island, finding it impossible to withstand the combined pressure from Canada and England, in 1873 agreed to enter the Dominion on condition of securing improved communications with the rest of the Dominion, an annual grant of $45,000, and an additional $800,000 with which to buy out the remaining absentee landholders. Newfoundland had been represented at Charlottetown in 1864. However, the majority of her fishermen, particularly the "out-harbour" ones, disliked the Canadians. They looked to Europe for their market. Nevertheless, those favoring union with the other colonies put up a stubborn fight, but were overborne by the anti-federationists led by Charles F. Bennett. Newfoundland still remains outside the Canadian federation.

Within the thirty years that separated the federation from the rebellions the population of North America more than doubled. Ontario, to use the new name for Canada West, experienced the most rapid growth. The land of her western peninsula was taken up, and her cities, especially Toronto, grew rapidly. The population of the colonies was still overwhelmingly rural, though Montreal with 100,000, Quebec with nearly 60,000, and Toronto with 50,000 could make metropolitan pretensions. A vast stream of immigrants had entered Canadian ports during this period, particularly in the late forties, the famine years in Ireland. In 1847 nearly 90,000 immigrants landed at Quebec, many of them destitute, diseased, and starved. This was more than Canada could absorb; increasing the head tax on new arrivals reduced the number of immigrants for the succeeding years. Both sections of Canada were anxious to attract desirable settlers and saw with chagrin tens of thousands of the best immigrants pass through to the western region of the United States. Many native-born Canadians also were attracted by the superior opportunities offered south of the border, losses only partially offset by the emigration of American farmers to Canada. The United States had a broad western front of contiguous territory well adapted for farming. Here expansion could take place both in the regular wavelike fashion and by sudden inrushes as new opportunities were afforded by lake, river, and railroad transportation. Canada had her Laurentian Barrier to the north and west. The lumbermen of the pineries resented the coming of settlers and thus aided nature in thwarting the attempts of colonization societies and the government to attract immigrants by building roads and offering free land. Hundreds of miles of infertile land separated the Huron Tract and the Georgian Bay district from the prairie lands of British North America, whereas the Mississippi Valley was within relatively easy access of farmers from Europe, New England, and the southern portion of the United States.

Upper Canada had overexerted herself with public works before the union. The larger resources of United Canada were devoted, to a considerable extent, to the same purpose. The canal systems of the Upper St. Lawrence and the Great Lakes were extended; it was hoped that the St. Lawrence would be the chief artery of trade for the interior of North America. The canal projects proved a boon to penniless immigrants and poor farmers; but the trade showed a perverse inclination to follow the new railroads and the Erie Canal route rather than that of the St. Lawrence, perhaps in part because of the Elgin Reciprocity Treaty.

This famous agreement, which bears the name and imprint of the great governor general, embraced all colonies on the mainland. Reciprocal advantages were extended to fishermen, to traders in fish and other natural products of British North America and the United States, and to the users of the lake, river, and canal routes. The trade of Canada flowed into north and south instead of east and west channels; and the Maritimes found markets in the United States for products of forests, shipyards, and fisheries hitherto sent to Britain and the British West Indies. In 1865 the United States served notice that the treaty would be abrogated after one year and Canada failed in her efforts to save it.

Nova Scotia, New Brunswick, and Quebec continued as centers for shipbuilding as long as wooden ships dominated. The Crimean War, the Reciprocity Treaty with the United States, and the American Civil War aided this industry. In 1855 fifty large ships were launched at Quebec; ten years later the shipyards of Nova Scotia and New Brunswick produced, in one year, vessels with an aggregate tonnage of 120,000. This was the last flourishing year for these yards. Exhaustion of the best wood for ships, the hackmatack, aided other forces in ending this era in ship-building. Industries such as the textile, farm implement, and carriage-making grew considerably but never approached in importance the primary ones of fishing, agriculture, and forestry. In the thirties seal hunting was added to fishing as an important source of income for the people of Newfoundland. The fisheries of Nova Scotia continued to be largely inshore, and the great fishery resources of the coast of British Columbia remained untouched. Coal and gold were mined in Nova Scotia and British Columbia. Canada West exported wheat; the discontinuance of the British preference on wheat, flour, and timber from British North America aroused dissatisfaction with the mother country in the late forties.

Canadians owned much shipping on Lake Ontario in the forties and fifties. The Cunard Line, though founded by a native of Nova Scotia, was at the time of the federation less Canadian than the Allan Line. In 1867 the Cunarders plying in the trans-atlantic mail and passenger trade ceased to call at Halifax, whereas the Allan Line maintained regular sailings from Liver-pool and Glasgow to Montreal.

The fifties witnessed great activities in the promotion of railroad companies and railroad-building. The Grand Trunk represented the largest single unit in the 2529 miles of rail-roads in British North America in 1867. The seaboard terminus for this line was Portland, Maine; the company made strong efforts to build up traffic with Detroit and Chicago. Though the colonies were short of capital, it has been estimated that they contributed 37 per cent of the $160,000,000 spent in rail-road construction before 1867. Capital was drawn from England and the United States. Canada's adoption of decimal coinage testified to the influence of her commercial and financial con-nections with her southern neighbor.

Education was one of the many topics that felt the touch of Lord Sydenham's short but energetic and constructive administration. The elementary schools received increased support from provincial funds. Nevertheless, denominationalism continued to be a dominant force in education, the British North America Act safeguarding the church schools in Quebec and Ontario. In Quebec, Laval University succeeded Quebec Seminary; McGill University at Montreal and King's College at Toronto were secularized; but denominational colleges soon grew up in connection with the University of Toronto. Queens University, Kingston, developed into a flourishing institution. Anglicans and Roman Catholics founded secondary schools in Newfoundland; the establishment by the Anglicans of St. John's College in the Selkirk settlement, 1866, marks the beginning of higher education in the northwest. As in the case of her population, Canada had drawn on many sources in founding her institutions of higher learning. Universities in England and Scotland, Trinity College in Dublin, Wesleyan University and Dartmouth College in the United States, and others have made contributions. Rather early the colleges of British North America developed something distinctive, something in their intellectual atmosphere that partook of both English and American characteristics but had a flavor of its own. Immigration had been heavy, yet out of a population of three and a half million in the Dominion of Canada in 1867, 83 per cent were native-born. A basis existed for a Canadian nationality.

William Lyon Mackenzie and Louis Papineau, the leaders of the agitation which preceded the rebellions of 1837, returned to Canada after 1841 but exerted little influence. Robert Baldwin and L. H. Lafontaine failed in their role as national leaders. Joseph Howe, the "uncrowned king" of Nova Scotia for several decades, pursued an unsteady course during the formative period of the federation. George Brown was too uncompromising to command a large following, though his paper, the Toronto *Globe*, wielded much influence. But in John A. Macdonald Canada found a leader who possessed the gift of statesmanship required to guide the Dominion. It was still a new and rough country. British statesmen feared that the Canadians might imperil their future by political jobbery and the adoption of a spoils system. Nevertheless, the mother country decided that self-government should be extended, not rescinded; and she helped to promote a strong federation of her colonies in North America, the formation of a new state with powers hitherto unknown in the transmarine sections of the British empire.

CHAPTER 13

THE WEST INDIES IN THE DOLDRUMS, 1838–1870

THE stirring days in the history of the British West Indies belonged to the past long before Queen Victoria ascended the throne. Sentries might still gaze from bastions of old forts, but no hostile fleet broke the horizon, for the sugar islands no longer caused wars. The West Indies seldom figure in the annals of Victorian diplomacy. Slavery came to an end in 1834, and its aftermath, the apprenticeship system, terminated four years later. The economic structure of the West Indies received another damaging blow when the duties on colonial and foreign-grown sugar were equalized. Vainly the West India interest sought aid from the English protectionists. Nothing could stem the tide of free trade, and the sugar monopoly was swept into limbo. The sugar islands received some assistance in the form of imperial guarantee of loans and the importation of cheap labor from India and China. But in the main they were left unaided to solve the problems created by the freeing of the slaves and the United Kingdom's destruction of their monopoly of the sugar market. The proportion of whites to black and colored declined within the period. When the West Indies showed little capacity in handling the machinery of virtual complete colonial autonomy which they inherited, Britain reversed the process applied in North America, South Africa, and Australasia. At a time when the colonies in those regions received more self-government, the older ones in the Caribbean declined to the status of crown colonies.

In Guiana the boundaries of the British empire were coterminous with those of South American republics. Less than one-seventh of the present area of British Guiana was effectively occupied, but Britain had inherited from the Dutch vast claims in the interior. No serious attempt had been made to define the boundaries until December, 1840, when the British government appointed a commission headed by a German traveler, Robert Schomburgk. After extensive surveys, the commission fixed a boundary known as the Schomburgk line. Venezuela objected to it. Lord Aberdeen did not insist on this boundary, and no final decision was reached until the last decade of the nineteenth century. With the discovery of gold in California attention was drawn to the Isthmus of Panama, and projects for a trans-isthmian canal were revived. Britain, whose connections with this region were of long standing, dating back to the time of Drake, now made arrangements to safeguard her interests, arrangements to which the United States took umbrage. But issues in dispute were settled by a treaty of 1850, wherein both powers agreed to respect each other's rights. During the American Civil War the Bermudas and Bahamas were havens for blockade runners. Their ports teemed with traffic; and these islands became parties in disputes concerning the duties of neutrals, the doctrine of continuous voyage, and other points in international law. For a period of four years they were of world importance; with the war over, they relapsed into obscurity.

The apprenticeship period, 1834–1838, which followed the abolition of slavery was on the whole an unhappy one for both the apprentices and their masters. Yet its termination, two years before it was due for the former field slaves, was resented by many planters, especially those of Jamaica. In law the Negroes now had the status of freemen; the transition was sudden, they were bewildered, and their friends in England showed little skill in guiding them. As in most cases of this kind, the manumitted slowly and painfully adjusted themselves to the new conditions. The old slave-holding interests continued to control the government wherever colonial autonomy existed, and it was only natural that they should try to use this power to their own economic advantage. However, the colonial office, missionaries, and the anti-slavery forces in England were vigilant. They frustrated attempts at legalized exploitation of the Negroes and the lowering of their status. Peonage never secured a foothold in the British West Indies.

Though it is customary to speak of the British sugar islands, including Guiana, as a unit, they differed widely in their social and economic problems. Barbados and Antigua had no unoccupied land and their supply of labor was plentiful providing it could be kept in the islands. Much of the soil in the coastal regions of Jamaica was exhausted; but large areas in the interior, still untouched, might supply livelihood for a Negro peasantry, though they were deemed unsuited for sugar-growing. Trinidad and Guiana had fertile soil in abundance but lacked labor. The planters occasionally combined in order to keep wages low; some of these combinations were effective in restricted areas, but for the sugar islands as a whole they failed. The daily wages of the plantation laborers varied greatly — 6*d.* in Barbados, 1*s.* in Jamaica, and 2*s.* in Trinidad might be paid in the same year for similar tasks. In all the colonies the planters objected to landholding by the Negroes, a question not serious in Barbados, but judged vital in Jamaica and Trinidad. Obstacles were raised to the ownership and leasing of land by Negroes, and it required much vigilance by the colonial office and James Stephen in particular to prevent legal discrimination based on race, color, and previous servitude. Other factors favored the Negroes: economic necessity often compelled owners of land to sell or rent it to Negroes, desire for private gain caused some whites to act contrary to race or class interests, and Negro squatters on crown land could not easily be dislodged. Negro villages sprang up; in Guiana former slaves sometimes co-operated in purchasing estates. Thus social and economic forces proved too strong for both sentiment and law.

Antigua stands practically alone in reporting an increase in the production of sugar in the early years after slavery was abolished. Decline was the rule. Much of this was due to the scarcity and irregularity of labor; slavery was not a good school for training in habits of industry and providence; old associations had left a stigma attached to field work on sugar plantations; and the sons of Africa have nowhere been remarkable for thrift. As a means of getting their work done, the planters introduced a system of piece or task work, each task being roughly equivalent to what a slave had been able to do in one day. When paid by the task, the Negro often completed it in less than a day; the pay for three or four tasks sufficed for his weekly needs – an inconvenience for employers, especially in the rainy season when weeds throve. On most of the plantations the Negroes continued to occupy the cottages they inhabited as slaves, and the owners tried to use the rent as a means of compelling the occupants to seek work. The results were disappointing. Small gardens, which satisfied some but not all the Negroes' wants, were usually attached to the cottages; more land was needed. When at the colonial office, Lord Grey believed that by keeping rents on land high a fairly steady supply of labor might be maintained; this conformed with the creed of Wakefield. Although the theory seemed sound logically, it failed in practice.

Since the creoles could not satisfy the demand for labor in the larger and more fertile colonies, the planters had to look elsewhere. In 1838 John Gladstone of Liverpool obtained permission to recruit coolies in India for his plantations in Demarara; this immediately aroused the suspicion of the anti-slavery people – an indentured coolie might be a slave in disguise. Not until 1845 were Indian coolies imported in considerable numbers for

Jamaica, Trinidad, and Guiana. Other possible sources of labor were suggested and some were tried. Among them were Portuguese from Madeira, Negroes released from captured slavers or recruited in Western Africa, and coolies from China. In the end India became the main source of labor for the British West Indies. Statistics of immigration, 1835–1871, show that out of 255,151 immigrants, 137,981 came from India, 34,364 from Madeira, 21,118 from Sierra Leone, and 16,222 from China. This importation of coolies was of both imperial and local importance. It interested the governments of the colonies, of India, and of Britain; consequently the imperial authorities assumed responsibility for supervising the recruitment, the transportation, the treatment of the coolies on the plantations, and their repatriation; the details, financial and otherwise, were left in the hands of the colonial governments. Many of the coolies settled in the colonies, and before long some of the colonies — Trinidad in particular — became veritable Babels, the newcomers adding new racial and social problems. Occasionally the arrival and settlement of foreign laborers caused disturbances like the anti-Portuguese riots in Guiana in 1856 and the coolie riots in the same colony in 1869, but on the whole the different races and racial mixtures in the British West Indies showed a remarkable capacity for getting along amicably.

In the late forties the economic situation in the British West Indies seemed more hopeless than either before or since. In 1841, when Peel came into power, the British customs duties on colonial sugar stood at 24*s.* per cwt.; the prohibitive duty of 63*s.* per cwt. was levied on foreign sugar. True, the West Indian sugar growers had those of Mauritius and India as competitors; but distance and other natural obstacles limited what could be imported from the east. Moreover, the consumption of sugar in the United Kingdom was increasing. A year later Peel began to lower the bar against foreign-grown sugar not the product of slave labor. The West India interest became alarmed but failed to effect an alliance with the English landlords who were fighting the new tariff policy in the great battle over the repeal of the corn laws. Shortly after these had been repealed, the Liberal government of Lord John Russell removed the preferences on colonial produce, and it was proposed that by 1852 the sugar duties should be equalized. The protectionists, led by Lord George Bentinck and Benjamin Disraeli, now assumed the role of champions of British colonial sugar against the slave-grown sugar of Cuba and Brazil. The anti-slavery forces did not rally to their side, cheap food for British laborers was a powerful battle cry, and a respite until 1854 was all that could be secured. After that date the sugar growers in the British colonies met the full force of foreign competition.

It was claimed in 1848 that the British import of sugar from the West Indies had fallen 50 per cent since the freeing of the slaves. Later, perhaps partly because of the importation of coolie labor, West Indian trade statistics showed improvement, but this was neither uniform nor general. The exports varied a good deal; thus while the Leeward Islands as a group could report progress during 1853–1872, one of them, Antigua, experienced a decline in both the volume and the value of her trade. The imports and exports of the Bermudas and the Bahamas rose phenomenally between 1860 and 1865, an increase due entirely to the American Civil War. With the war over, the trade dropped to its former low level.

In the early years of freedom the Negroes eagerly sought to satisfy their cravings for finery; hence the import of luxuries rose. It is significant, however, that the collections in the dissenting chapels also increased – the Methodist and Baptist missions now became self-sustaining. In the older colonies the Church of England, as we have seen, was established by imperial and local laws. But most of the funds for this church were raised locally, a situation resembling that in Ireland before 1869. In Jamaica the attendance at Anglican church services represented one-fourth of the total church attendance reported for the colony, and this church received £33,000 annually from imperial and local funds; all other churches received only £467, and the Baptists, who reported the largest church attendance, secured nothing. Similar conditions existed in most of the other old colonies. In Trinidad the Roman Catholics were given financial assistance by the government, though not in the same proportion to their number as in the case of the Anglicans. In the late sixties the Gladstone government began the work of disestablishing the church in the West Indies, a task that took years to complete. In several of the colonies aid to all the church bodies in proportion to their strength replaced the system of exclusive support for one of them.

Neither denominational nor public secular education made much progress in the period under review. Jamaica with a population of 450,000 in 1861 spent only £3700 for elementary education. In Trinidad, the governor, Lord Harris, in 1851 sponsored a system of tax-supported, secular, elementary education, but the Roman Catholics, who formed a majority, were hostile to this plan; out of a population of 100,000 only 3600 were enrolled in the public schools. Of educational institutions above the elementary grade Barbados in 1869 had Codrington College, Jamaica had St. Christopher's School, St. Vincent and Grenada had grammar schools, and Trinidad had two so-called collegiate establishments. The British West Indies, with a population of 1,120,000, had no institution that even pretended to offer university education. In this, as in so many other respects, the sugar islands lagged far behind the young colonies of North America and Australasia.

The proportion of whites to the Negro and colored population declined rapidly after the emancipation of the slaves. In the thirties, the whites in Jamaica formed about 10 per cent of the population; by 1870 this had dropped to about 3 per cent. Though the decline was uneven, and probably greater in Jamaica than in some of the other colonies, the relative decrease in the number of whites was noticeable everywhere. Socially and economically the Negroes and colored progressed, but not sufficiently to warrant intrusting them with control of the government. Consequently, the electorate in all the West Indian colonies remained ridiculously low. In 1864 Jamaica had 1903 electors, of whom 1457 voted; in St. Vincent, 47 voted in the election of 1856; and in Tobago in 1862 two representatives were elected by one illiterate voter. Occasionally districts were left unrepresented because of the absence of electors. Under such conditions representative institutions became a travesty. It could be argued with much justice that the West Indian assemblies were unrepresentative, costly, and a barrier to good government.

These assemblies, however, had a long history, some of them enjoyed extensive powers, and many had shown much independence in their attitude toward governors and the imperial authorities. In 1839 the Melbourne government sought without success to suspend the Jamaican assembly for five years. This narrow escape apparently made no impression on the Jamaicans. Ten years later, in retaliation against the proposed equalization of sugar duties, they refused to vote supplies. At about the same time the combined courts of Guiana, wherein the unofficial element outvoted the official two to one, followed a similar course of procedure. But though the West Indian assemblies were recalcitrant and often demonstrated their unfitness, the imperial government was loth to destroy them and so reverse the policy followed in North America, South Africa, and Australasia. When a petition from Trinidad asking for an elective assembly was discussed by the colonial office, James Stephen, who had often been sorely tried by the West Indian assemblies, wrote: "I must avow myself to be so much prepossessed in favour of the system of governing Colonies by Council and Assembly . . . that I should have regarded the governor's opposite opinion on this case with distrust but for what I have read and believe of the strong anti-Anglican feeling which animates the foreign population of Trinidad and of their great relative strength." The request was not granted. But later when a legislature was created for Honduras, it was composed of eighteen elected and only three nominated members. The separation of the executive and legislative councils, which took place in the North American colonies in the thirties, occurred in the Bahamas in 1840 and in Jamaica in 1854. In 1848–1849 Lord Grey was willing to extend responsible government to Jamaica, but the colonists refused the offer fearing that it would decrease their control over finance.

A new policy for the West Indian colonies was foreshadowed when the Turk and Caicos Islands were separated from the Bahamas in 1848 and given a council composed of a president, four nominated and four elected members. The miniature legislature of the Virgin Islands was made unicameral in 1854, three of its members to be nominated and six elected; five years later the number of elected members was reduced to four, and in 1867 elections ceased. A similar change took place in Dominica, 1863–1865. But the heaviest blow to self-government in the West Indies was struck in 1866 when the assemby of Jamaica voted itself out of existence.

The governorship of Jamaica, with a salary of £7000, was long considered one of the best in the colonial service. In the forties the post was held by men like Sir Charles Metcalfe and Lord Elgin. But the importance of the island declined both absolutely and relatively while the difficulties of its chief executive mounted. Financial embarrassment and perpetual conflicts with the legislature made the duties of the office onerous. Sir Henry Barkly, governor of Jamaica from 1853 to 1856, grappled with the complex governmental problems and tried to solve them by creating a small administrative body composed of three members from the council and one from the assembly. This worked during his term of office, but afterward confusion set in. The last governor of Jamaica under the old system, Edward John Eyre, was unequal to his task. Rising prices, rules and regulations governing landholding, the general economic situation in the island, and problems of race and color stirred up the Negroes. Grave disturbances took place at Morant Bay in October, 1865, in which thirty whites were killed. Governor Eyre acted promptly and peace was soon restored, but in effecting it nearly 450 Negroes were killed or executed, some of them in a barbarous fashion, and 1000 houses were burned. It was charged that Eyre had been unnecessarily severe, and he was attacked in England especially for the execution of a colored preacher and member of the legislature named Gordon. The Jamaica rebellion, the conditions in the island, and the conduct of Governor Eyre were investigated and hotly discussed at home. One of the severest among his critics was John Stuart Mill; one of his most ardent defenders was Carlyle. In Jamaica the whites were thoroughly frightened, and in a panic the assembly adopted Governor Eyre's suggestion to ask the crown to assume direct responsibility for the government of the island. The imperial authorities showed little enthusiasm for the task, but accepted an apparent necessity. The old constitution of Jamaica was abrogated; and at the time of the launching of the Dominion of Canada, Jamaica limped into port as a crown colony.

The large number of separate governments in the West Indies were expensive and seemed unnecessary in view of the smallness of many of the colonies. Arrangements whereby such groups as the Windward Islands were put under a governor general failed to solve the problem inasmuch as each island continued to have a legislature, a lieutenant-governor, and separate judicial and administrative establishments. When success crowned the efforts to federate the colonies of British North America, a movement was started to combine some of the West Indian islands under one government. The extinction of the elected assemblies of the Virgin Islands and Dominica aided in the establishment, in 1871, of a quasi-federation of the Leeward Islands, comprising Antigua, St. Kitts, Nevis, Montserrat, the Virgin Islands, and Dominica. There was no enthusiasm for it among the people concerned, but by using strong means of persuasion the imperial government succeeded in effecting the federation. The new legislature had ten elected and ten nominated members. It was expected that the governments of other islands might be combined in a similar fashion; some even dreamed of a federation of the British West Indies, but this was outside the realm of possibility. The islands continued to sink in the scale – more and more of them became crown colonies. Politically, socially, and economically they were completely outstripped by Canada, South Africa, and Australasia.

CHAPTER 14

BRITISH AFRICA, 1837–1870

BETWEEN 1837 and 1870 missionaries, traders, and explorers gradually lifted the veil that covered the interior of Africa. The great African lakes were discovered; the basins of the Upper Nile, the Zambezi, the Congo, and the Niger were explored; even the terrors of the Sahara failed to deter intrepid travelers. Lakes, rivers, and mountains replaced the blank spaces on maps of Africa. Reports of strange people, animals, and plants, of minerals and other resources attracted the curious and the greedy. The dark continent yielded its secrets. Of the European countries, Britain and France were most interested in the exploration of Africa. The list of English explorers is long. Headed by David Livingstone, it includes Samuel Baker, Richard Burton, and John Speke. The British government aided several exploring expeditions, and the work of British explorers and missionaries supplied the government with a basis for claims to African territory.

The English missionary activities in Africa increased greatly in this period. The Church Missionary Society labored in East Africa; the Universities' Mission to Central Africa established headquarters at Zanzibar; and in South Africa the Wesleyans and the London Missionary Society continued their work among the heathen. The L.M.S. missionaries were especially energetic, pushing northward from the Cape through Bechuanaland to the Zambezi. On the roll of this great organization appear the names of Robert Moffat, David Livingstone, and John Mackenzie — devout servants of God, but also representatives of Britain. Livingstone rather early became more of an explorer than a missionary. In his train followed explorers and empire-builders such as John Kirk and H. M. Stanley. Political considerations played a part in the successful efforts of the London Missionary Society to maneuver German missionaries out of Bechuanaland in the early sixties. Kuruman and Shoshong, the stations of Moffat and Mackenzie, were centers of British influence in the land of the Bechuana.

But apart from annexations in the southern part of the continent, Britain did little to push forward her African boundaries. Small additions were made to Sierra Leone and the Gambia. The Danish forts on the Gold Coast were bought; Dutch forts, first exchanged for British to effect consolidation, were finally taken over, for a small compensation, by Britain in 1872; and by securing Lagos she obtained a foothold in Nigeria. But a naval station which Britain had maintained at Fernando Po was abandoned in 1842, a house of commons committee of 1865 proposed that the Gambia be given up, and in 1871 it was suggested that Mauritius might be exchanged for Pondicherry. Nothing came of these proposals, but they indicate the sentiment of many in England. The suppression of the western sea-borne slave trade put an end to the anti-slavery stimulus to British annexations in Western Africa for the purpose of destroying the slave trade; medical science had not yet discovered effective means to combat the perils of the climate; and the trading interests on the coast of the Gulf of Guinea had not grown sufficiently strong to have a serious influence on imperial policy in that region.

The history of Mauritius, Britain's eastern sugar island, supplies a marked contrast to that of the West Indies. Though a crown colony, the planters of Mauritius intimidated successive governors to such an extent that the illicit importation of slaves continued openly for many years after 1814 — the Trinidad regulations for the treatment of slaves could not be applied here. Slaveowners in Mauritius received more than two million pounds as compensation for setting them free; but before the apprenticeship period was over the planters had begun to import Indian coolies. Discontinued in 1839, the importation of coolies was resumed in 1843. This supply of labor proved cheap and plentiful. Mauritius has a rich soil, and the equalization of British colonial sugar duties was a boon to her. In the forties, when the West Indian islands sank deeper and deeper into debt and financial chaos, she experienced a perpetual boom, checked only slightly by the removal of the preference granted to colonial sugar. As in the West Indies, a large number of the coolies chose to remain after the term of their indenture had expired. Soon the Indians outnumbered the older population of Mauritius and by 1870 the ratio in their favor was nearly two to one. Though, geographically a part of Africa, Mauritius became racially a part of India.

Britain's scattered possessions in various parts of Africa did not provide her statesmen with serious difficulties except at the Cape. But here problems of race and color, of landholding and government, of geography, rainfall, and climate formed a tangled skein which was made more complex by confused and conflicting views and policies held and applied by imperial statesmen six thousand miles away.

In June, 1837, if the young queen could have been transported to the South African frontier of her empire, could have taken a bird's-eye view of its northeastern portion, she would have beheld dozens, scores, perhaps hundreds of heavy, clumsy wagons drawn by slowly moving spans of oxen; women and children riding on the wagons or toiling behind; drivers, urging the oxen on with whip and shouts; herds of cattle and sheep surrounding the trains of wagons; dour men on horseback armed with heavy elephant guns watching, driving, scouting — Boers were on the trek. Nothing unusual that some should be, but strange that they should travel in groups numbering hundreds. They were in search of a land where they could live their own lives, free and unmolested. Scouts had reported grasslands on the plateau, the high veld to the north, denuded of its population by the depredations of Moselekatse and his fierce horde of Matabeles; rumors had also reached the Boers of fertile valleys and plains between the mountains and the sea, northeast of the land of the Kaffirs, a country left barren of inhabitants by those men of blood, the Zulu kings, Tshaka and Dingaan. The emigrants reached the villages of the Griquas on the banks of the Orange. Here was land, but not enough. Besides, the Bastaards were protected by missionaries and treaties with the government of England; they had horses and guns, could ride and shoot straight. On moved the Voortrekkers across rivers, up hills and mountainsides, braving heat and cold, rain and drought, dust and flies, wild men and wild beasts — on and on as if urged by some primeval force, in search of a land they could seize, build homes in, and call their own.

The Voortrekkers did not move as a compact body; the nature of the land through which they traveled, the need for pastures, the dissensions and jealousies — the inborn dissenting and individualistic tendencies of Dutch Calvinists and French Huguenots strengthened by generations of frontier life — made it impossible for them to unite under one leader. Only when grave danger threatened did they combine. Mounted scouts went ahead of the larger groups. Occasionally smaller bands, trusting too implicitly in their horses, their guns, and their God, pushed on too rapidly and came to grief. But disasters to their fellows only steeled the determination of the survivors. Winburg in the Orange Free State became an important center — by courtesy we may call it the capital — for the Voortrekkers. To the north, in modern Transvaal, Moselekatse had his kraal surrounded by thousands of braves. The Matabeles cut off stragglers among the Boers and harried the larger parties — their power must be broken. A raid on Moselekatse's kraal in April, 1837, failed to do this. In a second attempt in November of the same year, 135 hard-riding straight-shooting Boers, led by Pieter Uys and Hendrik Potgieter, went to the headquarters of the dreaded Moselekatse. A surprise night attack threw the kraal into confusion, but the Matabeles did not belie their reputation for bravery; the impis rallied and charged in close formation; thousands of blacks hurled themselves at the handful of whites who rode forward, aimed carefully, discharged their guns, and retired to reload. Ox-hide shields were valueless; the assegai fell short; the speediest Matabele was outstripped by the men on horseback. Vainly the Matabeles tried to encircle their foes. The shooting party lasted nine days. The dead among the Matabeles numbered perhaps in the thousands; although the Boers lost not one man, both men and horses were nearing physical collapse when Moselekatse sought safety in flight. As the year 1837 closed, the Matabeles were streaming across the Limpopo. The high veld belonged to the Boers by right of conquest.

Spacious was the plateau; still it alone did not satisfy Piet Retief, leader of the greatest body of Voortrekkers. To the east of the Drakensberg Mountains lay land devastated by the Zulus. On the coast was Port Natal, an outlet and a port of entry, a window to the world outside. To complete their independence, the Boer republics must have access to the sea. Retief sought to gain it. Down the slopes of the Drakensberg he led his followers; he approached Dingaan and asked for land. The Zulu was willing provided Retief could recover for him some cattle stolen by another native tribe. The condition was fulfilled; Dingaan agreed to cede land to the Boers and invited Retief to a feast. Suspicion lulled, Retief and his companions stacked their guns and went unarmed to the royal banquet. "Kill the wizard," shouted the king. In an instant the Boers were seized and clubbed to death. The nearest camp of the Boers, deprived of their leader and more than sixty other men, was surprised before a laager could be formed. Neither age nor sex was spared; the soil at Weenen (Weeping) was drenched with blood. However, one youth who escaped on horseback warned the larger body of Boers in time for them to go into laager; against it the Zulus charged in vain. Thus the die was cast. The title to Natal had to be won by wager of battle. The Boers, descendants of those who had defied Philip II and Louis XIV, would not turn back; they had put their hand to the plow. Reinforcements came from beyond the Drakensberg; aid was sought and received from the few Englishmen at Port Natal and from native enemies of the Zulus. Drawn battles were fought before the greatest of the Boer leaders, Andries Pretorius, appeared on the scene. With a force of 430 farmers he took the offensive against the Zulu army, estimated at more than 30,000. On December 16, 1838, came the day of reckoning for Dingaan. His impis fought with their usual reckless bravery, but to no avail, for the white man's magic was too potent. Dingaan's Day, a South African national holiday, commemorates the date, Blood River the spot where the power of the Zulu was broken. Diplomacy finished the task. Panda, half-brother of Dingaan, formed an alliance with the Boers; Dingaan, beaten anew by men of his own blood, fled and was killed. Panda submitted to Pretorius; and in 1840 the Boers held Natal and proclaimed the founding of a republic.

But the proclamation of the republic of Natal brought to a head the agitation for British annexation of the country. The emigration of several thousand Boers from the Cape, their wanderings farther north, and their dealings with the natives had aroused misgivings in many quarters. The trek broke down the ring-fence policy sponsored by Dr. Philip and Andries Stockenström and adopted by Glenelg. It was feared that the Boers might reestablish slavery and become a permanently disturbing element in South Africa. As an antidote, Dr. Philip suggested British annexation to the tropics. To this no imperial statesman gave heed; but the Cape of Good Hope Punishment

Act, 1836, extended the criminal law of the Cape to the 25th degree south latitude. Since the Boers could not divest themselves of British citizenship by migrating, they remained British subjects. But the Cape Punishment Act could not be enforced without annexations. The defeat of Moselekatse and occupation of his land by the Boers aroused little anxiety in England – a savage ruler had met his just desert. Nor did the crushing of Dingaan's power cause much regret. But with the establishment of the republic of Natal, Port Natal passed into the hands of a foreign power. In the twenties Port Natal had been occupied by the British and, to the regret of several governors at the Cape, later given up. Repeatedly they had urged its reoccupation. The home government vacillated. British troops held it from 1838 to 1839, but were withdrawn. The colonial office, and James Stephen in particular, frowned on the assumption of new responsibilities in Africa. However, the young republic of Natal clamored for recognition, promising to be a friend and ally of Britain. The promises made no impression on the governor at the Cape, Sir George Napier, who viewed with alarm the founding of an independent European state in South Africa. Glenelg shared Stephen's aversion to annexation, while Lord John Russell, colonial secretary, 1839–1841, was inclined to follow the suggestions of the Cape governor; though no definite step had been taken before Russell went out with the Melbourne government in September, 1841, his successor, Lord Stanley, adopted Glenelg's attitude. Meanwhile Napier had sent troops to Durban. When they clashed with the Boers, the governor redoubled his efforts to obtain imperial consent to the annexation of Natal. Among the reasons urged for such a step were the need for protecting the natives and the danger that a foreign power – Holland and the United States were mentioned – might establish relations with the Boers injurious to the interests of Britain in South Africa. Lord Stanley yielded to the pressure, and in December, 1842, consented to the annexation which was proclaimed officially on May 12, 1843.

The Boers offered resistance at first but, realizing the hopelessness of such a contest, soon surrendered. Pretorius tarried for a while in Natal, uncertain whether to stay on the newly won farms or seek independence on the high veld. Acts of the British authorities in Natal solved the problem for him. The earliest comers among the Boers were allowed farms of 6000 acres each, but later arrivals were limited to 2000 acres; natives were flocking in, and they were accorded legal rights in conformity with the spirit of the hated fiftieth ordinance at the Cape. It appeared that the Boers had trekked and fought in vain. A considerable number of them, refusing to admit defeat, recrossed the Drakensberg under Pretorius' leadership. With bitterness in their hearts they left in the hands of the English the land consecrated at Weenen, won at Blood River. Between the Orange and the Vaal new republics sprang up. They were left alone, but not for long.

Missionaries and governors in South Africa might urge a forward policy and occasionally force the hand of the government at home. Nevertheless, the imperial center was Downing Street. Here many forces were at work raising issues and shaping policies. British South Africa was but a relatively unimportant part of a far-flung empire. It mattered little to England whether the policies pursued in such an out-of-the-way corner were changed and reversed. Far from the Kaffir frontier and the high veld the fate of whites and blacks, of English settlers and Boer emigrants was decided. The missionary societies urged that Britain should become the trustee of the South African natives, protecting them against themselves and the Boers; but the Cobdenites repudiated this idea of trusteeship and advocated that Britain should restrict her territorial responsibilities overseas and reduce expenditures. The philanthropists and the economists clashed over the frontier policy in South Africa. It was a seesaw – at first the philanthropists won.

Since the thirties influential Englishmen had taken a keen interest in the natives of South Africa. Treaties of 1836 elevated black chiefs to positions of sovereign princes. But the Great Trek spoiled the effect of the treaties, and the exploits of Zulus and Matabeles had broken many tribes. The Matabele had withdrawn; the Zulu was checked. Remnants of tribes were scattered far and wide between the Kalahari Desert and the northwestern boundary of Natal, the land seized or claimed by the emigrant farmers. Dr. Philip, now nearing his journey's end, urged a renewal of the treaty policy. By it he hoped that Griqua and Bantu might be secured in the possession of their land and be made to keep the peace. His arguments appealed to both philanthropists and economists. In the mountainous section between the northwest corner of Natal and the southern limits of the region later organized as the Orange Free State, Moshesh, greatest among Bantu chieftains, was building the Basuto nation from fragments of many tribes. Other chiefs effected consolidations on a smaller scale. With some of these, with Moshesh, with Kaffir chiefs on the eastern border of the Cape Colony, and with leaders of the Griquas, new treaties were concluded. Their territorial rights were recognized; and the leaders promised to keep their followers in order.

But the ink was scarcely dry on the treaties when Kaffraria was ablaze. In 1846 the seventh Kaffir war broke out. It lasted more than a year and cost the British taxpayers about one million pounds. A new governor at the Cape, Sir Harry Smith, felt convinced that the solution of the South African problem lay in placing natives, Griquas, and Boers under British control. The matter was urgent, and he went ahead without awaiting instructions. The treaty policy was thrown to the wind. The Cape frontier was moved eastward to the Keiskamma and with much ostentation Smith declared himself supreme chief of the Kaffirs. He then hurried northward and on February 3, 1848, proclaimed the annexation of the entire region between the Orange and the Vaal rivers as far east as the Drakensberg Mountains. Recalcitrant Boers, led by Pretorius, were defeated at Boomplaats on August 28, 1848. Pretorius fled across the

Vaal with a price upon his head; his followers were fined; and the Orange River Sovereignty was organized. Retief's dream of a land wherein the Boers could dwell and call their own was again shattered. In his most flamboyant style, Sir Harry Smith assured Lord Grey, colonial secretary since 1846, that the "new deal" in South Africa meant peace and happiness for all, the end of Kaffir wars and of demands for money and troops. Grey was willing to try it, and public opinion in England sanctioned it. Philanthropists and economists were satisfied.

However, fate often plays strange tricks with human plans. Within six years after Boomplaats, the policy of Smith and Grey had collapsed and freedom had been granted to all Boers beyond the Orange. Reasons for the altered course are found both in England and in South Africa. Revolutions and wars disturbed Europe. Led by Wellington, the advocates of preparedness urged England to strengthen her military and naval establishments. Cobden scoffed at the panic but could not quell it, and by 1854 Britain was at war with Russia. The voice of philanthropy was lost in the tumult. Men were not in the mood to pay much attention to South Africa; nearly everyone felt that men and money should not be sunk in that hole. Just then the tocsin was sounded and beacons were lit where Smith had proclaimed peace.

Try as hard as he might, no repetition of a Coué formula that things were becoming better and better could disguise from Sir Harry Smith that his South African remedy had failed. He had cried peace, yet there was no peace. Less than three years after he had with pomp and circumstance proclaimed that he was their supreme chief, the Kaffirs rose — the eighth Kaffir war lasted more than twice as long and cost more than twice as much as the seventh. To this was added an uprising of the Hottentots and defections among their kinsmen serving as soldiers. Nor was this all. In the Orange River Sovereignty the British commissioner, Major Warden, became involved in a war with Moshesh; the farmers refused to obey the calls for commando; Warden's serious reverses made him fear that Pretorius might return and try to rouse the Boers.

That Sir Harry Smith's much-vaunted "new deal" had failed was understood by Lord Grey. Before he left the colonial office the independence of the Boers beyond the Vaal had been recognized by the Sand River Convention in January, 1852. But this

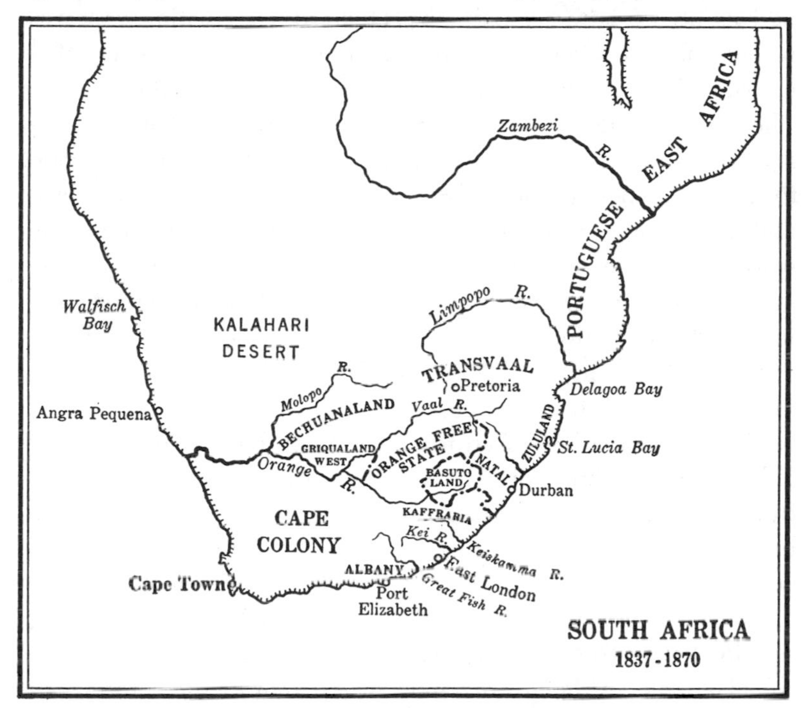

was only the beginning of the reversal of the policy adopted by Smith in 1847–1848. In England the philanthropists were no longer in the saddle. A special commissioner, Sir George Clerk, who was sent to the Orange River Sovereignty, reported that despite the land speculators, subsidized ministers, and a subsidized newspaper, public opinion favored independence. This was conferred upon the Orange Free State on February 25, 1854, by the Bloemfontein Convention. White South Africa was now definitely divided.

Then as now the interest of South Africa demanded a close union of the whites. This was perceived clearly by Sir George Grey, who arrived at the Cape as governor and high commissioner the year of the Bloemfontein Convention. Grey had achieved fame as governor in South Australia and New Zealand, and had been conspicuously successful in his dealings with the natives of the latter colony; the Duke of Newcastle, who was responsible for Grey's transfer to South Africa, believed that he was the man to solve the problems of the subcontinent. These were, indeed, both numerous and complex, with those involving the natives overshadowing the rest; they were common to all white communities, and they needed to be handled in a uniform fashion. Grey, perceiving this, proceeded to undo the work of the conventions. In 1856 he inquired whether the imperial government might be disposed to retrace the steps leading to the Bloemfontein Convention. The answer was in the negative. Nevertheless, he persisted in dreaming of and working for a South Africa united under the British flag. When the colonial office in 1858 asked for his opinion on the feasibility of federating the three British colonies — the Cape, British Kaffraria, and Natal — he seized upon this as an opportunity to invite overtures from the government of the Orange Free State and to introduce a resolution in the Cape parliament favoring a federation which should include this republic. In so doing he violated instructions; he was rebuked and recalled by the colonial office. Although restored as governor of the Cape when Newcastle returned to the colonial office in 1859, Grey was warned not to push his plans for a federation. When in 1861 he was removed to New Zealand, with a touch of sadness he confessed his belief that the opportunity for uniting white South Africa had been lost forever.

Events of the sixties widened the gap between Boer and Briton in South Africa. The republics were denied a share in the customs duties on goods in transit collected at the ports of the Cape and Natal; their efforts to secure an outlet to the sea were blocked; and plans to unite the Cis-Vaal and the Trans-Vaal Boers were frustrated by the British government. The Boers had trekked and fought to gain a freedom that proved illusory. Imperialism out-trekked them. Memories of old wrongs rankled; and new ones, real or fancied, made the Boers bitter. Moshesh, the Basuto, had long been a thorn in the flesh of the Free State. Finally the republic made a vigorous effort to crush him in 1865–1867; he was beaten and sued for peace. When the terms offered seemed to presage the destruction of the Basuto nation, Moshesh threw himself on the mercy of the English. The Cape governor, Sir Philip Wodehouse, sympathized with the Basuto and went beyond instructions from home when on March 12, 1868, he extended British protection to Basutoland. After some hesitation Downing Street approved the act. But the baffled and enraged Free Staters called it a breach of faith and a violation of the Bloemfontein Convention.

While the anger of the Free State was still at white heat a dispute arose over the ownership of a portion of Griqualand West where diamonds had been found in 1867. The land was claimed by a Griqua chief, Nicholas Waterboer, by the Free State, and, parts of it, by the Transvaal. English officials, adventurers, and concession hunters backed Waterboer's claims and induced him to offer the territory to the British government. A company was formed in London; and old and new stories of the slave-hunting and slave-holding proclivities of the Boers found their way into the British press and the colonial office. South Africa attracted attention, became a Mecca for concession hunters. Diggers, most of them British, poured into the diamond fields and threatened to resist by force the claims of the Free State; a government was needed at the diggings. Sir Henry Barkly, who had succeeded Wodehouse as governor, favored the annexation of the diamond fields; the staff at the colonial office assumed that Waterboer's claims were strong. This report was sent to Gladstone. But the diamond fields had no attraction for him because he thought that they ought not to become an English colony – Britain had enough land. Finally he gave his consent to their annexation to the Cape because the region was badly in need of a government and the claims of the Free State seemed weak. Barkly then hoisted the British flag on October 31, 1871, without awaiting formal authorization by the Cape parliament. Lord Kimberley, the colonial secretary, feeling that the governor must be sustained, sanctioned the act; Gladstone could not repudiate it. When the Cape parliament later refused to take over the diamond fields, Griqualand West became a British colony although the prime minister had opposed the annexation. The Free State suggested submitting the diamond field dispute to arbitration by a foreign ruler, but Britain – and to this Gladstone agreed – would not allow a foreigner to meddle in South African affairs. The Free Staters believed they had been robbed of the richest diamond mines in the world. They cursed England and the English.

By an irony of fate the annexation of the diamond fields with its resultant estrangement of the Free State took place at a time when British statesmen were casting about for ways to federate South Africa. Barkly was authorized to appoint a commission to study and report on this question. Downing Street now favored holding open a door for the republics to enter such a federation. But the opportunity, if such there was, for the formation of a South African federation was practically lost with the annexation of the diamond fields.

The relations between Britain and the Boer republics form an important chapter in the history of British South Africa. But other topics vie with it in interest. Of these perhaps the native question merits first place. Little thought was given to the natives and the problems their presence raised until the humanitarians and missionaries secured for them a definite legal status. Even then Cape colored folk and freed slaves were treated on the basis of *laissez faire.* But when hordes of Bantu became British subjects by the annexation of Natal and British Kaffraria, a definite native policy was evolved.

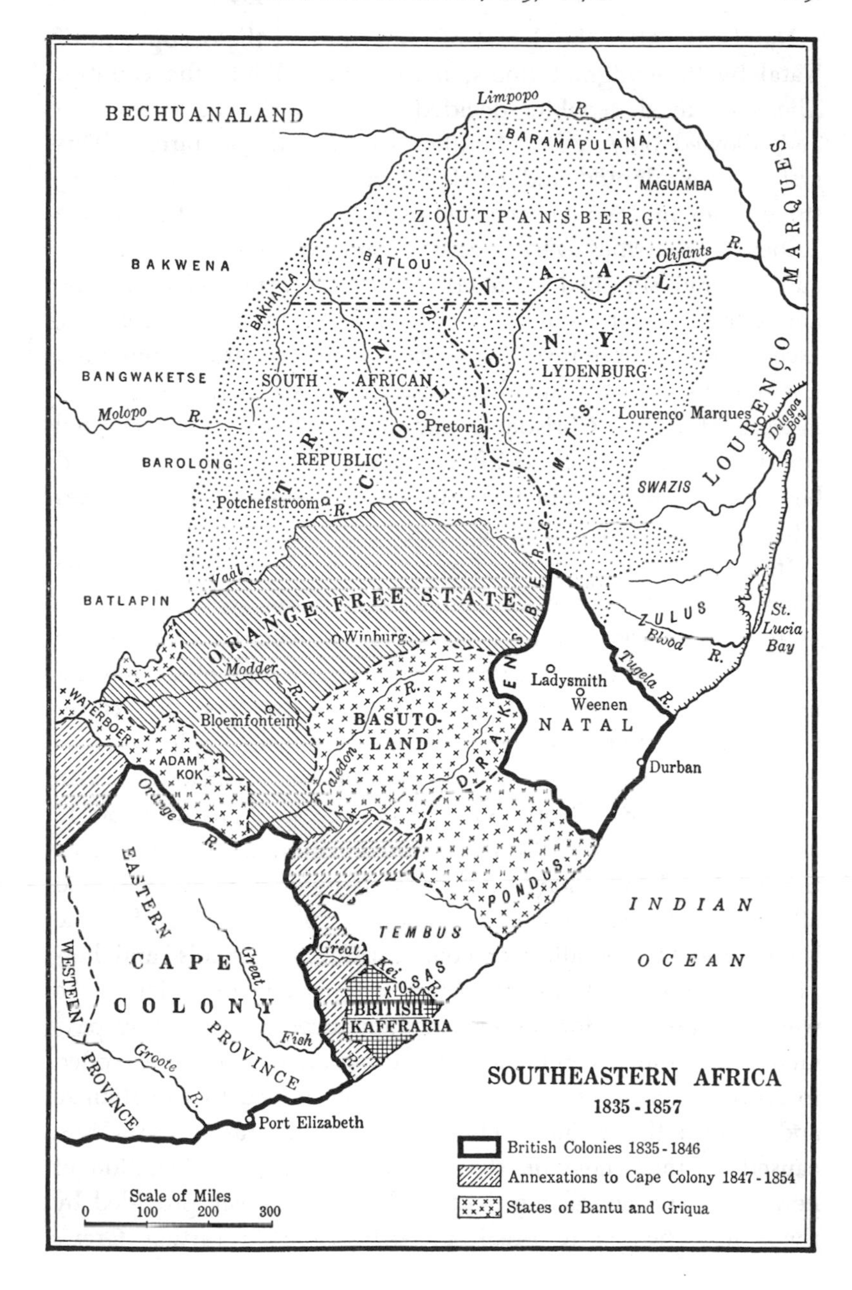
BECHUANALAND
Limpopo R.
BARAMAPULANA
MAGUAMBA
ZOUTPANSBERG
BAKWENA
BATLOU
Olifants R.
MARQUES
TRANSVAAL
BAKHATLA
SOUTH AFRICAN REPUBLIC
COLONY
LYDENBURG
BANGWAKETSE
Molopo R.
Pretoria
Lourenço Marques
LOURENÇO
Delagoa Bay
BAROLONG
SWAZIS
Potchefstroom
Vaal R.
DRAKENSBERG MTS.
BATLAPIN
ORANGE FREE STATE
Winburg
ZULUS
Blood R.
St. Lucia Bay
Tugela R.
Ladysmith
Weenen
NATAL
Modder R.
WATERBOER
Bloemfontein
BASUTO-LAND
Caledon R.
ADAM KOK
Durban
Orange R.
PONDUS
EASTERN PROVINCE
INDIAN OCEAN
TEMBUS
WESTERN PROVINCE
CAPE COLONY
Great Fish R.
Great Kei R.
XOSAS
BRITISH KAFFRARIA
Groote R.
Port Elizabeth
SOUTHEASTERN AFRICA
1835 - 1857
British Colonies 1835 - 1846
Annexations to Cape Colony 1847 - 1854
States of Bantu and Griqua
Scale of Miles
0 100 200 300

Natal led. After the defeat of Dingaan and the occupation of Natal by the emigrant Boers, natives rushed into the country. The short-lived republic decided to establish native reserves and allowed only a few families to live on the farms. This system was adopted and carried further by Theophilus Shepstone, who in 1845 became "Diplomatic Agent to the Native Tribes." The tribes were mostly fragments, but they were organized and supplied with chiefs wherever possible. On the native reserves the chiefs were sustained by native customs, excepting only those revolting to European standards of morality. Exemptions from the jurisdiction of the chiefs might be granted in case of native Christians, and only natives thus exempted could gain the franchise after representative institutions had been granted to Natal in 1856. Before 1872 only the missionaries attempted to Europeanize the natives in Natal.

It was otherwise at the Cape. When the district between the Fish River and the Keiskamma was reannexed in 1847, the natives were assigned to locations and given land for which they paid an annual quit rent. By prizes and other inducements they were encouraged to become farmers. Sir Harry Smith distributed tools and other European implements in British Kaffraria. These civilizing efforts were carried on with much vigor by Sir George Grey; the success of his attempts to civilize the Maoris of New Zealand encouraged him to apply the same methods among the Kaffirs. No sooner had he assumed office than he announced a policy of public works for the Kaffirs and the founding of civil institutions, schools, and hospitals for them. White magistrates replaced the chiefs, who were recompensed for the loss of their income by monthly payments from the government. This program was to be extended to all of Kaffraria. By these means Grey hoped to Christianize and civilize the Kaffirs. The famine in Kaffraria, 1857–1858, caused by the wholesale slaughter of cattle in anticipation of new herds and flourishing fields to be miraculously provided by the spirits, helped to break up tribes and to further Grey's work. Although not much progress had been made when he left, the policy to which he had given a powerful impetus became the native policy of the Cape.

The nominated legislative council at the Cape established in 1834 restricted somewhat the power of the governor. But the councilors were chosen by him, and the European population clamored for an effective voice in their government. The grant of autonomy to the British North American colonies strengthened the demand for self-government at the Cape, but many factors helped to retard the granting of it. The humanitarians in England feared the effects upon the treatment of the natives if the white minority should be intrusted with extensive political power; the rivalry between the eastern and western districts prevented the colonists from presenting a united front in demanding self-government; and distrust of the Boers as well as financial difficulties contributed to the postponement of its consummation. In rejecting a request for the granting of representative government to the Cape, Lord Stanley in 1842 stressed the cleavage of the community into two European elements and into whites and blacks, and expressed apprehension lest extensive political power in the hands of whites might be "perverted into a means of gratifying the antipathies of a dominant caste, or of promoting their own interests or prejudices at the expense of those of other and less powerful classes." Four years later Lord Grey, in a dispatch to the governor at the Cape, Sir Henry Pottinger, declared himself in favor of "the largest powers of self-government" in local affairs for the remote dependencies. But not until 1853 was an elective legislature granted to the Cape. The reasons for the delay were numerous; foremost among them stands the bitter jealousies that existed between the eastern and western districts. The east had the bulk of the English-speaking population of the colony; it was far removed from Capetown and communications were slow; and it was constantly exposed to the dangers of a Kaffir war. The easterners, claiming that they were neglected, wanted the colony divided or at least the seat of government moved from Capetown. Their allegations were denied and their requests blocked by the men from the west. And so they wrangled. Finally a new constitution, following in most essentials plans that had been drawn up at the Cape, was promulgated by order in council in March, 1853. A bicameral legislature with both houses elected was established. The franchise was low and there was no color bar. The members of the legislative council were elected for ten years and had to possess a considerable amount of property. The assembly was elected for five years. Both houses, in conformity with English precedents, could be dissolved before the expiration of the allotted time. Eight of the fifteen members of the legislative council and twenty-four of the forty-six members of the assembly were to be elected from the west. Thus the division of the colony was recognized. The new parliament was wholly elective, but was intrusted neither with full power of finance nor with control over the executive. The arrangement combined defects of the Canadian governments before 1837 with some of those inherent in the Canadian Union Act of 1840; and the grant to the Cape fell short of what had been and was being conceded to colonies in North America and in Australasia.

Demands soon arose for responsible government at the Cape. A leader in the movement was J. C. Molteno, a westerner, whom the majority of the easterners refused to support. They feared, or professed to fear, western and Boer dominance. Nevertheless, the agitation for responsible government made considerable progress in the prosperous years of the late fifties and early sixties The population increased, trade flourished, and there were no native disturbances. But from 1862 until the end of the decade droughts and other misfortunes befell the colony. A series of budgetary deficits and apprehensions concerning the effects of the opening of the Suez Canal upon Cape trade deepened the prevailing gloom, all of which coincided with the promulgation in England of the doctrine, "Self-government begets self-defense." Downing Street was now eager to give the Cape full control over local affairs, but what was given with one hand was more than outweighed by what was taken away with the other — a charter of liberty was bracketed with a recall of the imperial garrisons. Even Molteno was unwilling to accept responsible government under such conditions.

Meanwhile the government at the Cape approached chaos. Sir Philip Wodehouse, who succeeded Grey as governor, fell on evil times. He lacked the charm and brilliancy of his predecessor; he had little faith in colonial democracy; and he had to fight economic misfortunes and a prolonged depression. Before long Wodehouse openly expressed himself in favor of a change in the constitution whereby the executive would be strengthened; but a return to a crown colony form of government was unacceptable both to the colonists and to the home government. However, the other alternative, responsible government, was unwanted by the colonists because it would result in the withdrawal of the imperial troops.

At the beginning of the seventies nature and common sense cooperated in leading the Cape of Good Hope into the fold of colonies with responsible governments. Plentiful rains in 1870 broke the prolonged drought, trade improved despite the opening of the Suez Canal, and the budget showed a surplus. Molteno now reopened the agitation for responsible government and secured help from an eastern leader, Gordon Sprigg. The executive council continued to oppose it, but the new governor, Sir Henry Barkly, gave it his blessing, as did also Lord Kimberley at the colonial office. To those who raised the bogey of Boer disloyalty and unfitness for self-government, Kimberley replied that elsewhere the Dutch had shown political capacity and that the experience with self-government in Quebec had disproved assertions concerning French-Canadians similar to those now made in regard to the Boers. He further aided responsible government by promising to keep imperial troops at the Cape after the reform had been adopted. Barkly and Molteno increased their efforts, and in June, 1872, both houses of the Cape parliament, with narrow majorities, decided in favor of responsible government. Attempts by easterners to secure a division of the colony failed. With the grant of complete local self-government to the Cape, a nucleus had been formed for a future dominion.

After its annexation in 1843, Natal was a part of the Cape colony for three years; then a separate crown colony government was set up. Ten years later Natal secured a legislative council composed of four officials and twelve elected members. The colony was semi-tropical, and it failed to attract white labor—by 1870 the European population numbered less than 18,000. Efforts to obtain responsible government simultaneously with its grant to the Cape proved unavailing. Natal had to wait until 1893 before it reached the status of its sister colony.

The boundaries of the Cape were extended gradually. To the north there was no opposition on the part of the natives, but to the east the Kaffirs not only resisted encroachment on their own territory but often assumed the offensive. However, they were beaten in the field and their land was annexed. In 1847 the Cape frontier was moved to the Keiskamma and the territory between that river and the Kei was organized as a separate crown colony. The imperial government would at the time gladly have turned it over to the Cape, but the Cape legislature refused to accept a gift that might be an encumbrance; not until 1866 was consent given to annexing British Kaffraria to the Cape of Good Hope. British influence extended, of course, beyond the Kei, but twenty years passed before the Trans-Keian territory was annexed.

The Cape, unlike the Australian colonies, had little land available to offer immigrants or to sell in efforts to raise funds to pay their passage. Furthermore, the low wages paid the natives restricted the field for employing white laborers. Lord Grey tried to form military settlements along the eastern frontiers, using veterans from the old soldiers' home at Chelsea, but the pensioners were unfit both as soldiers and as settlers. However, special aid provided under an act of 1857 brought 9000 immigrants to the Cape, 1858–1862, and an additional 1000 paid for their own passage. In 1856 about 2000 Germans from the German legion that had fought for Britain in the Crimea were sent to the eastern province. Some of these reenlisted and saw service in India during the Mutiny, but most of the survivors returned to the Cape. Some hundreds of poor children from Holland and about 1300 Germans from Hamburg helped to increase the white population of the Cape and British Kaffraria. Although the emigration to South Africa was hardly a trickle compared with the flow of emigrants going to North America and Australasia, the European population at the Cape in 1872 was about 200,000 – an increase at least fourfold in a period of forty years. In Natal the actual increase of white settlers was small, but the native population was swelled by both natural increase and immigration. However, when the Bantu failed to satisfy the demand for labor on the sugar plantations of Natal, Indian coolies were brought in, beginning in 1860. Thus the seed was sown for the South African Indian problem of today.

Farming in various forms continued to be the chief industry of South Africa. In the western portion of the Cape Colony wheat-growing and some mixed farming prevailed; in the eastern province the land was best suited for sheep-raising. Disease of the vines and removal of the preferences granted wine from the Cape ruined the wine industry for the time being; its place as chief article of export was taken by wool. The discovery of diamonds changed the course of the economic history of South Africa. Greedy capitalists and adventurous prospectors were attracted to this distant land. The value of the export of diamonds increased from £153,460 in 1870 to £403,349 in the following year – and this was only the beginning. The detrimental effects of the opening of the Suez Canal on the Cape were more than offset by the diamond discoveries. As the period closes the Cape was brought within twenty-five days of London by the steamers of the Union and Castle lines, and a new breakwater at Table Bay and the Capetown docks, opened in 1870, made it possible for the city to continue as an important harbor and port of call even under modern conditions.

Among the social changes, those in the church and in education were of greatest importance. All church organizations became self-governing. The Anglicans ceased to be under the ecclesiastical control of England, and the Dutch Reformed founded their own training school and no longer had to import ministers from Holland or Scotland. The department of education, created in 1839, gradually extended the scope of its activities so that by 1871 it had supervision over 486 schools with 43,099 children. Mission schools and schools for natives benefited by the £51,063 19*s.* 6*d.* disbursed in that year from central and local government funds for elementary education. Nor was higher education neglected. The annual grant of £200 from the colonial treasury to the South African College, begun in 1834, was increased in 1837, and in 1841 the college received a land grant for building purposes. Under the stimulus of Sir George Grey, the Grey Institute at Port Elizabeth was founded in 1856 and the Graaff-Reinet College in 1860, each institution receiving £400 per annum. The Church of England maintained colleges at Rondebosch (1849) and Grahamstown (1856). An act of 1858 "stipulated that the qualifications for certificates in Science and Literature must, as far as conditions in the colony permitted, be equal to the qualifications for similar degrees in the United Kingdom." To secure the fulfillment of these conditions a board of examiners was created; this became a forerunner of the University of the Cape of Good Hope established in 1874. An act of 1865 created a system of inspection for all higher institutions receiving government grants. Far from remaining stagnant, British South Africa made rapid strides in government and in the development of economic and social institutions. No longer simply a "Tavern of the Seas" or a mere port of call, the colony on the subcontinent had by 1870 become a center for the spread of British influence and European civilization over the vast continent of Africa.

CHAPTER 15

AUSTRALIA, 1837–1870

UNKNOWN Australia was reduced to relatively narrow limits during the period 1837–1870. Winning less renown than their contemporaries who traversed Africa, the explorers of Australia were not inferior to them in skill, courage, and endurance. But Australia possessed no Victoria Falls, no lakes and rivers comparable to those of tropical Africa, no regions rivaling those of the Zambezi, the Congo, and the Niger, in stimulating the cupidity of European monarchs, governments, and capitalists. All too often the rivers of Australia disappeared in the sand or emptied into lakes that pleased the eye but repelled the taste. Vast stretches of sandy or stony wastes and salt pans frequently faced the explorers of her coasts and hinterland; and even where the soil was fertile and grassy plains and wooded hillsides gladdened the eye, the rainfall was uncertain and prolonged droughts might turn the region into a desert.

Nevertheless, in 1837 Australia had room and room aplenty for many times the 150,000 white inhabitants found there. She soon proved it. Little more than thirty years later her population had increased tenfold, and her wealth had grown at an even greater rate. Relatively, the progress of Australia in the first half of the Victorian era far outstripped that of British North America or South Africa. Her colonies rid themselves of convictism, made heavy inroads on the wilderness, forced the earth to yield great wealth, developed into self-governing communities, and laid the cultural and social foundations for an Australian nationality.

Testimony given before Molesworth's committee on the transportation of criminals, 1837–1838, laid bare many of the ghastly horrors of the system; prison reformers had already begun to doubt its efficacy as a cure for crime; the Wakefieldians were denouncing it; and a growing number among the free settlers of New South Wales resented the stigma that it placed on their land. It appears, however, that it was British rather than colonial opinion that caused the discontinuance of the policy of sending criminals to New South Wales in 1840. Still, half a dozen years later when Secretaries Gladstone and Grey wished to resume transportation to the northern portion of the colony, colonial opinion had become so hostile that the project failed. With New South Wales no longer available as a penal colony, the convict ships discharged their cargoes in Van Diemen's Land. In 1840 the island had 27,246 convicts as against 13,000 free adults, and 35,378 more convicts were landed between 1841 and 1852. It was a flood; the helpless and bewildered colonial authorities protested, but the mother country wished to get rid of her delinquents. Finally aid came from an unexpected quarter. With the gold discoveries of 1851, transportation to Van Diemen's Land ceased to be a punishment. Bass Strait, which separates the island from the gold colony, Victoria, is comparatively narrow, and escapes were frequent; hence transporting criminals to Van Diemen's Land seemed like sending them to Eldorado. Not without regret the home authorities in 1852 abandoned this means of ridding themselves of undesirables, but the colonists rejoiced and sought to wipe out old stains by changing the name of their home to Tasmania. Western Australia had asked for convict labor, and transportation thither lasted from 1849 until 1867. It was better regulated than the earlier to New South Wales; only males were sent and they were not assigned to private employers but were engaged on public works. The colony was remote; its labor shortage was acute; and the convicts doubtless aided in carrying Western Australia through a difficult period.

The total number of convicts sent to Australia during the eighty years the system lasted must have exceeded 150,000, the overwhelming majority of them males. In the early decades the

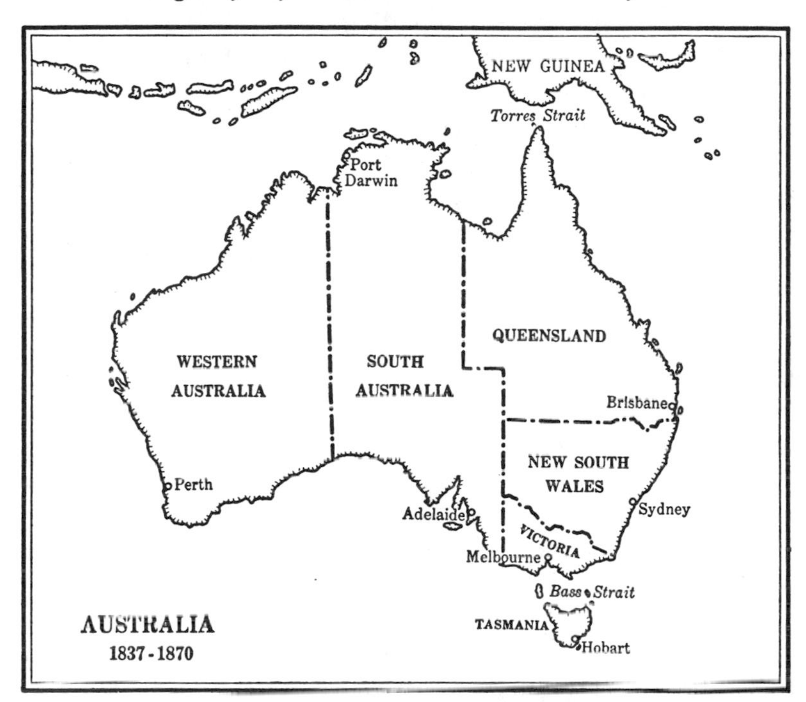

chances for emancipists to marry and beget offspring were comparatively rare. Thousands of the deportees left Australia as soon as they could, but tens of thousands remained and contributed to the racial stock of the land. This is something of which their descendants are not apt to boast. Indeed, the contrast between the apparent fecundity of the few Pilgrim Fathers that survived the first winter in Massachusetts and the alleged sterility of the many that were sent to Botany Bay is somewhat of a biological conundrum. But Australia has achieved a signal success in counteracting bad heredity.

However, convictism was not the only social danger that threatened Australia from without. No sooner had the transportation of criminals to New South Wales ceased than the colony's employers of labor began to ask for coolies. The millions of India and China offered an inexhaustible supply of drudges. The planters of Mauritius were importing Indians and those of the West Indies were soon to recruit laborers in India and China. But the Australian demands for coolies met with an emphatic veto by the colonial office. In a minute of July 17, 1841, James Stephen declared: "To expedite augmentation of wealth in New South Wales by introducing the black race there from India would, in my mind, be one of the most unreasonable preferences of the present to the future, which it would be possible to make. There is not on the globe a social interest more momentous, if we look forward for five or six generations, than that of reserving the continent of New Holland as a place where the English race shall be spread from sea to sea unmixed with any lower caste. As we now regret the folly of our ancestors in colonizing North America from Africa, so should our posterity have to censure us if we should colonize Australia from India." Two years later, when the question again came up, Stephen penned another vigorous protest. On both occasions his superiors agreed with him, and the danger was averted.

In the fifties the question of "white Australia" was raised in a different form. The gold discoveries attracted the Chinese, and by 1857 about 40,000 of them had found their way to Victoria. Serious racial riots broke out on the Buckland River gold field, and the colonial legislature imposed a heavy resident tax on the immigrants from the Celestial empire. Later South Australia and New South Wales passed similar laws against the Chinese. Australia had become conscious of the Asiatic danger, and the white Australia policy, foreshadowed by James Stephen, had become a reality.

Later attempts to bring in coolies to Western and Northern Australia were frustrated without much difficulty. However, in the sixties another aspect of the issue arose in Queensland. The sugar planters of northern Queensland recruited native laborers, the Kanakas, from the islands of the South Sea. Many of them were kidnaped and the conditions of their employment probably differed little from actual slavery. When the white laborers objected, the planters sought to divide the colony, but failed. The humanitarians of England then went into action and begged the imperial government to stop "blackbirding" in the South Pacific. This was achieved, but not without a prolonged struggle.

Meanwhile the James Stephen's dream of an Australia settled from sea to sea by British immigrants had begun to be realized. Starting in 1831, proceeds from land sales were set aside to aid immigration. The Australian colonies had the greatest amount of land to sell, and they were the greatest beneficiaries under the new policy. From 1831 to 1840 the aid generally took the form of bounties to shipowners. After 1840 the newly organized Land and Emigration Commission assumed the management of land sales, the selection of emigrants, and the chartering of ships. When the crown lands of Australia were handed over to the colonies, the work of the commission was curtailed and it ceased in the seventies; but between 1840 and 1870 this body sent more than 300,000 emigrants to Australia.

When gold was discovered in New South Wales and Victoria in the early fifties a heavy unassisted immigration set in. In five years the combined population of the two colonies rose from 264,000 to 617,000, with Victoria far ahead. The greatest gold rush took place in 1851; however, the Victorian gold fields were extensive and new discoveries were made for nearly a decade. In the late sixties, gold finds in Queensland resulted in a rush on a smaller scale to these fields. A goodly number of the gold diggers may have been birds of passage, but the majority of the immigrants who landed in Australia, 1837–1870, founded homes there. In no other way can we explain the growth of her population from perhaps 150,000 in 1837 to 1,668,371 in 1871.

At the latter date the six Australian states of today were full-fledged political entities. But in both wealth and population the poorest and least populous, Western Australia, was widely separated from Victoria, then the richest and most populous among the colonies. Western Australia, Thomas Peel's colony on the Swan River, ruined her founder and most of those who pinned their faith in her future. Nevertheless, a handful of settlers clung to the land, searched for and found spots more favorable for farming and the pastoral industry than the one first chosen, and secured a modest livelihood. Immigrants trickled in, some aid was obtained from the imperial government, the cheap convict labor proved a boon; in 1870 the population had reached 25,000. Large patches of grassland suitable for sheep pastures had not yet been found, and the Western Australian gold boom was still in the distant future. The colony lived in a state of chronic despondency.

South Australia had been founded on faith in a formula — that of Wakefield on systematic colonization. Here, too, bitter disillusionment awaited the early settlers who speculated in buying and selling land not yet under tillage. Two years passed before they realized that there is no substitute for hard work if a new settlement is to succeed. When Colonel George Gawler assumed the duties of governor in October, 1838, the colony was still in the doldrums. He brought it out by hastening the survey of agricultural land and insisting that the land should be occupied and tilled. Further assistance came from sheep-raising and the expenditure of funds for public works which enabled the immigrants to obtain much-needed cash. This policy was continued by his successor Captain (later Sir) George Grey, who compelled the home government to honor the promises to pay issued by him and Gawler. Fortunately, the soil was of the required quality to reward the farmer for his toil. The discovery and opening up of copper mines helped in providing employment and supplying an exportable commodity. Squatting, sheep-raising, and their concomitant — the accumulation of large areas of land in the hands of individuals — developed in South Australia, but not to the same extent as in Victoria and New South Wales. South Australia became a colony of moderate-sized farms devoted to wheat-growing. It soon replaced Van Diemen's Land as the granary of Australia; by 1862 "the area under wheat in South Australia and the wheat harvest were about equal to those of all the other colonies put together." The invention by John Ridley, a South Australian, of the "stripper" or header in 1843 reduced materially the cost of harvesting and made wheat-farming on a large scale profitable. The boundaries of the colony were extended to the northern sea, but the interior and the northern region added little to its natural resources.

Tasmania was heavily timbered, had an adequate rainfall, but few stretches of level, fertile land. Her climate left seemingly little to be desired, though neither climate nor soil equaled that of South Australia for the growing of wheat; and since large portions of her best land had been acquired for purposes of speculation, the development of farming was retarded. Furthermore, the excessive number of convicts sent to the colony deterred immigration, and before transportation came to an end the gold discoveries on the mainland drew off a large proportion of the island's able-bodied males. In the fifties emigration exceeded immigration, and in the following decade Victoria's protective tariff injured her neighbor south of Bass Strait. The close of this period found Tasmania laboring in heavy seas.

In 1870 four-fifths of the population and an even larger proportion of the capital and trade of Australia were concentrated in New South Wales and the colonies carved out of its territory, Victoria and Queensland. The progress of Victoria had been phenomenal. When separated from the mother colony in 1851 her population numbered 77,345; twenty years later it had risen to 731,526, exceeding that of New South Wales by more than 200,000. Melbourne, scarcely more than a crude frontier village in 1837, had by 1871 become a metropolis with 206,780 inhabitants, having outdistanced Sydney by about 75,000. At first the Port Phillip district, which was renamed Victoria in 1851, was a squatters' paradise. The early comers negotiated with the natives and claimed extensive areas by right of purchase of large areas. But the imperial government refused to recognize many of these claims and Wakefield's principles in a modified form were put into operation; land was sold to settlers who were *bona fide* farmers. The soil and climate proved attractive to immigrants and the population grew fairly rapidly until the discovery of rich gold districts, seventy to a hundred miles from Melbourne, drew immigrants from the other Australian colonies and from the world outside. At first the rush to the gold fields threatened to paralyze all other activities in the colony. Laborers, clerks, servants, shopkeepers, artisans, sailors, farmers, shepherds, shearers, cowboys — nearly the whole able-bodied male population of Melbourne, Victoria, and adjacent districts of New South Wales and South Australia flocked to the gold fields. Within a few months, 100,000 were at the diggings; and the problems of supplies, transport, and the maintenance of law and order became acute. Policemen left their beats, the colony lacked the funds to hire the required number of new ones, and Governor Latrobe had only 80 soldiers available. Efforts to make the miners pay for the increased cost of government by means of a license fee, raised to £3 a month in December, 1851, provoked resentment. Though later reduced, the loss in revenue being made good by an export duty on gold, the license fee remained both high and unpopular; it aided in causing serious riots on the Ballarat fields in 1854, the organization of the Ballarat Reform League, talk of a Victorian republic, and the building of a stockade at the Eureka camp. Soldiers were called in; they stormed the stockade and arrested 120 "insurgents." However, juries refused to convict the leaders of high treason; and some of the miners' demands, such as lower fees, an export duty on gold, taxes on the Chinese, and sale of land in small quantities, were conceded by the colonial government. Gradually the more restless spirits among the miners either left or quieted down. Order was established and economic and social life adjusted itself to the new conditions.

The gold discoveries made Melbourne for about one generation the financial and banking center of Australia. But they also established habits of reckless spending and stimulated the gambling spirit never far beneath the surface in any frontier community.

Comparatively speaking, the home counties of New South Wales and the city of Sydney were old and well established in 1837; they possess most of the "first" things in the history of Australia. A certain amount of wealth had been accumulated from farming, cattle- and sheep-raising, trade, and the rise in land values. Nevertheless, the early forties were a period of gloom, for over-speculation, drought, and withdrawal of funds to London brought about a long and severe depression. Credit ceased, values tumbled, banks failed, and sheep which fetched only 6*d.* apiece in the market were boiled down for their tallow. But the abundance of land, the active pioneering spirit, and a primitive economic structure made Australian society resilient. The economic recovery in England after 1842 also aided Australia. Matters had mended when gold was discovered in New South Wales, a few months before its discovery in Victoria. The gold fields in the mother colony were not as rich as those of Victoria, and the economic balance of New South Wales was not so much upset by the discovery, nor did her wealth increase in the same proportion. Moreover, New South Wales possessed more of an economic foundation than did her offspring; her structure was more solid.

The northern portion of New South Wales, the region around Moreton Bay, had early shown separatist tendencies; and Queensland, with Brisbane as her capital, was separated from the mother colony in 1859. A large section of Queensland is within the tropics and here efforts were made to cultivate products that require a warm climate. The Civil War in the United States with its resultant cotton famine in Lancashire led to experiments with cotton-growing in southern Queensland, but the results were disappointing. Greater success attended the efforts at cane sugar-growing farther north, and sugar became a staple product of Queensland. This colony too had a gold rush in the late sixties and early seventies. The establishment of sugar plantations gave rise to the problem of the Kanaka laborers, and the discovery of gold brought in the Chinese. By the end of this period, Queensland held a focal position in the struggle for keeping Australia "white."

Within the time limits fixed for this chapter, the population of Australia increased more than tenfold; her material progress may perhaps be gauged by the 3,690,000 tons of shipping that entered and cleared her harbors in 1871, the production of 211,-413,000 pounds of wool, weighed in the grease, that year, and the more than one thousand miles of railroads then in operation. The wool growers of Australia had overcome the handicap of distance, had defeated their German and Spanish competitors, and had successfully combated disease among sheep. But rural Australia was more than a mere sheep run. Cattle-breeding and wheat-growing had kept pace with the mounting population. By 1870 she produced wheat for an export market, and sugar-growing promised to become a thriving industry. The most spectacular events in the economic history of Australia were connected with the unlocking of her mineral wealth. Copper had been found in paying quantities, and the gold finds had drawn the attention of the world to the great southland. In the fifties the Australian gold mines produced more than 124 million pounds' worth of this precious metal; old mines were still being worked and new ones were being discovered as the period ends. Gone were the days when Australians used rum as the medium of exchange or had to resort to Spanish dollars for purposes of trade. Mints at Sydney and Melbourne turned out gold sovereigns, and Australia ranked first among the gold-exporting countries. In the dizziest period of the rush for the gold fields, when fabulous finds were reported, when shops closed and farms, sheep runs, and cattle stations were being abandoned in the mad quest for gold, Australia seemed threatened with the fate of Midas. Wages rose so rapidly and hands became so scarce that there was real danger lest the brush and the kangaroo might recover possession of the soil. However, matters soon became adjusted; disappointed gold seekers returned to the farms, thousands of the new immigrants bought land. Although prices had risen 50 to 100 per cent, an equilibrium was reached between them and wages; and in 1858, New South Wales had twice the area under cultivation that she had possessed in 1851. Eastern Australia had experienced a forced economic expansion which left many weaknesses; but real strength came with the years and 1870 found Australian colonies ready for new and vigorous growth.

The gold discoveries supplied stirring episodes, they changed the course of Australian history and left permanent traces; but even more fundamental for the economic history of the southland was the battle over land policies waged almost continuously from the time of the founding of New South Wales. In this struggle several issues were involved. A general one, one found in nearly every British colony, was whether the colonists or the imperial government possessed the right to control the unoccupied land; a more specific one dealt with the details of administering this domain — in particular, what should be done to the squatters who used vast areas without any legal right. As long as the colonies of Australia were governed as dependencies there could be no doubt but that the title to the land was held by the imperial government; but when New South Wales received representative government in 1842 the colonists began to claim control of the land and the proceeds of the sale thereof. This was denied by the home authorities. In the middle of the fifties, however, nearly all the Australian colonies were granted self-government and soon afterward they secured title to their crown land.

Meanwhile a large percentage of the funds obtained by selling colonial land had been utilized to assist immigration. The Colonial Land and Emigration Commissioners, a board of three members sitting in London, arranged the details of the recruiting of the aided emigrants and their landing in the colonies — a piece of paternalistic administration that contrasts strangely with the supposedly *laissez faire* policies of the British government during this period. The major part of the activities of these commissioners was devoted to the Australian colonies. Not only did the proceeds from colonial land sales not go into the imperial treasury, but from time to time the imperial parliament voted additional grants in aid of emigration.

Under the influence of Wakefield's theories the imperial government decreed in 1831 that land in New South Wales should be sold by auction at a minimum upset price of 5*s.* per acre. Squatting had already become prevalent, especially beyond the Blue Mountains. The land seized by the squatters was used largely as sheep runs; and since wool represented practically all that Australia had to sell, it was felt that the government should be careful lest the proverbial goose be killed. The squatter claimed certain rights to the land discovered by him and depastured by his sheep; some of these rights were recognized by a New South Wales act of 1836. Outside the nineteen home counties the land was divided into districts with a commissioner of crown lands for each one. In these districts the squatter could obtain for £10 a license which gave him the right to have one or more runs without limitation as to their size. Three years later a border police was established, paid for by a tax on the squatters' stock.

Meanwhile the South Australian venture had been launched, with provisions that the settlers in the new colony should pay at least £1 per acre for their land. The promoters of this enterprise criticized the low land price in New South Wales, and this criticism, combined with the fact that land in the latter sold rapidly and at prices well above the minimum price of 5*s.* per acre, caused Lord Glenelg in 1838 to raise the upset price to 12*s.* per acre. A wail went up in the colony, but the home government paid no heed, and in 1842 the upset price of land in New South

Wales was boosted to £1 per acre. This checked the sale of land until the gold discoveries had both increased the number of colonists and raised the general level of prices.

The squatters of New South Wales, however, were not satisfied with the position created for them by regulations of 1836 and 1839. They demanded security of tenure, compensation for improvements, and a preemptive right to buy their runs. These questions were settled for the time being by Governor Gipps. In April, 1844, he laid down the rules that each squatting license was to be limited to one run of not more than twenty square miles with a maximum of 4000 sheep; that after five years the squatter should buy 320 acres, the value of improvements being taken into account; after this purchase he should have undisturbed use of the land for eight more years, at the end of which he must buy an additional 320 acres. This right to keep a run with periodic purchases of land might continue indefinitely; but if a squatter failed to buy at the time stipulated, any other person might purchase the homestead and thereby secure the run. These regulations aroused a storm of opposition in the colony, public opinion arraying itself with the squatters; and their friends at home, merchants, wool buyers, shipowners, joined in the attacks on Gipps. The colonial office, however, sustained him. Further and more elaborate rules concerning squatting were laid down by an imperial order in council of 1847. The land of New South Wales was divided into settled, intermediate, and unsettled areas. Land in the first category could be leased for only one year, land in the second for eight years, but it might be offered for sale at the end of each year; leases for land in the third category would be for fourteen years during which time only the lessee could buy it. These rules were modified in detail, but the principle of squatters' leases, compensation for improvements, and certain preemptive rights to purchase the runs were applied in all the Australian colonies.

The popular party in New South Wales, led by Robert Lowe, had joined the squatters in the hue and cry after Governor Gipps, but before long it was discovered that both his regulations and those contained in the order in council of 1847 gave the squatters control over hundreds of thousands of acres of good farming land on the eve of a period of rising prices. The popular party now changed its tune – the squatter became the target for attack. The increase in the demand for land made the issue of squatters' rights one of paramount importance. In the early sixties New South Wales and Victoria had gained control over their crown lands, laws were passed permitting free selection of land by settlers within the areas held by squatters, and squatters in Victoria were denied renewal of their leases. The situation which arose strongly resembled the one later found in the western part of the United States when the homesteader began to encroach on the domains of the rancher and lumber baron. As in America, the squatters of Australia found means of evading the law – a favorite method being to "pick the eyes" of the land by having dummies select land with water holes and other strategic features, which they later sold to their employers. The struggle for the control of the land was not over by 1870; indeed, it is perhaps among those that never end.

We saw in an earlier chapter that in the thirties the question of continuing the transportation of convicts to New South Wales became linked with that of self-government. The colonists were told they could not have both, though that was what many employers of labor preferred. By discontinuing transportation the dilemma was removed, and in 1842 New South Wales was granted a legislative council composed of twenty-four elected and twelve nominated members. It was a hybrid body of a new species, exercising a limited amount of power. Among the most important topics withheld from it were the civil list, the crown lands, and the proceeds from the sale of land. The executive branch of the government remained independent of the legislative, the governor retained his veto power, and even bills dealing with purely colonial questions might be either vetoed by the governor or reserved by him for the signification of the queen's pleasure. With cessation of transportation, the old cleavage between the exclusionists and the emancipists of New South Wales disappeared. Both united in demanding the type of responsible government that had been granted to Canada; and in this they were supported by the new immigrants whose political education at home had often been supplied by Chartist orators. In 1846, when Lord Grey began his long and eventful term at the colonial office, the official imperial opposition to self-government for New South Wales came to an end. Grey shared the view, expressed a few years earlier by James Stephen, that the Englishmen of New South Wales "will never be at a loss to manage a large proportion of the details of Government for themselves, if invited, or permitted to do so." From 1846 to 1851 the home government devoted much attention to Australian problems, problems which supplied occasions for full-dress debates in parliament. Lord Grey and his colleagues wished to separate the Port Phillip district from New South Wales, to grant all Australian colonies extensive powers of self-government, and to provide the framework for a federated Australia. Some of these plans were opposed in the colonies. The colonists agreed that they were entitled to autonomy to an even greater extent than that contemplated by Lord Grey, but New South Wales resented the loss of the territory south of the river Murray, and the other colonies objected to any scheme of federation, fearing that it would perpetuate the ascendancy of New South Wales. The outcome of these discussions was the Australian Colonies Government Act, 1850. By this act, the Port Phillip district was separated from New South Wales; the proposal for a common government for Australia was dropped, the new title, governor general of Australia, to be borne by the governor of New South Wales being left as its sole trace; the representative government of New South Wales was extended to the other colonies; and to the colonial legislatures was delegated the power to frame new constitutions, subject, of course, to the approval of the home government.

The act provoked protests from New South Wales. Her legislative council objected to the imperial control over the crown land, the territorial revenues, and patronage, and to the continuance of the governor's veto power and the reservation of colonial laws. However, all the colonies, except Western Australia, proceeded to draw up plans for new legislative bodies. In doing so, New South Wales, Victoria, and South Australia followed suggestions made in the house of commons by Roebuck, Gladstone, and Molesworth, and tried to distinguish between local and imperial subjects. These plans were rejected at home. By 1855 four Australian colonies had bicameral legislatures that exercised large powers of self-government. They were intrusted with control over the crown lands, and responsible government was granted to these colonies, not by an act of parliament but, in good English fashion, by constitutional usage. When Queensland was created a separate colony in 1859, she received all the rights and privileges enjoyed by the others. Western Australia alone lacked political maturity.

The Australian colonies were by imperial statutes prevented from levying tariffs that might contravene imperial commercial treaties; this came to mean that they could not grant tariff favors to each other. The issue arose in the sixties when Victoria adopted a protective tariff and her neighbors felt injured thereby. They then proposed plans for differential tariffs on goods of Australasian origin, but this right the imperial government at first refused to concede. Successive colonial secretaries tried to impress upon the antipodean colonies the benefit they might derive from a customs union and the complications that would arise if they were granted the right to levy differential duties. By 1870 the colonial secretary, Lord Kimberley, had become convinced that the Australians must be given what they wanted, but Gladstone, the prime minister, feared that to do so would constitute a violation of treaties and a breach of international law. The discussion lasted several years, until it was found that Canada had been allowed to levy differential duties. Gladstone then gave way, and an act of 1873 granted the Australasians permission to establish differential duties.

During this prolonged dispute with the home government, several intercolonial conferences were held in Australia. The colonies realized the advantage of presenting a united front, though there was no real sentiment for a united Australia. They spurned the suggestion of forming a customs union as twenty years earlier they had rejected Lord Grey's plan for a council for Australia. Some Australian statesmen favored a federated Australia, notably E. Deas Thomson, Charles Gavan Duffy, and Henry Parkes; but not one staked his political future on the issue. Indeed, it would have been futile, for in the sixties Australian public opinion opposed federation. Even the title governor general of Australia was dropped in 1861. The colonies were widely separated and their lines of contact — human, economic, and financial — were with England instead of each other. The separation of Victoria and Queensland had left a certain amount of soreness and jealousies between these two colonies and their capitals and New South Wales and her capital. Each colony had its local problem which it desired to solve in its own way. The colonies might adopt similar measures concerning Chinese immigrants, but on tariffs and other issues they differed. The poorer and weaker among them feared that the wealthier and stronger would dominate under any form of a federal union. All of them felt secure against a foreign foe. There might be irritation with the French over New Caledonia and momentary apprehension when Britain was at war with Russia from 1854 to 1856 and when another Anglo-Russian war seemed likely in 1863. But these anxieties were of brief duration. Safe in their remoteness, the colonies of Australia saw no need for sacrificing their identity by creating a superstate.

The feeling of safety coupled with the belief that the colony possessed the required economic power to paddle its own canoe caused political leaders of Victoria to assume an independent tone toward the imperial government, 1869–1870. Victoria paid the cost of the imperial garrison and did not object strenuously to its withdrawal; she hastened to construct small naval vessels under the provision of the Naval Defense Act, 1865; and voices were heard demanding that communications between her government and the imperial authorities should pass through the British foreign office instead of through the colonial office, that the union between her and Britain should be a purely personal one, resembling the old union of Hanover and England 1714 to 1837, and that she might, if she chose, remain neutral in an imperial war. This was the high watermark of Australian particularism in the nineteenth century. Within the next generation, the people of Victoria began to think of themselves as Australians, and they found solace in being included in the British empire.

Viewed in the sense of control from the center of the empire, the churches of Australia may be said to have severed their connections with Britain before 1870. The Anglicans, the Presbyterians, and the Wesleyans of Australia had their own organizations. Nevertheless the Anglicans in Australia, with nine bishoprics and a metropolitan of their own, were probably linked much more closely in spirit with the home church in 1870 than when they had been under the ecclesiastical jurisdiction of the bishop of London. Relatively the Church of England was stronger in Australia than in either South Africa or British North America. It was conscious of its unity, and this feeling found visible expression in 1872 when a common constitution was drawn up and a synod for Australia was organized. The Roman Catholic Church was next to the Anglican in strength. This church showed a great deal of activity after the consecration of its first bishop for Australia in 1834. Anglicans, Roman Catholics, Presbyterians, and Wesleyans at first received state aid, but this was gradually withdrawn, South Australia leading by discontinuing government aid to religion in 1851, Queensland following in 1860, and New South Wales in 1862. The secular government assumed responsibility for education, and in 1871 Australia had

312,130 children at school. Nor was higher education neglected. The University of Sydney dates from 1852 and that of Melbourne is only three years younger.

Some Germans and a sprinkling of other non-British nationalities arrived in Australia, especially during the period of the gold rushes, but they were not sufficiently numerous to constitute an appreciable minority. Australia had no racial problem comparable to that of Canada and South Africa. She was essentially British. The Australian was also the only group of colonies wherein statesmen who later reached high office at home served a political apprenticeship. Robert Lowe, who played such an important role in the house of commons opposing parliamentary reform in 1866–1867, was a leader in New South Wales politics in the forties; Hugh Childers, afterwards a prominent member of two of Gladstone's ministries, spent several years in Victoria; and R. W. G. Herbert, who was brought to Queensland by her first governor, Sir George Bowen, to be the first prime minister, returned to England and served for many years as permanent undersecretary in the colonial office. Charles Gavan Duffy, a leader in the Young Ireland movement of 1848, migrated to Australia and became prime minister of Victoria. Other political leaders, native to or domiciled in Australia during this period, were W. C. Wentworth and the Presbyterian divine, Dr. John Dunmore Lang; leaders in a later period were E. Deas Thomson, John Robertson, and Henry Parkes. Like Upper Canada, Victoria had a political leader who was also a great editor. But otherwise there is not much resemblance between George Brown of the Toronto *Globe*, the prophet of the Grits, and David Syme of the Melbourne *Age*, the father of protection in Australia.

It is perhaps not surprising that in Australia, where so many and so perplexing social problems presented themselves, one of the greatest women pioneers in the field of social work should have appeared. Caroline Chisholm won the admiration and gratitude of her own and later generations by her welfare work in the interest of homeless girls, lonely men, children, criminals, the mentally defective, and immigrants. Australia led in the adoption of manhood suffrage and vote by ballot, and in a less conspicuous but no less useful way by the invention of the Torrens system, a rational method for registering land titles.

That Australia rose so quickly from being a prison farm and a vast sheep run to holding a leading position among the states of the world was mainly due to the type of immigrants that reached her shores in the forties and fifties. Some were adventurers in quest of gold; others were English Chartists defeated in their attempt to make England a democracy, or Irish radicals who had failed in their effort to free Erin from the foreign yoke. All were bold and enterprising, men influenced by mid-nineteenth-century idealism, who in Australia found a better field for political and social experiments than could be provided by the old countries of Europe. Freed from ancient traditions and without fear of external foes, the pioneers of Australia could devote themselves to building up a new society offering opportunity for all to reach positions of power and influence.

By transporting hordes of delinquents to Australia, Britain acquired a heavy responsibility and became a debtor to her chief colonies on this continent. Transportation of criminals started in an age when none doubted the wisdom of maintaining colonies for the benefit of the mother country, but it was continued for several years after that policy had theoretically been abandoned. There is, however, a credit side for Britain in her accounts with Australia. The fund raised from the sale of land in the Australian colonies was used solely for their benefit; from public and private sources much capital flowed from England to these colonies; Britain supplied them with leaders and early gave the antipodean settlements a free hand in developing their own institutions; British statesmanship saved them from being overrun by Asiatic coolies; and the strong arm of Britain protected Australia against encroachment by European powers.

CHAPTER 16

THE FOUNDING OF NEW ZEALAND

TWELVE hundred miles from Australia, surrounded by vast stretches of ocean, lies the archipelago of New Zealand. It includes two large and several small islands. North Island and South Island, forming the heart of the group, are nearly equal in size; their combined area is somewhat more than a hundred thousand square miles; they extend from the 34th to the 47th degree of south latitude; and unlike Australia, they have an adequate rainfall in all parts. For beauty and variety of scenery New Zealand is unsurpassed among the British dominions. It is a land of snow-capped mountains and fertile plains, of rushing waterfalls and thermal springs, of fjords and glaciers, of brilliant sunshine and bracing winds. Its soil and climate have facilitated the development of extensive and varied types of agriculture. The two main islands are long and narrow, resembling the physical configuration of Great Britain, and the present population is overwhelmingly of British origin. In a sea-girt spot under a sunny southern sky has arisen the youngest of the British nations.

Tasman, a Dutch navigator, was the first white man to sight New Zealand; but an Englishman, Captain Cook, was the first to explore and chart the islands, 1769–1777. He found them inhabited by a brown-skinned Polynesian people, the Maoris. The natives were intelligent and adaptable, a brave and skillful race of warriors. They possessed only stone implements, their agriculture was extremely primitive, and they had no domestic animal except the dog. They fished, hunted, fought, and practiced cannibalism. The introduction of the potato and the pig greatly augmented the food supply, and the population increased until by the early part of the nineteenth century it numbered perhaps 120,000.

The white man bestowed benefits on the Maori, but he also acted as an agent of destruction. The bulk of the native population was in the North Island, and here was established the most famous whaling and sealing station of the southern seas, the Bay of Islands, which became the headquarters for American and European whalers and seal hunters. The visitors introduced the vices, diseases, and weapons of the white man. The Maoris eagerly offered their few supplies and their daughters and wives in exchange for muskets, which they learned to use expertly in frequent internecine wars. The mixed settlement, Kororareka, which sprang up at the Bay of Islands was soon known as a veritable Sodom. The Maoris killed each other by the thousands and supplied white traders with a ghastly article, the tattooed skull.

The natives of New Zealand were being debauched and threatened with extinction when the missionaries appeared on the scene. In England the humanitarian and missionary movements waxed strong during the first quarter of the nineteenth century, their activities spreading far and wide. Samuel Marsden, senior Church of England chaplain in New South Wales, was gripped by missionary zeal. He learned with dismay of the plight of the Maoris, and he rescued many of them from ships that touched at Sydney. With a few of these and two white families he landed at the Bay of Islands in December, 1814, and founded a mission station. Marsden was thus the pioneer missionary of New Zealand, his work was supported by the Church Missionary Society, and he aroused the English nation to the need for rescuing a noble race, but he never made New Zealand his home. At Parramatta, near Sydney, he trained Europeans and Maoris for missionary work in New Zealand. Before the end of the twenties, some of the missionaries, notably Henry Williams, had acquired great influence over the Maoris. Marsden encouraged the Wesleyans to establish mission stations in New Zealand, and at first Anglican and Wesleyan missionaries worked harmoniously, having agreed to a division of the field. The arrival of Roman Catholic missionaries in January, 1838, marked the beginning of strife among the representatives of Christianity, the protestants resenting what they regarded as an intrusion. When the Catholic missionaries secured the support of France the religious rivalry assumed a political aspect.

The missionaries spoiled much of the nefarious business carried on by the white traders, who tried to rouse the Maoris against the harbingers of a new religion. In this they failed, for early, and rightly, the Maori learned to look upon the missionary as a guide and protector; and he in turn justified this confidence by enlisting all available support in efforts to save the Maoris from the encroachment of the whites. The missionaries urged the Maori chiefs to keep peace and to form some sort of political union; they were warned against land sharks. In England Dandeson Coates, secretary of the Church Missionary Society, and the Reverend J. Beecham, secretary of the Wesleyan Missionary Society, opposed plans for an English colonization of New Zealand. They were successful at first. The British government of the twenties and thirties saw little need for annexing new lands for the purpose of colonization, and by the middle of the thirties friends of the missionaries, Lord Glenelg and James Stephen, controlled the colonial office.

Nevertheless, the missionaries could not long preserve New Zealand for the Maoris. The islands possessed too many advantages of soil and climate to escape the attention of colonizers and of the governments which they represented, and the Maoris lacked the strength necessary to keep out intruders. An irregular colonization had begun almost as soon as the Bay of Islands became a station for whalers and sealers. Deserters from visiting vessels, traders, and escaped convicts settled among the Maoris. Many of these settlers were steeped in vice. Neither the missionaries nor the Maori chiefs could control the lawless element. In the early thirties the British government had already recognized the need for interference, and in 1833 James Busby was appointed British resident or agent in New Zealand; but he wielded no power except moral suasion. Testimony before the select committee on the aborigines, 1837, disclosed a state of affairs in New Zealand that cried for intervention by a civilized government. At that time the missionaries would have welcomed a proclamation of British sovereignty if it could have been linked with a prohibition of European colonization, but colonization had become so intertwined with annexation that disentanglement was impossible.

The colonization of New Zealand was discussed in England in the twenties; among those who showed an interest in the question was J. G. Lambton, later famous as the Earl of Durham. In the thirties, when French attention was drawn to the fair antipodean islands, British interest in them increased. By 1836 the South Australian venture of E. G. Wakefield, the English colonizer *par excellence,* had failed to develop in accordance with his plan. Undaunted he sought another chance to prove the value of systematic colonization. New Zealand seemed a likely spot for a new experiment, and he threw his great talents as promoter and propagandist into the scale for annexing and colonizing these islands. He found powerful supporters both in and outside parliament, and the opposition of the missionary societies and the colonial office was overcome. The time was propitious for Wakefield. Humanitarians stood aghast at the disclosures concerning New Zealand made before the aborigines committee; James Busby, the British resident, was powerless; and rumors of French designs on New Zealand — in particular, French plans to make the islands a penal colony — made even the missionaries desire British annexation. Wakefield skillfully used both facts and rumors. The battle was won in 1839. In March James Stephen had become convinced that Britain must seize New Zealand; in May Wakefield's organization, the New Zealand Company, sent out the *Tory* to prepare the ground for colonization; and in June the colonial secretary, Lord Normanby, announced the government's decision to send Captain Hobson on a warship to New Zealand to negotiate with the chiefs of the Maoris for the cession of their land to Britain. This was accomplished by the Treaty of Waitangi, February 6, 1840. In the following months Hobson proclaimed British sovereignty over the two large islands, apparently forestalling by about one day a similar French action at Akaroa in the South Island. New Zealand became British and was immediately thrown open to British colonization. On the main issue, the missionaries suffered a defeat, but the defeat was no rout. Their chief aim was to protect the Maoris; and by the Treaty of Waitangi the government of Britain formally guaranteed "to the chiefs and tribes of New Zealand, and to the respective families and individuals thereof, the full, exclusive, and undisputed possession of their lands and estates, forests, fisheries, and other properties which they may collectively or individually possess, so long as it is their wish and desire to retain the same in their possession." In order that the natives should not be victimized by unscrupulous land speculators, the treaty provided that the British government should have "the exclusive right of preemption over such lands as the proprietors thereof may be disposed to alienate." These provisions stirred Wakefield to anger; he and his associates denounced and ridiculed a treaty "with naked savages." But the treaty stands as a monument of an honorable desire to protect the weak from the strong and to safeguard a backward race from spoliation by Europeans.

In 1840 small white settlements existed in various parts of New Zealand, especially near whaling stations, the most important being that at the Bay of Islands. The New Zealand

Company obtained a monopoly on colonizing the new dependency, and the first shipload of emigrants had left England prior to the signing of the Treaty of Waitangi. The company's agent, Colonel William Wakefield, had negotiated directly with the natives for the purchase of land; the treaty stipulation that all such negotiations should be handled by the government was an unwelcome surprise. However, in the late autumn of 1840 the company made an arrangement with the colonial office whereby it would receive four acres of land for every pound sterling spent in connection with sending out emigrants and in other preparations for the settlement of New Zealand. The question of the land claims was left for future consideration. Although the interpretation of the terms of this agreement later led to violent disputes between the New Zealand Company and secretaries of state for the colonies, under it the company sent several thousand emigrants to New Zealand and founded settlements at Wellington, New Plymouth, and Nelson. But the company's capital, £300,000, was insufficient for such a vast undertaking as the colonization of New Zealand; and when, after the first burst of enthusiasm was over, land there ceased to find ready buyers, the company faced serious financial difficulties. Wakefield sought a way out by recruiting German emigrants, but James Stephen's insistence that New Zealand should be English put an end to the scheme. Greater success attended Wakefield's efforts elsewhere. In the early forties Scotland was torn by a dispute over lay patronage in the church, the Free Church was organized, and some of its members listened to Wakefield's proposal for a Free Church settlement in New Zealand. After four years of negotiations and preparations, Scottish immigrants led by Captain Cargill founded the Otago settlement in the South Island in 1848. In the previous year, Wakefield met an Anglo-Irish gentleman, J. R. Godley, who on a visit to Canada in 1842 had become interested in the colonies; his observations of the effects of the Irish famine had made him an advocate of emigration and colonization. Godley, a devout member of the Church of England, had excellent social connections. A result of his meeting with Wakefield was the formation of the Canterbury Association for the purpose of establishing a Church of England settlement in New Zealand. Godley went to New Zealand in 1849, and the settlement named after England's chief arch-episcopal see was founded. The Canterbury Association secured land from the New Zealand Company and spent much money in New Zealand, but the finances of the company were in such a state that its charter was surrendered in 1850. Shortly afterward, the affairs of the Canterbury Association were wound up with losses to the promoters. Although the New Zealand Company and its subsidiaries functioned for only a short time, they rendered yeoman service in the colonization of New Zealand, and they shaped the course of its development.

Even during the years when the New Zealand Company controlled the colonization of the islands, independent settlers came out, especially to Auckland, which Captain Hobson had chosen as the capital of the colony. In the neighborhood of Auckland the home government established a few small military settlements. The Colonial Land and Emigration Commission never played an important role in the settlement of New Zealand, less than a thousand emigrants going out under its auspices. The discovery of gold in Australia first caused dismay in New Zealand by attracting many of her laborers, but later brought benefits in the form of higher prices for the products of her farms. In the early sixties New Zealand had gold rushes of her own in South Island. Money became plentiful and immigrants poured in. Although the gains were not unmixed, the gold rushes helped the population to double in ten years; thirty years after the islands became a part of the British empire the census showed a population of a quarter of a million.

The white man took possession of the land of the Maori, but not without bloodshed. In the early days the natives of New Zealand welcomed the whites who brought money and goods, especially firearms, which the Maoris desired. When colonists began arriving by the thousands, the situation changed. The missionaries and the home government tried to protect the natives and earned obloquy thereby. Were they not retarding progress, denying the right of the white man to inherit the earth? And strive as they might, neither the missionaries nor the imperial government and its representatives could avert the results of the impact of western civilization upon that of Polynesia. The Maori lacked the white man's conception of landownership and the nature of land sales. Disputes were unavoidable, and disputes grew into conflicts. Maori leaders saw tribes breaking up, their social organization crumbling, and white farmers in possession of the land. Brave and high-spirited, appreciating only dimly the strength of the forces behind the invaders, the Maoris refused to surrender without a struggle. Some desultory fighting took place during 1843–1845, but Captain Grey's arrival in the latter year as governor of New Zealand temporarily put an end to hostilities.

Grey had served with distinction in South Australia. He was a born leader of men, and the manly qualities of the Maoris appealed to him. He learned their language, studied their customs and needs, listened to their complaints, righted their wrongs, and became to the Maoris what Sir Harry Smith vainly tried to be to the Kaffirs, their great chief. But in 1853 Grey left. His successors were less wise and less firm. Furthermore, in 1852 New Zealand received self-government, which soon meant responsible government. The crown land came under the control of the colonists, the hands of the governors were tied, the pressure on the Maoris grew more intense, and they sensed danger. In the late fifties the Maoris attempted, with some success, to combine for defense. In 1860 a war broke out in the Taranaki district in the North Island which lasted with short interruptions nearly a dozen years. The return of Sir George Grey in 1861 failed to appease the Maoris, for they realized that responsible government meant colonial control over their destinies. The war assumed such proportions that the British garrison at one time numbered 10,000 men aided by an equal number of colonists, volunteers, and friendly Maoris. Against them the hostile Maoris could apparently never muster more than 2000 men. As brave as the Zulu, the Maori was more skillful in constructing fortifications; his pahs, or intrenched camps, often aroused the admiration of British military engineers.

After several years of indecisive fighting the imperial government despaired of securing peace in New Zealand as long as the colonists did not bear the full responsibility for the results of their land and native policies. The garrison was withdrawn, and peace came in 1872, as much the result of wise diplomacy as of success in battle. The colonists had learned to respect their doughty foes, whose right to the land was recognized and who obtained four representatives in the parliament of New Zealand. The war destroyed much property, retarded the development of the North Island, saddled the colony with a heavy debt, and reduced the Maori population from 55,336 to 37,502; but from it emerged a native policy that has withstood the test of time.

The early colonists of New Zealand and Wakefield and his friends in England had denounced vigorously the safeguards for the native rights which had been erected by the Treaty of Waitangi. But circumstances compelled New Zealand to adopt a native land policy based on that of the treaty. A land act of 1862 stipulated that a careful inquiry into ownership must precede any transfer of land, and thirty years later the preemptive right of the crown to land owned by Maoris was restored. A special court created in 1865 was intrusted with the duty of inquiring into and settling titles to native lands, and the colony assumed responsibility for the education of the Maoris.

The British emigrants to New Zealand represented more of a cross section of the society of the mother country and were selected with greater care than those who had gone out as pioneers to any other British colony. The mixed and generally less desirable white settlers who had preceded British annexation were soon outnumbered by those chosen by the New Zealand

Company and its satellites. As good Englishmen, these colonists fretted under the paternalistic crown colony form of government created shortly after New Zealand was annexed. They felt capable of self-government, and the home authorities stood ready to let them have it. In 1845, Lord Stanley, the colonial secretary, announced his willingness to grant representative institutions to the settlements in New Zealand, and his successor, Gladstone, wrote in January, 1846: "The desire and purpose of Her Majesty's Government is, that the colonists of New Zealand . . . should undertake as early and with as little exception as may be, the administration of their own affairs." The tangible evidence of this "desire and purpose" was an act passed later in the year which set up a cumbersome system of municipal, provincial, and central government for New Zealand. It provided the colony with representative institutions, but Governor Grey considered them so unsuited for New Zealand that he asked for and received permission to suspend the operation of the act for five years. Before the end of this period, he had prepared proposals for a new constitution which formed the basis of the New Zealand Government Act of 1852.

This act bears the imprint of the liberal spirit that prevailed in the conduct of colonial affairs in the middle decades of the nineteenth century. Though no mention was made of responsible government, the act conferred upon the people of New Zealand ample power of self-government. The colony was divided into six provinces, with an elective council and an elective superintendent for each. The general legislature was of the usual bicameral type, with a nominated upper and an elected lower house. The latter, which exercised most of the power, was chosen by a liberal franchise. The civil list and native affairs were kept out of the hands of the legislature; but the new parliament was granted the power to amend the constitution, subject to approval from home, a power that was used frequently in the next ten years. The first New Zealand assembly passed a resolution demanding responsible government, the colonial office assented, and in 1856 responsible government began functioning in New Zealand. In 1862 the control over native affairs was turned over to the colonists.

However, the provincial system caused many complications. Although the general legislature was superior to those of the provinces, a superiority greatly increased in 1857, provincial jealousies, political logrolling, and disputes concerning the limita-

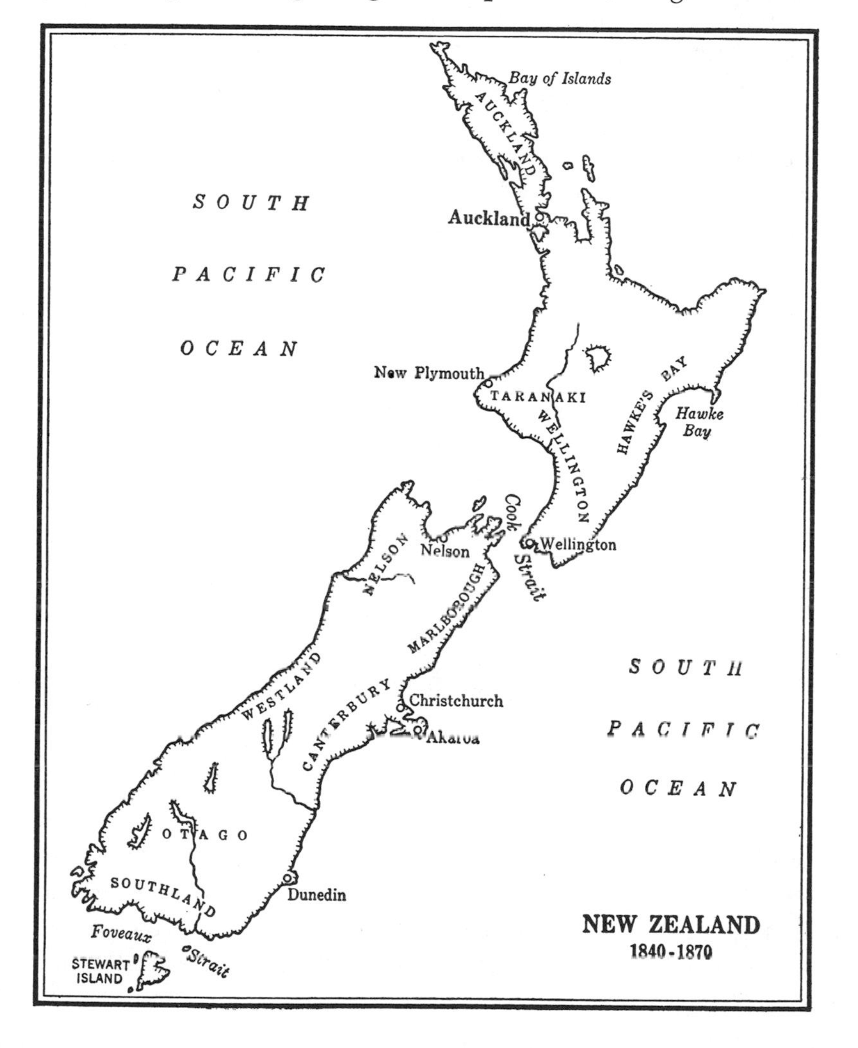

NEW ZEALAND
1840-1870

tion of power, the collection and distribution of revenues, commercial policy, and land and native affairs shortened the lives of New Zealand ministries and made the position of successive prime ministers anything but a bed of roses. The prevailing opposition to Auckland resulted in the seat of the government being moved to Wellington; demands for separate government for the two large islands threatened to disrupt the colony at one time; and requests for the creation of new provinces disturbed the political life. E. G. Wakefield emigrated to New Zealand in 1853 and was elected to the assembly, but his relations with the colonists were on the whole no happier than his earlier ones with British colonial secretaries. As a leader he was repudiated by the inhabitants of the colony he had founded. He died at Wellington on May 16, 1862. By 1870 the star of many of the old leaders had set or was setting, but that of a new one, Julius Vogel, was rising; for better or worse, his influence on the history of New Zealand became scarcely inferior to that of Wakefield.

In New Zealand, as in all other new colonies, the early history centers around land, landownership, land usage, and land policy. Wakefield insisted on the application of his principle of a high price on land, and the imperial government stressed its right to preemption and the need for protecting the natives. Neither succeeded in fully achieving the object desired. The government had to recognize purchases of native land by individuals and the New Zealand Company, and Wakefield saw his cherished principle of high upset price violated by private owners of large tracts of land and especially by the government. Governor Grey fixed a price of from 5*s.* to 10*s.* per acre. Moreover, the Australian system of leasing land for sheep runs was introduced in New Zealand; with it came squatting and dispersion of settlers.

Whaling and sealing at one time brought a certain amount of much-needed cash to New Zealand, but the flourishing period of this industry was over before settlement by whites began in earnest. The settlers faced the economic problems common to new communities — scarcity of money, of supplies, and of goods to sell. Nevertheless, New Zealand was in every respect more fortunate than New South Wales had been. For more than a decade promoters of colonization did not allow the British public and the British government to forget New Zealand. Britain possessed capital. Individuals and companies spent money on improvements in New Zealand, and the government had large outlays on account of the Maori wars. The Australian gold discoveries boosted prices and provided markets for the produce of New Zealand farms. The sheep throve and the owners of sheep runs benefited by Australia's experience. In 1853 New Zealand's export of wool was valued at £67,000 and that of grain at £19,000; twenty years afterward she exported £2,702,000 worth of wool, £67,000 of tallow, and £136,000 of grain. Between 1861 and 1871 her export of gold averaged in the neighborhood of £2,000,000 per annum. Other valuable articles of trade were timber and the resin, Kauri gum. Considering the size of the population, the figures on New Zealand trade – imports £7,000,000 in 1863 and £4,100,000 in 1871, exports £3,500,000 in 1863 and £5,300,000 in 1871 – are extraordinarily large. In the sixties the development of the North Island was retarded by the Maori wars; the South Island prospered. The Canterbury plains proved well suited both for general farming and for the pastoral industry. Otago and Canterbury profited by the gold discoveries, and these two provinces possessed an initial advantage in their selected population. Much of the profit accruing from the gold rushes went into permanent improvements, especially in Canterbury. Roads were built, and the small province undertook to tunnel the hills which separated Christchurch from Lyttelton and opened the first railroad in New Zealand in 1863. Part of the revenue obtained from the sale of land was set aside for educational and religious institutions; in this Otago and Canterbury led. New Zealand early made elementary education "free, secular, and compulsory," and the founders of the dominion laid the groundwork for the University of New Zealand.

Although both Wakefield and the New Zealand colonists often

complained of the unsympathetic attitude of the imperial government, the charges on that score seem ill founded. True, the home authorities tried to check the rapid alienation of land from the natives and apparently preferred the interests of the dusky savages to those of their own flesh and blood, but the motive behind these actions deserves praise rather than censure. The credit of Britain was used, not very generously though perhaps wisely, in guaranteeing loans of the new colony; the grant of self-government came early; and troops were supplied to fight wars caused largely by policies pursued by the colonial authorities. However, the recall of the imperial garrison before the great Maori war was over produced much bitterness in New Zealand; the colonists spoke of being betrayed. In the dispute between the Australasian colonies and the imperial government over differential tariffs, the spokesmen for New Zealand strongly insisted on the right of the colonies to control their fiscal policy. Indeed, New Zealand in the late sixties and early seventies was not far behind Victoria in presenting extreme claims of colonial autonomy. But with the adoption of the new public works policy sponsored by Julius Vogel in the seventies New Zealand forgot her irritation while seeking access to the money market of the mother country.

For some months in 1840 New Zealand was treated as part of New South Wales. The official separation came in November of that year, and although she later joined in tariff conferences with the Australian colonies she showed no desire to combine with them in a political union. Her early governors, Grey in particular, were keenly aware of the dangers lurking in having strong foreign neighbors. In 1848 he urged the annexation of Fiji and the Tonga Islands; four years later he advocated taking Tahiti from the French; and in 1853 he warned the colonial office of the risks connected with a French occupation of New Caledonia. But the imperial government would not act upon his suggestions for further annexations in the South Pacific. Better luck attended his later recommendation concerning the Auckland

Islands, which were included within the boundaries of New Zealand by an act of 1863. In 1871, Vogel continued Grey's policy by proposing the annexation of Samoa, but the government of Gladstone refused to consider it. Thus early in her history New Zealand felt the need of British dominance in the southern seas. Although she had no land frontiers, she proved no exception to the rule that the colonies of Britain have supplied a dynamic force for widening the frontiers of the empire. Perhaps that is only another way of proving that from the beginning New Zealand was truly British.

PART III

Commonwealth and Empire, 1870–1901; India, 1858–1905

INTRODUCTION

IN the last quarter of the nineteenth century the expansion of Europe reached its final stage. The great powers with the exception of Austria-Hungary appropriated vast areas in Africa, Asia, and Oceania; even the remotest corner of the earth felt the impact of aggressive European imperialism. The era was filled with diplomatic maneuverings; alliances were negotiated; a great race in armaments was launched; power politics became the order of the day. The economic activities were as intense as the political. Old as well as new industries expanded at an unprecedented pace; trade rivalries grew more intense; and dreams of national self-sufficiency strengthened demands for high protective tariffs. The mid-nineteenth-century ideals concerning a community of interests of all nations were discarded. A spirit of militant nationalism gripped racial groups, and imperially-minded statesmen sought to direct nationalistic aspirations into great pan-racial movements such as those of the Germans and the Slavs.

All the while people were taught that they were moving forward, that things were getting better and better. Science unraveled nature's mysteries and enabled man to harness new forces; education became more widely diffused; the luxuries of past ages were now necessities; and democracy was the political creed of all civilized men. But this progress failed to bring security and contentment. Class strife threatened to match international rivalry as disturber of the peace of nations.

Britain and her far-flung empire were deeply affected by the world-shaking forces. By degrees the British governmental system became more responsive to the popular will; class barriers were leveled, the door of opportunity opened. Each new decade found Britain more industrialized, but rivals began pressing on her heels and even to overtake her. Needs for guarding what she had and providing new opportunities for her growing population, capital, industries, and trade caused Britain to participate in the competition for new lands, markets, and sources of raw materials. She felt it necessary to attempt to strengthen and consolidate her empire.

Meanwhile, British nations were arising beyond the seas. The colonies of North America and Australasia gained more complete mastery of their own households. They had full control over internal affairs and were little by little moving in the direction of autonomy also in external relations. They were, however, not sufficiently strong to stand alone in an imperialistic age. Moreover, most of the self-governing colonies had been settled by British immigrants. To them Britain was the "old country," the home land. The pan-German and pan-Slavic movements had a counterpart in an increased attachment to Great Britain on the part of people of English and Scottish ancestry.

But nationalism was also a disruptive force within the British empire. Ireland clamored for autonomy; Irish people everywhere resented the English dominance over the land of their fathers; and the ancient races of India were growing restive. As the century closed, British complacency received rude shocks from defeats in the Anglo-Boer war and the realization that the diplomatic isolation of Britain involved great risks. British statesmen began to show apprehension, even fear of the future.

CHAPTER 17

BRITAIN AND THE LATTER HALF OF THE VICTORIAN ERA, 1870–1901

THE death of Queen Victoria on January 22, 1901, ended the longest and most eventful reign in English history. Although the United Kingdom during the sixty-three years of her rule did not face crises equal in intensity to those that confronted the England of Queen Elizabeth's time, the changes wrought in the life and conditions of the British people between 1837 and 1901 were more numerous and far-reaching than those which took place between 1558 and 1603, and the changes of the Victorian era represented a development which gained tremendously in momentum with every passing decade. The "gay nineties" were separated from the earnest sixties by a wider gulf than that which ordinarily separates a generation from the one immediately preceding it. The effects of the industrial revolution continued to accumulate and to them were added the alterations brought by the increased use of gas and electricity. The standards of life and the outward manner of living were altered completely in the latter half of the Victorian era, but these changes were hardly more striking than the common acceptance of new ideas and ideals between 1870 and 1901.

Many of the typically Victorian aspects in the life and views of cultured men and women had become outmoded long before the great queen breathed her last. The faith, earnestness, and self-discipline of the early Victorians were considered old-fashioned in the nineties. As the century closed, doubts were entertained concerning individualism as an economic doctrine; political democracy and free trade were no longer regarded as effective cure-alls for the ills of society; mention of the sentiments which had inspired the poetry of Browning and Tennyson and the oratory of Bright and Gladstone might provoke a pitying smile; the outstanding younger British statesmen of the year 1901 – Joseph Chamberlain, Lord Curzon, and Sir Alfred Milner – showed a tendency to abandon the principles of Burke and to stray from the path of Cobden. They were indeed further removed from the great mid-Victorians, Bright, Cobden, and Gladstone, than they were from the pre-Victorians, Castlereagh, Canning, and Wellington. Compared with the England of 1870, that of 1901 was a new England; but this new England was not created by a sharp and sudden break with the past; it was the result of a political, social, and economic evolution well under way at the high noon of the Victorian era which proceeded with accelerated speed during the next thirty years, an evolution which so transformed the United Kingdom and so profoundly affected the attitude of the people of Britain to the overseas empire that it amounted to a revolution.

At the beginning of the second half of the reign of Queen Victoria the great Liberal statesman William Ewart Gladstone was in office and in power. His first ministry, 1868–1874, had as a main object the pacification of Ireland, but the complicated Irish problems did not exhaust the energy or dampen the reforming zeal of Gladstone and his colleagues. They desired to remove special privileges based on religion and social caste and to open the door of opportunity to all Englishmen. As part of such a program they abolished religious tests at Oxford and Cambridge, established tax-supported elementary schools, discontinued the practice of buying commissions in the army, and extended the civil service system. A new Trade Union Act strengthened the position of organized labor, and a Ballot Act enabled the newly enfranchised workers in the towns to cast their vote without being subjected to the intimidation that had prevailed when voting was oral. Disraeli, the leader of the Conservative opposition, accused the government of having "threatened every corporation and endowment in the country . . . examined into everybody's business . . . criticized every profession and . . . vexed every trade." Allowance must be made for rhetorical exaggeration; nevertheless, it is significant that a considerable majority of the English electors agreed with Disraeli to the extent of driving the Liberals from power in the election of 1874 and placing him in Gladstone's seat.

But the great social forces were on the side of reform; and by acts dealing with trade unions and factories, the relations of master and servant, housing, and shipping, Disraeli's ministry during 1874–1880 continued the type of social and economic legislation that Conservatives had criticized when the bills were introduced by the Liberals. The work of leveling the barriers of religion and class, the development of political and social democracy, and the amelioration of the conditions of the poorer classes made considerable progress. Atheists were admitted to the house of commons and heavy onslaughts were levied at the established church in Wales and at the legal provisions which excluded Roman Catholics from the offices of lord lieutenant of Ireland and lord chancellor of Great Britain. By 1891 elementary education in England had become free and compulsory, and the aid granted by the government to education below that of university grade increased from about two million pounds in 1870 to more than twenty million in 1900. Slowly and grudgingly the equalization of rights and opportunities was extended also to women. An act of 1882 recognized the property rights of married women; women were gradually admitted to the professions; and they were prying open the portals of the great national universities.

However, this evolution of social democracy produced by the

far-reaching social legislation was overshadowed by the rapid progress made in the direction of political democracy. The Reform Act of 1884–1885 extended the franchise to the agricultural laborers, and acts of 1888 and 1894 created elective institutions for the local units of government, the counties, parishes, and districts. Simultaneously with these modifications in the governmental machinery, the laboring classes began to grow conscious of their political power, and their political education grew apace. The two old parties, the Conservative and the Liberal, had to bid for the votes of the masses; in his campaign in the Midlothian district of Scotland in 1879, Gladstone inaugurated the practice of discussing issues of high politics on the platform. This practice was deplored by some of his supporters and all his opponents, but it was one which once started had to be continued. The voting millions wielded great power; they had to obtain political education part of which was supplied by Conservative and Liberal orators who were not, however, the only mentors. In the seventies a Warwickshire farm laborer, Joseph Arch, carried on effective political agitation in favor of the franchise for his own class; in the early eighties the doctrines of Marxian socialism were spread through the efforts of the Social Democratic Federation and the Fabian Society; in the nineties Keir Hardie organized the Independent Labour Party; and in February, 1900, conferences of representatives of the Social Democratic Federation, the Fabian Society, the Independent Labour Party, and the Trades Union Congress afforded the first step in the formation of the Parliamentary Labour Party which twenty-four years afterward assumed office as His Majesty's Government. In 1880 Queen Victoria was much disturbed over the growth of the democratic spirit in the country and in parliament, and about the middle of the decade she sought unsuccessfully to create a center party to combat all dangerous democratic tendencies. But her fears for the safety of the monarchy were unfounded; its position was stronger in 1901 than it had been in 1870. Some of this new strength was due to the fact that the people of Britain had begun to realize that the crown was an important bond of union for the scattered portions of the British empire.

The position of organized labor improved greatly in the second half of the Victorian era. An act of 1871 legalized the position of the trade unions and safeguarded their funds, another in 1876 removed galling restrictions on their freedom of action in labor disputes. These acts gave vitality to the meeting of representatives of the unions, known as the Trades Union Congress; and when this body in 1890 opened its doors to representatives of the organizations of unskilled laborers, it could speak for more than one and a half million of workers. The political power given to the laboring classes by the Reform Acts of 1867 and 1884–1885, the strength of the labor unions, and a growing recognition of the principle that the government must be *for* the people resulted in improvements in the life and conditions of the poorer classes. Factories, workshops, and mines acts, master and servant acts, employers' liability acts, acts dealing with housing and sanitation, the new activities on the part of the municipal authorities inaugurated by Joseph Chamberlain in Birmingham in the seventies, and the relaxation of the old rules against outdoor relief bestowed numerous benefits on the laboring classes. Moreover, indications of an alert and active social conscience in England in the last decades of the nineteenth century are found in the widespread interest in Henry George's *Progress and Poverty* and Edward Bellamy's *Looking Backward,* in the organization of the Salvation Army and the founding of social settlements like Toynbee Hall, in the sympathy shown for the strike of the girls working in match factories in 1888, and in the investigations of life and labor in East London sponsored by Charles Booth and those of the sweated industries undertaken by a committee of the house of lords. The studies of social and economic conditions disclosed the prevalence of abject poverty and merciless exploitation amid the wealth and ostentation of the period. England might seem like heaven to the Polish and Russian Jews who entered and swelled the slum population of her cities, but to a large number of Englishmen life appeared hard and they looked longingly to the wider opportunities found in the United States and in British colonies beyond the sea.

The major industries of Britain, except agriculture, continued to make progress from 1870 until the end of the century, although the progress was relatively not so rapid as in the years between 1846 and 1870, nor did Britain in 1901 hold the preeminence in industry and commerce that she had enjoyed in 1870. The British agriculturists had vainly opposed free trade in grain, fearing that it would prove injurious to their interests; toward the end of the seventies their fears materialized. Enormous areas of virgin soil had been brought under cultivation in the Americas and Australasia, land which produced good crops with little labor; mass production of grain was made possible by the new agricultural machinery; and the improved means of transportation made the wheat growers of the Mississippi Valley direct competitors with those of Norfolk. Nor was the competition of English farmers with those of the Americas and Australasia limited to grain. Refrigeration soon brought the beef and mutton of Argentina and Australia and New Zealand butter and cheese fresh to the English market; nearer home the farmers of Holland and Denmark could undersell those of England. The results of foreign competition were aggravated further by a general fall in the price level from 1873 to 1895. British wheat which had sold for 60*s.* a quarter in 1873 declined to a record low of 23*s.* per quarter in 1893–1895. Farmers were ruined and the landed aristocracy suffered from the steady shrinking of their rent rolls. A few of them, like the Dukes of Bedford and Westminster, could subsidize their landed estates with the income from urban properties, others could do this with returns from business investments, and still others regilded tarnished coronets and replaced tattered ermine by wealth obtained through marriages with heiresses to commercial and industrial fortunes in England and America. Nevertheless, one result of the changed agricultural situation was that the land as such could no longer maintain the aristocracy; and it was no accident that the Tories of Britain who in former days had opposed imperial expansion became its advocates late in the Victorian era.

The coal, iron, steel, textile, and shipbuilding industries of Britain continued to expand after 1873, but they too felt the effects of falling prices, which did not commence to turn upward until 1895. In the eighties British economic interests began to sense that foreign competitors and foreign tariffs might have a harmful effect on Britain's trade and manufactures. Germany and the United States had been and continued to be good customers for British goods, but after 1870 the new German empire possessed large coal and iron deposits and its government encouraged the growth of industry. The natural resources of the United States seemed well-nigh inexhaustible and her people soon developed a high degree of technical skill and a marvelous capacity for organization and production on a large scale. Protective tariffs aided, or were supposed to aid, the new industries of the United States and Germany; tariff walls were erected by other countries, notably France and Russia. The hope for the universal adoption of free trade vanished; in the early eighties a modest "fair trade movement" was launched in England; and later in the decade a royal commission for the study of the depression of trade took cognizance of the foreign competition. Before the century ended both Germany and the United States had passed Britain in the annual output of steel, and well-equipped German steamship lines had become strong rivals of the British for the carrying trade of the world.

London remained the world's banking center throughout the period, but the export of British capital did not show the same proportional average increase per annum after 1873 as it had in the preceding decade. The drop may have been due to the reinvestment abroad of capital already exported and of its earnings, to the lower price level, and to the losses sustained by British investors in the Americas. However, Britain continued to accumulate capital, the profit motive remained strong, and owners or controllers of surplus capital began to study the opportunities for exploiting new lands, particularly those of Africa. When the British government seemed too slow in appropriating desirable territories, powerful companies were organized to undertake both the economic exploitation and the political control over vast areas. The most famous of these were the North Borneo Company, the Royal Niger Company, the Imperial East Africa Company, and the South Africa Chartered Company.

The economic forces which created demands for economic expansion were continually gaining in strength, and the maintenance of a high birth rate aided by a slowly falling death rate provided more human material for empire-building. The annual surplus of births over deaths in England and Wales rose from about 300,000 in 1875 to nearly 400,000 per annum twenty-five years later. England and Wales lost 3,680,333 persons through emigration to non-European lands between 1871 and 1901. Although these losses were in part made good by Irish immigration, it was largely the natural increase that caused the population to grow, despite the heavy emigration, by more than ten million in this period. The man-power of Britain remained unimpaired.

The political, social, and economic changes in Scotland paralleled in most respects those of England. The franchise bills were extended to Scotland, and the Scottish laborers were on the whole more politically-minded than the English. Scottish education had for more than a hundred years been in advance of the English, and it continued to improve; the position of the workers was appreciably bettered. Still, the conditions in the industrial regions of southern Scotland left much to be desired, and the men of the Clyde were ready to embrace more radical political doctrines than those preached by Liberals and Conservatives. The suffering among the crofters and cottars of the Highlands and the Scottish islands led to disturbances which in turn resulted in an investigation by a royal commission in 1883–1884. The commissioners stated that the increase in the size of the game preserves had not been an important cause of the prevailing distress; they recommended, however, that no further increases should take place. Among remedial measures they suggested emigration. More than 600,000 Scots left for non-European lands in this period, but thanks to a high birth rate and improved sanitary conditions the population of Scotland in 1901 showed an increase of 1,111,939 over that of 1871.

Beginning with the disestablishment and disendowment of the Anglican church in Ireland in 1869, successive governments sought to right the ancient wrongs of Ireland. Gladstone by acts of 1870 and 1881 tackled the land question; the position of the tenants was made safer by the first act; the second aimed at securing fixity of tenure, compensation for improvements made by the tenant, and a fair rent. But the benefits expected from these acts failed to materialize, partly because of the fall in prices of agricultural produce and the foreign competition in the English market. From 1885 until the end of the century, the British government provided large sums of money on easy terms for Irish farmers who wished to purchase the land they tilled; and ultimately it was asserted that land purchase had solved the Irish land question. In the nineties Sir Horace Plunkett, with encouragement from the government, began his great work for the improvement of agricultural education in Ireland and the development of the cooperative system and the dairy industry. It was hoped that some day Ireland might outrival Denmark in the production of eggs, butter, and bacon. The government tried to stimulate the Irish fishing industry, and aid was given to education.

But the concessions came too late or were suspected of being bribes to make Ireland forget her political grievances. Celtic Ireland never became reconciled to the Act of Union. In the forties Daniel O'Connell agitated for its repeal, in the sixties the Fenian Republican Brotherhood favored the establishment of an Irish republic, and during the last quarter of the nineteenth century the majority of Irishmen wanted a separate legislature at

Dublin. The fact that, in proportion to her population, Ireland was over-represented in the house of commons at Westminster did not dampen the ardor of the Irish Home Rulers. The movement was started by Issac Butt early in the seventies but did not assume formidable proportions until late in the decade when Charles Stewart Parnell became its leader. Parnell, a protestant and a landlord, gained a preeminence among the Catholic Irish politicians which exceeded that of O'Connell fifty years earlier. He secured control over the Irish Land League organized by Michael Davitt, and used it for the purpose of making unbearable the position of English landlords in Ireland; he enforced stern discipline among the Irish Home Rulers in the house of commons; and soon his phalanx of about sixty members worried and made life miserable first for the Conservative government of Lord Beaconsfield and afterward for the Liberal government of Gladstone. The Land Act of 1881 and repressive legislation proved unavailing — Ireland became the scene of continuous disorders and foul crimes. The Reform Act of 1884–1885 included Ireland, and the enfranchisement of the agricultural population strengthened Parnell. The election of November, 1885, resulted in a great victory for the Home Rulers, 86 out of the 103 representatives of Ireland following Parnell; this gave him the balance of power in the house of commons. For some years before 1885 Gladstone had been veering toward home rule for Ireland. Evidence was daily accumulating that the government in Ireland had broken down, and in the election of 1885 Ireland decisively demanded home rule. In surveying the experience of fifty years in official life, Gladstone saw how self-government had stilled discontent in the British colonies and made them loyal members of the British empire. This remedy might be tried near home; hence toward the end of 1885 he decided that self-determination should be applied to Ireland to the extent of giving her a parliament of her own. But a large portion of the Liberal party, headed by Joseph Chamberlain and Lord Hartington, afterward Duke of Devonshire, refused to follow Gladstone. They later organized as the Liberal-Unionists who eventually combined with the Conservatives to form the Unionist party. Gladstone's home rule bill of 1886 was defeated in the house of commons, and the Gladstonian Liberals were overwhelmed in the election of August, 1886. The election of 1892 gave Gladstone a small majority in favor of home rule, but the home rule bill passed by the house of commons after a prolonged struggle was thrown out by the house of lords, and the Liberal government dared not make this the chief issue in an effort to curb the lords.

When Gladstone adopted the cause of home rule for Ireland, the Conservatives aroused Ulster, the industrial, Scottish-Irish, and largely protestant section of northern Ireland, against the measure. From then on Ireland was definitely a house divided against itself. In 1890 the Irish situation became still more confused when Parnell, who had been proved an adulterer in a divorce case, was rejected as a leader by the majority of the Irish home rule group in the house of commons. Parnell, refusing to accept defeat, devoted the remaining months of his life — he died in 1891 — to a fierce campaign against his old Irish and English allies. His death did not end the feud among the Home Rulers. For a decade Parnellites fought anti-Parnellites and both fought Ulster; the Irish confusion became worse confounded.

The industrial north of Ireland made progress in the last thirty years of the nineteenth century, but despite remedial measures agricultural southern Ireland suffered in common with agricultural Britain, partly for the same reasons — falling prices and foreign competition. The rise in prices in the late nineties encouraged Sir Horace Plunkett and his agricultural reformers, but their work came too late to modify materially the dark picture presented by Ireland during the period under discussion. Although the prevailing crime and disorder may have pleased a few ruffians and the constant political agitation probably made politicians happy, the heavy emigration indicated that a large number of Irishmen preferred other surroundings. Ireland, like her sister kingdoms, maintained a high birth rate, yet her population declined from 5,414,377 in 1871 to 4,456,546 in 1901; within those three decades 1,737,953 sons and daughters of Erin left their old homes to seek new ones in non-European lands.

Between 1870 and 1901 the United States and the self-governing British colonies of North America, South Africa, and Australasia made strong and successful efforts to attract immigrants. New railroads opened vast areas of fertile land for settlement; improved steamship service made even the voyage to New Zealand comparatively easy and inexpensive; railroad companies and steamship lines vied with each other in extolling the beauties and opportunities of the new lands; Canada and the United States offered land free to those who wished to till it; some of the Australian colonies provided all or part of the passage money from Europe; and the member or members of a family who had migrated earlier often supplied steamship and railroad tickets for those who had remained behind. Although the position of the working classes of the British Isles improved greatly, it is significant that in 1886 there existed in Britain forty-nine private organizations which promoted emigration and that the total emigration in these thirty years from the United Kingdom to lands outside of Europe reached the high figure of 6,055,630. The largest outpouring took place in the decade from 1881 to 1891, when 2,593,226 people of British origin left the British Isles. A majority of the emigrants went to the United States, but a substantial minority, about 28 per cent, gave a British colony as their destination when they left home. If we omit the Irish, it is probably true to say that the majority of the emigrants left Britain not because of oppression but because the New World offered fairer prospects for themselves and their children, and that they cherished love, not bitterness, for the mother country. On the prairies of Canada, the high veld of South Africa, and the plains of Australia the immigrants dreamed of their old home; the memories could be kept fresh and the bonds sustained by the modern facilities for postal communication and travel. The new immigrants were not cut off from the land of their birth as the old ones had been; letters, newspapers, and books enabled them to keep in touch with people at home; they did not shed their nationality when they left England and Scotland for Saskatchewan or Queensland; they still gloried in the name of Britain and remained loyal to a common sovereign.

At the beginning of this chapter, attention was called to the transformation which took place in Britain between 1870 and 1901. Politically this is revealed in the decline of mid-nineteenth-century liberalism, the liberalism that had urged peace, retrenchment, reform, free trade, and *laissez faire.* The Liberals under Gladstone held office from 1868 to 1874 and 1880 to 1885, but they were in power for only a few months in 1886 and held a precarious tenure from August, 1892, until June, 1895. In March, 1894, Gladstone resigned because he stood alone in opposing increases in the naval estimates; he observed truly that the new generation differed profoundly from the one in which he had lived and had his being. This difference was shown in a striking fashion when three of the most prominent among the younger leaders of the Liberal party — H. H. Asquith, R. B. Haldane, and Sir Edward Grey — in 1899 confessed themselves Liberal-Imperialists. Although less spectacular, a change in the direction of an aggressive imperialism took place also among the Conservatives. Those of the older school, Lord Salisbury and Sir Michael Hicks Beach, viewed with misgiving the South African ventures of Joseph Chamberlain. They were out of step with the younger men, as Gladstone had been out of step half a dozen years earlier; and they could not share the prevailing enthusiasm for imperial expansion.

Joseph Chamberlain, the erstwhile radical, was the man of the hour as the century closed. He represented the new school that favored social legislation for the people and he was a leader in the movement for the expansion and consolidation of the British empire. The difference between the radical Joseph Chamberlain who was mayor of Birmingham in the seventies and the Chamberlain who was colonial secretary from 1895 to 1903 was more apparent than real. In his former capacity he had used the power and wealth of the municipality for the benefit of the people living therein — better houses and sanitation, improved facilities for recreation; as colonial secretary he used the power of Britain to improve the well-being of her colonies and to safeguard her interests. In both capacities he rejected *laissez faire*, appealed to corporate interests, and used the power of the whole for the benefit of the parts.

Chamberlain's conception of the duties and functions of the state harmonized with the growing tendency to favor collective action. The social and economic legislation of the latter half of the Victorian era trained the people to look to the state for aid and protection — the government existed *for* them. At the same time the growth in the political power of the masses and in their political consciousness made them aware of owning a share in the mighty structure known as the British empire. The sight of the vast areas colored red on the map of the world caused the heart of the propertyless as well as that of the wealthy to swell with pride. Queen and pauper alike could talk about "our empire."

The wide tolerance of the mid-Victorians had its root in a sense of security. However, toward the end of this era fear began to enter the hearts of Englishmen, and the prolonged debates over Irish home rule fostered apprehension. Gladstone urged his countrymen to practice what they had preached, to put their trust in freedom as a bond of unity between Irish and English. But a majority of them refused to listen to him because they feared that home rule meant destruction of the union between Ireland and England and that England would thereby be weakened. The dream of Bright and Cobden that the nations of the world would adopt free trade and that free trade in turn would usher in an era of universal peace failed to come true. Tariff walls confronted British exporters and foreign commercial and industrial competitors were gaining on or even overtaking Britain. Britain stood outside the two powerful alliances, the triple alliance composed of Germany, Austria, and Italy, and the dual alliance of France and Russia; she was viewed with envy by both these combinations, and her imperial frontiers were exposed. The new generation, which realized the need for social legislation for the purpose of keeping Britain healthy and strong, advocated also that she should protect her empire by consolidation and expansion and enter into an *entente* with a first-rate continental power. Britain was worried even before her disasters in the war in South Africa, 1899–1902, weakened her self-confidence.

For a brief period in the early nineties, Oscar Wilde, the exotic author of *Salome,* enjoyed great vogue, but he was soon forgotten and Rudyard Kipling, the manly author of *Plain Tales from the Hills,* became the popular favorite. In him the imperialists found a poet laureate whose songs and tales pleased both castle and cottage. The England of 1901 was an imperialistic England.

CHAPTER 18

IMPERIAL FRONTIERS AND IMPERIAL EXPANSION, 1870–1901

THE expansion of Europe which began in the fifteenth century was practically completed at the close of the nineteenth. When the present century opened, few regions of the earth, with the exception of those around the poles, had not been visited, reported on, and mapped by white men; and no people had escaped the impact of the ideas, religion, economic penetration, or political dominance of Europe and her offspring in America. The proselytizing spirit of Christianity was as active and more widely diffused in the last quarter of the nineteenth century as in the days of St. Xavier; the Christian missionaries brought not only the message of the Man from Galilee, but also modern ideas of health, sanitation, and manners of living, and occasionally they acted as political agents of the government to which they owed allegiance. The lust for gold and commercial gain was as strong at the end of the nineteenth century as it had been when the treasure troves of the Incas were plundered, when the shores of the Gulf of Guinea were first visited by European slave traders, and when Dutch, English, and Portuguese fought over the trade with the spice islands. Reports of the atrocities committed by the dealers in rubber in the Congo basin and the region of the Upper Amazon showed that eighteen centuries of Christianity had not softened the hearts of the worshipers of mammon. Changes in the standards and manner of living increased the demand for the old and created needs for new products of the tropics. Even the poor of Europe and America required and used the oil of the palm, the ground nut, and the cocoanut in their soap and oleomargarine; the world's requirement of rubber mounted every year; and thanks to refrigeration tropical fruits were no longer enjoyed solely by the inhabitants of the lands where they grew. Improvements in transportation and means of communication, progress in medicine, and new lethal weapons facilitated the subjugation of equatorial lands. The desire to possess them was greatly stimulated by the spread of a faith in a neo-mercantilistic economic policy of self-sufficiency and by the belief that national prestige would be enhanced with the building up of a colonial empire. Among the political results of the operation of these factors were the partition of Africa, the appropriation of the islands of Oceania, and attacks upon the Chinese empire. Because of her wealth, her population, her sea power, and her extensive colonial possessions and interests it was only natural that Britain, despite the reluctance and actual opposition of her statesmen, should play a dominant role in the new era of European expansion.

At the opening of this period, Britain, Russia, and France possessed large colonial empires, Holland had retained the greater part of her rich East India possessions, Spain maintained a precarious hold on islands in the West and East Indies, and Portugal kept her dead hand on large portions of Africa. Before it closed, Russia by a glacier-like advance had annexed new regions in central Asia and was threatening China; Britain and France had each added in the neighborhood of three million square miles to the African lands under their control, Britain had acquired Indian borderlands and had extended her sway over the Malay Peninsula, France had expanded in Indo-China, and both Britain and France had new acquisitions in the South Pacific. As a result of the Spanish-American War, 1898, Spain lost practically all that remained of her ancient empire; but thanks to the old alliance with Britain, the area which Portugal actually held in Africa was not diminished. Holland, despite her weak position in Europe, continued to be a great colonial power. The United States acquired control over or possession of the majority of the islands lost by Spain, but this had slight effect on British empire policies. It was otherwise with the actions and policies of Germany when in the eighties she entered the race for colonial prizes; indeed from 1884 until 1890 British expansionists were as much concerned over the colonizing activities of Germany in Africa and the South Pacific as they were over the forward movements of Russia in Asia. Italy, another newcomer among the colonizing powers, was too weak to be considered a serious rival for desirable lands.

Despite the keen competition for colonies, the partition of Africa, where the greatest prizes were obtained, was achieved by a series of conferences and bilateral agreements and without a European war. In this respect the expansion of Europe in the late nineteenth century differed greatly from that of preceding centuries. When and where the countries interested could not take possession immediately, they claimed spheres of interest or established protectorates — methods of occupation that proved effective in keeping rivals out. Much that was new in means and methods was utilized in the latest epoch of European expansion, but the reappearance of the chartered companies represented an interesting reversion to old ways. In 1847 no less authority than Sir James Stephen spoke of the well-recognized inability of such companies to act as colonizing agents; yet between 1881 and 1889 charters were granted to four British companies — the North Borneo, the Imperial East Africa, the Royal Niger, and the South Africa — which exercised wide powers over lands nearly as extensive as that of British India, and in which they represented the British empire. A principal reason for the organization of the companies was that Britain's leading statesmen refused to heed the clamor for annexations on the part of economic interests, newspapers, and the "forward" school of politicians at home and to listen to the Australasians and South Africans who urged the promulgation of Monroe doctrines for their respective regions.

If we except Disraeli, none of the older British statesmen of the late Victorian era embraced whole-heartedly the creed of the expansionists. In this respect no wide gulf separated Gladstone of the Liberals from Sir Stafford Northcote, Lord Salisbury, and Sir Michael Hicks Beach on the Conservative side. The generation of statesmen who had been brought up in the tradition of Waterloo and had in their early manhood seen Britain prosper under a policy of free trade and non-expansion felt confident that Britain's strength lay in Britain; they feared that weakness would follow dispersion of power and annexation of new lands. But the men of the later generation — Rosebery, Asquith, Chamberlain, Balfour, and Curzon — were not so sure of her ability to go it alone; some of them began to cast about for allies; and most of them believed that it was necessary to strengthen the more tangible economic and political bonds of union between Britain and her self-governing colonies and that new annexations would make the empire more powerful. The great forces favoring European expansion after 1870 strongly affected Britain. The wide and varied activities of her traders, explorers, and missionaries had supplied her with advance information and prior claims to distant lands, her wealth was sufficient to finance daring ventures, and her sea power insured protection to distant settlements. Moreover, the land frontiers of the British empire in Africa and Asia supplied points of contact with new and desirable regions or were exposed to attack which necessitated occupying new "key" positions in order to safeguard them. The latter factor operated powerfully in the regions bordering India and aided in bringing about the establishment of British control over Egypt and Cyprus. Viceroys of India, notably Lords Lytton and Curzon, were advocates of a forward policy for the purpose of insuring the safety of the Indian empire; and England ever sensitive on that point was always ready for action when India seemed threatened. Not in India alone, but in most of the African and in some of the Australasian colonies, the governors often became advocates of imperial expansion; their independent attitude in pressing for aggressive action caused Lord Salisbury to speak sarcastically about the obeying of orders as "an eccentric quality" in a governor; a governor could create situations, as in the case of the diamond fields in South Africa, which made it absolutely necessary for Britain to move her boundary posts forward. Sometimes the governors might act on their own initiative, but more often, if they served in self-governing colonies, they were urged onward by colonial opinion and colonial legislatures. The autonomous colonies of Australasia and South Africa held a semi-independent position; they were ardent advocates of British annexation of territories which might be called contiguous; they breathed vague threats of secession if their requests were not heeded; and both they and their sympathizers at home showed great annoyance if the foreign situation compelled the British government to let Germany or France acquire lands which the expansionists had wanted Britain to seize.

The question of British expansion, 1870–1901, therefore touched many complex economic, political, and constitutional issues; it was linked with domestic, intra-imperial, and foreign problems. None of these can be treated in detail, but most of them will be mentioned in the following discussion which will take up separately the various geographical divisions of the British empire.

In the western hemisphere, Britain had possessions in North, Central, and South America; if we except India, the longest continuous land frontier of the British empire in 1870 was that between Canada and the United States, but it caused the least anxiety. Fortresses and military posts were unnecessary along the three thousand miles of boundary that separated British North America from her neighbor. The two nations were busy developing their vast inland domains, and the movement of French-Canadians into the eastern states of the American union and of American farmers into the western territories of Canada gave no cause for worry on either side. In the far west disputes over the possession of San Juan Island at the beginning of this period and over the Alaskan boundary at its close were settled amicably. In South America things did not go quite so smoothly. In the nineties the unsettled state of the British Guiana-Venezuela boundary threatened to precipitate an international crisis of the first magnitude. The Schomburgk line, drawn up by a British representative in the forties, was not then accepted by Venezuela nor did Britain insist upon its acceptance. But about 1886 a boundary dispute flared up, both sides presented extreme demands, and for a while it looked as if Britain would use force in making good her claims. At this juncture, President Cleveland served notice that the United States was interested in the dispute and he invoked the Monroe Doctrine. Late in 1895 excitement ran high both in Washington and in London, but in the end arbitration was resorted to; the boundary as delimited represented a compromise. In the last quarter of the nineteenth century projects and plans for a trans-isthmian canal at Panama precipitated discussion of the Anglo-American agreement reached in 1850 known as the Clayton-Bulwer Treaty; in the eighties friction developed over this issue, but settlement was deferred until 1901.

The Pacific Ocean looms large in British imperial history, 1870–1901. In Hawaii British influence had preceded American and in the forties the islands were on the verge of becoming a British possession; however, they gradually passed under the control of the United States and her formal annexation of them in 1898 evoked no protest from Britain. A different situation developed farther south and east in this vast ocean. British explorers, whalers, traders, and missionaries had visited and established stations on various islands in the South Pacific and the Australasian colonies strengthened the British interest here.

The cotton famine resulting from the Civil War in the United States stimulated experiments in cotton-growing in the Fiji Islands and northern Queensland. The former were regarded as a no-man's land, but the establishment of cotton plantations caused disputes over land titles and labor which ultimately compelled Britain to interfere; the annexation of the islands took place in 1874. In Queensland the development of cotton and sugar plantations created a need for cheap labor which the planters sought to satisfy by recruiting natives from South Sea islands. Without supervision and restriction the hiring or indenturing of Kanakas — blackbirding it was commonly called — led to grave abuses and the indentured laborers could hardly be distinguished from slaves. When information about this reached England, two famous and influential organizations, the Aborigines Protection Society and the Anti-Slavery Society, became active. In 1872 parliament passed the Pacific Islander Protection Act; and after the annexation of Fiji its governor was made high commissioner for the Western Pacific. But neither the act nor the new high commissioner could curb the activities of French, German, and American traders. The situation called for annexation or the establishment of a British protectorate over Polynesia.

Actions of this sort were desired by the Australasian colonies. Sir George Grey, when governor of New Zealand, 1846–1853, had advised annexation of New Caledonia and the expulsion of the French from Tahiti, and the Australians greatly resented the French occupation of New Caledonia as a penal colony. In the seventies rumor began to fly about that France would seize and use the New Hebrides for this purpose; German traders became suspiciously active in the neighborhood of Australia; and Australians and New Zealanders united in demanding a Monroe doctrine for the South Pacific, requesting Britain to annex Fiji, New Guinea, the New Hebrides, Samoa, Tonga, and numerous other islands scattered far and wide over the South Sea. After some delay Fiji became British, but both Conservative and Liberal statesmen hesitated to accede to the Australasian demands for contiguous territory.

What to do with New Guinea became a very embarrassing question in the eighties. The Dutch had occupied western New Guinea and had gradually extended their area to 141° east longitude, leaving approximately 130,000 square miles as a no-man's land. In 1793 representatives of the English East India Company had visited and claimed the island for Britain, and in 1846 Lieutenant Yule of the royal navy hoisted the Union Jack at "Cape Possession"; but these as well as other efforts to make New Guinea British received no encouragement from the imperial government. In the seventies the Australians became interested in New Guinea; companies were formed for the purpose of exploiting the resources of the island; Australian legislatures petitioned for its annexation; and in 1878 reports that gold had been found there stimulated the discussion of the annexation question. At home, the Royal Colonial Institute supported the Australian demand, but the government moved with great circumspection. On July 31, 1876, the colonial secretary, Lord Carnarvon, asked the foreign office to obtain through the British ambassador in Paris French recognition of the paramountcy of British claims to New Guinea; however, the French limited themselves to a disavowal of any design of their own on the island. With this Carnarvon was content; he made no further attempt to claim New Guinea for Britain and he refused to approve the acquisition of land there by British subjects. Still, the admiralty surveyed its coast and the Australians would not drop the question. They magnified the importance of the gold boom of 1878, and when that collapsed German commercial activities supplied a basis for alarmist reports. But neither the Conservative secretaries of state for the colonies, Lord Carnarvon and Sir Michael Hicks Beach, nor their Liberal successors, Lords Kimberley and Derby, paid much attention to the Australian clamor for British annexation of New Guinea.

Despairing of action by the authorities at home, Queensland

sent an agent to New Guinea, who hoisted the British flag and took possession of portions of the island April 4, 1883 – a bold step which created consternation in Downing Street. Apart from the merits or demerits of this particular act, the imperial govern-

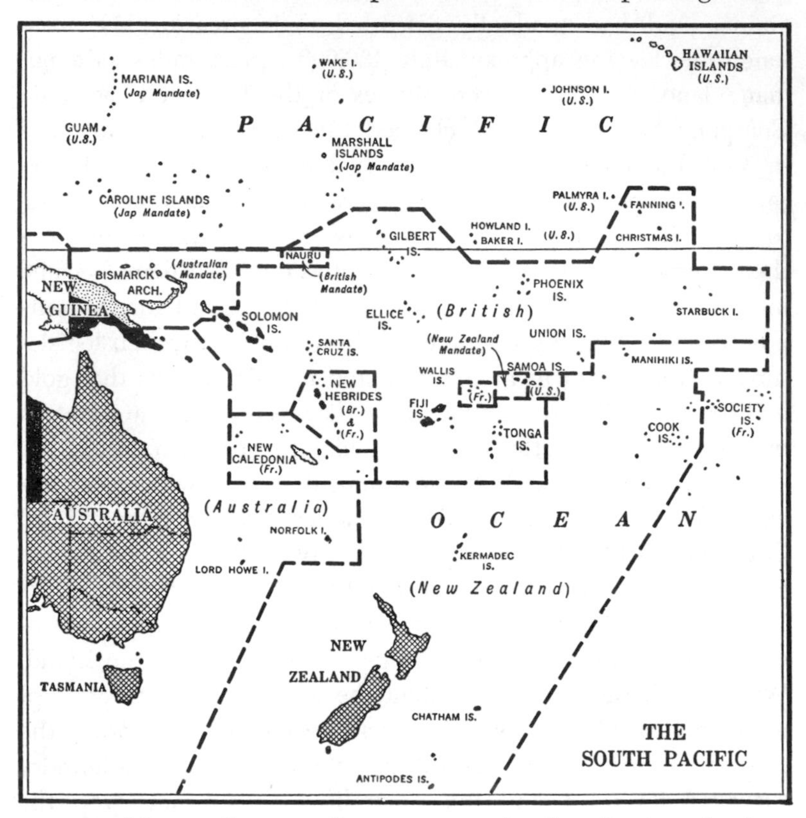

ment could not allow a colony to annex land without authorization. Although Queensland was supported by her sister colonies, she was sternly rebuked by the colonial office and her annexation of New Guinea was declared null and void. Meanwhile the foreign office investigated whether any power except Holland had claims to New Guinea; and Sir Edward Hertslet reported that neither Spain nor Portugal had tried to seize the island. When rumors of German colonization activities reached England,

Lord Ampthill, the British ambassador at Berlin, in the spring of 1883 asked Count Hatzfeldt, the German foreign secretary, about the attitude of the German government toward colonization; Hatzfeldt then disclaimed any German design on New Guinea and said that as everyone knew Bismarck was not interested in colonization. France gave assurances that she had no interest in New Guinea; and when Italy made inquiries concerning the island Britain told her to stay away. Thus fortified, Lord Granville, the British foreign secretary, assured the colonial office on May 3, 1883, that no foreign government had designs on New Guinea, and this information was conveyed to the Australian colonies.

In the British cabinet's discussions of the New Guinea question, 1883–1884, much weight was given to the opinion of Sir Arthur Gordon, governor of Fiji and high commissioner for the Western Pacific, 1875–1880, and governor of New Zealand, 1880–1882. He could speak authoritatively on conditions in the South Pacific and besides he was a close personal friend of Gladstone. In private letters to the prime minister, Gordon argued strongly against the annexation of New Guinea by Queensland, mainly on the ground that it would lead to exploitation of the natives who, being numerous and warlike, would resist and armed conflicts would follow; he doubted the strength of the Australian annexation movement, which he attributed to the sugar growers of Queensland and the people engaged in the so-called "island trade." He admitted, however, that something should be done concerning New Guinea and he recommended that the authority of the high commissioner for the Western Pacific should be extended so as to include the unoccupied part of the island. Gladstone and Lord Derby, then colonial secretary, agreed that the annexation of New Guinea by Queensland should be quashed, but in May, 1883, the former showed himself willing to consider annexation to Australia "if the Australian colonies would combine into some kind of political union." However, when representatives of the seven Australasian colonies met in conference at Sydney in November and December, 1883, they presented such extravagant demands for keeping all foreign powers from acquiring islands in the Pacific south of the equator that Gladstone lost faith in them. He feared also that if Britain took steps to declare a protectorate over New Guinea the Australians "would begin to hook more to it, and our position would be a false one."

The year 1883 ended without a settlement of the New Guinea question. But the Australians continued to press their arguments in favor of annexation, and Lord Derby grew alarmed lest persistence in refusing to grant this request should impose too severe a strain on the connection between the Australasian colonies and Britain, an alarm not shared by Gladstone. H. C. E. Childers, chancellor of the exchequer and a former resident of Australia, supported Derby's demand for action in the matter of New Guinea. Toward the end of July, 1884, the cabinet decided to proclaim a British protectorate over the non-Dutch portion of the island without specifying its limits. No sooner had this decision been reached than Count Münster, the German ambassador to London, informed Granville that Germany wished to protect her interests in the South Pacific and that she considered the northeast coast of New Guinea a suitable field for German colonization. An awkward situation soon developed; neither Granville nor Gladstone opposed German colonization, and Bismarck, then at the zenith of his power, might create embarrassment for Britain in Egypt if his wishes were not gratified. On the other hand, British statesmen could not submit to bullying by Bismarck; and the Australasian demand for sole British control over New Guinea east of the 141st parallel received strong support from expansionists at home. The foreign office wished to let Germany have northeastern New Guinea, the colonial office opposed it. Delays caused by this disagreement within the cabinet and by the need for correspondence with the Australian colonies irritated Bismarck whose position grew stronger when it became evident that Britain must appeal to the powers in arranging a new financial settlement for Egypt. Finally he made it clear to the British government that concessions to the German demand for colonies was his price for supporting Britain's effort to rehabilitate the finances of Egypt. Since he held strong cards, the non-Dutch portion of New Guinea was divided in April, 1885; Britain secured 63,000 and Germany 67,000 square miles, the latter including New Britain and other islands to the northeast of New Guinea. A suggestion by Governor Loch of Victoria that Britain should try to appease the Australians by an offer to buy Dutch New Guinea was rejected by Gladstone who refused to submit to a small state a proposal which Britain would not wish to make to a great power. British New Guinea was annexed formally in 1888; it was governed by a high commissioner, the Australian colonies contributing £15,000 annually toward the cost of its government.

To many Australians, the question of the New Hebrides was scarcely less important than that of New Guinea. This island group lay relatively close to New Caledonia, which had been annexed by France in 1853 and since used by her as a penal colony. British missionaries complained of high-handed actions by the French authorities, the French penal colony was a source of grievance to the Australians, and it was feared that if France succeeded in acquiring the New Hebrides the trouble with escaped convicts would increase and the security of Australia might be endangered. Consequently, Australian legislatures and Australian intercolonial conferences pressed strongly for British annexation of the New Hebrides. The imperial government, while sympathizing with the colonists on the matter of escaped convicts and seriously attempting to persuade France to discontinue transportation to New Caledonia, absolutely refused to seize the New Hebrides. The matter was temporarily settled in 1887 by an agreement whereby a joint Anglo-French naval commission was intrusted with the duty of maintaining order in the islands. This arrangement lasted until 1904 when the treaty of the Anglo-French *entente* paved the way for a new settlement of the question.

Samoa and Tonga were included in the extensive claims for territory put forward by New Zealand. In the eighties the latter group of islands was virtually governed by an English Wesleyan missionary, Shirley Baker; in Samoa Germany and the United States had developed interests which provided foundations for claims to political influence. By a tripartite agreement of 1889, involving Britain, Germany, and the United States, a joint protectorate was established which in fact meant a threefold division of the islands. This settlement satisfied no one, least of all the Germans. After prolonged negotiations, Germany in the autumn of 1899 took advantage of Britain's difficulties in South Africa to press for a new settlement in Samoa. In November, 1899, Britain withdrew from the islands, and as a partial compensation Germany surrendered claims to Tonga, over which Britain proclaimed a protectorate in the following year. Other Anglo-German agreements of 1886 and 1899 divided the Western Pacific into British and German spheres of influence. To Britain fell the Gilbert and Ellice Islands, some of the Solomon Islands, and the Cook Islands; the last-named was annexed to New Zealand in 1901.

In Asia and territories adjacent thereto, Britain's policy was determined largely by her concern for the safety of India. Indeed it may be said that this factor shaped British foreign policy throughout the Victorian era. For the purpose of safeguarding India Britain bought shares in the Suez Canal Company, established herself in Egypt, opposed Russia's attempt to reach Constantinople, acquired Cyprus, gained control over Baluchistan, annexed Upper Burma, and became involved in a war with Afghanistan, 1878–1880. In 1884 the Russian occupation of Merv on the Afghan frontier caused great excitement in England; and when the Russians in 1885 drove the Afghans from Penjdeh even Gladstone spoke of war. In the nineties the no-man's land that separated the British Indian and Afghan frontiers was added to India, whose boundaries were pushed northward toward the Pamirs; and under the viceroyalty of Curzon, 1898–1905, Britain strengthened her hold on the Persian Gulf and made an effort to establish control over Tibet.

In the Malay Peninsula and nearby islands Britain in 1870 held Penang, the Province Wellesley, Malacca, and Singapore. The tin mines of Malaya attracted European and American capitalists; and the disorders that prevailed in its small states, the prevalence of debt slavery, and the need for protecting merchants, mainly Chinese, who were British subjects caused Britain to extend her authority over the peninsula. Penang, the Province Wellesley, Malacca, the Dindings, and Singapore were organized as the Straits Settlements with a crown colony form of government. Several islands in the Bay of Bengal, among them the Cocos Islands and Christmas Island, were attached to this colony. The Malay states of Perak, Negri Sembilan, Pahang, and Selangor were brought together as the Federated Malay States under British protection. Each of these states retained its native ruler but was in reality governed by a British agent or resident, with a high commissioner and a chief secretary forming the nucleus of the federal government. The unfederated states—Johore, Kedah, Perlis, Kelantan, and Trengganu—also came under British control; and the three regions were ultimately organized as one economic unit.

East of the Strait of Malacca, the influence of Britain grew more by the extension of her trade, by control over mineral resources, and by grants of loans on the part of British banks than by annexations. The North Borneo Company, chartered in 1881, acquired land in Borneo; and in 1888 Sarawak, North Borneo, and the sultanate of Brunei, which occupy the northern portion of the island of Borneo, were declared British protectorates. Farther north, Port Hamilton on the Corean peninsula was seized in 1885 and surrendered two years later; in May, 1898, the British flag was hoisted at Weihaiwei; and in June of that year Britain leased for ninety-nine years Kowloon, a strip of territory on the mainland opposite Hongkong. But the extent of these acquisitions do not provide an adequate measurement of Britain's power in China toward the close of the nineteenth century. At that time about 70 per cent of China's foreign trade was with Britain; an Englishman, Sir Robert Hart, was

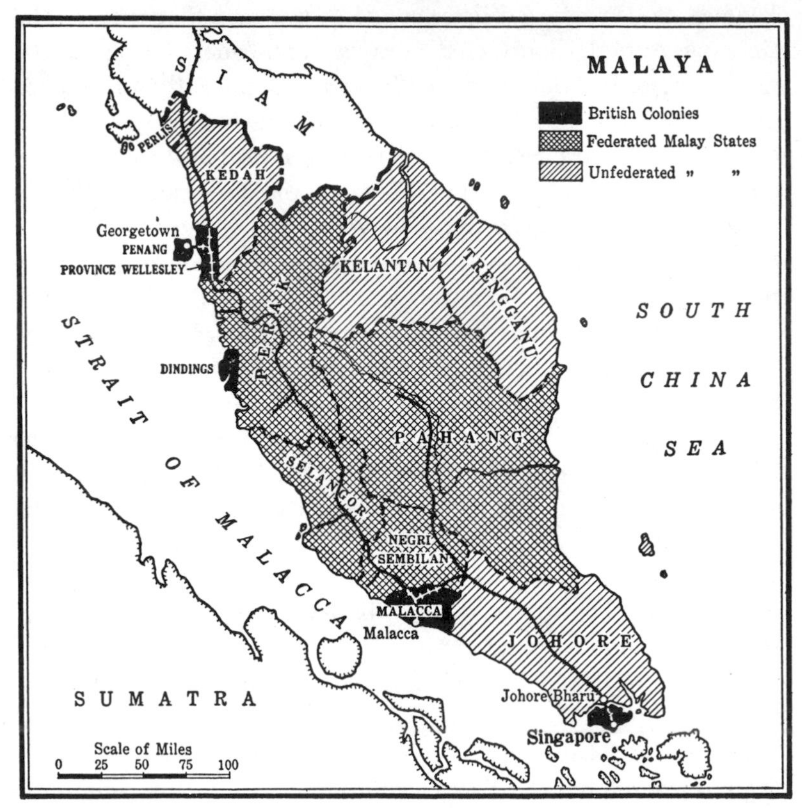

inspector-general of the Chinese customs; Shanghai was practically a British port; and British influence predominated in the rich Yangtse Valley. Because of the importance of her trade with China, Britain was anxious to keep the Celestial empire intact, and it was hoped that China would prove strong enough to resist the growth of Russian influence in the Far East. But the Sino-Japanese war, 1894–1895, revealed China to be a giant with feet of clay. Britain had striven to avert the war and had sympathized with China; however, with the disclosure of China's appalling weakness the object of British policy became not to antagonize Japan and to prevent China from sharing the fate of Africa. In pursuance of these aims, Britain refused to join Russia, France, and Germany in coercing Japan to revise the Treaty of Shimonoseki, 1895, which concluded her war with China, and Britain secured from China a pledge that the Yangtse region would not be alienated. In the latter half of the nineties France encroached upon China from the south, Russia from the north; French gold enabled Russia to extend loans to China and obtain concessions in return. Keen competition arose for the privilege of lending money to China and the right to build her railroads. Although receiving some support from Germany, Britain was clearly on the defensive and she was barely able to hold her own against Russia and France. In 1897–1898, when Russia secured Port Arthur, Germany Kiaochow, and France Kwangchow, Britain obtained Weihaiwei and Kowloon; each of these powers had one or more provinces earmarked as a sphere of influence. Nevertheless, Britain, still hoping to avert a partition of China, joined the United States in 1899 in wresting from the powers a recognition of the principle of the "open door" in China. While this principle applied only to commerce, its acceptance tended to deter the powers from encroachments upon Chinese territory. In 1900 an anti-foreign outbreak, the Boxer Rebellion, resulted in the occupation of Peking by an international force, and for a time it looked as if China might be divided; she was saved largely because of the jealousies among the powers. As the period closes, Britain sought to obtain assistance from Germany and Japan in efforts to prevent China from passing under the control of Russia.

The Mediterranean coastal lands of Africa had for all practical purposes formed a part of Europe since time immemorial. The climate, the forbidding aspects of her coasts, the absence of good harbors and navigable rivers, and lack of knowledge of the interior had, except in the extreme south, prevented Africa from becoming a field for European colonization. By the beginning of the last quarter of the nineteenth century explorers, traders, and missionaries had penetrated most of Africa; their reports of her climate, peoples, and resources whetted the appetites of European governments and capitalists for opportunities to exploit the dark continent. The race for African possessions started in 1876 when Leopold II, king of the Belgians, convened at Brussels an unofficial conference on Africa; this led to the organization of the International African Association with King Leopold as president which in time gained control over the extensive region in Central Africa known as the Congo Free State. International conferences dealing with Africa were held at Berlin in 1884–1885 and Brussels in 1890, at which agreements were reached on general rules of procedure in claiming and occupying African lands. The work of the conferences was supplemented by numerous treaties delimiting the boundaries of the colonies, protectorates, or spheres of influence of Britain, France, Germany, Italy, and Portugal in Africa. In addition to these agreements between European powers a large number of treaties were concluded between concession hunters and native chiefs, although the latter seldom if ever understood the meaning of the documents to which they affixed their crosses. Occasionally a king with superior intelligence like Mtesa in Uganda and Lobengula of the Matabeles made a clumsy attempt at matching his wit and diplomatic skill with those of the white "empire-builders" or at playing one of them off against the other. Although the inevitable outcome might be thus postponed for a brief span of time, the end was never in doubt; the rulers of Africa, except Emperor Menelik of Abyssinia, were like the proverbial fly in the spider's net.

Because of her possessions in West and South Africa, the widespread activities of her citizens, her wealth, and her command of the sea, Britain enjoyed great advantages in the scramble for African lands, but until 1895 her government showed no eagerness for these lands. In the seventies a governor at the Cape, Sir Bartle Frere, was censured by a Conservative government for his forward policy in South Africa; the Transvaal, annexed in 1877, was restored in 1881; when the sultan of Zanzibar in 1881 asked Britain to become guardian and protector for his son the request was refused; and neither Liberals nor Conservatives were eager to enter or anxious to remain in Egypt. Nevertheless, Britain secured control over about three million square miles of African territory within the years 1870–1901. A small factor in this expansion was the forward thrusts of settlements limited to South Africa. Occasionally Britain seized control because if the land in question fell into other hands British possessions or trade routes might be endangered; this motive acted powerfully in the case of Egypt (the occupation of which brought Britain into the Sudan), Somaliland, Zanzibar, coastal lands in South Africa, Bechuanaland with its missionary road leading to the interior of Africa, and the Boer republics. Enormous areas were ultimately incorporated in the British empire because of actions of individuals and private companies. Among British statesmen, Lord Carnarvon and Joseph Chamberlain took by design a leading part in extending the British empire in Africa; governors such as Sir Bartle Frere and Sir Alfred Milner were not simply agents of the home government, but themselves initiated policies and created situations which made aggressive action necessary. An even greater role in the drama of the extension of Britain's African empire must be assigned to men like Cecil Rhodes, Sir Harry Johnston, Sir George Goldie, Sir William Mackinnon, and Captain (later Lord) Lugard. Largely because of the initiative of these men, the Royal Niger Company, the Imperial East Africa Company, and the South Africa Chartered Company gained upward of a million square miles of African territory for Britain; they have as monuments the Kenya Colony, Uganda, Nigeria, and Rhodesia.

Although the partition of Africa was effected without a European war, it often created tense diplomatic situations. Until

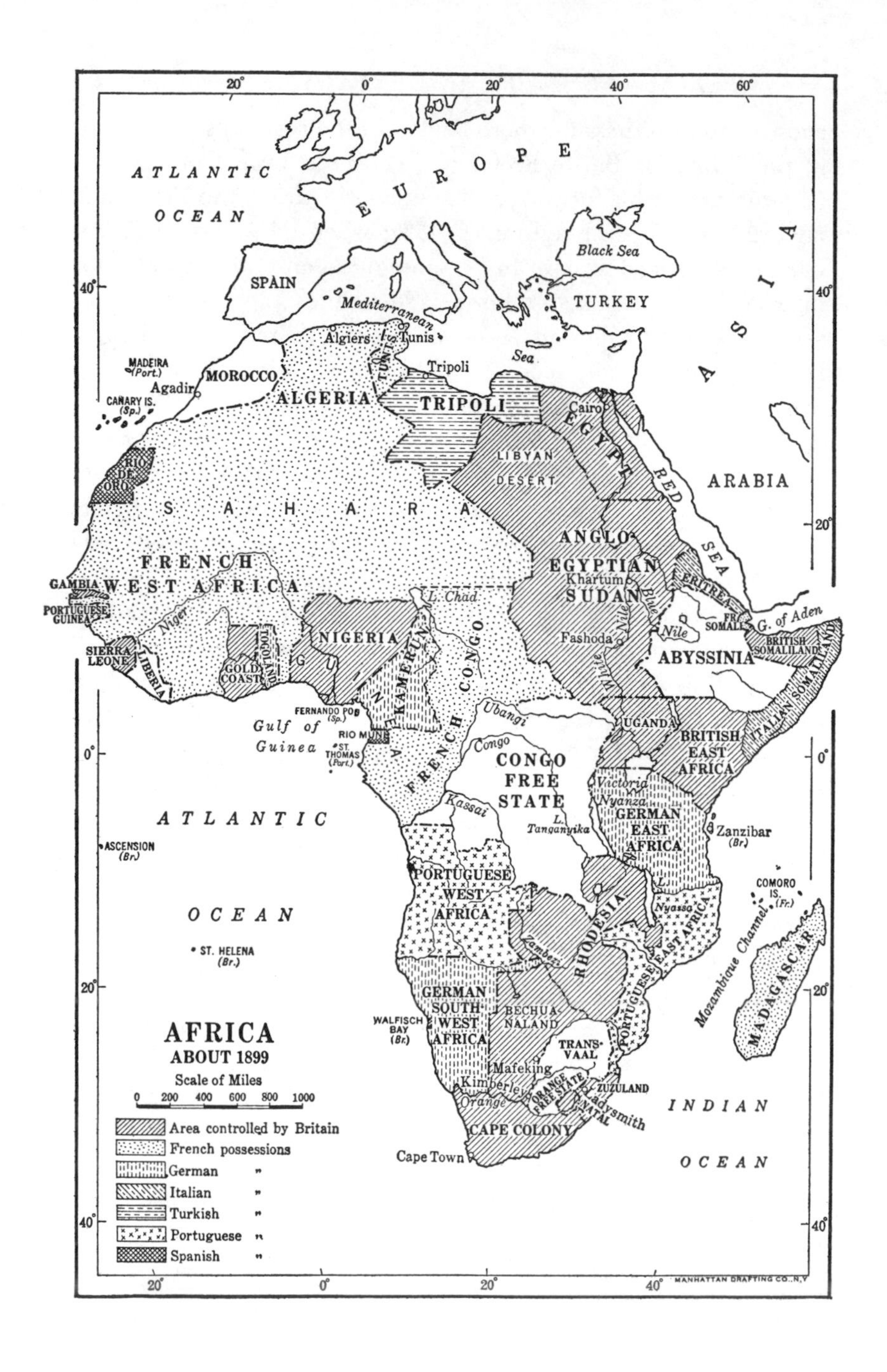

AFRICA
ABOUT 1899
Scale of Miles
0 200 400 600 800 1000
Area controlled by Britain
French possessions
German "
Italian "
Turkish "
Portuguese "
Spanish "
ATLANTIC OCEAN
EUROPE
ASIA
SPAIN
TURKEY
Black Sea
Mediterranean Sea
Algiers
Tunis
TUNIS
Tripoli
MADEIRA (Port.)
CANARY IS. (Sp.)
Agadir
MOROCCO
ALGERIA
TRIPOLI
Cairo
EGYPT
LIBYAN DESERT
RED SEA
ARABIA
RIO DE ORO
SAHARA
ANGLO EGYPTIAN SUDAN
Khartum
FRENCH WEST AFRICA
GAMBIA
PORTUGUESE GUINEA
ERITREA
FR. SOMALI
G. of Aden
BRITISH SOMALILAND
Niger
L. Chad
NIGERIA
TOGOLAND
GOLD COAST
SIERRA LEONE
LIBERIA
KAMERUN
FRENCH CONGO
Fashoda
Blue Nile
White Nile
Nile
ABYSSINIA
ITALIAN SOMALILAND
FERNANDO PO (Sp.)
Gulf of Guinea
RIO MUNI
ST. THOMAS (Port.)
Ubangi
Congo
CONGO FREE STATE
UGANDA
BRITISH EAST AFRICA
Victoria Nyanza
Kassai
L. Tanganyika
GERMAN EAST AFRICA
Zanzibar (Br.)
ASCENSION (Br.)
PORTUGUESE WEST AFRICA
RHODESIA
Nyassa
EAST AFRICA
COMORO IS. (Fr.)
Mozambique Channel
MADAGASCAR
ST. HELENA (Br.)
Zambezi
PORTUGUESE
GERMAN SOUTH WEST AFRICA
WALFISCH BAY (Br.)
BECHUANALAND
TRANSVAAL
Mafeking
Kimberley
Orange
ORANGE FREE STATE
ZULULAND
Ladysmith
NATAL
CAPE COLONY
Cape Town
INDIAN OCEAN
MANHATTAN DRAFTING CO., N.Y.

her agreement with France in 1904, Egypt was an Achilles' heel for Britain. France resented the British control of Egypt and consequently created difficulties elsewhere in Africa, in the South Seas, and in the Far East. During the eighties and nineties Britain was often dependent upon the good will of Germany; but on account of public opinion at home, in Australasia, and in South Africa the British government did not gracefully pay the price in colonial lands that Germany demanded for diplomatic support against France or Russia. This price was exacted largely in Africa; much bickering preceded Anglo-German agreements concerning colonies in West, South, and East Africa. In exchange for withdrawal of German claims in Zanzibar, Britain was forced to cede Heligoland to Germany.

During the thirty years 1870–1901, much territory was added to the British empire by annexation or conquest; and in the same period settlers in North America, South Africa, and Australasia pushed forward the boundaries of fields, meadows, and grazing land. Millions of acres of virgin soil were made to yield untold wealth; farmsteads and thriving cities sprang up in the wilderness. By increases from natural sources and immigration from the British Isles and other European lands, British nations developed rapidly beyond the seas, nations destined to exercise a powerful influence both on the affairs of the British empire and the outcome of world conflicts.

CHAPTER 19

IMPERIAL RELATIONS AND IMPERIAL POLICY, 1870–1901

BRITAIN took long strides in the direction of true democracy during the latter half of the Victorian era. As it closed, manhood suffrage was almost universal; British labor was organizing for independent participation in politics; educational opportunities from the kindergarten through the university were available even to those of limited means, irrespective of religion and social status; to a greater extent than before in the history of Britain the state was assuming responsibility for the welfare of all the citizens, and the British people were learning to rely upon collectivistic action by either private organizations or the state or subdivisions thereof for economic improvements and social well-being. Similar changes at varying rates of speed and degrees of success took place in practically every other European country. The great nation states moved forward at a rapid pace; and Britain, who in the middle years of the nineteenth century had held undisputed leadership in finance, industrial organization, commerce, and as a colonizing power, found herself at its end pressed by rivals and competitors. Gladstone, the greatest of the Victorian statesmen, wrote in 1894: "The world of today is not the world in which I was bred and trained and have principally lived." This was more than a mere recognition on the part of an octogenarian that to live is to outlive; it was the diagnosis by a wise man that the ideas and ideals of an earlier generation had been shelved. *Laissez faire* had been given up, free trade was in danger, doubt and fear had replaced confidence and optimistic idealism, and leading British statesmen stood ready to abandon her time-honored policy of no entangling alliances. These changes in the Old World and Old World relations left deep marks upon Britain's policy toward, and her relations with, the empire beyond the seas.

British imperial policy and the intra-imperial relations have a close and often a causal connection. No attempt will be made to treat them separately except in so far as may be necessary for a clearer understanding of special episodes or a particular course of action. In the discussion of this dual topic, the constitutional changes achieved or attempted will be treated first; then will follow the economics and the defense of the empire; and finally the various threads of imperial policy will be brought together in considering the work of Joseph Chamberlain as colonial secretary from 1895 till the end of the reign of Queen Victoria.

While the most significant constitutional developments were along the line of granting more freedom to the overseas possessions, warning voices called attention to certain disintegrating tendencies, and determined efforts were made to group neighboring colonies into federations and to draw all of them more closely to the mother country. The principle of giving the inhabitants of the overseas empire a share in their own government was applied widely in the last thirty years of the nineteenth century. Even India secured a modest gift of local self-government during the viceroyalty of Lord Ripon, 1880–1884, and this was extended somewhat in 1892. Jamaica, proudest of Britain's West Indian islands, had lost her ancient assembly in 1866 and was thereby reduced to the status of a crown colony. Eighteen years later her institutions and administration had been sufficiently modernized to permit the restoration of popular representation on a small scale. Her legislative council was changed from one wholly nominated to one in which half of the eighteen members were elected. After the enlargement of the legislative council to twenty-eight in 1893, the governors for six years left in abeyance their power to nominate the full quota of fourteen; thus the elective element, temporarily at least, remained in control. The new council of government for Mauritius, created by letters patent of September 16, 1885, contained twenty-seven members of whom ten were elected; and a new constitution for Malta in 1887 provided for an assembly of twenty-one, including the governor; of these a majority, fourteen, were elected. Cyprus, administered by Britain although not yet a part of her empire, in 1882–1883 secured a legislative body with an elective majority. In recognition of the religious division of the island, the Mohammedans were given three, or one-fourth, of the elected members, thus introducing the principle of communal representation destined later to cause so much difficulty in India.

As crown colonies were moved upward by being granted representative government, so those already in this category advanced the further step to the status of colonies with responsible government. At the Cape this evolution was completed in 1872, after some doubt and hesitation by both the colonists and the colonial office. At this time the imperial government was removing the garrisons from colonies with responsible government on the ground that self-government begets self-defense. Consequently the colonists at the Cape hesitated to accept a boon coupled with such an unpalatable condition. Furthermore, those who opposed the introduction of responsible government claimed that risks would be incurred because of the strong Boer element in the Cape population. But the Gladstone ministry scoffed at these fears and showed its eagerness to extend colonial autonomy by agreeing to maintain an imperial garrison at the Cape of Good Hope even though the colony had been given responsible government. These grants were not made indiscriminately. Natal was refused responsible government in the early seventies because of the smallness of her white population. Indeed the Conservatives, whose long lease on political power in England began in 1886, showed no alacrity in giving to the colonies what Lord Salisbury once derisively styled "the Liberal nostrum called responsible government." Western Australia negotiated with the colonial office from 1883 till 1890 before she obtained what her sister colonies had secured so readily thirty years earlier; and conditions imposed by the Salisbury government postponed the grant of responsible government to Natal until after the Liberals had returned to power in England in 1892.

Under the system of responsible government the ministry must have the support of a majority in the popularly elected branch of the legislature. The amount of self-government connected therewith varied during the period with place and time, though the general tendency was to extend it. Thus the Dominion of Canada was considered as occupying a more elevated position than other colonies with responsible government like Newfoundland and Tasmania. The rank later labeled dominion status evolved gradually. But in none of the colonies with responsible government would the colonial office interfere in purely local affairs. Hence Gladstone refused in 1873 to take any action in connection with the Canadian Pacific Railway scandal; and twenty-five years later Chamberlain made it plain that he considered unwise the contract which Newfoundland had concluded with R. G. Reid of Montreal for taking over a railroad, the telegraph, and other public utilities, but since it concerned only Newfoundland the colonial office would keep hands off.

It was, however, difficult to determine the dividing line between colonial and imperial questions. Extreme advocates of colonial autonomy like George Higinbotham of Victoria proposed a purely personal union in the king between a self-governing colony and the mother country such as that which had formerly bound Hanover to England. From this proposition it followed logically that the position of the governor of a self-governing colony would be identical with that of the sovereign of England and that therefore in all matters he would be bound to accept the advice of his ministers — a view which failed to win general acceptance even in Victoria. The question of the relations between the governor and his ministers on the one hand and between him and the colonial office on the other was one of great practical importance. Australian governments insisted that the governor must dissolve the legislature when advised to do so; this some governors, including Lord Canterbury of Victoria, refused to do. When a crisis over this issue developed in Victoria in 1872, Canterbury asked for instruction from home. The colonial secretary, Lord Kimberley, declined to give advice since the question was a local one, although privately he believed that Canterbury should have granted the dissolution desired by his ministers. But when the Australian assemblies and governments demanded that the governors aid them in overcoming the opposition of legislative councils by adding new members where they were nominated as in New South Wales and Queensland or by dissolution where they were elective, the colonial office generally told the governors not to grant the requests. Yet on these as on many similar points involving the governor's authority versus that of his ministry, the victory in the end rested with the latter. Thus despite the resistance of governors the legislative council of New South Wales was increased gradually from 31 in 1870 to 65 thirty years later.

Both in Canada and in Australia opposition developed against the detailed instructions which the colonial office, following old precedents, issued to each governor upon his appointment. In Canada, Edward Blake, minister of justice from 1875 to 1877, led the attack upon this policy, and the colonial secretary, Lord Carnarvon, gave way. A somewhat similar change was made in 1892 in the formal instructions issued to the governors of the Australian colonies and Newfoundland. In 1888–1889 all the colonies of Australia except Victoria supported a request presented by Queensland and South Australia that they should be consulted on the selection of their governors. Lord Knutsford, then colonial secretary, refused the request. The particular case which gave rise to this controversy, the appointment of Sir Henry Blake to the governorship of Queensland, was settled by Blake's voluntary withdrawal; and it seems evident that the practice already followed in choosing the governor general of Canada — making certain beforehand that the new chief executive would be acceptable to the Dominion — was extended to Australia. Although the political power of the governor declined, still he could, if possessed of tact, ability, and experience, wield much influence as did Lord Dufferin in Canada, 1873–1878. Moreover, the colonial governors continued to use their veto power and to reserve certain bills for "the signification of Her Majesty's pleasure."

The latter provision was applied to various types of laws including those which aimed at excluding immigrants because of race or color. Australasia, Natal, and British Columbia wished to keep out Asiatics; this gave rise to complications because China was a friendly nation that offered a vast field for British trade and economic exploitation, and India was a part of the British empire. When the Chinese flocked to the Australian gold fields in the fifties the colonies concerned passed discriminatory tax laws; these, coupled with the white miners' hostile attitude to the Chinese and the exhaustion of the mines, solved the problem temporarily. In the middle seventies gold discoveries in Queensland brought another influx of Chinese, and when the colony attempted to stop it by special immigration laws, the colonial office offered objections on the basis of unfair discrimination against subjects of a friendly power as well as against Britain's Asiatic and African subjects. Queensland countered with the claim that immigration belonged to the topics which might be called local and could therefore be dealt with by the colonial government. The Conservative colonial secretaries, Lord Carnarvon, 1874–1878, and Sir Michael Hicks Beach, 1878–1880, upheld the imperial prerogative; a Liberal, Lord Derby, 1882–1885, conceded the point to the colony. However, for the sake of imperial interests and international harmony the colonies were urged to find a way out that did not hurt Chinese national pride. The final solution of the Chinese immigration question for Australia was an educational test first devised in Natal for the purpose of keeping out the natives of India. Indian coolies had in the sixties been invited to Natal as indentured laborers, but when as traders they began to become an important factor in the economic life of the colony and threatened to outnumber the whites the colonial legislature passed discriminatory laws. After 1893, when Natal secured responsible government, imperial interference gave rise to a constitutional issue which in the end was dodged by the invention of the above-mentioned educational test given in a European language and so flexible that those whom the colonial authorities wished to keep out were kept out.

British Columbia shared the fear of and hostility toward Asiatic immigrants prevalent along the Pacific coast of America from Alaska to the Mexican border. Chinese laborers had been brought in by the Canadian Pacific Railway Co. during the early eighties; and when the United States adopted a policy of rigidly excluding Asiatics British Columbia, fearing that the stream would be diverted in her direction, passed immigration bills for their exclusion. Again a constitutional question was raised. But behind British Columbia stood the Dominion of Canada; in the end face-saving solutions were found, which, however, left as a legacy the question of the status of the natives of India within the British empire.

The various dodges and subterfuges invented to solve the constitutional issues raised in the discussions between Britain and the self-governing colonies over Asiatic immigration somewhat concealed the fact that victory rested with the colonies. In matters pertaining to tariffs, however, their successes were plain to all. From 1867 until 1873 the imperial government refused the Australasian colonies' demand for permission to discriminate in their tariffs between goods of Australasian origin and goods from the outside. After the Liberals came into power in England in December, 1868, the chief opponent of the concession was the prime minister, Gladstone, who feared that Australasian differential tariffs would violate British commercial treaties with Belgium and Germany. Charges of bad faith on the score of treaties would have been awkward at this time, for Britain was taking a strong stand on the question of the sanctity of treaties and inviolability of international law in diplomatic controversies with Russia and the United States. Gladstone resisted the Australasian demands after these issues had been settled; not until it was shown that the point in dispute had been conceded earlier to the colonies of British North America did he give way. Thus a power granted to the American colonies for the purpose of fostering their economic union became a lever for securing greater tariff autonomy for the British colonies of Australasia. The "casual" have continued in the modern period, as they were so often in the medieval, to be "causal" factors in British constitutional progress.

The statesmen of Australasia, particularly Charles Gavan Duffy of Victoria and Julius Vogel of New Zealand, resented the fact that their tariff policies were restricted by imperial commercial treaties. In the heat of the differential tariff disputes they demanded full tariff autonomy and the abrogation of restrictive treaties. Both points were gained before the close of the century. British statesmen had vainly striven to prevent first Canada and then Victoria from adopting protective tariffs. By the seventies the battle was lost; one after the other the self-governing colonies abandoned the fiscal creed of the parent state. Consequently, if Britain did negotiate commercial treaties suitable to conditions in these colonies her spokesmen had to practice ventriloquism. To avoid compromising situations, the colonial secretary, Lord Kimberley, decided in 1882 that it would be better to let the Canadian high commissioner in London, Sir Alexander Galt, negotiate directly for a commercial treaty between Canada and France. Thence the evolutionary process was easy and rapid. In 1897 Britain agreed to abrogate the Belgian and German commercial treaties that hampered the freedom of the colonies to adopt preferential tariffs. And by the end of the decade it had been decided that a self-governing colony could conclude separate tariff agreements with foreign countries and be bound by those of Britain only when the colonies had specifically declared their adherence thereto.

Although fiscal autonomy had thus been achieved, little progress was made in the direction of securing colonial participation in determining the foreign policy and foreign relations of the empire. True, Canada's prime minister, Sir John A. Macdonald, was one of Britain's five representatives on the Joint High Commission which negotiated the Treaty of Washington in 1871. However, he quite correctly looked upon himself as a hostage. It was recognized beforehand that a settlement between Britain and the United States would include topics such as the fisheries on which agreement could not be effective without Dominion legislation. Since expediency therefore required that Canada be represented at the Anglo-American negotiations of 1871, a precedent was established for colonial participation in international settlements vital to them. Nevertheless, imperial interests continued to outweigh colonial, as was evident from the refusal of the British government to heed requests from the Cape and Australasia for the annexation of contiguous territory in South Africa and the Pacific area. Given the choice of offending a colony or a group of colonies or offending either France or Germany, Britain chose the former; the colonies as the weaker party had to pocket their pride. In diplomacy Britain did not yet admit the self-governing colonies to her counsels.

Among the attempts to counteract the centrifugal tendencies inherent in the extension of colonial self-government must be mentioned the efforts at federating groups of colonies, the agitation in favor of imperial federation, and the use of colonial conferences. The first of these, the federating of colonies, was sponsored or supported by the imperial government as means for strengthening the empire at reduced cost to the British taxpayers. Aid and encouragement were given to efforts at enlarging the Dominion of Canada so as to include all of British North America. This was achieved, except for Newfoundland which preferred to go it alone. Despite protests from some of them, the colonies of the Leeward group in the West Indies — Antigua, Dominica, Montserrat, Nevis, St. Kitts, and the Virgin Islands — were federated in 1871, but attempts to federate the Windward Islands and plans for a greater West Indian federation failed. We have seen that an effort by the Cape governor, Sir George Grey, to unite the white communities in South Africa was frowned upon by the colonial office. When, somewhat later, the dissatisfaction in the eastern province of the Cape Colony threatened to split that colony, the colonial office suggested in 1871 as a possible solution a federal arrangement which might include Natal and even the Boer republics. But the people of South Africa showed no desire to form a federation, and Lord Kimberley refused to listen to the suggestion by Robert W. Herbert, permanent undersecretary in the colonial office, that a federation might be achieved by an imperial act. Kimberley's successor, Lord Carnarvon, a less wise and more impatient man, had in 1867 steered through parliament the British North America Act which created the Dominion of Canada; upon his return to the colonial office in 1874 he was eager to effect a similar federation for South Africa. Unfortunately he did not wait until the people concerned inaugurated such a movement; he prejudiced them against it by sponsoring both agitation at home and an enabling act passed by the imperial parliament. The annexation of the Transvaal in 1877 for the purpose of promoting federation had the opposite effect. By a remarkable series of blunders committed by friends of a South African union like Cecil Rhodes, the split between the Boer republics and the British empire grew wider until in October, 1899, they became locked in the great Anglo-Boer war.

Success ultimately crowned the efforts at federating the Australian colonies. The suggestion by the colonial office in 1849 that a council should be provided for all the colonies of Australia met with no response there, nor did they act upon an imperial proposal for an Australian customs union. The colonial office then decided to follow Burke's dictum — to let "a beneficent nature take its own course to perfection." Intercolonial conferences, 1867–1871, for the purpose of discussing the preferential tariff question failed to draw the colonies together. But similar conferences held in the early eighties because of French and German colonizing activities in the South Pacific resulted in the establishment of a federal council for Australia in 1885. The undertaking received the blessing of the home government together with an expression of regret because the most powerful of the colonies, New South Wales, had not joined the council. Late in the eighties, however, the realization that the British empire in the South Seas was exposed to dangers from the outside gave a powerful stimulus to the federation sentiment in the Australian colonies. Beginning in 1890 a series of constitutional conferences, debates in the colonial parliaments, and elections fought on the issue of federation resulted in agreement on a plan for an Australian constitution which, like that of the Dominion of Canada, had been worked out by the people themselves, the colonial office observing strict neutrality. This plan was passed as an imperial act in the summer of 1900; the Commonwealth of Australia dates from the first day of the present century.

While colonial federation was encouraged and even initiated by the British government, the schemes for imperial federation were sponsored wholly by private organizations; none received support or even encouragement from the imperial government until the end of this period. Late in the sixties the imperialistic sentiment revived in Britain. The rise of Prussia under the guidance of Bismarck caused forebodings of the approach of an age less liberal and less spacious for Britain and her empire. Conservative Englishmen viewed with misgivings the withdrawal of the garrisons from the self-governing colonies. Unable to see that this was a necessary result of the autonomy which these colonies now enjoyed, they preferred to interpret it as evidence of a wish to abandon overseas possessions. The alarmists found support in the protests against the new colonial defense policy which came from Australia and New Zealand, in the irritation caused by the refusal to grant the Australasian colonies permission to pass differential tariff laws, and in the resolutions discussed in the assembly of Victoria favoring a personal union with Britain. Although these storms blew over, the uneasiness over the future of the empire grew during the seventies and eighties, waxing especially strong after both France and Germany began pursuing an active policy of colonial expansion. The revival of demands that Britain too should push forward her imperial boundaries coincided with discussions of ways and means of checking imperial disintegration.

The extension of the franchise by the reform bills of 1867 and 1884 probably contributed toward the rise and growth of the new British imperialism. The laboring classes felt that they too had a share in the imperial patrimony of Britain and they were anxious to have it enlarged and made secure. The knowledge of the empire was increased and interest in it was stimulated by a number of remarkable books, foremost among which were *Greater Britain* by Sir Charles W. Dilke, published in 1868, *The Expansion of England* by J. R. Seeley, 1883, and *Oceana or England and Her Colonies* by J. A. Froude, 1886. Other proofs of the revival of an imperialistic spirit were public meetings and magazine articles devoted to the discussion of imperial problems, and the organization in 1868 of the Colonial Society, soon to be renamed the Royal Colonial Institute, which early became a potent factor in stimulating interest in and spreading knowledge concerning the empire.

Earl Russell, former leader of the Liberal party and twice prime minister, wrote in 1869 that he favored a colonial representative assembly, apart from the British parliament, which might vote contributions to the imperial army and navy. The question was discussed in the house of commons on May 31, 1872, when it was moved to appoint a commission to study means whereby the colonies might be admitted to participation in the government of the empire. But neither of these propositions aroused much attention. Later W. E. Forster, one of the most prominent among the leaders of the Liberal party, advocated imperial federation and was supported by other Liberals such as Lord Rosebery and James Bryce. The Imperial Federation League, with branches in both Britain and the colonies, was organized in 1884, and it waged a vigorous campaign for several years. But these discussions were purely academic. When challenged to produce a concrete program the movement collapsed, partly because Britain and the colonies did not see eye to eye on the tariff issue but principally because no satisfactory federal machinery of government could be devised. Though Gladstone and Salisbury differed on many things they agreed that imperial federation was impracticable. The latter believed that the self-governing colonies would soon proclaim their independence. Writing to Arthur Mills, November 21, 1891, he said: "I doubt that the self-governing Colonies will stay with us — *Amour propre* is too strong — & the difficulties of our managing their foreign relations is a real one."

Four years earlier he had spoken in a different tone when he opened the first colonial conference, precursor of a series of similar gatherings since called imperial. These conferences owed their inception to Edward (later Earl) Stanhope, who held the seals of the colonial office for a brief period from August, 1886, to January, 1887. True, something of the kind had been suggested by the Royal Colonial Institute in 1870 but had found favor neither with the colonial office nor with the colonies. By 1886, however, the situation had changed in important respects. Home rule for Ireland had been scotched in the election of that year, partly at least because of a surge of imperialistic sentiment; the self-governing colonies had showed their loyalty in the Sudan crisis of 1885 by offering aid to the mother country; the international situation was threatening; and a study of the existing economic depression had shown that Germany and the United States were becoming serious commercial rivals to Britain. In 1887 the empire would celebrate the golden jubilee of the reign of Queen Victoria, a splendid occasion for pageantry demonstrating imperial wealth and power. Surely no more propitious time could be found for a conference between representatives of the colonies and British ministers to discuss such vital questions as defense and "the promotion of commercial and social relations." So at least thought Stanhope, and the prime minister, Lord Salisbury, agreed. Consequently, in a circular dispatch of November 25, 1886, a gathering was suggested for an "interchange of knowledge" principally on the topics mentioned above. Political federation would not be debated because "there has been no expression of Colonial opinion in favour of any steps in that direction." The suggestion for a conference was well received. The conference held its first session April 4 and met intermittently until May 9, 1887; included were representatives of the crown colonies as well as of those with responsible government.

In the opening speech Lord Salisbury emphasized that the purpose of the conference was to see how far it was possible to overcome the effects of the physical disunion of the empire "by agreement and by organisation." He ruled out for the present imperial federation and an imperial customs union, the important business in his judgment being "the Union for the purposes of mutual defence." In addition to plenary sessions in which the general as well as the particular aspects of this and related questions were discussed, a secret session was devoted to the special problems of the South Pacific, New Guinea, the New Hebrides, and Samoa. Although Salisbury at this session stressed the need of placating France, this did not appear very urgent to at least one of the Australian delegates, Alfred Deakin, from Victoria. The immediate practical results of the conference were meager. The colonies admitted the principle of sharing the cost of defense, and those of Australasia agreed to an annual contribution of £126,000 for the upkeep of the imperial squadron in their waters. Sir Samuel Griffith of Queensland and Jan Hofmeyr from the Cape broached the question of an imperial tariff on goods imported from outside the empire, the proceeds from which should be used for imperial defense. While these proposals later received a good deal of attention, their discussion at the time brought no result. At the 1887 conference Lord Salisbury and the other British delegates were patronizing and condescending in their attitude toward the representatives of the colonies — the sovereign power had called a meeting of the vassals. This feeling was perhaps natural. Although Salisbury in his youth had visited Australia and studied some of the colonial problems, he had been out of touch with them for a long time; the acquaintance formed more than thirty years earlier was on the whole rather a handicap for an appreciation of the Australia of 1887. Both British and colonial statesmen needed education in the affairs of the empire. In that respect the conference was valuable. Moreover, the ice was broken, a precedent had been established for future gatherings of delegates from the far-flung portions of the British empire.

The next meeting was held at Ottawa in 1894. Called for the purpose of discussing a Pacific cable and commercial relations between Australasia and Canada, the Ottawa conference was limited as to both membership and scope. Delegates came from Canada, Australasia (except Western Australia), and the Cape. The imperial government sent no official representative, but only an observer, the Earl of Jersey, ex-governor of New South Wales. One reason for the abstention of the home government was that the conference would most likely discuss an imperial preferential tariff which the strongly free trade Liberal government then in office in England could not consider. The prognostication proved correct; during the conference the discussion of broad questions of imperial policy took precedence over the narrower ones which appeared on the agenda. Resolutions were passed favoring preferential tariffs, the abrogation of the commercial treaties with Belgium and Germany, and permission for the colonies to negotiate their own tariff treaties. All these points were gained within a few years.

Shortly after the Ottawa conference Joseph Chamberlain entered the colonial office. Since his administration forms a distinct epoch in British empire history, it will be treated separately; but for the sake of continuity a résumé must be given of the third colonial conference, held in 1897. This, too, came in a jubilee year, the diamond jubilee of Queen Victoria. The colonial conference had not yet become an established institution; hence a special occasion had to be utilized for calling one. This meeting, which included representatives from only self-governing colonies and Britain, with Joseph Chamberlain presiding, was held behind closed doors; only sketchy reports of its proceedings have been published. It met as the disputes in South Africa were rapidly reaching their fateful climax and when Canada had taken the first step toward a new tariff arrangement by granting a 12½ per cent preference on goods of British origin. That political relations were no longer to be excluded from the deliberations of the conference became clear when in his opening speech Chamberlain placed this topic first, followed by defense and commerce. He boldly proposed the establishment of an imperial council "to which the Colonies would send representative plenipotentiaries." It was his hope that such a council might ultimately grow into "that Federal Council to which we must always look forward as our ultimate ideal." But the response was not favorable. The colonial premiers considered the existing political relations satisfactory, and refused to commit themselves further than recommending extension of the principle of the federation of geographical united colonies and the continuance of periodic conferences between "representatives of the Colonies and Great Britain for the discussion of matters of common interests." Australasia agreed to increase her naval contributions to £200,000 per annum, the Cape offered a battleship, later changed to an annual contribution of £30,000, and Natal pledged £12,000 annually toward naval defense, but Canada refused to promise military or naval contributions. There was general agreement at the conference that the principle of preferential tariffs should be extended and that all hampering commercial treaties should be denounced.

Thus the Victorian era came to an end without any definite progress in the direction of drawing the self-governing colonies closer to Britain by means of new political bonds. But the aid which these colonies spontaneously gave to the mother country in her South African war greatly encouraged those who hoped for a new political arrangement, and Chamberlain convened the conference of 1902 in the belief that something in the nature of a federation might be accomplished. Meanwhile the economic relations between Britain and her overseas empire had become increasingly important; this topic will next engage our attention.

Although the annual percentage growth in the accumulation of British capital slowed down after 1873, it was still large; and British investors were anxious to find employment for their savings within the empire, having had disastrous experiences with loans to the Americas. Britain's surplus wealth became a factor in imperial expansion with the organization of the great chartered companies, the British North Borneo Company, 1881, the Royal Niger Company, 1886, the Imperial British East Africa Company, 1888, and the British South Africa Chartered Company, 1889; all added extensive domains to the empire. The chartered companies represent the most spectacular uses of British capital for empire-building, but even larger sums went more prosaically into the building of railroads, docks, and breakwaters and the financing of private ventures in crown and self-governing colonies alike. The opening up of the Canadian northwest as well as of the interior of Australia could not have been accomplished at this time had not private capital been available on the money market of London. And though British investors sometimes suffered losses as did those in Australia when the financial collapse came in 1891 to 1893, they felt safer within than outside the British empire. This preference was shown in a striking fashion in the attitude toward loans to British colonies as compared with those to foreign countries; the latter had to pay a higher rate amounting on the average to nearly one per cent. The interest on colonial bonds was, indeed, so low that *The Economist* doubted whether the colonists obtained a substantial saving when in 1900 their loans were made available for trust investments.

In contrast to the confidence in British colonies shown by private investors was the caution exercised by the British government in guaranteeing or extending loans to them. The loans outstanding in 1901 guaranteed by the imperial government included £1,000,000 of New Zealand loans, a £600,000 loan of Mauritius, and Canadian loans for railroads and the purchase of Rupert's Land. The Colonial Loans Bill, 1899, met with considerable opposition although the aggregate was only £3,300,000. The government had to stress the need for aid especially to the West Indies because of hurricanes and low sugar prices, and to promise that these loans would not constitute a precedent. Those were the days when British chancellors of the exchequer were unusually careful in handling the money of British taxpayers.

The imperial government could not check the tendency of the self-governing colonies to adopt protective tariffs, but India was in a different category. When the financial needs of India necessitated an import duty of 5 per cent ad valorem on cotton goods, Lancashire offered strong opposition on the ground that this meant a preference for goods made in India. The duty was abolished in 1882; when reintroduced twelve years later, an excise on Indian manufactures kept the balance even. In the crown colonies Britain maintained an open-door commercial policy, with no special advantage for British traders. The depression of the early nineties caused a slump in British exports, and shortly after Chamberlain became colonial secretary an inquiry was instituted to ascertain whether foreigners were capturing Britain's colonial markets. The information gathered was disquieting – between 1884 and 1894 the percentage of foreign imports into British colonies had increased from 25.79 to 31.50. The rise had been especially sharp during the years of the depression and was slightly higher than the drop in colonial purchase of British goods. On the basis of the yearly average for the triennium 1893–1895 as compared with the average for 1888–1890, the import of British goods into her own colonies fell by £4,616,446 while that of foreign goods rose by £4,694,122. These figures explain why the question of trade loomed so large in the discussions at the colonial conference of 1897. There was no real upswing in intra-imperial trade until the last two years of the century and some of this can be attributed to rising prices and the war in South Africa. Board of trade statistics for the fifteen years 1886–1900 showed that, the slump of the nineties being disregarded, Britain's imports from Canada, Australasia, Ceylon, and the Straits Settlements had increased, while her exports to British North America had remained stationary and those to Australasia had increased though not so much as her imports therefrom. Her favorable trade balances were chiefly with the African colonies, India, and Hongkong; but imports from and exports to India were shrinking, the former by £4,742,401 and the latter by £1,607,380. The trade with the colonies like the trade with foreign countries showed a distinct tendency to a balance adverse to Britain. Exports to her colonies in 1886 exceeded imports to the extent of £448,432, while in 1900 her imports from them, exclusive of Cape diamonds, topped her exports to them by £7,506,578.

Loans and trade constituted the old forms of economic connections between the various parts of the British empire; but new times demanded new methods and new types of contact, several of which had been developed before the advent of Joseph Chamberlain. In the seventies the Royal Botanic Gardens at Kew, London, cooperated with the colonial office in working for afforestation, investigation of oil-producing nuts, improvements in the breeding of such plants as cotton and sugar cane, the fight against plant diseases, and the spread of the cultivation of tobacco, indigo, sisal and rhea grass, and, what later attracted so much attention, the rubber tree. The great rubber plantations in Malaya owe their origin to seed sent thither from Kew. Nor did the colonial office neglect stock-breeding and the fight against animal diseases. Economic planning by the imperial government was a large factor in developing the agricultural possibilities of West Africa and the Malay Peninsula. "The Imperial Institute of the United Kingdom, the Colonies and India, and the Isles of the British Seas" set up at South Kensington in 1888 had among its objects to study the economic interests common to the entire empire, to spread information and give advice, and to summon conferences for the discussion of economic, technical, and scientific problems of a practical nature. In line with this program was the work of the chambers of commerce, the first general conference of which was held in London in 1886. From 1890 on, the Liverpool chamber of commerce became especially active in the development and exploitation of West Africa. These were all signs of the new British imperialism that spread and grew stronger in the closing decades of the nineteenth century.

But in modern times as in days of old, the trader, the farmer, and the scholar work behind the shelter provided by the fighting services. Their importance in the empire and for empire policy loomed larger as the international situation became more alarming; hence they must be explained and traced in an historical account of the British empire, 1870–1901. The recall of the imperial garrisons from the colonies with responsible government was deemed completed by March 7, 1873, when an announcement to this effect was made in the house of commons by Edward Knatchbull-Hugessen, the parliamentary undersecretary of state for the colonies. An exception had been made, however, in the case of the Cape, where imperial troops were kept because of the strength of the native population both within the colony and outside. Because colonial responsibility was limited to local defense whereas protection against a foreign foe remained a duty of the imperial government, the naval stations of Halifax and Esquimalt in Canada continued to be garrisoned by imperial troops. The Canadians, however, had agreed in 1865 to spend at least one million dollars annually on military defense, an obligation that was assumed by the Dominion. Moreover, a Colonial Naval Defense Act of 1865 authorized the colonies to make provisions for naval forces.

As already indicated, the new colonial defense policy was interpreted as an effort on the part of the Liberal government to disintegrate the empire. Discussions on this issue provoked striking statements concerning empire policy by Disraeli and Gladstone, leaders respectively of the Conservatives and the Liberals. Speaking at the Crystal Palace June 24, 1872, Disraeli said: "Self-government when it was conceded, ought to have been conceded as a part of a great policy of Imperial consolidation. It ought to have been accompanied by an Imperial tariff, by securities for the people of England for the enjoyment of the unappropriated lands which belonged to the Sovereign as their trustee, and by a military code which should have precisely defined the means and the responsibilities by which the Colonies should have been defended, and by which, if necessary, this country should call for aid from the Colonies themselves." This statement was a clever political pronouncement, but it proved that the speaker did not understand the spirit of the self-governing colonies or conditions there. He doubtless appreciated the hollowness of his own argument inasmuch as he never made an attempt to realize the program embodied therein. In vivid contrast to the principle enunciated by Disraeli was that of Gladstone, proclaimed in a debate in the house of commons on a motion to invite each colony "to contribute, in proportion to its population and wealth, such annual contingents of men and money towards the defence of the Empire as may, by arrangement between the Home and Colonial Governments, be hereafter deemed just and necessary." In opposing this motion Gladstone said: "What we wish is not that the Colonies should under pressure from this country be brought to make, probably not insignificant, but at any rate grudging, contributions towards the expenses of the Empire; what we wish is to see the growth of the true spirit of freedom in the colonial communities which would make them not only willing, but eager, to share all the responsibilities of freedom and to take a part in the common burdens."

But the colonies showed no eagerness to do this. They all seemed safe from foreign attacks, at least so long as Britain remained mistress of the sea, and as new communities they had little capital. There was not enough available for their social and economic needs, and none to spare for unproductive military and naval armaments. Hence, until 1896 when an Anglo-American conflict seemed within the range of possibilities, Canada spent only little more than a million dollars on her militia, only a small portion of which received a semblance of military training each year. The cost of the militia jumped to $2,500,000 in 1900 and more systematic training was begun. Of naval forces Canada had none except what was needed for fishery patrol. Australia showed a similar lag, although New South Wales and Victoria had a few gunboats as part of a coast defense system. The recurrent wars with the Kaffirs boosted the military expenditures at the Cape, reported in 1887 at £450,000 a year, "or between one-sixth and one-seventh of the whole of our resources." Statements prepared for the colonial conference of that year showed that the self-governing colonies and Natal then had wholly or partially trained forces numbering 78,000 officers and men, with large reserves. By 1899 the number had grown to 86,486. The imperial government occasionally tried to create or stimulate interest in naval defense by presenting the colonies with old warships. Canada was given the *Charybdis,* New South Wales the *Wolverine,* and Victoria the *Cerberus* and the *Nelson.* All were obsolete; although used occasionally for ceremonial purposes, they were a failure as a means of making these colonies interested in a navy of their own.

Meanwhile, the imperial government began to show concern for the defense of the colonies, especially those of Australasia. A royal commission on colonial defense with Lord Carnarvon as chairman was appointed in 1879, its special task being to investigate "in what proportions the cost . . . of measures of defence should be divided between the Imperial Government and the Colonies to which they relate." The commission presented its final report in 1882, in favor of colonial participation in the cost of imperial defense. Three years later a colonial defense committee came into existence, which in 1895 became a part of the larger body known as the Committee of Imperial Defence. The defense needs of Australia were studied in the seventies by two royal engineers, Sir W. D. Jervois and Colonel Scratchley; in 1885 Admiral Tryon presented a report on Australian naval defense. The investigation of Australian preparedness for war conducted in 1889 by Major-General Bevan Edwards deserves special mention because his report gave impetus to a federation movement culminating in the establishment of the Commonwealth of Australia. Imperial defense was one of the major topics for discussion at the 1887 and 1897 colonial conferences, discussions which resulted in contributions for naval defense from Australasia and South Africa.

In the meantime proofs had been forthcoming showing that Gladstone's confidence in colonial "voluntaryism" in matters pertaining to defense had not been misplaced. The threat of war with Russia in 1878 produced spontaneous demonstrations of loyalty to the empire in Australia and Canada. Volunteers presented themselves in sufficient number to warrant the belief that in case of war at least 30,000 Canadians would have given their services. Similar demonstrations took place during the Sudan crisis of 1885, with offers from Canada, Victoria, and New South Wales. The offer of the last was accepted and on April 4, 1885, a military contingent of nearly 800 embarked at Sydney amid strong demonstrations of imperial loyalty. Though it returned from the Sudan without having seen active service, the expedition was nevertheless epoch-making as being the first dispatched from a self-governing colony for the purpose of fighting in an imperial war. The precedent set was followed during the Anglo-Boer war of 1899–1902. Before the war broke out, messages of loyalty from overseas poured into the colonial office. In Canada the French element in the population held back, and a vigorous opposition against sending troops to South Africa was started by M. Henri Bourassa; but the French-Canadian prime minister, Sir Wilfrid Laurier, stood firm in advocating aid to the imperial cause. About 8000 Canadians served the empire in various ways during the South African war. The number includes a cavalry regiment, Strathcona's Horse, raised and equipped at the expense of Lord Strathcona, then Canadian high commissioner in London, but not the battalion which relieved for duty in South Africa the imperial forces that till then had garrisoned Halifax. The Australian colonies sent more than 16,000 and New Zealand contributed 6500 officers and men to the British army in South Africa. "Voluntaryism" triumphed at last.

Toward the close of the nineteenth century imperial relations grew more complex, and additional burdens were thrown upon the colonial office. The improved means of communications, particularly the telegraph, altered the position of the colonial governor. Instead of being "the man on the spot" left free to make important decisions and even to formulate policies, he became "the man at the end of the wire" whose activities were controlled and directed from Downing Street. While on the outposts there was less room for personalities of the type of Lachlan Macquarie and Sir George Grey, the colonial office stood in greater need of forceful men like Joseph Chamberlain. Of the permanent staff, Sir Robert W. Herbert, undersecretary from 1871 to 1892, has the distinction of having occupied that important office longer than any other man. Moreover, before he reached the top in the civil service, he had held positions as private secretary to Gladstone, prime minister of Queensland in 1860–1865, and assistant undersecretary first at the board of trade and then in the colonial office. He could therefore speak with the authority acquired from intimate knowledge of and long association with colonial problems. He favored the annexation of New Guiana and recommended that South African federation should be promoted by the colonial office; and in constitutional disputes he, like his predecessors, was generally willing to let the colonists have their way. Perhaps his greatest service to the empire lay in his encouragement of scientific investigations and aid of the type rendered by the Botanic Gardens at Kew. The post of colonial secretary was held during this period by distinguished statesmen like Lord Granville and Sir Michael Hicks Beach, and by Henry Holland, later Lord Knutsford, who had occupied a subordinate position in the office before he became its political head. But none of them made outstanding contributions to imperial policy like those rendered by Lord John Russell, 1839–1841, and Earl Grey, 1846–1852, until Joseph Chamberlain assumed control in June, 1895.

Chamberlain at an early age had made a fortune in the screw-manufacturing business at Birmingham, his principal contribution being in connection with marketing the finished product. As mayor of Birmingham, 1874–1876, he made that city the "Municipal Mecca," with its excellent municipally owned gas and waterworks, its parks and recreation grounds, and its success in slum clearance. The city's wealth and resources were used for the benefit of all its citizens. The same energy and genius for organization and getting things done he carried into the arena of national politics where his caucus system, borrowed at least in part from America, contributed materially to the Liberal success in the election of 1880. He was first elected to parliament in 1876, where he was known as a radical because of his advocacy of free, compulsory, and secular education, social and economic reform, and his scant respect for the monarchy. As a member of the Gladstone government, 1880–1885, he was president of the board of trade and leader of the radical wing of the cabinet. He broke with Gladstone over Irish home rule and thus added the advocacy of imperial unity to his other causes. Chamberlain remained throughout life an ambitious, hard-hitting business man, a "go-getter." As colonial secretary he became chairman of the board of directors of Britain's greatest business enterprise at a time when trade statistics and the political trend seemed to indicate that it was headed for liquidation.

As mayor of Birmingham he had championed efficiency and government *for* the people; as colonial secretary he pursued the same goals. The colonial office was reorganized and a system introduced whereby each clerk spent at least one year in a colony, the vacancy thus created being filled by a colonial. Shortly after Chamberlain assumed control a special inquiry was sent to all the colonies aimed at eliciting information about the state of trade, especially the growth of foreign competition; and in the following year a royal commission was appointed to investigate conditions in the West Indies, particularly the sugar industry. The name of Joseph Chamberlain is associated with imperial expansion, agreements with France concerning West Africa, the successful promotion of road and railroad building in crown colonies and protectorates, the establishment of imperial departments of agriculture for the West Indies and West Africa and of schools of tropical medicine at Liverpool and London, the organization of the Colonial Nurses Association, the appointment of a malaria commission to study this scourge of West Africa on the spot, the creation of a special commercial intelligence branch of the board of trade, the grant of assistance and development loans to crown colonies, and the admission of colonial loans to the investments available for trust funds. He showed an amazingly wide range of interests and fertility of resource in devising ways and means for developing Britain's great overseas "estate." No wonder that the special appropriations in the British budget for crown colonies and protectorates rose from £217,570 in 1895–1896 to £890,240 in 1899–1900.

In dealing with the colonies having responsible government Chamberlain scrupulously refrained from interfering with their local affairs; but when New Zealand passed a Shipping and Seaman Act which impinged on imperial legislation he immediately called a halt. Nor was he unmindful of imperial obligations to the natives of Australia and South Africa. He urged the federation of Australia, but guarded against having the Commonwealth sever a bond of union with Britain such as provided by the appeals to the judicial committee of the privy council. His chief efforts were, indeed, directed toward securing closer political connections between the self-governing colonies and the mother country and a greater amount of cooperation in matters pertaining to commerce and defense. Hence the emphasis on these topics at the colonial conference of 1897 and the great appreciation shown of the aid which the colonies gave Britain in the Anglo-Boer war.

Chamberlain was an imperialist both in the sense of tightening the bonds within the empire and in that of favoring aggression on the frontiers. His actions indicate that he considered an offense the best defense. Hence his support of the Cape-to-Cairo railroad scheme and the claims of the Uitlanders in the Transvaal which precipitated the Boer War, 1899–1902. In common with several of the middle-aged statesmen of the late Victorian era, Chamberlain felt the need of ending the diplomatic isolation of Britain, and from 1898 on he made several unsuccessful efforts to establish an Anglo-German *entente*. This, too, was part and parcel of his general policy to strengthen and make safe Britain's vast empire.

In comparing the intra-imperial relations and the imperial policy of Britain as the twentieth century opened with those of

1870, one is impressed on the one hand by the growth of freedom and on the other with the extent to which new contacts and purposeful planning had replaced drift and *laissez faire.* Not only had crown colonies advanced to the status of colonies with representative government and colonies in this class moved the further step and secured responsible government, but those in the last category had progressed in the direction of political sovereignty by attaining complete control over immigration and the right to negotiate commercial treaties. The high commissioner for the Dominion of Canada and the agents-general for the colonies with responsible government held positions of undefined rank which, however, began to approximate that of a hybrid between the consular and the diplomatic representatives of independent states. Even where the old arrangements still prevailed as in the appointment of a governor or a governor general and appeals to the judicial committee of the privy council, changes showing an unmistakable tendency to greater freedom had crept in. The government of Canada was now consulted in the choice of the governor general, the wishes of the Australian colonies could not be ignored in the selection of their governors, and colonial judges might take their place by the side of British judges on the judicial committee. The latter privilege might, of course, be taken as a move toward imperial consolidation in line with the colonial conferences, contributions to imperial defense, and the Canadian preferential tariff; on the other hand, it indicated also a growing recognition of equality of status with Britain. Canada and the self-governing colonies were ceasing to be dependent units; the character of the empire was changing.

As a complement to the advance toward the later commonwealth ideal of the intra-imperial relationship there had grown up within Britain a greater appreciation of the value of the overseas empire. Private organizations advocated the maintenance and strengthening of the sentimental, racial, and cultural bonds of empire; imperial statesmen and royal princes went on tours of the empire; and colonists visited and were welcomed by

Britain. Efforts were made to safeguard Britain's position as the cultural center of the empire as well as the center whence were sent financial assistance, advice concerning the health of men, beasts and plants, and suggestions for the utilization of the soil, the introduction of new plants, and the improvement of the old. Under a former dispensation the colonies had existed for the benefit of Britain; under the new, the emphasis was laid on the services that Britain could render them. Thus further ties were created; and all the while one old link of empire — the queen, wearer of the royal and imperial crown — added to its strength with the advancing years. By January, 1901, few could remember any British sovereign but Queen Victoria. She had become their *alma mater,* an institution, a symbol of devotion to duty, and the ideal of an empire one and indivisible. The variety of races, languages, interests, and political, social, and economic institutions within that empire almost passed human comprehension, but there was only one *Queen.*

CHAPTER 20

BRITISH NORTH AMERICA, 1867–1901

IN 1867 the Dominion of Canada included the two provinces, Ontario and Quebec, into which old Canada had been divided, Nova Scotia, and New Brunswick. Rupert's Land was purchased from the Hudson's Bay Company in 1869 and out of it was carved, in 1870, the Province of Manitoba; in the following year British Columbia and in 1873 Prince Edward Island joined the new federation; and the imperial government in 1880 formally annexed to it all the British possessions in North America except Newfoundland and its dependencies. Today the Dominion embraces an area of 3,745,000 square miles. In 1871 this vast domain had a population of barely 3,500,000. With the exception of old Canada and the Maritimes, the Dominion at this time was an empty land and one divided by natural barriers into four sections — the Atlantic border, the region of the St. Lawrence and the Great Lakes, the plains of the northwest, and the Pacific coast. Canadian statesmen faced the problem of overcoming these barriers by means of railroads; they had to develop a governmental machinery suitable to the needs and claims of sections, of provinces, of two racial groups, British and French, of diverging religions, and of a rising Canadian nationalism. The period from 1867 to 1901 was one of Canada in the making. Politically, economically, and socially, the Dominion experienced growing pains.

A Conservative-Liberal coalition in old Canada under the leadership of Sir John A. Macdonald was largely responsible for the creation of the Dominion. Sir John became its first prime minister; and except for a break of five years, 1873–1878, he served in this capacity until his death in 1891. Between 1867 and 1891 he fought seven elections, losing only one, that of 1874. The coalition broke up early in the period, and Macdonald became leader of the Conservative party. Several of his allies of the Confederation days, such as George Brown of the Toronto *Globe*, parted company with him and returned to their former position as his bitter critics; but he was on the whole remarkably successful in maintaining himself as a *national* leader. In forming and reforming his cabinets he was able to solve the jigsaw puzzle of provincial, racial, and religious rivalries; and not until his declining years and the elevation of a French-Canadian, Wilfrid (later Sir Wilfrid) Laurier, to the leadership of the Liberals did that party become intrenched in the province of Quebec in a manner analogous to the intrenchment of the Democratic party in the southern states of the American union.

In the election of 1872, Sir John committed the blunder of personally soliciting campaign funds from Sir Hugh Allan, who later secured a contract for the construction of the Canadian Pacific Railway. This made necessary his retirement from office in 1873 and caused the defeat of his party in the election of 1874. Otherwise Macdonald was seldom guilty of political blunders. Wary and supple, a past master of political strategy and tactics, a hard and not overly scrupulous fighter, he was without a peer in the arena of the Canadian politics of his day. He had mastered the art of the politician and he had the vision of a statesman. In the hectic days of the agitation for a Canadian federation as well as in the even more trying years that followed, he never lost sight of the need for laying a solid economic and constitutional foundation for the new nation. He urged the construction of the railroads that linked the coast of the Atlantic with that of the Pacific; he insisted on asserting the supremacy of the federal government over the provinces; the "Canada first" cry had been raised by the Liberals, but outwitting his opponents he capitalized on the sentiment underlying this slogan by making a national tariff policy the chief issue in the election of 1878; when a dozen years later a demand arose for closer commercial relations with the United States, he stood forth as the champion of Canadian nationalism within the British empire. Macdonald generally succeeded in compelling his opponents to give battle on issues chosen by him. For this reason the Liberals of his day became supporters of provincial rights and a low tariff.

Between 1867 and 1873 a French-Canadian, Sir George Cartier, was Macdonald's trusted ally and lieutenant, but after Cartier's death Sir John was the boss of the Conservative party. Sir Charles Tupper of Nova Scotia came nearest to being a second in command; however, he was sent to London in 1884 as Canadian high commissioner and hence ceased to have much influence in Dominion politics until after Macdonald's death. Joseph Howe, who had played a brilliant role in the politics of Nova Scotia in the thirties and forties, caused Macdonald some annoyance during 1867–1869 by reversing his stand on federation to the extent of advocating the secession of his province. But Macdonald persuaded Howe to join the government; on the latter's death in 1873 he was lieutenant-governor of Nova Scotia.

The opposition to Macdonald crystallized in the late sixties under the leadership of George Brown, Alexander Mackenzie, and Edward Blake in the organization of the Liberal party. Mackenzie was chosen its first leader. He was, like Macdonald, a native of Scotland; honest, industrious, and a capable administrator, he lacked the political adroitness and ruthlessness required in the warfare against Macdonald. When the latter was compelled to resign in 1873 because of the Canadian Pacific Railway scandal, Mackenzie became the head of the Liberal government which won a great victory in the election of 1874. Mackenzie apparently was bewildered by the victory; the depression which swept Canada at that time added to his worries; as minister of public works he found it difficult to handle contractors; and he was unable to enforce discipline among his colleagues. The most brilliant and erratic among these was Edward Blake, who in 1880 succeeded Mackenzie as leader of the Liberals. Although an able lawyer, Blake was too unstable and thin-skinned for the rough and tumble game of Canadian politics. Sir Oliver Mowat, Liberal prime minister of Ontario, 1873–1896, at times showed himself a match for Macdonald, but he preferred to exercise his talents on the provincial stage. When Wilfrid Laurier succeeded Blake in 1887, the Liberals at last secured a leader comparable to Macdonald. With a charming personality and great oratorical gifts Laurier combined political skill, courage, and sagacity. As a French-Canadian and Roman Catholic he was especially acceptable to the population of Quebec which soon voted almost solidly for the Liberal party in the federal elections. The rise of Laurier and the Liberals was aided by the confusion which beset the Conservatives following the death of Macdonald on June 6, 1891. Charges of corruption, the difficulties connected with the Manitoba school question (to be discussed later), inability to rally behind the new leaders, and losses by death among these leaders resulted in defeat for the Conservatives in the election of 1896. Laurier then began his career as prime minister which lasted until 1911.

Despite earnest and strenuous efforts to the contrary, religion and race crept into Canadian politics. In Ontario the Orange Lodge was strong and inclined to chant "To hell with the pope," which of course offended the French-Canadian Roman Catholic element of Quebec. When one of their compatriots, Louis Riel, leader of the Red River rebellion in 1870 and the Northwest rebellion in 1885, was hanged, French-Canadians asserted loudly that his crimes had been only political, and that he was executed because of his religion and his race. Three years later the legislature of Quebec voted to pay $400,000 to the Society of Jesus as compensation for the estates seized by the government when that order was suppressed late in the eighteenth century. This vote was accompanied by increased grants to the protestant schools of the province; nevertheless, the Orangemen of Ontario tried to force Macdonald to disallow the Quebec act, but he refused to interfere. Shortly afterward an issue involving religion and provincial rights was raised in Manitoba. In 1871 this province established a system of separate tax-supported denominational schools similar to those in Ontario and Quebec which had been safeguarded by the British North America Act. But a Manitoba act of 1890 discontinued the provincial aid to denominational schools and inaugurated a system of free secular education based on American models. In this instance the Roman Catholics wished to invoke the power of the federal government to disallow provincial acts. The issue proved troublesome for the four Conservative prime ministers who succeeded Macdonald. Laurier settled it temporarily in 1896 with an arrangement whereby religious instruction might be given after school hours in separate rooms in the tax-supported schools of Manitoba.

The changes in the political structure of Canada in the years 1867–1901 were connected chiefly with a clearer definition of the relations between the federal government and those of the provinces, reforms in the government of the federal territories, alterations in the provincial governments, and efforts to free Canada from imperial restrictions imposed by law, custom, and foreign treaties.

The power of the federal government was strengthened when it secured control over bankruptcy legislation and when a supreme court was created for Canada in 1875. The judicial committee of the privy council in England, however, remained the court of last resort to which appeals might be taken from both the supreme court of Canada and the higher courts of the provinces. In 1888 an attempt was made to abandon such appeals in criminal cases, an effort which did not succeed until 1931. Sir John A. Macdonald, eager to assert the supremacy of the federal government over the provinces, secured the veto of provincial laws dealing with landholding and the regulation of railroads, and other acts which allegedly violated property right and the sanctity of contract. As a champion of centralization he had the support of economic and financial interests in Montreal and Toronto; his most formidable opponent on this issue was Sir Oliver Mowat. The provinces scored several victories in appeals to the judicial committee, which, in 1895, laid down that within the sphere defined as provincial the provincial governments were supreme. After this decision and the Liberal victory in the election of 1896 federal disallowance of provincial acts became less frequent.

By the purchase of Rupert's Land and the cession to Canada of the North-Western Territory, the Dominion acquired a large federal domain. Part of it became the province of Manitoba in 1870 and the rest was organized as the North West Territories. The Territories were given a partially elected legislative council in 1875, an elective assembly in 1888, and responsible government in 1897. The discovery of gold in 1897 in the extreme northwest, the Klondike, was followed by a great inrush of gold miners and the consequent organization of the Yukon as a separate territory in 1898.

Among other changes of a political character are to be noted that British Columbia obtained responsible government at the time of her admission to the Dominion, and that Manitoba in 1876 and New Brunswick in 1892 abolished the second chamber. The only serious political disturbances with which the Dominion had to deal were the Riel rebellion at Fort Garry (Winnipeg) in 1870 and the Northwest rebellion in the valley of the Saskatchewan in 1885. Both were disturbances by half-breeds who feared that under the new surveys they would lose their land. Louis Riel figured as leader of these uprisings. The former came to an end before imperial military forces with a Canadian contingent reached Fort Garry; the latter was put down by a Canadian force after some fighting. In 1870 Riel fled to the United States; he returned later to Canada and was elected to and expelled from the Canadian house of commons. When the half-breeds of the Northwest prepared to rise in 1885 they invited Riel, then living in Montana, to become their leader. He accepted, was captured by the Canadian forces and executed at Regina, November 16, 1885.

No spectacular changes took place in the relations between the Dominion and the mother country, but the trend of developments was unmistakably in the direction of greater autonomy for Canada. Canadians, notably Edward Blake when Dominion minister of justice from 1875 to 1877, objected to statements in the royal instructions to governors general concerning the reservation of bills, the exercise of the power of pardon, and other matters deemed within the purview of the Dominion government. The instructions were changed in 1878 in conformity with the wishes of Canada. The reservation of Canadian acts for the signification of the queen's pleasure, which of course meant the pleasure of the home government, became a mere formality; and the imperial government was careful to choose governors general who were acceptable to the Canadians. Appointed to this post were generally noblemen of ancient lineage; one of them, the Marquis of Lorne, 1878–1883, was a son-in-law of Queen Victoria. The governor general continued to be the official agent for communications between the governments of Canada and Britain, a situation not materially altered after the appointment in 1879 of a Canadian high commissioner in London, whose duties were in the main commercial. The first occupants of this post, Sir Alexander Galt and Sir Charles Tupper, were, however, statesmen of great ability, experience, and force of character; they therefore elevated it to one of considerable importance, especially in matters pertaining to the commercial position of the Dominion.

In 1867 and for many years afterward all portions of the British empire were bound by commercial treaties negotiated by the home government. The restrictions thus imposed were irksome to the colonies; but they were relaxed so as to permit special tariff arrangements among the British North American colonies. The adoption of protective tariffs by Canada and the other self-governing colonies, except New South Wales, while the imperial government adhered to free trade, created awkward situations. This was realized by Lord Carnarvon, colonial secretary from 1874 to 1878, who in 1877 admitted that although the old commercial treaties must bind all colonies, adherence to new ones might be made optional for those who possessed self-government. When in the late seventies Canada desired a commercial treaty with France, the British ambassador to France, Lord Lyons, was instructed to leave the negotiations for it mainly in the hands of Sir Alexander Galt lest the treaty, which of necessity must recognize Canada's protective tariff policy, might compromise the free trade policy of Britain. A result of this logic was that in 1893 Sir Charles Tupper signed a Franco-Canadian commercial treaty as joint plenipotentiary with the then British ambassador, Lord Dufferin.

At the colonial economic conference in Ottawa in 1894, the colonies demanded freedom to negotiate their own commercial treaties and the abrogation of Britain's commercial treaties with Belgium and Germany which prevented self-governing colonies from granting tariff favors to each other or to Britain. The Liberal colonial secretary, Lord Ripon, in a dispatch of June 28, 1895, refused to allow Canada to negotiate directly in commercial matters with a foreign power, but his Unionist successor, Joseph Chamberlain, was more lenient. The treaties with Belgium and Germany to which the colonies had objected were denounced in 1897, leaving Canada free to grant preferential tariff treatment to certain classes of goods of British origin. At first the preference amounted to 12 1/2 per cent; it was later raised to 25 and ultimately to 33 1/3 per cent.

Sir John A. Macdonald was one of the British representatives on the high commission that negotiated the Treaty of Washington in 1871, not because Britain wanted to grant Canada a share in the conduct of foreign relations but because it was foreseen that Canadian legislation was required to put the treaty into operation. Macdonald described his position as that of "a hostage"; without his support the parliament of Canada would hardly have accepted the provisions of the treaty dealing with the rights of American fishermen in Canadian waters and American use of Canadian waterways. Canada was also represented on the American-British fisheries claims commission in 1874, and at the international cable conference in Paris in 1883. Thus by slow degrees the colonial status was left behind and approaches were made toward a national status. Matters of high politics, however, were of less concern to the average Canadian than those dealing with communications, the public land policy, the settlement of the open spaces, and the growth of industry and commerce. These topics will be treated in the order given.

In the sixties the Maritimes demanded an intercolonial railroad as part of their price for entering the federation desired by Canada. The request was granted. At the first session of the Dominion parliament an act was passed authorizing the construction of such a railroad by the federal government, and by 1876 it had been completed from Halifax, Nova Scotia, to a point near Levis, on the southern bank of the St. Lawrence opposite Quebec. This western terminus, however, proved unsatisfactory; and by purchase and agreements with other lines the Intercolonial finally gained entrance to Montreal.

British Columbia followed the example set by the Maritimes in demanding a railroad, a transcontinental road. Although in 1871 Sir John A. Macdonald agreed to have it built within ten years, the enterprise seemed too large to be undertaken by the Dominion government. Following the American precedent set in the case of the Union Pacific, the government of Canada promised liberal subsidies in the form of land grants and money for the building of a Canadian transcontinental railroad. The bait was alluring, and a keen competition for the contract developed between rival syndicates headed respectively by D. L. Macpherson of Toronto and Sir Hugh Allan of Montreal. The latter won in 1872. Later, when it was discovered that he had contributed about $300,000 to the funds of the Conservative party during the election campaign of that year, Macdonald's political opponents and Allan's business rivals united in a cry of corruption that drove Macdonald from office and caused the cancellation of the railroad contract. During the Liberal administration of Mackenzie, 1873–1878, the government tried to redeem its pledge to British Columbia by building sections of the railroad and filling gaps between them by arranging for water transportation by lakes and rivers. This policy was continued for a short time by the Conservatives after their return to power in 1878, but it was deemed a failure and abandoned. Consequently, in 1880 an agreement was concluded between the Dominion government and the Canadian Pacific Railway Company for the construction within ten years of a line connecting Callander, near Lake Nipissing in Ontario, with Vancouver. The aid promised by the government included transference to the company of the sections of the railroad already built, $25,000,000 in cash, 25,000,000 acres of land along the route, the privilege of importing materials duty free, a monopoly on traffic and on the construction of branch lines for a period of twenty years, and tax exemption for a similar period on the land held by the railroad. When this support proved insufficient, government loans totaling $27,500,000 were granted to the company which pushed the construction with so much vigor that the last spike of the Canadian Pacific Railway was driven on November 7, 1885. As the Intercolonial had been compelled to extend westward, so the C.P.R. had to extend eastward; ultimately it succeeded in entering not only Montreal and Quebec but also Halifax. The men most prominently connected with the building of these two railroads were William Van Horne, Sanford Fleming, Donald Smith, later Lord Strathcona, and George Stephen, afterward Lord Mount Stephen.

The railroads superseded the canals as the means for uniting British North America and as aids for the spread of settlements;

nevertheless, the older system of transport continued to be of great economic importance from the head of Lake Superior eastward. The Welland Canal and the canals of the St. Lawrence were deepened to fourteen feet during 1885 to 1901, and the lock at Sault Ste. Marie was enlarged to take care of the increased traffic. This traffic, at least in part, was due to the growing population of the Canadian northwest.

By the Public Lands Act of 1872, homesteads of 160 acres were granted from the public domain to persons over 21 years of age. This method of attracting settlers was adopted also by the provinces of British Columbia, Ontario, and Quebec. *Bona fide* settlers might obtain additional land on easy terms, the limit being 640 acres. By a system of passenger warrants the cost of the ocean passage was lowered for desirable immigrants, aid was extended to defray the expense of their inland transportation, and the head tax on them was abolished in 1873. The liberal support offered by the Dominion to settlers on its land evoked some criticism in the older provinces; consequently the subsidy for inland transportation was discontinued in 1885 and that for ocean transportation was abandoned in 1888 but revived two years later. Private companies were organized for the purpose of bringing in settlers, the best known among them being the Commercial Colonization Company of Manitoba; but none of these companies played a role comparable to that played by those that had operated in the Canadas early in the century. Considerable success did, however, attend the efforts of the Canadian Pacific Railway Company to attract settlers for its land. As the nineteenth century closed, this company was engaged in a vigorous advertising campaign, thereby securing both land purchasers and passengers for its trains.

Another feature of the peopling of western Canada in the late nineteenth century was the religious and nationalist group settlement. Primitive Methodists, German-American Roman Catholics, German-speaking Mennonites from Russia, Russian Doukhobors, Ukrainians, and Icelanders established communities in Manitoba or the North West Territories. The opportunities for free land and economic betterment were, of course, utilized by young men and women in the older provinces; thus settlers from Ontario early took land along the route of the Canadian Pacific Railway. In Quebec, however, the Roman Catholic Church viewed with disfavor the scattering of its flock either to the Canadian northwest or to the United States. In an effort to check the tendency to dispersal, Father Labelle in the seventies and eighties made strenuous and fairly successful efforts to extend the frontier of settlement northward in Quebec.

To the chagrin of patriotic Canadians, the progress of the Dominion in wealth and population, 1867–1901, failed to keep pace with that of the adjoining sections of its southern neighbor. At the close of the century the population of Canada totaled 5,371,315; of these, 4,671,815 were Canadian-born. By this time the tide of European immigration to Canada was swelling every year, bringing many non-British settlers. The census of 1881 showed that 478,235 Canadians had been born in the British Isles or in British possessions other than those in North America; by 1901 the number had fallen to 405,883. Within the same period the number of other foreign-born had risen from 131,083 to 278,788; to these the United States contributed 77,753 in 1881 and 127,899 in 1901. The migration of people from this country to Canada was, however, more than offset by a stronger movement in the opposite direction. The United States census of 1900 disclosed about 1,100,000 residents born in Canada, many of them French-Canadians who had moved into Vermont and New Hampshire.

Generally speaking, Canada welcomed immigrants except those from Asia. Already in the seventies British Columbia was apprehensive because of the influx of Chinese immigrants; and their number increased considerably in the eighties when contractors engaged in the construction of the Canadian Pacific Railway found it profitable to import Chinese coolies. In 1901 British Columbia had 17,000 Chinese. Early provincial acts for the exclusion of Chinese were disallowed by the Dominion; later, however, the Dominion passed similar acts and became involved in controversies with the imperial government which deprecated discriminatory legislation against the subjects of a friendly power. Despite opposition from Downing Street, the Dominion head tax of $50 on Chinese immigrants, authorized in 1885, was increased to $100 in 1901. The self-governing colonies secured the right to control immigration; like Australasia, Canada was determined to be a white man's country.

British Columbia, the North West Territories, and Manitoba grew rapidly in the years 1871–1901, while the Maritimes, especially Prince Edward Island, showed but a small increase. Old Canada was relatively nearly as dominant in 1901 as in 1871. At the earlier date the joint population of Quebec and Ontario was 2,812,367 out of about 3,500,000; in 1901 it was 3,831,845 out of 5,371,315. Montreal and Toronto were the financial and commercial centers of Canada. The population of the former rose from 115,000 in 1871 to 267,730 thirty years later; that of Toronto increased from 59,000 to 208,040. Within the same period the population of the city of Quebec grew from 59,699 to 68,840; a striking contrast to the slow growth of the old city was the population figure for Winnipeg, 241 in 1871 and 42,340 in 1901.

Despite the growth of urban communities and the efforts of the Dominion government to foster manufactures by means of the "national policy" of protective tariff, Canada in 1901 as in 1867 was largely an agricultural country. Between 1891 and 1901 the area in field crops, with wheat and oats leading, increased by 4,100,929 acres; the number of milk cows increased 29.9, other horned cattle 40, hogs 35.7, and poultry 27 per cent in the last decade of the nineteenth century. Dairying which ranked eighth among manufactures in 1891 had reached third place in 1901; and the latter census disclosed that agriculture contributed 85 per cent of the value of the finished products of Canadian industries. Forests and mines came next to agriculture in economic importance, the value of the output of the mines being boosted by the rich gold finds in the Klondike. In 1871 the output of gold in the Dominion was given as 22,941 and in 1901 as 862,000 ounces. The miners of the Klondike produced in 1897 two and a half and in 1900 twenty-two million dollars' worth of gold.

In common with the rest of North America, and indeed the world, Canada suffered from the economic depression of the seventies and nineties and from the fall in the price level. For Canada this drop has been computed as being from 111 in 1873 to 61 in 1896; in terms of the price of a bushel of wheat the decline was from an average of $1.75 for the ten years 1867–1876 to $0.88 for 1887–1896. The debtor class suffered, of course, from the rise in the value of gold, although the suffering was mitigated somewhat by the demand for labor in the construction of railroads and the abundance of cheap or free land.

The close of the Victorian era found Canada in the early stages of a boom period characterized by heavy immigration, extensive railroad-building, and rapid growth of the settlements in the northwest. This boom may be attributable to the general rise in prices, easier credit, and economic policies adopted by the new Liberal government under Wilfrid Laurier. But the period of expansion and prosperity belongs to the twentieth century, and its story will be told in a later chapter.

The Dominion and the new provinces admitted to it took as great an interest in the promotion of education as had the older colonies. Following an American example, the Dominion set aside for educational purposes two sections of the public lands in every township in the northwest. Manitoba established a tax-supported public school system in 1871 and a university six years later, the latter organized as a federation of colleges modeled somewhat upon the University of London. The various religious denominations of old Canada sought to minister to the spiritual and educational needs of their co-religionists in the northwest before the Dominion was "extended from sea to sea," and they increased rather than relaxed their efforts afterward. The churches were responsible for the development of higher education in Manitoba, and the seriousness with which they viewed their educational activities may be gauged by the bitterness aroused by Manitoba's effort to establish secular tax-supported elementary schools. Outstanding among the religious leaders of the pioneer period were the Roman Catholic Père Lacombe, the Methodist John MacDougall, the Anglican Robert Machray, and the Presbyterian James Robertson. These men, their assistants, and collaborators did much to enrich and make human the lonely life of the frontier.

The external relations of the Dominion of Canada touched chiefly Britain, the other portions of the British empire, and the United States. Changes in her status within the empire have already been discussed, Canada obtaining a position aptly described by Kipling: "Daughter am I in my mother's house, But mistress in my own." As a daughter she borrowed in the mother country's money market and relied upon the protection of the imperial navy. Although the imperial garrison was withdrawn from Quebec in 1871, imperial troops continued to occupy the naval stations, Halifax and Esquimalt. Apart from small vessels used in the fisheries protection service, Canada made no effort to build a navy; and despite proddings from home her militia continued to be badly organized and trained until 1896 when the possibility of an Anglo-American war aroused Canadians to realization of the need for a better system of defense. In 1878 and again in 1885, when a war between Britain and Russia seemed within the range of possibilities, Canadians showed readiness to volunteer for service against the foes of the British empire; and in 1899 when the Anglo-Boer war broke out Canada raised and equipped a volunteer force that served the empire in South Africa. This action stirred up great resentment among French-Canadians and caused a cleavage within the Liberal party.

Only rarely was Canada concerned about her relations with other British colonies. Suggestions for closer economic and perhaps political relations with Newfoundland and the West Indies met with little response. In 1894 the first British colonial economic conference was held at Ottawa; it discussed the need for an all-British Pacific cable and a better steamship service between Australasia and Britain via Canada. The Dominion supported the demand for these improvements, which held hopes of increased traffic for Canadian harbors and railroads. The effects of the conference upon the Dominion's fiscal position have already been discussed.

Apart from the field of government, the relations of Canada with the United States were closer than her relations with Britain. They touched politics, boundaries, fisheries, and commerce. The United States did not welcome the formation of the Dominion, congress denouncing it as a violation of the Monroe Doctrine; Irish Fenians in the United States in 1870 repeated their attempt of 1866 to invade and seize Canada; the United States government refused to indemnify the Dominion for the cost of guarding against and repelling these raids; and highly placed men in the government of the United States such as Senator Charles Sumner, Reverdy Johnson, the American ambassador to London, and Secretary of State Hamilton Fish, spoke openly of the desirability of Britain's ceding Canada to their country. Such a union was favored in 1870 by a small group in Canada, the most prominent among whom was Alexander Galt; and in the late eighties supporters of closer commercial relations between Canada and the United States – for example, Goldwin Smith, erstwhile regius professor of modern history at Oxford and now residing in Toronto – spoke of a union of the two countries as a manifest destiny. But the republic showed no eagerness for it; and in Canada descendants of the United Empire Loyalists of Ontario and French-Canadians of Quebec agreed in opposing it.

Boundary disputes between Canada and the United States were settled amicably. On October 21, 1872, the German emperor, as arbitrator in the controversy over the ownership of San Juan Island, awarded that island to the United States. In the preceding year doubts as to the location of the northwestern point of the Lake of the Woods mentioned in the demarcation of the boundary in 1826 were removed by a commission consisting of one Canadian and one American. In 1867 the United States bought Alaska from Russia. The subsequent expansion of Canada established a Canadian-American boundary in Alaska about which discussion grew keen after gold discoveries had given the remote northwest economic significance. The most important point at issue was how to trace a boundary described as following the sinuosities of the coast ten leagues from the shore along the crest of the mountains. The Canadians wanted this traced in such a way as to give them a harbor on the Lynn Canal, the natural ocean outlet for the Yukon territory; the Americans insisted upon a literal interpretation of the phrase "the sinuosities of the coast." The question engendered a good deal of ill feeling in Canada which lasted even after a commission of six (three Americans, two Canadians, and one British) in 1903 voted 4 to 2 (the Canadians in the minority) in favor of the American claims.

Disputes concerning the rights of American fishermen in the inshore fisheries of British North America were of long standing. When the United States in 1866 abrogated the Elgin Reciprocity Treaty this issue came to the front. In the negotiations preceding the conclusion of the Treaty of Washington the Canadians wished to barter fishery rights for commercial concessions, but the strongly free trade British government headed by Gladstone refused to participate in such a deal. The right of Americans to fish in Canadian waters was recognized in the treaty; and seven years later, by the so-called Halifax award, Canada received about $4,500,000 of the $5,500,000 paid by the United States to British American fishermen as compensation for the losses they suffered because of the rights enjoyed by American fishermen.

In the eighties controversy arose over the hunting of fur-bearing seals in the Bering Sea. Seal hunters from British Columbia found this hunting profitable, but their activities threatened the fur seal with extermination. The United States then forbade all such hunting, claiming in effect that the Bering Sea was a closed sea, and seized Canadian ships engaged in it. This issue was settled in 1893 by the decision of a tribunal composed of two representatives from the United States, two from the British empire (one of whom was a Canadian), and three neutrals. The Bering Sea was declared open outside the customary three-mile limit and Canadians were given compensation for the ships seized; but the contentions of the United States concerning the need for restricting the hunting of fur seals were upheld.

Resentment against Britain because of alleged friendliness toward the Confederacy during the American Civil War was largely responsible for the abrogation by the United States of the Elgin Reciprocity Treaty which Canada was anxious to have renewed. However, she received no help from Britain, whose statesmen believed that Canada would benefit by the adoption of free trade without a reciprocal trade arrangement with the United States. Nevertheless, Canadians made repeated attempts to conclude a new reciprocity treaty; one was agreed upon in 1874 but defeated in the American senate. During the years 1887–1891 the Liberal party of Canada supported a plan for close commercial relations with the United States which became a main issue in the Canadian election of 1891. The government of Sir John A. Macdonald strongly opposed a commercial union, stating that if one were arranged it should be with Britain or other portions of the British empire. Macdonald won. After the Liberal victory of 1896 the Canadian minister of finance, Sir Richard Cartwright, mentioned to Joseph Chamberlain the possibility of a Canadian-American commercial union, but Chamberlain opposed it. Ultimately the Laurier government adopted an alternative tariff plan by which preferential treatment was accorded British goods. In office the Liberals soon became as nationalistic as the Conservatives had been under Macdonald. Both parties adopted a "national policy."

As we have already seen, in 1869 Newfoundland voted against

joining the Dominion of Canada, a position she maintained despite occasional urgings from London. Charles F. Bennett led the opposition to a union with Canada, the prosperity enjoyed by the island, 1869–1873, making his task easy. Yet even when hard times returned in 1873 the Newfoundlanders refused to reverse their stand on federation; they clung to it in the nineties when the imperial government showed a strong disposition to regard a union with the Dominion as the best solution for the difficulties which beset the island. These were chiefly economic and financial, although disputes with France and with the United States over fishery rights added materially to the embarrassments of the government of Newfoundland.

The attempts to develop agriculture in Newfoundland met with scant success. The cod continued to be the mainstay of her economic structure. A small catch or a drop in the price of the cured fish, especially when these calamities coincided, spelled hard times or even ruin. To relieve a depression that struck the island in the late seventies, the government, headed by Sir William Whiteway, encouraged by land grants and cash subsidies the construction of railroads, built a large dry dock at St. John's, and extended the telegraph lines. But prices continued to fall, the new railroads operated at a loss, and the government had to take them over. By the early nineties the public debt had risen to $14,000,000, a crushing amount for a population of about 200,000, the majority of whom were desperately poor. To add to their misfortune, a great fire swept St. John's in July, 1892, leaving 10,000 homeless and inflicting property damages estimated at $20,000,000, of which only $5,000,000 was covered by insurance. The series of disasters was climaxed with the closing of the Commercial and the Union banks at St. John's on December 10, 1894. Appeals to the imperial government for financial assistance brought no result because, it was alleged, the issues involved were local and the colony possessed complete self-government. A conference at Ottawa aiming at a federation with Canada also failed. Driven to desperation, the government of

Newfoundland decided in October, 1897, to hand over to a Canadian contractor, Robert G. Reid, its railroad, the telegraph lines, the dry dock at St. John's, public land, and other assets in return for a cash payment of $1,000,000 and promises to maintain these public services, including the coastwise mail, for which, however, Reid would receive an annual subsidy.

This "selling out" to private interests provoked a great furore. The governor, Sir Herbert Murray, opposed it. When he asked the colonial office to interfere, he was told that although Her Majesty's government considered the Reid contract unwise and one that might have serious consequences, the colony was self-governing and the imperial government could therefore not interfere. Greater success attended the local opposition led by Robert (later Sir Robert) Bond, who won the election of 1900 and in the following year bought back from Reid the railroad, the telegraph, and the dry dock. These were then leased to the Newfoundland Company, of which Reid and his sons were directors. By this deal Newfoundland recovered part of the economic independence lost as a result of the financial collapse. The recovery was, however, not complete. The Bank of Montreal and the Bank of Nova Scotia had become and remained dominant factors in the financial life of the island.

The problems connected with the fishery rights of French and American citizens in the waters of Newfoundland were complex — involving as they did economic interests, the interpretation of various treaties, the general international interests of the British empire, and the intra-imperial status of Newfoundland. The disputes connected with the French rights were the older — dating from the Treaty of Utrecht, 1713, and of Versailles, 1783.

France owned two small islands, St. Pierre and Miquelon, off the southwestern coast of Newfoundland, and French fishermen had been granted fishery rights along certain portions of both the eastern and the western coasts, designated as the "Treaty Shore." In the eighties France subsidized her Newfoundland fisheries, thus giving her fishermen an advantage over those of Newfoundland. When the latter sought redress by making it difficult for the French to purchase bait, the act was disallowed by the imperial government. A new act, modified so as to remove the objections which Canada had advanced against the act of 1886, went into effect in 1888, but by then new issues had arisen over the lobster factories established by British subjects on the "Treaty Shore." It now became necessary to determine whether the lobster was a fish and whether the French rights meant the complete exclusion of British fishermen from the "Treaty Shore." The issue was further complicated when it was discovered that the imperial naval officer who had destroyed the lobster factories had acted on the authority of a law repealed in 1830. Feeling ran high in Newfoundland, but the colony was too small to exert effective pressure upon either Britain or France. A temporary Anglo-French agreement of 1890 allowed both British and French subjects to participate in the lobster fishery along the "Treaty Shore." Final settlement was reached by the Anglo-French treaty of April, 1904, which terminated the right of the French to land but recognized the equal rights of British and French fishermen to fish in the waters along this shore.

The rights of American fishermen had been restricted to fishing, without permission to utilize the land. The Treaty of Washington, 1871, recognized that in the case of Newfoundland as in the case of Canada the reciprocal right to fish in the waters of the United States north of the 39th degree was not adequate compensation; hence the fishermen of Newfoundland secured about $1,000,000 of the Halifax award. However, friction between American fishermen and the local authorities of Newfoundland, especially over fishing on Sundays, caused riots and resulted in diplomatic "episodes." The anti-English attitude of American statesmen, due largely to the importance of conciliating the Irish vote, caused the United States congress to pass a resolution in 1883 denouncing the Treaty of Washington and thus reopening the question of the fisheries. Newfoundland would have been satisfied with an arrangement giving her fish free entry in the United States market, but, as in the French fishery dispute, the colony was not allowed to arrange the matter. A joint Anglo-American commission of 1888 reached a temporary settlement, but the imperial government refused to ratify the

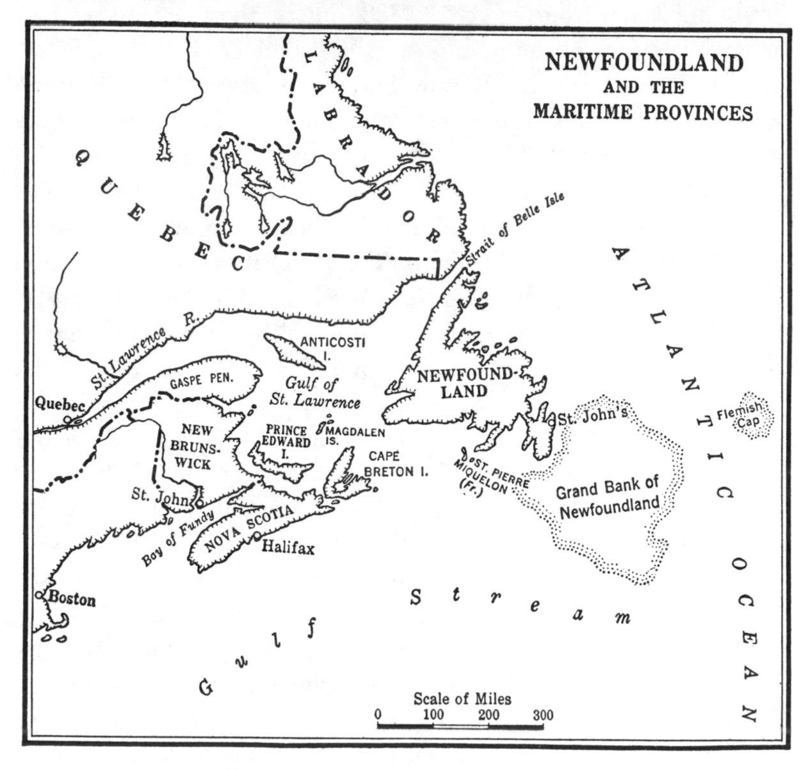

Newfoundland-American reciprocity treaty of 1890 known as the Blaine-Bond convention. No final agreement was reached until the present century.

The population of Newfoundland grew from 146,536 in 1869 to 220,948 in 1901. Poverty and religious rivalry were bars to educational progress. The denominational schools were small and struggling; those above the elementary grades suffered from lack of equipment. An event of much importance for the fishermen of Newfoundland and Labrador was the founding of the Grenfell Mission in 1892. The opening of the great iron mine at Bell Island in 1895 held promise of diversifying the economic life of Newfoundland. Nevertheless, the close of the Victorian era found England's oldest colony facing an uncertain future.

CHAPTER 21

THE WEST INDIES, 1870–1901

By repealing the sugar preferences Britain administered a staggering blow to the posperity of her West Indian possessions. Yet they strove with laudable courage but doubtful wisdom to maintain their old economic system despite labor shortage, falling sugar prices, and the competition of bounty-fed sugar from continental Europe. The economic history of the British colonies in the region of the Caribbean during the latter half of the Victorian era is therefore a tale of woe, cries for imperial aid, and only slight adjustments to changing times. Socially there was some progress in the field of elementary education; otherwise stagnation prevailed. Politically all the colonies, excepting the Bahamas, Barbados, and Bermuda, had sunk to or remained at the level of a crown colony; there were few changes upward. Vested interests coupled with the innate conservatism of the governing classes defeated practically all efforts at federating island groups, although this was strongly favored by the imperial government.

At various times the relations between the British West Indies and the United States called for exchange of notes and special tariff arrangements; the boundary dispute between British Guiana and Venezuela in 1895 precipitated a sharp Anglo-American diplomatic conflict in which the Monroe Doctrine was invoked.

Twice, in 1883 and again in 1897, the conditions of the West Indies were studied by royal commissions, and in 1901 this region received special attention from the colonial office then in charge of Joseph Chamberlain. Since the old sugar colonies were no longer among the more valuable of Britain's overseas dependencies, our account of their history from 1870 to 1901 must be brief. For the sake of clarity it will follow the topical arrangement already indicated – economic and social, political, foreign and imperial relations.

Apart from the asphalt lake in Trinidad and gold-bearing ore in British Guiana, the economic resources of the West Indies are limited to the products of the soil. Among these sugar continued to hold the first place. In 1896 it furnished 53 per cent of all the West Indian export; with Jamaica excluded, this figure is 75 per cent. The decline of Jamaica as a sugar producer is one of the important aspects of West Indian economic history; in 1896 sugar supplied only 18 per cent of Jamaican export. Lord Olivier writes: "In 1882, when I entered the Colonial Office, the value of sugar exported [from Jamaica] was £910,000. In 1886 it had fallen to £387,000 and in 1897, when I first went to Jamaica, it was down to about £300,000." The loss was in part made good by the export of dyewoods. The logwood which grew as a weed in Jamaica had by 1893 become more important as an article of export than either tea or coffee. Unfortunately, however, the natural dyes were soon to be replaced by the synthetic, in the production of which Germany excelled. The Jamaican export trade in bananas dates from 1867, but it developed slowly until the end of the century when the United Fruit Company of New Jersey began to supply the growers with proper marketing facilities. By this time the value of Jamaica's fruit export was more than double that of sugar and rum.

British Guiana and Trinidad by virtue of a greater supply of fertile virgin land and coolie labor forged ahead of Jamaica as producers of sugar. But even for these colonies the export figures on sugar dropped 50 per cent or more between 1870 and

1901. The British Guiana export fell from £2,190,510 to £1,038,-165 and that for Trinidad from £938,000 to £453,304 in this period. The West Indies like the rest of the world experienced many fluctuations in foreign trade in the latter half of the Victorian era, with 1897 as the low year. A comparison of the terminal years, 1870 and 1901, shows an increase of approximately 15 to 20 per cent in the foreign trade. During the eighties British Guiana became a gold-producing country, the metal being found in various places. From a modest beginning of 250 ounces in 1884 the output reached 138,528 ounces in 1893–1894.

For the primary products of tropical agriculture — sugar, coffee, cocoa, and fruit — the questions of land, labor, and prices continued to be of basic importance. In all the colonies large estates owned by individual planters had been the customary mode of landholding in the days of slavery, and so it continued with only a few modifications. In British Guiana, shortly after emancipation, freed Africans established communal holdings by pooling their money resources, electing headmen, and buying estates. These agricultural villages called for cooperative efforts in maintaining the dikes where the land lay below sea level at high tide, draining off the surplus water in the rainy season, and providing roads and other common needs. Jamaica remained a colony of large estates. A survey and scrutiny of land titles led to resumption by the government of considerable tracts of land which in the nineties were parceled out and sold to the Negroes and Indians desirous of becoming peasant proprietors. Barbados with a plentiful supply of resident black labor and Trinidad with her gangs of imported coolies continued to be capitalistic in their agricultural organization. Nor was this system weakened with the introduction of improved machinery for cane-crushing and sugar-refining. The companies that owned sugar mills bought and operated estates in order to insure a regular and plentiful supply of cane. Similarly fruit-farming in Jamaica developed along capitalistic lines.

Consequently the West Indian type of agriculture required a

large supply of labor working regularly in the cane fields, fruit orchards, or on coffee and cacao plantations. As mentioned in an earlier chapter, the freed Negroes were unwilling to continue toiling at tasks associated with memories of their slave status, nor would they bind themselves to report regularly for work five or six days a week. In Jamaica they had been accustomed as slaves to grow their own food, and they retained the provision grounds which though small satisfied their most urgent wants; the others were met by casual employment or pilfering. Stealing from gardens and orchards, under the rather high-sounding name of "praedial larceny," was common in Jamaica until peasant proprietorship became more prevalent. The Jamaica Negro was a good worker on his own land but an unreliable employee for the owners of sugar estates. He would rather emigrate and work on a railroad in Nicaragua or a canal in Panama than hire out to a sugar planter. Besides, the pay of the navvy was better than that of the field laborer.

Hence there was a considerable migration of Jamaican laborers to South and Central America. Twenty-five thousand of them were working for the de Lesseps Panama Canal Company at the time of its collapse in 1889. Barbados had a dense resident population and hence was an exception; but most of the other colonies, particularly British Guiana and Trinidad, continued like Jamaica to need imported labor, the majority of which came from India. Despite assertions by the enemies of slavery that the indentured coolies were practically slaves, thousands were annually transplanted from India to the West Indies. Many died and some returned at the expiration of the five-year period of indenture, but enough remained to contribute materially to the polychrome character of the population of several West Indian colonies. In British Guiana in 1901, more than 100,000, or about 40 per cent of the population, and in Trinidad around 80,000, or upward of 30 per cent, were natives or descendants of natives of India. The Jamaican import of coolies had been smaller, averaging approximately 500 annually; hence her Indian population numbered only 15,000 at the close of the century. Physically weaker than the creole Negroes, the Indians proved docile and dependable under indenture, thrifty and industrious as free laborers, a people who in the West Indies have shown love of and aptitude for work on the land. Rarely have they created trouble for the civil authorities, the most disastrous exception being the Trinidad riot of October 30, 1884, which caused the death of eighteen rioters and the wounding of about one hundred.

With an economic organization dependent on an export trade, the West Indies were of course affected by world prices and general economic conditions and policies. When gold appreciated, the value of West Indian sugar moved downward. The prices in the United Kingdom on sugar in lumps or loaves declined from shillings 29.14 per cwt. in 1881 to 14.75 in 1896, on beetroot from 21.15 to 10.34, and on cane and other sorts from 21.09 to 10.85 for the same period; the 1897 prices were still lower. The production of beet sugar in Europe rose from 1,783,000 tons in 1882 to 3,840,256 in 1894. This production was subsidized so that when the prices fell during 1895–1896, the governments doubled the export bounties; by 1896 these reached £4 10*s.* per ton in France and in Germany £1 5*s.* per ton on raw and £1 15*s.* per ton on refined sugar. As in the middle years of the nineteenth century when the sugar preferences were discussed and the issue of free versus slave-grown sugar was raised, the British consumers bought in the cheapest market. The United Kingdom's import of refined beet sugar rose from 185,000 tons in 1885 to 738,000 in 1896. The distress caused in the West Indies by low prices on sugar, the subsidies awarded the beet sugar growers, and the effects of the open market on sugar in the United Kingdom did not escape the watchful eye of Joseph Chamberlain. The result was the appointment in December, 1896, of the sugar commission, about which more will be said later.

Countries do not progress socially in periods of economic stagnation or decline, and the West Indies were no exception to this rule. The growth of the population averaged about 10 per cent per decade and may be estimated (there was no general census) at 1,850,000 in 1901; the figures include the population of British Guiana, Honduras, and Bermuda as well as the West Indies proper. An important factor in this growth was the Indian coolie immigration which brought undoubted economic benefits but perhaps complicated social problems. Little progress was made in the promotion of public health. In 1897 a medical officer in Trinidad called attention to the prevalence of yaws, a filth disease, and the difficulty of combating it because of the low standards of cleanliness. Similar conditions existed in the other colonies. The villages in British Guiana presented knotty problems because of the flat, low country. Education advanced very slowly. Thus in Jamaica it was found in 1883 that although expenditures for elementary education and the number of children enrolled in the schools had increased considerably during the last twenty years, the average yearly salary for teachers had fallen from £38 to £33, and that out of 250,000 adult Negroes only 22,000 could write. The census of 1891 disclosed that about one-half of the West Indian population over five years of age could neither read nor write. The Indian coolies helped to swell the percentages of illiterates; moreover the language problem made it difficult to reach them by any system of adult education. The expenditures for education rose from £95,000 in 1882 to £180,000 in 1896, a gain of about 90 per cent, yet the figures were low considering the size of the population. Some of the educational needs were satisfied, however, by the various churches and by private endowments. The depression of 1896–1897 led to a reduction in the expenditures for education except in Jamaica where the elected members of the legislative council opposed curtailment.

Among the trends to be noted in the history of education in the West Indies is the fact that the state gradually assumed responsibilities for education formerly shouldered by religious bodies and that after the middle of the nineties a sudden upswing took place in the teaching of manual training and agriculture.

This was to a considerable extent a result of imperial aid and encouragement. A manual training school was started in Jamaica in 1897, agriculture was introduced in the elementary schools, and special efforts were made to train teachers for this subject. Secondary education, such as it was, received support from endowments dating from the eighteenth century. Teachers' training schools supported by the Mico Trust operated in Jamaica, Antigua, and British Guiana; Shortwood College, Jamaica, for the training of women teachers, was founded in 1885. In 1876 Codrington College, Barbados, became affiliated with Durham University and tried to satisfy the need for education at the university level. However, in this as well as in the other branches of education the West Indies remained relatively backward.

The reasons for this backwardness must be sought in the poverty, the character of the population, the distances which separated the colonies, and their political disunion. Despite the fertility of the soil in some of the colonies, Trinidad and British Guiana in particular, the majority of the inhabitants lived perpetually on the margin of destitution. The white element continued to decline; with the Bahamas and Bermuda omitted, it constituted in the nineties from only 2 to 9 per cent of the population in the various colonies. As noted earlier, Jamaica lost her elected assembly in 1866 and several of the other colonies declined similarly in political status. Barbados, the Bahamas, and Bermuda on the other hand kept their institutions practically unchanged which meant that they remained as inefficient and unprogressive as of old. For Jamaica the era of crown colony government was inaugurated by Sir J. P. Grant, governor from 1866 to 1872, who with the aid of a nominated legislative council reorganized the system of finance and the judiciary, and organized a constabulary, government savings banks, the immigration service, a medical department, and a government medical service. Lord Olivier, a competent critic, says that "Sir J. P. Grant laid the administrative foundations of modern Jamaica, with as great efficiency and foresight as could be expected of any man." Several of his successors, notably Sir Anthony Musgrave, 1877–1883, Sir H. W. Norman, 1883–1889, and Sir Henry Blake 1889–1895, also receive high praise from the same authority. Nevertheless, it was recognized that a crown colony form of government was an anomaly for Jamaica in the British empire of the nineteenth century. In 1884 the legislative council, composed of nine official and nine non-official members, was altered by making the non-official members elective and giving them power over finance. The governor withdrew from the council in 1893, two years later the number of elected members was increased to fourteen, and the governor refrained from appointing an equal number of nominated members until the financial crisis of 1899.

In British Guiana the government and administration of the villages received much attention partly because of the communal system of landholding and partly because of the nature of the land which required dikes to keep out the sea and drainage for the surplus water in the rainy season and hence created special problems for agriculture and the health services. After various experiments and changes, an ordinance of 1883 placed all the villages under the department of public works and made the village inspectors subject to the authority of a central board of health. The villages had no elective officials; but two cities, New Amsterdam and Georgetown, in 1891 secured elective councils which in turn chose the mayors. The cumbersome central government of British Guiana, with a college of electors on life tenure choosing the five elective members of the court of policy, which with six additional special representatives formed the combined court that had control over finance, was a source of dispute and embarrassment. Since the indirect system of election provided voting power for only a small minority, the elected members of the court of policy could not claim to represent the people; and when in 1887 they went on strike as a protest against a medical report by a certain Dr.

Williams, public opinion supported the governor. After lengthy discussions a thorough reorganization was effected in 1891. The college of electors was swept away, a separate executive council created, the court of policy enlarged from ten to sixteen – eight nominated and eight elected – and both the elected members of the court of policy and the financial representatives who joined this body to form the combined court were now chosen directly by the voters. Though the franchise remained narrow the government of British Guiana became more representative in character as a result of these changes.

The question of federating some or all of the West Indian colonies occupied the minds of successive colonial secretaries, members of royal commissions, and other people interested in their welfare. Despite protests from the colonies concerned, Lord Kimberley, colonial secretary from 1870 to 1874, effected in 1871 a federation of the Leeward Islands – Antigua, Dominica, Montserrat, Nevis, St. Kitts, and the Virgin Islands. Since each retained its local government, the anticipated saving in expenditure and gain in efficiency were not achieved. Except for the combining of St. Kitts and Nevis in 1882, the federal arrangement failed to bring harmony and cooperation among these colonies. The royal commission of 1883 advocated unification for both the Leeward and the Windward Islands. In preparation for the latter's federal organization, Barbados was separated from them in 1885, and a governor-in-chief residing at Grenada was appointed for the Windward Islands including Grenada, St. Lucia, St. Vincent, and Tobago; but they refused to be federated. In 1889 Tobago was separated from the Windward Islands and joined with Trinidad. Ten years later these two islands united, their union representing the only real success scored during this period by the advocates of closer political connections between the British colonies in the West Indies. Nor did the far-fetched proposals for a closer commercial union between Trinidad and Canada bring any results.

As the United States grew in wealth and population she became the principal market for West Indian sugar; hence changes in American tariff policies were watched lest they have injurious effects upon these colonies. Thus in 1884, after the United States had concluded commercial treaties with Hawaii and Mexico which accorded favored treatment to their sugar, the British foreign office sought to have these favors extended to the British colonies in the West Indies. The American secretary of state, Frelinghuysen, replied with a draft treaty embodying reciprocal trade arrangements. However, since the treaty seemingly aimed at drawing the colonies within the economic orbit of the United States, it was rejected by Britain on the grounds that it violated the most-favored-nation principle, restricted the freedom of the West Indies to make other tariff arrangements, and limited the tariff favors to goods carried in American or British ships. No serious results followed the failure of this treaty. In 1891 a new alarm was raised over the possible effects upon the West Indies of the McKinley tariff which allowed free import of sugar, molasses, coffee, and tea, provided the exporting country granted tariff favors to goods imported from the United States. An attempt was made to negotiate on the basis of 1884. But Secretary of State Blaine in a long dispatch of October 30, 1891, pointed out that the open door policy claimed for the British West Indies was illusory. The United States bought 58 per cent of the West Indian produce whereas only 32 per cent of the latter's imports came from America. Britain, which took only 40 per cent of the export of the colonies, supplied 65 per cent of their import. The purchases from the United States were foodstuffs and other necessities, those from Britain were luxuries; yet American goods were subject to ad valorem custom duties of 60 per cent or more as against only about 12 1/2 per cent levied on the luxuries of British origin. Blaine therefore demanded that the West Indies lower their tariffs on American produce. The British minister to Washington, Sir Julian Pauncefote, countered by pointing out that Blaine had chosen only a small segment of the British empire, the question of reciprocity was one between the whole empire and the United States, and that when viewed from this angle the trade balance favored the latter to the extent of $243,725,400 for the year ending June 30, 1890. The idea of a special commercial treaty was then abandoned; but in an exchange of notes it was agreed that no new tariff burdens would be imposed on West Indian produce in return for certain reductions in the latter's tariff schedules on goods imported principally from the United States. However, later American tariffs imposed 50 per cent ad valorem duties on West Indian sugar.

Apart from questions pertaining to tariffs, the West Indies affected Anglo-American relations slightly in matters pertaining to Central America and strongly in the British Guiana-Venezuela boundary dispute. The British interposition with Nicaragua in the early eighties in behalf of the Mosquito Indians aroused suspicion in the United States, which in 1882–1883 registered a belated protest against the occupation of British Honduras. This was small beer. The Guiana boundary dispute on the other hand resulted in a diplomatic crisis that threatened to assume large proportions. As related earlier, the British government in the forties had not insisted on the British Guiana-Venezuela boundary line drawn up by Schomburgk, the matter being left in abeyance for a generation. However, in the late seventies Venezuela became anxious over this boundary and for ten years tried to reach a settlement with Britain. Meanwhile gold had been discovered in the disputed area, settlers and prospectors moved in, and mining concessions were granted. Angry because of Britain's dilatory and somewhat superior attitude, Venezuela in 1887 withdrew her minister from London and ordinary diplomatic relations were suspended for three years. When they were resumed, she presented extravagant demands but declared her willingness to arbitrate. To this Britain agreed, provided the Schomburgk line was accepted beforehand; this Venezuela declined to do.

Thus the matter stood when the government of the United

States decided to intervene. The basis for her claim of the right to do this was the allegation that Britain by her refusal to have arbitrators decide on the lawful boundary between British Guiana and Venezuela had exhibited a desire to extend her possessions in South America in violation of the Monroe Doctrine. Among the motives assigned to President Cleveland and his secretary of state, Richard Olney, for their aggressive attitude was a desire to court favor with the anti-English voters in the United States and to aid Americans who had secured concessions from Venezuela in the disputed territory. After some preliminary warnings, the American case was stated at considerable length, aggressively though not skillfully, in a note submitted on August 7, 1895, to Lord Salisbury, then foreign secretary as well as prime minister. Reply was delayed until November 26, which of course did not mend matters in the eyes of Cleveland and Olney. In the replies (there were two notes) Salisbury refused to recognize the validity of the Monroe Doctrine, denied that Britain was claiming territory which did not belong to her by right, surveyed the whole history of the boundary dispute with Venezuela, and repeated the refusal to arbitrate claims to land inside the Schomburgk line. President Cleveland submitted these dispatches to congress on December 17, 1895, with a message asking that provisions be made for an American commission to determine the true boundary between British Guiana and Venezuela and declaring that the boundary thus traced should be maintained by the United States. The belligerent tone of this message and the unprecedented methods recommended by President Cleveland and supported by congress and the American press, created the tensest situation in Anglo-American relations since the *Trent* affair thirty-four years earlier. Britain was surprised, shocked, and bewildered. A few voices cried no surrender, but the majority wished to maintain friendly relations with the United States to which so many were bound by the closest personal ties. A few thousand square miles in the interior of South America, even though they might contain gold mines, were deemed not worth the risk of a war; moreover, the situation in South Africa in which the German emperor seemed to take a keen interest presented risks not to be ignored. Salisbury therefore abandoned his intransigent attitude in the matter of the Schomburgk line. Time and reflection calmed the minds of Cleveland and his secretary of state. When both sides showed a willingness to recede from the forward positions, little difficulty was experienced in concluding a treaty between Britain and Venezuela for the arbitration of the boundary dispute, excluding only such area as had been occupied fifty years or more. The delimitation of the boundary, completed in 1899, gave Venezuela a little territory inside the Schomburgk line and assured her control of the mouth of the Orinoco River; on the whole, however, Britain was the gainer.

The imperial government was dilatory but not neglectful of colonial claims in the Guiana-Venezuela boundary dispute. Yet as we view all the colonies and the period as a whole, we find little genuine interest in the problems of the West Indies until Joseph Chamberlain took the helm at the colonial office. True this office had facilitated the importation of coolies from India and aid was forthcoming to islands swept by hurricanes; but the problems of landholding, public health, and education were neither studied carefully nor supported generously. Nor were efforts made to supply the capital necessary to develop fruit-growing and market the fruit, to provide modern machinery for the sugar industry, to explore and exploit the resources of British Guiana, and to build much-needed roads, bridges, railroads, and docks. A royal commission to study public finance and taxation visited the West Indies in 1883 and issued a report the following year. The commissioners gave a broad interpretation of their duties and collected a mass of valuable material concerning economic and social conditions in the islands, but their work produced little in the way of tangible results.

The low prices on sugar, the economic depression in the West Indies, and the advent of Joseph Chamberlain to the colonial office brought about the appointment on December 22, 1896, of another royal commission composed of Sir Henry W. Norman, ex-governor of Jamaica, Sir Edward Grey, later famous as foreign secretary, and Sir David Barbour, an expert on finance. Attached to the commission as agricultural adviser was Dr. Daniel Morris, assistant director of the Kew Gardens, who had been in Jamaica as director of public gardens and plantations. The special duty of this commission was to investigate the state of the sugar industry and the alleged effects of the competition with the bounty-supported beet sugar of Europe. Like their predecessors fourteen years earlier, the commissioners investigated the general social, economic, and political situation in the West Indian colonies and in 1897 issued a valuable report with minutes of the evidence presented to them. The commission recommended better facilities for sending West Indian fruit to England, improvement of rural credit, the establishment of a department of economic botany and a system of agricultural education, and reduction of public expenditures. The commissioners noted that both the Negro and the Indian liked to own land, but that peasant proprietorship had been discouraged. This they believed should be reversed, aid being extended to all who wished to purchase small farms. On the question of the sugar bounties the commission advised renewed efforts to secure their abolition; but while the majority opposed countervailing duties on beet sugar, the chairman, Sir Henry Norman, urged that duties equal to the amount of bounties paid by the exporting country should be levied on all beet sugar entering Britain. Attention was called to the fact that special British obligations had been incurred for the West Indies because "we have placed the laboring population where it is, created for it the conditions, moral and material, under which it exists, and we cannot divest ourselves of the responsibility for its future."

Chamberlain shared this point of view, and the effort to put an end to the export bounty on beet sugar was crowned with success in 1902. A West Indian department of agriculture was established, with stations in several colonies, at a cost of £17,500 per annum borne by the imperial exchequer, and special aid was extended for the development of agricultural education and for experiments aimed at benefiting the agricultural industries. Imperial subsidies amounting to £10,000 annually were awarded a steamship company for maintaining a fortnightly direct service between Jamaica and the United Kingdom, and an annual grant of £13,500 for five years was promised for a similar service between Canada and the West Indies providing the Dominion contributed an equal amount. A special grant-in-aid was extended to St. Vincent for a compulsory purchase of undeveloped land to be distributed in small holdings, and large contributions from both private and public sources were made to the islands devastated by hurricanes in 1898 and 1899. Chamberlain's Colonial Loans Bill of August, 1899, included loans totaling £663,000 to the West Indies. Of this amount £453,000 was lent to Jamaica; this enabled her to complete a railroad and other public works. A good business man, the colonial secretary did not extend this aid to Jamaica without a stricter supervision of the public finances. After a sharp struggle the island had to accept an increase in the number of the nominated members of the legislative council so as to give them, and thereby the governor and the colonial office, effective supervision of revenues and expenditures. At the turn of the century the West Indian colonies were receiving much attention and aid from the imperial government; the outlook seemed hopeful.

CHAPTER 22

THE BRITISH EMPIRE IN AFRICA, 1872–1902

IN 1872 the British empire in Africa consisted of four small possessions in Western Africa and on the coast of the Gulf of Guinea, three in South Africa, and several islands rather distant from the African coast of which the most important was Mauritius. For more than fifty years British colonial expansion in Africa had in the main been limited to the southern part of the continent, but after 1880 a great change took place. Between that date and 1902 approximately two and a half million square miles were brought under British control, so that at the close of this period the African lands annexed to the British empire or included in the British spheres of influence exceeded Australia in area. These lands were held under many different kinds of tenure. Some were self-governing, others were crown colonies; Rhodesia was held by a chartered company; in the eastern, central, southern, and western portions of the continent vast regions were under British protection, which meant that the native chiefs were nominally in control but Britain ruled; Egypt was a part of the Turkish empire although administered by the British agent and consul-general at Cairo; and the Anglo-Egyptian Sudan was in theory governed jointly by Britain and Egypt, the latter being a sleeping partner.

Except in the case of the Cape Colony and Natal, the history of the African dominions of Britain, 1872–1902, will be limited to the account of how they came under British rule, the international rivalries and agreements connected with the partition of Africa, struggles with the natives, the work of missionaries, the beginnings of exploitation by Europeans, and the establishment of government. Egypt supplied the statesmen of Britain with the greatest number of international complications, and the Boer republics of South Africa offered the stoutest opposition to being incorporated in the British empire. For the sake of convenience, the story will be grouped under the headings, Egypt and the Sudan, East Africa, Central Africa, West Africa, the islands, and South Africa. A considerable amount of space will be devoted to the internal development of the South African colonies, especially the Cape; otherwise attention will center on how and why Britain obtained control, the government of the various possessions, and the changes effected by the British administrators.

Britain gained control over Egypt in 1882. Since the sixteenth century the land of the Pharaohs had formed a part of the Ottoman empire; and in Egypt as elsewhere within that empire foreigners had acquired certain privileges under the "Capitulations," the most important being exemption from taxation and the right to be tried by their own consular courts. Since by the Treaty of Paris, 1856, the powers guaranteed the integrity of the Turkish empire, they could claim the right to be consulted when important changes took place within it. Until the opening of the Suez Canal in 1869, France alone had taken a special interest in Egypt; but no sooner had that waterway been completed than Britain realized that it was a main artery for her trade and her highroad to India. In 1875 the British government under Disraeli bought nine-twentieths of the shares in the Suez Canal Company. Shortly afterward the financial difficulties of the Egyptian government led to the establishment of joint Anglo-French control over Egypt. The two governments agreed in 1879 to keep the other powers out of Egypt; nevertheless, other powers still had opportunities to interfere by virtue of the privileges enjoyed under the Capitulations or by invoking the Treaty of Paris or using the sultan as a tool for this purpose. Furthermore, the powers had arranged for mixed courts to try civil cases in which their nationals were involved and these courts could render judgments against the Egyptian government; an international debt commission was established to administer revenues assigned to the services of the debt; and an international agreement, which regulated the finances of Egypt and was known as the Law of Liquidation, went into effect in 1880. Consequently, only when Britain and France worked harmoniously in Egypt could the other powers be kept out – a rift between these two might lead to a reopening of the whole Egyptian question.

Opportunities for reopening it came in 1882. Egyptian nationalists had chafed under the foreign control of their country and in 1881 the ranks of the disaffected were swelled with discharged and unpaid army officers. A native Egyptian colonel, Arabi Pasha, became the leader of a hybrid nationalist-military movement that caused many disturbances in the country. Gladstone, who became prime minister in 1880, had opposed the Egyptian ventures of his predecessor; he preferred international to dual control over Egypt, but he was confronted with a secret Anglo-French treaty which compelled him to follow the lines fixed by Beaconsfield and Salisbury. When the cry "Egypt for the Egyptians" was raised, Gladstone was inclined to lend a sympathetic ear; but when Gambetta, who became French prime minister in November, 1881, scoffed at it and advocated strong measures in Egypt, the British government decided to accept his lead. He fell from power at the end of January, 1882; his successor, M. Freycinet, showed little inclination to cooperate with Britain. The English government, wishing to stay out of Egypt, desired to invite the Turks to restore order in the country, but this was vetoed by Freycinet. A joint Anglo-French squadron was sent to Alexandria; Britain and France wrangled over what to do with it; the Egyptian government fell into the hands of Arabi Pasha, whom Britain refused to recognize; riots broke out in Alexandria in June, 1882; the French squadron was withdrawn. When shore batteries, which presumably threatened the British fleet riding at anchor in the harbor of Alexandria, were strengthened despite British protest, the British bombarded the forts on July 11, 1882. This act precipitated fresh riots, the burning of the city, and the landing of British forces to restore order. A British expeditionary force commanded by Lord Wolseley defeated Arabi Pasha in the battle of Tel-el-Kebir, September 13, 1882; Cairo was occupied; and Britain thereby became *de facto* the mistress of Egypt. France had refused to cooperate in overthrowing Arabi; Britain regarded this as tantamount to withdrawal from the dual control and so informed her. For the next twenty-two years French statesmen harbored resentment against Britain for occupying Egypt; they strove by hook and by crook to make her work of restoration in Egypt impossible; and they revenged themselves by creating difficulties for her in the Far East, in the South Seas, and in Central Africa.

This estrangment between Britain and France made Bismarck practically a dictator in international affairs from 1882 to 1885. Egypt became linked with the Anglo-German colonial rivalry in Africa and the South Seas; by refusing to assent to British proposals for reforming Egypt's finances Bismarck compelled Britain to yield on colonial issues. Gladstone did not object to German colonization, but Australasians and South Africans demanded Monroe doctrines for their respective regions and British expansionists wished to color the map red. A formal annexation of Egypt by Britain might have cut the Gordian knot, but Liberal election pledges and party principles forbade such action; hence in order to put Egypt's finances in shape Bismarck must be given his colonies. The British concession came grudgingly, and the colonial disputes left bad blood between Britain and Germany and created bitterness toward the British government in the hearts of Australians.

Sir Evelyn Baring, later elevated to the peerage as Earl of Cromer, was appointed British agent and consul-general to Cairo in 1883 and remained at this post until 1907. During these years he was virtually the ruler of Egypt. Among the British achievements in Egypt in that period we may mention that the country was saved from bankruptcy; irrigation works, notably the great Assuan Dam completed in 1902, trebled her cotton and doubled her sugar production; taxation was more evenly distributed; the peasants were largely relieved from the corvée or forced labor; the kurbash, the terrible whip made from the hide of the hippopotamus, was no longer used on their backs; sanitation was improved; and corruption in high places came to an end.

The administration of Egypt under Cromer bore strong resemblance to the British rule in India. The civil service was recruited largely in England, it followed Indian traditions, and the government was benevolently despotic. In 1892 a new khedive, Abbas Hilmi, tried to assert a certain amount of independence but was speedily and effectively put in his place by Cromer. Gladstone declared in September, 1882, that attempts should be made to develop self-government in the country, and the Egyptian constitution promulgated in 1883 seemed to point in that direction by providing for elective councils; but the councils were ineffective—Egypt was given good government, not self-government. It cannot, however, fairly be charged that Britain obtained undue direct advantages for herself through the occupation of Egypt. Her exchequer gained nothing thereby and the Egyptian trade was open to all nations on equal terms. Although time and again Britain with the best of intentions assured the powers that her stay in Egypt was only temporary, the country's internal condition did not warrant withdrawal; furthermore, the growing tension in international relations made her loth to abandon a country strategically so important for the British empire.

The occupation of Egypt led Britain into the Sudan. Before

her collapse in 1882, Egypt had established her authority over more than a million square miles of the Sudan, the land of the Negroes. Her rule was oppressive and hated by the Sudanese; therefore when a religious leader, self-styled the Mahdi or guide, raised the standard of revolt in 1881 he was joined by hundreds of thousands of disaffected Sudanese, Egyptian armies were defeated, and garrisons were either converted by or put to the sword. In 1883 the question whether this revolt should be quelled and Egypt's rule reestablished in the Sudan confronted the British government. Since the Egyptian army had been disbanded and the treasury was empty, the issue narrowed to whether Britain should send her army into a vast country with a pestilential climate to crush an opposition so widespread that it seemed truly national. Gladstone thought that it was national; he was appalled by the forecasts of the cost in lives and treasure connected with a war in the Sudan; he did not want this region added to the British empire; he thought that a war there would greatly complicate the financial situation in Egypt, and that if Britain undertook such a war all the world could bully her. But in a weak moment in January, 1884, he agreed to send General Charles Gordon, who had been governor in the Sudan in the seventies, to report on the condition of and means for saving the remaining Egyptian garrisons in the Sudan; from this he was led to consent to Gordon's appointment as governor general of the Sudan for the purpose of evacuating the country. Gordon was bottled up at Khartoum, the Sudanese capital, in the spring of 1884; the fact that he was one of England's greatest heroes aroused a violent clamor that he must be saved. Meanwhile Gordon had decided that the Mahdi had to be crushed. Finally in the autumn of 1884 a relief expedition was sent under Lord Wolseley. It moved slowly; two steamers were finally sent in advance; but when they reached Khartoum on January 28, 1885, it was too late. Two days earlier the Mahdists had stormed the city and killed Gordon. Now the cry arose, "Avenge Gordon," and for a moment Gladstone bowed before it and agreed to let Wolseley remain for war in the Sudan. But the arrival of the news that Russia had taken Penjdeh on the western border of Afghanistan produced the specter of Russia threatening India. A war with her seeming unavoidable, the British army was withdrawn from the Sudan except the Red Sea coast, and the greater portion of the former Egyptian dependency passed into the hands of the Mahdi and his successor, the Khalifa.

For about ten years the Sudan was left alone but not forgotten. Englishmen remembered and thirsted for vengeance on the slayers of Gordon; the rapid progress in the scramble for Africa made it clear that the Sudan would soon cease to be a no-man's land, and time increased her importance for Egypt. If a hostile European power should seize the Upper Nile, the results for Egypt might be disastrous. France was known to have designs on the Sudan and Britain decided to forestall her. By the middle of the nineties the condition of the finances and of Egypt's new army made it possible to begin the work of reconquering the Sudan. The task was intrusted to Sir Herbert (later Lord) Kitchener, who after careful and systematic preparations advanced southward with an Anglo-Egyptian army and defeated the Khalifa at Omdurman across the river from Khartoum on September 2, 1898. No sooner had Khartoum been occupied than news arrived of the presence of a small French force under Major Marchand at Fashoda farther up the Nile. Kitchener hastened thither and Marchand was persuaded to withdraw. After a dispute which threatened to precipitate an Anglo-French war, France agreed to leave the Valley of the Nile in British hands. In 1899 a boundary was drawn between the Anglo-Egyptian and the French Sudan, the former being held jointly by Britain and Egypt under an arrangement known as a condominium. But the partnership was unequal — as the nineteenth century closed, the Valley of the Nile from Lake Albert to the Mediterranean was virtually under British control.

In Eastern Africa parts of Somaliland were seized by Britain in 1884–1885. The campaign against the local chiefs was undertaken with Aden as a base, the purpose of the conquest being to safeguard further the route to India. For that reason, until 1898 the new possession was governed from India. The area obtained was relatively small, not much larger than that of England and Wales; the population of British Somaliland was and is scant; and this crown colony lacked the possibilities for further development found in British East Africa and Uganda.

Geographical features help to explain why the east coast of Africa from Cape Guardafui to Mozambique so long escaped the concession hunters and other so-called pioneers of empire. The paucity of harbors, the absence of navigable rivers, and the low-lying tropical coastal belt about one hundred miles in width prevented Europeans from learning about the salubrious climate and the other natural advantages of the East African highlands. In 1823 the British flag was hoisted at Mombasa but was soon hauled down voluntarily. However, the trade between India and Zanzibar was of considerable importance in the nineteenth century, and their connection was so close that in a dispute over the division of the lands of the sultan of Oman in Arabia, to whom Zanzibar then belonged, the viceroy of India, Lord Canning, was asked to act as arbiter. His decision separated Zanzibar from Oman in 1861. In the following year Britain and France agreed to guarantee the territories of the ruler of Zanzibar, a state which then included the islands of Zanzibar and Pemba and a long strip of coast on the mainland. Shortly after the completion of the Suez Canal the British India Steam Navigation Company, of which Sir William Mackinnon was chairman, established regular steamship service between Zanzibar, India, and Europe; and Mackinnon gained so much influence that in 1877 the sultan of Zanzibar offered him the concession of collecting the customs and administering the government, but the British government frowned on the project and it was dropped. Four years later the sultan proposed that in the event of his death the government of Britain should be the guardian and protector of his son; since this was deemed a violation of the Anglo-French treaty of guarantee, the proposal was rejected.

Meanwhile British, French, and German explorers began to reach the highlands of Eastern Africa where Mount Kilimanjaro and Mount Kenya tower. The year 1884 found an Englishman, Harry (later Sir Harry) Johnston and a German, Dr. Karl Peters, busily engaged in getting dusky potentates of Eastern Africa to put their crosses to treaties the contents of which they probably did not understand. Johnston arrived, ostensibly on a scientific expedition, in the Kilimanjaro district in the summer of 1884 and in July sent Lord Edmond Fitzmaurice, undersecretary in the British foreign office, a glowing account of the healthfulness and resources of the region and extolled its value as a field for colonization. The report so impressed Lord Granville and several of his colleagues in the ministry that they proposed that Britain should reconsider her rejection of the offer made by the sultan of Zanzibar a few years earlier and that he should be encouraged to extend his dominions westward since this would be the cheapest and most convenient method whereby she could establish her power in the East African highlands. Gladstone demurred; despite the arguments presented by Clement (later Sir Clement) Hill of the foreign office and Consul Holmwood, then in England on leave from Zanzibar, the prime minister refused to acknowledge that a German specter haunted the slopes of Kilimanjaro or to sanction any extension of British responsibilities in East Africa. His objections carried the more weight since Sir John Kirk at Zanzibar appeared lukewarm toward the projects of Johnston and the British foreign office.

These discussions took place in November and December, 1884. Soon after New Years, 1885, Dr. Peters emerged on the coast with a portfolio full of treaties and hastened to Germany where he was welcomed by a colonization company that ultimately received the support of Bismarck. Thereupon British interests, deeply disappointed over the government's failure to seize a portion of East Africa, organized a company with Mackinnon as chairman. This company, which was chartered in 1888 as the Imperial East Africa Company, aided in the establishment of the East African Protectorate and included Uganda within the field of its operations. Here British protestant and French Catholic missionaries had flourishing missions. At first they had combined against the Mohammedans but later they disagreed among themselves, and native Christians engaged in actual warfare. This brought the possibility that France might interfere. When the resources of the chartered company proved unequal to the strain imposed by the necessity of building a railroad and keeping order among the natives, appeals for aid were sent to the British government. Lord Salisbury, who was prime minister when the situation began to grow threatening, showed little enthusiasm for Uganda, and Gladstone, who succeeded him in 1892, was opposed to intervention; but Lord Rosebery, Gladstone's foreign secretary, became convinced that Britain must act. After a sharp struggle with the prime minister and his lieutenant, the redoubtable Sir William Harcourt, Rosebery had his way. In June, 1894, Uganda was proclaimed a British protectorate. The company surrendered its charter in 1895. Its main purpose had been achieved — the East African and Uganda protectorates with an area of more than three hundred thousand square miles had been won for Britain. Agreements with Germany in 1886 and 1890 arranged boundaries between the British and German spheres of influence; by the 1890 agreement Germany recognized a British protectorate over Zanzibar in return for Heligoland. France consented to the abrogation of the treaty of 1862 in exchange for the withdrawal of British opposition to her activities in Madagascar. Thus the European powers bartered in African lands.

In the fifties, Livingstone explored the Zambezi and is tributary the Shiré River which forms the outlet of Lake Nyasa. Missionaries had followed the exploration and in 1861 the Universities Mission began work among the natives of the Shiré highlands but soon abandoned the field. In the seventies the work was taken up anew in the region of Lake Nyasa by Scottish missionary societies, and in 1878 the African Lakes Company began trading in that area. Henry O'Neill, British consul at Mozambique, visited Blantire, a missionary station in the Shiré highlands, in 1884; he considered the country superior to the Congo basin, and he found British settlers there. However, Portugal's occupation of Mozambique and Angola had given her certain claims to the country between the two colonies, although she had neither explored nor formally annexed the region. In 1887 she attempted to close the Zambezi, announcing that the interior belonged to her. But by this time British traders and missionaries had been active north of the Zambezi for about a dozen years, and Cecil Rhodes had formulated plans for British expansion into the lands of the Matabele, the Mashona, and the Barotse partly for the purpose of exploiting the country and partly in pursuance of his scheme for a Cape-to-Cairo railway through all-British territory. Hence, the opposition to an extension of Portuguese control across Africa came from many quarters, and Lord Salisbury informed Britain's "oldest ally" that her wish could not be granted. The limits of the British and Portuguese spheres of interest were agreed upon in 1891; Nyasaland with an area of about 40,000 square miles west and south of Lake Nyasa became a British protectorate, and the bulk of the region claimed by Britain in Central Africa, approximately 300,000 square miles, was handed over to the South Africa Company organized by Cecil Rhodes.

The British stations in Western Africa had had for three centuries the dismal reputation of being the white man's grave. Not until the end of the nineteenth century did medical science advance sufficiently to be of help against the effects of the climate; and if we exclude the traffic in slaves and ivory, not until that time did a brisk demand arise for the natural products of this part of Africa. Consequently, a house of commons committee of 1865 advised the abandonment of the Gambia and retrenchment in other places. Although the recommendations were not put into effect, the Gambia remained a mere enclave in French West Africa and but little territory was added to Sierra Leone. The Gold Coast Colony on the Gulf of Guinea was enlarged through the acquisition of Dutch stations in 1872 and as a result of wars with the Ashantees in 1873–1874 and the nineties. Germany and France annexed adjoining territories to which Britain might have presented prior claims; hence when the boundaries of the British sphere of influence were delimited, the Gold Coast Colony and Protectorate embraced only the relatively modest area of 90,000 square miles.

Lagos, on the old Slave Coast, was acquired by Britain in 1861 for the purpose of stopping the traffic in slaves. With this post as a nucleus she extended her influence eastward over the delta of the river Niger, but her statesmen showed no eagerness to increase her territorial responsibilities. British traders had, however, been active in the Niger region since the seventeenth century, and in order to meet French competition they organized in 1879, under the leadership of George (later Sir George) Goldie, the United African Company which in 1886 received a charter as the Royal Niger Company. At the Berlin congress on Western Africa, 1884–1885, Britain claimed the coastal lands of Nigeria, then called the Oil Rivers district; this was proclaimed a British protectorate in June, 1885. Meanwhile, Goldie and his associates had negotiated and continued to negotiate treaties with the Mohammedan rulers of the interior. The territory thus acquired was regarded as a British sphere of interest and frontiers with the adjoining German and French possessions were settled by agreements of 1886, 1890, 1893, and 1898. The transfer of this territory to the crown took place on January 1, 1900. At that time Britain held Lagos, which was a colony, and the protectorates of Southern Nigeria, formerly the Oil Rivers Protectorate, and Northern Nigeria; the the three were later united to form the Nigeria of our own day – a rich and populous possession of 335,000 square miles.

The islands which may be reckoned geographically as belonging to Africa need not detain us long. Madagascar, where Britain for a considerable length of time had had both trading and missionary stations and whose rulers had been friendly to her, was allowed to become French. Of the islands belonging to Britain, Mauritius was the most populous and was steadily becoming more Indianized. The census of 1901 gave the population as 371,023, of whom 259,086 were Indians. Sugar continued to be the main crop of the island, but her sugar growers like those of the West Indies suffered from the competition of the bounty-supported beet sugar of central Europe. Fires, disease, and hurricanes caused great losses in Mauritius, gloom and depression replacing the optimism and speculation of the mid-nineteenth century. In 1870 the governor, Sir Arthur Gordon, suggested that the island might be returned to France in exchange for Pondicherry, but the suggestion found no favor with the Gladstone government. Although yielding no revenue for the British exchequer and small if any return to British capitalists, Mauritius still held too important a position strategically to permit her retransfer to France. West of Africa St. Helena was used as a place of detention for Boer war prisoners. For about two years her population of less than 3500 was augmented by 4500 of these prisoners, prices rose, and the island enjoyed a brief spell of illusive prosperity. The war over, her poverty-stricken inhabitants continued to fight unobtrusively their unceasing battle with nature.

In 1872 Britain's South African possessions included the Cape Colony, Natal, and Griqualand West. Of these the first had a comparatively long history, the second was tropical and had failed to attract European immigrants, and the third consisted of a mining camp, Kimberley, on the edge of the desert. On the plateau of South Africa between the Orange River and the Limpopo emigrant Boers from the Cape had founded two republics, the Orange Free State and the South African Republic; northeast of the latter lay Portuguese East Africa, whose boundaries were still undefined. The white communities contained a large colored and native population and on their borders hovered unsubdued native tribes, the most important of whom occupied the regions between the Cape Colony and Natal, between Natal and Portuguese East Africa, and to the west and north of the South African Republic. The discovery of diamonds in Griqualand West in 1867 signaled the opening of a period of prospecting for and discovering rich diamond and gold mines; these discoveries, the mining camps that sprang up, and the hope of new finds profoundly altered the course of South African history. In the eighties and nineties the powers of Europe coveted South African possessions; the natives were subdued and their lands appropriated, and the chief gold mining center of South Africa, Johannesburg, in the Transvaal or South African Republic, became the economic center of the subcontinent and the focal point for financial and political intrigues. The importance of the foreign competition for South African land and of the gold discoveries must not, however, be allowed to overshadow the effects of British colonial policy generally, of the native question, and of the relations between Briton and Boer on the course of South African history. Although the various forces which shaped her destiny during 1872–1902 often operated simultaneously and were closely related, for the sake of clarity we shall discuss them in the following order: the Anglo-German rivalry in South Africa, British expansion, Britain and the Boer republics, the native problem, and the internal development of British South Africa, tracing these topics more or less separately until the outbreak of the Boer War in 1899.

Until the last quarter of the nineteenth century Britain was reluctant to extend her boundaries in South Africa. Capetown was considered valuable as a port of call, but otherwise South Africa was viewed with indifference, an indifference that Cape politicians and a handful of expansionists at home strove hard to overcome. The Guano Islands off the coast of Namaqualand were annexed by Britain in 1861 and 1866, and some of the colonists at the Cape began to clamor to have the western coast of

South Africa from the Orange River to the southern boundary of Angola proclaimed a British sphere of interest. Yielding to these importunities, Sir Bartle Frere, governor at the Cape from 1876 to 1880, annexed Walfisch Bay, but requests for further annexations were vetoed by the imperial government. Meanwhile German missionaries had established stations in Namaqualand and Damaraland, and the question of protection for them had been discussed by Britain and Germany in the late sixties and early seventies. Shortly afterward German traders appeared on the scene, and in 1883 a merchant from Bremen, F. A. C. Lüderitz, bought land and hoisted the German flag at Angra Pequeña. Downing Street was perplexed. The colonial secretary, Lord Derby, was inclined to heed the clamor at the Cape; but Gladstone had no intention of proclaiming a Monroe doctrine for South Africa, he thought Germany was entitled to colonial possessions, and he believed that with German colonies in the vicinity it would be easier to keep the Cape and deal with its politicians. In this Granville, the foreign secretary, agreed with his chief. There was delay; Bismarck, growing impatient, began to employ bullying tactics which made Gladstone and Granville hesitant to yield, but the Egyptian situation was so dangerous that the British statesmen had no choice. Germany secured a West African colony extending from the Orange River in the south to the Kunene River in the north; the Guano and Ichaboc Islands and Walfisch Bay remained British.

On the eastern coast of South Africa the activities of the Boers beyond the Vaal had caused Britain in 1861 to revive old claims to Delagoa Bay, which Portugal refused to surrender. In 1872 the question was submitted to the arbitration of the president of France who three years later decided in favor of Portugal. Southwest of Delagoa Bay, in the land of the Zulus, lay St. Lucia Bay which offered possibilities as a harbor. In 1879 Britain broke the power of the Zulu but did not annex his land. A few years later Boers and Germans began to cast covetous eyes on St. Lucia Bay, and to forestall action by either one Lord

Derby advised in 1884 that Britain make her colonial boundary in southeast Africa coterminous with that of Portugal, but Gladstone was unwilling. However, shortly after New Years, 1885, it looked as if Bismarck would repeat at St. Lucia Bay the tactics employed at Angra Pequeña; moreover, by joining hands with the Boers the Germans might block British expansion northward from the Cape. Faced with this possibility, Britain annexed St. Lucia Bay in 1885. In the same year and for the purpose of driving a wedge between Germans and Boers, Britain declared Bechuanaland a British protectorate, thereby securing control over the great northern or missionary road from the Cape to the interior along which Cecil Rhodes and his pioneers were soon to travel in quest of the land of the Matabele and the Mashona.

The powers of Europe agreed to arbitrate or to settle by negotiations their disputes concerning African lands, but the Bantu refused to surrender without a struggle. In 1877 white met black in battle array in Kaffraria; the outcome, of course, was never in doubt. British authority continued to be extended in the land of the Kaffirs, their territory was gradually added to that of the Cape Colony, and in 1894 its boundary became coterminous with that of Natal. By the middle of the seventies a new Zulu power had grown up to the north of Natal. Cetewayo, last of the great Zulu war lords, had built up a formidable military machine and his young men were eager to dip their spears in blood. He quarreled with the Transvaal, this republic was annexed by Britain in April, 1877, and the Boer–Zulu boundary dispute became her concern. Sir Bartle Frere, governor at the Cape and high commissioner for South Africa, arrived at the conclusion that the Zulu power must be broken, and without formal authorization from home he demanded in December, 1878, that Cetewayo disarm. Choosing war rather than dishonor, the Zulu destroyed a British force consisting of about 800 regulars and an equal number of native allies at Isandhlwana on January 22, 1879; among the later victims of the war was the prince imperial of France, the son of Napoleon III. Although the Zulus under Cetewayo upheld the fighting traditions of their race, the superior skill and equipment of the British soon told against them; their defeat at Ulundi, July 4, 1879, ended a hopeless struggle. The home government, having censured Frere for his rashness in precipitating the war, now refused to annex Zululand, which was divided among thirteen petty chiefs. This arrangement was unsatisfactory, and after an attempt to restore Cetewayo his land was formally annexed by Britain in 1887 and later added to Natal. Basutoland was joined to the Cape Colony in 1871, but efforts to disarm the Basutos caused an uprising in 1880, and Basutoland was finally separated from the Cape and organized as a British protectorate.

British missionaries had worked among the Bechuana tribes since early in the nineteenth century and had gained much influence over them. But in 1882–1883 adventurers from the Transvaal entered Bechuanaland, seized territory, and founded the republics of Stellaland and Goshen. Cape politicians had earmarked this region as a field for northward expansion; and Cecil Rhodes, who in the short span of a dozen years had risen to a position of financial and political leadership in South Africa, spoke of Bechuanaland as the Suez Canal to the interior. A missionary, the Reverend John Mackenzie, went to England to agitate in favor of extending British influence in Bechuanaland, for it appeared possible that if nothing was done Boers and Germans might unite, a consideration that stirred a reluctant British government to action. In 1884–1885, General Warren entered Bechuanaland with an army of 5000 men; a British protectorate was proclaimed on September 30, 1885. The portion of Bechuanaland lying between the Orange and Molopo rivers was annexed and joined to the Cape Colony in 1895, but the larger part of the territory, a region of 275,000 square miles, is still a protectorate.

North of the Limpopo the Matabele king, Lobengula, held sway. In the late eighties keen competition arose among British,

Boer, Portuguese, and other concession hunters for permission to exploit and seize his land. In 1886 rich gold mines were discovered in the Witwatersrand area in the Transvaal; prospectors began to hunt for new finds elsewhere; and Rhodes, one of the greatest among British empire-builders, dreamed of a Cape-to-Cairo railroad through British-controlled territory. Events moved swiftly during 1886–1893. In 1887, Portugal attempted to join Angola with Mozambique, an effort which Britain frustrated. Partly as a result of Rhodes' entreaties, the Reverend J. S. Moffat, son of the famous missionary to the Bechuana, was sent to Lobengula's kraal as British resident; and in February, 1888, he concluded a treaty whereby the king pledged himself not to cede territory without the consent of the British high commissioner to South Africa. Later in the year emissaries of Rhodes obtained from Lobengula exclusive rights to hunt for minerals within his domain. This, the famous Rudd concession, "was upheld by the Imperial Government." With the foundation thus laid, Rhodes proceeded to organize the British South Africa Company, including among its directors the Duke of Fife, son-in-law of the Prince of Wales, and Albert Grey, later Earl Grey and governor general of Canada. A royal charter was secured in 1889; the "pioneers" moved into Mashonaland and founded the town of Salisbury in 1890; and in 1891 an Anglo-Portuguese convention delimited the boundaries of the company's territory and obtained for it an outlet by railroad to Beira in Portuguese East Africa. In 1893 Lobengula made a hopeless effort to rid himself of the intruders. When, three years later, his people rose again, Rhodes persuaded them after some fighting to lay down their arms. In recognition of his great services, the inland African empire, an area of about 475,000 square miles, which Cecil Rhodes had won for Britain was named Rhodesia in 1895.

Distrust of the Boers acted as a powerful stimulant for British expansion in South Africa, 1872–1899; as the century closed, the mutual suspicion of the two white races on the subcontinent culminated in the great Anglo-Boer war. In the early seventies the Orange Free State nourished resentment against the British on account of the annexations of Basutoland and Griqualand West; Britain's subsequent payment of £90,000 as compensation for Free State claims to the diamond fields did not heal the wounds to pocketbook and dignity. The Transvaal, too, had claimed portions of the diamond fields, but an award by R. W. Keate, the lieutenant-governor of Natal, as arbiter in a boundary dispute between the Transvaal and Bantu and Griqua chiefs, excluded the Boers from the diggings. The decision was probably just but it was unsatisfactory to the losing side. While these disputes were still fresh in the minds of the Boers a British colonial secretary, Lord Carnarvon, decided to federate all white communities in South Africa. He was in a hurry and so was his agent, Sir Theophilus Shepstone, when he annexed the Transvaal in April, 1877. The president of the republic, the Reverend T. F. Burgers, and a small group at Pretoria acquiesced in and probably desired annexation, but the backveld farmers saw no need for it and resented losing their hard-won independence. They protested and sent a deputation to England, only to be told that the annexation was final; they were, however, promised local autonomy.

Then came Gladstone's Midlothian campaign in 1879. With burning eloquence the great Liberal leader denounced and repudiated the annexation of the Transvaal. When the British election of 1880 restored him to office and power, the disaffected Boers of the Transvaal expected that he would immediately reverse the act he had repudiated. The distinction between reversal and repudiation was not so clear to them as it was to him; it grew clearer to him when he was informed that the Transvaal Boers were becoming reconciled to British rule and that there was still hope that the governor at the Cape, Sir Bartle Frere, might carry confederation. This hope was dashed in the summer of 1880; the governor was recalled; time passed before his successor was sent out; and the Boers of the Transvaal, receiving neither self-government nor independence, took up arms to secure the latter. Small British forces suffered reverses that culminated in the defeat and death of their commander-in-chief, Sir George Colley, at Majuba Hill on February 27, 1881.

Before this disaster the British government had decided to negotiate with the Boers; the decision was adhered to although comparatively large reinforcements had been ordered to South Africa. Gladstone withstood the clamor to avenge Majuba. By an agreement known as the Pretoria convention the Transvaal was restored, her boundaries defined, her independence recognized (subject to the vague proviso that the queen's suzerainty remained), and specific limitations imposed on her power to deal with the natives and with foreign states. Three years later an Anglo-Boer convention concluded at London made no mention of "suzerainty"; "native legislation was freed from the Queen's veto, the powers of the [British] Resident were cut down to those of a consul and the debt reduced by a third." But safeguards concerning the civil rights and equal taxation of Europeans and the prohibition of treaties with foreign states, other than the Orange Free State, and with neighboring native tribes without British consent were retained in the London convention.

The retrocession of the Transvaal has been described as the right thing done in the wrong way; but even this handicap might have been overcome if new factors had not enormously complicated Anglo-Boer relations and if representatives of British interests, especially Cecil Rhodes, had been less hurried. Among the most potent new factors were the scramble for Africa by European powers and the discovery of gold in the Transvaal. The first brought Germany to South Africa. Efforts by Transvaal Boers to expand to the west or east were suspected by Britain as moves to effect a combination with the Germans and to block her own road to the interior. On the west the Transvaal obtained only about 2000 square miles of Bechuanaland; the two Boer republics, Stellaland and Goshen, were taken over by

Britain. To the east the "New Republic" founded by Boers in Zululand was kept within narrow limits before it was allowed to unite with the Transvaal in 1888. Seven years later the Transvaal was permitted to establish control over Swaziland, but direct outlet to the sea was prevented by British annexations. North of the Limpopo Cecil Rhodes' chartered company completed the encirclement of the Transvaal, whose only contact with non-British lands was with Portuguese East Africa, which made possible direct railroad communication to Delagoa Bay.

In 1886 rich gold finds in the Witwatersrand area attracted adventurers from all quarters of the globe, and the city of Johannesburg sprang up. Placer mining gave way to the sinking of shafts and the digging of tunnels, work which required capital. Consequently the Transvaal soon found that she had both a large foreign population, mostly British, in her midst and powerful capitalistic mining interests intrenched within her borders. All South Africa began to look toward the Rand. From Cape and Natal ports government-owned railroads were constructed for the purpose of tapping the traffic of Johannesburg. The Transvaal government, becoming affluent overnight, signaled its financial independence by refusing to join a customs union with the Orange Free State and the Cape, and it started to open a window to the outside world via Delagoa Bay. Cecil Rhodes, who had become prime minister of the Cape in 1890, saw that white South Africa must be united, and to this end he worked harmoniously with Jan Hendrik Hofmeyr, the great Boer leader at the Cape. The refusal of the Transvaal to enter a South African customs union and to conclude a railroad agreement with the Cape was interpreted by Rhodes as meaning that she would never voluntarily unite with the other white communities in South Africa. Rhodes, realizing that only a comparatively brief span of life remained to him, took time by the forelock when in 1895 he entered into a conspiracy against the Transvaal. The plot embraced an uprising by disaffected foreigners in Johannesburg, an appeal from them for protection against the Boers, and a dash into the city of armed forces collected in Rhodesia and concentrated at or near Mafeking on the Bechuanaland-Transvaal border across the veld. The plan miscarried; Dr. (later Sir) L. S. Jameson, who in December, 1895, led the raid was captured with his whole force. The "Raid" convinced President Kruger of the Transvaal that Britain intended to seize his country and feverishly he began to arm. Worse still, in 1896 the German emperor, William II, sent him a clumsily worded New Year's greeting congratulating him upon having met a dangerous situation "without appealing to the help of friendly Powers." This greeting encouraged Kruger to think that the Transvaal had friends who might give aid in case of need, but it created consternation in England and strengthened the suspicion that Germany was plotting against Britain in Africa. The stage was being set for an Anglo-Boer war.

The events sketched above were largely instrumental in shaping the course of the history of the Cape Colony and Natal, 1872–1899. The boundaries of the former were extended by the annexation of Griqualand West in 1880, British Bechuanaland, and the Transkeian territory, 1879–1895. A decrease in area was sustained when Basutoland was severed from the Cape and put under imperial protection in 1884, but inasmuch as the Basutos had been both strong and turbulent the loss could be counted a gain. The frontier posts of Natal were moved forward by the acquisition of Zululand and Tongaland in 1897. By these annexations and transfers of land from imperial to colonial authority, the Bantu population of the Cape and Natal was greatly augmented. A special native penal code was passed for the Transkei, the social status of the chiefs was recognized, and "legislation was enacted by Proclamation of the Governor." In 1894 the first step was taken to establish district councils on which natives were represented in both the Ciskeian and the Transkeian portions of Kaffraria.

Natal continued to apply the native policy formulated by Theophilus Shepstone in the middle of the nineteenth century.

His power as secretary for native affairs was modified somewhat in 1875 when the Natal native high court was created; a Natal code of Bantu law prepared in 1878 was supplemented and supplanted by a code of native law promulgated in 1891. At the Cape efforts were made to accustom the Bantu to European methods of agriculture and industry, and those who could pass the educational test and possessed the necessary property qualifications might vote; but in Natal the natives were left more to themselves, and at least in theory sufficient "reserves" were set aside to take care of this population. Whites and natives alike were affected by the discovery of the diamond mines at Kimberley and the gold mines on the Rand. Next to the Great Trek this discovery is the most significant event in the history of South Africa.

About the time Griqualand West was annexed by Britain, Kimberley had a population of more than ten thousand; this soon doubled. The economic center of gravity thus began to move inland and need arose for a railroad to link the diamond city with the coast. The political rivalry between the eastern and western portions of the Cape Colony and the commercial rivalry between its chief ports resulted in the building of railroad lines which gave Kimberley three outlets to the sea – Capetown, Port Elizabeth, and East London. The colony's railroad mileage increased from 73 in 1874 to 1600 in 1885; the lines were government-owned, and the same political considerations which had resulted in three lines being built where one would have sufficed gave rise to bitter fights over the rates to be charged from the interior to the coast. But the complications due to the competition for the Kimberley traffic were insignificant compared with those that arose when Johannesburg reached metropolitan proportions and investigations disclosed that the gold-mining on the Rand had a long future. The gold district was 952 miles from Capetown, 494 miles from Durban in Natal, and 369 miles from Delagoa Bay in Portuguese East Africa. The last route was favored by the government of the Transvaal, but the question of capital for constructing it caused complications. In 1886 Natal had two hundred and twenty miles of railroads in operation, but the intransigence of President Kruger of the Transvaal delayed the completion of the line from Durban to Johannesburg. The distance of the Cape ports from the Rand had been reduced by the railroads built to or toward Kimberley; furthermore, the colony had the advantages of experience in the building and operation of railroads and of credit for further construction as the need might arise. But the shortest route to Johannesburg lay through the Orange Free State and her consent must be secured before that city could be linked with Cape ports. Although the farmers of the Orange Free State profited greatly from hauling supplies to the mines, it proved easy to reach an agreement with this republic whereby the Cape lent her the money necessary for building the line through her territory. The route to Delagoa Bay was favored by President Kruger; however, an early concession granted to an American, Colonel McMurdo, by the Portuguese authorities and afterward cancelled by them led to disputes and international complications that delayed the building of the railroad.

Negotiations between the colonies and states over railroad concessions and rates embraced the question of customs tariffs. In the old days duties were collected on the coast, the republics being denied a share in them or a refund at their border. The gold discoveries changed this. Both the Cape and Natal were anxious to barter tariffs for railroads. In 1889 the Cape and the Orange Free State formed a customs union; but the Transvaal, which two years earlier had proposed such an arrangement, now stood aloof as did Natal. Economic factors tended to divide South Africa into the Cape-Free State and the Natal-Transvaal groups; and both between and within these divisions disputes over traffic rates and customs tariffs complicated and embittered the relations of the white communities.

The diamond and gold mines drew thousands of adventurers to South Africa, attracted capital, and produced capitalists.

Among the last, Cecil John Rhodes soon reached towering heights. The tubercular youth of seventeen who landed in South Africa in 1870 had by the beginning of the eighties become a financial magnate and a power in politics at the Cape. The virtual monopoly which he acquired over the diamond industry combined with the influence wielded by his control over one of the great gold-mining companies supplied him with capital for his Rhodesian ventures, for railroad construction in Bechuanaland, and for political, cultural, and humanitarian enterprises. His connections with Cape and South African politics generally will be discussed in some detail later.

The economic development of South Africa from 1872, the year of the granting of responsible government to the Cape Colony, to the outbreak of the Anglo-Boer war may be gauged to some extent by the increase in railroad mileage — the 63 miles in operation at the end of 1872 had grown to 3834 miles in 1899. The average yearly export from Cape ports for the period 1870–1874 was valued at £4,648,092; by 1895–1899 it had risen to £20,171,390, and the import had increased from £4,002,930 to £16,294,329. Trade statistics for Natal reveal an annual average of exports, 1870–1874, of £594,111 and imports of £777,527, but for the years 1895–1899 the export and import figures averaged £1,834,067 and £4,845,715 respectively per annum. The annual export of gold from the Cape during 1895–1899 was valued at £11,286,016, and diamonds furnished £4,515,672. Beginning in the eighties these two products supplanted wool as the chief article of export; however, measured in quantity the yearly export of wool increased 50 per cent between 1872 and 1899. Wine, which led the field of Cape exports early in the nineteenth century, dropped so far behind that in the nineties less than 100,000 gallons were shipped out annually. Among the new export articles besides gold and diamonds Cape statistics for 1895–1899 list copper, £295,121; ostrich feathers, £648,560; and mohair, £677,430. The rapid growth of the mining centers and the construction of railroads to provide them with direct outlets to the sea were largely responsible for heavy imports of machinery and foodstuffs. The United States supplied a large share of the former; the value of the imports from that country rose from less than £500,000 in 1890 to £2,767,000 in 1898. Foodstuffs, meat, wheat, and canned goods came chiefly from the various parts of the British empire. Although Britain in 1898 held a comfortable lead over all the other countries combined in supplying the needs of South Africa, her exports to that country increased only about 25 per cent between 1890 and 1898, whereas those of Germany quadrupled and those of the United States increased more than fivefold.

Both the British colonies and the Boer republics experienced a rapid growth in their white population from 1872 until the outbreak of the Boer War. The number of Europeans at the Cape rose from 236,000 in 1875 to 336,000 in 1891; by 1899 it was nearing the half-million mark. Natal had about 20,000 white inhabitants at the opening of the seventies; the census of 1891 recorded 46,000, and by 1904 this had risen to 97,000. Besides her large native population the coming of Indian coolies provided Natal with a new racial element destined to prove embarrassing; in 1904 the Indians outnumbered the Europeans there. In 1873 the Orange Free State had 27,000 and the Transvaal approximately 40,000 European inhabitants; on the eve of the outbreak of the Anglo-Boer war the figures for the former had risen to about 100,000 and for the latter to 250,000. Included in this new Transvaal population were many non-Boers, chiefly British, who constituted the foreign-born, the Uitlanders, and provided such formidable domestic and foreign political problems for the republic.

Much of this increase in population represented urban growth. The railroads which existed before 1899 did little to aid the rural agricultural areas of South Africa, for it was cheaper to bring wheat to Johannesburg from Australia than from most of the farming regions in the Transvaal or the Cape. There were few incentives to extend the agricultural possibilities of the subcontinent nor were efforts made to check the gradual impoverishment of the pasture lands by the drought-resisting grasses as a result of overstocking. Moreover, in the eighties and nineties phylloxera, a disease on the vines, and the rinderpest among cattle greatly embarrassed two large classes of South African agriculturists.

Population figures and trade statistics reveal changes in the tangible phases of South African life during 1872–1899, but other phases of vital importance in the history of Britain's South African colonies are less easy to gauge. True, figures on expenditures show that the Cape government's outlay for education rose from £25,268 in 1872 to £270,758 in 1899; but a Cape education commission of 1891 found only 41,037 of the 99,280 white children between the ages of 5 and 14 in aided or private schools, leaving nearly 60 per cent unaccounted for; attempts to introduce compulsory education failed. Nor did Natal present a more favorable picture. In the field of higher education the founding of Victoria College at Stellenbosch raised the number of collegiate institutions at the Cape to two; the University of the Cape of Good Hope, modeled upon that of London, received a royal charter in 1879. Cecil Rhodes, whose dreams were those of Napoleon, not those of Midas, showed an interest in education and the arts, and he strove to create enthusiasm for a South African style of architecture. Nor, in considering South Africa, 1872–1899, should it be forgotten that Olive Schreiner, born in Basutoland in 1855 of missionary parents – the father German and the mother English – produced in *The Story of an African Farm*, 1883, the only novel of British colonial origin that gained world-wide recognition within this period.

The Cape Colony secured responsible government in 1872 and twenty-one years later a similar boon was conferred upon Natal. In the seventies Sir John C. Molteno was the dominant figure in Cape politics, but a quarrel with the masterful governor general, Sir Bartle Frere, over the control of the colonial forces in the Kaffir war of that decade led to his resignation as prime minister in 1878. He was succeeded by Gordon (later Sir Gordon) Sprigg, who continued active in Cape politics until after the Anglo-Boer war. Among others who played prominent roles on the political stage at the Cape were John X. Merriman, J. W. Sauer, T. Upington, and Sir Thomas Scanlen. Sir John Robinson was prime minister of Natal from 1893 to 1897. None of these men compare in importance with J. H. Hofmeyr and Cecil Rhodes. Hofmeyr in 1883 gained control over the Afrikander Bond which had been founded as a Sinn Fein Boer and anti-English organization. Under his leadership the Bond dropped its narrow nationalistic program and became a dominant factor in South African politics, supporting Rhodes for premier at the Cape, 1890–1895. Hofmeyr seems to have envisaged a future for South Africa and the British empire resembling that which Generals Botha and Smuts sought to realize after 1907, and Hofmeyr's political views were sufficiently near those of Rhodes to provide a solid basis for a political alliance; this, however, was shattered by the Jameson raid. Both men worked for a united white South Africa; to Hofmeyr, a Cape Boer, the British flag was no obstacle.

But before Hofmeyr and Rhodes began their work for a South African union a British secretary of state, Lord Carnarvon, had blunderingly and clumsily sought to undo the work of the Sand River and Bloemfontein conventions. In an earlier chapter we saw that Sir George Grey attempted to reunite white South Africa in the fifties and that Lord Kimberley in 1870 instructed Sir Henry Barkly to consider federation as a possible solution for South African problems, more especially that of the ceaseless friction between the eastern and western portions of the Cape Colony. However, the efforts of Grey and Kimberley were fruitless. In 1874 Lord Carnarvon succeeded Lord Kimberley at the colonial office. For about twenty years he had been interested in Britain's intra-imperial problems, in 1867 he had steered the British North America Act through parliament, and in 1874 he considered the federalization of South Africa a primary object of imperial policy. Like Rhodes at a later date, Carnarvon was in a hurry. In 1875 he suggested that representatives from the South African colonies and republics should meet in a confederation convention; and to expedite matters he arranged for the payment of £90,000 to the Orange Free State as compensation for the loss of the diamond fields, replaced Sir Henry Barkly with Sir Bartle Frere as governor at the Cape, and sent J. A. Froude, the historian, to South Africa to agitate in favor of federation. The last step was a capital blunder, for Froude by his tactlessness exposed himself to the accusation of fomenting discord between the eastern and western districts at the Cape and attempting to undermine the position of the Molteno ministry. It soon became evident that no confederation convention would be held in South Africa. Thereupon Carnarvon, disregarding the lessons that might have been deduced from the federating of British North America, called a phantom South African confederation convention in London and had the colonial office prepare a constitution for a federal South Africa. An even more drastic method for furthering this end was the annexation of the Transvaal by Carnarvon's agent, Sir Theophilus Shepstone, in April, 1877. Carnarvon's confederation project was dead even before he left the colonial office early in 1878; and Frere's crushing of the Zulus in 1879 helped destroy the desire that Transvaal Boers may have harbored to be British subjects on account of the protection offered by Britain. The colonial office, however, proved slow at learning; all hope for accomplishing a South African federation had not faded when the Liberals returned to power in Britain in April, 1880. But an adverse vote by the Cape parliament finally dispelled the illusion; Frere was recalled; in December, 1880, the Boers of the Transvaal rose against Britain; and in the following year the republic beyond the Vaal was restored.

Carnarvon's efforts to federate white South Africa were hasty and poorly executed; although they failed, they embodied an ideal not wholly lost sight of by British statesmen and governors at the Cape. Cecil Rhodes in the first and last periods of his career in South Africa dreamed of and worked for a purely British control over the subcontinent, whereas in the middle period, the period when J. H. Hofmeyr was his ally, his aim seems to have been to found a South African nation bound to the British crown by an arrangement similar to that which exists today.

To these two ideals for South Africa which envisaged the British flag dominant south of the Zambezi must be added a third, that of Paul Kruger, president of the South African Republic from 1882 to 1900. As a child Kruger had participated in the Great Trek; he could remember the days of Piet Retief, Weenen, and the events at Blood River; as a young man he had been present at the signing of the Sand River Convention in 1852; and thirty years later he had been a leader in the successful effort, 1880–1881, to restore the independence of the Transvaal. Deeply and passionately he felt that South Africa belonged to his people by all rights founded on the laws of God and man; he dreamed of a day when his people's flag, the Vierkleur, should be the flag of a united South Africa. Between this ideal held so fervently by the strong man of the Transvaal and the British imperialists' ideal in the latter half of the nineties no compromise was possible. The "South Africanism" represented by Hofmeyr ceased to be an effective force; and as the century closed, Briton and Boer were locked in a deadly struggle for dominance — a struggle generally called by historians of South Africa the Anglo-Boer war, 1899–1902.

In tracing the origins and causes of this war one must go back to the early days of the British occupation of South Africa. The rebellion at Slachter's Nek, the ordinance granting civil rights to the natives, the policies adopted at the instigation of Dr. John Philip and his friends, the freeing of the slaves, the Great Trek, the British annexation of Natal, Boomplaats, and other incidents in the early history of the relations between Briton and Boer were as potent factors in causing this war as were the annexation of the Transvaal in 1877, Majuba Hill, the British encirclement

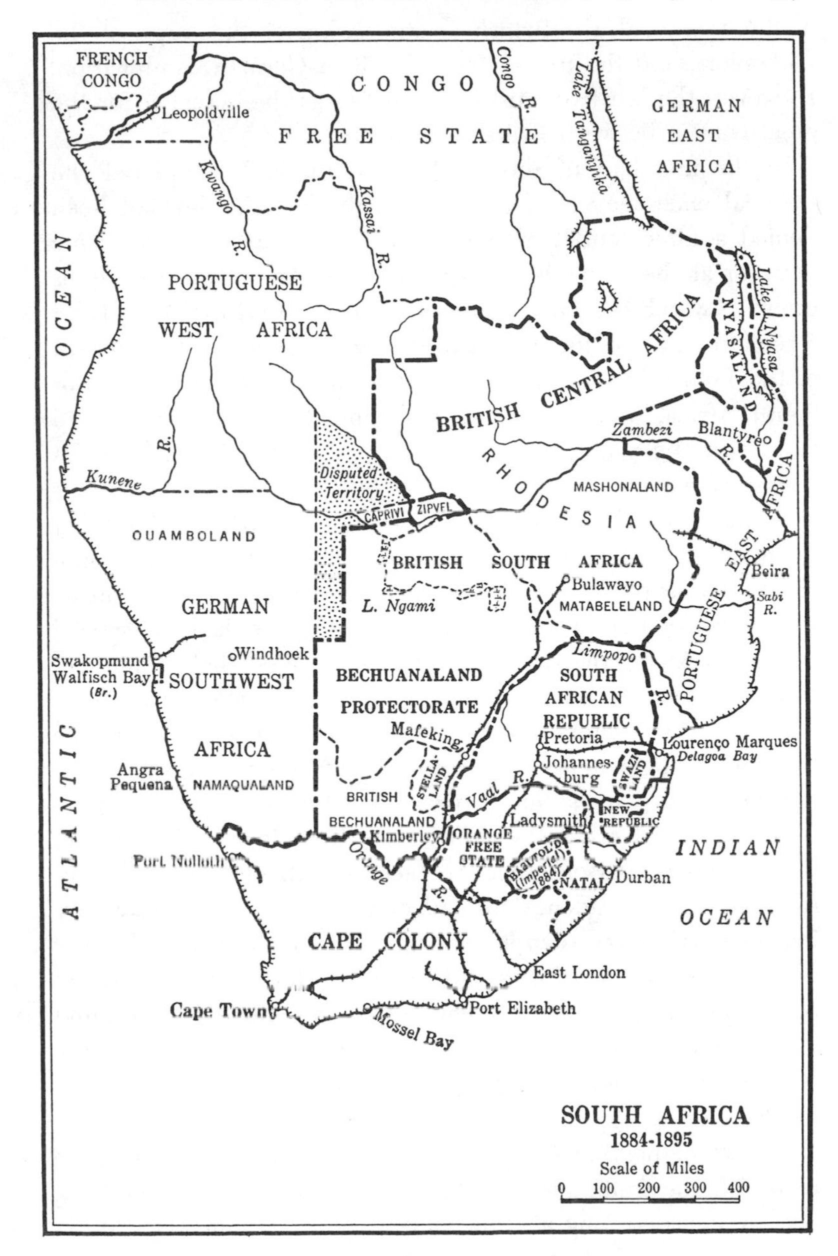
FRENCH CONGO
Leopoldville
CONGO FREE STATE
Congo R.
Lake Tanganyika
GERMAN EAST AFRICA
Kwango R.
Kassai R.
OCEAN
PORTUGUESE WEST AFRICA
BRITISH CENTRAL AFRICA
NYASALAND
Lake Nyasa
Zambezi
Blantyre
R.
Kunene
Disputed Territory
CAPRIVI ZIPVFL
RHODESIA
MASHONALAND
OUAMBOLAND
BRITISH SOUTH AFRICA
Beira
Bulawayo
MATABELELAND
Sabi R.
GERMAN
L. Ngami
PORTUGUESE EAST AFRICA
Swakopmund
Walfisch Bay (Br.)
Windhoek
SOUTHWEST AFRICA
BECHUANALAND PROTECTORATE
Limpopo
SOUTH AFRICAN REPUBLIC
Mafeking
Pretoria
Lourenço Marques
Delagoa Bay
Johannesburg
SWAZI LAND
STELLA LAND
Angra Pequena
NAMAQUALAND
BRITISH BECHUANALAND
Vaal R.
NEW REPUBLIC
Ladysmith
Kimberley
ORANGE FREE STATE
ATLANTIC
INDIAN OCEAN
Port Nolloth
Orange R.
BASUTOLAND (Imperial) 1884
NATAL
Durban
CAPE COLONY
East London
Cape Town
Port Elizabeth
Mossel Bay
SOUTH AFRICA
1884-1895
Scale of Miles
0 100 200 300 400

of the Transvaal, the British championship of the cause of the Uitlanders, and the British fear of a Boer-German combination. However, the last two must be reckoned as the occasion for the great contest between British and Boers.

In the first half of the nineties Britain had completed the political encirclement of the Transvaal; the republic had been denied a direct outlet to the sea; and Cecil Rhodes, as prime minister at the Cape, had built up a British-controlled customs union to which the Transvaal and even Natal refused to adhere. The gold mines on the Rand supplied wealth for the government of the Transvaal, made it dominant among the political units of South Africa, and brought a government of farmers face to face with the problems presented by strangers in their midst who were partly safeguarded by pledges given in the conventions of Pretoria and London and who raised the specter of foreign dominance. Kruger knew that the Transvaal belonged to him and to his people; behind the Uitlanders loomed Britain; and he sought counsel from Dutch and Germans who had no special reason for loving the British. At first he treated the foreign element at Johannesburg generously. Liberal gold laws were passed and state support was granted to English schools, but the increase in the number of the foreigners and perhaps his own advancing years made him fearful. The state aid was withdrawn from the English schools; Dutch became the sole official language; a foreign-born person could not acquire citizenship until after fourteen years' residence instead of the former and customary five years, and even then he was ineligible to the first and really dominant Volksraad, the second Raad, to which foreigners could be elected, being practically without power. But the mines and the foreigners paid nearly all the taxes in the Transvaal and the British-born citizens were subject to call on commando or military service.

The foreigners had grievances, and Kruger, by trying to choke off the traffic between the Cape ports and Johannesburg and by concentrating all the political power in the republic in his own hands, created powerful enemies. Intrigues by the Uitlanders in Johannesburg and by Dr. Jameson, the administrator in Rhodesia, Cecil Rhodes, and a few of their friends culminated in the Jameson raid which has already been mentioned. Sir Hercules Robinson, governor at the Cape and British high commissioner for South Africa, and Joseph Chamberlain, the British colonial secretary, knew of the possibility of an outbreak in Johannesburg and believed that if it took place Britain might and should intervene, but they had no knowledge of the projected raid. Nevertheless, when it occurred, Kruger considered Jameson Chamberlain's agent, and the German emperor's ill-advised telegram to Kruger was accepted by the British as proof of plans involving an anti-British Boer-German combination. The raid by Jameson made the Anglo-Boer war inevitable.

Between January, 1896, and October, 1899, many serious efforts were made to iron out the differences between Kruger and the Uitlanders as well as between Kruger and Britain; but all controversies narrowed to the paramount issue: should Kruger and his Boers or Britain dominate South Africa? Since neither would or could give way no agreement was possible. Sir Alfred (later Lord) Milner, who in 1897 succeeded Robinson as governor at the Cape, seems to have felt certain from the beginning that a war could not be avoided, but Chamberlain was slow to admit this. The Uitlanders in Johannesburg organized, drew up a statement of grievances, pointed to pledges broken by the government of the Transvaal, and invoked the aid of Britain. A dispute then arose between Britain and the Transvaal over whether the "suzerainty" mentioned in the Pretoria but not in the London convention had been given up, over the extent of the powers Britain could claim under the conventions, and over the rights of the foreigners in the Transvaal.

During the three and a half years of negotiations Britain suggested among other things that Johannesburg should be given municipal self-government, and Kruger tried to barter concessions to the foreigners for complete independence for his country. Meanwhile he armed vigorously. Somewhat belatedly Britain began to send troops to South Africa. Steyn, president of the Orange Free State, de Villiers, chief justice at the Cape, and Hofmeyr tried in vain to prevent an appeal to arms. A conference at Bloemfontein, June 1–3, 1899, between Kruger and Milner brought no results. In September the military preparations of the Transvaal seemed complete; the republic had arms for about 80,000 men. The alliance with the Free State, the hope of a rising in the Cape Colony, a belief in God's aid, the weakness of the British military forces in South Africa, and a knowledge of the other foreign complications facing Britain at this time led Kruger to assume that the moment had arrived for settling once and forever the issue between Briton and Boer. On October 9, 1899, the Transvaal presented an ultimatum to Britain demanding withdrawal of British forces from the frontier within forty-eight hours. The request was ignored and war broke out.

A pigmy had challenged a Titan; the former put much trust in the favor of the God of Battles, the latter was as astonished as Goliath was when challenged by David; and for a while the world beheld a combat reminiscent of the famous contest between the Philistine giant and the Hebrew shepherd boy. The British forces were driven back and hemmed in at Ladysmith, Kimberley, and Mafeking, and the road through Natal lay open to the Boers. To the British public which had anticipated an early and easy victory the steady reports of disasters during the first three months of the war came as stunning blows. The British had miscalculated, but so had their adversaries — the English were not driven into the sea, the rising in the Cape Colony occurred too late and was too small to affect the outcome, and the great powers although generous with their sympathy offered no material assistance. In January, 1900, Russia started conversations with France and Germany that apparently had for their object the embarrassment of Britain, but nothing happened. The Boers had underestimated the tenacity of their foes. Defeat steeled Britain's determination to settle finally the South African issue.

Volunteers flocked to the recruiting stations; and the self-governing colonies, especially those of Australasia, aided generously. Of the 300,000 men mobilized by Britain about one-tenth came from overseas.

In the early stages of the Anglo-Boer war Sir Redvers Buller was British commander-in-chief; General P. J. Joubert commanded the Transvaal forces and General Christian de Wet those of the Orange Free State. Lord Roberts soon replaced Buller, and Lord Kitchener, who came to South Africa as Roberts' chief of staff, succeeded him as commander-in-chief. On Joubert's death in 1900, Louis Botha became generalissimo of the Boer forces. In February, 1900, the Boers suffered their first great reverse with the surrender of General Cronje and 4000 men. They had mustered their full strength at the beginning, had no reserve population to draw from, and with the tightening of the British blockade of Delagoa Bay were cut off from supplies from outside. In March, 1900, Roberts occupied Bloemfontein, the capital of the Free State, and two months later he entered Pretoria, the capital of the Transvaal. Although the republics were annexed, resistance continued, the guerilla war dragging on until May 31, 1902, when Kitchener and the Boer leaders signed the Treaty of Vereeniging. The vastness of the country and the extreme mobility of the Boer forces had compelled the British, in fighting their foes, to adopt an elaborate system of blockhouses and barbed-wire entanglements, to destroy a large number of farmsteads, and to concentrate the Boer women and children in camps. Because of the difficulty in establishing and enforcing proper health and sanitary regulations in these camps, the death rate was high and 4000 women and 16,000 children died; this about equaled the number of British soldiers killed in the war. The generous terms granted the Boers at Vereeniging did not obliterate the memories of the war or efface from the records the long list of innocent victims of the struggle.

The Anglo-Boer war, 1899–1902, was epoch-making in the history of the British empire, especially in the history of that empire in Africa. The war revealed Britain's isolation and the dangers connected therewith, and British statesmen began in earnest to seek friends and allies; the support which the colonies overseas gave the homeland disclosed the strength of their attachment and encouraged Chamberlain to think that it would be possible to create tangible political and economic ties between Britain and the self-governing colonies; and the outcome of the struggle decided the issue of a South African union south of the Zambezi.

CHAPTER 23

AUSTRALIA, 1870–1901

ON April 19, 1870, Australia celebrated the centenary of her discovery by Captain Cook. Appropriately enough, an exposition at Sydney directed the attention of the world to the progress made in Australia since January, 1788, when the first shipload of convicts landed at Port Jackson. From this unpromising beginning had developed six colonies with a total population of 1,600,000. All the colonies, except Western Australia, were now self-governing, and since 1867 the continent had ceased to be the dumping ground for the delinquents of the British Isles. The agricultural and mineral wealth of Australia was gradually being unlocked; and Australians could with pardonable pride point to their flourishing cities, thriving farming communities, and teeming sheep ranches.

Rapid and even spectacular progress had been made by Australia in the first half of the Victorian era. Still, it was only the beginning. Unknown regions in the west-central and northern portions of the continent challenged explorers; the empty spaces of known fertility and resources invited settlers; and social, economic, and political life had hardly passed the initial frontier stage. Exploration, immigration, prospecting for minerals, the pushing forward of the pastoral and agricultural frontiers, and the adjustment of the political and economic institutions to the needs and conditions of Australia continued to occupy the attention of the colonists. When the period was half over, however, new situations developed from the colonizing activities of non-British peoples in the neighborhood of Australia. From those situations arose the need for the federal union that came into existence on January 1, 1901.

The governments of Western and South Australia, which controlled the least-known areas of the continent, were anxious to unravel the mysteries of the great lone land of their section. The former sent out several exploring expeditions, among which the most successful were led by John Forrest, afterward Lord Forrest of Bunbury. These paved the way for the building of the telegraph connecting Perth with Adelaide and revealed the agricultural and grazing possibilities of the Hampton Tablelands and the Murchison district in the southern and northwestern portions of the colony respectively. In 1870 South Australia undertook the construction of a telegraph line linking Adelaide with Port Darwin in the extreme north. The surveying and building of this line increased the knowledge of the dry or desert land of central and northern Australia. A new incentive to exploration came with the discovery of several artesian basins; this raised hopes that water from them might make the desert blossom and become fruitful. The old motives for exploration – the need for new pastures and the hope of finding gold – continued to spur men on to brave the heat, the sand, and the thirst of the arid and semi-arid regions of Australia. Nor were all the prospectors chasing a will-o'-the-wisp. "Strikes" at Mount Morgan, Queensland, in 1882, and at East Kimberley, Coolgardie, and Kalgoorlie, Western Australia, in the years 1883, 1892, and 1893 respectively, brought rewards to some and advertised that Australia was still a land of gold.

The gold discoveries of the eighties and nineties, like those of the early fifties, attracted immigrants to Australia; but as means of augmenting the permanent population they were overshadowed by the governmental policy of granting free passage from Europe, by promises of free or cheap land to prospective settlers, and by the public works which provided employment for the new arrivals at wages that seemed high to Europeans. Until the low prices and hard times of the late eighties and early nineties produced unemployment even in Australia, all the colonies, but Queensland in particular, were anxious to obtain settlers. The white population of the Australian colonies grew from 1,668,377 in 1871 to 3,771,415 in 1901; about two-fifths of this is attributable to immigration. Western Australia recorded the largest growth, measured by percentage — from 25,000 to 184,-000, concentrated mainly in the decade 1891–1901 when gold was discovered within her borders. But in this case the newcomers came from the eastern colonies as well as from overseas. Gold rushes in the seventies and eighties brought immigrants to Queensland; moreover, this colony had both grassland for cattle and sheep and a fertile coastal belt suitable for tropical agriculture. Anxious for settlers, she not only used the proceeds from land sales but even borrowed £3,000,000 during 1860–1890 for the purpose of aiding immigration. Her population increased from 120,000 to nearly 500,000 in the period under discussion. The need for labor on the sugar plantations caused Queensland planters to bring in South Sea islanders, the Kanakas, contrary to the principles of the white Australia policy; Western Australia attempted to secure oriental laborers for her northern sections. However, the Australian labor unions offered stout and successful opposition to these efforts to dilute the labor market with non-Europeans. Between 1870 and 1885 the self-governing colonies of Australia borrowed large sums for public works, principally railroads, which served the double purpose of providing employment for immigrants and opening up new areas for farming. Then came a ten-year period of drought, depression, and collapse of borrowing. Low prices, unemployment, the contraction of settlements caused by the drought, and opposition by organized labor led the colonies with the exception of Queensland to discontinue the policy of aided immigration for the time being.

The growth of the population and their special economic needs moved the planters of northern Queensland to ask for a division of the colony and the settlers of Western Australia to demand responsible government. The separatist movement in northern

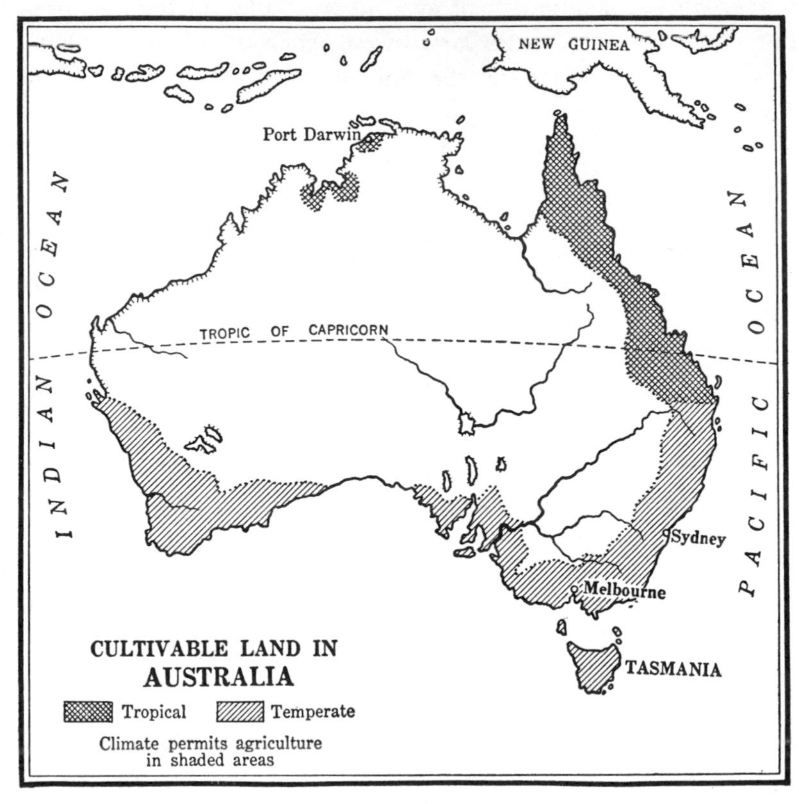

Queensland was linked with the development of tropical agriculture and the need for cheap non-European labor. The colony was large, more than 670,000 square miles, and the capital, Brisbane, is located in the far south. The sugar planters claimed that their interests were neglected; certain it is that the laborers of southern Queensland opposed the employment of Kanakas anywhere in the colony. Labor was powerful politically and the colonial legislature flatly refused the separation plea of the north.

The planters then appealed to the colonial office but without avail. English humanitarianism as represented by the Aborigines Protection Society and the Anti-Slavery Society opposed the indenturing of Kanakas for the sugar plantations of northern Queensland; they believed that the indentured Kanakas were practically slaves; and they saw in the separatist movement an effort to perpetuate the employment and exploitation of this labor without too strict supervision. Moreover, the Conservative government of Lord Salisbury, 1886–1892, in power when the Queensland separation question became acute, was bitterly hostile to home rule for Ireland; for the sake of consistency it could hardly approve a separatist movement in Queensland. It is also possible that English investors in Queensland bonds opposed a division of the colony on the ground that it might lessen the security behind these bonds. The upshot was that despite the precedents established by the division of New South Wales, quoted by the planters, and their assertions of neglect, the colonial office refused the request for a separate colony of northern Queensland.

In the case of Western Australia, on the other hand, the imperial government for a time demanded the division of the colony as the price for granting it complete self-government. The only crown colony in Australia, it had a legislative council, two-thirds of the members being elected and one-third nominated. The census of 1881 showed a population of 29,708 – larger by 4000 than Queensland's had been when she was granted a separate existence and responsible government. A request for self-government was sent to the colonial office in 1883, but its occupant, Lord Derby, refused to make a decision. Shortly afterward gold was discovered at East Kimberley, and the population increased by 18,000 in the eighties. Western Australia was anxious to be freed from the limitations which the colonial office imposed upon her power to borrow for public works and desired to have the same political stature as the other colonies of Australia. The conditions laid down by an imperial statute for the grant of autonomy to an Australian colony were fulfilled, yet Downing Street still hesitated. Reasons for the hesitation are to be found in the imperialistic views of the Salisbury government. In 1888 a committee on colonization sent a circular to all the colonies of Australia with suggestions concerning immigration and colonization. Those with responsible government refused to cooperate in plans to further British emigration; they would not accept the thesis that they should help in relieving unemployment and distress at home. Hence the colonial office in 1890 tried to impose as conditions for conceding self-government to Western Australia that no barrier should be erected against British immigration, that the territory north of the 26th degree south latitude should be separated from the rest and become a crown colony, and that a fixed sum should be set aside for the care of the natives. Western Australia accepted the last stipulation but refused to consent to a division. The other Australian colonies supported her, as did also a select committee appointed to study the whole question. Western Australia remained intact and obtained responsible government in 1890.

As we saw in an earlier chapter, New South Wales, Victoria, South Australia, Tasmania, and Queensland in the fifties secured two-chamber legislatures with the executive responsible to the popularly elected lower house or assembly. The first chamber, the legislative council, was nominated for life in New South Wales and Queensland, and in the other colonies elected on the basis of a narrower franchise than that fixed for elections to the legislative assembly. This tended to make the legislative councils more conservative than the assemblies. The legislative councils were elected for a long term — in Victoria ten years, reduced in 1881 to six; in South Australia twelve years, reduced to nine — with provisions that one-third should retire every second or third year as the case might be. The terms for the assemblies were three or five years (after 1893 they were all elected for three years), with the result that their political complexion changed more rapidly than did that of the legislative councils. Moreover, the limitations of the spheres of power for the two bodies had nowhere been fixed, nor had provisions been made for ending the deadlocks that became a regular feature of the Australian political scene, 1870–1901. The legislative councils objected to lavish expenditures for public works, to payment for members of the assembly, and to parts of the labor reform programs of the nineties. Where the legislative councilors were nominated by the governor his ministers, who were of course responsible to the assembly, demanded that deadlocks should be broken by the appointment of additional councilors. To this the colonial office objected, and the governors of New South Wales were thus caught between two fires. The result was a seesaw, with a gradual increase in the number of councilors — in New South Wales from 31 in 1871 to 65 thirty years afterward. Though the conflicts were at times bitter in the case of a nominated council, they were even more violent when the council was elected. Both houses could then claim support of a considerable body of public opinion; furthermore, an elective council stood on firm ground in its refusal to be reduced to political impotence. A solution of the frequent deadlocks was devised by South Australia in 1881, when she provided that if a bill passed twice by the assembly with an election intervening were rejected by the legislative council, the governor might either dissolve both houses or have additional members elected to the council. A result of the conflicts between the two houses was that the governments in the Australian colonies were generally short-lived, which in turn tended to strengthen the influence of the permanent civil service. Nevertheless, political democracy made visible progress. The power of the assemblies increased at the expense of the governors and legislative councils; after 1893 all assemblies were triennial; their members received salaries; and the advent of organized labor into politics gave new impetus to political and social democratic movements.

The character of the Australian labor movement has been shaped by the historical background and the peculiarities of the economic and social structures of that continent. Most of the colonies had started with convict establishments which supplied unfree labor to private employers. From the outset this system created a deep social cleavage and a distinct employing class. With the development of sheep-raising and squatting on government land appeared relatively large-scale employers who seized control of the machinery of government especially in New South Wales. The "squattocracy" prevented close settlements of small landowners. Consequently when immigrants flocked to Australia in the years of 1860–1890 they were generally forced to seek employment either on the public works or with the sheep magnates. Australia offered the individual less opportunity to become economically independent than was the case in the corresponding period in the history of the American northwest. Australian labor therefore became either concentrated in the urban centers which offered employment at the docks or in factories, or attached to two large industries, sheep-raising and mining. The earliest attempt at concerted action among Australian workers came when employers proposed to import coolies after the transportation of convicts to New South Wales had ceased. Labor found an ally in the colonial office, the latter formulating the white Australia policy. Later the gold and coal miners resisted the intrusion of Chinese; their methods were generally mob action and pressure upon the legislatures to exclude Chinese immigrants.

Gold miners and sheep shearers organized the first effective labor unions. When the period of placer mining was over, the claims passed into the hands of companies that employed miners for wages. The miners began to establish unions, and since many of them worked seasonally as shearers, the miners' union gave a direct impetus to the organization of a shearers' union. W. G. Spence, pioneer labor leader of Australia, was instrumental in starting unions in both fields. The fact that shearing is a seasonal occupation and the labor engaged in it was largely migratory made the maintenance of an effective union difficult. On the other hand since sheep-shearing like wheat-harvesting must be done within a limited period lest the product be spoiled — in the case of wool by seeds and matting — the shearers had certain advantages in bargaining for better pay, food, and living conditions. The immediate cause for the formation, on June 3, 1886, of the Amalgamated Shearers Union, which later became so powerful, was a proposed cut in the piece rate. The early history of this union is characterized by great violence, at times amounting practically to guerilla warfare. To be effective it had to spread both geographically and vertically so as to include not only shearers but also those engaged in handling the clip. In the early eighties Australian unionism received a fillip when shipowners engaged Chinese as crews aboard steamers. Again Australian labor was called upon to resist an invasion of orientals. Moreover, a stimulus came from the mother country with the rise there of the new unionism, the great dockers' strike in London in 1889 to which Australian labor gave monetary assistance, and the socialistic doctrines preached by H. M. Hyndman. His slogan, "England for all," had an Australian counterpart in William Lane's "Socialism in our time." By 1890 the world-wide slump in prices hit Australia; the early nineties brought low wages, low prices, and much unemployment. During the early stages of the depression Australian labor sought to check the fall in wages by widespread strikes, thereby hastening the financial crisis of 1891–1893.

The strikes failed, but the years of strife and misfortune created a feeling of solidarity among Australian labor. When the ordinary weapons of the laborers proved ineffective they turned to political action. Although the laborers of New South Wales led, those of the other colonies were not far behind. Scoffed at in the beginning by veteran politicians like Sir Henry Parkes, the leaders of the new Labour party demonstrated their skill as tacticians by obtaining the balance of power in the legislative assembly of New South Wales. Among principal early demands of Australian labor were restriction of immigration with exclusion of orientals, wages and arbitration boards, and an old age pension.

In Australia as in New Zealand labor's entrance into politics marked the beginning of an era of state intervention in social and economic life.

That peculiar phenomenon of Australian society and special product of Australian conditions, the squatter, owner of many sheep and controlling by lease or occupation much government land, secured at an early date a dominant position in New South Wales and Victoria. All the colonies attempted, by various systems of selecting land before or after survey, to increase the number of *bona fide* settlers. But the laws were evaded so successfully that the areas held by many Australian squatters make the baronies of medieval Europe look puny. Thus in 1883, 96 persons held more than 8,000,000 acres of land in New South Wales; and even in South Australia where the squatters were comparatively unsuccessful 130 estates were found to average more than 20,000 acres in 1891. By this time the best land in Australia had become private property and much of it was not used for agriculture; in the Hunter district of New South Wales 14 persons held 227,000 acres, of which only 331 were cultivated. The homestead system of the United States and Canada was never fully adopted by Australia. Not until the middle of the eighties, when the public works policy was suspended, did the governments of Australia begin seriously to consider the desirability of small farms and closer settlements. The land hunger was great. "In New South Wales, over three thousand persons applied for 312 blocks [i.e., allotments] while, in one instance in South Australia, there were 136 applicants for one block." Instead of looking upon the land mainly as a source of revenue, the governments now realized its value as a means for taking care of the needy and unemployed. They began to take over land from private owners or lessees and to found labor colonies and village and communal settlements; but none of these experiments were successful. Realizing the evils and dangers connected with the large holdings, South Australia in 1884 began to impose a special tax on unimproved land. Her example was followed by

Tasmania, 1889, New South Wales, 1895, and Victoria, 1895. As an aid in furthering settlements Western Australia in 1894 set up an Agricultural Bank that granted long-term loans at easy rates for agricultural improvements. Both methods – breaking up the large estates by a system of taxation and helping the small farmers by easier credit – were extended after the economic recovery at the turn of the century.

Meanwhile the lords of the vast sheep ranches had been engaged in fighting many other enemies besides the farmer occupier and hostile legislation. The rabbit pest became threatening in the late seventies and a veritable scourge during the succeeding decade, to be checked only by an expensive network of fences. Fences were also used for sheep; although many hands could thereby be dispensed with, the fences necessitated heavy capital outlay. Moreover, refrigeration created a demand for new breeds of sheep producing a heavier carcass – another need for capital outlay. These changes occurred in a period of falling prices and recurrent labor troubles. This, however, does not complete the tale of woes for the squatter and agriculturalist of Australia. The rabbit, overstocking, and drought brought in the early 1890's sandstorms and dustbowls similar to those that afflicted southwestern United States in the 1930's. In New South Wales 6,000,000 acres and in South Australia 30,000 square miles of land had to be abandoned, mainly, of course, on the fringes of the settlements, the land of the pastoralist. The number of sheep declined from 106,400,000 in 1891 to 70,600,000 in 1901. Still, wool valued at £15,237,454 led the field of Australian exports for the year 1901.

The squatter was not the only capitalist farmer of Australia who fell upon evil times in the nineties. The sugar planters of northern Queensland failed in their efforts to establish a separate colony, the price of sugar fell, partly because of the competition offered by the subsidized beet sugar of Europe, and colonial legislation deprived them of their Kanaka labor. However, shifts were effected in the sugar industry. Large refineries with modern machinery supplanted the old plantation mills. Cane-growing and refining were separated; plantations were broken up and replaced with small farms.

Although the distance from world markets hindered agricultural progress in Australia, the industry moved forward with the aid of modern inventions and discoveries. The double and triple furrow plow and the stripper which reaped and threshed the grain enabled the wheat farmer to crop larger areas at reduced labor cost; similarly, new varieties of hardy rust-resisting wheat and the introduction of artificial fertilizers meant larger yield. The "mallee roller" and the "stump jump" plow helped to put under cultivation a large section in Victoria covered with "mallee" or scrub. In the eighties much had been expected from the tapping of the underground waters and at one time there was a boom in well-drilling. Though most of the wells proved disappointing, the five thousand or so that flowed were of assistance to the pastoralists. More success attended the husbanding of surface water for irrigation by methods copied from California. Among those who took a keen interest in this development was the Victorian statesman Alfred Deakin. By using the California system at Mildura, Victoria, 8225 acres, used chiefly for fruit and vine growing, had been reclaimed by 1894. Mixed farming became more common; and aided by the rise in prices the area under crops took a sharp upturn between 1895 and 1900. The gain, more than 2,000,000 acres, about equaled the entire area under crops in 1871. Refrigeration made possible the shipment of mutton, beef, and butter to England. The sheep, hitherto valued almost solely because of the wool and tallow, now supplied another article for export—the value of exported meat rose from £566,780 in 1871 to £2,611,240, in 1901. Even more significant was the increase in the export of butter from 1,812,700 to 34,607,400 pounds.

In 1901 the mineral output of Australia was valued at £21,816,770, to which gold contributed £14,017,540, copper £2,265,440, and silver-lead £2,248,600. During the depression years the high value of gold and the new cyanide process of extracting it from the ore made mining profitable at lower levels. At several of the old diggings companies took up the work when placer mining ceased; although the annual yield fluctuated, the average was around 5,000,000 pounds exclusive of the new strikes. The most important of the latter were at Mount Morgan and East Kimberley in the eighties and at Coolgardie and Kalgoorlie in the nineties. The last two were providential not only for Western Australia but also for the other colonies. In 1890 Western Australia secured responsible government and immediately launched an ambitious public works program, borrowing for that purpose £1,336,000 in 1891 just as depression hit the antipodes. The gold discoveries of the following years enabled her not only to carry on but to expand this program. Her gold production rose from £115,200 in 1891 to £6,749,830 in 1901. During the hungry nineties unemployed from Eastern Australia flocked to the hitherto only slightly regarded colony in the west.

Although Australia remained a land where the primary industries — the pastoral, the agricultural, and mining — continued to be of the greatest importance, all the colonies with the exception of New South Wales made efforts to stimulate manufacturing by means of protective tariffs. Victoria led in this. The gold discoveries of 1851 caused a great influx of immigrants. When gold mining by their primitive methods ceased to be profitable, the labor market became glutted and the unemployed demanded that work be provided. Among remedies suggested was governmental encouragement of industry by a protective tariff. David Syme, owner and editor of the Melbourne *Age,* became the high priest of protectionism. After a sharp tussle with importers and politicians he won. The other colonies followed Victoria's lead largely because the tariff supplied a supposedly painless method of extracting revenue. New South Wales, however, remained faithful to free trade principles partly because of the political power wielded by the squatters and partly because her most influential statesman, Sir Henry Parkes, believed as passionately in the economic virtues of free trade as David Syme did in those of protection. Changes in the price level made it difficult to appraise the effects of the Australian tariffs, since the progress of manufactures in New South Wales nearly kept pace with that in Victoria and the depression of the nineties disclosed that the former held a stronger economic position. The growth of Australia's foreign trade paralleled her increase in population. Rated at £23 2*s.* 9*d.* per head in 1870, her trade fell to a record low of less than £16 in 1894 when the depression was at its nadir, but rose rapidly and had reached £24 6*s.* 1*d.* per head in 1901.

Government borrowing for public works was an important feature in Australia's economic history during 1871–1885. The interest rates on the London money market were low, particularly in the quinquennium 1876–1880; British investors, having sustained heavy losses in the Americas, turned their eyes to Australia. New South Wales, Victoria, Queensland, and South Australia availed themselves of this opportunity, each borrowing £5,000,000 in those years. The confidence of the British investing public was extended to Australian banks and private ventures with the result that money poured into Australia during the eighties. Cheap money stimulated speculation and when the crash came, 1891–1893, it was found that many of her banks and other enterprises were of the wild-cat variety. London, shaken by the failure of a great banking house, the Barings, in November, 1890, began to recall overseas deposits. Nevertheless, those in Australia rose until 1893. In May of that year many of the British deposits were due and were certain to be withdrawn. Numerous financial structures had already toppled. To save something from the threatening wreck every bank in Victoria except one underwent "reconstruction" in April, 1893. Heavy losses were sustained by both English and Australian investors. New South Wales bore up better than Victoria, and Sydney resumed its old position of financial preeminence.

Railroad-building formed an important part of the development programs of the Australian colonies. Lacking navigable rivers, only by extending the railroads into the interior of the continent could they bring new land under cultivation and its produce to market. But private promoters steered shy of Australian railroads; consequently they were state built, owned, and operated. Radiating from the seaports which were also the capitals, they served the needs of the separate colonies. Particularism was strong in Australia, each colony looking to its own capital as the center of the antipodean universe. The strength of this separatist feeling is revealed by the difference in the railroad gauges — 5 feet 3 inches in Victoria, 4 feet 8½ inches in New South Wales, and 3 feet 6 inches in the other mainland colonies. Adelaide, Melbourne, and Sydney might have connection by rail, but they could not have through trains.

With responsible government the colonies of Australia secured complete control over finance and other local matters. They were, however, not entirely freed from imperial supervision. Their legislation must not violate fundamental principles of English law; the governors appointed and instructed by the imperial government had the power of veto and could reserve bills for the signification of "Her Majesty's pleasure"; even the self-governing colonies were bound by imperial commercial treaties; and, of course, they had no independent status in the eyes of international law. At times they were made keenly aware of the fact that their sovereignty was limited. Now and then Victoria and New South Wales protested loudly though unavailingly because their governors, backed by the colonial office, refused to overawe or pack their legislative councils. Australians asserted that, with reference to his ministers, the position of a governor in a colony with responsible government was analogous to that of the queen in Britain, a doctrine which the colonial office refused to accept. Though there were few formal concessions to the demands made by the colonies in this field, they gained ground. Lord Carrington, governor of New South Wales from 1885 to 1890, bowed to colonial will in the matter of increasing the nominated legislative council; and the instructions to newly appointed governors were revised in 1892 to make them more conformable to the wishes of the colonists. The most extreme demands for colonial autonomy, such as that for a purely personal union between Victoria and the United Kingdom, were put forward, 1869–1871, in the heated controversy between the Australasian colonies and the colonial office over the differential tariff issue. The colonies desired power to differentiate in their tariffs between goods of Australasian origin and goods from outside. This had been prohibited by the Australian Colonies Government Act of 1850, and was considered contrary to British commercial treaties with Belgium and Germany. The Australians challenged the doctrine that they were bound by imperial commercial treaties and asserted that they had the right to control completely everything pertaining to trade and commerce. In 1873 the imperial government yielded on the differential tariff issue.

The extent to which imperial treaties might fetter the Australian colonies was revealed further in the disputes over the exclusion of Chinese immigrants. This issue rose first when Chinese flocked to the gold fields of Victoria and New South Wales. The colonies passed stringent laws against them, which, coupled with the decline of placer mining, effected a temporary solution of the problem. But the issue flared up anew in 1875 with the discovery of the Palmer gold fields in northern Queensland — within two years there were 17,000 Chinese as against 1400 whites at the diggings. The discovery, shortly afterward, that cheap Chinese labor was replacing the white on ships plying the Australian waters widened the front. Chinese immigration thus touched the interests of several groups of laborers and more than one colony. In 1876 Queensland passed a bill which excluded Chinese immigrants from the colony; but the bill was reserved "for the signification of Her Majesty's pleasure," the colonial secretary, Lord Carnarvon, pointing out that it violated Anglo-Chinese treaties and discriminated against British subjects of Asiatic and African origin. Queensland contended, however, that immigration was a local question and therefore completely under the jurisdiction of the government of the colony; she also made efforts to enlist the support of all the self-governing colonies of Australia for her interpretation of the constitutional issue. The replies from her sister colonies were discouraging, and Queensland was compelled to pass an amended bill which achieved the desired object without specific mention of the Chinese. In the eighties, however, Australia became alarmed lest the exclusion of the Chinese from the United States turn a flood of these emigrants to Australia. This question occupied a prominent place on the agenda and in the discussions of the Australian intercolonial conferences of the eighties. A Liberal colonial secretary, Lord Derby, admitted that the Australian colonies had full power over immigration; but he pointed out that from the point of view of imperial interests it was inexpedient to antagonize the government of China which now, more than heretofore, endeavored to protect its nationals. Consequently the home government suggested that Australia follow the lead of Natal and impose an educational test in a European language on all immigrants. The wisdom of this method was recognized and the educational test was adopted by the first parliament of the Commonwealth of Australia.

The controversies arising from the attempts of the Australians to exclude Chinese and other orientals from their continent brought home to them the fact that their interests were weighed on an imperial scale, that united action might bring results not obtainable by individual colonies, and that their isolation was ended. These lessons were reinforced by experiences growing out of the disturbing appearance of France and Germany as colonizing powers in the South Pacific. The former had been active since the second quarter of the nineteenth century and rumors of her designs on the New Hebrides caused an excitement in Australia surpassed only by that aroused when Germany in 1884 annexed the northeastern portion of New Guinea and several islands adjacent thereto. Western New Guinea had long been claimed by Holland, but the eastern part had been looked upon as a no man's land. Consequently British naval officers and forward-looking Australians had urged the colonial office to seize this portion; companies for colonizing New Guinea had been organized in both Australia and England. In 1875 the government of Victoria proposed an ambitious scheme for the annexation of New Guinea, the New Hebrides, and several other groups of islands in the South Pacific, but the Disraeli government gave it a cold reception especially since it involved saddling the mother country with heavy expenses for the government of colonies whose economic or strategic value was doubtful.

The second Gladstone administration, which succeeded that of Disraeli in 1880, came into office and power on an anti-imperialist platform. Hence Queensland's action in proclaiming southeastern New Guinea British in April, 1883, met with instant disavowal and a stern rebuke — to sanction an unauthorized annexation by a colony was contrary to established practice. Moreover, in long private letters to Gladstone, Sir Arthur Gordon, afterward Lord Stanmore, lately governor of Fiji and New Zealand and high commissioner of the Western Pacific, warned the imperial government against the aims and policies of Queensland. For appeasement purposes Lord Derby assured the Australians in July, 1883, that no foreign power had any design on New Guinea. This was belied by events; for a year later when Britain finally decided to proclaim a protectorate over the southeastern and parts of the northeastern coasts of the island, Bismarck announced the latter as falling within a German sphere of interest. In the ensuing diplomatic conflict Britain gave way, Gladstone finding some consolation in the thought that with Germany in the neighborhood the Australian colonies might prove less recalcitrant. They were indeed deeply disappointed; Sir Henry Loch, then governor of Victoria, was so impressed with the widespread feeling of resentment against the mother country that on January 7, 1885, he suggested a British purchase of Dutch New Guinea as a peace offering; this was promptly vetoed by Gladstone. The eastern colonies of Australia undertook to guarantee £15,000 per annum toward the cost of governing British New Guinea, formally annexed in 1888. The administrator, later advanced to the rank of lieutenant-governor, was subject to instructions from the government of Queensland. Thus Australia secured her first dependency.

In 1885 Britain appeared to be on the brink of war with Russia; although this was averted, the international situation continued threatening. Imperial defense formed the chief topic for discussion at the colonial conference of 1887, the Australian colonies agreeing to make a small annual contribution toward the cost of maintaining an imperial squadron. Shortly afterward their defense systems were inspected by an imperial officer, Major-General Bevan Edwards; his report, issued in 1889, called attention to the exposed position of the Australian colonies in case of a general war, and their inadequate defense forces on land and sea. This alarmed the Australian colonies and gave an impetus to the move for an Australian federation. As discussed in an earlier chapter, the imperial government had already in 1849 envisaged a federal system for the colonies of Australia, but the plan then suggested was badly received and dropped. The particularism of these colonies increased during the next thirty years because of a variety of factors, among which may be mentioned the geographical distribution of the settlements along the fringe of the continent, the distances separating them, and the jealousies among the capitals, Adelaide, Melbourne, Sydney, and Brisbane. Moreover, when Victoria adopted a protective tariff, a fiscal barrier was erected which proved a serious obstacle to an Australian federation. In the sixties, tariff disputes led to a series of intercolonial conferences dealing with the traffic and collection of customs on the river Murray, questions which concerned New South Wales, Victoria, and South Australia. With the rise of the differential tariff issue later in that decade and the resultant controversy with the home government, another series of conferences took place, which brought together representatives from all the colonies of Australasia. After the desired right was obtained, the conferences were discontinued without having brought federation a step nearer.

The next issue which caused the convening of representatives from the Australian colonies was the expansion of foreign powers in the South Pacific. Australia as a whole had approved the action of Queensland in annexing a portion of New Guinea. When it was annulled by the colonial office, an Australasian conference met at Sydney and declared in favor of a federal council for Australasia; the plan was not accepted by New South Wales and New Zealand. Nevertheless, a federal council was created by an imperial act of 1885. The council was composed of two representatives from each colony and it met every other year from 1886 to 1899; however, it was little more than a debating assembly and it had no appreciable influence upon the federation movement. The real stimulus for this came from Major-General Edwards' report showing the defenseless state of the Australian colonies. Sir Henry Parkes, now the grand old man of New South Wales, put his shoulder to the wheel of the federation movement. A conference at Melbourne in 1890 was followed by a convention at Sydney in 1891, consisting of representatives elected by the colonial parliaments. This convention prepared a draft constitution that formed the basis for the discussions which followed.

The principal difficulties to be overcome had their roots in the particularism of the colonies, the jealousies between the small and the large, the fear of the richer that they would have to carry an increased burden of taxation, and the difference in points of view on the tariff question. The outcome was, as always when federal arrangements are adopted, a compromise. Following the American model the powers of the federal government were enumerated, the residue being left in the hands of the states; the senate was established on the basis of true federal principles, six senators being elected from each state; representation in the house of representatives was based on population. As a further concession to the states, governors continued to be sent out by the imperial government instead of, as in Canada, being chosen by the federal government. Free traders and protectionists alike yielded on the tariff issue to the extent of leaving it in the hands of the new federal government, which also was given control over excise and other taxes; however, for a period of ten years and as long thereafter as the federal parliament might decree, three-fourths of the revenues raised by customs and excise were to be returned to the states. The question of the division of powers between the two houses had long been debated in the Australian colonies. In the federal or Commonwealth parliament, the house of representatives secured full control over the purse, including all matters pertaining to taxation and appropriations. Deadlocks between it and the senate were to be ended by joint sittings at which the senators would be outnumbered approximately two to one. The long-standing rivalry between Sydney and Melbourne made the choice of a federal capital difficult. The solution, copied after the one followed in the United States, was the creation of a new capital at least one hundred miles from Sydney near the border of Victoria. Here a district was set aside and a new city, Canberra, was eventually built. In the meantime Melbourne served as the capital of the Commonwealth. The work of completing this constitution was done by a statutory convention consisting of elected representatives meeting in several sessions, 1897–1898, at Adelaide, Sydney, and Melbourne. The draft was then submitted to and approved by plebiscites in all the colonies.

Following the precedent set in the case of the Dominion of Canada, the imperial government had left the Australian colonies free in working out a plan for the federation. Advocates of federation in Australia, however, had claimed that among the advantages it would bring was more freedom from imperial control and supervision. This was not entirely to the liking of the colonial secretary, Joseph Chamberlain. The Australian constitution had to be passed as an imperial act, and during that stage Chamberlain introduced amendments aimed at safeguarding the position of the judicial committee of the privy council as the supreme court for the whole empire. The Australians wished to make their new high court the final court of appeal except in certain very unusual cases which in no way concerned the interpretation of the federal and state constitutions. On this point a compromise was effected; disputes dealing with constitutional relations between the Commonwealth and states or between states were not to be appealed to the imperial tribunal; others might be if the appeal was approved by the high court of Australia. The constitution for the Commonwealth of Australia received royal assent July 9, 1900. Meanwhile, Western Australia, which had kept aloof during the later stages of the work for the federation, completed her arrangements for joining it. On August 17, 1900, the Commonwealth of Australia embracing New South Wales, Victoria, Queensland, Tasmania, South Australia, and Western Australia was proclaimed as established from January 1, 1901.

The new federation possessed a homogeneity of population lacking in Canada and South Africa. Except for a small minority, the Australians were of British origin with the English element dominant. Though they were tenacious in demanding their rights, their attachment to the homeland was strong and made manifest on many occasions. In January, 1885, when Britain's difficulties in the Sudan multiplied, Victoria placed her newly built gunboats at the disposal of the imperial government, and New South Wales' offer of a military contingent was accepted, the troops being dispatched to the Red Sea. At the colonial conference of 1887 Australian delegates favored imperial federation in some form and agreed to pay £126,000 annually toward the cost of maintaining an imperial squadron in the waters of Australia; and Sir Samuel Griffith, then prime minister of Queensland, first suggested the possibility of an imperial preferential tariff. At the conference of 1897 the Australian contribution to naval defense was increased; during the Anglo-Boer war, 1899–1902, Australia sent 16,000 men to South Africa to fight for the empire.

Australians took an active part in the discussions at the Royal Colonial Institute which tried to devise ways and means to strengthen the bonds between the colonies and the mother country. Although by 1901 Australia had four universities of her own, her youth still preferred to complete their education in England, and scholars trained at British universities were sought for teaching positions in Australia.

Politically, economically, and socially, the Australia of 1901 had grown in stature and political experience. Though her institutions had been borrowed from England, they had been remolded and shaped to fit Australian conditions. Australia evolved her own pattern, and the new federation, the Commonwealth of Australia, was to develop along lines peculiar to itself. Except for perhaps a few small patches, there was no longer an unknown Australia, but the results of the explorations of the late nineteenth century had been disappointing in many ways. Though the area of the continent practically equaled that of Europe or the United States, its natural resources were vastly inferior. Still they were ample for a population several times larger than the 3,771,715 persons enumerated there in 1901. That the future like the past would show growth and development none could doubt. The mineral and agricultural resources of Australia, her railroads, telephone, telegraph, and manufacturing industries were pledges of progress. Generally speaking, her progress had been in the direction of the conventional democratic type of political and social institutions, but in the nineties she began to experiment with new ventures in state enterprise and regulation and soon outpaced the United Kingdom. Still the new nation of the antipodes was a British nation, nursed in the traditions of the British Isles, and bound to the mother country with the strongest of racial, linguistic, social, economic, and sentimental ties.

CHAPTER 24

NEW ZEALAND, 1870–1901

GLOOM prevailed in the North Island of New Zealand at the close of the sixties: the Maori war dragged on, settlements had been deserted, immigration had ceased, the imperial troops were being withdrawn, and the debt burden was mounting. The South Island, on the other hand, had benefited by gold rushes and immigrants had flocked in. Yet even there the outlook was far from bright – the Otago gold rush was over, the province was discovering that the aftermath of a gold rush is not pleasant, and only Canterbury was relatively prosperous. But the South Island was in duty bound to help shoulder the cost of the Maori war. In general, the people of New Zealand felt uncertain and apprehensive about the future.

At this juncture a leader appeared in the person of Julius Vogel, a Jewish immigrant who had settled in Otago. Under his direction the colony launched an audacious public works program. From 1870 until about 1878 New Zealand experienced a boom; money flowed freely, prices were high, and work was plentiful. This was succeeded by a period of depression that lasted well into the nineties. At the turn of the century, however, she was again riding the crest of the wave; prices rose, and the feeling was strong that this time economic prosperity had a solid foundation. Indeed, by looking backward from 1900 to 1870, one discovers a rate of progress that justified confidence in the future. A loosely bound aggregation of settlements with a population of less than 250,000 had become a well-knit state containing more than 800,000 inhabitants. Roads and bridges, telegraph and telephone, railroads and steamships, and new social and economic institutions had by 1900 effectively linked the old provinces. Furthermore, the islands were no longer isolated from the greater world outside. Submarine cables and steamship lines provided regular communications between New Zealand and Europe and America, and the new methods of refrigeration had widened the market for her produce. The colony had become an integral part of a world-embracing economic order; the ebb and flow on world markets affected financial and economic conditions in Auckland, Wellington, Christchurch, and Dunedin. But New Zealand, although small and often dragged along by powerful outside forces, continued to manifest that spirit of independence, ingenuity, and resourcefulness so often found in frontier communities. Far from being a mere dinghy in the wake of the great outside world or a slavish imitator of the methods and means employed in the old countries, she bravely laid out a new course and tried a new tack. At the beginning of the twentieth century, Europe and America considered New Zealand a laboratory for testing new ideas – a probable guide toward social righteousness and industrial peace.

Julius Vogel holds a place in the colony's history in the seventies analogous to that occupied by E. G. Wakefield thirty years earlier. Wakefield founded the colony; Vogel brought it out of a slough of despond. Both were born promoters – energetic and resourceful, not overly scrupulous in their choice of means, bent on achieving complete and immediate success. Vogel diagnosed the ills of New Zealand in 1870 as due to a lack of settlers, of capital, and of a strong centralized government. With evangelistic zeal, he preached "faith in New Zealand" and converted both a majority of his fellow colonists and influential financiers in England to a belief in a great future for the colony. His elixir was the expenditure of money on public works. He "sold" New Zealand to English investors, and the flourishing condition of the London money market at that time enabled him to increase the colony's public debt from £7,000,000 in 1869 to about £20,000,000 in 1879. Roads, bridges, telegraph lines, railroads, and other public utilities were promoted on a large scale. Critics of the new policy accused Vogel and his associates of waste and corruption. Although some of these charges were no doubt true, Vogel could point with pride to the achievements of his glorious decade — the population doubled, large new areas of land brought under cultivation, 4000 miles of telegraph, 1100 miles of railroads, a large number of roads and bridges, and the destruction of the noxious provincial system of government.

The last achievement ranks probably as Vogel's greatest service to New Zealand. The Constitutional Act of 1852 had divided the colony into provinces with legislatures of their own that possessed wide powers, and had created a weak central government. Perhaps this system was the best that could be devised for New Zealand at that stage of her development, but by 1870 the evil results of decentralization were clearly evident. Log-rolling and provincial jealousies impeded progress; a narrow particularism often blocked the adoption of necessary reforms; and the emphasis on local interests proved inimical to the general good. Vogel early realized that the provinces must cease to exist as powerful political units. With the adoption of a far-reaching public works program parliament put an effective weapon into his hands. In fighting the opponents of centralization, he interspersed his arguments with promises of tangible benefits in the form of roads, bridges, and other local improvements. Sir George Grey, who now lived in New Zealand as a private citizen, entered politics to lead the defenders of the provincial system, which was largely his creation; but he was defeated in parliament, the voters ratifying the constitutional change in the election of 1876. With the destruction of the provinces as political entities, a new system of counties and smaller administrative units was created to meet the need for local government; the machinery of the central government remained practically as before, only immeasurably stronger.

In the era of the Vogel prosperity, private borrowing and spending in New Zealand kept pace with the public efforts in that respect. Despite recent assertions to the contrary, prosperity by spending cannot endure; and when the slump struck New Zealand toward the end of the seventies the load of private and public indebtedness was crushingly heavy. A general fall in prices made the load still heavier — she had to pay interest and amortize loans with dear money. Now buoyant optimism gave way to a disillusionment bordering on despair. For a dozen years the government pursued a policy of retrenchment coupled with high taxes. Immigrants had flocked to New Zealand during the fat years. Although some of them had been placed on land, the majority had found employment on public works or in private enterprises. When the collapse came, thousands of laborers were thrown out of work; unemployment reached alarming proportions; soup kitchens and other relief measures failed to ward off suffering; and in the eighties New Zealand became a land of emigration. Julius Vogel went to England in 1876 as agent-general for the colony; eight years later he returned and reentered politics; but the old magic failed — his work ended in the seventies — and the ungrateful task of guiding New Zealand during the long depression fell largely to one of his old colleagues, Sir Harry Atkinson.

In the depressed eighties refrigeration provided a ray of hope for the people of New Zealand. The first shipment of frozen meat left the colony for England in 1882. The success was almost immediate; a regular fortnightly steamship service was inaugurated, and by 1903 New Zealand shipped home frozen meat valued at more than £3,000,000. Refrigeration also created New Zealand's great dairy industry. In 1883 she exported butter and cheese valued at £49,000; twenty years later the figure had risen to £1,513,000. The success of dairying in turn stimulated the demand for small farms, which soon developed into a great political and economic issue.

In the early days of New Zealand, Wakefield had tried to check the growth of large estates by imposing a high upset price on land; but sheep-raising and grain-farming, aided by the new agricultural machinery, had resulted in the accumulation of land in the hands of a few to such an extent that by 1894 "less than one-eightieth of the country land holders had two-fifths (in value) of the land." The unemployment of the eighties created a back-to-the-land movement; it was found that dairying could be carried on most profitably on small farms provided the farmers learned to cooperate, and this the farmers of New Zealand learned very quickly. But when the landless agriculturists sought to obtain farms they discovered that most of the best land was in the hands of a few, sometimes absentee, landowners. The small farmers thus had a serious grievance, and they joined with organized labor, which had suffered a crushing defeat in the maritime strike of 1890, in overthrowing "the continuous" ministry of Sir Harry Atkinson. A Franchise Act of 1889 abolished plural voting and introduced manhood suffrage, and thus facilitated the victory of the farm-labor group over a prime minister who was not a blind reactionary but had acquired odium as the advocate of high taxes and retrenchment during the weary years of financial liquidation, and who was, perhaps rightly, suspected of being the tool of the landowning oligarchy. The success of the radicals in the election of December, 1890, was completed in the following year when the tenure of office of the legislative councilors was reduced from life to seven years, and the size of the council was increased from thirty-four to forty members.

The reforms adopted by the Liberal-Labor party in New Zealand, 1891–1906, aroused world-wide interest. But before we consider them in detail, we need call to mind that a certain paternalism had characterized economic and social developments in New Zealand from the beginning. Immigration had been subsidized both in the early days and during the regime of Julius Vogel; the New Zealand Company and the Canterbury Association had made special efforts to assist the original settlers; and later the state had built and operated railroads and the telegraph, founded hospitals and asylums, and provided postal savings banks, life insurance, and a trust office for the administration of estates of deceased persons. Perpetual leases of crown land with periodic revaluation had been tried in 1882; experiments with state-aided village settlements were carried out on a small scale in 1884–1887; and the state had encouraged the organization of cooperative dairy companies. But these excursions into fields which Europe and America generally reserved for private enterprise were few and halting compared with those attempted after 1891.

John Ballance and Richard John Seddon shared the leadership of the progressives in 1891; the former's death in 1893 left Seddon as the guiding spirit of the reform movement. He was ably assisted by a number of younger men, prominent among whom was W. P. Reeves, author of several books on New Zealand and later high commissioner in London. Although Seddon was not born in New Zealand and, from the point of view of time, does not belong among her pioneer statesmen, he had the characteristics of the frontier, and many of the traits of his Canadian contemporary, Sir John A. Macdonald, the difference being that Seddon was a radical who seldom hesitated to leave the beaten path. He had had little formal education but much experience in life when he became the leader of the Liberal-Labor party of New Zealand. A rough and ready fighter, Seddon was on occasion rash but usually shrewd, cool-headed, and resourceful in a crisis.

Among the legislation of a somewhat general character passed after 1891, we may note the adoption of woman suffrage, the higher protective tariff, the revision of the system of taxation, and the establishment of old age pensions. In New Zealand, as elsewhere, the radicals supported the agitation for woman suffrage in the mistaken belief that the women would align themselves with the forces of the left; the protective tariff was expected to stimulate employment and raise wages; and the new system of taxation struck directly at the big landowners. Organized labor in New Zealand was aided by the new restrictions that the government imposed on immigration, by far-reaching laws for the regulation of wages, hours, and other conditions of labor, by the adoption of new acts governing employers' liability, and by the new machinery for conciliation and arbitration in labor disputes which at first worked uniformly for the benefit of the employees. In some cases, contracts for public works were let directly to organizations of laborers. A newly created department of labor assisted the workers. The new laws were administered in a spirit friendly to labor; and luck favored Seddon and his supporters inasmuch as the rise in prices after 1895 eased the tension their reforms might have engendered between employers and employees.

The small farmers were benefited by the break-up of large estates, the new arrangements for securing crown land, and the easier terms for farm credit. Graduated land and income taxes replaced the old tax on general property, and special taxes were levied on the land of absentee owners. Moreover, the government obtained the power to compel an unwilling proprietor of a large estate to part with it, although in every such case the owner received fair compensation. An act of 1892 appropriated £50,000 yearly for the purchase of land by the government; this was raised to £250,000 in 1894 and to £500,000 in 1897. By March 31, 1902, the government had bought 107 separate holdings totaling 448,350 acres, at a cost of £2,117,352. The land so acquired was made available to settlers.

When disposing of crown land, the government of New Zealand offered the farmer a choice of three alternatives — he might buy the land outright, he might lease it for twenty-five years at a rent fixed at 5 per cent of the value and with the right to purchase after ten years, or he might occupy it on a 999-year lease, the rent being fixed at 4 per cent of the value at the beginning of the occupation and not subject to change. No farmer could acquire more than 640 acres of first-class or 2000 acres of second-class land. The limited-term lease with right to purchase proved most popular with the farmers; in New Zealand, as practically everywhere else, they craved to own the soil they tilled. Among special means of furthering landownership that received government support were the cooperative buying of land by associations of farmers, the founding of village settlements, and the placing of unemployed laborers on land. Opponents of the government often denounced its land policy as socialistic; but its aim was peasant proprietorship, or at least the establishment of an equity in the land for those who worked it — the most effective barrier against the founding of a Marxist state. Seddon's land policy owed nothing to Karl Marx, although it may have owed something to Henry George.

Before the government began to aid borrowers, the legal interest rates on farm loans in New Zealand had been from 7 to 9 per cent, but brokerage and commissions often brought the actual rate nearer 15 per cent. To remedy this, the government borrowed money in London at 3 or 3½ per cent and loaned it to farmers at 5 per cent, with no brokerage or commission charges and only a small fee for appraisal. Loans ranging from £25 to £3000 could be obtained from the local post office, and repayment could be arranged in installments covering 36½ years. This method of financing the purchase of land was popular from the beginning, and between February 23, 1895, and March 31, 1902, 11,312 loans aggregating £3,736,620 had been authorized.

The many new activities undertaken by the state caused the debt of New Zealand to increase on the average somewhat more than £1,000,000 per annum during 1891–1901, but the lower rate of interest and the growing prosperity enabled the colony to carry the new load easily. As the century closed, her trade was flourishing. The export for 1900 exceeded £13,000,000, with a favorable trade balance of about £3,000,000. Wool and frozen meat accounted for more than 50 per cent of the value of her exports; butter, cheese, and other agricultural products supplied the bulk of the remainder, although gold valued at £1,437,600 formed an important item. The banks of New Zealand had had a checkered history until 1893, when the government began to supervise them more carefully. When the period closes, bank deposits amounted to between £28 and £29 per capita, and the banking institutions appeared sound.

The pioneer English and Scottish settlers in New Zealand showed great zeal for the establishment of a democratic system of education. Those at Nelson began preparations for such a system while on their way to their new home, and shortly after landing they organized a literary and scientific society. The founders of Otago and Canterbury showed a similar interest in the training of their children. At first elementary education was denominational and under the control of the provinces; but in 1877 a national system was created which made education "free, secular, and compulsory." Although denominational schools still continued, especially among the Roman Catholics, and some of the well-to-do settlers had private tutors for their children, these methods took care of only a relatively few children and their number declined steadily during the nineties. Secondary schools were established early at Nelson, Otago, and Canterbury. The University of Otago was founded in 1869, and in the following year the general assembly made provisions for the University of New Zealand, to which that at Otago surrendered its right to confer degrees. Colleges were later founded at Canterbury, Auckland, and Wellington; these, with the pioneer institution at Otago, were federated in the University of New Zealand, the latter functioning as a purely examining and degree-granting body. The growth of technical education kept pace with that of the academic; the needs of the Maoris were supplied by special government schools. In 1900, 150,000 children and young people were being educated, largely at public expense, and great efforts were being made to enable the youth of New Zealand to play their part in the new era.

Other agencies for public education such as mechanics' institutes, libraries, and athenaeums had been encouraged from the beginning; and the New Zealand Institute, with branches in the larger towns, did yeoman's work in stimulating an active scientific interest in the geology, flora, and fauna of the islands. Missionaries and churchmen like the Reverend W. Colenso and Bishop W. Williams and Governor Sir George Grey made valuable studies of the anthropology, language, and mythology of the Maoris. New Zealand, however, was too small to develop an art and literature of her own at this early date.

Although outsiders often look upon New Zealand as a part of Australia, her people were keenly aware of their separateness from their sister colonies more than one thousand miles away. They occasionally cooperated with the Australians. Representatives of New Zealand met with those of the Australian colonies to discuss differential tariffs; and they joined in efforts to exclude Chinese immigrants from Australasia and in urging the British government to annex Fiji, New Guinea, Samoa, and other islands in the South Pacific. New Zealand also participated in the discussion leading toward the creation of a federal council for Australia in 1885 and she sent delegates to the Australian federation conference of 1891. When asked to federate with the Australian colonies the spokesmen for New Zealand could conveniently mention the 1200 miles of intervening ocean as a great obstacle to a political union, though they might also have spoken of New Zealand's pride of origin and institutions that made her unwilling to give up her identity.

In 1870 New Zealand nursed a grievance against the mother country because of the recall of the garrisons, and a few reckless voices were heard favoring special commercial arrangements with the United States. But this irritation subsided when the Maori question was settled and New Zealand found easy access to the London money market. However, criticisms of the imperial government were frequent and at times bitter in the eighties when requests for adding New Guinea and Samoa to the British empire went unheeded and Australasian plans for excluding Chinese laborers were vetoed by the colonial office. But the wishes of New Zealand concerning annexation were realized in part when the Kermadec and Cook Islands were added to the colony in 1887 and 1901 respectively; and the educational test suggested by the imperial government proved fully as effective in keeping out unwanted immigrants as the vetoed poll tax could have been. Although New Zealand now and then grumbled at the mother country, the invisible "silken ties" between them — those of race, language, culture, and institutions — showed no sign of weakening with the passage of time; on the contrary, they were reinforced by the concrete ties of self-interest. Britain was New Zealand's best customer and the well-filled coffers of the mother country stood open for loans. With the increased activities of foreign powers in the South Pacific, the political isolation of New Zealand was broken, and she put her trust in the British navy to safeguard her against foreign foes. The discussions in the eighties in favor of imperial federation aroused a considerable amount of interest in New Zealand; she agreed to pay a portion of the cost of the imperial squadron in the South Pacific; and during the Boer War she sent 6500 officers and men to South Africa.

The people of New Zealand developed an intense devotion to their own island home, at the same time maintaining a loyal attachment to the island home of their fathers. In blood the most English of all the colonies of Britain, New Zealand remained English in style of architecture, in customs, in thought, and in feeling. Thanks largely to the work of its early representatives, Samuel Marsden, the brothers Henry and William Williams, and Bishop Selwyn, the Church of England remained strong there. The census of 1901 disclosed that of the people in New Zealand 40 per cent called themselves Anglicans, 22 per cent Presbyterians, 14 per cent Roman Catholics, and 10 per cent Methodists; thus even the relative strength of the religious divisions followed fairly closely those in Great Britain. New Zealand was in many respects a "little England," but an England with a difference not accounted for by census figures. It was an England bathed in sunshine, an England minus smoke and dirt, an England without the glaring differences between those who have and those who have not, an England less shackled by tradition, an England politically, socially, and economically more of a democracy than the mother country in the northern seas.

CHAPTER 25

INDIA, 1858–1905

THE Mutiny in 1857 ended the fiction of "John Company's" control over India. After prolonged discussions the act which effected the transfer of India to the crown received royal sanction in August, 1858, and on Nevember 1 following, Queen Victoria announced the change in a famous proclamation to the peoples and princes of India. In this historic document the queen promised to fulfill all treaties and engagements that the company had concluded with the native princes, to abstain from territorial expansion, and to work for the prosperity and social advancement of the peoples of India. "We hold ourselves," the queen was made to say, "bound to the natives of our Indian territories by the same obligations of duty which bind us to our other subjects, and those obligations, by the blessing of Almighty God, we shall faithfully and conscientiously fulfill."

In solemn and sonorous language the queen disclaimed "alike the right and desire to impose our convictions on any of our subjects." "We declare it," she continued, "to be our royal will and pleasure that none be in anywise favoured, none molested or disquieted, by reason of their religious faith or observance, but that all shall alike enjoy the equal and impartial protection of the law; and we do strictly charge and enjoin those who may be in authority under us that they abstain from all interference with the religious belief or worship of any of our subjects on pain of our highest displeasure. And it is our further will that, as far as may be, our subjects, of whatever race or creed, be freely and impartially admitted to offices in our service, the duties of which they may be qualified by their education, ability, and integrity, duly to discharge."

The extent to which these pledges have been kept in letter and in spirit will appear in part from the subsequent history of India. For the sake of clarity the discussion will be grouped under the following topics: external affairs, British India and the native states, the government set up in 1858 and modifications thereof, economic and social changes, the rise of nationalism, and the work of Lord Curzon, 1898–1905.

The parts of India which in 1858 passed under the immediate control of the British crown were known as British India. Most of them lay in a continuous stretch of territory extending from the eastern boundary of Assam to the foothills of the mountains that formed the northwestern boundary of Punjab and thence southward to the Indus delta. Except for three small posts held by the French, the entire eastern coast, the greater portion of the western seaboard of India, and all of Lower Burma were included in British India. In the southwest some of the native states were bounded by the sea; the others were surrounded by territory directly controlled by Britain.

Of the land frontiers, that to the north caused the least trouble because a great mountain wall, the highest and most extensive in the world, formed an effective barrier; and Nepal, the only independent state on the southern slope of the Himalayas, was attached to the British by bonds of friendship and political alliance. To the east, Upper Burma in 1858 was still independent, but clashes on the frontiers marred Anglo-Burmese relations, traders complained of ill treatment by Burmese officials, and the wholesale massacre of rival claimants to the throne by King Thibaw of Ava caused humanitarians to demand that Britain seize the remainder of Burma. This event was hastened by the activities of France in Indo-China. Fresh annexations by the French resulting from a war with China in 1884–1885 made the boundaries of French Indo-China approach those of Upper Burma; Anglo-French relations were strained at this time because of the British occupation of Egypt; and French political and commercial agents avidly seized opportunities to obtain a foothold in Upper Burma. Thus France on the eastern frontier of India began to play the role held so long by Russia on the west and northwest frontier. The danger seemed imminent to Lord Dufferin, then viceroy of India, and in 1885 British troops moved swiftly along "the road to Mandalay." The third Burmese war lasted only a fortnight; Upper Burma was annexed, attached to India like the earlier Burmese acquisitions, and given a government modeled upon that of India. It took, however, about five years for the new province to become quiet and orderly.

The difficulties on the eastern boundary were of relatively short duration and they seem small in comparison with those on the west and northwest. The Pathan and Baluch tribes to the west of Sind frequently raided their neighbors, and counter raids by the British proved a poor remedy for a chronic ailment. British official opinion of the sixties being opposed to annexations, the English non-expansionists formulated for India the closed frontier policy generally held by the Liberals throughout the remainder of the nineteenth century. In support of it they cited the high authority of Lord Lawrence who as Sir John Lawrence had won great renown as administrator of the Punjab in the days before and during the Mutiny and had served as viceroy of India, 1864–1868. Even while Lawrence governed India, the situation on the western frontier of Sind became so intolerable that his subordinates began negotiations with local chieftains which resulted in the boundary of British India being moved westward. This proceeded slowly at first, but with Disraeli's advent to power in England in 1874 and his appointment of Lord Lytton as viceroy of India in 1876, the closed frontier policy was shelved. Quetta, one of the various

CHINA
INDIA
BURMA
Mandalay
I-rrawaddy
Salween
R.
Rangoon
Sikiang
Canton
Hong Kong
Macao (Port.)
TAIWAN
Hanoi
Kwangchow (Fr.)
HAINAN
FRENCH INDO-CHINA
Mekong R.
THAILAND
Bangkok
Saigon
PHILIPPINE ISLANDS
Manila
ANDAMAN IS.
NICOBAR IS.
Gulf of Siam
SOUTH CHINA SEA
Strait of Malacca
PENANG
FEDERATED MALAY STATES
Malacca
Singapore
SUMATRA
LABUAN I.
BR. NORTH BORNEO
BRUNEI
SARAWAK
BORNEO
CELEBES
INDIAN OCEAN
JAVA SEA
Sunda Strait
Batavia
JAVA
BALI
SUMBAWA
CHRISTMAS I.
COCOS I.
SOUTHEASTERN ASIA
British Dependency
Scale of Miles
0 100 200 300

"keys" to India, was occupied in 1877; and before the Conservatives were hurled from office in 1880, parts of Baluchistan had been added to British India and the remainder had become dependent upon the British.

India was an important factor in shaping the foreign policy and foreign relations of Britain under Disraeli, 1874–1880. Concern for the safety of India was given as the explanation for his purchase of nine-twentieths of the shares in the Suez Canal Company in 1875, for his Near Eastern policy during 1875–1878, for the Cyprus convention of 1878, and for the course pursued by Beaconsfield and Salisbury at the Congress of Berlin. In those years the British public learned a good deal about some old and several new keys to India; they were regaled with discussions in the press, on the platform, and in parliament of the strategic importance of Kabul, Kandahar, Quetta, Herat, the Hindu Kush Mountains, the Suez Canal, and the Russo-Armenian frontier. Constantinople continued to be one of the major "keys"; and when Russia found that Britain blocked her advance in the Balkans she quite naturally retaliated by thrusts in Central Asia that might be viewed as endangering India's safety. A romantic prime minister in Downing Street, a similarly-minded viceroy at Calcutta, and even the unromantic Lord Salisbury, secretary of state for India, 1874–1878, and for foreign affairs, 1878-1880, envisaged serious danger resulting from Russian activities in Turkestan; they began to tremble for the safety of India, and they saw great need for supplying her with "a scientific frontier." Lord Lytton initiated a series of maneuvers intended to checkmate Russia and establish British hegemony over Afghanistan. Sher Ali, the amir of Afghanistan, placed so uncomfortably between the Russian bear and the British lion, strove to the best of his limited ability to escape the clutches of both. His unpopularity with his own people encouraged Lord Lytton to think that he could pursue a forward policy with impunity. The amir's polite refusal to accept an official British mission to Kabul was treated by the viceroy as an insult.

A case, though not a strong one, was built up for a war with Afghanistan, and toward the close of 1878 British armies invaded the country, entering Kabul early in 1879. By the Treaty of Gandammak Yakub Khan, a son of the recently deceased Sher Ali, who had been proclaimed amir, ceded some territory to the British and agreed to accept a permanent British agent at Kabul and to conduct his foreign relations in accordance with British views. Neither the treaty nor the new amir nor least of all his foreign masters won approval among the Afghans. They found a capable leader in Abdur Rahman, a nephew of Sher Ali, and killed the British resident at Kabul, Sir Louis Cavagnari, and his escort. Cavagnari's murder was avenged in a primitive fashion but with scientific thoroughness when an Anglo-Indian army under Lord Roberts reoccupied Kabul. For a while both Lord Lytton and his superiors at home considered a partition of Afghanistan. However, a somewhat belated though very beneficent ray of wisdom entered his mind when shortly before his recall in June, 1880, he accepted Abdur Rahman as ruler of Afghanistan. The details of the arrangements were completed by the new Liberal viceroy, Lord Ripon. Afghanistan, including Kandahar, was evacuated and recognized as a valuable buffer state; and although Abdur Rahman accepted a pension from the British, he preserved his country's independence with great skill and success until his death in 1901.

In the early years of his reign, Abdur Rahman was aided in his work by the non-expansionistic policy of the Gladstone government, 1880–1885. But the queen disliked the evacuation of Kandahar; and she, a large section of the British press, and a considerable body of opinion in and outside of parliament were ready to take alarm at any report of Russian activities in Central Asia. In the cabinet one of the staunchest opponents of the alarmists was Lord Northbrook, who as an ex-viceroy of India carried much weight in the discussions of Indian problems. In a long memorandum of 1882 he asserted that the Russian advances in Turkestan should be welcomed as a means of ridding the country of the slave traders and that the greatest need was a delimitation of the Afghan-Russian boundary. To effect this a joint Anglo-Russian commission was appointed; it finished its task in 1895. Meanwhile the Russian occupation of Merv, on the western frontier of Afghanistan, in 1884, and their expulsion of the Afghans from Penjdeh in 1885 aroused great excitement in England. The latter incident led Gladstone to deliver a warlike speech in the house of commons and to ask for and receive a vote of money for war. But Abdur Rahman, knowing that in the event of an Anglo-Russian war his country would be the chief sufferer, chose to regard the Penjdeh incident as a trivial affair, and in the spring of 1885 Britain and Russia agreed to arbitrate their differences concerning Penjdeh.

Between British India and Afghanistan lay a strip of territory occupied by Waziris, Afridis, Mohmands, and other warlike tribes over whom no one had been able to establish effective control. In the early nineties expansionistic sentiment waxed strong in England and demands arose for a definitive settlement of the Indian boundaries. A commission headed by Sir Mortimer Durand drew the Afghan-Indian frontier line which bears his name; this awarded to India the greater share of the former no-man's land. The work of the commission was supplemented by efforts to place British garrisons in the far northwest, but the tribes resented these threats to their independence; and in 1897 Afridis, Mohmands, Swatis, and Orakzais took up arms, captured several forts, and raided Punjab villages. Although at one time more than 35,000 troops were engaged against the Afridis, the outcome was never in doubt.

The frontier war had just closed when a new viceroy, Lord Curzon, arrived in India in December, 1898. A member of the forward school of English statesmen, he lost no time in consolidating and strengthening Britain's power in northwestern India by enlisting frontier tribes under British officers to guard and keep order in the disturbed areas, by separating nearly all the trans-Indus territory from Punjab and organizing it as the

North West Frontier Province under his direct control, and by pushing the construction of roads and railroads in this province.

As already mentioned, the northern frontier of India had presented no important problem since the war with Nepal, 1814–1815. But at the opening of the present century Curzon saw or imagined he saw an increase in the Russian influence in Tibet. This theocratically governed, semi-independent province of China had been and wished to remain closed to foreigners, and its ruler, the Dalai Lama, refused Curzon's request to receive a British mission at his capital, Lhasa. Following the precedent set by Lytton in dealing with Afghanistan twenty-five years earlier, Curzon insisted that the unwanted mission be accepted, and in 1903 he obtained from a reluctant British cabinet consent to dispatch an armed force into Tibet. The Russo-Japanese War broke out early in 1904, and while Britain's old rival more than had her hands full Curzon sent a military mission headed by Colonel Younghusband into Tibet in the spring of that year. After some hundreds of poorly armed Tibetans had been shot down, Younghusband entered Lhasa and forced the regent, the Dalai Lama having fled, to sign a treaty that granted commercial and other concessions to the British and imposed a rather heavy war indemnity.

Curzon's watchful eye discovered dangers to India from the situation in the Persian Gulf. To avert them, he forestalled possible French action by seizing Muscat in southeastern Arabia, and he blocked suspected efforts of the Russians to establish a naval station at Bandar Abbas on the Persian side of the entrance to the gulf. At its head, close by the expected terminus of the German-controlled Berlin-to-Bagdad railroad, lay the tiny realm of the sultan of Koweit. The strategic importance of this territory was appreciated by both the British and the Germans; but thanks to Curzon, the British entered the field first and negotiated a treaty with the sultan in 1900 whereby he pledged himself to grant no concession to which Britain might object. British warships warded off Turkish attempts to assert supremacy over

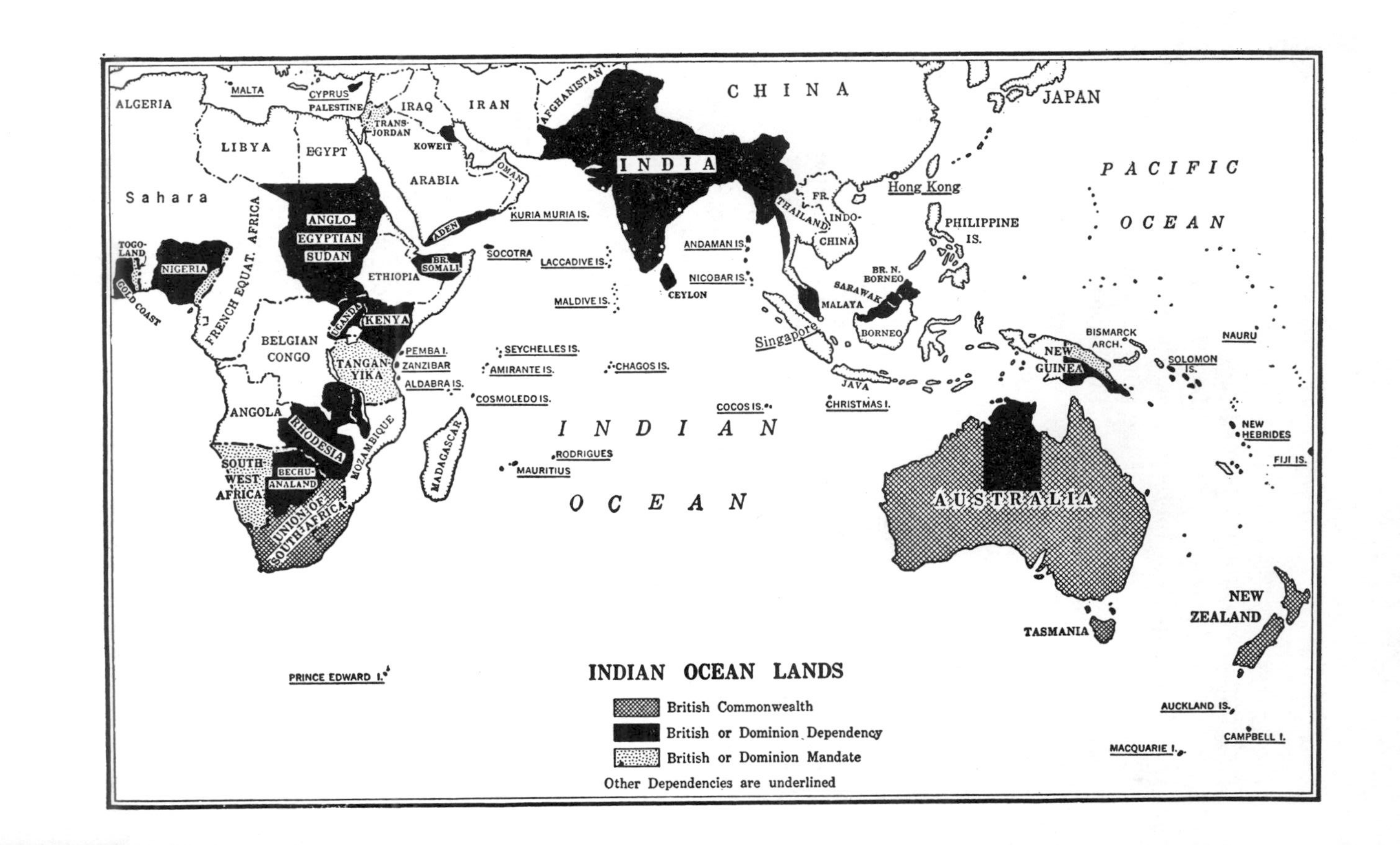
INDIAN OCEAN LANDS
British Commonwealth
British or Dominion Dependency
British or Dominion Mandate
Other Dependencies are underlined
ALGERIA
MALTA
CYPRUS
PALESTINE
IRAQ
IRAN
TRANS-JORDAN
KOWEIT
LIBYA
EGYPT
ARABIA
OMAN
ADEN
Sahara
ANGLO-EGYPTIAN SUDAN
TOGO-LAND
NIGERIA
GOLD COAST
FRENCH EQUAT. AFRICA
ETHIOPIA
BR. SOMALI
SOCOTRA
KURIA MURIA IS.
BELGIAN CONGO
UGANDA
KENYA
TANGAN-YIKA
PEMBA I.
ZANZIBAR
ALDABRA IS.
ANGOLA
RHODESIA
MOZAMBIQUE
SOUTH WEST AFRICA
BECHU-ANALAND
UNION OF SOUTH AFRICA
MADAGASCAR
SEYCHELLES IS.
AMIRANTE IS.
COSMOLEDO IS.
MAURITIUS
RODRIGUES
LACCADIVE IS.
MALDIVE IS.
CHAGOS IS.
AFGHANISTAN
INDIA
CEYLON
ANDAMAN IS.
NICOBAR IS.
CHINA
JAPAN
Hong Kong
FR. INDO-CHINA
THAILAND
PHILIPPINE IS.
BR. N. BORNEO
SARAWAK
MALAYA
BORNEO
Singapore
JAVA
CHRISTMAS I.
COCOS IS.
INDIAN OCEAN
PACIFIC OCEAN
BISMARCK ARCH.
NEW GUINEA
SOLOMON IS.
NAURU
NEW HEBRIDES
FIJI IS.
AUSTRALIA
TASMANIA
NEW ZEALAND
AUCKLAND IS.
CAMPBELL I.
MACQUARIE I.
PRINCE EDWARD I.

Koweit. Thus under the guidance of a masterful viceroy, India's interests were fitted into the pattern of Britain's imperial policy.

In the days when the East India Company represented Britain east of the Cape of Good Hope, all British-controlled territory in that region was administered by the company. It was therefore partly as a heritage from the past and partly as a means of relieving the British government and taxpayer that new eastern territorial acquisitions were attached to India. The Indian army was used to fight battles that were not the exclusive concern of India. For example, British economic interests and imperial policies were fully as important as the need for safeguarding India in causing the wars with Burma which were fought by India's army and paid for by her. That many of the islands in the Indian Ocean should be attached to India was perhaps to be expected. The Andaman and Nicobar Islands and the Laccadives were penal settlements which helped to insure Britain's naval supremacy in the eastern waters. In Malaya, Singapore, Penang, the Province Wellesley, and Malacca were under the government of Bengal until 1867; in Africa, British Somaliland was a dependency of Bombay from 1884 to 1898; and Aden on the southwestern tip of Arabia was a part of that presidency until 1932 and was later put under India. Indian troops fought the Abyssinian War of 1867–1868, were sent to Malta in 1878 when a war with Russia seemed imminent, and were used on the Red Sea coast of Egypt in the early eighties. At that time Gladstone sought unsuccessfully to convince the viceroy of India, Lord Ripon, that Indian interests in connection with Egypt and the Suez Canal justified charging her with some of the cost of British military expeditions to the Red Sea. Gladstone's government departed from earlier practices, however, when it contributed £5,000,000 from the imperial exchequer toward the cost of the second Afghan war.

Turning from the external affairs of India to her internal problems, we must mention briefly those connected with the relations between Britain and the native states of India. In her proclamation of November, 1858, Queen Victoria pledged Britain to observe the treaties that the company had concluded with the Indian princes. This promise was kept; no attempt was made to employ Dalhousie's methods in dealing with the native states. Although chronic misrule necessitated the removal of the Gaekwar of Baroda in 1875, and the murder of a British commissioner and his escort in Manipur in 1891 caused the dispatch of a punitive expedition and the deposition of the native ruler, members of the ruling houses were enthroned in both places and the position of the states was not altered. Indeed, in 1881 Lord Ripon departed so far from Dalhousie's practice as to restore Mysore, a state of about 30,000 square miles, to a prince of the old governing family. Although the company's treaties were kept, several proclamations, called sanads, emphasized the British overlordship, and none of the native princes were allowed to claim independence. They could not have commercial or diplomatic relations with a foreign power; their troops, if they had any, were to be at the disposal of the suzerain; and the growing complexity of social and economic life facilitated the strengthening of Britain's supremacy over the feudatory states. This was especially true during the viceroyalty of Lord Curzon, 1898–1905.

The governmental changes made necessary by the transfer of India to the crown were effected by the Government of India Act, 1858, and the India Councils Act, 1861. The former provided that the duties of the court of directors and the board of control should be taken over by a secretary of state in council. The secretary of state was of course a member of the cabinet, which now became more directly responsible for the affairs of India, subject to the supreme authority of parliament. The council of India in London was at first composed of fifteen members, seven of whom were elected by the court of directors of the East India Company; vacancies were filled by cooption by the council. The remaining eight were nominated by the crown, which in practice meant the secretary of state. The councilors were appointed for life; and a majority among them, which came to mean nine, must have resided or served at least ten years in India and not been absent from the country more than ten years previous to their appointment. Originally the council of India held a semi-independent position and exercised a considerable amount of authority, particularly over finance; but its power of initiation was limited, it had no voice in determining India's foreign relations, and its decisions could be overriden by the secretary of state. Moreover, its power was weakened in 1869 when all the councilors became royal nominees and their term of office was limited to ten years with a possible extension to fifteen. By an act of 1876 the secretary of state was empowered to appoint not more than three experts under the old life tenure and in 1889 he was given authority to leave vacancies unfilled until the number of councilors had been reduced to ten.

Among the outstanding secretaries of state for India, 1858–1905, were Sir Charles Wood, afterward Lord Halifax, author of the India education dispatch of 1854; the Duke of Argyll, Lord Salisbury, Lord Hartington, Lord Kimberley, and Lord Randolph Churchill. The post was generally held by men in the front rank of their parties, men who possessed more than average ability as statesmen and administrators. But as in the case of the other departments of the government, much of the work of the India office devolved upon the staff, especially upon the permanent undersecretary whose influence is generally great though hard to measure. From 1883 until 1909 this post was held by Sir Arthur Godley, afterward Lord Kilbracken. The council of India was intended to take the place of the court of directors as a buffer against the British economic interests which demanded that India should be governed for their benefit, but as such it was not very effective. The limitations on its powers and its subservience to the secretary of state prevented able and ambitious men from seeking appointment to it, although councilors like Sir Henry Maine and Sir Alfred Lyall are an exception to the rule; those with Indian experience were often old; and British chambers of commerce could generally exert more direct pressure upon the secretary of state and parliament than was possible for the council of India.

The act of 1858 stipulated that the governor general of India and the governors of Madras and Bombay be appointed by the crown; the lieutenant-governors were to be chosen by the governor general, subject to the approval of the crown; the ordinary members of the governor general's council and the councils for Madras and Bombay were selected by the secretary of state in council; and many other appointments were made by the same authority on the recommendation of the civil service commissioners. The change in the royal title in 1876, whereby the queen was made empress of India, in no wise affected the machinery of government. When the governor general represented the sovereign he was called the viceroy; in common parlance this title superseded that of governor general. The work of governing India was intrusted to the governor general in council. The phrase "in council" is misleading during this period inasmuch as the governor general dominated the council. With the exception of Sir John Lawrence, governor general from 1864 to 1868, the occupants of this office lacked previous experience in India, but had usually held positions in the British government or acquired administrative and diplomatic experience before they went to India. Partly because of accidents, the majority of the governors general appointed as successors to Lord Canning were Liberals or ex-Liberals: the two Lords Elgin, Lawrence, Mayo, Northbrook, Ripon, and Dufferin were Liberals at the time of their appointment; Lansdowne was an ex-Liberal. The Conservative viceroys were Lytton, 1876–1880, and Curzon, 1898–1905, the latter ranking with Warren Hastings and Dalhousie among the great rulers of India. Although subordinated to the secretary of state, the governors general of India continued to maintain an independent position which did not diminish with the opening of direct telegraphic communication between Britain and India in 1870. Indeed Lord Curzon often acted as independently of his official superiors as Lord Dalhousie had fifty years earlier. The government of India was more centralized by the act of 1858, but its dual character persisted.

The periodic investigations of conditions in and the affairs of India which had preceded each renewal of the company's charter ended when India was transferred to the crown. Although yearly reports by the governor general and parliamentary debates on Indian budgets supposedly took the place of the earlier studies and reports, they were not so revealing. Domestic, Irish, and other imperial issues generally absorbed the entire attention of the house of commons until after the turn of the century, when an Indian nationalist sympathizer, Sir Henry Cotton, and an occasional Labor member began to ask awkward questions. The retired governors and viceroys of India seldom disturbed the placid atmosphere of the house of lords with criticisms of the government's India policy. The interest shown by parliament in questions concerning India lacked vitality to such an extent that in 1894 the secretary of state and the government of India ignored a house of commons request that Indian civil service examinations be held in India as well as in England. Queen Victoria was not unmindful of her duties toward her Indian subjects, but lack of knowledge, insight, sympathy, and power prevented her from being a vital factor in the government of these teeming millions.

The government created for India in 1858 was a despotism — benevolent, but despotic all the same. Slight changes in the direction of representative government were made by the Indian Councils Acts of 1861 and 1892 and by alterations in the municipal and district government of India during the seventies and eighties. The act of 1861 prescribed a council for India consisting of five members, three of whom should have served at least ten years in India; the fourth member was to be a financial and the fifth a legal expert. A sixth member, to have charge of public works, was added in 1874. To this body, which bore a strong resemblance to the executive councils in the British crown colonies, were to be added, for purposes of lawmaking, from six to twelve members, of whom not more than half should be officials; this enlarged council was the legislative council for India. Although its work was restricted to legislation, it could not initiate laws, the governor general possessing this power; furthermore, he could veto the laws passed by the council, and in an emergency he could issue ordinances which had the force of law for six months. The Indian legislative council could not pass laws which affected the supremacy of parliament or English laws applicable in India; acts signed by the governor general might be disallowed in England. It was suggested in the debates on the India Councils Act of 1861 that some of the "additional" members of the council should be native Indians, but the government refused to have such a provision embodied in the bill; however, Indians were from the beginning included among the "additional" members, although being chosen from the nobility they could hardly be said to represent the people of India. The act of 1861 reinstated the legislative councils for Madras and Bombay and made provisions for that of Bengal, created in 1862; similar councils were established in the North Western Provinces in 1886, and in the Punjab and Burma in 1898. The laws passed by the provincial legislative councils required the sanction of both the governor and the governor general, and they might be disallowed at home.

In 1888 Lord Dufferin, then viceroy of India, recommended that the native sons of India be given "a wider share in the administration of public affairs." Although this recommendation was endorsed by his successor, Lord Lansdowne, not until 1892 did the Conservative government of Lord Salisbury see its way to a timid application of this principle. The India Councils Act of 1892 raised the maximum number of "additional" members of the India council to sixteen, of whom ten were to be non-official; of these, four were to be chosen by the non-official members of the provincial legislative councils and one by the Calcutta chamber of commerce. The act also enlarged the non-official elements in the provincial councils, and provided that some of these councilors were to be nominated by district boards and the universities.

The government of India was so highly centralized in 1858 that governmental units smaller than the province hardly existed; except for the maintenance of watch and ward in some of the villages the people had no share in their local administration. However, by degrees the most important cities acquired some self-government and rural districts were created. In the local units of government representative institutions made their first appearance, elective members being introduced in the municipal council of Bombay in 1872, of Madras in 1878, and of Calcutta in 1882. Lord Ripon, 1880–1884, extended the functions of the administrative boards of the rural districts and made them partly elective. High hopes were entertained as to the extent to which the peoples of India could be trained for self-government in these local units, but as with so many well-laid plans the results were disappointing.

The assumption of the reins of government by the crown, the creation of legislative councils, and an increased realization of the need of serving India if her government were in some measure to keep abreast of modern developments resulted in a multitude of new laws and the establishment of a variety of new services. The penal code upon which Macaulay had spent much time and labor in the thirties was put into effect in a modified form in 1860. A number of similar codes soon followed, the aim of which was to make India's legislative system more logical and more scientific. In this process of codification much was borrowed from English, French, and American law; but in thus modernizing the laws it was realized that the Indian family law, varied and largely religious in origin, must be kept. Hence Hindu, Mohammedan, Buddhist, and Parsee law continued to exist side by side with law originating from or embodied in European ideas and experience. The foreign surface currents grew strong; but although the depths of Indian society were barely stirred by them, they were not untouched. Health, sanitation, medicine, forestry, police, and education were either organized from the beginning or reorganizd shortly after the Mutiny; the peasant escaped most of the effects of the innovations, but the city dweller could not. One immediate result of the many changes was to make the government more bureaucratic; this in turn meant a great increase in the number of government employees.

The Charter Act of 1833 had affirmed that race, color, religion, and place of birth should not bar Indians from employment in government service. This promise was reaffirmed in the Indian Civil Service Act of 1861, and again by Queen Victoria when she stated in 1858 "that, as far as may be, our subjects, of whatever race or creed, be freely and impartially admitted to offices in our service, the duties of which they may be qualified by their education, ability, and integrity duly to discharge." The last clause implied certain tests; about them controversies arose. Indians studied at the new university colleges and East met West at the government's "pie counter," but the jostling was kept within bounds by an arrangement whereby the qualifying examinations for the Indian civil service were given only in England. In 1868 the government of India tried to redress the balance by creating nine scholarships of an annual value of £200 to be used in England by Indians wishing to prepare for entrance into their country's civil service. An imperial act of 1870 made it possible to appoint natives of India who had not passed the prescribed tests, a backdoor that was opened wider by Lord Lytton when he established the "statutory civil service" whereby sixty-nine Indians could be nominated for certain appointments without a qualifying examination. But the experiment failed, and attempts by Indian well-wishers in the house of commons to have examinations for the Indian civil service given simultaneously in England and India came to nought. In the lower grades, called the uncovenanted civil service, the Indians formed a majority; but the opportunities for advancing from this to the superior covenanted civil service were few. To the ranks of the latter around forty Englishmen were admitted every year, whereas, after 1870, in some years there might be one or two or three Indians; in many years there were none. Britannia continued to rule India.

In a country that is governed under a system of benevolent despotism the government occupies and is expected to occupy the place of providence. India was, and is, a poor country; over vast areas the government was virtually the landlord; taxation however light was sure to bear heavily on the population; and the government had to take the lead in the country's economic development. Behind the government of India was that of Britain which had to be increasingly sensitive to an electorate that held its needs superior to those of any other portion of the empire and had learned to look upon India as a land to be exploited. Moreover, beyond the control of the governments of India and Britain were economic forces that made themselves felt when, for instance, the Civil War in the United States raised the price of Indian cotton, the Suez Canal was opened for traffic in 1869, and the price of gold rose and of silver fell in 1873–1895. Thus it was that peasants on the banks of the Ganges experienced the effects of the Federal blockade of the Confederacy in the United States in 1861–1865, and the success or failure of the monetary policies urged by senators from Nevada. India, 1858–1905, was a part of a world economic order that Britain could not regulate, but for whose workings her government was often blamed. Even further removed from British control was the monsoon, the life-giver for India, whose failure to appear made her a favorite field of operation for the death-dealing furies — famine and plague.

The new government of India inherited a debt of nearly £100,000,000 — a staggering load in the early sixties — a tradition that taxes on land should form the government's chief source of revenue, and the practice of not borrowing even for productive public works. At the beginning of the period, the land tax supplied about 40 per cent of the revenues; at its end, in the neighborhood of 25 per cent. For a little more than twenty years there was hot debate on whether a permanent settlement of the land tax, such as had been made in Bengal, should be extended to all of India; but this discussion virtually ended in 1883 with no drastic change in the system of assessing and collecting the land tax that had been in effect under the company. Other sources of revenue causing little dispute were the salt tax and the tax on opium. On the other hand, the income tax and the customs duties aroused violent controversies. The former was imposed after the Mutiny, discontinued in 1865, reintroduced in 1869, and in 1886 definitely became a part of India's financial policy. Customs duties averaging about 10 per cent ad valorem were levied in the early sixties. Since cotton goods supplied 60 per cent of India's import the duties on cotton excited lively interest in Lancashire; Lancashiremen quoted Bright, Cobden, and the other major prophets of free trade and cited England's experience. In 1877 the house of commons gave support to Lancashire's demand for the abolition of India's duty of 5 per cent ad valorem on cotton. But the Afghan War made this revenue tariff necessary, and it was not abolished until 1882. Reimposed in the early nineties, the duty on cotton goods again stirred Lancashire, which demanded and in 1895 secured the imposition of a countervailing duty or excise on Indian cotton goods equaling that on the products of its own looms. The following year the countervailing duty was reduced from 5 to 3½ per cent.

Rising prices and returning prosperity in the late nineties made the Indian duties of slight economic importance; but they were used effectively for political purposes by Indian nationalists who later received aid from the Indian cotton interests. Although Lancashire's motive in urging the imposition of excise duties on India's cotton manufactures was, of course, selfish, this cannot be said of all who advocated free trade for India. Sir John Strachey, financial expert on the council in India and a confirmed free trader, sincerely believed that free trade would benefit India. Ripon, under whose viceroyalty the Indian cotton duties were repealed, acquired a great and deserved reputation as a well-wisher of India; his motives were beyond reproach. It is also worth remembering that a protective duty for India's cotton industry meant dearer cotton goods and that the fall in the value of the rupee, amounting to nearly 50 per cent between 1873 and 1895, had the effect of a protective tariff. Statistically the growth of the Indian cotton industry may be gauged by the following figures: In 1879–1880 India had 58 cotton mills employing 39,537 workers; by 1894–1895 the number of mills had reached 114 and workers numbered 139,578; for 1914 the figures are 264 and 260,847 respectively. British capital was plentiful; and this, together with the fall of the rupee and the prospect of profiting by the cheap labor in India, helped to build up her cotton industries. At the turn of the century neither this industry nor the Indian nationalist movement appeared formidable; combined, they formed a cloud presaging a storm that later spread havoc far and wide amid the vales of Lancashire.

Before we consider the public works policy of the India government, its causes and results, we may briefly call attention to the effects upon India of the fluctuation in world prices. As already noted, the Civil War in the United States created a brisk demand for Indian cotton, prices rose, and the cash nexus was introduced into India. As on so many similar occasions at other times and in other parts of the world, the Indian cotton growers spent their earnings, contracted debts, and fell into the clutches of the money lenders. The period of prosperity was but a St. Martin's summer. With the war over, American long-staple cotton easily recaptured the English market; neither the shortening of the sea route to England by the Suez Canal nor the fall in the value of Indian money could offset the advantages enjoyed by American cotton growers. After 1873 the price of silver, the basis of India's currency, began to drop. The rupee valued at 2*s.* in the early seventies stood at about 1*s.* 1*d.* in 1894–1895. Among the factors responsible for this were the rise in the value of gold and the demonetization of silver by the Latin monetary union and Germany. In those far-off days when no respectable government deliberately juggled with its currency such a decline was considered a disaster. And a disaster it was because India's export trade could not expand in proportion to the decline in the value of her money, and her liabilities such as debt charges, the cost of her administrative services, and pensions were payable in sterling. For a while Indian financial experts hoped for salvation from the silver policies discussed in the United States; then they recommended that India adopt a gold standard and discontinue the free coinage of silver. An Indian currency commission prepared a plan which embodied the second and a modified form of the first proposal. The British sovereign was made legal tender in India at the rate of 15 rupees to the sovereign, making the rupee equivalent to 1*s.* 4*d.* Shortly after this plan had been suggested prices rose as a result of the large amount of gold produced in South Africa, the Klondike, and Alaska, and the rupee was kept stable until the outbreak of war in 1914.

In the late sixties the government of India inaugurated the policy of borrowing for public works. Much of the money so borrowed was used for the construction of railroads and for irrigation, the interest in both being greatly stimulated by the famines which recurrent failures of the monsoon brought upon India during 1860–1900. Because of the economic importance of these calamities we shall discuss them first. The rainfall over the larger section of India depends chiefly upon the southwest wind, commonly called the monsoon; when it fails, drought and famine follow. These disasters befell the North Western Provinces in 1860, Orissa in 1867, Bihar in 1873 and 1877, and Central India in 1896–1900. In Orissa, a province southwest of Calcutta, only a comparatively small area was affected; but cut off by jungles and a harborless coast, Orissa was practically inaccessible and the famine resulted in a great loss of life. Appalled by the disaster, the viceroy, Sir John Lawrence, vowed that in the future there should be no loss of life due to famine; and successive famine commissions strove earnestly to formulate effective plans for coping with the threat. Railroads were built for the specific purpose of reaching areas that frequently suffered from drought; irrigation works sought to repair nature's deficiency; administrators were supplied with detailed plans for meeting emergencies; and efforts were made to establish a form of famine insurance. Nevertheless, in the latter half of the nineties a drought of four years' duration, affecting 400,000 square miles and making approximately 60,000,000 people dependent upon government aid, made the task of such magnitude that it would have more than strained the resources of a richer country than India. Aid came from the United Kingdom and other portions of the British empire and India's relief and health services fought bravely against famine, disease, and death; still, people succumbed in large numbers from lack of food and from the diseases that feast on undernourished bodies. At the opening of the present century a new famine commission with Sir Anthony MacDonnell as chairman was engaged in preparing plans which included provincial famine codes. The new "famine strategy" was put to a test in 1907–1908 and proved quite effective.

Lord Dalhousie had dreamed of a day when a vast railroad system would cover India, and had made a start in that direction by surveys and the actual construction of about 150 miles of lines. Since India lacked capital, the first railroads were built by English companies using imported material under a system whereby the government guaranteed a return of 5 per cent and reserved the right to purchase the lines. This system did not encourage economy in construction on the part of the companies, and in 1869 the government undertook to build railroads. There was a return to the guarantee system a few years later;

nevertheless, the greater portion of the 25,000 miles of railroads in India in 1900, including all the trunk lines, belonged to the government, which also owned and operated factories and shops for construction and repair of equipment. As already mentioned, the railroads aided in combating famines and furthered the growth of Indian industries, especially iron and coal. The Suez Canal had so cheapened freight rates that for several years after 1869 English coal could undersell that of India at Bombay; but thanks largely to the extension of the railroads India grew more and more independent of imported coal.

Irrigation has been resorted to in India since time immemorial; its rapid extension along scientific lines was due to the decision of the government to borrow money for irrigation works. The recurrent famines and the growth of the population made it urgent to increase the cultivated area and to make the grain crop more certain. Within the period under discussion, the Punjab and the North Western or United Provinces were the chief beneficiaries of the government's irrigation policy. In the Punjab, the area under government irrigation increased from 1,025,166 acres in 1867–1868 to 5,211,249 acres thirty years later; the increase during the same period in the United Provinces is shown by the figures 716,000 and 2,345,486 acres. In all of India the area under government irrigation in 1905 totaled 14,676,000 acres. But irrigation was only one phase of the problem of increasing the amount of foodstuffs for the people of India; the other was the question of improving Indian agriculture by making it more scientific. Here the innate conservatism of the people and their religious taboos made progress difficult. Where unprofitable animals and destructive vermin are not permitted to be removed, the yield of field and pasture can hardly be increased.

Sanitation, health education, and medical service are complementary to the food supply in the work of saving human lives. All three were and are sorely needed in India. The great problems connected with their improvements involved numbers, age-old customs and beliefs, and finance. In the sixties the heavy death rate among the British troops in India caused the government to establish a sanitary commission for Madras, later supplanted by the sanitary commission of India; in 1883 the civil medical service was greatly extended. It has been observed that while the Indian may not be filthy in his home and cleanliness may form a part of his religious rites, he finds it hard to understand matters of public hygiene, pure water, the disposal of refuse, sewage, and healthful building sites. Progress was made in fighting a disease like smallpox where vaccine plays an important role, but to combat cholera was more difficult; and when the bubonic plague appeared in Bombay in 1896 the battle against it touched ancient taboos to such an extent that it became a political issue. Moreover, it was not until the close of the period that the connection between the rat-flea and bubonic plague and between the Anopheles mosquito and malaria were definitely established; both discoveries were of immense significance for India. The progress in sanitation and health education was so slow that deaths exceeded births by 125,000 in Calcutta, 1891–1901. That progress had been made where the authorities could exercise unchallenged control was shown by the declining death rate among soldiers and prisoners. The death rate per thousand among European troops in India fell from 26.95 in 1861–1865 to 16.52 in 1896–1900; that among the jail population from 48.86 in 1879–1883 to 29.97 in 1896–1900. Despite the prevailing high death rate, the population of India grew from 206,000,000 in 1872 to 294,000,000 in 1901. Although some of this gain was due to annexations, it is significant that the decade 1901–1911 showed a natural increase of nearly 20,000,000. A mere glance at these figures will convey an impression of the tasks facing a government that attempted to educate the Indians in accordance with west European standards of the late nineteenth century.

We have seen that education became a concern of the government shortly after the British assumed control in India; the educational program outlined in Wood's dispatch of 1854 was restated in 1859. In the midst of the turmoil of the Mutiny, universities were founded in the three presidency cities, Bombay, Calcutta, and Madras; and to these were added the University of Punjab, 1882, and that of Allahabad, 1887. By 1882 more than 2,225,000 pupils were attending public educational institutions; twenty years later the number had grown to 3,887,493, of whom 558,378 were enrolled in secondary schools. An Indian education commission of 1902 reported the existence of 104,622 institutions for public instruction; of these, 97,854 were primary schools, 145 were arts colleges, and 46 were professional schools. The government of India realized that the responsibility for education must by a process of devolution be laid at the door of the smaller units of government, especially the provinces and municipalities, and that for financial reasons use must be made of private donations, religious and charitable organizations, and the fee system. Consequently, of the 401 lakhs of rupees — $12,-964,370 — expended for public education in 1901–1902, less than one-half came from the various government units and about one-third was derived from fees. Similar compromises were arranged in the operation and management of the schools, so that of the 104,622 institutions 22,250 were under public and 82,372 under private management; of the latter, 62,747 received aid from the government and the remaining 19,625 were subject to some form of inspection. Christian missions maintained 3778 schools, among which were 40 colleges which had affiliations with the Indian universities. The language question was also treated in a spirit of compromise. The lower schools, of course, used the vernacular, and English was taught as a foreign language in the majority of the secondary schools. But since English was the only common language among the educated Indians, and since it was a requirement for public employment, especially in the higher grades of the various services, it was a popular subject. In the secondary schools and in the colleges the culture of the West was brought to India; it was emphasized in the examinations at the universities, which, with the exception of that of the Punjab, were not teaching but examining institutions.

Although the results of the efforts to provide India with proper educational facilities may be judged meager, an appreciation of the difficulties to be overcome — financial, linguistic, racial, and religious — will put the matter in a different light. The filtration theory held by some of the pioneers of Indian education proved fallacious; university graduates were more eager to secure government employment than to spread sweetness and light among the masses, especially the depressed classes. Among the latter Christian missionaries did quite effective work, with some encouragement from the government and as a rule opposition from the educated Hindus. General education made most rapid progress in Burma where Buddhism presented no obstacles of caste and sex; and the number of female scholars, which in 1901–1902 for all of India represented less than one-ninth of the whole, was greatest in that province. The upper- and middle-class Hindus took an interest in education, but caste and sex prejudices hindered this. The Mohammedans were least responsive. The 46 professional colleges, which included law, medicine, engineering, agriculture, commerce, forestry, and art, were maintained by the state. Although the need for such education was great, the average Indian preferred arts colleges to professional schools. The educational system of India, especially in its upper branches, reinforced the effects of government and of economic and social development in producing a national movement in India. That it should appear was more natural than that it should not; nevertheless, when it did appear and gained strength, Britain seemed as surprised as the proverbial hen with a duckling.

Like other great movements in history, Indian nationalism is a result of the spread of general ideas and of conditions in the nineteenth century, as well as of the special religious, racial, political, and social situation found in India. The national awakenings which so profoundly stirred the peoples of Europe and transformed Japan could not leave India untouched, especially when her youth was nurtured in the ideas of Locke, Burke, and J. S. Mill. The English had always been sojourners in India, and time increased the awareness of a difference between them and the natives. The Mutiny destroyed the English feeling of security — a volcano which had erupted so violently once might erupt anew. On both sides, the victims and memories of the Mutiny formed a barrier. The appearance of a small European planter and trader class made possible a European society and fostered racial exclusiveness. In days of old, the representatives of a trading company had lived among the people without being so racially conscious as the Indian civil servants of the late nineteenth century were apt to be. The Suez Canal and the steamship made it easier for the Europeans in India to live a family life and harder for them to become identified with the land wherein they dwelt. These factors did not create Indian nationalism, but they stimulated its growth.

Hinduism is a religious and social system for four-fifths of the people of India. At first it recoiled before the impact of the West. Somewhat bewildered, Hindu religious leaders of little more than a hundred years ago attempted to reach a spiritual compromise in a sect, the Brahmo Samaj, which sought to establish an eclectic religion embracing some of the best features of leading eastern and western religions. The sect never numbered many adherents, but it exercised an intellectual influence out of all proportion to its numerical strength. Among its leaders was Debendranath Tagore, father of the famous poet Rabindranath Tagore. However, the compromises of the Brahmo Samaj did not satisfy many of the young Hindu intellectuals of the latter half of the nineteenth century; and some of them founded the Arya Samaj, an organization uncompromisingly Hindu and certain that the classics of Hindu literature contain everything or the germ of everything needful for a complete life. As the leaders in the later Irish revival preached going back to the old Celtic literature, so the great Indian religious leader, Swami Vivekananda, emphasized the need for "going back to the Vedas." Nor was the Indian spiritual revival without encouragement from the West where religious skepticism combined with social unrest made many earnest men and women uncertain of the much-vaunted superiority of Europe over Asia. Indeed, a few Europeans like Mrs. Besant and Mme. Blavatsky were convinced of the opposite and so told the Indians. In its origin the Indian national movement was spiritual and intellectual and had no political aim. This came later.

Political movements are generated by concrete grievances; and these Indians had. Educated Indians were conscious of inequalities based on race and color – they frequently experienced them in social intercourse and travel. Individual Englishmen flaunted their belief in a racial superiority and, especially in the case of army officers, forgot the results of the greased cartridges; they compelled servants to perform tasks that necessitated religious defilement – a great empire and bad manners go not well together. India had received a solemn promise that for employment in government service none should be discriminated against because of race, color, religion, or place of birth; yet the qualifying examinations for the superior civil service were given only in England and arbitrary age limits acted as a further bar against Indians. Lord Lytton's Vernacular Press Act, 1878, put the native press under censorship, thereby causing an irritation which its repeal by Lord Ripon could not remove. This well-meaning but not very competent viceroy was responsible for the so-called Ilbert Bill of 1883, which made it possible to have Europeans tried by Indian judges. This was welcomed by the Indians as a charter of racial equality, a fulfillment in letter and in spirit of the queen's proclamation of 1858; but it provoked such a violent outburst of rage among Anglo-Indians that, aided by superpatriotic Englishmen at home, they forced the government to emasculate the bill. Indian leaders considered this a slap in the face; dissatisfaction grew, and in 1885 the first India National Congress met at Poona.

An Englishman, A. O. Hume, was active in the organization of the first congress, and the viceroy, Lord Dufferin, pronounced something of a benediction upon it. The discussions were moderate in tone and the resolutions adopted asked for legislative councils for the North Western Provinces and the Punjab, that elected members should be added to all the legislative councils, that these should have the power to discuss budget and administrative questions, and that civil service examinations should be held simultaneously in India and in England. Although the tone tended to grow more peremptory, the program of the congress changed little in character between the first meeting and the arrival of Lord Curzon in India. Prominent at the early annual meetings of the India National Congress were Gopal Krishna Gokhale and Surendranath Banerjea — moderate, wise, strong men who had been deeply influenced by Gladstonian liberalism.

Forgetful of the parable of the mustard seed, Lord Dufferin in 1888 sneered at the "microscopic minority" represented in the congress. The movement grew, and various factors helped to strengthen the uncompromisingly nationalistic element within it. Legislative councils were established in the North Western Provinces and the Punjab; but in the nineties Gladstonian liberalism was a vanishing quantity in English politics. The statesmen responsible for the India Councils Act, 1892, lacked the faith of Edmund Burke and the courage of Lord Durham — the representation granted to the Indians by this act was truly microscopic. Men like Gokhale were grievously disappointed. The revived Hinduism represented by leaders of the type of Bal Gangadhar Tilak took offense at an act of 1891 which raised the age of consent to twelve years, and used this act to arouse hostility against British rule. Tilak in south-central India and Lajpat Rai in the Punjab worked hard to turn religious enthusiasm into political channels, showing much of that curious blending of religious mysticism and political shrewdness which have since characterized the Indian nationalist movement. Meanwhile, Indian industrial interest had begun to appreciate the need for some form of political action. Religion, Locke, Machiavelli, and mammon combined to shape the destiny of India.

This strange though historically not uncommon union was furthered by the work of Lord Curzon. During his viceroyalty the British rule in India reached its apogee. The last of the benevolent despots, he shares with Warren Hastings and Dalhousie the first place among Anglo-Indian rulers. For six years he devoted his great gifts as legislator and administrator, his magnificent power of concentration, and his "daemonic energy" to the work of enriching the life, furthering the welfare, and safeguarding the position of India within the British empire; yet he left India in disgrace, dismissed by his friends at home and execrated by leaders among the people for whom he had worked.

Not more than a bare summary of Lord Curzon's achievements can be attempted. No other viceroy had taken such pains to prepare himself by study and travel for the task of governing India; in spite of this, his Indian administration has been adjudged a failure. Curzon's external and frontier policies have already been discussed; though he was interested in imperial issues, the more humdrum ones connected with internal reforms were not less to his liking. Someone said that he "took to government as other men took to pleasure." For twelve or more hours each day he delved into old records, examined current problems, and sketched solutions. When he found that the administrative machinery stood in his way he cut red tape and reduced dispatch-writing; he tried to infuse the whole establishment with his conception of deep responsibility for the peoples of India and his own zeal for efficiency and justice. Even the princes of India were sternly told that their position involved functions and responsibilities which must be faithfully discharged. As he entered upon the duties of his office, a fearful famine was ravaging a great portion of the land. The famine commission of 1902 was appointed by and received encouragement from him; but not content merely with plans for relief, he sought to avoid the need for it by formulating new irrigation schemes involving millions of acres, creating an imperial agricultural department, easing the taxes on land and curbing the money lenders, providing easier agricultural credit, and encouraging village credit associations. "Before Lord Curzon left India he had done more to prevent and combat famine, than any two of his predecessors or successors." The currency was stabilized, taxation reduced, and a department of commerce and industry established. The railroads were extended by about six thousand miles; the police system was overhauled; and the educational system reformed and reinvigorated. With Lord Curzon education was a deep and abiding passion, and he strove to free that of India from the grip of formalism and mere cramming for examinations and to make the Indian universities a vital force in the intellectual life of the empire. No former viceroy of India had taken such a deep interest in the art and civilization of the land and had sought so earnestly to revive and stimulate others to take an interest in these great subjects. He encouraged archeological research and restored ancient monuments, including the famous Taj Mahal at Agra. A lover of pomp and circumstance, he arranged a great durbar for the crowning of Edward VII as emperor of India in 1903; a thoroughgoing believer in efficiency, he sought unsuccessfully to reduce the position of the presidencies to greater dependence upon the central government. He divided the great province of Bengal and encouraged army reform, but resisted the attempt of the commander-in-chief, Lord Kitchener, to make the military independent of the civil power. The division of Bengal and the quarrel with Kitchener contributed much to the alleged failure of Curzon's administration. By adding a portion of eastern Bengal to Assam and Chittagong, he split asunder an old and historic province of India; although the act was defensible from the standpoint of reason and good government it was unwise because it aroused fierce nationalistic agitation against the British in general and Curzon in particular. In his quarrel with Kitchener, Curzon was doubtless in the right. The conflict partook somewhat of the familiar English one between the war office and the commander-in-chief; but here he encountered a will as masterful as his own. Curzon was largely to blame for the prevailing nervousness about the defense of India; Kitchener was what Curzon never became, a popular English hero. The home government failed to support Curzon, and he left India a defeated and disillusioned man.

When Curzon enters, to borrow his own phrase, "the cold dissecting chamber of history," the prober will find and give unstinted praise to his great achievements. He loved righteousness and hated iniquity; justly and even-handedly he dealt with Europeans and with natives; it was no idle boast when he declared that his eyes had been fastened on the people of India as a whole; and none can doubt that his aim had been: "To fight for the right, to abhor the imperfect, the unjust, or the mean, to swerve neither to the right hand nor to the left, to care nothing for flattery or applause, or odium or abuse . . . never to let your enthusiasm be soured or your courage grow dim, but to remember that the Almighty has placed your hand on the greatest of His ploughs, in whose furrow the nations of the future are germinating and taking shape, to drive the blade a little forward in your time, and to feel that somewhere among these millions you have left a little justice or happiness or prosperity, a sense of manliness or moral dignity, a spring of patriotism, a dawn of intellectual enlightenment, or a stirring of duty where it did not before exist." One must agree with him when he said: "That is enough, that is the Englishman's justification in India. It is enough for his watchword while he is there, for his epitaph when he is gone." Proudly Curzon said: "Let India be my judge."

But India has judged Curzon harshly. With all his knowledge of and sympathy for her, he had not plumbed her soul — the soul of an ancient people with an ancient culture and deeply ingrained traditions and beliefs, a proud and sensitive people who had imbibed some of the generous teaching of the English liberals, who felt restless under restraint, their restlessness not so much a measure of England's failure as of England's success.

Into the soil of this land Curzon drove the blade deep and fast; his hand was that of a master; his manner was superior; he conveyed an impression of personal and racial arrogance; he could not delegate authority; in his reverence for facts he forgot the imponderables of human relations; and with the vision of the statesman he failed to combine the art of the politician. "Wrapped in the dignity of self-dependent virtue," Curzon left India, defeated, not by Kitchener or by Tilak, but by time and tide.

PART IV

Storm and Stress, 1901–1939

INTRODUCTION

STORM and stress fell to the lot of the British empire in the twentieth century. It faced dangers from without unparalleled since the days of Queen Elizabeth, and it experienced unusual strains on its social and economic system. In Britain the laboring classes began to exert their political power and became a directing force in the government, and the social services were extended so as to make that government one that really functioned *for* the people. Overseas the dominions of Australasia developed state socialism to such an extent that they were rightfully considered true social democracies.

Shortly after the opening of the century the threatening aspects of the international situation caused Britain to abandon her time-honored policy of diplomatic isolation, to make great efforts at strengthening her naval defense, and to attempt to convert her empire into a great defense league. For more than four years, 1914–1918, the empire was engaged in a world conflict. It stood the test. The dominions and colonies rallied magnificently to the support of the mother country. United in war, the dominions nevertheless insisted upon securing recognition of their status as free nations; and this was accorded them at the negotiations for peace, in the organization of the League of Nations, and by formal declarations and legislation by Britain.

For twenty years the British empire enjoyed external peace.

These years were filled to the brim with internal problems and legislative activity. Depression, unemployment, demands for relief furnished the leaders in all the British countries with tasks often too heavy for their strength and skill. In the early thirties the British empire reintroduced the system of imperial tariff preferences abandoned ninety years before. The British empire had become both a commonwealth of nations and an economic organization based on mercantilistic principles. India received a large measure of self-government and Celtic Ireland became a virtually independent republic.

The dominions were fully occupied with their own affairs and refused to take an active part in shaping the foreign policy of the British Commonwealth of Nations. They hoped and worked for world peace. But this was not to be. Japan, Italy, and Germany proclaimed that they lacked their legitimate share of economic resources and proved their determination to redress the balance by force. Thus the security of the British empire was threatened. When all efforts at satisfying the dictators failed and Britain reluctantly took up the sword, the British nations overseas again rallied to her support. In September, 1939, the British Commonwealth entered a fateful struggle in which its existence was at stake.

CHAPTER 26

BRITAIN IN THE NEW CENTURY

THE age of Queen Victoria enjoyed orderly progress; that of her successors was marked by wars, the preparation for and the liquidation thereof. Political democracy won great victories in Britain in the first four decades of the twentieth century, and social legislation proceeded beyond the limits imagined by reformers of the preceding era; but neither advance so touched the lives of the people of the British Isles as did the great international conflicts, all of which were of fundamental importance for the British empire.

When Queen Victoria died the Anglo-Boer war was half over; before it ended, diplomatic maneuvers heralded the international tension and the race in armaments which culminated in the Four Years' War, 1914–1918, when Britain, heroically aided by the dominions beyond the sea, battled for her existence as a world power. Then followed an effort to build a new world order by means of a league of nations, a grapple with widespread economic depression, a twilight of democracy in leading countries of Europe, and the frustration of hopes for a richer civilization and a better world. Deceit, savagery, slaughter, and destruction were the chosen instruments of national policy as Nazi Germany spread her baleful shadow over Central Europe; her assault on Poland, August 31, 1939, plunged the world into new disasters.

The effect of Britain's foreign relations upon the empire will be traced in later chapters; this one will deal with the domestic affairs of the British Isles and show their relation to empire history. However, the war of 1914–1918 exerted such profound influence upon domestic as well as imperial affairs that it will be necessary to divide our treatment of the epoch 1901–1939 into three parts: the first dealing with the period of transition, 1901–1914; the second treating the war and post-war years, 1914–1924; and the third calling attention to significant developments in the era of hope and frustration, 1924–1939. In each part the discussion will center upon political changes, economic problems, and social legislation, special emphasis being given to the connections between these and imperial policies and relations.

On the political scene the outstanding events of the years 1901–1914 were the retirement of Lord Salisbury from the prime ministership in 1902, the resignation of the succeeding Balfour government in December, 1905, the smashing victory won by the Liberals in the election the following January, the bitter struggle to limit the power of the house of lords during 1909–1911, the growth in the influence of the Parliamentary Labor party, and the resurgence of an old issue, home rule for Ireland, 1911–1914.

When Salisbury retired, his nephew Arthur J. (later Lord) Balfour succeeded to the prime ministership. The younger man was a staunch Conservative, a clever debater, and a successful house of commons man who had won fame as chief secretary for Ireland in the late eighties. A Cecil on his mother's side, Balfour had in the fullest measure the intellectual acumen and proud self-assurance associated with the members of this famous family, and more than his share of their aloofness. The uncle had enjoyed prestige by virtue of being the head of an old house, possessing great intellectual power, and having long been associated with the government. He carried great weight in the country and he exercised a control over the house of lords unequaled since the day of Wellington. The nephew was a commoner whose brilliant intellect and dialectical skill had gained him admirers and enemies but no substantial following in the country. In a democratic age the prime minister of Britain made no efforts to conceal that he was a born aristocrat, one who was proudly conscious of "effortless superiority." Lord Salisbury had in his youth been rated as a colonial reformer and to the end of his life he retained an interest, though a rather languid one, in the overseas empire. Balfour on the other hand was an intellectual somewhat bored by things mundane, a man with wide interests but no real grasp upon the imperial and economic problems which in the early days of the present century clamored for solution.

In 1906 imperial issues played an important role in bringing to an end the ten-year reign of the Unionists. The khaki election of 1900 had given them a substantial majority largely because voters held it both unpatriotic and unwise to change government in the midst of the war. The criticism of the conduct of the war waxed louder as the struggle ran its bloody and wearisome course from October, 1899, to May 31, 1902. Britain won; Boer republics no longer threatened the safety of the communications between the Cape and Rhodesia; the dream of an all-red route for a railroad linking Capetown with Cairo had presumably been brought a stage nearer realization. But the victory was dearly bought in blood, treasure, and self-esteem. Britain had learned with a shock that a large number of her young men were physically unfit for military service, that her generals had blundered, and that although outnumbered ten to one the Boers had kept her forces at bay. Moreover, she did not relish being in the dock before the public opinion of Europe and America for assaulting two tiny states and employing "methods of barbarism" in breaking their resistance. Painfully Britain awakened to the fact that she had no friend among the powers and that she had narrowly missed having to face a hostile European coalition. The government was naturally blamed for all this unpleasantness and humiliation. With the war over, ministers could no longer use the large cloak of patriotism as a protection against criticism.

Indeed they supplied their attackers with a most potent weapon when the colonial office sanctioned Lord Milner's plan for restoring the pre-war output of the Johannesburg gold mines by importing coolies from China. "Chinese slavery" to enrich South African magnates proved a potent slogan for the enemies of the Balfour government; it united middle-class humanitarians and the masses of British laborers and contributed mightily to the discomfiture of the Unionists in the election of January, 1906.

Another imperial issue helped to make this defeat almost a rout — imperial preference. Joseph Chamberlain brought to the colonial office the instinct, habits, and training of a business man. He found that foreign rivals were making inroads on the colonial markets and that the colonies were willing to grant tariff preference to British goods. Canada had led the way, thereby arousing Germany who, declaring the preference unfair to her, retaliated by imposing discriminatory duties on Canadian produce. An awkward situation arose; Chamberlain wished to aid Canada and tell Germany "hands off," but since Britain had free trade this could hardly be done without creating a diplomatic incident. However, Joseph Chamberlain was an imperialist and a fighter. A tariff could be used as a weapon to teach unmannerly Germans not to touch the cubs of the British lion. Moreover, he was genuinely disturbed by Germany's industrial progress, which might be attributed to her protective tariff. Returning early in 1903 from a brief visit to South Africa, Chamberlain decided that Britain must revamp her tariff system. Free trade was outmoded; by granting preference to goods of empire origin a ring fence might be built that would keep foreigners from trespassing on a British preserve. Thus he believed that home industries would prosper, the colonies would be protected against tariff wars with foreign countries, and the empire consolidated in a customs union. Chamberlain's preferential tariff program caused an explosion in British politics; the Unionist party split wide open. Balfour sought to save the situation by vague statements, metaphysical subtleties; but plain-speaking Englishmen would have none of this tomfoolery. The country had prospered under free trade; it was of English origin and therefore hallowed. Embarrassing to the Unionists, the tariff issue was a godsend to the Liberals; gone were their war-time dissensions, they could all unite under the old banner of Richard Cobden. By resigning before the election Balfour gambled on the possibility that Liberals might again fall out among themselves, but he lost. In January, 1906, when the votes were counted the Liberals under Sir Henry Campbell-Bannerman numbered nearly 400 in the house of commons. Undaunted by the defeat and a paralytic stroke Chamberlain continued the fight until his death in 1914. By then the Conservatives had accepted his views on the tariff.

Campbell-Bannerman was a Gladstonian — a believer in freedom for the colonies. But this faith was not popular; some of the strongest among his colleagues — Asquith, Grey, and Haldane — had been Liberal imperialists during the Boer War. A test came in 1906 when the new South African possessions, the Transvaal and the Orange River Colony, were to be given new constitutions. For a while Campbell-Bannerman apparently wavered between the Conservatives' proposal of giving them representative government and the demand for responsible government voiced by the Boer leaders Generals Botha and Smuts. Deciding in favor of the latter, he won his colleagues over to this plan; from then on the two great Boer generals were staunch supporters of the British empire. By his generosity to the Boers Campbell-Bannerman earned distinction as a great imperial statesman.

Neither the grant of self-government to the Boers nor the changes in the government of India in 1909, which extended the principle of representative government, caused serious political controversy in Britain. It was otherwise when the Irish Nationalists compelled the Liberals under Asquith to take up the cause of home rule for Ireland. The fight over the budget of 1909, thrown out by the house of lords, led to an election in January, 1910, which had the disappointing result of giving the Irish the balance of power in the lower house. Their price for supporting the government was the Parliament Act of 1911 curbing the power of the lords, and a new home rule bill. The former was forced through the upper house by the threat of creating enough peers to swamp the opposition; the latter went on the statute book in 1914 under the provision of the new Parliament Act that a bill passed unaltered by the house of commons in three separate sessions covering a period of not less than two years shall receive royal assent even though rejected by the lords.

The years 1906–1911 were remarkably fruitful in social legislation. The Liberals abandoned *laissez faire* and proceeded to enact laws safeguarding the health of the nation, improving the condition of the laboring classes, devising machinery to combat unemployment, and establishing pensions for the aged. In particular, the great National Insurance Act of 1911, providing for sickness, disability, and to a more limited extent unemployment benefits, was a landmark in British social legislation. Thus the lower classes were made conscious of a stake in the country and its prosperity, which in turn depended in no small measure upon its imperial position.

The social legislation failed, however, to bring contentment. Wages barely kept pace with the rise in prices, and the demands for the good things in life mounted faster than the earnings of the laboring classes. Luxuries of earlier times became necessities; the motor cars and display of wealth by the "haves" stimulated the discontent of the "have nots." Strikes grew more frequent, and in the years 1911–1913 emigration reached record figures. It was a boom period overseas, especially in Canada, and Chamberlain's arrangements for keeping British emigrants within the empire now brought results. In the decennium 1891–1900, only 26 per cent of the emigrants from the British Isles went to empire countries; this percentage rose to 56 in the years 1901–1910, reaching a high of 80 in 1911. British immigrants swelled the population of Australia, Canada, and New Zealand; and when war brought calls for volunteers they set a good example to their fellow citizens by flocking to recruiting stations. More than 60 per cent of the first expeditionary force to leave Canada in 1914 was born in the British Isles.

In Scotland politics and economic and social developments followed the same lines as those in England with the exception that the northern kingdom was more radical in politics. The industrialization of southern Scotland proceeded rapidly. Glasgow, second among the cities of the United Kingdom, had the largest shipyards in the world, but it also enjoyed an unenviable reputation as a slum center. Here agitators found ready listeners; "the wild men of the Clyde" were in the van of the British labor movement.

Ireland seemed strangely quiet at the opening of the present century. Agrarian outrages were less frequent than formerly, and British Conservatives entertained the delusion that home rule was dead. The peace in the rural areas was due largely to the increased prosperity resulting from progress in agriculture and the spread of peasant proprietorship. Sir Horace Plunkett and his associates promoted agricultural cooperation and made strenuous efforts to familiarize the Irish peasants with scientific farming. Dairying assumed greater importance in Irish rural economy; it was hoped that Ireland might rival Denmark as a producer of bacon, eggs, and butter for the English market. The Unionist government was suspected of plans to kill home rule with kindness, as more money was made available for land purchase. The Liberals continued this policy so that by 1910 about £100,000,000 had been used for land purchase; by then approximately one-half of the land of Ireland had passed into the hands of peasant proprietors. Economic conditions improved, but the outflow of young men and women continued. In Australia especially, the Irish element became an important factor in politics.

As the nineteenth century closed, the conflict between Parnellites and anti-Parnellites subsided, and the Irish Nationalists united under the leadership of John Redmond. In 1904 George Wyndham, chief secretary for Ireland in the Balfour government, explored the possibility of solving the island's political problem by a system of local government which did not impair the Act of Union. But the government's supporters would have none of such a plan. The Ulsterites, who were especially bitter in their opposition to home rule in any form, found a skillful though unscrupulous leader in the eminent barrister Sir Edward (later Lord) Carson. Balfour refused to stand by Wyndham, who was forced to resign.

After the death of Gladstone the Liberals were lukewarm toward Irish home rule. Although Sir Henry Campbell-Bannerman rated as a Gladstonian Liberal, nothing was done for Ireland during his premiership, 1905–1908. With an independent majority in the house of commons the government ignored Ireland's supplications while granting self-government to distant Transvaal and the Orange River Colony. However, the elections of 1910 altered the political map. Now the Irish Nationalists held the balance of power in the house of commons. They demanded curtailment of the veto power of the house of lords and home rule for Ireland. Experience had shown that the latter could not be won without the former. By the Parliament Act of 1911 the house of lords could defer the passage of a non-financial measure two years; under this provision the Government of Ireland Act, 1912, was put upon the statute book in 1914. Stormy scenes marked its passage through the house of commons the three separate times required under the new Parliament Act. Moreover, guided by Carson the Ulsterites organized and drilled for armed resistance to home rule. Somewhat later Celtic Ireland took similar action, and early in 1914 conflicts between the Ulster and the National volunteers seemed inevitable. A ban upon importation of arms into Ireland enraged the Nationalists; the situation became ominous in March, 1914, when officers of British troops stationed at Curragh, Ireland, let it be known that they would resign if ordered to coerce Ulster, an action in which they had been encouraged by leading members of the Unionist party. Although the Curragh incident led to no outbreak of disorders, the Conservatives had set a dangerous precedent and Ireland seemed on the brink of civil war until August 4, 1914, when Britain's entrance into the Four Years' War caused the Irish factions to bury their hatchets for the time being. Subsequent events showed that the burial places had been carefully marked.

Meanwhile, unnoticed by the political leaders of England as well as those of Ireland, a new Irish movement had been launched, one with a broader basis and more truly national than the party led by John Redmond — Sinn Fein, "We ourselves." The Irish leaders of the nineteenth century had concentrated on political and, to a more limited extent, on economic objectives; at first Sinn Fein aimed simply at arousing pride in and love for the old Irish culture, literature, language, and at fostering an intellectual renaissance akin to the many similar ones then stirring suppressed peoples from the Baltic to the Aegean. Sinn Fein started in the nineties when Irish politicians were furiously engaged in internecine strife. The Gaelic League, dating from 1895, was non-political; from it sprang the Irish Literary Theater. Arthur Griffith's *United Irishman,* launched in 1899, differed from the earlier publication bearing this name by being devoted to cultural instead of political topics. Men of genius in fields of literature and scholarship — J. M. Synge, W. B. Yeats, Douglas Hyde, John MacNeill, and others — devoted their talents to an Irish cultural revival. But here, as in the spheres of politics and economics, Irishmen encountered what seemed to them the dead hand of English influence. The ruling race claimed superiority all around; the Irish language had ceased to produce literature; its ancient monuments were half-forgotten or despised; and as a spoken tongue it lingered mainly on the lips of peasants in out-of-the-way places. The cultural renaissance therefore brought new attacks upon the English. In 1905 Sinn Fein held its first national convention; the movement spread, gained momentum, and became ruthlessly hostile to England and the English. One of the leaders, Constance Gore Booth, imitated Baden-Powell's Boy Scout movement by organizing bands of Fianna boys and instilling in them deep hatred of the dominant partner in the Anglo-Irish union. Ireland must rise and be free culturally, economically, politically – such by 1914 was the belief and the program of Sinn Fein. But as yet neither Dublin Castle, seat of the administration of Ireland, nor John Redmond, the leader of the Irish Nationalists, deigned to take notice of the new movement; its sponsors were regarded as cranks and visionaries – the old story of the cloud not larger than a man's hand destined to fill the sky. The war supplied opportunities fully utilized by Sinn Fein.

It is not the purpose of this book to present a complete history of Britain at war and of the post-war era until the French evacuation of the Ruhr in August, 1924. But this conflict and its aftermath affected Britain and her empire so profoundly that some of the more salient features must be noted. Hopes for a speedy victory were soon dispelled; the war which began as a struggle between Germany and Austria-Hungary on the one side with Britain, France, Russia, Belgium, and Servia on the other reached world-wide dimensions, engulfing most of the countries of Europe, Africa, America, and Asia. Britain's task was threefold – to maintain control of the sea, supply her allies with money and credit, and provide expeditionary forces for the main battlefront in France as well as for the numerous "side shows" of a world war. The first part involved driving the enemy's warships and raiders off the high seas, safeguarding the transport of huge quantities of supplies and large armed forces to and from distant regions; the second necessitated heavy taxation and large-scale borrowing at home and in the United States; and the third caused the combined armies of the British empire to swell from a modest beginning of perhaps half a million to a grand total of more than seven and a half million men, of whom Great Britain contributed about four million.

The gigantic efforts of the Four Years' War had momentous repercussions at home. In 1915 the Liberal government under Asquith became a coalition government; in December, 1916,

Asquith was supplanted by David Lloyd George, who concentrated all the power in a small war cabinet of five, representing the Conservative, Liberal, and Labor parties. Lloyd George, once the bogeyman, now became the darling of ultra-patriotic Englishmen. His unflagging energy and courage bolstered the drooping spirit of the Allies and contributed mightily to the final success. The ink was still fresh on the agreements that stilled the guns on the front in France on November 11, 1918, when David Lloyd George, aided and abetted by the leader of the Conservative party, Andrew Bonar Law, dissolved parliament and issued writs for an election held early in December. The two leaders asked for a vote of confidence and a mandate for concluding peace abroad and effecting reconstruction at home. A nation with nerves on edge after more than four years of war, who had suffered more than two million casualties, who had lived in terror of sea and aerial bombardments, and whose normal life had been interrupted more completely than at any other time since the civil war of the seventeenth century, listened with delight to campaign slogans like "Hang the Kaiser," "Make Germany pay," "Squeeze them till the pips squeak." The government prepared lists of candidates who could be trusted to be safe and patriotic. Dissentients such as the followers of the former premier, H. H. Asquith, who had ventured to examine critically some of the acts of the government, and those arrayed under the banner of the Labor leader J. Ramsay Macdonald were accused openly or by implication of being "softies" unmindful of the real interests of the British people and empire. As a further inducement to support his government, David Lloyd George promised relentless war upon poverty and other social ills — Britain should be made "fit for heroes to live in." Such promises at such a time could not fail to bring the desired result. Critics and opponents were snowed under. In the new house of commons the coalition government had 526 supporters against 63 Laborites and 33 Independent Liberals, Asquith being rejected by even his old constituents. Labor now became His Majesty's loyal opposition; the Liberal party, the historic party of Gladstone, was shattered beyond repair. There was, however, one fly in the ointment for the government, for the Irish Nationalist party also vanished. Sinn Fein captured the majority of the Irish seats and these M.P.'s, 74 in all, refused to go to Westminster; instead, they formed a republican convention in Dublin.

Controlling and controlled by this huge majority, Lloyd George went to Paris as head of the British delegation at the peace conference. Successful party leaders seldom take preelection pledges too seriously, acting on the principle that "none can keep all that he promises"; to this Lloyd George was no exception. Little attempt was made fully to honor what electors had taken to be the government's promises concerning the punishment of Germany. Still it was unreasonable to expect that representatives of democracies stirred to frenzied hatred by the war, meeting at Paris, the capital of the only one of the great powers that had suffered enormous damages in the war, and led by the "tiger of France," M. Clemenceau, would make a peace based on the precept "Forget and forgive." The terms inflicted upon Germany by the Treaty of Versailles, 1919, were more severe than those dictated to France in 1814 and 1815; Castlereagh's principle of leaving the former enemy with a "balanced empire" was lacking in the peace which ostensibly was to end war and safeguard democracy. However, even the most captious critic must admit that the terms imposed upon defeated Germany were of the milk and water variety compared with those that would have been dictated had the roles been reversed. But this faint praise does not conceal the fact that the treaty of 1919 failed to bring peace.

For three years David Lloyd George strove manfully to appease the French, to wrest reparation from Germany, and to make Britain fit for heroes to live in. Nothing worked. New conferences, fresh formulas, and ingenious wheedling failed to allay French fear and suspicion of Germany. A tripartite treaty by which the United States and Britain guaranteed France against

Germany collapsed because the American senate refused to endorse it. Similarly the League of Nations, launched so confidently by President Wilson at Paris, lost in seaworthiness when his country disowned him. Nor did Lloyd George fare better on the domestic front. The plans for a gradual demobilization of the armed forces and their absorption in the country's industries went awry. Soldiers and sailors insisted upon being released soon after the armistice; the labor market was glutted; and a serious economic collapse followed a short-lived post-war boom. In 1922 ex-soldiers went begging in the streets of London; and when Britain in September of that year faced the possibility of a war in Asia Minor after a resurrected Turkey had driven the Greeks, Britain's allies and friends, into the sea at Smyrna, Conservative supporters of Lloyd George deserted him, demanding his resignation. He complied; and the reins of government fell into the somewhat palsied grip of Andrew Bonar Law.

The ensuing election in October, 1922, gave Bonar Law a strong majority. However, he had promised peace when there was no peace; his watchword, "tranquillity," described spitefully but not inaptly as "a yawn," failed to bring results. France grew more truculent; in January, 1923, accusing the Germans of default and bad faith, she occupied the Ruhr, richest of Germany's industrial areas. This stopped all payments of reparations, hastened the collapse of the German monetary system, and checked the industrial revival of Britain. Harsh words were exchanged by Britain and France; in the house of commons Bonar Law's foreign policy was labeled one of "benevolent impotence." A debt agreement with the United States negotiated by the then chancellor of the exchequer, Stanley Baldwin, was accepted with misgiving for the terms seemed harsh. A majority of Englishmen favored cancellation all around, including some of the German reparations. On paper Britain and the United States would have lost much by this; and since the latter refused to listen to such a proposal, all discussions of it were purely academic. By spring, 1923, the prime minister resigned on account of ill health, and the position of the government was rather unhappy. Baldwin, who succeeded Bonar Law, struggled through the summer; in the autumn he decided that the country ought to adopt Joseph Chamberlain's preferential tariff program but declined to put it into effect without a mandate from the people. This was refused. The Conservatives retained their position as the largest party, but the Labor-Liberal supporters of free trade had a majority. Defeated on a motion of no confidence, Baldwin resigned and the king sent for the Labor leader, J. Ramsay Macdonald. Early in 1924 he formed Britain's first Labor government, which with the support of the Liberals held office until the autumn when a new election, the third in two years, gave the Conservatives a majority of 211 in the house of commons. Shortly afterward the second Baldwin government replaced that of Macdonald.

In foreign affairs the Labor government of 1924 scored notable triumphs. Investigations by an American, General Charles G. Dawes, resulted in a scaling down of German reparations, and the new agreement enabled the French to withdraw from the Ruhr without an official admission that this venture had been a tragic blunder. With Macdonald's approval the British representative at Geneva, Arthur Henderson, agreed to a proposal which provided a perfect paper scheme for collective security. Although the Geneva protocol was disavowed by the Conservatives as imposing too heavy obligations on Britain, Baldwin's foreign secretary, Austen (later Sir Austen) Chamberlain, was nevertheless willing to sponsor Germany's admission to the League of Nations and to join in the treaties for mutual security known as the Locarno pact. At the end of 1924 it looked as if the Four Years' War was nearly liquidated.

In the troubled war and post-war years the British government assumed more complete control over the nation's economic and social life and became inclined toward imperial preferences. War needs made necessary elaborate and detailed regulation of trade, shipping, industry, labor, railroads, and consumption of necessary supplies. After much hesitation and prolonged debates Britain adopted conscription for the army and established a national service registry for all males between 16 and 65. Women entered industry and other occupations in large numbers, and trade unions suspended important rules and abrogated hard-won rights. With few exceptions, the people of England, Scotland, and Wales united in heroic efforts to make Britain win the war. High taxes and heavy borrowing had as corollaries free spending and a laxity in financial administration shocking to older statesmen.

As a war measure Britain in 1915 abandoned free trade. The then chancellor of the exchequer, Reginald McKenna, secured the adoption of ad valorem duties of 33 1/3 per cent on automobiles, motor cycles, moving picture films, musical instruments, and a few other articles on the ground that they were luxuries and that curtailing their import saved money and cargo space for necessities. Incidentally, the new tariff protected certain home industries and the McKenna duties became the opening wedge for a new tariff policy. Events favored its advocates. In preparing the budget of 1919, Austen Chamberlain retained the war duties and provided tariff reductions on certain goods of empire origin. Thus he brought a step nearer realization the preferential tariff program dear to his father as well as himself. A post-war boom in industry and trade ended in 1920. Then came severe depression, unemployment, and inflation of foreign currencies. The last provided excuses for protection in the guise of safeguarding home industries against those of countries with cheap money and offered opportunities for an extension of imperial preferences. Furthermore, overseas markets lost during the war proved difficult to recover; and the dominions who had rendered valuable services in the war and had granted preferences to British goods demanded reciprocal favors from the mother country. Tariff reformers lost the election of 1923 but returned to power in 1924. From then on, the free traders fought a losing battle.

Emigration was another important issue in intra-imperial relations. In 1913 British emigration exceeded immigration by a quarter of a million. When the war broke out the tide turned; first came refugees from Belgium, then loyal Britishers returned to the homeland. The call "Your king and country need you" helped to bring them home; moreover, the mother country needed men not only for the armed forces but for shops, factories, and shipyards. Peace came, refugees left, and in 1920 the balance favored emigration by 166,688; then the outward flow slowed down. It took much encouragement to get Britons to leave home. In the war period, although they suffered privations along some lines, laborers became accustomed to new comforts, entertainments, and conveniences. The majority of Britain's unemployed were industrial workers unused to the toil and hardships of frontier communities; furthermore, at home they were taken care of. In 1918 Lloyd George promised to better living conditions for the people of Britain; though reality fell short of anticipation, the jobless were kept from starving. A life of ease without plenty, with cheap entertainment and social services, seemed more attractive to the unemployed than did the prospects of long hours of unaccustomed work in the colonies or dominions. The period of large-scale emigration was over.

In Ireland the years 1914–1924 provided a series of exciting episodes. On the eve of the outbreak of the war Redmond and Carson proclaimed a political truce — Ireland seemed then the bright spot in a dark sky. Redmond encouraged enlistments in the British army, his son and his brother leading the way. But the war office suspected the Nationalist Irish and this hostile attitude cooled Ireland's enthusiasm for the war. Sinn Feiners seized the opportunities supplied by the war; they welcomed a German victory. At first little heed was paid to their propaganda. Redmond felt uneasy, however, and urged the government to put Irish home rule into operation. This stranded on the opposition of Ulster. Its champion, Sir Edward Carson, became attorney general in the coalition government of 1915, an appointment not calculated to allay Irish distrust. In April of the following year matters came to a head, when a fanatical Sinn

Feiner, Sir Roger Casement, landed from a German submarine for the purpose of starting a rebellion. Although both he and a cargo of arms destined for the rebels were seized, this did not prevent an uprising. Easter week saw bitter fighting in the streets of Dublin, but regular troops suppressed the rebellion without much difficulty. The government then faced a perplexing situation. Since the rebellion had occurred while the Allies were striving desperately to halt German assaults at Verdun, it was felt that Britain had been stabbed in the back, that Ireland was a traitor. In vain the prime minister, H. H. Asquith, urged leniency; Casement was hanged and leaders of the rebellion were shot. Thus Sinn Fein was provided with martyrs; the movement spread like wildfire. Despairing of securing home rule for Ireland, Redmond withdrew from the house of commons. He died in March, 1917, a leader deserted by his people.

Buoyant as ever, Lloyd George believed that he could solve the Irish question. In 1917 he summoned a convention of leaders of the various shades of Irish public opinion except Sinn Fein; it failed to find a solution. Early the following year he coupled an announcement that military conscription would be introduced in Ireland with a promise that home rule would be put into operation. Neither pleased the Irish, and both were given up. In the election of 1918 Sinn Fein replaced the Nationalists but their members refused to go to Westminster; instead they constituted themselves a parliament for Ireland at Dublin. A fourth home rule bill in 1920 provided for the separation of Ulster with a joint council for the whole island. The north accepted this and six counties organized as Northern Ireland with fifteen members in the British house of commons; the rest set up a republican government independent of Britain. By then civil war was raging over large areas in southern Ireland. The murder of policemen and individuals suspected of English sympathies became everyday occurrences. The Royal Irish Constabulary could not cope with the situation and the government hesitated to employ the regular army. For the purpose of restoring order a semi-military force was created, known from their uniform as the black-and-tans. In ferocity they were a match for the secret Irish republican army whose hideouts could not be found. The war was carried on as a series of ambushes with retaliations and counter retaliations. Creameries were destroyed; homes, banks, and stores looted. The island relapsed into primitive savagery. A large body of British public opinion objected to and felt humiliated by the government's Irish policy; protests came from the dominions as well as from the United States.

On June 22, 1921, George V in person opened the new parliament of Northern Ireland and presented an earnest "appeal to all Irishmen to pause, to stretch out the hand of forbearance and conciliation, to forgive and forget, and to join in making for the land they love a new era of peace, contentment and goodwill." General Jan Smuts, the prime minister of South Africa and an erstwhile enemy of Britain, lent a helping hand in the work for conciliation. The result was a conference in London between Irish republican leaders and members of the British cabinet. Active on the government's side were the old die-hard opponents of home rule for Ireland, Lord Birkenhead and Austen Chamberlain. After prolonged negotiations a treaty was signed on December 6, 1921, conceding dominion status to southern Ireland, which was to be known as the Irish Free State. The size of her army was restricted; certain ports were set aside for the use of the royal navy; and the new dominion was to enjoy all the rights and privileges accorded to Canada. The treaty was approved by a majority in the Sinn Fein parliament; but Eamond de Valera, who had participated in the negotiations, refused to accept it. Styling himself president of the Irish republic, he led a revolt of the irreconcilable Sinn Feiners against the new government. Irish fought Irish; murders, shooting from ambush, reprisals made their bloody rounds. The fight was as bitter as the old one with the British armed forces now watching on the side lines. Among the victims of the second civil war were Michael Collins, former commander of "the Irish republican

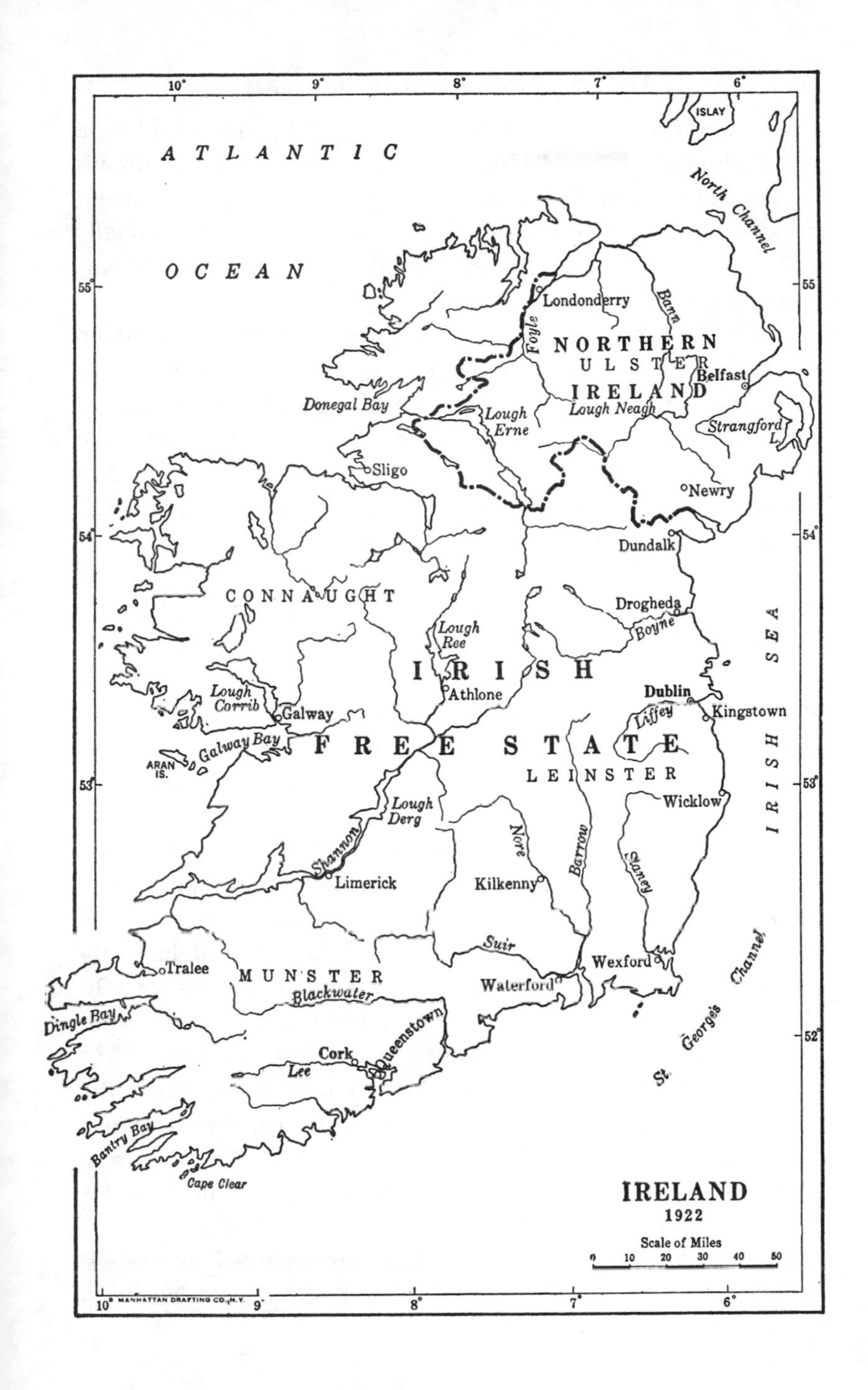

ATLANTIC
OCEAN
ISLAY
North Channel
Londonderry
Bann
Foyle
NORTHERN
ULSTER
IRELAND
Belfast
Donegal Bay
Lough Erne
Lough Neagh
Strangford L.
Sligo
Newry
Dundalk
CONNAUGHT
Drogheda
Boyne
Lough Ree
IRISH
IRISH SEA
Athlone
Dublin
Lough Corrib
Galway
Liffey
Kingstown
Galway Bay
FREE STATE
ARAN IS.
LEINSTER
Wicklow
Lough Derg
Nore
Barrow
Shannon
Slaney
Limerick
Kilkenny
Suir
Wexford
Tralee
MUNSTER
Waterford
St. George's Channel
Blackwater
Dingle Bay
Queenstown
Cork
Lee
Bantry Bay
Cape Clear
IRELAND
1922
Scale of Miles
0 10 20 30 40 50
MANHATTAN DRAFTING CO., N.Y.

army," shot from ambush by the rebels; and Erskine Childers, a singularly gifted and attractive Englishman who threw in his lot with the irreconcilables and was executed by a government firing squad. However, the Free State government gradually gained the upper hand and in 1924 the Anglo-Irish treaty was formally ratified by its parliament.

In 1924 Europe seemed to be on the road to recovery; fifteen years later the war drums were beating. In the interval, except for a two-year period from 1929–1931, the government of Britain was in the hands of the Conservatives. On three occasions — the general strike, 1926; the change from a Labor to a National government, 1931; and the abdication of King Edward VIII, December, 1936 — the country passed through crises of the first magnitude; and the economic situation underwent rapid and startling changes, though these were less catastrophic than the changes on the international stage. An era of peace seemed assured with the conclusion of the Locarno treaties and the admission of Germany to the League of Nations, 1925–1926. Hopes were dashed early in the thirties with Japan's adoption of an aggressive policy in the Far East, Hitler's advent to power in Germany, and the launching of large-scale imperialistic ventures by both Italy and Germany. Britain had a strong desire to satisfy Germany's legitimate demands, but this appeasement policy failed. The masters of the Third Reich sought world dominion; talking peace, they prepared for war. Reluctantly the British government entered the race in armaments. In March, 1939, Germany broke solemn pledges and seized Czechoslovakia, an act of perfidy that aroused the British empire. War became inevitable. Five months later Hitler threw down the gauntlet by attacking Poland, and for the second time within a quarter century Britain and Germany were at war. These shifting scenes will be sketched, with emphasis on their significance for the British overseas empire.

The Macdonald government of 1924 disappointed its friends. Radical demands for the nationalization of industry were ignored; the unemployed found less sympathy than they had expected; and the economic policy of the Labor government was orthodox. Macdonald, who had traveled more extensively within the British empire than any other prime minister, showed no inclination to reverse policies his predecessors had pursued in Egypt and India. On the tariff issue Laborites and Liberals agreed — they refused to adopt imperial preferences. Macdonald's coldness toward demands presented by the dominions was contrasted with his readiness to grant favors to Russia. A Russian trade treaty and a proposal for Russian credit aroused bitter comment and contributed largely to the defeat of Labor in the election of 1924.

In foreign relations the period of the second Baldwin administration, 1924–1929, was one of hope. Germany was admitted to the League of Nations; treaties of mutual guarantee boded well for the future; agreements for judicial arbitrament of differences among the powers were designed to outlaw war; and the League of Nations promised to become an effective instrument in furthering human progress. The Italian dictator cooperated with the western powers, but Russia remained an outlaw. The Soviet government was suspected of conducting subversive propaganda in Egypt and India; and on May 12, 1927, fear of Communist intrigues caused London police to raid the offices of the Russian Trade Agency ("Arcos"). Although nothing of importance was found, this exploit, carried out on the authority of the ultra-Conservative home secretary, Sir William Joynson-Hicks, led to the severance of both trade and diplomatic relations with the Soviet Union. In harmony with Conservative traditions, the second Baldwin government opposed demands of Egyptian and Indian nationalists but followed Liberal traditions when it acceded without demur to dominion requests for equal status with the mother country. Old dreams of an imperial federation were labeled visionary and imperial preference made little progress during these years when dominion trade flourished. However, mindful of possible dangers to British possessions and interests in the Far East, the Conservatives resumed the work, suspended by the Laborites, of making Singapore *the* great imperial stronghold in that region.

The second Baldwin government was less successful at home. Aided emigration failed to relieve unemployment and some of the British key industries, especially coal and textiles, remained in a state of chronic depression. The militant element of British labor suffered defeat in the general strike of May, 1926, as well as in the long-drawn-out coal strike of that year; but dissatisfaction with the economic state of the nation continued, and the Conservatives lost the election of 1929.

With 290 followers in the house of commons Mr. Macdonald for the second time headed a Labor government. Although he lacked a clear majority his party was now the strongest in the lower house and he could count upon aid from the Liberals, numbering nearly 60, in his efforts to produce happier conditions for the people of Britain. But fate was unkind. Shortly after Macdonald took office a crash on the New York stock exchange ended a hectic period of American prosperity. During the Four Years' War New York supplanted London as financial center of the world, and the prosperity of the twenties was in no small measure founded upon easy American credit. This stopped abruptly. In 1928 alone more than one billion United States dollars had been invested abroad; after October, 1929, this outward flow of money ceased. Debtors were now asked to pay up; prices fell; accounts had to be met with dear money; the world's economic life was upset.

To Britain, suffering with the rest of the world, came colonies and dominions in distress. Demands arose for cancellation of debts owed the mother country and for tariff preferences. Neither could be granted in the face of mounting deficits and declining trade. Dissatisfaction overseas matched that at home. In 1931 heavy withdrawals of foreign deposits caused a near panic in Britain. The Bank of England, long considered the rock of solidity among financial institutions, went begging for credit.

Paris and New York told Britain to reduce expenditures and balance her budget. Worried and humiliated, she exchanged her Labor government for a coalition government labeled National. It was supposed to save the pound which Winston Churchill in 1925 had put back on a gold basis. This proved impossible, and on September 21, 1931, the Bank of England suspended gold payment, an act sanctioned by parliament. Macdonald led the new National government, but the majority of his supporters were conservative and believed in tariff reform; they pressed for dissolution. The result of the elections, giving a majority of 502 to the government, was interpreted as a verdict against free trade. In November, 1931, began a series of sweeping tariff changes which within a year left Britain with a fiscal policy related to mercantilism. Preferential duties at home and in the dependencies, reinforced by a system of import quotas, marked a radical departure from Cobden's principles. Pressure from overseas played a role in this change, and old-style Liberals grumbled because the United Kingdom sacrificed foreign markets which took nearly three-fourths of British exports in the interest of the imperial markets. It was evident that the daughter nations now told the mother country what to do. In financial matters, however, the reins were tightened, imperial authorization being required for dominion and colonial loans floated in London.

At the time the British Commonwealth of Nations seemingly drew together in a customs union, the constitutional bonds were loosened. In 1926 Balfour, the Conservative ex-prime minister, drafted a resolution affirming the equality of status as between the dominions and Britain; four years later an imperial conference presided over by a Laborite endorsed this principle; and it was implemented in December, 1931, by a parliament containing a huge Conservative imperialistic majority. The constitutional change enhanced the position of the crown — placed heavier demands upon the wearer of it, made him more of an institution. For King-Emperor George V the new situation created no embarrassment. In him British subjects everywhere could see the man in the king and the king in the man. But when his son Edward VIII demanded freedom to marry the woman he loved, the fact that this woman must divorce a subject to marry him and that she had still another ex-husband living blocked the royal will. He found his desires as a man in conflict with his duties as a king. Public opinion at home and overseas deemed it unseemly that Mrs. Simpson should become the royal consort. In December, 1936, Edward VIII sacrificed the crown for love; sadly the British people took leave of their king whose human qualities had endeared him to his people. Henceforth he was known as the Duke of Windsor. The second son of George V succeeded to the throne as George VI. The change was effected without straining intra-imperial relations, and the new sovereign fitted naturally into the position created by the constitutional evolution within the empire.

Since 1931 the Conservatives have controlled the British government. The sudden shift to the right was caused by fear that national institutions were threatened by Communists and Fascists. Old-style liberalism ceased to be a separate political force in British politics; and the Labor party could not recover from the loss suffered in 1931, when their trusted leaders, J. Ramsay Macdonald, Philip Snowden, and J. H. Thomas, allied themselves with the Conservatives in the National government. Because of the prevailing confusion in socialist ideology and the lack of leaders who combine constructive thinking with an ability to make emotional appeals to the masses, labor remained in the wilderness. The cleavage of the Russian Communists into Trotskyites and Stalinists, the ruthlessness with which the latter crushed opponents, transferred the state into one huge capitalistic organization, and adopted imperialistic policies reminiscent of the tsarist regime were as bewildering to British left-wingers as was the collapse of the German socialist republic and German trade unionism under the impact of Hitler's National Socialism. Dissensions between intellectuals and trade unionists added to the discomfiture of the British Labor party. Its endeavors to attract support under the banner of disarmament and pacifism proved singularly ill-timed in the thirties when forces from within and without threatened the British empire with destruction. Macdonald continued as the nominal head of the National government until June, 1935, when he was replaced by Stanley Baldwin. Although a general election later in the year increased to 154 the Labor representation in the house of commons, the Conservatives were seated firmly in the saddle. In the summer of 1937 Baldwin quietly handed the reins of government over to Neville Chamberlain, second son of the famous Joseph Chamberlain.

In the thirties economic conditions at home and abroad favored the growth of imperial policies based on the principles of the elder Chamberlain. Attention has been called to the change from free trade to protection and imperial preferences. Faced with loss of markets as results of the industrialization of India, China, and Japan and the economic policies of Nazi Germany, British traders, investors, and industrialists tried to save themselves by expanding home and overseas markets. Great slum clearance projects benefited both capital and labor; aid to agriculture had the dual aim of strengthening a basic industry and expanding the purchasing power of those engaged in it. Recovering from the shock of the 1931 crisis, British investors resumed the old practice of exporting capital. The managed currency which replaced the pound based on gold proved a help rather than a hindrance to economic expansion. A great sterling block, embracing besides the British empire countries in Europe and South America, had London as its financial center. While pegging its pound to the sterling, Australasia kept its money somewhat lower, thus favoring exports and helping to attract British capital. In 1937 the new British rearmament program checked the outward flow of capital; and as this race grew keener the dominions were encouraged and aided in their efforts to strengthen their defenses, Britain supplying by loans or direct grants a considerable part of the necessary funds. Thus the empire became not only a customs union but also a union for mutual protection.

The hopes of the twenties that law, justice, and order would replace force, banditry, and anarchy in international relations were dashed shortly after the opening of the thirties. Japanese aggression in Manchuria in 1931 was followed six years later by attacks on China proper. In 1935–1936 Italy seized Ethiopia; and in March of the latter year Germany scrapped the Locarno treaties by remilitarizing the Rhineland, offering as substitutes non-aggression pacts that later proved worthless. Civil war in Spain, 1936–1939, furnished opportunities for intervention by Germany, Italy, and Russia, Britain rather pathetically sponsoring a program of non-intervention. Meanwhile, Hitler and Mussolini had forged the famous Berlin-Rome axis; Italy seized Albania and Germany occupied Austria and Czechoslovakia. The last outrage led Britain to guarantee Poland, suspected of being the next victim of aggression, and to open negotiations for a military pact with Russia. In the midst of these negotiations, the announcement, on August 23, 1939, of a Hitler-Stalin pact startled the world. The two dictators agreed upon a division of Poland. Hitler found a pretext for an attack upon Poland, and Britain and France honored their treaty obligations by declaring war on Germany.

Slowly, too slowly, Britain had awakened to a realization of the fact that Hitler's Germany constituted a greater menace to the safety of herself and her empire than had the Germany of William II or Napoleonic France. In its early stages Hitlerism found defenders in England. True, the persecution of the Jews and the Nazi purge of 1934 aroused revulsion and disgust; on the other hand some Englishmen had lost faith in republican Germany and many more felt that, in view of the fact that France had failed to disarm, Germany was entitled to have a war machine. In the early thirties pacifism was fashionable in England. As late as 1935 the League of Nations Union conducted a "Peace Ballot" in which ten and a half of the eleven and a half million

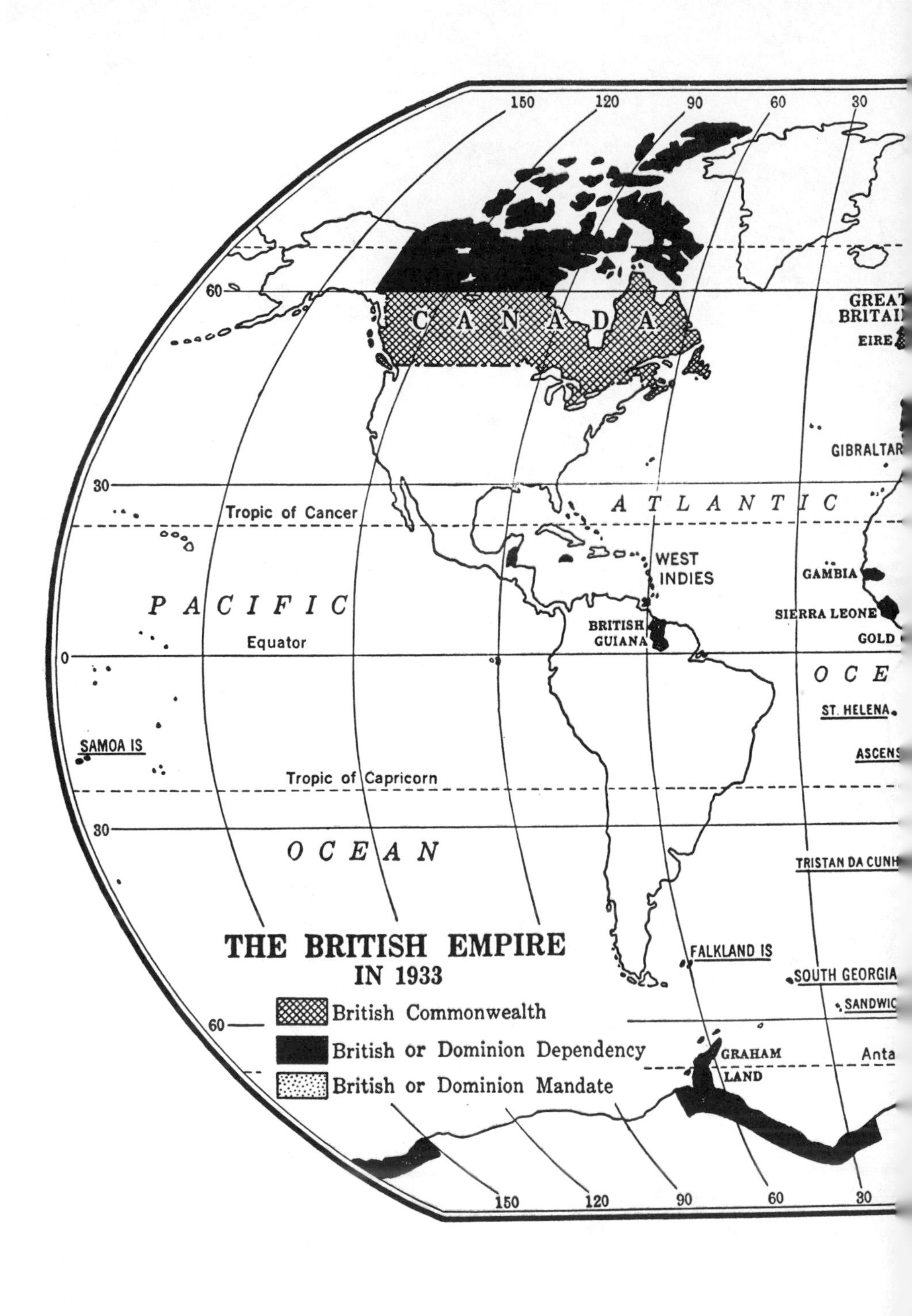

150
120
90
60
30
60
30
0
30
60
CANADA
GREAT BRITAIN
EIRE
GIBRALTAR
ATLANTIC
Tropic of Cancer
WEST INDIES
GAMBIA
SIERRA LEONE
GOLD
PACIFIC
Equator
BRITISH GUIANA
OCE
ST. HELENA
SAMOA IS
ASCENS
Tropic of Capricorn
OCEAN
TRISTAN DA CUNH
THE BRITISH EMPIRE IN 1933
British Commonwealth
British or Dominion Dependency
British or Dominion Mandate
FALKLAND IS
SOUTH GEORGIA
SANDWIC
GRAHAM LAND
Anta
150
120
90
60
30

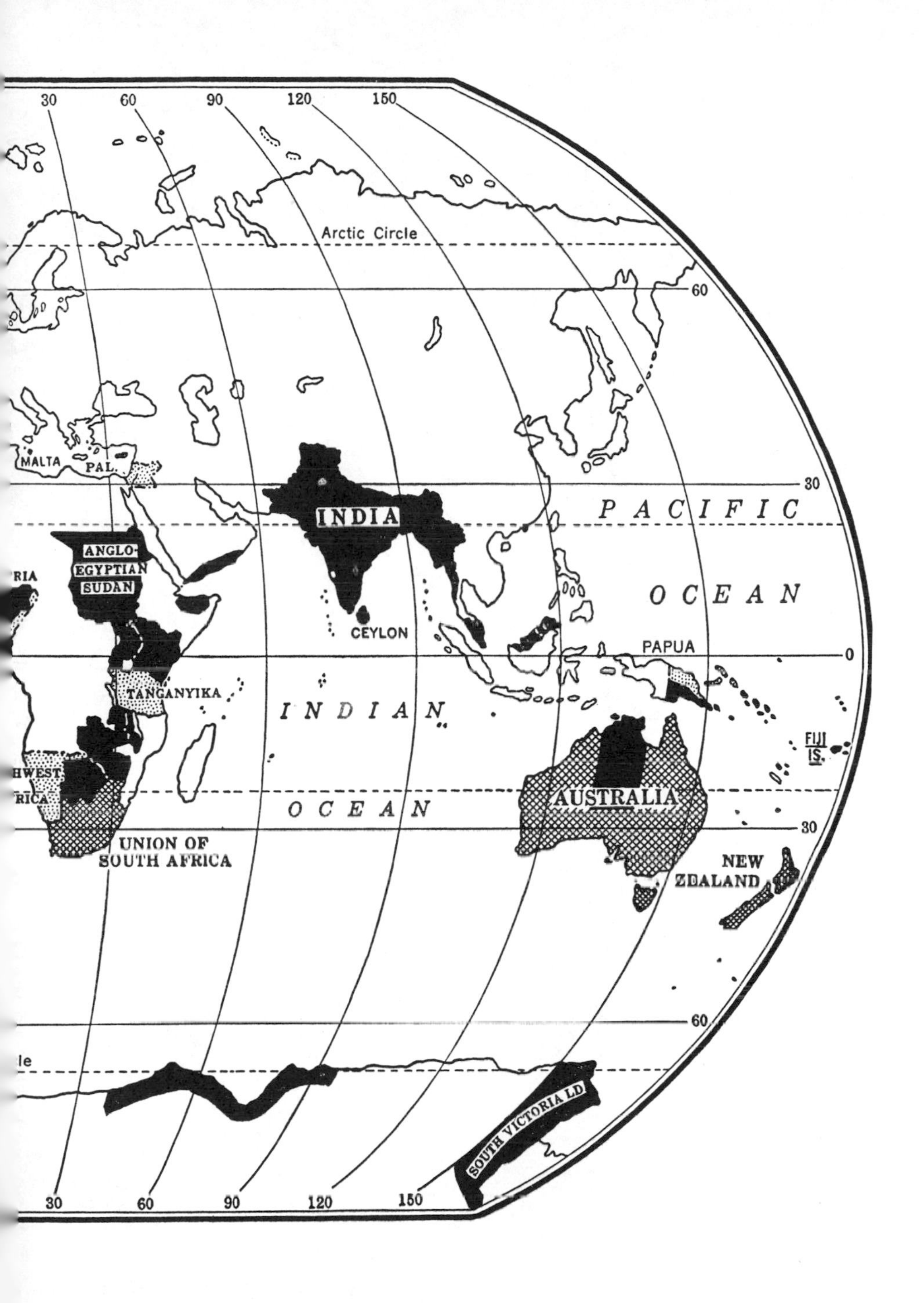
30
60
90
120
150
Arctic Circle
60
MALTA
PAL.
30
P A C I F I C
INDIA
ANGLO-
EGYPTIAN
SUDAN
O C E A N
CEYLON
PAPUA
0
TANGANYIKA
I N D I A N
FIJI
IS.
AUSTRALIA
O C E A N
30
UNION OF
SOUTH AFRICA
NEW
ZEALAND
60
SOUTH VICTORIA LD
30
60
90
120
150

votes favored disarmament. Britain was still suffering from the war-weariness engendered by the Four Years' War. She was a power sated with territory, loaded with responsibilities and commitments; a war could only bring loss; hence she was willing to pocket her pride and tolerate "incidents" both in the Far East and nearer home which at other times might have brought war. Moreover, the British Commonwealth was a league of nations, each having special interests, all being loth to assume responsibility for such issues as the integrity of China and Czechoslovakia, the independence of Ethiopia and Albania, or the success of left-wing republicanism in Spain. An aggressive act by the home government might, besides failing because of lack of power, have the further result of developing rifts within the British empire, disclosing a house divided. As the realization of danger became clearer to the people of Britain it spread to the dominions. Lukewarm to the idea of saving Spain against itself and Sudetenland for Czechoslovakia, dominion opinion became galvanized in March, 1939, when the Germans occupied Prague. Clearly, in the eyes of the German dictator small nations had no rights; Hitler evidently aimed at the mastery of Europe, perhaps of the world. Soon he would attempt the destruction of the British empire. With this contingency in mind the overseas dominions chose to stand by the mother country on September 3, 1939, when she entered the war against Germany.

CHAPTER 27

THE INTERNATIONAL SITUATION, 1901–1939

THE frontiers played a very important role in the history of the British empire in the twentieth century. Gone were the spacious days of the Victorian era when Britain led the world in industry and commerce, when overseas colonies might be secured with little effort, and when the outposts were comparatively free from danger from foreign foes. In the new age European, American, and Asiatic rivals challenged the British empire and caused contractions and shifts in its spheres of material interest. In the years 1902–1914 fear for the safety of political frontiers compelled Britain to abandon her traditional policy of diplomatic isolation; during the Four Years' War, 1914–1918, a considerable share of her war efforts were expended on non-European fronts; the peace settlements of 1919–1920 greatly extended the responsibility of the British empire in Africa, Asia, and Oceania; and in the post-war epoch empire development became a popular British slogan. Events on and the significance of the economic, political, and settlement frontiers of the British empire, 1901–1939, will be discussed in the order given.

At the turn of the century the pressure of foreign competition in overseas markets began to worry British statesmen. The most energetic and resourceful among them, Joseph Chamberlain, colonial secretary from 1895 to 1903, advocated meeting this challenge by a drastic revision of the British tariff policy, suggesting an elaborate system of protection and imperial preferences. But his proposal suffered a crushing defeat in the general election of January, 1906, for Britons refused to abandon free trade or to be alarmed by reports of German trade advances in South America. They pointed to the prosperity enjoyed by the United Kingdom under the existing tariff system, and to the expansion of industry and commerce after the reversal following the war in South Africa. Protection might suit the needs of Germany and the United States, but a large majority of the British voters were convinced that Britain should remain a free trade country.

The Four Years' War changed the economic frontiers of Britain. Concentration on the prosecution of the war made it difficult for her to supply the wants of foreign customers and take advantage of the temporary disappearance of Germany as a trade rival. The United States and Japan captured German markets and made heavy inroads upon British ones; and London yielded to New York the proud position of banking center of the world. In the post-war years money plus efficiency aided the Americans and cheap labor plus efficiency strengthened Japanese industry and trade, while British industrialists and traders were hampered by the unsettled situation in Europe, internal taxation, labor unrest, and the effort to restore the pound to its former gold parity. Although the United States suffered a great setback as a result of the New York stock market crash in October, 1929, and the subsequent collapse of thousands of American banks, Britain could not benefit by the discomfiture of her competitor because of the world-wide economic depression which in 1931 caused a British financial crisis of the first magnitude. During the thirties, however, London did regain its old place of leadership among the financial centers of the world, but it no longer had a large surplus of capital for investment abroad; furthermore, tariff barriers, monetary experiments, and political disturbances in foreign countries narrowed the orbit of British economic influence.

The shrinkage of the economic frontiers was especially noticeable in the Far East. In India and China domestic manufacturing aided by widespread anti-British political agitation and the boycott of British goods caused serious losses to British trade and industry. The most dangerous threat came from Japan. While the great powers of Europe were engaged in a suicidal war, Japan developed commercially and industrially. In the early thirties her cotton industry, financed in part by British capital, was rated the most efficient in the world. Pursuing an aggressive economic imperialistic policy she gradually replaced Britain as producer of the coarser grades of cotton cloth for the markets of Africa and Asia. Not content with her success in this field, Japan in 1931 started a drive for absolute control over China. First she attacked the weakly held province of Manchuria, separated it from China, and formed the puppet state of Manchukuo. In this northern region British economic interests were comparatively unimportant; hence Britain watched with misgiving but without alarm the forward move by her former ally. In 1937, however, the Japanese attacks were shifted to central China. Here Britain had long enjoyed a preeminence bordering on complete economic control. China resisted the invader while withdrawing her forces farther and farther inland, leaving the Japanese masters of both the rich Yangtse Valley and southern China. British sympathies were with the Chinese, but, fully occupied near home, Britain was unable to render assistance except by sending a limited amount of supplies. British investors in Chinese enterprises and British traders suffered heavy reverses. Britain "lost face" in the orient. A century after she had begun her advance to secure economic mastery over the Chinese empire, Britain was in full retreat, her Far Eastern outposts lost to Japan.

Elsewhere the advances on the economic frontiers of the British empire were linked with the need to control sources of oil. With the discovery of rich oil fields in Persia (now Iran) the

British government bought shares in the Anglo-Persian Oil Company and aided this concern in getting the concessions necessary to drill wells and construct pipe lines to the sea. In the twenties Britain showed a similar interest in the oil fields of Iraq and in the construction of the pipe line thence to Haifa, seaport of Palestine. The fields of Persia and Iraq were important sources of fuel oil for the royal navy in the Indian Ocean and the Mediterranean; hence the alliance between the British government and the oil companies. Less mixed with political interests was the expansion of British control over oil fields in Rumania; apart from the usual protection afforded British enterprise abroad, the government had no definite connection with the British oil companies operating in Mexico. Here Britons as well as Americans suffered serious losses in 1937 when the government seized the wells.

No definite boundaries delimited the spheres of British material interests; the use of new devices for disguising political control made nebulous even the political boundaries of the British empire. In the last quarter of the nineteenth century the employment of various types of protectorates, of the condominium – as in the case of the Anglo-Egyptian Sudan – of chartered companies, and of so-called spheres of interest complicated the problem of defining the frontiers. In 1919 and 1920 they were further confused by the adoption of British mandates for former German and Turkish possessions. Nevertheless, in this period problems connected with these political frontiers deeply affected British policy in peace and war. In 1919 the British empire reached its greatest extent.

Threats to the imperial frontiers were responsible for the British diplomatic revolution, 1902–1914. Abandoning isolation, Britain became the ally of Japan and formed an *entente* with France and Russia. Alarmed over the safety of her economic frontiers in the Far East, in 1902 she concluded an agreement with Japan which by treaties of 1905 and 1911 evolved into an alliance for the mutual protection of political frontiers in the orient, including India. In the eighties and nineties disputes concerning African frontiers, particularly Egypt, had caused friction between Britain and France; confronting a common danger from Germany, the two western powers decided to settle them. By the treaty of April 8, 1904, Britain recognized the paramountcy of French rights in Morocco in return for a similar recognition by France of British rights in Egypt; France exchanged fishery privileges in Newfoundland for territory in Central Africa; the spheres of interest of the two powers in Siam were delimited; and arrangements were made for a condominium over an island group, the New Hebrides, in the South Pacific. Germany's efforts to test this *entente* made it stronger; by 1914 Britain and France were allies *de facto* though not *de jure.*

In August, 1907, Britain and Russia reached an understanding concerning the Middle East. The British political mission was withdrawn from Tibet and the Russian from Afghanistan. The former was recognized definitely as an integral part of the Chinese empire, and Russia admitted that Britain held a special position in Afghanistan. Persia was divided into three zones: in the northwest Russia was dominant; in the southeast, Britain; in the region between neither power claimed exclusive privileges. Thus by clarifying the situation on the frontiers, withdrawing in some areas, advancing in others, Britain defined the limits of her political influence more clearly and broke the ground for cooperation between herself and the powers of the dual alliance, France and Russia.

Although the main cause of friction between Britain and Germany was naval rivalry, the settlement of frontier issues during 1912–1914 promised to restore friendly relations between them. These issues pertained to German efforts to expand in the Near East and South Africa. Early in the twentieth century a German concern held the right to build a railway across Anatolia and Syria to Bagdad on the Tigris. German influence being then in the ascendancy at Constantinople, Britain feared that with the control of the Bagdad railroad Germany would endanger her position in Mesopotamia and at the head of the Persian Gulf. Here her privileges were of long standing but ill defined. After the Bagdad railroad question had been discussed in the British press and parliament, Sir Edward Grey, the British foreign secretary, took it up directly with the German foreign office. In 1913 an agreement was reached which defined the Bagdad railroad system and arranged details concerning its management, termini, and port facilities. Thus British commercial and political rights in this section of the Turkish empire were placed on a firmer basis. In Africa Germany had long cast covetous eyes at the colonies of Portugal, Britain's oldest ally. Finally in the early months of 1914 an arrangement was made between Britain and Germany which gave the latter an option to purchase a large portion of these colonies. It was expected that these agreements would lessen the tension between Britain and Germany and perhaps even bring them together.

But hopes for an Anglo-German *entente* were dashed. In July, 1914, Austro-Serbian friction culminated in Austrian threats to destroy the smaller neighbor. Behind Serbia stood Russia; behind Austria stood Germany. France was drawn in as the ally of Russia, and the possibility that France might be overwhelmed aroused Britain. While the issue of peace and war still hung in the balance as far as Britain was concerned, Germany invaded Belgium, thus supplying Britain with a *casus belli* in harmony with traditional policies as well as current interests. During the night of August 4–5, 1914, war broke out between Britain and Germany. At first it was generally believed that Britain's chief and perhaps only contribution to the cause of her allies — Belgium, France, Russia, and Serbia — would be made on the sea. British sea power was a vital factor in bringing them victory, but soon the British empire was compelled to mobilize its man power as never before. Of the 7,500,000 soldiers called within the empire during the Four Years' War more than 3,000,000 were supplied by British countries overseas. While the outcome of the conflict was finally decided on French soil, it was a world war not simply because every country was involved in or affected by it but because of the numerous campaigns in non-European lands. These "side shows" were of the utmost importance for the British empire beyond the sea.

British forces fought in Samoa, New Guinea, in West, South, and East Africa, in Egypt, Palestine, Arabia, Mesopotamia, and Persia. When Turkey entered the war as an enemy of Britain the latter took formal possession of Cyprus and declared Egypt a protectorate. Australian troops seized German New Guinea; New Zealand captured German Samoa; British and French forces took German Togoland and the Cameroons; the newly established Union of South Africa conquered the German colony in her neighborhood; and soldiers from the dominions, colonies, and India made up the greater part of the armies that fought in and captured German East Africa, Palestine, and Mesopotamia. British diplomacy, British gold, and a few troops aroused and armed the Arabs against the Turks and established a short-lived British hegemony over Persia.

When the peace conference at Paris, 1919–20, sought to bring order in a world scrambled by war and revolution, the British empire could by right claim a strong voice in negotiations dealing with lands captured by its soldiers and sailors. German and Turkish possessions were divided among the victors, but non-European lands were to be held not in ownership but as trusts under the newly formed League of Nations. For this purpose the mandate system was invented. Thus Britain obtained control over portions of the German colonies of Togoland and the Cameroons, of German East Africa, now christened Tanganyika, of Palestine, and Mesopotamia; under the same system the South African Union kept German South-west Africa; Australia, German New Guinea and adjoining islands; and New Zealand, German Samoa. These mandates and other regions like Arabia and Persia were within the orbit of the British empire.

The shrinkage of the British political frontiers began in 1921. The scene was the Middle East; the causes were complex.

Clearly the empire was over-extended and the burden of the cost and of the responsibilities connected therewith was too heavy for the British taxpayers. Moreover, the "no annexation" slogan and the doctrine of self-determination proclaimed from the housetops in 1918 were not lost upon the peoples over whom Britain had secured ascendancy. In the Middle East their opportunity came when Bolshevik Russia grew sufficiently strong to pick up the threads of tsarist diplomacy. Persia and Afghanistan illustrate these points.

In 1916 Persia despite her neutrality became a battleground for British, Russian, and Turkish forces. The collapse of her ally, Russia, and her enemy, Turkey, left Britain dominant in the country. In 1919 this dominance was signalized by the conclusion of a formal treaty which, although affirming Persia's independence, allocated to Britain such tasks as the reorganization of railroads and defense whereby she obtained both economic and political control of the land. In vain a Persian delegation sought a hearing at the peace conference. Lord Curzon was proud of the Anglo-Persian treaty, his handiwork, but the triumph was short-lived. Persia wished to be relieved of British overlordship, anti-British feeling grew, and in 1920 Russia appeared on the scene. Entrance of her troops into Persia led to the conclusion of a Russo-Persian pact. The British military forces were withdrawn, and in February, 1921, the Persian government declared the treaty of 1919 null and void.

A similar diplomatic defeat was suffered by Britain in Afghanistan. Despite urgings from Germany and Turkey, Afghanistan remained neutral during the war; but in April, 1919, when disturbances broke out in the Punjab an Afghan army appeared in the Khyber Pass. Although the pass was held by only a weak British force, the attack was not pushed vigorously and British reinforcements equipped with armored cars and airplanes soon routed the enemy. This Afghan war, the third, was of short duration and a cheaply won military triumph for the British. Nevertheless, by the ensuing peace Britain surrendered control over Afghan foreign relations, held since 1880 and recognized by Russia in 1907. Afghanistan now became completely independent, her ruler boasting openly that he had won the war; actually he had won the peace. The solution of the riddle was again Russia. On March 1, 1921, Afghanistan and Russia signed a treaty of friendship and alliance. The situation in India and war-weariness at home barred the possibility of a forward British policy in Afghanistan. Britain chose to retreat, bide her time, await the course of events. For Afghanistan the nineteen-twenties was a troubled period, with revolutions and three changes of dynasties. Finally in 1929 a very able member of the old ruling family, Nadir Shah, gained the throne and established order. The British diplomatic mission, withdrawn from Kabul during the disorders, returned in 1930. From then on, Anglo-Afghan relations improved steadily. King Nadir Shah, assassinated in 1933, was succeeded by his son, Zadir Shah. Like his father, the new king regarded with apprehension the pushing of Russian motor roads and railroads toward his country's frontiers; to him as to his father, Britain was less dangerous than the Soviet Union.

On the dismemberment of the old Turkish empire, Mesopotamia, later called Iraq, came into existence as a separate political entity. Using Indian troops, Britain had expelled the Turks from Mesopotamia, and the peace conference turned her into a class "A" British mandate. The rather ill-assorted collection of tribes that made up the greater part of the Iraqi was none too well pleased with British rule; a rebellion that broke out in 1920 was quickly suppressed. Imperial-minded Englishmen described Iraq as a "key" to India, a slogan ineffective in view of the fact that the country's frontiers were open to attack from all sides. Moreover, the occupation of Iraq and the suppression of the rebellion had cost a great deal of money. Consequently Britain lost little time in making arrangements for a withdrawal. In 1921 the Emir Feisal, the third son of the king of Hedjaz, was proclaimed king of Iraq. During the following years a dispute with Turkey over the ownership of Mosul oil fields created much difficulty. A League of Nations commission assigned the disputed area to Iraq — a decision attributed by Turkey to British machinations. However, an Anglo-Turkish treaty of June 6, 1926, mollified the Turks by a promise of 10 per cent of Iraq's oil royalties from Mosul, and Britain then proceeded rapidly with the liquidation of her responsibilities in this region. A treaty of 1930 safeguarded her interests in oil fields and pipe lines, assigned bases for her air force, and made other provisions for mutual assistance in case of war. With these details arranged, Iraq was two years later admitted to the League of Nations as an independent and sovereign state.

The Four Years' War deeply affected Britain's position and policies in the Levant. In November, 1914, Turkey joined Germany against her old ally and protector, Britain. This resulted in the British annexation of Cyprus and the declaration of a protectorate over Egypt. Furthermore, the logic of the new situation caused Britain to assign Constantinople and the Straits to Russia in the event of a victorious termination of the war. In 1915 Britain tried to defeat Turkey by assaults upon the Dardanelles and a campaign on the Gallipoli peninsula at the southern exit of the Straits. When these failed, resort was had to slower methods — campaigns against Turkey in Mesopotamia, in Palestine with Egypt as the base, and in Arabia. The Arabs of western Arabia, long restless under Turkish dominance, were incited to revolt by an Oxford don, Colonel T. E. Lawrence, who became the great hero of the desert war. The autumn of 1918 found Britain in control of Syria and of extensive regions of the Turkish empire to the south and east of that country. Completely exhausted, Turkey sued for peace, but the arrangement of the final terms had to wait nearly two years. Although the promises to Russia were considered canceled by virtue of her separate peace with Germany, other pledges and secret treaties and claims, sentimental as well as nationalistic, made the disposal of Turkish lands, the estate of the famous "sick man," a delicate and complicated task. Finally by the Treaty of Sèvres, 1920, Turkey was shorn of all her European possessions except Constantinople and a small strip of land by the Bosphorus and the Sea of Marmora, and of all her Asiatic territory except Anatolia. The Straits were demilitarized and put under international control; Smyrna and the surrounding area were assigned to the Greeks, who also assumed the task of pacifying western Asia Minor from Smyrna to the region of the Straits.

Meanwhile the defeated Turks had found an unusually able and resourceful leader in an army officer, Mustapha Kemal. With Angora (later Ankara) as his headquarters he organized an army from the ragged starved remnants of the old Turkish forces. Some help was received from Russia and, after 1921, surreptitiously from France and Italy. The Greeks, anxious to seize control over all of western Asia Minor, scoffed at the Kemalist movement and vowed to crush the government at Ankara. In encouraging the Greeks, the British put their money on the wrong horse. In September, 1922, the Turks drove the Greeks into the sea at Smyrna; the withdrawal of the French and Italian detachments guarding the region of the Straits on the Asiatic side left but a small British force to face the victorious Turks. In vain the British government tried to rally its allies; help was sought from the dominions, but only Australia and New Zealand gave encouraging replies. However, the skill and firmness of General Harington, the British commander in Asia Minor, saved the situation. No untoward incident occurred; the question of the Turkish peace settlement was reopened, and a new treaty was negotiated at Lausanne, Switzerland, by which Turkey recovered Thrace, all of Asia Minor, and parts of Armenia.

Under the vigorous leadership of Kemal Pasha, rightfully called Ataturk (father of the Turks) Turkey experienced an amazing national revival. The new Turkey, with Angora (Ankara) as capital, rid herself of the sultan, the caliphate, and numerous ancient ideas and customs. Constantinople, the famous old capital on the Bosphorus, was relegated to the position of a provincial city. The center of the new Turkey was Anatolia, organized economically, politically, and socially along modern lines. At first this revitalized country considered Britain its enemy, but gradually a better understanding arose between them.

THE NEAR EAST

Among the great powers, Britain alone had no design upon Turkish territory. Though the British government issued a protest in 1936 against the resumption of full Turkish control over and refortification of the Straits, this was in reality only a form. The two powers needed each other. In the face of strenuous German efforts to build up a following in the Middle East, the non-aggression pact of July, 1937, between Turkey, Iraq, Iran

(Persia), and Afghanistan was considered a victory for British diplomacy. When war broke out in September, 1939, Turkey was a non-belligerent ally of Britain and France.

British relations with the Mohammedan states of the Near and Middle East were deeply influenced by consideration of their effects upon the Mohammedans of India. In the early twenties Indian Mohammedans were angered by the harsh treatment accorded Turkey, the leading Mohammedan state, and this sentiment promoted cooperation between them and the Hindu Nationalists, a cooperation extremely embarrassing to the government of India. However, Kemal Pasha's abolition of the caliphate and other unorthodox reforms eased the situation in India. In spite of this Britain had to step warily, for her empire contains more Moslems than have ever before been gathered in one political unit, and her statesmen were forced to reckon with the possibility that a Pan-Islamic movement might disturb *pax Britannica* in both Asia and Africa.

This religio-political problem was of special importance in Palestine. In November, 1917, as British forces were advancing toward Jerusalem, Balfour, then secretary of state for foreign affairs, announced that Britain would reestablish Palestine as a national home for the Jews—a plan later endorsed by the League of Nations. Palestine therefore became a British mandate. At the outset, Transjordan was detached from it and erected into a separate state with a son of King Hussein of Hedjaz as its ruler. In the rest of Palestine, an area of about 10,000 square miles, place had to be found for the tens of thousands of Jews who flocked thither, without ousting the resident Arab population. The stream of immigrants became a flood especially after the advent of Hitler to power in Germany, and restrictive measures were necessary. Although the Jews brought capital, energy, initiative, and resourcefulness to their new home and Palestine soon prospered as never before in the Christian era, a considerable proportion of the Arab population resented the invasion. Before the end of the twenties violent anti-Jewish outbreaks marred the peace of Palestine and presented the British government with a problem of great complexity. Forcible suppression of Arab discontent might stir up Arabs elsewhere and perhaps arouse the whole Islamic world against Britain. On the other hand, failure to give adequate protection to the Jews and the curtailment of their immigration exposed her to the charge of having broken solemn promises and to the hostility of the Jewish world. In 1937 a plan for a division of Palestine met with opposition in both camps; a later proposal to restrict Jewish land purchases was condemned bitterly by the Jews and refused sanction by the mandates commission of the League of Nations. Meanwhile the growing tension in Europe tended to ease relations between Arabs and Jews in Palestine. Despite vigorous Italian propaganda, the Arabs suspected Italy; the spread of anti-Semitism and the intensification of the Jewish persecution in Europe perhaps softened the Arab attitude toward the Jews, who on their side realized that Britain was their only friend among the powers. They sided whole-heartedly with her against their German and Italian tormentors. In September, 1939, Palestine was quiet.

During the Four Years' War the Arabs were stirred to revolt against the Turks. In June, 1916, Hussein, Sheriff of Mecca, declared his independence of Turkey and later assumed the title king of Hedjaz; Hedjaz is a strip of territory in western Arabia along the Red Sea. Hussein and his sons, especially the Emir Feisal, rendered valuable aid against the Turks, but to Colonel Lawrence's utter disgust the promise of an independent Syria with Damascus as capital was not kept—Britain broke faith with the Arabs. The conclusion of the war found three Arab kingdoms in former Turkish territory, Hedjaz, Iraq, and Transjordan. Another formidable power soon appeared. Ibn Saud, sultan of Nejd in central Arabia, extended his sway westward and ultimately overthrew the king of Hedjaz. In the later stages of the Four Years' War the India government had prudently subsidized Ibn Saud; hence his conquest of Hedjaz did not leave the British high and dry. On May 20, 1927, a treaty of friendship between Britain and the new kingdom of Hedjaz and Nejd (later renamed Saudi Arabia) was signed. This change in the political map did not alter the British position in Arabia. Aden in western and Muscat in eastern Arabia remained under British control, as did also the sultanate of Koweit at the head of the Persian Gulf and the Bahrein islands near its entrance. Although Italy gained the friendship of Yemen, a kingdom north of Aden, Britain remained the dominant power in the Arabian peninsula and the seas bordering thereon; in this region of the world the imperial boundaries did not recede.

Complicated as were the Anglo-Arab relations they were relatively simple compared with the Anglo-Egyptian. As the period opens, Lord Cromer, British agent and consul-general at Cairo, was the real ruler of Egypt although she was still nominally a part of the Turkish empire and paid tribute to the sultan at Constantinople. The Anglo-French treaty of April, 1904, though strengthening the British position in Egypt, failed to clarify it. Nor did the proclamation of a British protectorate prove of much help in this respect. Britain became the suzerain of Egypt — what this meant nobody knew. During the war Egypt provided training grounds for troops from Australia and New Zealand, bases for the Gallipoli and Palestinian campaigns, and was a source of supplies and labor. Money poured into the country, but the fellaheens were not protected so carefully as in Cromer's time; moreover, the number of Englishmen in the Egyptian service multiplied. These grievances gave added strength to Egyptian nationalism.

The Egyptian national movement dated from the early eighties; it made little progress under Cromer, 1883–1907; but because his successors lacked his skill and the prestige derived from long service and intimate knowledge, it grew formidable. Nationalist leaders became stronger and bolder during the war, which according to the professions of the Allies was fought in the interest of national self-determination. This slogan was shelved when Egyptians demanded a hearing at the peace conference; their leader, Zahglul Pasha, was arrested and sent to Malta. Resentful over these actions, Egyptians in 1920 boycotted a commission headed by Lord Milner and sent from England to study and report upon the problems of Egypt. Nevertheless the commissioners gathered a good deal of evidence and presented a report strongly recommending the termination of the status of protectorate, full independence for Egypt, and an Anglo-Egyptian alliance. Although the recommendations bore the signature of Lord Milner, an old imperialist and a high authority on Egypt, and had the support of Lord Curzon, another statesman of even greater eminence, the British government refused to act. Not until February, 1922, was Egypt offered independence subject to the following reservations:

"(*a*) The security of the communications of the British Empire in Egypt;

"(*b*) The defence of Egypt against all foreign aggression or interference, direct or indirect;

"(*c*) The protection of foreign interests in Egypt and the protection of minorities;

"(*d*) The Sudan."

A liberal constitution was promulgated; the ruler of Egypt, styled sultan since the separation from Turkey, now took the title of king; and Zaghlul Pasha was permitted to return. But he and his party, the Wafd, declined to accept the reservations cited above; and since they won elections with embarrassing regularity, deadlocks ensued. The main points in dispute between the British and the Wafd dealt with the presence of British troops in Egypt, and the position of the Sudan. To the Egyptians a foreign garrison was a token of dependence. They insisted on their right to be the guardians of the Suez Canal and they demanded complete control over the Sudan. The situation became critical in 1924 when Sir Lee Stack, commander-in-chief of the Egyptian army and governor general of the Sudan, was murdered in Cairo. This outrage caused the British government to demand an apology from Egypt, punishment of the criminals, payment of £500,000, and the right to use an unlimited amount of Nile water for irrigation in the Sudan. Egypt had no choice but to comply. However, King Fuad showed considerable skill in maintaining at least a semblance of constitutional government, preventing on the one hand a return to the status of a British protectorate and on the other open rebellion. At last, when both British and Egyptians became alarmed in 1935 over the Italian attack on Ethiopia, a treaty was negotiated and signed on August 26, 1936, whereby Britain again affirmed the independence of Egypt and promised aid in securing the abolition of the Capitulations and Egypt's admission to the League of Nations. British troops were to garrison the canal zone, the defense of which was to be a joint duty of the two countries. They were to be allies, and Britain received the right to use Egyptian air bases and the naval base at Alexandria, while the Sudan continued to be administered jointly by Britain and Egypt. The governor general of the Sudan was to be appointed by the king of Egypt on the nomination of the British government; Egyptians became eligible for appointment in the Sudan; restrictions upon Egyptian emigration thither were removed; and Egyptian troops were to share in its defense. When the new king, Farouk, who succeeded his father in April, 1936, reached majority he showed a desire to draw closer to the Asiatic group of Mohammedan powers, and in March, 1939, his sister married Mohammed Reza, heir to Iran. Egypt, like Turkey, feared Italy, and this fear kept the country within the sphere of British political influence. Though in name independent, the land of the Pharaohs remained within the orbit of the British empire.

Apart from Egypt and the Sudan, the British empire in Africa faced problems connected with Italy's imperial ambitions and with the former German colonies held as mandates by Britain and the Union of South Africa. By the Treaty of London, April, 1915, which fixed the terms for the Italian entrance into the war on the side of the Allies, Italy was promised territories in Africa if Britain and France acquired new areas on that continent. The peace settlement gave the two western powers mandates over German colonies; technically this did not match the conditions laid down in the treaty, nevertheless in 1924 Italy obtained a portion of Kenya on the border of Italian Somaliland. This territory, known as Jubaland, had an area of 33,000 square miles and a population estimated at 12,000. There was also a slight rectification of the Eritrean frontier. But these concessions did not satisfy the Italians, for their territorial ambitions reached Napoleonic proportions after the Fascist order had been firmly established. The revival of Turkey frustrated hopes for Italian acquisitions in western Asia Minor, nor was there then any possibility that France would relax her grip on Tunisia. Hence the attention of Italian imperialists turned toward Ethiopia, the only native state in Africa enjoying an independent existence.

In the early thirties Italy posed as a friend of Ethiopia and sponsored her admission to the League of Nations, but in 1935 Mussolini threw off the mask and demanded control over the country. The Ethiopians refused to surrender, trusting to the security offered by the League and by the climatic and physiographical conditions of their land. They were disappointed. Britain tried to save Ethiopia — if this could be done short of a European war. The British interest in the country was based on the fact that within its borders lies Lake Tsana, source of the Blue Nile which supplies much of the water used for irrigation in the Sudan and Egypt; that with Ethiopia in Italian hands the security of the Sudan, Kenya, Uganda, and British Somaliland might be menaced; and that it was necessary to prove that membership in the League of Nations meant protection. At first the British foreign secretary, Sir Samuel Hoare, sought to placate Italy by offering to summon a world economic conference to consider the distribution of raw materials, but his proposal fell on deaf ears. On September 11, at a meeting of the assembly of the League of Nations, Sir Samuel spoke brave words, declaring that Britain would uphold the authority of the League of Nations; but when Mussolini defied the League, Hoare and the French prime minister, M. Laval, urged virtual surrender to the Italians. However, the Hoare-Laval pact was disavowed by the British prime minister, Mr. Baldwin, and Anthony Eden succeeded Hoare at the foreign office. The Italian attack upon Ethiopia was condemned by the League of Nations whose members were urged to impose "sanctions," i.e., an economic boycott, on Italy. Several League as well as non-League members refused to comply — even Britain did not go the whole way on oil and war material. Air power gave Italy an immense advantage over the Abyssinians, whose resistance was broken after a brief campaign. Recognizing their failure, the British government in June, 1936, abandoned the sanctions against Italy. Thus Britain suffered a great diplomatic defeat; Italian hostility had been aroused; the famous Rome-Berlin axis was formed; and the prestige of the League of Nations suffered irreparable damage. Established in the center of eastern Africa, the Italians threatened Britain's African interests and frontiers.

In 1919 Britain obtained control of the major portion of Germany's colonial empire in Africa. No leading statesman at the peace conference advanced the views held by Castlereagh a century earlier, when France was in the dock, that the defeated enemy should be left with a "balanced empire." In the British election of December, 1918, successful candidates had promised to "squeeze Germany till the pips squeak." British economic interests favored grabbing all that could be had, and humanitarians pointed to Germany's bad record as a colonial administrator. Protests against depriving her of all her colonies were ignored; the mandatory system, it was argued, offered the ideal solution of the colonial problem. Thus Britain secured the mandate of portions of Togoland and the Cameroons and of German East Africa, and the Union of South Africa became mandatory power for German South-west Africa. For purposes of administration the British section of Togoland was attached to the Gold Coast

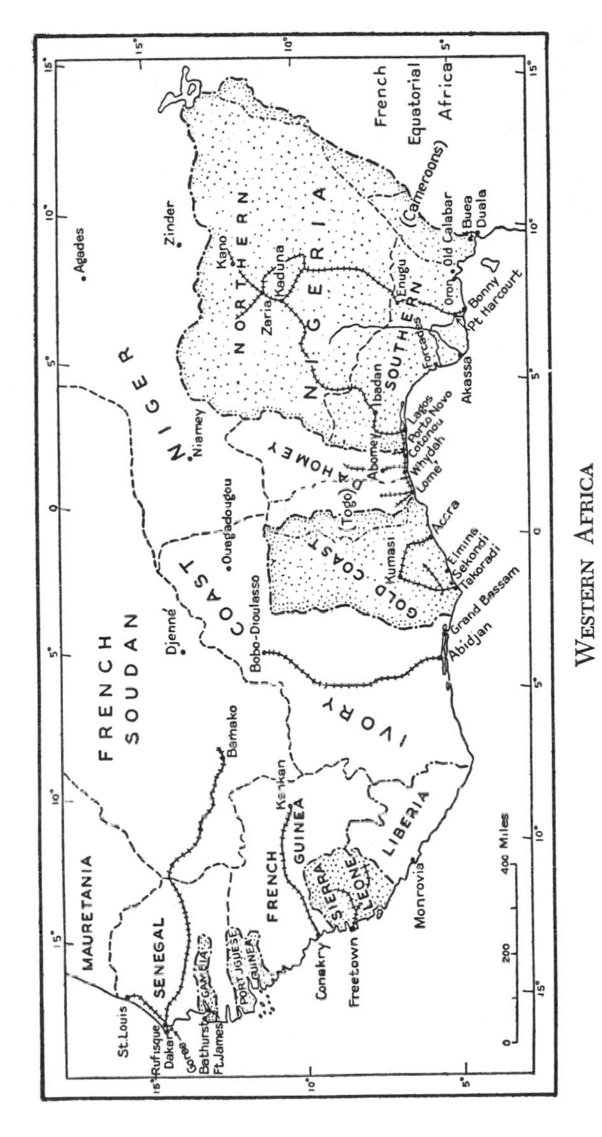

WESTERN AFRICA

(From Colby's *Geographical Aspects of International Relations*, University of Chicago Press.)

Colony, and that of the Cameroons to Nigeria. A proposal to unite German East Africa, now called Tanganyika territory, with Kenya was vetoed by the mandates commission of the League of Nations. The former German colony between the Orange River and the southern boundary of Angola was conquered by the Union of South Africa without outside help. Since imperialists at the Cape had demanded British annexation of this area in the eighties, the conquest fulfilled long-cherished ambitions. South Africans chafed somewhat under the restrictions imposed on them by the League of Nations; they looked upon their mandate as a permanent acquisition and considered formal incorporation of it into the Union as a mere matter of time. Similar views were held in Australia concerning German New Guinea, and in New Zealand in regard to German Samoa. With a collapse of the mandatory system these dominions were ready to claim ownership of the mandated territories.

The region of the Pacific had little direct contact with the Four Years' War. The campaigns against the German colonies, the Japanese capture of the German-controlled Shantung peninsula, and even the naval battle of Coronel off the coast of Chile in which a British squadron was destroyed were insignificant in comparison with the contests fought elsewhere. Nevertheless, the war formed a turning point in the history of the Pacific. The temporary withdrawal of European powers including Russia from the Far East provided Japan with both economic and political opportunities. Her trade expanded and in 1915 she presented a series of demands on China which made that country virtually a vassal state. Britain and the United States, traditional upholders of the open door in and the integrity of China, viewed the Japanese maneuvers with misgivings, but the former was fully occupied with the war and the latter was content with a formal protest. In the last stages of the war Japanese forces in Siberia, ostensibly operating in support of White Russians against the Bolsheviks, bade fair to eliminate Russia from the Far East.

The Washington conference, 1921–1922, changed this situation. Shortly after the conclusion of the Four Years' War, wiseacres predicted that the scene of the next conflict would be the Pacific — a contest between the United States and Japan. This possibility was of great interest to Britain and the dominions of Australasia and Canada. The Anglo-Japanese alliance was due to expire in 1921 and speculations were rife as to its future. It had been valuable for the British empire, and a strong sentiment for its renewal existed in both Britain and Australasia. On the other hand Canada objected to its renewal, and those who advocated Anglo-American cooperation in international affairs considered the alliance a serious obstacle to the realization of their desire. In spite of the opposition of Australia, who grumbled at making sacrifices for the sake of American friendship, the British empire accepted with alacrity President Harding's invitation to a conference to be held in Washington for the purpose of discussing disarmament and problems of the Pacific region. Britain, Canada, Australia, India, and New Zealand participated in this conference with the United States, France, and Japan. A four-power pact between Britain, the United States, France, and Japan replaced the old Anglo-Japanese alliance. Japan agreed to evacuate Chinese territory held by her, the *status quo* was to be maintained in the Pacific, and Britain promised not to maintain a first-class naval base east of Singapore. Subsequently Britain transformed Singapore itself into the strongest naval and air base outside the British Isles; it became the guardian of British interests in that part of the world, the Gibraltar of the East.

Unemployment at home caused Britain to take a keen interest in emigration to empire lands. During the twenties plans for pushing forward settlement frontiers in Australia and Canada received much attention. The Empire Settlement Act, 1922, contained provisions for financing emigration in cooperation with the dominions. But the results were disappointing. Unemployed industrial laborers were unwilling to leave Britain and unfit for the hard life on the frontiers. These frontiers were ultimately

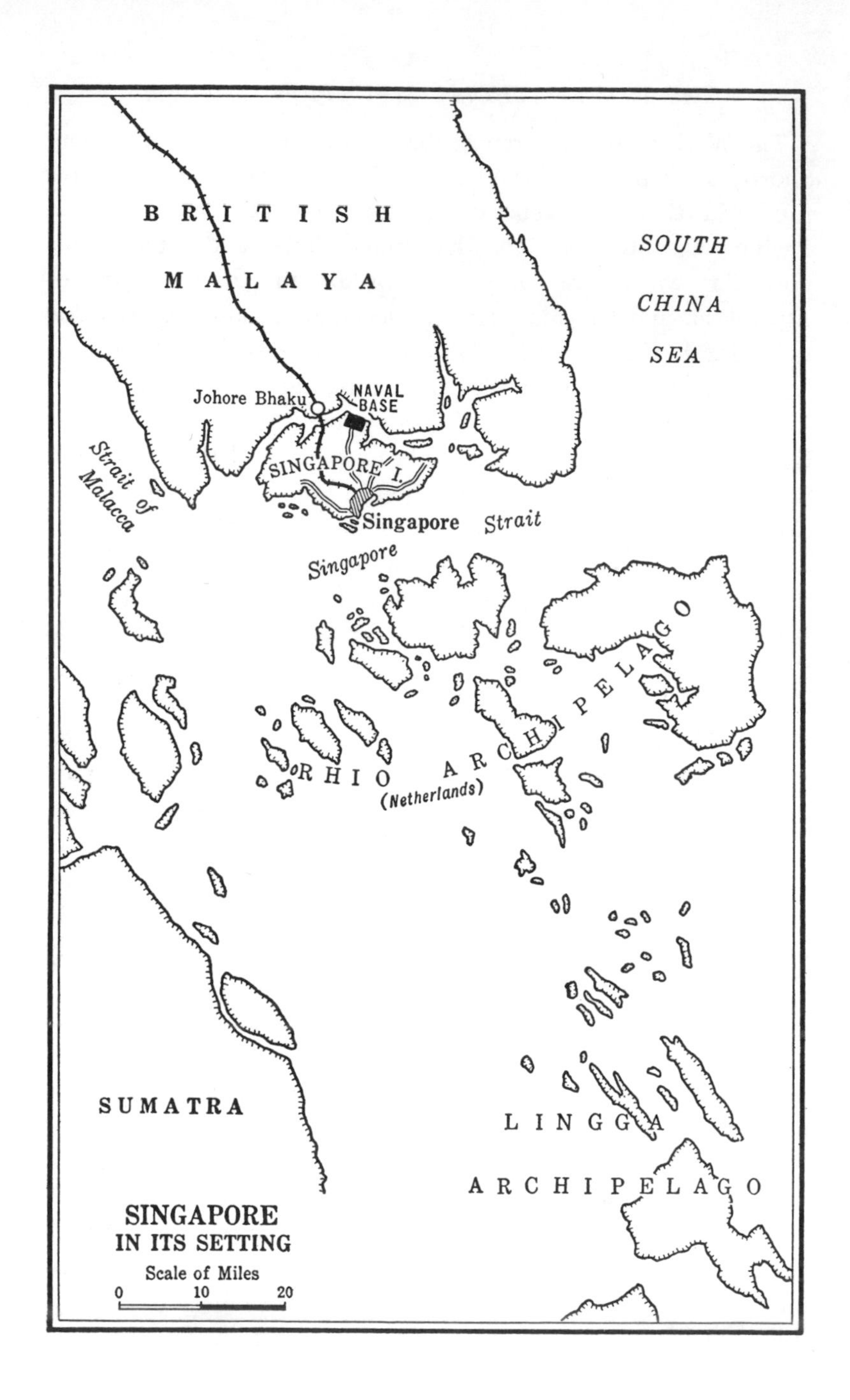

SINGAPORE
IN ITS SETTING

pushed forward, especially in Canada, but the pioneers were more often natives of the dominion or colony than immigrants from the British Isles. As in earlier epochs, dynamic forces were found on the periphery of the British empire; here also British interests clashed with those of foreign powers. But domestic problems and political situations arising in Europe engaged the major attention of British statesmen. In 1914 quarrels in the Balkans lit the torch of war; twenty-five years later the overweening ambition of the German Fuehrer, Adolf Hitler, his lust for glory and conquest, upset the balance of power in Europe. British peace efforts failed, and the empire again became involved in a life-and-death conflict.

CHAPTER 28

EQUALITY OF STATUS, 1901–1939

IN the Victorian era British statesmen seldom focused their attention on the problems of the overseas empire. Now and then crises such as the rebellions in the Canadas, the Indian Mutiny, or Kaffir wars in South Africa compelled them to abandon the habits of *laissez faire,* ponder the whys and wherefores of imperial issues, and try to find solutions; but generally speaking, the tendency was to drift and let "a beneficent nature take its own course to perfection." This attitude changed in 1895 with the advent of Joseph Chamberlain to the colonial office. A businessman, an organizer, a man with ideas and plans, Chamberlain put purpose and direction into British imperial policy. He was anxious to safeguard, defend, consolidate, and develop Britain's overseas interests. With his retirement in 1903 the guidance from the imperial center became less purposeful for the master's hand had been removed; nevertheless, events at home and abroad compelled the people of Britain to think imperially.

After the death of Queen Victoria British imperial policy followed seemingly divergent paths. On the one hand self-government increased in the British lands beyond the sea to such an extent that the great dominions reached a status of equality with the mother country; on the other the older idea of the empire as an estate revived so that directed emigration, empire development, and imperial tariff preferences engaged the attention of British statesmen. Consequently, the British empire became an example of "unity in diversity."

In tracing the history of the British empire, 1901–1939, the years 1901–1914 will be treated as a unit. The war during 1914–1918 created new problems, complicated older ones, and left various types of issues to vex the post-war generation. Hence a brief survey of the empire in the Four Years' War will be followed by a more detailed discussion of events and policies in the period 1919–1939. Topically the Britannic questions will be grouped under expansion, defense, emigration, trade, imperial development, political and constitutional problems, and the efforts to reconcile unity with diversity.

As the nineteenth century closed, Britain acquired control over the Egyptian Sudan and annexed the South African Republic and the Orange Free State. It was then understood that territorially the British empire was "sated." And well it might be. Nearly one-fourth of the habitable surface of the globe was now within the wide-sweeping orbit of this empire. In the years 1901–1914 Britain followed a non-expansionist policy and was even willing to contract her political frontiers. She opposed plans for the partition of China; her treaties with Japan, France, and Russia aimed merely at safeguarding what she already had. By the treaty with France in April, 1904, Britain relinquished title to land in Central Africa in exchange for the French surrender of fishery rights on the coast of Newfoundland; the Anglo-Russian treaty of August, 1907, stipulated that the British political mission should be withdrawn from Tibet which was to be recognized as an integral part of the Chinese empire.

The alliance with Japan and the *entente* with France and Russia were motivated by fear for the safety of the outposts of the empire. Defense problems became all-important, for as the twentieth century advanced the specter of war came nearer. It was then that Britain considered the possibility of securing military and naval assistance from the dominions. In the sixties British statesmen were content to have the self-governing colonies assume responsibility for local defense, naval protection and defense against foreign foes remaining as imperial duties. But shortly after the turn of the century the international situation grew menacing for Britain. Germany, the strongest military power in the world and allied with two first-class European powers, Austria-Hungary and Italy, launched a naval program designed to challenge British naval supremacy. To meet the danger, British men-of-war were withdrawn from distant stations and concentrated in home waters; colonies were left without naval protection, and the dominions were urged to contribute toward imperial defense. The aid rendered Britain in the Anglo-Boer war by Australasia and Canada encouraged British statesmen to think that it might be possible to organize the British countries in a union for defense; and this issue figured prominently in the discussions at the colonial conference of 1902 and at the imperial conferences of 1907 and 1911; in 1909 it occasioned the convening of an emergency defense conference.

Although the discussions of defense failed to bring an imperial defense union into existence, they helped materially in strengthening the dominions' naval and military establishments, and they promoted coordination of imperial forces. At the conference of 1902 Australasia agreed to increase the annual contribution for the maintenance of a British naval squadron in the South Pacific; and Canada, who during the Anglo-Boer war had taken over the naval stations at Halifax and Esquimalt, announced her readiness to establish a navy of her own. In the succeeding years the merits, from the standpoint of imperial defense, of cash aid versus those of separate dominion navies were hotly debated. The heads of the British fighting services and British public opinion generally favored the former; the dominions veered more and more toward the latter, for to them the cash contribution seemed a tribute — a badge of inferiority.

By 1906 the bulk of the British naval forces were in home waters; but the Liberal government, trying to avert a race in naval armaments, did not press the issue of defense at the imperial conference held the year following. At this conference Thomas Smartt of the Cape Colony vainly sought acceptance of the principle that the dominions should contribute to naval defense. New Zealand was willing, but Australia joined Canada in a declaration favoring separate naval units, on which plan imperial authorities then bestowed their blessing. Two years later a near panic swept the British empire upon disclosures in the house of commons that the admiralty believed that Germany was outbuilding Britain in battleships of the latest type, the *Dreadnought.* Offers of contributions for naval defense poured in from overseas, and a defense conference was hastily convened in London. South Africa, not yet united, agreed to continue the annual payment of £85,000 for naval defense and New Zealand's offer of a battle cruiser was accepted by the British government. Australia and Canada promised to proceed with plans for navies of their own. Australia implemented this pledge with orders for warships to be built in Britain, and by 1914 her navy consisted of one battle cruiser, two light cruisers, and several smaller craft. In Canada naval defense became a party issue. Laurier's program of two Canadian naval units, one for the Atlantic and one for the Pacific, met with strong opposition – from French-Canadians because of its cost and tendency to involve the Dominion in a British war, and from Conservatives because of its alleged impracticability. When the latter won the election of 1911 the new Borden government proposed a gift to Britain of $35,000,000 for the building of battleships. A bill for this purpose passed the Canadian house of commons, only to be thrown out by the senate where the Liberals still held a majority. In 1914 the war found Canada with two old cruisers and a few smaller surface vessels and submarines, two of the latter bought in the United States just as war broke out. In 1913 the first lord of the admiralty, Winston Churchill, suggested the organization of an imperial naval squadron, with Gibraltar as its base, maintained jointly by Britain and the dominions; but this proposal found no support overseas. Even New Zealand decided in favor of a separate navy. In August, 1914, only one dominion naval unit, that of Australia, had been completed. It had been understood that all naval establishments belonging to colonies and dominions would in case of war pass under the supreme jurisdiction of the British admiralty; hence the British empire entered the war with unity of naval command.

The program for imperial military defense was worked out along lines entirely different from the naval program. At home Britain refused to adopt compulsory military service in time of peace, though this was urged by eminent military authorities headed by the renowned Field Marshal Lord Roberts. Instead the small standing army was constituted as an expeditionary force which could be sent overseas at short notice. At the universities and other great schools arrangements were made for training reserve officers, and a volunteer "territorial" army was organized for home defense. The dominions were as opposed to anything savoring of militarism as was England; besides, they were all busily engaged with schemes for internal development. Nevertheless, they subscribed to the principle of military training for all able-bodied males. Canada's militia dated from the French period, but only a small portion of it was called up annually for brief periods of training. Australia and New Zealand on the other hand adopted a system of military training for boys, modeled after the citizen army of Switzerland, the training to be completed before the young men had reached the age of twenty-five. In 1912 the Union of South Africa replaced the old commando system with a defense organization based on the principle of compulsory military service.

During these years the imperial government made determined efforts to improve the various systems of military defense. To secure uniformity of training and organization within the empire high British officers were sent to the dominions on tours of inspection, young men from the dominions were given commissions in the British army, and military and naval colleges were established overseas. In 1907 an imperial general staff was created. The work of the Committee of Imperial Defense embraced not only planning for the coordination of military and naval defense for the entire empire but also a certain amount of correlation between foreign policy and preparedness for war. In 1911 at a meeting of this body the foreign secretary, Sir Edward Grey, disclosed the state of the international situation to the dominion prime ministers assembled in London for the imperial conference; and the following year a similar procedure was followed when the mysteries of Britain's foreign relations were revealed to the new Canadian premier, Robert L. Borden.

The attempts to build up British empire defense for war were supplemented with the endeavor to preserve and augment its strength in man power and economic resources. With only slight deviations, the years 1901–1914 were a period of prosperity, one in which Canada in particular made determined efforts to get settlers for her public lands, and one of mass emigration from Europe to the New World. In those years British emigration figures averaged about 200,000 annually. The imperial government desired to send these emigrants to empire lands, and the dominions, especially Australia and New Zealand, were anxious to receive them; the dominions wished to be British countries. The imperial conference of 1907 declared "that it is desirable to encourage British emigrants to proceed to British colonies rather than to foreign countries." This policy, advocated by Chamberlain, was popular in Britain, although apart from a hesitating attempt to settle soldiers in South Africa the imperial government at this time gave no direct aid to its furtherance. But in 1905 local authorities were empowered to aid unemployed persons desirous of going to British colonies, and about forty voluntary organizations were engaged in similar tasks. Prominent among these was the Salvation Army, which in the years 1904–1912 helped 70,000 to emigrate, the majority of them to the dominions. The Canadian government as well as private companies, especially the Canadian Pacific Railway Company, advertised widely the attractions of the Dominion, whose offer of 160 acres of free land was especially alluring to the land-hungry people of Europe. Early in the twentieth century Australia and New Zealand resumed the practice of granting aid to immigrants, discontinued during the depression of the nineties, offering special inducements to those from the British Isles. The result of these efforts was that about three-fourths of the British emigrants went to British countries. These newcomers formed a living link with the mother country. They promoted empire unity in both peace and war.

Early in the twentieth century discussions of British empire unity for defense were often bracketed with discussions of the need for empire economic unity. In the late nineteenth century the self-governing colonies, except New South Wales, had protective tariffs while the United Kingdom clung to free trade. The colonies were released from obligations imposed by British commercial treaties unless they specifically declared their adherence to such treaties, and they received the right to negotiate trade agreements with foreign countries. At the same time a movement started overseas in favor of granting preference to goods of British origin. In 1897 Canada led the way by providing a tariff reduction of 12 1/2 per cent on certain articles imported from the United Kingdom, a preference that was later increased to 33 1/3 per cent. The principle received endorsement by the colonial conference of 1902 and was subsequently put into practice by the South African customs union, New Zealand, and Australia. It was also extended to trade between dominions and British colonies. The new tariff arrangements between Canada and British West Indian colonies were of special significance inasmuch as these regions supplemented each other's needs, instead of being rivals and competitors as was ordinarily the case with the dominions. But the preferential or reciprocal trade agreements did not abrogate the protective tariff systems which had become common in the dominions.

The tariff preferences remained a one-sided affair. The mother country had none to offer as long as she adhered to free trade. The colonial conference of 1902 went on record as favoring United Kingdom preference for empire goods, and a year later Joseph Chamberlain started a vigorous campaign for such a policy. Early in his career as colonial secretary he had made special efforts to discover how British goods fared in competition with articles of foreign origin in British colonies overseas. The results were disquieting — British export seemed to be losing ground. During the war in South Africa a duty of one shilling per quarter was levied by Britain on imported wheat. This was a revenue tariff, but with the war over Chamberlain proposed to retain it for wheat of non-empire origin, thus converting it into a preferential tariff measure. He failed to persuade his colleagues in the government and the duty was repealed.

Chamberlain had become convinced of the need for strengthening the empire by means of a new British fiscal policy. In his judgment, an endeavor should be made to reserve the empire market for British manufactures as far as possible. From such a policy he expected a growing feeling of empire unity, a great increase in intra-imperial trade, and safer and steadier markets for both British and colonial exports. Aided by a number of famous British economists such as Professors William Ashley and W. A. Hewins, Chamberlain in May, 1903, launched his famous campaign for a British preferential tariff. With all the strength and resource at his command, he warned Britain of the dangers lurking in a continued adherence to free trade in a world that had gone protectionist, he showed how Britain was outdistanced industrially by the United States and Germany, and he exhorted his countrymen to act before it was too late. By converting her empire into a customs union Britain might avert calamities and she could go on growing in prosperity and strength. The campaign stirred the British empire. Although the dominions welcomed British preferences, they were cautious in their support of Chamberlain. Laurier, speaking for Canada, the premier dominion, said in substance: we believe in the policy of imperial preference, we have granted preferences to British goods, but as we claim tariff autonomy for ourselves we concede it to you; it is a question for *you* to decide. Britain decided against Chamberlain's plan. The Unionists split on the tariff issue and the Liberals became united as never before since 1880. In hoisting the old free trade banner of Cobden, Liberal orators called attention to the fact that Britain had prospered and was prospering under free trade, that statistics showing percentage increases in the export trade of foreign countries were misleading inasmuch as these had started from scratch whereas Britain had for a long period been a heavy exporter, and that the proposed tariff policy would mean dearer food for British workmen. Labor opposed Chamberlain and old Conservatives like Lord St. Aldwyn denounced his program. Practically all Englishmen favored strengthening the bonds of unity within the empire, but only a minority believed that a preferential tariff would promote this end.

Chamberlain's program of tariff preferences failed to win in the general election of 1906. Shortly afterward he was laid low by a stroke of paralysis, but he continued the fight, loyally aided by his elder son, Austen (later Sir Austen) Chamberlain. Trade flourished, 1908–1914; nevertheless, after 1911 when Andrew Bonar Law was chosen leader of the Unionists, the Conservatives of Britain subscribed to the Chamberlain program.

Despite a certain lukewarmness on the part of sections of the Liberal and Labor parties toward the problems of empire, the British people waxed imperially-minded. Apart from the private organizations which aimed at fostering interest in the overseas possessions, the home government made decided efforts to spread knowledge and promote the empire's economic development. In 1907 the Imperial Institute at Kensington passed under the control of the colonial office. Its well-trained staff of scientists bent their energies to the solution of such problems as the promotion of cotton-growing in Uganda, the cultivation of cocoa on the Gold Coast, rice in northern Nigeria, and tea in Natal, as well as searching for ways and means to combat sleeping sickness, the great scourge of tropical Africa. In April, 1912, a royal commission consisting of representatives from Britain and the dominions was appointed to inquire into the natural resources of the latter, with special emphasis on trade and the production of raw materials and foodstuff. Indicative of imperial interests of that time was this commission's careful investigation in 1912 of imperial immigration and emigration.

The new tendencies in British imperial policy, stressing defense and economic problems, did not obliterate the old interest in promoting self-government overseas. The most significant changes of this nature took place in India and South Africa. The India Councils Act, 1909, enlarged the representation of Indians on the provincial legislative councils, and Indians were appointed to both the council of the governor general and that of the secretary of state. But Lord Morley, who was chiefly responsible for these changes, had no intention of extending the system of responsible government to the provinces of India. Greater courage was shown in dealing with the new South African possessions. At first organized as crown colonies, the Orange River Colony and the Transvaal were offered a plan of representative government by the Balfour ministry. This had not been put into operation when the Liberals under Sir Henry Campbell-Bannerman took office. The new premier, a stout-hearted Gladstonian Liberal, was persuaded to accept the principle that in South Africa Boers were partners with the British. Consequently he courageously bestowed complete self-government to the people lately at war with Britain. This courage and generosity were amply rewarded in 1914 when

Generals Botha and Smuts arrayed themselves without hesitation on the British side in the war with Germany.

The term colony denoted an inferiority of status poorly suited to states like Canada and Australia; accordingly the label "dominion" was affixed to them, to New Zealand, and to the Union of South Africa. The dominions were irked by anything that savored of dictation by the mother country. In complete control of their local affairs, they slowly advanced toward a status of equality with the United Kingdom, gradually acquiring some of the attributes of nationhood. In 1907 it was decided that the periodic conferences between representatives of Britain and the dominions should be held regularly every fourth year and be styled imperial conferences, and that they should consist of prime ministers presided over by the British premier, not as heretofore by the colonial secretary. Furthermore, it was understood that at these gatherings the position of the British prime minister was to be only that of a "first among equals," *primus inter pares.* At the same time the creation of a separate dominion division within the colonial office embodied a recognition of the fact that the dominion status differed from that of a self-governing colony. Separate naval and military establishments under the direction of dominion officers were among the other indications that the dominions were becoming distinct states.

In the nineteenth century the dominions acquired fiscal independence, in the twentieth they demanded diplomatic freedom. Discussions on the latter point arose in connection with the Anglo-French agreement of 1904 concerning the New Hebrides and the British demands for dominion aid in imperial defense. Australians objected to the principle that the control of the New Hebrides could be decided without consultations with them. This question was discussed at the imperial conference of 1907; and it was understood that in the future Britain should consult the dominions if matters of vital interest to them were involved in diplomatic negotiations with foreign countries. Another dominion, Canada, was keenly interested in the Anglo-Japanese alliance for she feared that in the event of a war between the United States and Japan Britain might be obligated to aid the latter. Consequently, Canada's wishes were ascertained in 1911 before the renewal of the alliance, and the new treaty contained a provision guarding against British intervention in case of an American-Japanese war.

Intra-imperial discussions of the defense question brought up the topic of dominion share in the conduct of Britain's foreign relations. Too glibly Laurier said, "If you want our aid call us to your council," for he was absolutely opposed to imperial federation in any form. The best that could be hoped for was that the dominions would be consulted on matters pertaining to foreign policy, but the manner in which this consultation should take place presented obstacles well-nigh insuperable. Suggestions that one member of each dominion government should reside in London for the purpose of discussing foreign affairs or that the high commissioners of the dominions should be used for this purpose were ruled out as impracticable. Makeshifts were resorted to such as Grey's speech to the dominion premiers in 1911 and the disclosures made to Robert L. Borden in 1912. Foreign affairs continued to be handled by the imperial government exclusively, and in 1914 it was generally conceded that the dominions were at war when Britain was at war, although this did not commit them to active participation in the conflict.

Though the possibility of dominion neutrality in an imperial war was considered so remote as to be practically unthinkable, many Englishmen felt concern over what they considered evidence of a loosening of imperial ties. Efforts at creating a customs union failed; more and more the dominions were approaching nationhood, grumbling even over the position of the judicial committee of the privy council as a supreme court because the judicial appeals detracted from their dignity as autonomous states. Therefore numerous attempts were made to check the tendencies toward disintegration within the empire, and various types of intra-imperial contacts were established. Organizations like the Daughters of the Empire, the Victoria League, and the Over-Seas Club emphasized the sentimental bonds of British unity. Indirectly, imperial press conferences and the imperial chamber of commerce served the same purpose. The Rhodes Trust, established by the famous millionaire-imperialist, Cecil Rhodes, provided scholarships at Oxford for the purpose of exposing superior young men from British dominions and colonies, the United States, and Germany, to the amenities of England, English intellectual life, and English culture. The Royal Colonial Institute continued its work of spreading knowledge of the British empire, its problems, and its peoples; it worked quietly, unobtrusively, and perhaps not very effectively for empire unity. In the judgment of several of the men who early in the century had been associated with Lord Milner in South Africa, new efforts were required and therefore in 1910 they launched a quarterly, *The Round Table,* devoted exclusively to imperial affairs. The aim of the founders appears to have been the promotion of imperial consolidation in some form, but their immediate objective was to spread knowledge of imperial economic, social, political, and constitutional issues.

As the day of the fatal conflict with Germany drew near, the imperial policy of the British government embraced not only efforts to mobilize the entire empire for war and develop all its resources but also to conciliate public opinion in the dominions and colonies by grants of political concessions and material aid, by increased emphasis upon the fact that the mother country stood ready and willing to serve and guide the overseas communities. Improved communications and a general growth in wealth promoted travel within the empire. Social and intellectual contacts became more numerous; the union of hearts was furthered. In August, 1914, the fondest hopes of official and unofficial empire-builders were realized, for the great crisis found the British empire united as never before. The British nations beyond the sea were determined to stand by the mother country irrespective of cost.

Though warned repeatedly that a crisis was pending, its rapid development in the first days of August, 1914, came as a shock and surprise to the overseas empire. In the previous year conferences in London, it was believed, had adjusted Balkan problems, and early in 1914 Lloyd George had spoken optimistically of the outlook in foreign affairs; hence the news of the assassination on June 28 of the heir to the Austrian throne (the Archduke Francis Ferdinand) was at first considered just another addition to the long list of tragedies in the annals of the Habsburgs. However, with the recession of the hope of preserving peace in Europe, the dominions informed the home government of their readiness to send aid in case of war, an aid that ultimately surpassed expectations. The reasons for this attitude were many and complex. True, when Britain was at war the empire was at war, but this did not compel the dominions to become active participants. Furthermore, overseas "isolationism" was strong and all the dominions were busily engaged with domestic problems, fundamentally un-warlike. Even so, the resentment at the actions of the aggressor powers, Austria and Germany, was immediate and strong. Both began the war by attacking small states, Serbia and Belgium, the latter an entirely innocent bystander who suffered simply because her territory supplied the most convenient highroad for the German assault on France. In 1914 a belief in law and fundamental rights was widespread and deeply rooted in the consciousness of the British nations; moreover, they too were small states whose existence was imperiled by the doctrine that "might makes right." Economically all of them benefited by their connections with Britain, politically their position was satisfactory, and the majority or near majority of the population in all of them was sentimentally strongly attached to Britain. A defeat of Britain meant dominion loss of the feeling of security, and injury to pride, prestige, and pocketbook. The stake of the dominions in the outcome was considerable; their war contributions were great.

At the beginning of the war the overseas empire was exposed to the risk of attacks on ports and shipping from German cruisers at large on the high seas, the strongest force being the squadron in the Far East stationed at Kiao-chau. Leaving its base shortly after Japan entered the war, this squadron in the Pacific spread nervousness far and wide from Vancouver to Auckland, Sydney, and Singapore. The feeling of apprehension was heightened when the news came that on November 1, 1914, the Germans under Admiral von Spee had met and destroyed a weaker British fleet unit under Admiral Cradock at Coronel off the coast of Chile. Cradock and 1600 men perished. If, as was highly probable, the fast German ships entered the Atlantic they might inflict incalculable damage. Enter they did, but at the Falkland Islands on a bright sunny day in December, 1914, they encountered a strong British squadron under Admiral Sturdee. It was Coronel in the reverse; von Spee shared Cradock's fate. Meanwhile the cruiser *Emden,* most destructive of commerce raiders and listing among her exploits a bombardment of Madras, had on November 10 been defeated and chased ashore by the Australian cruiser *Sydney* at the Cocos Islands in the Indian Ocean. By 1915 the danger to the empire from German naval operations, except those of the submarines, had vanished. Thereafter the scene of naval action was limited to European waters.

Among the dominions, South Africa alone was imperiled by the action of German land forces, and here largely because a considerable number of Boers harbored resentment against Britain. A rebellion broke out, but thanks to prompt and energetic action taken by an old enemy of Britain, General Louis Botha, now prime minister of the Union of South Africa, it was quickly suppressed and German Southwest Africa captured. Egypt and the Suez Canal were at one time harassed both by the Senussi, tribesmen from the western desert, and by Turkish forces approaching the canal from the east, but neither attack assumed serious proportions. Because of the British control of the sea the dominions had few direct contacts with the Four

Years' War, and their participation in it was largely voluntary. The overseas empire supplied more than 3,000,000 men for war service, of whom one-third came from India. In addition gifts in money and in kind from individuals and organizations, colonies and Indian princes were of substantial benefit to British war efforts.

Compulsion played a minor role in producing help from the lands beyond the sea. Toward the end of the war Canada and New Zealand resorted to conscription, but even in those dominions the number of conscript soldiers was small compared to that of volunteers. That sentimental attachment to the old home was a powerful factor in causing men to enlist is evident from the large number in the early contingents from Canada and Australasia who had been born in Britain. New Zealand, most English of the dominions, sent to the various battlefields a higher proportion of her manhood than did any of the others. Boers and French-Canadians lagged behind their compatriots of British origin in volunteering. French Canada opposed conscription and in Australia the Irish vote and influence were chiefly responsible for its defeat. Sikhs and Gourkhas formed the great majority of Indian volunteers; these men enlisted because they liked soldiering rather than because they loved Britain. As the war dragged on for more than four years, overseas opposition to participation in it became more voluble and took various forms. Non-British dominion statesmen like M. Henri Bourassa of Canada and General Hertzog of South Africa joined with political and economic leftists in denouncing the war as imperialistic, fought in the interest of the ruling classes. War-time restrictions on civil liberties irked some; the limitations on profits, modest though they were, irritated others. Money flowed freely from London to remote parts of the empire, but the few reaped more benefits than did the many; much blame was heaped upon the mother country for the conflict and the way it was conducted. During the war party lines were blurred in Canada, Australia, and New Zealand, coalitions replacing governments based on party; but in South Africa party strife waxed more bitter with Boers discussing the possibility of establishing a republic; and in Egypt and India nationalistic movements grew mightily.

The war changed the British attitude toward concessions to India and Ireland. Various factors contributed to this change. In India the loyalty of Nationalists like Gandhi and Tagore, the generosity of princes, the response to calls for volunteers merited rewards. Nor could the reverse of this picture be ignored. The activity of anti-British agitators spurred on by German and Turkish agents made the Indian situation extremely critical. A study of the failure of the Mesopotamian campaign of 1916, which had been conducted from India, revealed grave defects in the Indian administrative system — the case for a new Indian policy was strong and extremely urgent. A change came in 1917, when at the imperial conference representatives of India took seats side by side with those from the dominions. On August 20 the new secretary of state, E. S. Montagu, announced in the House of Commons that the British government aimed at "the progressive realization of responsible government in India as an integral part of the British Empire" — an announcement taken to mean that at a date not far distant India would acquire dominion status. As preparation for implementing this policy Montagu visited India and prepared jointly with the viceroy, Lord Chelmsford, a great report which formed the basis for the Government of India Act, 1919. This act extended the representative system in both the central and the provincial governments of the country.

Ireland presented problems as perplexing as those of India. Solved they were not, although brave attempts at this were made throughout the war period. The end of the war found the greater part of the island in a state of open revolt and British public opinion gradually crystallizing on the following points: (1) Ireland should be divided; (2) Ireland, exclusive of Ulster, should be given more self-government than was contemplated in the

Home Rule Act of 1912, even to the extent of dominion status; (3) Ulster should remain an integral part of the United Kingdom with representation in the parliament at Westminster. British Conservatives as well as Liberals receded from pre-war positions and were searching for new ones that might prove tenable.

Superficially the war united the empire as never before and enthusiasts for imperial federation thus believed that it greatly promoted their cause. Actually the reverse was true. The war hastened the evolution of equality of status and brought into existence the British Commonwealth of Nations consisting of the United Kingdom and the dominions.

Attention will be focused first upon the unifying process of the war period. Despite opposition to the war in some quarters, it produced within the British empire unprecedented unity of effort, of management, and of purpose; great exertion was made in a common cause. All naval establishments were under the British admiralty, and the military forces were directed from the imperial center. Nor was this all. The British war-time control of finance and supplies led to the imperial government's purchases, at fixed prices, of the entire stock of essential materials produced in the dominions. In 1917 the dominion premiers plus the British war cabinet formed the imperial war cabinet, which presumably had complete direction of the empire's war policy. When the imperial conference of 1917 passed a resolution favoring the convening of a special conference after the war for the purpose of discussing constitutional changes within the empire, old-style imperialists considered this a first step toward imperial consolidation. It was expected that the unity of hearts in the world conflict would prove permanent and lead to unity of action in meeting peace-time problems.

But the hope of a constitutional consolidation of Britain and the dominions proved visionary, for inexorable facts produced an evolution in the opposite direction. Nor is this surprising. Each dominion individually decided to aid the mother country during the war; her naval and military forces were combined, not amalgamated, with those of Britain. Each had a separate army which, except in the case of Newfoundland, was supplied and maintained by the dominion. Deeds of valor, victories won by Canadians, Australians, or New Zealanders were extolled at home, caused the hearts of their friends and relatives to swell with pride. The victory of an Australian cruiser, the *Sydney,* over the *Emden,* the heroism shown by the Anzacs at Gallipoli, by the Canadians at Ypres all contributed toward the growth of a spirit of nationalism within those dominions. Fighting side by side with British Tommies, associating with them behind the lines, visiting the old homeland revealed to dominion soldiers differences unsuspected by men whose knowledge of Britain had come from tales told by parents and grandparents who idealized her. Blunders at Gallipoli, in Mesopotamia, and elsewhere destroyed illusions regarding the superiority of British leadership; dominion soldiers and statesmen felt themselves to be the equals of those of Britain. As the war continued and with all immediate danger to themselves gone, the dominions began to think that they were fighting only Britain's battles, rendering services that merited rewards. With war contributions equaling those of sovereign states like Belgium, Portugal, and Serbia, the British dominions demanded that they should participate on terms of equality with those states in arranging the terms of peace. This claim was advanced by Sir Robert L. Borden of Canada, seconded by other dominion statesmen, and granted by Britain.

By 1919 that part of the British empire which included the United Kingdom and the dominions had become the British Commonwealth of Nations — an association of equals. The dominions had their own delegations at the peace conference and in it dominion statesmen like Borden of Canada, Hughes of Australia, and Smuts of South Africa held important posts and exercised considerable influence. Hughes, though British to the core, was no respecter of persons, had no hesitancy in battling for the rights of Australia even though his views might be displeasing to the British premier, David Lloyd George, or to President

Wilson. General Jan Smuts, ex-member of the British war cabinet and for two years past the British empire's handyman, had a large share in drafting the Covenant of the League of Nations. In the League the dominions and India were given representation in the assembly and were eligible for election to non-permanent seats on the council on a basis of equality with independent states. Moreover, Australia, New Zealand, and South Africa were given mandates over former German colonies. In 1919 the complete diplomatic independence of the dominions came appreciably nearer when Canada was granted permission to appoint her own minister to the United States.

Postponing till later the further discussion of the growth of equality of status *de jure,* we shall now focus our attention upon British imperial policy at the peace conference and on imperial problems of the years 1919–1939, an epoch during which men toiled in the shadow of one war just finished and another soon to come.

While the Four Years' War lasted, security was extolled as its ultimate aim — a prize worthy of heroic effort and sacrifice. This desideratum gave meaning to the slogans "A war to end war," "A war to save democracy." When firing ceased on November 11, 1918, new complications arose. How was security to be obtained and made lasting? By aggrandizement, said some; by faithful adherence to the war-time pledge, "No annexations, no punitive indemnities," and the establishment of a new world order, replied others. During the war imperialists bemoaned the British failure in the Victorian era to seize land in Africa and Oceania, the neglect to block German imperial expansion. The war saddled Britain with an enormous debt; hence one school of thought held that political and economic security could be obtained only by expanding the imperial boundaries. The final solution would have done credit to a Solomon. Lands outside Europe taken from Germany and Turkey were placed under the League of Nations and assigned as mandates to some of the victors. The British countries received the lion's share; and since few people understood the degree of independence enjoyed by Australia, New Zealand, and South Africa the areas assigned to them were generally believed held by Britain. Similarly, the representation accorded the dominions in the League of Nations led to Britain's being accused of a desire to dominate that organization, which was described as camouflage for British hegemony over the world. Support for the charge that Britain was still imperialistic in the old manner was adduced from the nature of the Anglo-Persian treaty of 1919, and her reluctance to grant Egyptian and Indian demands for freedom.

In the early twenties hope ran high that security might be obtained through the League and by multilateral treaties outlawing war. Negotiations for disarmament were conducted under League auspices; the pacts bearing the names of Locarno and Kellogg or Paris were expected to usher in an era when sweet reasonableness would guide relations between nations. In Britain the generation that had fought the Four Years' War suffered from extreme war-weariness; the succeeding one was bitterly opposed to war largely from a sense of futility, a belief that nothing was worth fighting for. This combination of skepticism and inertia was partly a reaction to the emotional strain of the war years and partly the effect of the prevailing unemployment. Busy with domestic problems, the people of Britain as well as of the dominions refused to consider the need for defense programs. Indeed, during the twenties Germany appeared to be prostrate and the Russian talk of world revolution faded. Even the Nazi revolution failed to rouse the British peoples. Hitler was regarded by some as a mountebank and by others as a bulwark against Bolshevism; they were willing to accept his professions of peaceful intentions without a closer examination of German economic, industrial, and military rearmament. Britons failed to gauge the strength of the revenge motive in the minds of the Germans and believed that the Italians had buried their resentment over not sharing in the control of ex-German and ex-Turkish territories. The Anglo-French alliance was considered to safeguard Britain in Europe, and treaties with Mohammedan states were expected to protect her interests in the Middle East and her route to India. Under these circumstances the Singapore naval base was the only great defensive work undertaken by the British empire in the twenties. Dominion navies fell into decay, the Australians even abandoning compulsory military training.

The Italo-Ethiopian war and the formation of the German-Italian alliance in 1936 jolted British complacency. The former was alarming to the dominions because it demonstrated the inability of the League to protect a weak member from aggression. Moreover, early in 1936 an Anglo-Italian war seemed within the range of possibilities, and in 1937 Anglo-Japanese friction in the orient raised the specter of war in that quarter. Australia and New Zealand were particularly interested in these developments, the former because a loss of British control of the Mediterranean would affect her trade and shipping. The prospects of attacks by Japan aroused both; Australia had two 10,000-ton cruisers, two smaller ones, four destroyers, and some lesser vessels; New Zealand had two cruisers on loan from the British navy — forces which, of course, could not do much against the naval strength of Nippon.

The imperial conference of 1923 devoted much attention to imperial defense, especially to the new problems arising because of the development of air power. In general, agreement was reached on the pre-war basis that local defense was a primary duty of each member of the British Commonwealth, but that the protection of lines of communication including air bases demanded cooperation. The system of exchanging officers was continued; the opening of an Imperial Defence College in 1927 facilitated uniformity of training. In 1937 Britain and the dominions, however, formed less of a union for defense than they had in 1914 since the latter's status of equality with Britain enabled them to remain neutral in an imperial war. That Britain must protect the dominions was accepted, but not the reverse. Despite the Simonstown agreement whereby South Africa provided the land defense of this important naval base, the Union might choose not to fight; and in 1938 a new Anglo-Irish agreement cancelled the right, under the treaty of 1921, of British warships to use certain Irish harbors. After the opening of the Sino-Japanese conflict in 1937, Australia began seriously to discuss plans for improving her defenses; in the following year other dominions did likewise. The tempo quickened after the Munich crisis in September, 1938, although preparations did not really get under way until the German occupation of Prague, in March, 1939, called to mind the old sinister slogan, "Might makes right." Faced with the possibility of a war between Britain and Hitler's Germany the small nations of the British Commonwealth began to speed work for rearmament. Realizing the importance of air power they paid special attention to this arm. In 1938 the personnel of the Australian air force numbered more than 2000 men as against a peace-time army strength of 2300; the Canadian air force had a permanent personnel of 1730 and a non-permanent one of 1062 men and the navy had only 77 officers and 1344 men; situations in New Zealand and South Africa were comparable.

While the interest in imperial defense languished, considerable attention was bestowed upon empire development. At home the old conception of the empire as an estate revived; faced with stagnation in trade and heavy unemployment, empire "planners" devoted a great deal of thought to the possibility of fighting depression by means of intra-imperial cooperation. Efforts along this line fell into three main categories: (1) scientific study of imperial resources, (2) imperial migration, and (3) imperial trade. The first and the third dealt with the empire as a whole, while the second was limited to the dominions since the dependencies and India did not attract emigrants from the United Kingdom.

Reckless exploitation of outlying lands has no place in modern British imperial policy. It has been supplanted by concern for the welfare of all portions of the empire, and planning for the purpose of improving the social and economic well-being of the peoples therein. For this reason scientific inquiries into the problems and needs of the dominions and colonies in the new age occupied a role of increasing importance. Imperial institutes of entomology and mycology were established to combat insect pests and fungus diseases of plants; an Imperial College of Tropical Agriculture was founded at Trinidad in 1919; a Colonial Advisory Council of Agriculture and Animal Health was established in 1929; and in that year was also organized the Imperial Advisory Bureau with an executive council to administer and act as a clearing house for research in eight special fields of agriculture. These and other institutions of a similar nature extended and supplemented the scientific work carried on for the benefit of the empire by the Royal Botanic Gardens at Kew and the Imperial Institute at Kensington. Although they performed experiments and collected data of great value for the progress of pure science, their primary purpose was to apply modern scientific knowledge and equipment in the solution of overseas economic problems. Maintained by Britain, the dominions, and the colonies, these scientific institutions were modern links of empire.

Imperial migration held an important place among the plans for British imperial development. Emigration from Britain practically ceased during the Four Years' War, and in the post-war era the United Kingdom faced a serious problem of unemployment. Crude statistical studies of the populations of the dominions seemed to show that they had room and room to spare for British jobless. During the war it had been foreseen that peace would bring the difficult task of reabsorbing a vast number of discharged soldiers and sailors into the nation's economic life. The Dominions Royal Commission of 1912, in its final report in 1918, devoted much attention to this problem and recommended the establishment of a central body with full control over emigration from the British Isles. This led to the creation of an overseas settlement office as a branch of the colonial office.

On initiative taken by the Royal Colonial Institute a special study was made of the opportunities for settling ex-service men overseas. Out of these efforts grew a scheme whereby the imperial government provided free passage, third class, to ex-service men and their families who were assured of employment overseas, or of land, under plans set up by overseas governments. By the end of 1922, when the privilege of free passage was abandoned, a total of 86,027 men, women, and children had received this assistance in emigrating from the British Isles to a dominion or colony. The scheme was not intended to introduce a system of aided emigration; it was simply a device to help people with special claims upon the bounty of the government.

Meanwhile unemployment had become so extensive as to call for drastic remedies. The one which seemed readiest to hand was emigration – but whither? The dominions refused to serve as dumping grounds for the industrial proletariat of Britain. After protracted conferences between the secretary of state for the colonies, Lord Milner, and dominion representatives and discussions by the imperial conference of 1921, a solution was found, later to be embodied in the Empire Settlement Act, 1922. It was none other than planned emigration and the founding of settlements overseas on a scale undreamed of by E. G. Wakefield and his friends ninety years earlier. The imperial government was to defray not more than one-half of the expenses connected with the selection, training (if necessary), transportation, and establishment in their proper place of emigrants suitable for the particular needs of a dominion or colony. The total cost to Britain was not to exceed £3,000,000 annually. Agreements under this act might be negotiated between the imperial government and either one or more local governments or private organizations.

The Commonwealth and state governments of Australia were first in the field with plans for taking advantage of the bounties provided by the aided empire migration. Among the most ambitious of the several agreements negotiated was one whereby

Western Australia undertook to find a place for 75,000 settlers from the British Isles within a period of three years, and another under the terms of which the Commonwealth proposed to care for 450,000 British immigrants in ten years. Although these agreements could not be fulfilled, in 1926 the number of assisted emigrants reached 65,523, with a total of 302,000 for the years 1922–1929, a figure not far short of the total for the forty years during which the Colonial Land and Emigration Commission of the Victorian era helped send emigrants from the United Kingdom to British colonies overseas.

With the opening of the thirties the dominions had their own unemployment problems and like Britain faced a situation in which the urban population increased at the expense of the rural. Land was being abandoned, especially in Australia; the apparent over-production of agricultural produce caused the government of the United States to pay farmers to leave their land fallow. Under these circumstances, the Empire Settlement Act became practically a dead letter. Moreover, population experts worried about the falling birth rate in the United Kingdom. Britain needed her men at home; the belief grew that other means than emigration must be found to cure unemployment.

Trade depression was, of course, recognized as a cause of unemployment, and trade revival was therefore a main objective of efforts by governments as well as by private enterprise. The task proved difficult; indeed, the obstacles were insuperable in a world devastated and impoverished by war, revolution, and the destruction of empires. The desperate economic situation in Europe was made worse by repudiations of national debts and currency inflation. In this new and confused world British statesmen and financiers sought by orthodox methods to find a way to economic recovery. Laborites and Liberals hesitated to abandon free trade; the Conservatives, on the other hand, were willing to take the plunge. During the twenties nothing decisive was done on this issue. American credit promised to revive trade, but Britain was handicapped by industrial unrest, which culminated in the general strike of May, 1926, and the coal strike the same year which for upward of eight months had a paralyzing effect upon industry and trade. Moreover, in 1925 the British government decided to return to the gold standard; this meant a dear pound and comparatively high costs for British manufactures. However, the world generally enjoyed a certain amount of prosperity until the end of 1929 when the American stock market broke and New York bankers began to collect instead of just handing out money and credit. Confusion prevailed; and in September, 1931, Britain abandoned the gold standard – an unprecedented act in times of peace. The British tariff revisionists then had their innings; after a lapse of eighty-five years tariff preference became a part of British imperial policy. In the election of October, 1931, the National government asked for a "doctor's mandate," for permission to use any remedy including tariffs that might cure the economic maladies. Receiving a majority of 502, it immediately passed the Abnormal Importations Bill which made possible a customs duty of 50 per cent ad valorem on articles suspected of being "dumped" on Britain. This provisional measure was followed in March, 1932, by an Import Duties Act which established protection for British goods as against foreign but continued the free import of goods of empire origin.

Supplementary to this system, preferential tariffs in favor of British goods were established in the British dependencies not prevented from so doing by the Berlin Act of 1884–1885 or by regulations governing British mandates. In July, 1932, an imperial economic conference met at Ottawa. After prolonged discussions a series of agreements were reached whereby Britain promised to extend her preferences to empire goods by raising existing duties on foreign goods and imposing duties on some articles still on the free list. Moreover, by quantitative regulations of import, known as the quota system, dominions were assured of a fixed share of the British market. The dominions on their part agreed to maintain or increase their preferences on British goods, but these were still subject to relatively high duties in the dominion markets. Hopes for an economic union of the British empire were dashed. The dominions were the great beneficiaries under the new system; Britain footed the bill. In a hundred years the relations between Britain and the daughter nations had been reversed; she no longer issued orders, she received them. This was a natural outcome of a constitutional evolution whereby Britain and the dominions had been transformed into a league of British nations.

The old policy of granting political autonomy to dependencies was applied in the period between the Four Years' War and the Nazi War. Responsible government was established in Malta in 1921, and in Southern Rhodesia in 1923, but in Malta growing disorders, allegedly due to Italian intrigues, caused suspensions and finally the abrogation of the new constitution. Representative government was granted Southwest Africa, a mandate under the Union of South Africa, in 1925; and the following year Kenya, Tanganyika, and Zanzibar received legislative councils containing a considerable number of unofficial or elected members. Tropical Africa came in for much attention in the twenties. In Kenya the white minority clamored for permission to control the colony, and several plans were discussed for uniting Kenya, Nyasaland, Tanganyika, and Uganda. Out of these discussions arose, in 1926, the East Africa Governors' Conference, participated in by the chief executives of Kenya, Tanganyika, and Uganda, with provisions for participation by those of Nyasaland, Northern Rhodesia, and Zanzibar. The object of the conference was to secure cooperation and coordination in all efforts to solve the problems of this region. However, these changes were all relatively insignificant compared with those affecting the dominions.

As already indicated, the dominions had their own representatives at the Paris peace conference and in the assembly of the League of Nations; and this principle was followed in the selection of delegates to the Washington conference of 1921 and to other international gatherings. In 1923 Canada negotiated a treaty with the United States for the regulation of the halibut fishery in the Pacific without utilizing the services of the British ambassador in Washington, nor was the treaty submitted to the British government for ratification. It was a startling innovation, one discussed at considerable length by the imperial conference of 1923. This body agreed that in the future the procedure followed by Canada in negotiating the halibut treaty should be followed if the subject for negotiation concerned only one dominion, but if it touched others including Britain, these should participate; in any case, all members of the British Commonwealth should be informed of it.

By 1923 the Irish Free State had joined the dominions. The Anglo-Irish Treaty of 1921 assured the new member of the British Commonwealth a status equal to that of Canada, and since a large party in the Free State demanded full independence this dominion was sure to be in the van among those pressing for equality of status. In 1924 General Hertzog, an advocate of a republic, replaced General Smuts as prime minister of the Union of South Africa. Consequently, as preparations went forward for the imperial conference of 1926, imperial statesmen realized that two of the dominion premiers — Cosgrave of the Irish Free State and Hertzog of South Africa — must be handled with care lest they raise the banner of independence in their respective states, and that Mackenzie King of Canada was a strong supporter of dominion rights. Among the preliminaries of the conference was the unveiling in France of a memorial to South African soldiers who had fought in the Four Years' War. Hertzog, participating in the ceremonies, was made aware of the community of interest within the British Commonwealth. In addressing the assembled premiers at the opening session, Stanley Baldwin called attention to the establishment the previous year of the secretaryship of state for the dominions. No longer would their affairs be handled by the colonial office with its unpleasant associations of inferiority. Emphasis was laid on the prevailing method of direct communications between the prime minister of Britain and those of the dominions. The British empire represented "unity in diversity," a condition recognized by the new title, the British Commonwealth of Nations. This matter received further attention in the committee of status with Lord Balfour as chairman. Its report, which reveals the deft hand of this master of English diction, contains the following celebrated definition of the position of the dominions and the United Kingdom: "They are autonomous Communities within the British Empire, equal in status, in no way subordinate one to another in any aspect of their domestic or external affairs, though united by a common allegiance to the Crown, and freely associated as members of the British Commonwealth of Nations." The report states further: "Equality of status, so far as Britain and the Dominions are concerned, is thus the root principle governing our Inter-Imperial relations." The report and the proceedings at the imperial conference pleased General Hertzog; on his return to South Africa, he declared himself satisfied with the existing status of his country.

Further study and discussions were needed before equality of status could be established in law. A special committee deliberated at length upon the necessary legislation and reported to the imperial conference of 1930, the substance of this report forming the basis for the Statute of Westminster, 1931. This great act supplied, as nearly as could be, a constitution for the British Commonwealth of Nations. The principle that the law of the dominions cannot be repugnant to English law was formally abrogated. The dominions were empowered to repeal any British act or part thereof which might have become embodied in their laws and "to make laws having extra-territorial operation." The further stipulation that no act passed by the parliament of the United Kingdom should extend to a dominion without its consent apparently put an end to the age-old right of the imperial parliament to legislate for every portion of the British empire. The sole remaining constitutional bond of unity within the British Commonwealth of Nations was the crown. This enhanced the position of the king-emperor; all legislation, the enforcement of justice, the conduct of foreign affairs, etc., continues in his name, but in each dominion he acts only upon the advice of ministers responsible to an elective parliament.

Australia and New Zealand showed little enthusiasm for equality of status and they were exempted from the operation of several sections of the Statute of Westminster until their own parliaments adopted them. On the other hand, South Africa and the Irish Free State made haste to carry the interpretation of equality of status to its farthest limits. The former by an act of 1934 repealed any provision in the South Africa Act of 1909, which forms the constitution for the Union, that might in any way detract from her position "as a sovereign independent state." The Irish Free State strove to go even further, if possible. In 1932 Eamon de Valera replaced William Cosgrave as head of the government of this dominion. De Valera had long been a professed republican, and was recognized by his followers as head of an Irish republic. Shortly after his accession to office he secured parliamentary sanction for a refusal to pay land annuities due Britain under an agreement of 1923. This led to a tariff war lasting five years. Moreover, de Valera denied the validity of the Anglo-Irish Treaty of 1921 and repudiated the constitution based upon this instrument. In quick succession he secured the abolition of the oath of allegiance to the king prescribed for members of the Irish parliament by the 1922 constitution, put an end to appeals from the Free State to the judicial committee of the privy council, and abolished the office of governor general. The constitution of 1937 removed the king as part of the Irish legislature, retaining him solely for external relations, especially those with the British Commonwealth. The active head of the government was to be a president elected for seven years; upon him devolved the duty of appointing the prime minister on nomination by Dail Eireann, or assembly. The name

Eire, or Ireland, replaced the old Irish Free State, thereby emphasizing the unity of the island which de Valera and his followers hoped to achieve in the near future. Special stress was laid on describing Eire as a "sovereign," "independent," and "democratic" state. Although this government was republican in everything but name, the extreme republicans were not satisfied; in 1939 they tried, by bombings in England, to extract further concessions from a British government seemingly bent on appeasement all around.

Equality of status did away with the supremacy of the British parliament over dominion legislation and practically ended dominion appeals to the judicial committee, but the fact that all had a common sovereign caused disputes over whether the crown was one or divisible. Practically this was the question of whether all the dominions were at war when Britain was at war. This was the view of Australia and New Zealand; the contrary opinion was held by Eire and the Union of South Africa, both insisting on their right to remain neutral in a British war. When the test came in September, 1939, the parliament of the Union decided by a rather narrow majority to fight on the side of Britain; Eire chose to remain neutral. Thus arose the paradox that as king of Eire His Majesty George VI remained at peace with Germany while as sovereign of the other sections of the British empire he was at war with the Reich.

Britain's imperial relations have represented less a system than a way of life. Weakness of logic but fertility in devising methods of meeting emergencies has been a leading characteristic of her political thinking. New economic situations compelled a return to mercantilistic policies for trade and tariffs. A unity was established by the new tariff preference and by cooperation in the control of the marketing of goods, the regulation of shipping, and the preservation of the empire's natural resources and the fight against diseases of plants and animals. But all the while the political relations among the various parts of the empire grew more diverse. "Unity in diversity" described the situation in a telling phrase. With all its newness in political thought and conception, the imperial policy of Britain seemed hopelessly archaic to the dictators of Europe. In September, 1939, began the test of Britain and the British system of government.

CHAPTER 29

CANADA AND NEWFOUNDLAND, 1901–1939

THE history of Canada since the death of Queen Victoria divides naturally into three periods: the pre-war years, 1901–1914; the war and post-war era until the retirement of Sir Robert Borden in July, 1920; and the recent period. There are of course overlapping topics, especially in the fields of social and cultural history; nevertheless, each of these epochs has features sufficiently distinct to warrant separate treatment. The Liberals dominated Canadian politics during eleven of the fourteen years of the first period. The Conservatives who came into power in 1911 held it, despite a certain blurring of party lines by Borden's Union government of 1917–1920, until their defeat in the election of December, 1921. Since then Canada's political life has been characterized by the seesaw struggles which seem normal under a two-party system of government. Sir Wilfrid Laurier refused to join the coalition of 1917 and led the Liberals until his death on February 19, 1919. In the following summer William Lyon Mackenzie King was chosen leader of the Liberals and has held that position since then. When Sir Robert Borden resigned, the Conservatives elected Arthur Meighen their leader; he was in turn succeeded by R. B. Bennett in October, 1927. In Canada as elsewhere the Four Years' War changed the current of economic and social life and left difficult legacies for the post-war generation. It seemingly halted the Dominion's progress toward national status. Although cooperation within the empire during the war encouraged advocates of imperial union to think that their goal was within reach, this proved an illusion. Actually the role played by Canada in the war and at the peace negotiations speeded up the evolutionary process which made her an independent state and produced the British Commonwealth of Nations.

Fate, which in 1873 brought the Liberals under Mackenzie into office as a depression settled upon Canada, redressed the balance in 1896. Economic recovery coincided with the return to power of the Liberals under Laurier, the era of prosperity outlasting the ministry by one year. Rising world prices was the biggest single factor in ushering in and maintaining this prosperity; for Canada it was greatly aided also by the Laurier government's policies concerning immigration and internal improvements. Never before had the Dominion made such systematic efforts to attract new settlers from Europe and the United States. The government vied with steamship and railroad companies in calling attention to the free land, the excellent climate, and the other physical and social advantages of western Canada. At the turn of the century a rate war in the passenger service of the North Atlantic aided immigration from Europe; and the coming of age of sons of the pioneers in the prairie states of the United States produced an exodus thence to Canada.

The immigration figures for 1901 stood at 49,542, of whom 11,810 came from the United Kingdom; those for 1912, the highest in the history of Canada, were 150,542 from the United Kingdom, 402,432 from all countries. Of the contributions to this stream, that from the United States was the most significant. From less than 2500 in 1897 the number of immigrants rose to nearly 60,000 in 1907 and 125,000 in 1911. While many of them were farmers' sons with little capital but much knowledge of and skill in the type of farming suitable for northwestern Canada, a goodly number were older farmers who sold their farms in

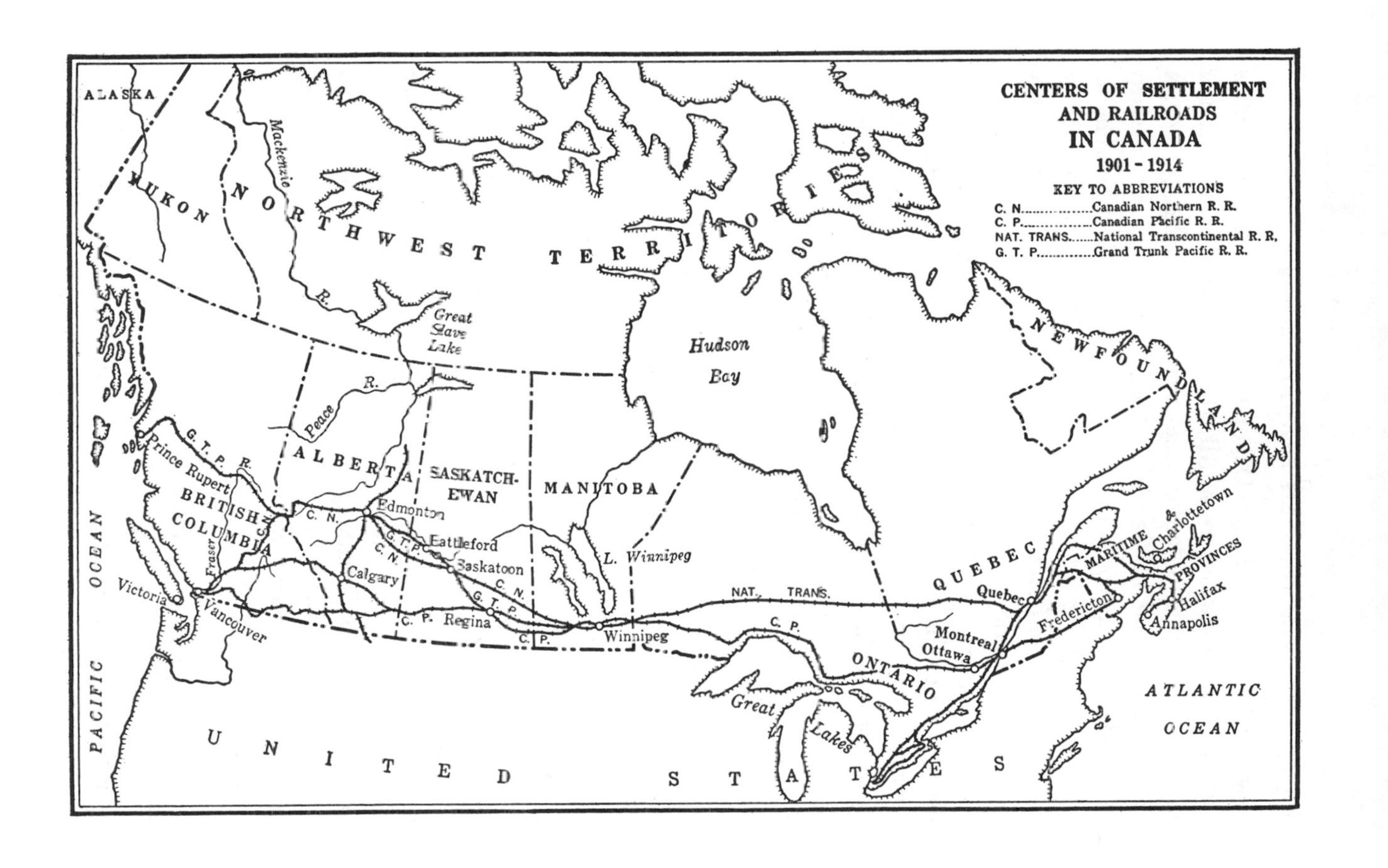
CENTERS OF SETTLEMENT AND RAILROADS IN CANADA 1901 - 1914
KEY TO ABBREVIATIONS
C. N. .... Canadian Northern R. R.
C. P. .... Canadian Pacific R. R.
NAT. TRANS. ...... National Transcontinental R. R.
G. T. P. .... Grand Trunk Pacific R. R.
ALASKA
YUKON
NORTHWEST TERRITORIES
Mackenzie R.
Great Slave Lake
Peace R.
Hudson Bay
NEWFOUNDLAND
ALBERTA
SASKATCH-EWAN
MANITOBA
L. Winnipeg
BRITISH COLUMBIA
Prince Rupert
G. T. P. R.
Fraser
Edmonton
Battleford
Saskatoon
Calgary
Regina
Winnipeg
Victoria
Vancouver
C. N.
G. T. P.
C. P.
NAT. TRANS.
QUEBEC
Quebec
Montreal
Ottawa
ONTARIO
Fredericton
MARITIME PROVINCES
Charlottetown
Halifax
Annapolis
Great Lakes
PACIFIC OCEAN
ATLANTIC OCEAN
UNITED STATES

Iowa, Minnesota, and the Dakotas, moved with their entire family into Saskatchewan or Alberta, and for the price of the land they had sold obtained free and by purchase four to six times that amount of Canadian land. Moreover, the married sons and daughters could establish their independent households fairly close to the parental roof. It was simply a continuance of the old American frontier movement in a region where there was no language barrier and the political boundary was no hindrance. The newcomers were welcomed with open arms, and in the early years of the present century they were full of enthusiasm over the economic opportunities and the excellent law enforcement north of the international line. Alberta and Saskatchewan, which became separate provinces in 1905, registered a remarkable growth in population during the decade 1901–1911; that of the former rose from 73,022 to 374,295, and of the latter from 91,279 to 492,432. Manitoba and British Columbia also showed unusually large increases — from 255,211 to 461,394 and from 178,657 to 392,480 respectively. Although emigration continued from eastern Canada into the United States, the loss was more than offset by the movement in the opposite direction farther west and the immigration from Europe. The Dominion census of 1901 showed a population of 5,371,315; that of 1911 recorded 7,204,838. The extent to which the west dominated in Canada's progress during the first decade of the present century is revealed even more graphically when economic statistics are used as the basis for comparison. The area of occupied farm land increased in Saskatchewan by 24,809,551 acres or 647.18 per cent, and in Alberta by 15,016,269 acres, equivalent to 548.91 per cent; the increases for the same period in the eastern provinces ranged from 0.65 of one per cent in Prince Edward Island to 8.09 per cent in Quebec. When the value of all farm property is considered, the rise in Alberta was 1319.71 and in Saskatchewan 1773.14 per cent. These figures were, of course, affected by the general rise in prices and the speculation in farm land in the decade 1901–1911.

The farms of western Canada were much larger than those of the east, the average size being for Alberta 288.66, for Saskatchewan 297.2, and for Prince Edward Island 83.68 acres. The size of farms increased less than one per cent in Alberta and 15.59 per cent in Saskatchewan, while in Manitoba it decreased 4.01 per cent. The big industry of the west was wheat-growing; in 1910 the prairie provinces — Alberta, Manitoba, and Saskatchewan — produced 110,166,704 of the 132,077,547 bushels of wheat grown in Canada. Saskatchewan forged far ahead of Ontario in wheat-growing, although in value of all field crops combined the older province led the younger by a wide margin. Among the consequences of the one-crop farming in the west were a need for urban distributing centers and a sparse rural population. Early in the twentieth century western cities like Calgary and Edmonton had booms of the type generally associated with mining towns south of the international boundary.

The high annual average of rainfall which followed the drought period of the nineties was an important factor in the settling of western Canada; yet without the railroads and easy credit the development recorded above could not have taken place on such an unprecedented scale. In the prosperous years at the turn of the century the Canadian Pacific Railway Company built branch lines, extended its steamship services both on the ocean and on inland waterways, and erected hotels. Since the company reported profit — the dividends rising from 2 per cent in 1896 to 10 per cent for each of the years 1912 and 1913 — it found no difficulty in enlarging its working capital by new stock issues and by borrowing. Some aid was secured from provincial sources, particularly from British Columbia; but in the main the C.P.R. stood on its own feet, benefiting from local monopolies and from being first in western Canada.

Prospect of profit brought rivals. In Manitoba the Canadian Northern Railway system was built up by combining several small local lines. Branching out from Winnipeg, this system in 1901 secured connections with United States lines by leasing the

Canadian section of the Northern Pacific; Port Arthur on Lake Superior provided an outlet for western wheat; and extensions east and west provided outlets at Quebec and at Vancouver via Edmonton. In addition to generous provincial and Dominion subsidies, the Dominion government took over $40,000,000 of common stock of the C.N.R. and guaranteed $45,000,000 of its bonds. In the west this company served a large area to the north of the territory of the Canadian Pacific Railway Company.

Generous as the Laurier government was to the Canadian Northern, it was even more so to the Grand Trunk. Early in the century this old company of eastern Canada negotiated with the Canadian Northern for joint services in the west. When these negotiations broke down, the Dominion government encouraged the organization of the Grand Trunk Pacific Railway Company as a subsidiary of the old Grand Trunk. By an agreement of 1903 the Dominion undertook to build the National Transcontinental from Winnipeg eastward, through the northern sections of Ontario and Quebec, to the Atlantic via the cities of Quebec and Moncton, New Brunswick. This new line was to be operated under lease by the Grand Trunk Pacific. The western section from Winnipeg to Prince Rupert was to be built by the Grand Trunk Pacific, the Dominion guaranteeing 75 per cent of the bonds issued to cover the cost of construction and limiting the company to $13,000 per mile on the prairies but no fixed limit in the mountains. Since this ambitious program of railroad-building was launched in a period of rising prices and wages, estimates of costs were exceeded by huge sums — for the Transcontinental, by nearly $100,000,000. Although it was known that the railroad to Prince Rupert would traverse large stretches of country without settlements, hope ran high that Prince Rupert with its spacious harbor might rival Vancouver and Seattle as a Pacific port. The railroad mileage of Canada rose from 18,693 in 1901 to 30,661 in 1913. Much of this increase was due to the railroad policy of the Laurier government which in the end proved a cause of and a prelude to the Dominion's taking over two of the country's three big railroad systems.

The financing of the new ventures in railroad and business expansion was achieved to a considerable extent by bond issues which for the years 1910–1913 totaled more than $1,144,000,000. British money developed western Canada; however, the United States soon showed a tendency to invest in Canadian securities. In 1910, 81.50 per cent of the new Canadian bonds were taken in Great Britain as against 1.50 per cent for the United States; the percentages for 1913 were respectively 74.24 and 13.56. Despite the sudden growth of American investments in Canada, New York had not yet replaced London as the center for the Dominion's foreign borrowing. Her debt to Britain in 1914 has been estimated at $3,000,000,000. The foreign trade of Canada trebled between 1900 and 1914, with imports outdistancing exports. In the last year of the nineteenth century she had a favorable trade balance of $10,000,000, but for the year ending in March, 1914, imports exceeded exports by $164,000,000. By this time, however, the tide of prosperity had receded. A fall in wheat prices in 1912 precipitated financial liquidations which might have reached alarming proportions but for the outbreak of the Four Years' War in August, 1914.

Meanwhile Alberta and Saskatchewan had in 1905 been carved out of the North West Territories and organized as provinces. In an effort to avoid the dispute that had proved so troublesome in Manitoba, denominational schools were recognized as eligible for state aid. The Dominion retained control over the public land and the mineral resources and agreed to make cash contributions to the new provinces. By the Extension of the Boundaries Act of 1912, the Dominion detached 662,079 square miles from the northern territories, of which 349,108 were added to Quebec, 145,371 to Ontario, and 167,600 to Manitoba. The last secured in addition an increase in the federal subsidy from $840,000 in 1911 to $1,350,000 in 1912. British Columbia, which experienced much political confusion culminating in 1900 in the dismissal of the lieutenant-governor, Thomas R. McInnes, and struggled with unbalanced budgets for a number of years, in 1906 obtained a larger annual subsidy from the federal government. This was of less importance than the new development and exploitation of her fisheries, mines, forests, and agricultural resources. Seven fat years, 1905–1912, enabled the province to reduce its debt from $12,500,000 to less than $8,000,000 and to accumulate a surplus of more than $11,000,000. The greater part of this surplus had been devoured by two lean years when the war intervened.

During the colonial conference of 1897 Laurier delighted English audiences by sonorous phrases about the might and majesty of the British empire. He gave concrete evidence of his imperial sentiments by increasing the preference on goods of British origin to 33 1/3 per cent and extending it to the British West Indies, the Straits Settlements, India, Ceylon, and New South Wales. In 1903 Canada concluded a preferential tariff arrangement with New Zealand. The Dominion aided Britain with about 8000 men in the South African war and assumed permanently the duty of garrisoning Halifax and Esquimalt. But Laurier turned a deaf ear to appeals for direct Canadian contributions to imperial defense, always insisting that Canada should have her own navy. Steps in that direction were delayed until 1910 when two cruisers, the *Niobe* and the *Rainbow*, were bought from Britain and a Naval Service Act was passed. A link between the militia of Canada and the British army was broken in 1904 when an imperial officer, Lord Dundonald, was dismissed from the supreme command of the Dominion's military forces and a Canadian appointed in his place. New military contacts were provided by the adoption of British methods of training and organization, the sending of young Canadians to England for their military education, and a system of imperial inspection of the Canadian militia.

Both at the imperial conferences and in the negotiations dealing with defense, Laurier upheld Canada's autonomy. He refused to support plans for an imperial council; he insisted that no imperial treaty was binding on Canada without her consent and that the Dominion had full power to lay down rules for immigration. Canada was represented in the negotiations for a Boundary Waters Treaty with the United States in 1908–1909; a department of external affairs was created in 1909; and a special provision in the new Anglo-Japanese Alliance Treaty of 1911 safeguarded Canada in case of war between the United States and Japan. The Dominion made use of her fiscal independence by concluding commercial treaties with France, Belgium, the Netherlands, and Italy; by carrying on a tariff war with Germany during 1903–1910; and by negotiating a commercial arrangement with the United States in 1911 which led to the defeat of the Laurier government in the elections that year.

By 1911 Laurier had led the government for a longer continuous period than any other Canadian premier. There had been disagreements over policies within the ministry resulting in the resignation of three powerful members — Israel Tarte in 1902, A. G. Blair in 1903, and Clifford Sifton in 1905. The support given Britain in the South African war caused the brilliant and energetic Henri Bourassa to break with Laurier and organize a Canadian Nationalist party, consisting mainly of French-Canadians, which attacked him in Quebec on the charge of pro-British sympathies. On the other hand, the leader of the Conservatives, Robert (later Sir Robert) Borden, alleged that Laurier failed to appreciate the need for cooperation with Britain in defense.

Thus it came about that Laurier was caught in a pincer, one handle being the French-Canadian nationalism of Quebec, the other the imperialism of Ontario. During the fifteen years of power old friends had been disappointed and young men were growing restive and desirous of a change; the list of government mistakes real or alleged increased each year, its railroad policy in particular being open to attack from various angles; and the reciprocal trade agreement with the United States provided an excellent target. This was especially true after American statesmen, including President Taft and the speaker of the house of representatives, Champ Clark of Missouri, spoke as if the new tariff was but a prelude to commercial and ultimately political union. Against such a destiny for Canada diverse elements — French-Canadians, Orangemen, the United Empire Loyalists Association, Navy Leaguers, Daughters of the Empire, and many others — could combine in a common front. Borden, the opposition leader, lacked the brilliance, personal magnetism, and splendid oratorical gifts of Laurier, but he was honest, dependable, a man of character. Bourassa and his fiery nationalists seemingly preferred him to Laurier, the man of their own blood but unfaithful to their cause. Quebec was no longer solidly Liberal; when the votes were counted in 1911 it was found that the Liberals had poled 36,620 more than in 1908 but that the Conservative gain was 121,063; in the Dominion as a whole the Conservatives topped the Liberals by nearly 45,000. The change in the political complexion of the house of commons was even more decisive. The election of 1908 returned 134 of Laurier's supporters to 87 for Borden, that of 1911 gave Borden 133 and Laurier 88.

Laurier went out, Borden came in. He was in office but not absolutely in power. A bill providing for a cash contribution of $35,000,000 to imperial naval defense passed the house of commons but was defeated in the senate where Laurier's followers still held a majority. Borden visited England in 1912, attended a meeting of the Committee of Imperial Defence, learned of the grave international situation, and was strengthened in his determination to support Britain if and when the storm broke.

The outstanding events in the history of Newfoundland, 1901–1914, were connected with the settlement of the fishery disputes and the establishment of great paper mills at Grand Falls on the Exploits River to supply the Northcliffe press. The old quarrels over the French fishery rights were ended by the Anglo-French convention of 1904 whereby French claims on the west coast of Newfoundland were surrendered in return for territorial compensation in Central Africa and cash payments to cover losses sustained by individuals. No sooner was this settled than the controversies between the fishermen of Newfoundland and those of the United States assumed new aspects. The former tried to prevent the latter from securing bait, using purse-seines, and hiring crews in Newfoundland. When in 1906 the imperial government arranged a compromise whereby purse-seines might be used for the coming season and Newfoundlanders hired by Americans outside the three-mile limit, the colony protested against interference with its internal affairs. The question was discussed at the imperial conference of 1907 and finally submitted to the Hague Tribunal for arbitration. The decision, handed down in 1910, recognized the power of Newfoundland or Britain to fix regulations governing the fisheries, but stated that matters such as the use of purse-seines were to be governed by rules fixed by a body of fishery experts.

With the erection of the great paper mills on the Exploits River in 1905 a new important industry was established in Newfoundland. Coming at a time when the iron mines on Bell Island were being developed, the paper industry helped to lessen the island's dependence upon the fisheries, although these continued as the chief basis for its economic prosperity. In 1901 Newfoundland's export of iron ore was valued at £159,315; by 1913 it had risen to £281,101. During this time the total exports rose from £1,717,804 to £3,016,094 and imports from £1,536,268 to £3,291,431, with Britain's share in the exports, about 22 per cent, remaining constant but her share in the imports growing. The building of branch railroads boosted the mileage from 656 to 821 in the years 1901–1914, so that by the end of this period Newfoundland had sufficient railroads for her reasonable needs and too much for her financial structure. Immigration and emigration practically balanced, each averaging about 10,000 per year; hence the growth in population from 217,037 in 1901 to 238,670 in 1911 represented a natural increase. The

Newfoundlanders continued to be overwhelmingly British. Although at times they chafed under the restrictions which the imperial government imposed upon their freedom to deal with fishermen from France and the United States, nevertheless they were ready to assist Britain with naval defense, and without hesitation they threw in their lot with the empire when war broke out in August, 1914.

The sudden and fatal development of this crisis caught British North America unprepared. For more than a decade Canada had been too deeply engrossed with the task of developing and exploiting the great northwest to pay much heed to warnings of a coming struggle emanating from the British government and propagandist organizations like the Navy League. The reply that a western farmer was reported to have made to an advocate of a strong Canadian navy—"Damn the battleships, it's box cars we want"—pretty well summed up the sentiment of Canada. Consequently in 1914 she had only two old cruisers and a few smaller vessels, and her militia was not trained for modern warfare. In 1907 preparations were made for a central mobilization camp at Valcartier, sixteen miles northwest of Quebec city, and when Sir John French, later the Earl of Ypres, visited Canada in 1910 he made valuable suggestions concerning the organization of an expeditionary force. In 1911 Colonel (later Sir) Sam Hughes succeeded Sir Frederick Borden as minister of militia; under his energetic leadership much was done to improve the training and equipment of the militia and plans were worked out for an expeditionary force to be sent to Europe if the empire were at war.

But such a war did not seem imminent in the spring of 1914. The Canadian parliament prorogued on June 12 had no anticipation of the coming crisis. All Canada was stunned when one of the crack Canadian Pacific steamers, the *Empress of Ireland,* collided and sank in the St. Lawrence with the loss of a thousand lives; the economic depression that had settled upon the west two years earlier worried some; and the multifarious activities called forth by the summer occupied all, when the news came that the heir to the throne of Austria-Hungary, the Archduke Francis Ferdinand, and his consort had been murdered. Apart from the usual sentimental newspaper blurbs, the event aroused neither attention nor apprehension in Canada. It was another of the many tragedies which had befallen the house of Habsburg, a new addition to the long list of European political crimes. Life was running its normal course on July 23 when the Austrian ultimatum to Serbia warned the prime minister of Canada, Sir Robert Borden, as well as the leader of the opposition, Sir Wilfrid Laurier, of a serious crisis. The latter in 1911 and the former in 1912 had been appraised by British statesmen of the dangers that threatened the peace of Europe and the world. Borden hastened to Ottawa, and on August 1 he assured the imperial government of the Dominion's desire to assist the mother country in case war broke out. Shortly afterward Laurier cancelled all engagements, returned to the capital, and promised the government the support of the opposition in a policy of aiding Britain's cause. The issue was simplified by the fact that Germany was the aggressor and had attacked both Britain and France, the homelands of the two great racial groups of Canada. Even Bourassa, who had so strenuously opposed the assistance which Canada gave Britain in the Boer War, in August, 1914, supported the war efforts of the Dominion. When it was decided to send a volunteer expeditionary force to Europe, a united Canada asked her sons to come forward. The response was magnificent; soon more than thirty thousand men were encamped at Valcartier.

The Canadian parliament was summoned for August 18; meanwhile the government proceeded by orders in council and proclamations to put the country on a war footing. In addition to the work connected with the raising, training, and provisioning of an expeditionary force, regulations were issued concerning trade, finance, the treatment of enemy subjects, and other topics relating to the new situation. The war regulations were ratified by parliament in a five-day session, August 18–22; a war credit of $50,000,000 was voted; and the War Measures Act gave the government wide powers to deal with problems which might arise in connection with the emergency. The Canadian legislation, like the British Defence of the Realm Act, made possible, as far as might prove necessary as a war measure, the abrogation of freedom of speech and of the press, the right of habeas corpus, and other cherished liberties.

The history of Canada in the war years, 1914–1918, centers around the aid, principally military, that she rendered and the effects of the war upon her domestic, political, and economic situation, upon her relations with Britain and the other members of the British Commonwealth of Nations, and upon her international status. The war efforts attracted most attention at that time, and they had causal connections with the progress of events in the other fields.

When Canada entered the Four Year's War her military forces that could be called a standing army numbered barely 3000 officers and men. Since her militia could not be used for overseas service, it was necessary to create a separate organization for the expeditionary force. The plans for a contingent of 25,000 men were completed by August 10, and shortly afterward volunteers considerably in excess of this number had assembled at Valcartier. The first Canadian division embarked at Quebec, September 22–24; leaving Gaspé Bay October 1 it arrived at Plymouth two weeks later and thence proceeded to Salisbury Plain for the intensive training required for actual war service. As the first contingent left Canada, a new one was being organized; thus the raising and equipping of new units for replacement or reinforcement continued as long as the war lasted. By the end of 1917 the Canadian army in France numbered 140,000 and it was maintained at practically this strength until the armistice. More than 590,000 enlisted in Canada for active military service; 500,000 of these were volunteers, the rest being secured by conscription during the last year of the war. The additional units raised to serve as garrisons at Bermuda and St. Lucia and for non-combatant services, such as forestry, brought the total Canadian contribution in man power well above 600,000.

The first Canadian division, although organized and equipped as a separate unit, formed part of a British army corps. When there were two more divisions, the Canadians were organized as a distinct corps with its own general staff. A Canadian ministry of overseas forces was created in November, 1916. The organization of this department coincided with the removal of Sir Sam Hughes from the ministry of militia, his growing disinclination to cooperate with or take orders from the cabinet and the prime minister having created embarrassments. He was replaced by Sir Edward Kemp.

The Canadian soldiers received their baptism of fire in the second battle of Ypres in April, 1915, when unprepared they had to withstand the first German gas attack. Afterward they participated in much heavy fighting in some of the greatest battles of the war on the western front and covered themselves with glory, especially in the capture of Vimy Ridge in April, 1917. But for many of the young Canadians the path to glory led to the grave for of the 418,000 who went overseas, 51,000 were killed in action or died from wounds and 4000 died from other causes; Canadian casualty lists totaled 150,000 men. Ontario, the most populous of the Canadian provinces, contributed one-half of the enlistments, a ratio below that of British Columbia but higher than the average for Canada, which was low because of the relatively small number of enlistments from Quebec. Ontario with a population of 2,527,292 contributed 245,677, while Quebec with 2,005,776 supplied only 82,793. Of the various national groups, the British, as might be expected, contributed by far the largest percentage of enlistments. Indeed, the majority of the men in the first Canadian contingent were born in Britain; and of the 365,000 of all ranks sent overseas before March 31, 1918, 172,000 were reported as British-born and 147,000 were

Canadians of British descent. The disparity of enlistments both as between provinces and as between racial groups shows that the French-Canadians, representing 29 per cent of the population and concentrated largely in the province of Quebec, fell far behind their British-Canadian brethren in making sacrifices in a war in which Britain and France were fighting on the same side, the latter facing the graver risks.

The explanation for the reluctance of the French-Canadians to fight in a war which involved both the British empire and France is to be found in their attitude toward the imperial connection, their lack of interest in the homeland of their race and culture, and special domestic situations and problems. With a hard-headedness worthy of their Breton and Norman ancestry the French-Canadians accepted the guarantees and safeguards for their language and institutions provided by membership in the British empire without acknowledging reciprocal duties. They opposed the sending of troops to South Africa during the Boer War and the proposal to contribute to the imperial navy, and they accepted only half-heartedly Laurier's plan for a Canadian navy. "Canada for the Canadians" they approved for they regarded themselves as the only true Canadians, and they considered themselves safe behind the double protection of the British navy and the Monroe Doctrine. Since the empire was not likely to become involved in a war because of problems raised by Canada, the French-Canadians felt under no obligation to make sacrifices for imperial or European causes which did not touch them directly. Nor did they recognize obligations toward France. She had planted their ancestors in Canada for her own interests, and like the Boers of South Africa the French-Canadians had built up a society of their own which differed in important respects from that of the homeland. They had perpetuated an old order in which the Roman Catholic clergy held a dominant place, an order left behind and even despised by the governing element in modern France. French republicanism had a long tradition of hostility toward the church to which the *habitant* clung with unswerving loyalty. While members of the wealthier and professional classes might go or send their children to Paris to get a veneer of French culture, the French-Canadian farmers were satisfied with the old ways and their old *patois*, and suspicious of the godless land whence their ancestors had come in a past that seemed infinitely remote. France had no real claim on their devotion.

Nevertheless when war broke out, the advocates of Canadian participation in it made great show of the Anglo-French comradeship in Europe and used it with telling effect in appealing to mixed British and French-Canadian audiences. There was apparently unanimous agreement on the issue that when the empire was at war Canada was at war and that she must shoulder her share of the burden that the war entailed. Church, press, and politicians of French-speaking Canada rallied behind Laurier and Bourassa in support of the government's early war efforts, and French-Canadians responded well to the first call for volunteers. But the government failed to appreciate at the outset that the language difficulty made distinct French military units necessary. The mixing of French- with British-Canadians put a damper on a not too strong enthusiasm for war service and precipitated discussions on the status of the French language, discussions which assumed large proportions when an Ontario school law of 1915 refused to recognize bilingual schools except in the elementary grades.

Meanwhile Bourassa had returned to his earlier position of viewing with alarm Canada's participation in an imperial war. Soon his paper, *Le Devoir*, issued blast upon blast, asserting that Canada was being sacrificed on the altar of imperialism, that it was the patriotic duty of Canadians to remain at home, and that independence offered the best solution for the problems of Canada. By 1916 the Ontario language question seemed more important to a large number of French-Canadians than did the war. Moreover, the stories of hardships and suffering at the front coupled with the realization that high wages and prices offered opportunities for money-making at home supplied further motives for resisting the call to arms. One by one, French-language newspapers followed the lead of Bourassa and *Le Devoir* in discouraging or opposing the attempts to secure volunteers; provincial politicians in Quebec and the lower Catholic clergy began to waver; in vain distinguished French-Canadian officers gave aid to the recruiting campaign.

The spring of 1917 found the Allies in a precarious position. Russia was dropping out, France was growing weary, and it would take months before the strength of the United States could be brought to bear on the military situation. Borden returned from a visit to Europe deeply impressed with the need for more men. An attempt to raise a Canadian home defense force to release regulars for overseas service failed; an intense recruiting campaign which covered the whole province of Quebec produced only 92 volunteers. In 1916 Britain adopted conscription; the United States passed a compulsory military service law shortly after she entered the war in April, 1917; still Borden hesitated. In May, 1917, he invited Laurier to join a coalition government, but the Liberal leader refused; he was unalterably opposed to conscription which he saw coming. A month later a bill making all male British subjects between the ages 20–45 resident in Canada liable to military service was introduced in the house of commons and passed with large majorities despite opposition from Laurier, who was deserted by some of his Liberal followers but supported by a small group of Nationalists. The men liable to conscription were divided into several classes; unmarried men and childless widowers were to be called first. Although efforts to enforce the conscription law caused riots in Montreal and Quebec, French-Canada as a whole complied, largely because early marriages put her young men into deferred classes.

As already mentioned, the Liberal party supported the war but was watchful lest the Conservatives reap political benefits therefrom. The house of commons elected in 1911 expired in

1916; however, since a war-time election was judged undesirable, all parties united in a request to the imperial parliament for an extension of one year, which was granted. The party truce did not prevent the Liberals from watching and at times criticizing the government's way of conducting the war — scandals connected with the purchase of war supplies offered excellent opportunities. Since the French-Canadians formed the backbone of the Liberal party, Laurier could not ignore the political advantages accruing from the language dispute in Ontario or from the split between Borden and his French-Canadian allies. These tactics alienated western Liberals and in 1917 they began clamoring for a National Union government. Prominent as a leader in this movement was Sir Clifford Sifton, who had been minister of railways in the Laurier government, 1896–1905. When Laurier declined Borden's invitation to join a coalition government, negotiations were taken up with other prominent Liberals; in October, 1917, these resulted in the formation of a National government composed of thirteen Conservatives and ten Liberals. Meanwhile preparations were made for an election. These included the passage of a War-time Election Bill which disfranchised natives of Germany and Austria naturalized since 1902 and also conscientious objectors, and enfranchised the mothers, wives, and sisters of soldiers and women engaged in war industries. Furthermore the bill made provisions for the soldiers at the front to vote; however, they could vote only for or against the government without reference to candidates. Laurier vainly offered stout opposition to this measure. The ensuing election in November, 1917, gave the National government a majority of about 300,000. The Liberals swept Quebec, winning 62 of its 65 seats, but in Ontario they secured only 8 out of 82; farther west only 2 Liberals were elected. With this mandate Sir Robert Borden finished the war and concluded peace for Canada.

The Dominion contributions to the war efforts of Britain and her Allies were not limited to military aid. At the outset Canada presented the mother country with a million bags of wheat flour; the products of her fields, forests, and mines were valuable additions to the economic strength of the combination fighting Germany. Nor was this all. Britain's unpreparedness in arms and munitions was as serious as her lack of trained soldiers, and here the industrial skill and power of Canada proved of immense importance. By the end of 1917, 15 per cent of the expenditures of the imperial munition board went to Canada, and at the close of the war it was estimated that between 600 and 700 plants and upward of 300,000 workers in the Dominion had been employed by this board and that the imperial government had spent $1,100,000,000 in Canada. In addition to the sums raised by special taxes during the war, the Canadian national debt increased by $1,600,000,000 between March 31, 1914, and March 31, 1920. A large proportion of this debt was held in Canada, high prices on Canadian produce and the war expenditures having enabled her citizens to take over loans which in earlier times were usually floated in London. Thus while the war left Canada with a heavy debt it helped to make her financially more independent.

The war expenditures and the increased debt burden compelled the Dominion to levy new and heavier taxes and to extend the functions of her government. An income tax, a special business profits tax, and increased customs duties were among the means employed for raising additional revenues. By an act of 1916 Canadian life insurance companies were compelled to invest in Canadian securities and the government made arrangements to increase the production and regulate the distribution of foodstuffs. While these paternalistic measures were temporary, the government's taking over of the Canadian Northern in 1917 inaugurated the Canadian National Railway system.

Canada gained strength and stature as a nation through the storm and stress of war. She entered the conflict as a satellite of Britain; at its end her representatives sat at the council table as the equals of those from sovereign states. By degrees she built up an independent administration of her army; even in the field of high command she became emancipated. The Canadian troops in France were at first commanded by Sir Edwin Alderson, then by Sir Julian (later Lord) Byng, both Britishers; but on June 9, 1917, Major-General (later Sir Arthur) Currie, a native of Canada, was given command of them. In July, 1915, when Borden visited England, he was present at a meeting of the British cabinet; less than two years later he became a member of the imperial war cabinet, a deliberative body on which the prime ministers of the dominions were the equals of the prime minister of Britain. Although enthusiasts for imperial consolidation looked upon the imperial war cabinet as a precursor of an imperial council, this was not to be. Canada and the other dominions by their contributions and sacrifices earned recognition as states. Hence during the war period the dominions and Britain became known as the British Commonwealth of Nations. Sir Robert Borden made substantial contributions to the growth of the commonwealth idea by insisting upon and gaining separate Canadian representation at the peace conference. Canada signed and ratified the treaty of peace with Germany and was admitted to the League of Nations on the basis of an independent state with representation in the assembly of the League and eligibility to a seat on its council. Furthermore, Britain conceded to Canada the right to appoint her own minister to Washington.

Newfoundland in peace and war is overshadowed by Canada. In 1914 the island had no military establishment, but unlike Canada it had been contributing a small sum annually toward imperial defense and had maintained a royal naval reserve force of about 500 men. This body was of course called into service on the outbreak of the war and later augmented, so that in all nearly 2000 men were enlisted in Newfoundland for the imperial navy. In addition a regiment of 500 was raised and sent to England with the first Canadian contingent, though not forming a part of it. Later calls for volunteers and a system of conscription for men between 19 and 40 adopted in 1917 brought Newfoundland's military contribution up to 6300, of whom nearly 5000 were sent overseas. The Newfoundland regiment, incorporated with British divisions, saw service at Gallipoli toward the end of that ill-starred campaign, and on the western front. Few military units suffered heavier losses in battle; one-fourth of the Newfoundlanders who crossed the sea died in action or from wounds.

In Newfoundland there was practical unanimity on the war issues. The only political crisis of the war period occurred in 1917, when the legislative council defeated a proposed business profit tax bill, thus challenging the assembly's control over finance; but the appointment of four new members to the council broke the deadlock. The life of the assembly was extended twice by special legislation so that Newfoundland went through the war without an election. The commercial depression which she experienced in the early part of 1914 gave way to an unexampled prosperity. Her foreign trade in 1917 was double that of 1914; her fish oil, lumber, cellulose, and iron were in brisk demand at high prices. Recognizing the comparative poverty of Newfoundland, Britain maintained her troops after they had reached Europe; consequently England's oldest colony passed through the war with only about $13,000,000 added to its public debt and many private fortunes greatly increased.

The war over, British North America like the rest of the world strove to regain the equilibrium of the pre-war era. Reconstruction became a popular slogan in America as in Europe. Canada decided to reward her discharged soldiers with a bonus – $600 to married and $400 to unmarried men who had fought throughout the war, with gradations in proportion to length of service. Moreover, unoccupied land was offered to ex-soldiers, either free or at a low price, with easy annual payments over a period of twenty years. Each soldier-settler was granted $2500 for buildings, stock, and implements. Pensions were awarded war victims or their dependents. To facilitate the absorption of soldiers in the labor market, arrangements were made for the establishment of labor bureaus along the line of the English labor exchanges, and employers were urged to rehire employees who had left to join the army. As further aid during the transition from war to peace, the Dominion government granted credit of $25,000,000 for the building of homes, the sum to be divided among the provinces on condition that the provincial governments granted an equal amount. These loans were repayable at 5 per cent in twenty annual installments. A special Canadian trade commission was set up in London and $100,000,000 was made available to aid exports to Britain, Belgium, Greece, and Rumania. Moreover, a new reciprocal trade agreement between Canada and the British West Indian colonies granted mutual preferences ranging from 10 to 50 per cent.

These arrangements failed to stave off discontent among the laboring and farming classes. In the years 1918 and 1919, labor in western Canada was deeply influenced by the Industrial Workers of the World, a radical organization commonly known as the I.W.W. and flourishing south of the border, by the Russian revolution, and by sundry political, social, and economic grievances engendered by the war. The result was a series of strikes culminating, in June, 1919, in the general or red strike at Winnipeg. With the collapse of this strike, labor in Canada discontinued the use of militant tactics and sought the cooperation of the farmers in organizing for political action. In western Canada as in western United States, a certain amount of discontent with credit, transportation, and marketing systems has been endemic in farming communities. During the 1890's the Populist movement in the United States had its counterpart in the political activities of the Patrons of Industry of Ontario who in 1894 elected sixteen representatives to the provincial and in 1896 six to the federal parliament. The movement disappeared in the era of prosperity at the turn of the century. But the old elements of discontent were only dormant, and new grievances arose during the war — dissatisfaction with the operation of the conscription act, especially the exemptions granted sons of farmers, complaints against the tariff. Consequently in November, 1918, representatives of western farmers prepared a National Farmers Platform which favored free trade with Britain, reciprocity with the United States, heavier taxes on unoccupied land, large incomes, and inheritance, public ownership of utilities, proportional representation, the admission of women to the federal parliament, the initiative and referendum.

The discontent among the farmers grew in the early twenties with the sharp decline in the prices of agricultural products. Led by E. C. Drury, the United Farmers of Ontario captured the government of that province in the election of 1919. In January of the following year the farmers in convention at Winnipeg baptized their party the National Progressive Party which, thanks to aid secured from organized labor, in the federal election of 1921 secured 37 of the 43 seats of the three prairie provinces in the Canadian house of commons. With a total of 66, it became the second strongest party in that body. Ably lead by T. A. Crerar, the Progressives held the balance of power in the Dominion parliament. But when their leader retired temporarily from politics in 1922, dissensions tore ranks and the influence of the Progressives waned almost as rapidly as it had waxed. Farmers and laborers could not be welded into a strong political party. Moreover, the economic upswing of the mid-twenties cut much ground from under the new third party. In the election of 1925 the Progressives secured 25 seats; in the following year three farm-labor groups elected 31 members of the house of commons, but this was reduced to 15 in 1930.

In the early thirties depression and drought rekindled the flames of discontent. An Alberta schoolmaster-evangelist, William Aberhart, became convinced that the social credit gospel preached by a Britisher, Major Douglas, held the long-sought-for cure of the economic ills that beset western farmers. With the aid of the radio and promises of a social dividend of $25 a month to all citizens of the province, Mr. Aberhart swept the provincial election of Alberta on August 22, 1935, securing 56 of the 63 seats in the provincial legislature and 196,000 of the 300,000 votes cast. The once all-powerful United Farmers polled only 30,000 votes and failed to elect any of its candidates. In the subsequent federal election 15 of the 16 members chosen by Alberta for the house of commons represented Social Credit. At Ottawa they were joined by two from Saskatchewan. The province of Alberta became somewhat of an oddity in Canadian politics — the influence of the new creed was seemingly restricted to the province that gave it birth.

The political upheavals in western Canada had their counterparts in the Non-Partisan League, the Farmer-Labor, and the Progressive movements in the adjoining states of the American union. But unlike these, the third-party groups in Canada came within a measurable distance of being dominant factors in national politics. With the war over, the Nationalist or Union government headed by Sir Robert Borden suffered loss in popularity, a loss aggravated when ill health compelled Sir Robert to retire and his place was taken by Arthur Meighen. The new prime minister, although honest and capable, had been minister of the interior during 1917–1920, and therefore had to bear all the odium attached to the Conscription Act and its enforcement. The French-Canadians in particular were bent on his political destruction. Sensing the drift of public opinion, Liberals gradually withdrew from the government, their representation in the coalition soon being reduced from about one-half to one-fourth. The new name — the National Liberal and Conservative party — adopted by Meighen's supporters proved no help; in popular judgment they were the Conservatives, and before long they assumed their old name. Meanwhile the Liberal party revived under the skillful leadership of Mackenzie King. Without committing themselves strongly to any definite program except tariff reductions, the Liberals capitalized on the disaffection and unpopularity of the government. In the election of December 6, 1921, Quebec voted solidly Liberal, but outside this province the new Progressive party scored the greatest gains, electing 66. Since Mr. Meighen had only 50 followers in the new house of commons, as against 117 for Mackenzie King, he resigned without meeting parliament. Although Mackenzie King had a majority of only one, he maintained himself in office even after an election on October 29, 1925, wiped out this slim margin and reduced his party to 101, sixteen less than the Conservative. Besides his dexterity as a political tight-rope walker, he was aided by the fact that the Progressives preferred the Liberals to the Conservatives. However, in June, 1926, his position had become so uncomfortable that he asked the governor general, Lord Byng, to dissolve parliament. The refusal of this request precipitated an acrimonious debate over the position and power of the governor general. Australian precedents of the seventies favored Lord Byng, but the English were against him; the general constitutional development in Canada had been in the direction of the English type of relations between the prime minister and the nominal head of the government.

Mr. Meighen obeyed the governor general's summons to form a government; however, he was defeated in the house of commons and advised dissolution, which was then granted. The constitutional dispute was a handicap for Mr. Meighen and his party, for in the new house the Conservatives numbered 91 as against 118 Liberals. Mackenzie King returned to office and was again supported by the progressive groups as well as by the prevailing prosperity. His luck held until 1930, when depression hit Canada and R. B. Bennett succeeded Mr. Meighen as leader of the Conservatives. The election of July 28, 1930, returned 136 Conservatives and 89 Liberals; of the remaining, 18 represented left-wing groups and 2 were independents. But the depression proved a too heavy liability for Mr. Bennett also. The new American tariff bill of 1930 — the Smoot-Hawley — had disastrous effects on Canada's trade which were not counterbalanced by the benefits the Dominion received from the intra-imperial tariff program adopted in 1932 by the economic conference at Ottawa. One of the strongest of the Conservative leaders, H. H. Stevens, broke with the prime minister on the question of regulations for big business and formed the Reconstruction party. The parties of the left, on the other hand, tried to combine in the Co-operative Commonwealth Federation which had a socialistic program. The Liberals meanwhile secured control over all the provincial governments except that of Alberta. The parliament chosen in 1930 expired in 1935 and in the election of that year the Liberals scored their first real victory since 1908. When the votes were counted the Liberals had 177, the Conservatives 39; the Social Credit group with 17 was the strongest of the smaller parties in the new house of commons. Mackenzie King returned to office for the third time; both he and his party had been intrusted with power.

Despite electioneering promises of economy, Canada's public debt increased by nearly $1,500,000,000 between 1919 and 1936; even though her population had grown by more than 3,000,000 between 1911 and 1931, she had a larger foreign debt per capita than any other country save New Zealand. Meanwhile the boundaries of the settled areas had been pushed northward, especially in Alberta and British Columbia where the newly settled Peace River region proved especially well suited for wheat-growing. The output of minerals – particularly gold, nickel, and copper – rose rapidly in the post-war era. Comparison of the production of these metals in 1931 with that in 1921 shows an increase for gold of nearly 250 per cent; of nickel, 340 per cent; and of copper, more than 600 per cent. The subsequent abandonment of the gold standard while the demand for the metal continued heavy at greatly inflated prices benefited the gold-mining interests of Canada, and the race in armaments brought profit to the owners of nickel mines. Although drought and rust on wheat often reduced the quantity of this important export staple, foreign trade showed a fairly steady growth until 1929, the trade figures for the year ending March 31, 1929, being exports $1,363,709,672 and imports $1,265,679,091. Then came the financial collapse which was made worse for Canada by the new American tariff act. The exports from Canada to the United States dropped from $150,000,000 in 1929 to $17,000,000 in 1933, the total exports for that year being slightly more than one-third and the imports less than one-third those of 1929. The index figures, with 100 for 1913, reached 149.3 in 1929 and fell to 104.8 in 1933. Consequently the decline of trade was less in quantity than in value. Nevertheless the economic situation became serious, and for this reason Mr. Bennett insisted upon a new imperial tariff arrangement with a preferential treatment for Canadian produce in the British market. But the Ottawa agreements of 1932 were not entirely to the liking of the Canadians who believed in fostering the trade with the United States. Therefore in the election of 1935 the Liberals stressed the need for tariff revision downward, changes in the Ottawa agreements, and a reciprocal trade arrangement with the United States. The last was secured in part on November 15, 1935, when the two countries agreed on mutual reduction of duties on a large number of articles. In 1937 the Ottawa agreements were revised; Britain guaranteed the lists of free goods and increased the number of Canadian products to which she accorded preference. Mackenzie King was less rigid than Mr. Bennett in his trade policy with reference to other countries. The embargo against Russian goods was lifted, a trade war with Japan was ended, and the restrictions governing exchange with Germany were modified. The improvements in trade during 1936–1937 seemed to justify Mackenzie King's policy and earned political credit for the Liberal government.

The financial structure of Canada withstood the shock of the depression in a manner that aroused the envy of stockholders and depositors in the thousands of defunct banks in the United States. The centralized system — ten chartered banks operating through 3488 branches in Canada and 149 abroad — so often a target for attacks by western radicals, seemed justified. In the post-war era large American industrial concerns like the Ford

Motor Company established branches in Canada, and by the mid-twenties American exceeded British investments in Canada, the figure for 1926 being $2,597,800,000 of British as against $3,161,-200,000 of American capital; in 1930 the margin favoring the United States exceeded $1,500,000,000. After 1932 American investments declined while the British rose, so that four years later the difference in favor of the United States had been deduced to $1,250,000,000. Because of her connections with the two greatest financial powers in the world, Canada is naturally affected by changes in their monetary policies; this became painfully apparent when they followed different monetary policies for about two years. In September, 1931, Britain went off the gold standard, the American dollar appreciated, and Canada found it easy to make payments in London but hard in New York. For a while after the United States followed Britain's example in the spring of 1933, the pound was high in terms of dollars and the Canadian difficulties continued though in the reverse order. To meet the situation Canada has attempted to keep her dollar somewhere midway between the American dollar and the British pound whenever they depart widely from the old ratio of $4.86 to the pound. This task has tested the skill of Canadian financiers since despite, or may be because of, the huge stabilization funds of the United States and Britain their exchange fluctuated in a manner unheard of in the halcyon days at the opening of the century.

A decision of the judicial committee of the privy council in 1896, mentioned in an earlier chapter, checked for the time being the process of centralization of power at Ottawa. But the social and economic trends of the twentieth century, with numerous calls for financial aid and the need of policies applicable to all the provinces, caused a large increase in the functions of the federal government. The establishment of a Dominion department of labor in 1900 was followed seven years later by the passage of an Industrial Disputes Investigation Act, disallowed by the judicial committee in 1925 as not falling within the Dominion's power.

Meanwhile, the federal government had intervened in the Winnipeg strike of 1919, and its activities had been extended by a Workmen's Compensation Act, 1914, and a Minimum Wages Act for Women, 1930. A department of health and a Royal Commission on Industrial Relations came into being in 1919, a year which also saw the passage of a Technical Education Act. Shortly after the war, federal aid was granted to housing and the Dominion set up employment offices. Although the relatively prosperous years of 1921–1929 reduced the need for direct aid for unemployment relief, it rose sharply in the early thirties and increased to such an extent that the Liberals found it expedient to include reduction in federal relief expenditures as a plank in their platform in the election of 1935. Returning to office, they discontinued the labor service relief camps, the Canadian equivalent of the American Civil Conservation Corps, which had been operating under the direction of the department of national defense. The most common form of unemployment relief was grants to the provinces which in turn made allocations to the local units of government. The Dominion also made direct contributions to relief projects such as road construction, and the official *Labour Gazette* published monthly surveys of the employment situation.

The greatest of the Canadian economic experiments were in cooperatives such as those of grain growers in the west and the Hydroelectric System of Ontario. The former grew out of farmers' complaints against prevailing grain prices, charges for storage, and the grading of wheat. The elevator companies working in conjunction with railroad companies controlled the marketing facilities for grain. Appeals by farmers to provincial and federal authorities resulted in the appointment of numerous commissions — thirteen in all between 1897 and 1914 — to study marketing problems and the passage of a Grain Act in 1912 that established a Dominion Grain Commission. In the meantime the grain growers of Manitoba in 1906 organized a cooperative society operating grain elevators. Similar organizations sprang up in Alberta and Saskatchewan; later they developed into the great Wheat Pool which in 1929 included 140,000 wheat farmers. While this cooperative organization grew from small nuclei toward a center, that dealing with the purchase and utilization of hydroelectric power owed its origin to an Ontario act of 1906 creating a Hydro Commission that ultimately obtained control of plants at Niagara and other rivers and supplied the power to municipalities on a cooperative basis, the commission performing the services of a trustee. In 1910 the commission supplied 10 municipalities with 750 horse power; by 1927 the figures had grown to 252 and 673,000 respectively. Besides serving the needs of householders, the Hydroelectric System of Ontario has been an important factor in the industrial development of the province.

Canada made great strides in the direction of federal ownership of railroads. The Dominion took over the Canadian Northern in 1917, the Grand Trunk Pacific in 1918, and the Grand Trunk in 1921. It then had 22,000 miles of railroads. Since that date a railroad from Winnipeg to Fort Churchill on Hudson Bay has been built by the federal government and other lines have been secured; by 1935 the Canadian National Railway system included 23,880 miles. Several of these lines, notably that from Winnipeg to Fort Churchill, have run at a loss; hence the National Railway became a heavy drain upon the federal treasury — a drain which in 1933–1934 averaged $1,000,000 per week.

In 1927 the Dominion established a system of old age pensions; otherwise Canada has been more conservative than Australia and New Zealand in the field of social legislation. Some of this conservatism has been due to the political influence of the French Canadians. A large number of them are small landowners, nearly all are strongly attached to the Roman Catholic Church, and the parish priest and the hierarchy largely shape the views of the *habitant* on social and economic questions. Scenting the possibility of an infiltration of Marxism through labor unions, the church encouraged the organization of separate Catholic labor unions, an action which in part explains the comparative weakness of the Canadian labor movement. Moreover, the size and geographical configuration of Canada and the large percentage of her population engaged in farming have retarded the growth of such a movement.

The rapid growth in population during the first decade of the present century was not maintained. Immigration slowed down in the depression which preceded the war, dwindled to almost nothing during the war years, and even during the prosperity of the twenties never reached the 1912 level. The best farming land had been taken, there was less railroad construction, and some hundreds of thousands of returned soldiers had to be absorbed in the labor market. Canada supported the efforts of the United Kingdom to transplant part of its surplus population to the Dominion, but with little success. In 1930 unassisted immigrants from the continent of Europe constituted 55 per cent of those entering Canada. As in earlier periods, the Canadians discriminated against orientals. Even though the head tax on Chinese immigrants was raised to $500 in 1904, they still continued to come until their entrance for permanent settlement was prohibited in 1923. In 1908 arrangements were made with Japan to admit annually only 400 of her nationals; this was reduced to 150 in 1929. The natives of India have been as unwelcome as other oriental immigrants. When Indians began arriving in considerable numbers the dodge was invented that immigrants from the orient must arrive in Canada by a continuous voyage from their native land. Since there was no direct steamship service between India and Canada, this expedient served the purpose until the spring of 1914 when a specially chartered steamer with a load of Hindus arrived at Vancouver. The local labor unions demonstrated violently against their landing and ultimately they returned to India, where they helped to fan their countrymen's discontent with British rule.

The nativistic movement largely responsible for the post-war American immigration legislation favoring immigrants of the older racial stocks had a counterpart in Canada. In 1921 a Native Sons of Canada organization was founded in British Columbia; later it spread to the other provinces. Attempts were made to check the influx of newcomers from southeastern Europe; population experts discovered to their alarm that the Slovaks exceeded even the French-Canadians in fecundity. When the great depression settled upon Canada in 1929–1930, steps were taken to halt immigration. An order in council of August 14, 1930, limited immigration, except from Britain, a British dominion, or the United States, to close relatives of settlers and to agriculturists with sufficient capital to start farming. About 1,500,000 immigrants entered Canada during 1921–1931; but since 1,250,000 Canadians emigrated — mostly to the United States — the net gain from this population movement was only 250,000. It should be borne in mind, however, that the emigrants were chiefly natives of Canada; hence the population chart was materially altered during the decade. It showed among other things that the percentage of foreign-born, other than those from British countries and the United States, increased from 5.87 in 1921 to 7.50 in 1931, while that of British origin fell from 55.40 to 51.86 within the same period.

The newer provinces of the Dominion showed the same interest in higher education as had the older. Even before Saskatchewan became a separate province, attempts had been made to establish a university within her borders; the act authorizing the founding of the University of Saskatchewan passed the provincial legislature April 3, 1907, and the new institution opened its doors at Saskatoon in September, 1909. But Alberta had stolen a march on her sister province by passing the necessary legislation in 1906. The actual work of her university, located at Edmonton, dates from September, 1908. British Columbia lagged behind in providing an independent university for her youth. From 1899 until 1915 a college at Vancouver was affiliated with McGill; in the latter year the University of British Columbia formally began its work. The provinces endowed their universities with grants of land and made provisions for them in the provincial budgets. As might be expected, the prairie provinces made special efforts to build up strong agricultural colleges and experiment stations. Excepting in French Canada, the English influence continued strong in the academic branches of Canadian education. In the professional schools of agriculture, engineering, and medicine American models and methods have had a strong following, but in the more basic educational subjects from kindergarten through university the ideas of England and Scotland have prevailed over those in vogue in the United States.

The census of 1931 showed that a large percentage of Canadians were affiliated with some church. Among the churches, the Roman Catholic, claiming 41.3 per cent, was far in the lead; next came the United Church of Canada, organized in 1925 by a fusion of Congregationalists, Methodists, and Presbyterians, with 19.4 per cent; the Anglican communion with 15.8 per cent ranked third. The protestant churches of Canada have generally been active in fostering a nativistic spirit, urging the exclusion of non-British immigrants. The Canadian Roman Catholics were overwhelmingly French — 97 per cent. They have been strong for separate schools and for the avoidance of close connections with the League of Nations, and have helped to shape Canada's policy toward Russia, the Italian invasion of Ethiopia, and the civil war in Spain. Bitterly opposed to communism, the French-Canadian Roman Catholics of Quebec were at times accused of favoring the principles of *Fascismo.*

As already noted, Sir Robert Borden, though genuinely loyal to the cause of the British empire in the Four Years' War, insisted on the recognition of Canada as a separate state. As such she was represented at the peace conference, admitted to the League of Nations, signed and ratified the treaty of peace with Germany. Borden secured the promise of an independent Canadian representative in Washington, and by the middle of the thirties Canadian ministers had been appointed to Washington, Paris, and

Tokio. In 1921 his successor, Arthur Meighen, worked successfully against the renewal of the Anglo-Japanese treaty and in favor of the Washington agreements of 1921–1922. When the need arose for negotiating a treaty with the United States to regulate the halibut fishery on the Pacific coast, Canada insisted on having her own representatives treat directly with those of the United States without interference or participation by the British ambassador at Washington and on having the final agreement ratified by the crown upon the advice of her government. This was an important step toward the diplomatic freedom of the dominions, and the imperial conference of 1923 sanctioned by implication the method employed by Canada in negotiating the Halibut Treaty.

Although cooperating within the British Commonwealth of Nations as well as in the League of Nations, Canada kept aloof from steps and policies that might link her fortune too closely with that of either Britain or the League. Consequently the Dominion did not respond favorably in September, 1922, to Lloyd George's appeal for support at the time of the Chanak crisis, and it declined to approve the Anglo-Turkish treaty of 1923. Similarly Canada steered clear of agreements reached under the auspices of the League of Nations, such as the Geneva protocol of 1924 and the Locarno pact of 1925. Like the United States, she was afraid of European entanglements. In the questions pertaining to Japan's invasions of Manchuria and China, the Italo-Ethiopian war, and the Spanish civil war, the Dominion government avoided commitments, thereby perhaps acting as a brake on the British foreign office.

The policies of the Conservative and Liberal governments of Canada have been practically identical on problems of intra-imperial and foreign relations. Mr. Bennett was strong in his advocacy of imperial preferences; he was also the first prime minister of Canada to advise the king directly and officially on the appointment of a governor general. Both parties had a hand in making the arrangements necessary for the passage of the

Statute of Westminster and in shaping the foreign policy of Canada. Nor is it conceivable that Mr. Bennett if in office would have acted differently than Mackenzie King did in the Edward VIII–Mrs. Simpson crisis of 1936 or the Czechoslovak crisis of September, 1938.

Isolationism was strong in Canada, particularly among the French-Canadians, and a feeling of frustration and disillusionment replaced the enthusiasm and idealism of the years 1914–1919. Europe was far away, and Canada should not assume responsibility for her quarrels. Such was the feeling common to most Canadians, irrespective of racial background, until March, 1939, when Germany seized the remainder of Czechoslovakia. Evidently the prophets of evil, those who had depicted Hitler in the darkest colors possible, had been correct. Nazi Germany had no intention of keeping pledges and respecting the right of small nations. In the summer of 1939 George VI and Queen Elizabeth visited the Dominion. The tour was a great success — the king and queen received an enthusiastic welcome everywhere; they captivated the Canadians by their charm and affability; the feeling of solidarity with Britain was greatly strengthened. In August came the Hitler-Stalin pact; the ultimate aim of Germany — destruction of the ideals represented by the British Commonwealth — stood clearly revealed. Canadian public opinion became more consolidated. Since Mackenzie King had promised not to let Canada enter a war without authorization of parliament, the Dominion parliament was convened on September 7, 1939. Isolationist demonstrations in Quebec failed, the leaders of the opposition in parliament outdoing the spokesman for the government in their denunciations of Hitlerism. The most telling speech in favor of Canada's entry into the war on the side of Britain was made by M. Lapointe, the minister of justice. At no time was the outcome of the debate in doubt. On September 10, 1939, with the sanction of parliament as well as of public opinion, Canada was at war with Germany.

While the economic and social connections between Canada

and Britain continued to be close, those with the United States were in many respects even closer. Millions of American tourists visited the Dominion every year, American magazines and newspapers circulated freely, American movies were popular in Canada, and American broadcasts did not stop at the international boundary. Since 1896 Canadian imports from the United States never fell below 50 per cent of the total, rising in one year—1918—as high as 82.3 per cent. The last important territorial boundary dispute between the United States and Canada, that concerning the limits of Alaska, was settled by a joint commission in 1903; but the development of hydroelectric power, the question of water levels in lakes adjoining or divided by the boundary, and the importance of the great inland water traffic from the head of Lake Superior to Montreal necessitated delicate negotiations of far-reaching importance and the creation of special machinery to adjust disputes. The Boundary Waters Treaty of 1909 opened Lake Michigan to Canadians, provided a code of law for use in boundary waters and created the International Joint Commission to decide on such issues as the diversion of Lake Michigan water by the Chicago Sanitary District and the development of the Great Lakes-St. Lawrence waterway. The latter aroused much interest in the middle west, the advocates of facilities for large ocean going vessels to reach Chicago and Duluth loudly proclaiming the benefits accruing therefrom. But the project met opposition from the Atlantic seaboard and the railroads. Although Canada in 1932 completed the enlargement of the Welland Canal with locks 30 feet deep, the Dominion government was not enthusiastic over plans similarly to enlarge and deepen other sections of this waterway and to engage in ambitious electric power projects.

The Dominion of Canada proceeded from strength to strength during the period 1901–1939; Newfoundland, on the other hand, moved in the opposite direction. The prosperity of the war years engendered a spirit of optimism which seemed justified by events of the twenties. Labrador was definitely attached to Newfoundland; much was said and written about the wealth of the dominion; and the government proceeded with a program of extravagant public expenditures which brought its nemesis in 1931 in the form of an exhausted credit. When default threatened, Britain stepped in to save her offspring, so that one hundred years after representative institutions were first introduced in Newfoundland this dominion asked for a suspension of its constitution and the temporary abrogation of its status in the British Commonwealth of Nations. An imperial commission replaced the self-governing institutions of Newfoundland. This receivership is to last until the island becomes financially solvent.

The war prosperity stimulated heavy spending by the government of Newfoundland as well as by individuals. Habits were quickly formed that proved difficult to break; the politician who could promise extensive public works and who painted her present and future position in the rosiest colors was most certain of being elected to the legislative assembly. There were indeed signs that seemed to indicate that the poverty and hard times of the past were gone forever. In 1927 the judicial committee of the privy council decided that Labrador, an area of 110,000 square miles, of which 30,000 were covered with forests, belonged to Newfoundland. The fisheries of this region had long been exploited, the forests contained great potential wealth, and the water power and mineral resources held untapped reserves that promised further riches. In 1923 a new paper mill and a model town were erected at Corner Brook in Newfoundland. Together with the older one at Grand Falls, this mill normally employed 1400 men, with an additional 3000 during the cutting season; the annual payroll of the two mills totaled $6,000,000. It was believed that there was room for a third mill of dimensions comparable to those of the existing ones. In 1930 the iron mine on Bell Island furnished work for 2200 men; the lead and zinc mine at Buchans on Red Indian Lake employed 350 men even in the depression year of 1933. Considering that the population of the island was only slightly above a quarter of a million,

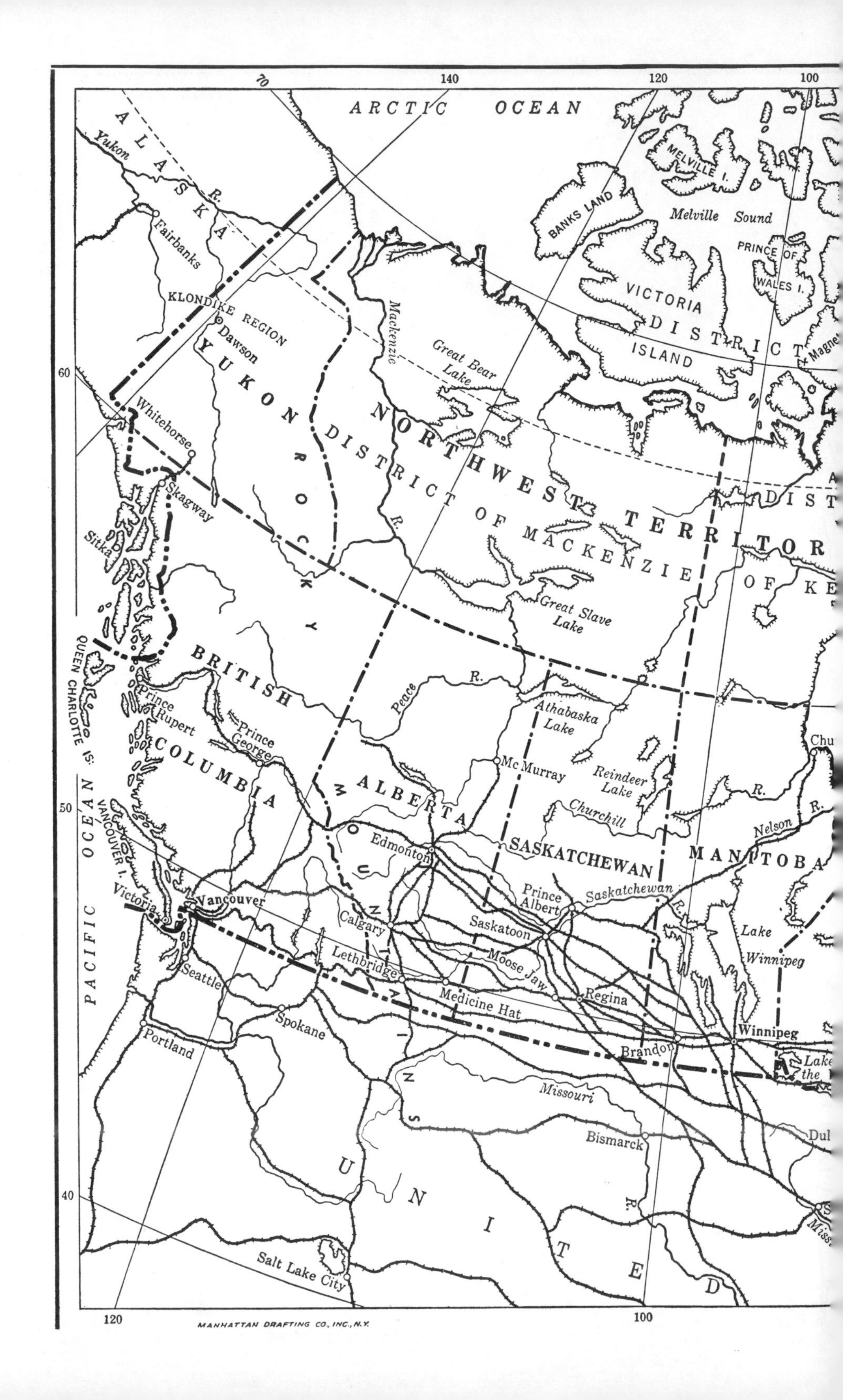
ARCTIC OCEAN
ALASKA
Yukon R.
Fairbanks
KLONDIKE REGION
Dawson
YUKON
Whitehorse
Skagway
Sitka
BANKS LAND
MELVILLE I.
Melville Sound
PRINCE OF WALES I.
VICTORIA ISLAND
DISTRICT
Mackenzie R.
Great Bear Lake
NORTHWEST TERRITORIES
DISTRICT OF MACKENZIE
ROCKY MOUNTAINS
Great Slave Lake
QUEEN CHARLOTTE IS.
BRITISH COLUMBIA
Prince Rupert
Prince George
Peace R.
Athabaska Lake
Mc Murray
Reindeer Lake
Churchill
ALBERTA
Edmonton
SASKATCHEWAN
MANITOBA
Nelson R.
PACIFIC OCEAN
VANCOUVER I.
Victoria
Vancouver
Calgary
Prince Albert
Saskatchewan R.
Saskatoon
Lake Winnipeg
Lethbridge
Moose Jaw
Regina
Medicine Hat
Seattle
Spokane
Portland
Winnipeg
Brandon
Missouri
Bismarck
UNITED
Salt Lake City
MANHATTAN DRAFTING CO., INC., N.Y.

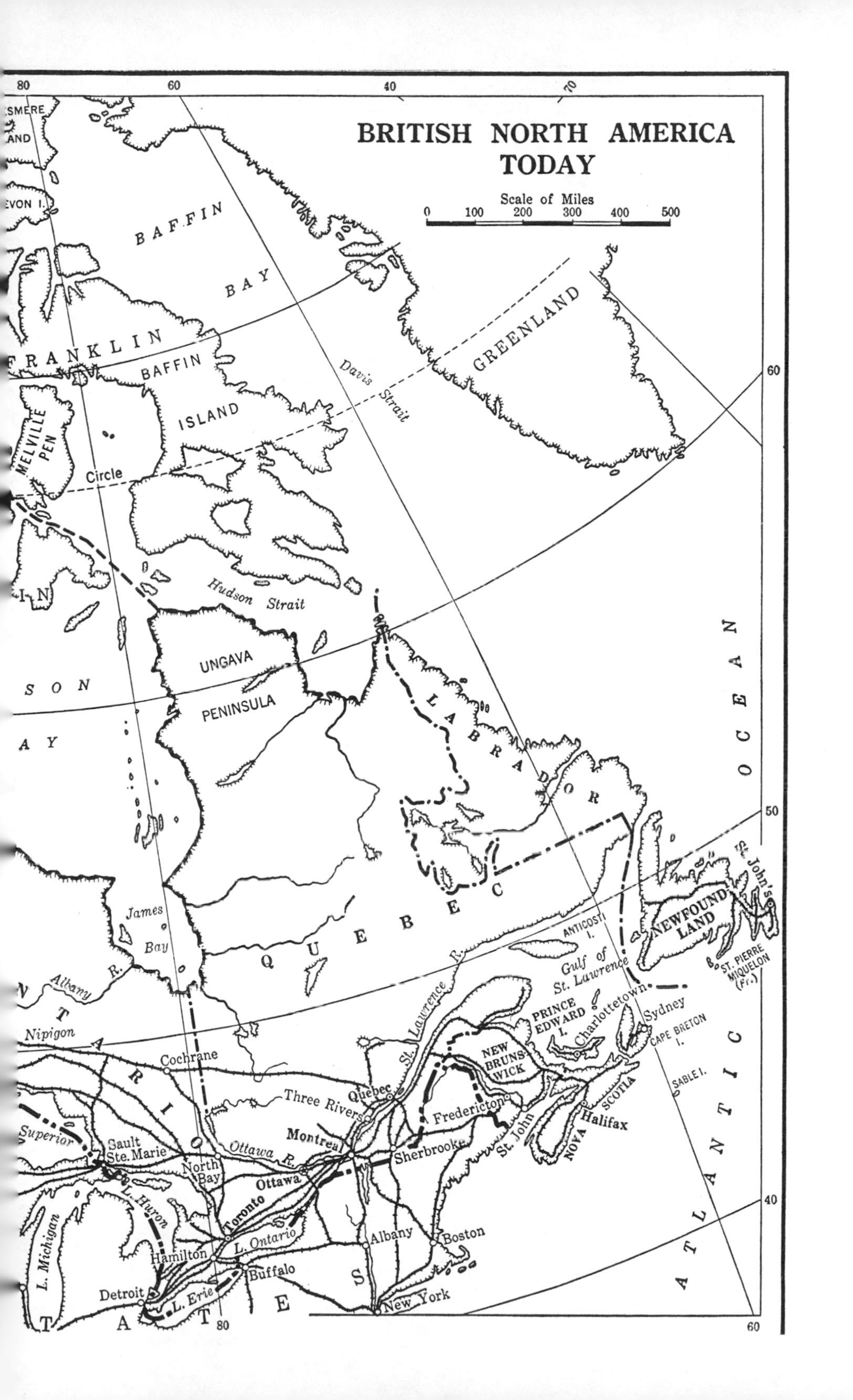
BRITISH NORTH AMERICA
TODAY
Scale of Miles
0 100 200 300 400 500
BAFFIN BAY
BAFFIN ISLAND
FRANKLIN
MELVILLE PEN
Circle
GREENLAND
Davis Strait
Hudson Strait
UNGAVA PENINSULA
LABRADOR
QUEBEC
James Bay
Albany R.
NEWFOUNDLAND
St. John's
ST. PIERRE MIQUELON (Fr.)
ANTICOSTI I.
Gulf of St. Lawrence
PRINCE EDWARD I.
Charlottetown
Sydney
CAPE BRETON I.
SABLE I.
NEW BRUNSWICK
NOVA SCOTIA
Halifax
St. John
Fredericton
Quebec
Three Rivers
Montreal
Sherbrooke
Ottawa
Ottawa R.
St. Lawrence R.
Cochrane
Nipigon
Superior
Sault Ste. Marie
North Bay
L. Huron
Toronto
L. Ontario
Hamilton
Buffalo
Detroit
L. Erie
L. Michigan
Albany
Boston
New York
ATLANTIC OCEAN
STATES

the industrial and mining developments were of great economic importance.

The institutional and public works programs of the government of Newfoundland were based on the assumption of a rapid growth in the future. Woman suffrage was introduced in 1925 and a redistribution act of that year increased the number of electoral districts from 18 to 40. While education in the lower brackets continued to be in the hands of the churches — among which the Anglican, Roman Catholic, and United Church of Canada dominated, practically dividing the field into three equal parts — the government in 1921 established a general training school for teachers and in 1925 it founded the Newfoundland Memorial University College offering two years of university work. In 1923 it resumed control of the railroads and proceeded to spend $6,000,000 on capital improvements. The means of communications were further extended by an ambitious roads program adopted in 1925; hence by 1933 the island could boast of about 3575 miles of fairly good highways.

Most of the public works financed by loans yielded no revenue. The Canadian and American tourists to be attracted by the roads failed to come; branch railroad lines did not earn operating expenses — to say nothing of interest on capital and charges for depreciation. Annual deficits in the budget, averaging $2,000,000 during 1920–1933, were covered by fresh loans. The credit was good until 1931; then neither London nor New York would take up new loans totaling $8,000,000. Newfoundland had now reached the end of her financial tether. Her public debt had risen from $43,000,000 in 1920 to $100,000,000 in 1933. In 1918 1919 the export of salted codfish brought $25,860,112.00, but only a little more than $5,000,000 in 1931–1932; in 1915–1916 Newfoundland had exported 76,060 barrels of herring frozen or in bulk, and 165,527 barrels of pickled herring; in 1931–1932 these figures fell to 4462 and 43,526 respectively. A general decline in prices on fish in the world market together with dietary changes that practically eliminated herring as a food for humans had disastrous economic effects upon Newfoundland. The demand for paper remained constant, but the iron mine on Bell Island, which in 1930 paid out more than $2,000,000 in wages and salaries, was forced to curtail to such an extent that in 1933 less than one-fourth of that amount reached its employees. The government of Sir Richard Squires, in office since 1928, was defeated in 1932; expenditures were curtailed on an heroic scale. The number of post offices was reduced from 663 to 313, of telephone offices from 347 to 214, of telegraph offices from 71 to 31; 160 miles of unprofitable railroad branch lines were abandoned; the house of assembly was reduced from 40 to 27 members and the sessional allowance for each was fixed at $600 instead of the former $1000; reductions of from 20 to 45 per cent were effected in salaries and pensions; and the government's aid to education was cut from $1,000,000 to $500,000. Although the savings thus effected amounted to more than $5,000,000, these were offset by falling revenue, the demand for relief resulting from unemployment, and the low price on fish.

Faced with the danger of defaulting on interest due January 1, 1933, the government appealed to Canada and the United Kingdom for aid. The two together advanced $1,250,000 for the January payments, and the latter supplied $1,850,000 to meet obligations maturing on July 1, 1933. Benefits were expected to accrue to Newfoundland from preferences such as the 1*s.* 4*d.* per gallon on cod liver oil and the 1½*d.* per pound on chilled or frozen salmon granted by Britain under the Ottawa agreements; on the other hand there might be a fall in her customs revenues under the new intra-imperial tariff system. A sale of Labrador or a union with Canada were solutions suggested but ruled out immediately. Newfoundland then begged the mother country for advice and aid. A royal commission visited the island in 1933, made an exhaustive study of past and present events, financial policy, and economic difficulties, and presented a comprehensive report. The financial policies of successive governments of Newfoundland were denounced in scathing terms, and the public debt was considered beyond her capacity; but the commission was favorably impressed with her wealth and found some comfort in the fact that savings deposits in the banks had risen from about $8,000,000 before the war to $26,000,000 in 1936. To lessen the immediate financial burden the commission recommended refunding the debt under an imperial guarantee, thereby effecting a yearly saving of $1,750,000; as a means of recovery it suggested that the constitution should be suspended and the existing machinery of governor, executive council, nominated legislative council, and elected house of assembly should be replaced by one consisting of the governor and six commissioners, three from Newfoundland and three from Britain, to be appointed by and responsible to the imperial government. This recommendation was accepted, and the necessary legislation was passed first by the legislature of Newfoundland and then by the imperial parliament. The new government by commission took office on February 16, 1934.

The change, though drastic and unprecedented, had less direct effect upon local institutions in Newfoundland than a similar change would have had in any of the other dominions. The island had no system of municipal or local self-government except in the capital, St. John's; the 4000 whites residing in Labrador were entirely without representative institutions. The people therefore had been accustomed to government of a paternalistic type from a distance. Under the new arrangement the regular government will be restored when the dominion has become financially solvent. However, the commission has been unable to balance the budget and Newfoundland may remain under imperial tutelage for a long time to come.

CHAPTER 30

THE WEST INDIES, 1901–1939

AS the twentieth century opened, the British colonies in Australia formed a federation; at the close of its first decade those of South Africa amalgamated into a union; shortly after the beginning of its second quarter the dominions were proclaimed of equal status with the mother country; but the West Indian possessions of Britain neither united nor advanced politically. They continued to be fragments scattered over a large area with no political bond among them except a common dependence on the imperial government. The political stagnation of these ancient colonies was matched by their economic and social backwardness. Despite careful study of their problems by experts sent from home, earnest efforts to help them onward, and a few sporadic advances, the British Caribbean dependencies stayed in the doldrums.

Geographical, historical, economic, and anthropological factors were responsible for this stagnation. The British colonies in the West Indies, unlike those in North America, South Africa, and Australia, were divided by vast stretches of ocean, by independent and semi-independent island states, and by colonial possessions of the United States and France. They had been established as separate units whose economic interests linked them to the mother country, not to one another. All were engaged in the primary industries common to tropical regions — rival producers of goods for the markets of Europe and America. These colonies had been founded in the era of mercantilism and encouraged to grow cash crops to satisfy the needs of Britain; their economic system remained unchanged after she abandoned mercantilism for free trade. The purchase of foodstuffs and manufactured goods and the need of securing ready money to meet debt charges prevented the West Indies from developing economic self-sufficiency. Their life moved in a vicious circle. Poverty caused the energetic and enterprising young men to leave the islands; those who remained were indifferent laborers; coolies had to be brought in from India and China; and the indenture system perpetuated the economic and social organization of the slave-holding period. Large estates and gangs of workers wholly dependent upon their employers remained leading characteristics of West Indian rural economy. Nor did this system change materially after the abandonment, in 1917, of the importation of coolies. The racial composition of the population grew more complex with the advent of the East Indians. British Guiana and British Honduras as well as the islands exhibited a mosaic of races; the white element decreased; and apart from a certain amount of particularism fostered by the vested interests of local officeholders, all the usual elements of a nascent nationalism were wanting. The Caribs, Chinese, Europeans, East Indians, and Negroes with various and perplexing degrees of intermixtures could not produce anything resembling a West Indian nationality. Despite charges of neglect, the problems of the West Indies occupied the minds of British statesmen from the time when Joseph Chamberlain held the seals of the colonial office to that when his son, Neville, controlled the destiny of the British empire.

In the period under discussion divergence and dependence marked the political situation in the West Indies. Plans and discussions for consolidation of some sort brought practically no results. Like the rest of the empire, the islands were deeply affected by the war of 1914, by the high prices in the war period, by the slump that followed, and by the economic reorganization of Britain's imperial system in the early 1930's. The topics indicated will be discussed in the order given.

Political dependence of the kind associated with crown colonies continued to be the badge of the governments of the British West Indies. Three of them — the Bahamas, Barbados, and Bermuda — had elective assemblies. Outwardly the governments of these colonies conformed to the pattern that existed in the Canada of the mid-nineteenth century and to that established in Southern Rhodesia in 1923, but their executives remained under the control of the representatives of the imperial government instead of being responsible to the elected branch of their legislatures. None of the West Indian islands was sufficiently mature politically to be granted self-government of the most advanced type. Jamaica made no political progress in this period. Although the constitution made an elective majority possible, her legislature continued to have a nominated majority. This island, the most populous of Britain's West Indian possessions, was unable to produce political leaders of the stature required to take full charge of local government. In 1928 British Guiana lost her cumbersome legislative machinery of a court of policy and a combined court, receiving instead the standard crown colony model with a mixed legislative council in which the elective element constituted a minority. This change showed more clearly the power of the crown over legislation and removed from the government of British Guiana one of the last vestiges of the Dutch period.

The problem of federating all or some of the colonies in the British West Indies was considered by both the imperial government and unofficial organizations. The undersecretary of state for the colonies, E. F. L. Wood (later Lord Halifax), visited the West Indies during December, 1921 to February, 1922, to study the possibility of extending the elective principle in the local governments and the practicability of federation. He reported negatively on both points. In 1926 a West Indian conference appointed by the then colonial secretary, Mr. L. S. Amery, recommended the establishment of a standing conference with representatives from all the colonies in the West Indies; but apart from a conference meeting in 1929 the plan was not put into operation. Early in the twentieth century individuals as well as voluntary bodies interested in the West Indies discussed the feasibility of either federating them or attaching them to the Dominion of Canada. Neither suggestion came within the range of practical politics. Nor did the West Indian National League, organized in 1932, succeed in being accepted as an organ for these dependencies. The possibility of uniting adjoining colonies was investigated by the Closer Union Commission of 1932. The federation of the Leeward Islands dated from 1871; in 1885 the Windward Islands had secured a common governor; and four years later Trinidad and Tobago had been united. The commission, considering whether it would be possible to bring these three units together in a federation of some sort, found that great dissatisfaction existed in the Leeward federation and that it would be impossibe to create a similar political entity embracing more colonies. Indeed the commission recommended weakening the federation of the Leeward Islands by detaching Dominica and joining her to the Windward Islands, thus allowing more autonomy to the local governments. This change took place in 1939.

Despite the failure of attempts to effect a political consolidation of the British West Indies they were treated more and more as a unit and were joined informally in common enterprises. Reciprocal trade agreements with Canada tended to assimilate their tariff systems, and in 1913 all the West Indian colonies agreed to grant preferences to British goods. Of even more significance from the standpoint of a union was the establishment of a West Indian court of appeals. Common problems connected with agriculture, the fight against diseases of plants and animals, education, law enforcement, and kindred subjects were discussed and agreements were reached at conferences of representatives from several of the colonies. The Associated West Indian Chambers of Commerce tried to further common interests; and the old West India Committee, thanks to its energetic and efficient secretary, Sir Algernon Aspinall, was active and alert in all matters pertaining to the welfare of the region often unkindly referred to as "the backwater" of the British empire.

The outbreak of the war in 1914 stirred up excitement and had a direct effect upon the economic situation in the British West Indies. It was feared that they might be attacked by German cruisers at large on the high seas or by raiders that had slipped through the Allied blockade. The fears proved groundless, although the situation might have been different had not the *Karlsruhe* blown up mysteriously on November 4, 1914, only 300 miles from Barbados. The West Indies were also particularly concerned with the tragic fate of Admiral Cradock and his squadron because he had been in command of the West India station; stokers from St. Lucia went down with the *Good Hope*. The people of the West Indies — whites, blacks, and colored — eagerly supported the empire. The famous West India regiment, recruited mainly from this region, saw service in West and East Africa; and a new body of troops called the British West Indies regiment was raised during the war. More than 15,000 West Indians joined this organization, which served in nearly every theater of war except Gallipoli. Among other contributions were cash gifts totaling £2,000,000, and supplies of various kinds.

The war disorganized the transportation service in the West Indies through the withdrawal of ships for other purposes, but otherwise it brought a prosperity unknown since the great days of the eighteenth century. Although the position of the sugar planters, so desperate in the late 1890's, improved somewhat after the Brussels convention of 1902 secured the abolition of the special aids granted by European countries to the exporters of beet sugar, the price dropped from 19*s.* in 1912 to 12*s.* 3*d.* per cwt. in 1914. Prices on other West Indian products such as cocoa and cotton suffered a similar heavy decline. This was reversed on the outbreak of hostilities in Europe. The price on sugar ultimately rose about 500 per cent above the early 1914 level, and the value of cocoa, cotton, and other articles doubled. But the benefits derived from the high prices were reaped largely by the employers; the rise in the cost of food often more than equaled the advance in the wages of labor. In the years of prosperity wise estate owners paid off mortgages and made improvements; the foolish spent money lavishly or bought land at inflated values — in Barbados land prices rose from £30 to £200 per acre. Speculators sowed the wind; the whirlwind was not long in coming.

The economic history of the British West Indies, 1919–1939, reveals the evil effects of war-time inflation, of too much reliance upon outside markets, and of an inelastic social and economic system. The war boom collapsed shortly after peace had been proclaimed and with it slumped the prices of West Indian produce, especially sugar. In 1919 sugar sold at 60*s.* per cwt.; four years later this price had been halved, and in 1935 it stood at 5*s.* 3*d.* per cwt. The price on cocoa fell from 112*s.* per cwt. in 1919 to 37*s.* in 1933; the market value of most of the other articles of export — fruit, coffee, cotton, and tobacco — similarly suffered a sharp decline. Moreover, in the period under discussion plant diseases caused heavy damages in the West Indies; even the sponge in the waters of the Bahamas fell victim to ailments, causing a heavy drop in the export of this article. The completion of the Panama Canal and economic depression in adjoining sections of South and Central America terminated the pre-war demand for West Indian labor. No longer could the young men of Jamaica go to the Isthmus of Panama, Venezuela, Colombia, and Cuba and get employment. On the contrary, migrants were returning home. In 1917 the importation of West Indian coolies ended, but the majority of the indentured laborers remained.

Estate owners who had over-extended or spent money extravagantly during the fat years of the war now went bankrupt, as did many others whose fixed expenses exceeded their shrinking income. The population grew rapidly, increasing from nearly two millions in 1901 to more than three millions in 1936; unemployment and the drift of laborers to the towns added to the woes. Soon began the weary round of appeals for aid, investigations by representatives of the imperial government, and reports of committees and commissions. Lack of local initiative made well-nigh hopeless the task of making the West Indies prosperous.

As mentioned earlier, the sugar islands had been encouraged to grow tropical produce and to buy provisions from the outside. Launched on this course they stuck to it although ruin resulted therefrom. Despite good advice and much encouragement to grow their own food and utilize the fish in their own waters, the West Indies continued to import about £5,000,000 worth of foodstuffs annually; even the rice for the East Indian laborers was bought from abroad. The purchase of food and manufactured goods and the overseas indebtedness of private individuals as well as public bodies made constant the need for a relatively heavy export of goods to be sold in a competitive market.

Sugar remained the principal article of export. The war was disastrous for the European producers of beet sugar, whose share in the total world production of sugar fell from 45.3 per cent in 1913–1914 to 20.1 per cent in 1919–1920; hence the inflation of prices and the great profits for the producers of cane sugar in the war period. With the war over, beet sugar made a rapid recovery, the annual production rising from 3,326,000 to 8,316,000 metric tons in the years 1919–1924. Furthermore, in the post-war era the cane sugar countries increased their output tremendously, Cuba leading the world. Favored with a plentiful supply of capital and a preferential treatment in the United States market, Cuban sugar growers increased the crop from about 1,000,000 tons at the opening of the century to 5,250,000 in 1929.

Ensconced in the American market, Cuban exporters could dump their surplus in other countries. During the 1920's sugar-producing lands — notably Australia, Hawaii, Java, the Philippines, Puerto Rico, and San Domingo — extended their output from 50 to 100 per cent. Compared with the world production, the export of sugar from the British West Indies was small, averaging only about 300,000 tons in 1926–1928, but it was the chief cash crop of these colonies. Although their produce was favored by Britain and Canada with preferences — respectively 3*s.* 8*d.* and 4*s.* 8*d.* per cwt. — this aid was insufficient for their need. In spite of wages being depressed to the lowest possible level, it was found that the West Indian growers produced sugar at a loss. Consternation gripped them when Lord Passfield, colonial secretary in the new Labor ministry, announced in 1929 that the sugar preferences would be abandoned. Interested parties put pressure on the home government; as a result a sugar commission headed by Lord Olivier, ex-governor of Jamaica and secretary for India in the first Macdonald government, left England in October, 1929, to make a fresh study of the West Indian situation. The plight of the sugar growers seemed so desperate that the commission advised the imperial government to increase the sugar preference to 4*s.* 8*d.* per cwt., establish a single imperial sugar purchasing agency, and set a minimum price that would cover the cost of production. To this Britain could not agree. However, the home government promised to compensate West Indian bankers or local government units to the extent of one-half of losses sustained on advances to sugar growers, £300,000 being the maximum. This offer was not accepted and the West Indies sank deeper in the slough of despond. Gone were the days when sugar made fortunes for planters and for the merchants of Bristol and Liverpool.

Ill luck has pursued the West Indies for more than a century. Royal commissions as well as private visitors advised them to abandon sugar and diversify their industries. Although most of them found it impossible to give up old ways, some did. Fruit-growing seemed well suited to these tropical islands; in 1914 Jamaica produced one-third of the world's supply of bananas and had large orange groves. The citrus industry spread to other islands, but hardly was it well under way before competitors in Florida and California crowded the West Indian fruit out of the American market. Canada came to the rescue and since 1927 she has begun to outstrip the United Kingdom as a market for West Indian produce. The trade with Canada was furthered by preferential tariffs and improved banking and transportation facilities. The trade agreement of 1925 between the Dominion and the British colonies in the West Indies provided substantial Canadian tariff preferences on bananas, raw cocoa, cocoanuts, grapefruit, coffee, and other West Indian exports, in return for preferences on Canadian produce like flour, beef, fish, butter, lard, cordage, boots and shoes, boards, and shingles. The Bank of Nova Scotia, the Canadian Bank of Commerce, and the Royal Bank of Canada have branches in the important trading centers of the British West Indies; and subsidized steamers with specially designed cold storage facilities for fruit ply between their ports and those of eastern Canada.

Only British Guiana and Trinidad have industries other than those connected with tropical agriculture. In 1936 the former supplied about one-eleventh of the world's output of bauxite, her export being valued at £212,428. She was benefited by the rise in the price of gold in the 1930's; her export of the precious metal increased from 4264 oz. in 1928 to 39,047 oz. in 1937. In the same period the value of this export mounted from £16,000 to £211,000. The demand for Trinidad's asphalt and oil continued brisk. In 1936 the famous pitch lake accounted for $959,759, and crude oil and its by-products supplied $15,910,638, or about 60 per cent of the colony's total export.

Although the British West Indies lost out in the competition with Cuba, Hawaii, the Philippines, and Puerto Rice for the American sugar market, their economic relations remained close. Some of the islands, notably the Bahamas, imported more from their great neighbor than from either the United Kingdom or Canada, and as late as 1936 the United States was far and away the best customer for special products like the arrowroot of St. Vincent and the chicle of British Honduras. The American tourist traffic with the West Indies increased greatly while prohibition was in force in the United States. The islands, particularly Bermuda and the Bahamas, were important "oases" for thirsty Americans, a fact that explains the sudden rise in the government revenues of the Bahamas from £254,019 in 1919–1920 to £852,573 in 1922–1923. Since the repeal of prohibition West Indian cruises have become fashionable; it has been estimated that in 1937 more than 80 per cent of Bermuda's income was derived from tourists.

But the contributions made by tourists have been a mere drop in the economic bucket for the principal colonies of the British West Indies. In the thirties unemployment and low wages prevailed. The improved connections with the outside world and its advanced ideas, the return of West Indian laborers from employment elsewhere, and the growing consciousness among the working classes of the social backwardness of the islands brought strikes and disorders. In 1935 clashes between police and rioters resulted in 10 dead and 60 wounded; in 1937 these figures stood respectively at 29 and 115; and from January 1 till June 22, 1938, the lists totaled 10 and 123. Trinidad, St. Kitts, St. Vincent, and Jamaica were the centers of these outbreaks. Alarmed at the seriousness of the disorders, the imperial government sent Major St. J. Orde Browne to investigate and report on labor conditions in the West Indies. Between the time of his arrival in Trinidad on September 7, 1938, and his departure from Bermuda on April 12, 1939, he visited all the colonies. He found that trade unions in the modern sense were practically unknown and that only a few of these colonies had regulations concerning the employment of women and children, hours and condition of labor, minimum wage, and workmen's compensation. Where such existed they were of recent date and in many instances not yet in operation. However, several of the colonies prepared labor codes which went into effect in 1938 and 1939, and some of them had ambitious plans for establishing old age pensions, unemployment insurance, and other devices designed to improve the lot of laborers.

Education made relatively little progress in the period under discussion. Moreover, despite urging by imperial authorities, the schools of the West Indies continued to be of the academic rather than of the vocational type; little was done to prepare young men and women for their future occupations. In general the colonies were decidedly backward in education; thus in British Guiana in 1937, more than 10 per cent of the children of school age did not attend school. Higher education in the West Indies took a long step forward with the opening in October, 1922, of the Imperial College of Tropical Agriculture at St. Augustine, Trinidad. Funds for its establishment and maintenance were provided by private contributions, grants from the imperial government, and appropriations of the governments of Antigua, Barbados, British Guiana, Grenada, St. Kitts-Nevis, Trinidad and Tobago, and St. Vincent. The purpose of the college was to provide practical education for planters and administrators, to train technological specialists in the various branches of tropical agriculture, and to study the plant and animal diseases peculiar to the West Indies. The college rates as a higher institution of learning, offering research facilities for experts as well as for students who have had general scientific training in other institutions.

Though a century has passed since the West Indian Negroes were emancipated, their progress has been slow and they retain many traces of their former bondage and even of their African origin. They lack enterprise and cling to outworn and baneful traditions. A hovel will do for a home; a fear of ghosts haunts them as it did their forbears in the jungle. Their ideas of sanitation are primitive; though many of the islands have a healthful climate the death rate is high. Their dietary habits are still those of the day of predial servitude, with salt meat, salt fish, and starchy foods forming the staples. Nor have the moral principles inculcated by the representatives of the various religious denominations made much impression on the West Indians. In some of the islands 70 per cent or more of all the children are illegitimate; this may help to explain the appalling rate of infant mortality — when the child is not wanted little care is bestowed upon it.

The West Indies constantly appealed for aid from the imperial government. In 1932 the tariff preferences on their goods were increased and extended; but financial stringency at home, the tense international situation, and the competition in armaments precluded large grants to these distressed colonies. Meanwhile the greater preoccupation with their affairs led to increased control and supervision by the colonial office. Except in Bermuda and the Bahamas the whites formed but a small minority of the population, and the West Indians showed little aptitude for self-government. Whether a more complete mingling of the many races in these colonies will ultimately produce a new race better able to handle their own affairs remains to be revealed. The colonists have been content with their membership in the British empire. In 1936 some of them criticized Britain for failure to save Ethiopia, and occasionally voices were heard demanding a greater share in the government for the inhabitants of the islands; but by and large they preferred to remain British subjects. The status of Puerto Rico, Cuba, San Domingo, or Haiti seemed not to promise them greater prosperity and happiness than they enjoyed as citizens of the British empire.

CHAPTER 31

THE UNION OF SOUTH AFRICA, 1902–1939

THE Treaty of Vereeniging, May 31, 1902, rang down the curtain of a great drama, the Anglo-Boer war. The long bitter struggle ended at last — the scattered Boer commandos laid down their arms and were forced to recognize that their republics had ceased to exist. In return the victorious British pledged assistance in rebuilding and restocking farms and promised self-government in a not too distant future. To some of the Boer leaders the cup of submission was too bitter, rather than drain it they went into exile; but the greatest among them, Generals Louis Botha, J. H. de la Rey, J. B. M. Hertzog, and Jan Smuts did not desert their people. They considered the Boers — or Afrikanders as they prefer to be called — a nation; they knew that their blood was dominant among the whites south of the Zambezi; and some of them hoped that a return of the Liberals to power in Britain might mean freedom. Perhaps if they were patient, Kruger's dream of a United South Africa might yet come true. It did sooner than they had dared hope, but in 1902 there was no political union except the common allegiance to the British crown. The country was divided into four political entities — the Cape, Natal, the Orange River Colony, and the Transvaal — and besides there were three native protectorates and Rhodesia. As the war ended, the Cape was under martial law and the suspension of her constitution was being considered; the two former republics were now crown colonies; and only Natal enjoyed full self-government. Moreover, the possibility of a union of hearts of Boers and British seemed remote. The war had sundered old ties of blood and friendship; and the defeated Boers returned sullenly to charred homesteads, and visited with burning resentment in their hearts graves of women and children at the concentration camps. Indeed the memories of these innocent victims of the war have been as effective in keeping Boers and British apart in the twentieth century as were the ghosts of the Bezuidenhout brothers and their fellow victims of the Slachter's Nek rebellion in the first and second quarters of the nineteenth century.

Nevertheless, the barriers against a political union of South Africa were broken down in a surprisingly short time. On the eighth anniversary of the Treaty of Vereeniging a unitary state replaced four separate colonial governments. From that time until 1924 the government of the Union was in the hands of two of the foremost of its architects, Generals Botha and Smuts. But their insistence upon forgetting the past — the burying of racial animosities among the whites — alienated a large number of Boers. Under the leadership of General Hertzog this latter group secured control of the government in 1924. The pro-Afrikander and anti-British policy foreshadowed by the new premier before he took office was afterward modified; yet he continued to represent many of the ideals dear to the old republicans of the Orange Free State and the Transvaal, and he resisted attempts to identify South Africa closely with British aims and aspirations. The test came in September, 1939, when Britain was again at war with Germany. Hertzog favored neutrality for South Africa, whereas Smuts believed that when the British empire was at war the Union of South Africa was at war and should act accordingly. The governor general refused Hertzog's request for a dissolution and asked Smuts to form a new government. He complied, and after an absence of fifteen years returned to his old post as prime minister of the Union of South Africa. It is convenient to divide South African history since the Anglo-Boer war into three periods — 1902–1910, 1910–1924, 1924–1939. The narrative of events will follow the customary topical arrangement — domestic, political, social, and economic problems, intra-imperial relations, and foreign affairs.

The reconstruction after the war and the formation of the new union form the main themes in chronicling events in South Africa, 1902–1910. Although some had profited by the war, for South Africa as a whole, for whites and blacks alike, it had been an unmitigated calamity. Much property had been destroyed. Large areas of the two republics had become literally a "scorched land," with houses burned, cattle, sheep, and horses killed, and the fields overgrown with weeds. The mines on the Rand had been reopened in 1901, but lack of labor crippled operations. The British contributed about £10,000,000 toward the cost of rebuilding the farms which they had laid waste, and a loan of £35,000,000 guaranteed by the imperial government and chargeable to the joint revenues of the two new colonies was used for repairing damaged railroad lines, supplying rolling stock, and providing other much-needed improvements. When these sums were inadequate for the needs, Generals Botha, de la Rey, and de Wet went to Europe in 1903 to ask aid for their stricken country. They hoped to get something from France, Germany, and Holland, who had been so generous with their sympathy during the war, but they were disappointed. In England they were lionized by society, shown the strength of British sea power in a magnificent naval review, and then told by Joseph Chamberlain that the peace terms could not be modified though some further aid might be extended to Boer families in distress. The generals returned home disillusioned and convinced that the people of South Africa must rely upon themselves. Even nature double-crossed them — the drought of 1903 was one of the worst on record.

Lord Milner, now governor of both the Orange River Colony and the Transvaal, was anxious to restore the finances of the new colonies and make all South Africa prosperous. This could be achieved only by increasing the output of gold, which again depended upon the supply of labor. Before the war 100,000 natives, mostly from Portuguese East Africa, had been employed at the mines. They had been dispersed; and despite the labor agreement of 1901 with the Portuguese, less than 30,000 natives were working on the Rand when the war ended. Moreover, building and restoration work created an unprecedented demand for labor. Wages were high and the mines failed to attract the natives. A suggestion that more whites should be employed ran afoul the color bar against certain types of manual labor. The mine owners then turned their attention to the world's greatest reservoir of unskilled manual labor — China. Milner and the colonial office agreed to a plan for bringing in Chinese coolies under an indenture system. The Boers objected and so did Australia and New Zealand, who had helped to win the war and were strongly opposed to Asiatic immigration. British Liberals, Laborites, and humanitarians denounced the "Chinese slavery" in South Africa. They were outvoted for the time being, but the issue supplied an excellent slogan for the approaching British elections. Meanwhile Milner worked energetically at bringing in coolies. Before the end of 1904, 23,000 of them had arrived in South Africa; within the next year the number reached nearly 50,000. However, British voters in January, 1906, decided against the Chinese labor policy and the coolies were shipped back to their old homes, but not before prosperity had returned to South Africa. With it came another set of problems — the prosperity was confined to the Transvaal.

The minds of men again turned to an old issue — the union of all the white communities. Some of the enthusiasts for such a union believed that it might be achieved as soon as the war was over. The Cape was then under martial law and the former republics were crown colonies. Natal had self-government, but the ministry of the day desired a South African federation. By suspending the constitution of the Cape it might be possible to federate the four colonies by an imperial fiat. Rhodes had favored such action. After his death this policy was advocated by his former lieutenant, Dr. Jameson, now a leader of the pro-English Progressive party at the Cape. The Afrikander Bond opposed the suspension of the Cape constitution, as did also prominent leaders of English origin, notably J. X. Merriman. To their support came premiers Barton of Australia and Laurier of Canada meeting in London, 1902, at the colonial conference. Milner, always resolute and energetic, advocated the establishment of federation by the proposed short cut. Chamberlain wavered—the business man in him urged action, the statesman suggested caution. The latter won. Regular political institutions were re-established at the Cape, and South Africa was left free to work out her political destiny.

Some aid came, however, from the outside. Young men brought by Milner to South Africa to aid in the reorganization and administration of the new colonies (dubbed his kindergarten) worked and agitated unceasingly for a South African federation. Moreover, the generosity shown by the imperial government in bestowing self-governing institutions upon the Transvaal less than five years after the termination of the hostilities proved a great boon to the federation movement. As soon as the peace treaty had been signed, the two former republics were given the crown colony form of government with a nominated legislative council wholly dependent upon the governor. Milner gave the colonies an efficient government but he was an autocrat; furthermore, the Boers hated him, believing him to be the principal author of their misfortunes. Milner's departure from South Africa came as a relief to the Afrikanders. His successor, Lord Selborne, was tactful and conciliatory, anxious to heal the wounds caused by the war and bring the two white races together. At this time Alfred Lyttelton, who in 1903 had succeeded Chamberlain at the colonial office, promulgated constitutions establishing representative governments in the new colonies. Before these went into effect the Unionist government in England had been replaced by a Liberal one headed by Sir Henry Campbell-

Bannerman, who had been pro-Boer during the war. His government scored a great victory in the election of January, 1906, partly because of the unpopularity of his predecessor's Chinese labor policy. The repatriation of the coolies was a necessary fulfillment of election pledges, but no definite commitment had been made concerning self-government for the Boers. The British ministry included the leading Liberal imperialists – Asquith, Grey, and Haldane – and there was a possibility that the Lyttelton constitutions though distasteful to the Boers might be put into effect.

At this juncture General Jan Smuts, who had resumed law practice in Pretoria after the war and with Botha been instrumental in forming a new political party, Het Volk (the People), went to London and presented the case of the Boers to the prime minister. This sane, large-hearted, strong-minded Scot listened intently, asked a few pointed questions, but said little. Speech he reserved for the cabinet, where in a ten-minute oration he turned a hostile majority into one favoring the proposition that a fresh start must be made in South Africa – the Boers were to be the partners of the British. A colleague who was present described Campbell-Bannerman's speech on this occasion as "the most dramatic, the most important ten-minute speech delivered in our time." The Lyttelton constitutions were canceled and the Boers given responsible government. In December, 1906, this boon was granted to the Transvaal, and a few months later to the Orange River Colony. The magnanimity shown by the British made a profound impression upon Botha and Smuts. "They gave us back," said Smuts at a later day, "in everything but name – our country. After four years, has such a miracle of trust and magnanimity ever happened before? Only a people like the English could do it. They may make mistakes, but they're a big people." The first election in the Transvaal gave a majority to Het Volk; Botha became premier and represented the colony at the imperial conference of 1907, where he was received with marked attention. During his absence Smuts presided over the government of the Transvaal. The two represented a remarkable combination of courage, sincerity, initiative, breadth of view, and solid common sense. They were willing and indeed anxious to bury the past and to unite all whites in common efforts for the welfare of South Africa.

Meanwhile at the Cape the old political institutions had been restored and amnesty granted to those engaged in or suspected of treasonable activities during the war. The Boers regained their earlier political influence in the colony; and their leaders, Messrs. J. H. Hofmeyr, F. S. Malan, and W. P. Schreiner, no less than the leaders of the English element in the population, Dr. Jameson and Messrs. Smartt, Sprigg, and Merriman, agreed on the desirability of a political union of all British colonies south of the Zambezi. In 1908 J. X. Merriman replaced Dr. Jameson as prime minister at the Cape. He led the newly organized South African party which, as its name implied, strove to bring together all the whites. The leaders in the small colonies, Natal and the Orange Free State, also supported the agitation for a South African union or federation.

The political development as well as social and economic factors pointed toward a united South Africa. The Native Affairs Commission appointed in 1902 made careful studies of the problems presented by the non-European races, especially the Bantu. The tribal system was disintegrating, causing bewilderment. A rebellion in Natal in 1906 showed that the Zulu had not lost his prowess as a fighting man. This uprising caused nervousness among the whites and forced them to take stock of the situation — they were outnumbered about four to one. The native population increased faster than the white, and encouragement from America had resulted in the development of the so-called Ethiopian movement with the slogan "Africa for the Africans." It was realized that the different systems of native administration, the vexatious poll and hut taxes, and the irritating pass regulations tended to stir up dissatisfaction among the non-Europeans. If the white was to continue as the governing race, it seemed imperative that all Europeans should unite. Economic factors pointed in the same direction. The Rand quickly recaptured its old position as the economic center of South Africa, and this revived the former competition for its traffic. The Cape ports and railroads competed with Durban and Delagoa Bay for the traffic to Johannesburg. The Delagoa Bay route presented great advantages to the Transvaal. Moreover, since the Transvaal government had to look to Portuguese Africa for labor, the Portuguese authorities took care to combine the question of recruiting labor within their territories with that of securing traffic for the port of Delagoa Bay.

The economic boom which followed the cessation of hostilities soon collapsed at the Cape. In a spirit of optimism this colony constructed 1100 miles of railroads between 1902 and 1906 which during the depression years added to the woes of its treasury. The Progressives under Dr. Jameson held office from 1904 till 1908 and increased the public debt by more than £13,000,000. The veteran statesman, J. X. Merriman, who succeeded Jameson in 1908, was pledged to economy and a balanced budget. A disciple of Gladstone in finance, Merriman reduced the number of railroad and civil service employees and effected economies in nearly every branch of the government, but still the budget would not balance. The diamond industry suffered from the economic slump of 1907–1908 in America and Europe; extension of the income tax to the brackets below £1000, as well as new taxes on cigarettes and patent medicines, failed to yield the necessary revenue. Natal and the Orange River Colony suffered from financial difficulties — the Transvaal alone prospered. With the native protectorates and Rhodesia the colonies formed a customs union in 1903. The duties on imported goods were intended to serve the double purpose of protecting South African industries and providing revenue. Although duties were raised in 1906, the industrialists at the Cape and in Natal were not satisfied; they combined with the advocates of a revenue tariff in urging further revisions upward. To this the Transvaal was resolutely opposed; this colony wanted a lower tariff and threatened to break away from the customs union. A pooling of interests as regards both the railroad traffic and the tariff seemed the only alternative to suicidal economic rivalries and conflicts.

During the period of reconstruction in the two new colonies several of the most essential services were administered in common. Their railroads were combined into one system, as were also the constabulary and a number of minor services. The guaranteed loan of £35,000,000 was used for the benefit of both colonies and was a charge on common revenues. Lord Milner, governor of both, provided them with identical institutions. The South African customs union of 1903 embraced all the white communities. Lord Selborne, who was strongly in favor of a South African unitary state, was given an opportunity to present his views on this question when Dr. Jameson as prime minister of the Cape in a minute of November 28, 1906, invited the high commissioner to "review the colonial situation in South Africa in such a manner as may enable the people of this country to appreciate the difficulties of administration under the present system, and to consider whether (and if so by what means) it is advisable to establish a central national government embracing all the British Colonies and Protectorates." Lord Selborne forwarded this minute to the governments of Natal, the Orange River Colony, and the Transvaal, and to the administrator of Southern Rhodesia. When they concurred in the request, action followed quickly. On January 7, 1907, Lord Selborne issued his famous federation memorandum. This great state document presented in a clear, concise, and convincing manner the difficulties and dangers which confronted South Africa because of her lack of political unity. It was shown that these could not be overcome by piecemeal measures. Three roads were open: "the makeshift regime of the High Commissioner, the jarring separation of the States of South America, the noble union of the States of North America."

Although Lord Selborne carefully refrained from assuming a dictatorial attitude, it was perfectly clear that in his judgment a South African federation was an absolute necessity. The memorandum stimulated activity. Educational propaganda developed on a large scale; in this the young men who had been associated with Lord Milner's administration of the Orange River Colony and the Transvaal took a leading part. These men were responsible for the publication of two important books, one entitled *The Government of South Africa* presenting a well-written and well-documented argument for a federation, and the other, *The Framework of the Union,* depicting the characteristics of the leading federated governments then in existence. Thus the stage was set for the discussion of the future of South Africa which became inevitable when the Transvaal in 1907 demanded the abrogation of the existing customs and railroad agreements.

A customs conference at Pretoria in May, 1908, agreed to a series of resolutions to be submitted to the parliaments concerned, declaring that "an early union under the Crown of Great Britain" was desirable. It was suggested that delegates be appointed with power to consider and report on the form of such a union and to prepare a draft constitution. The resolutions were well received in South Africa. Leaders of all political parties supported the call for a national convention. Among the most out-spoken supporters of this move was the president of the Afrikander Bond, who expressed a belief that the Pretoria resolutions "would be a powerful factor in speedily establishing a united South Africa." Mr. Lionel Curtis organized a number of closer union societies and established a periodical, *The State,* which supplied a forum for the discussion of all problems connected with a South African union. M. T. Steyn, ex-president of the Orange Free State, threw the weight of his great influence behind the movement for union, as did also Generals Botha, de Wet, Hertzog, and Smuts, as well as the Cape political leaders, Jameson, Merriman, and Sauer. The press in South Africa and Britain pronounced their blessing upon it; British statesmen gave it their support. On the eve of the national convention General Botha issued a stirring appeal to the people of South Africa. The former comander-in-chief of the Transvaal army, now the colony's prime minister, warned his fellow citizens that "South Africa has its opportunity now"; he expected South Africa "to do its duty." His own views as to the form of the proposed government were clearly stated. "I expect," he said, "the result of the Convention to include unity and therefrom to arise and develop a happy, prosperous, strong, and healthy nation."

The convention that decided the fate of South Africa met at Durban on October 12, 1908. It consisted of 30 representatives elected by the colonial parliaments — 12 from the Cape Colony, 8 from the Transvaal, and 5 each from the Orange River Colony and Natal. All political parties and shades of opinion were represented; of the outstanding leaders the only absentees were J. H. Hofmeyr and W. P. Schreiner. The former had refused to become a member of the Cape delegation, and the latter had resigned because the meeting of the convention coincided with the trial of Dinizulu, the Zulu chief, accused of incitement to the Natal rebellion of 1906; Schreiner defended him. The chief justice of the Cape Colony, Sir (later Lord) J. H. de Villiers was chosen president and M. T. Steyn of the Orange River Colony vice-president of the convention. Unification was urged by the best-organized groups present, namely, the Transvaal delegation and the representatives of the Progressive party at the Cape, both of whom brought staffs of experts. General Smuts and Mr. Lionel Curtis were the guiding spirits of these groups. The convention worked behind closed doors. It moved to Capetown November 23, meeting there in two sessions and adjourning February 3, 1909. It convened again at Bloemfontein May 3 to consider amendments which were offered to the original draft. The unionists had practically a clear field inasmuch as their chief opponents Hofmeyr and Schreiner were absent. It was agreed that the new state should be a legislative union with the four colonies as provinces subordinate to the central government.

The question of the franchise caused a great deal of difficulty because the representatives from the Cape were pledged to maintain the franchise for the colored people while those from the other colonies were strongly opposed to granting votes to non-Europeans. It was finally agreed to keep the existing arrangement for voting in each colony and to count only males of European descent in allocating representatives from the provinces in the Union parliament. This parliament was made bicameral — a senate of 40 members of whom 8 were elected by a system of indirect elections from each of the four provinces, the remaining 8 being nominated by the governor general, and a house of assembly to consist of 121 members, with 51 from the Cape, 36 from the Transvaal, and 17 from each of the other two provinces. This arrangement was to remain undisturbed for ten years and to be changed later by an automatic redistribution following each census. The language question aroused much controversy and even threatened to disrupt the work of the convention. Under the guidance of General Hertzog, the delegation from the Orange River Colony fought strenuously for absolute language equality. The question was settled by affirming that the Union was to be bilingual without going into details as to how this bilingualism would be safeguarded. Compromises were reached on the questions of location of the capital and the distribution of the railroad traffic. The executive capital was to be Pretoria, the legislative capital Capetown; the appellate division of the supreme court was to sit at Bloemfontein. Natal was to receive 30 per cent of the railroad traffic, Delagoa Bay 50 to 55 per cent; the remainder would go to Cape ports.

After the draft of the constitution had been completed, the closer union societies carried on an active propaganda in its favor. Hofmeyr and Schreiner failing to mobilize a strong opposition, the constitution was approved by three of the colonial parliaments and by a popular referendum in Natal. The high commissioner, Lord Selborne, remained studiously fair and correct throughout this period. His own views were well known, but he felt strongly that the question was one for the people of South Africa to settle in their own way. The imperial government and the British press had likewise been friendly and sympathetic while following a strict hands-off policy. The new South African constitution met with general approval in Britain. *The Times* described it as a "proud achievement of which the statesmen who modelled it and the people who introduced it have every reason to be proud."

A delegation from South Africa headed by W. P. Schreiner tried in vain to arouse the friends of the aborigines in England to exert pressure on members of the British parliament to amend the clause barring non-Europeans from holding seats in the parliament of the Union. Their cause was championed in the house of commons by Sir Charles W. Dilke; but since it was clear that the "colour bar" represented the wishes of the overwhelming majority of the whites in South Africa, the imperial government refused to accept amendments to the completed document. The prime minister, Mr. Asquith, and the leader of the opposition, Mr. Balfour, praised the task accomplished by the statesmen of South Africa and warned the house of commons "not to wreck this great work . . . of freedom and reconciliation." The constitution bill passed both houses of the British parliament without division.

The Union of South Africa was announced officially by a royal proclamation of December 2, 1909, and the eighth anniversary of the end of the Anglo-Boer war was fixed as the date for putting the new government into operation. Lord Gladstone, youngest son of the great Liberal leader, was appointed the first governor general of the Union, and General Louis Botha became its first prime minister. Four members of his government came from the Cape, three from the Transvaal, and two each from the Orange Free State (the old name was restored) and Natal. Botha and Smuts had reorganized their own party, baptizing it the South African National party. It held 66 seats in the Union's first parliament, and since the British or Unionist party strongly supported General Botha the new government was launched with an overwhelming majority in the legislature.

Although deeply occupied with domestic affairs, 1902–1910, the colonies of South Africa did not neglect imperial problems. At the colonial conference of 1902 the prime minister of Natal, Sir Albert Hime, supported Joseph Chamberlain while Sir Gordon Sprigg from the Cape sided with Barton of Australia and Laurier of Canada in opposing him. The Cape agreed to an annual contribution of £50,000 and Natal to one of £30,000 for naval defense. Joseph Chamberlain made a short visit to South Africa in January, 1903, and what he learned there strengthened his belief in the need for an imperial preferential tariff. The South African customs union fell in with his plan to the extent of granting a 25 per cent preference on British goods; this was followed by preferential tariff agreements with Canada in 1904, Australia in 1906, and New Zealand in 1907. At the imperial conference of 1907 General Botha, representing the Transvaal, struck a responsive chord by his advocacy of cooperation within the empire, although this was coupled with a warning that the self-governing colonies must have an absolutely free hand in internal affairs. The point was of special significance for the Transvaal which, contrary to the wishes of the imperial government, insisted on passing discriminatory laws against Asiatics.

The colonial defense conference of 1909 was held before the Union had been established; hence no decision could then be made concerning the part to be taken by South Africa in any scheme for imperial defense. However, it was understood that her military organization would be based upon British models, and a program of military training stood high on the list of tasks to be accomplished by the first government of the Union.

South Africa differs from Australia and Canada in being a unitary state. Her constitution provides for the continuance of the four colonies as units of administration completely subordinated to the central government. The provinces cannot challenge the supreme authority of the Union on any point. Questions such as education, agriculture, roads, markets and pounds, fish and game preservation are handled by the provincial councils, but all their ordinances are subject to the approval of the government of the Union. Four-fifths of the senators are elected in equal numbers from each province by the members of the provincial council and its representatives in the house of assembly. Four of the eight senators appointed by the governor general are chosen because of their familiarity with the problems of the natives. The parliament of the Union consists of the king, the senate, and the house of assembly, the last being the dominant power. The executive council must be supported by a majority in the assembly. Deadlocks between the two houses may be broken by joint sittings. The house of assembly is elected for five years but, as is the case in the other dominions, it may be dissolved before that time. In South Africa the legislative is superior to the judicial branch of the government; the framers of the constitution made definite efforts to create a strong central government.

As already indicated, General Botha was chosen by Lord Gladstone to head the first government of the Union. Although events proved the choice a fortunate one, at the time of the appointment many felt that the ex-prime minister of the Cape, J. X. Merriman, had a better claim to the premiership by virtue of long experience in high office and because the oldest colony had also the longest parliamentary tradition. Merriman, declining Botha's offer of a place in the ministry, assumed the role of a discriminating critic of the government, which despite its large majorities in divisions faced a difficult situation. The Union had been launched on a wave of emotional enthusiasm that could not endure — the idea of a unitary state had been "sold" to the people of South Africa by high-pressure salesmanship the effects of which soon wore off. The native danger had been exaggerated and the depth of Boer resentment to the English minimized during the agitation. Jealousies and rivalries between some of the leaders, especially between Botha and Smuts on one side and Hertzog on the other, helped to block the much-hoped-for union of hearts. General Botha was one of the great statesmen of the present century, great as Lincoln was great when he pleaded for the healing of the wounds of the United States following the Civil War, but he lacked experience; the tasks which confronted the Union were of exceptional magnitude, and they had to be accomplished under the shadow of and during the great war of 1914–1918.

Botha and Smuts wished to bury the past and trust the British. Herein in their judgment lay the salvation for South Africa as a white man's country. Hertzog's vision was more limited and he was tormented by an inferiority complex which made him bitterly resentful of anything that might be construed as a slight to either himself or his racial group. As a member of the Transvaal government, Smuts had aroused the ire of Dutch Reformed preachers by putting education under government control, making English compulsory and Dutch optional in the schools. Moreover, he had proposed the purchase of the great Cullinan diamond as a present to the king. Hence the Boers of the backveld suspected him of toadying to the British. Hertzog was different. In the Orange Free State where he was the actual leader, both European languages were compulsory in the schools. He had accepted the portfolio as minister of justice in the Union government, but Botha, apparently reluctant to have him, had negotiated through Smuts. This rankled. In the early days of the Union, Hertzog praised the British empire and seemed satisfied with the new political arrangement, its ideals and aims. But before long he began to accuse Botha of weakness and joined the chorus that ridiculed his wearing knee breeches and silk stockings at royal levées during the imperial conference of 1911; the vision of their leader in court dress offended backveld Boers with their memories of burned farmsteads and children's graves. To them Hertzog seemed *the* man — no mealy-mouthed wishy-washy toadying to the English about *him.* The Union government refused to make both English and Dutch compulsory in the elementary schools; the parents were to decide. The backvelders saw in this a slap at their mother tongue, Afrikaans. Hertzog agreed with this interpretation, criticized his colleagues, and announced that the British and Boers formed two streams in South Africa which could never unite. The union of hearts was an idle dream. Called upon by Botha to explain or withdraw from the government, Hertzog refused to do either. The premier then had the government resign in December, 1912, and reorganized it leaving Hertzog out. From then dates a new national movement among the Boers of South Africa.

Some of the difficulties which beset Botha and his colleagues were inherent in the conditions of South Africa, but others may be attributed to their inexperience. The latter accounts, at least in part, for the conflicts with organized labor, 1913–1914. Before the union Smuts had taken a strong stand against the demands of labor in the Transvaal, offering the unemployed 3*s.* 6*d.* when they demanded 5*s.* a day, and calling out troops belonging to the British garrison against miners who had fought under him in the war. This happened in 1907. Since then labor organizers had been active among the white laborers on the Rand, some of whom were recent arrivals from England imbued with radical ideas while others had drifted in from South African farms and villages ready from the beginning to fight the mine owners who carried away the riches of the subcontinent. Although white laborers constituted only about one-tenth of all labor employed at the mines on the Rand, they held a monopoly of the managerial positions and of all tasks requiring special training. However, both Chinese and Bantu laborers could be trained to replace them in many posts. Consequently the whites had to organize both for the purpose of improving laboring conditions and in order to maintain a color bar.

Legislation of 1911–1912 aimed at checking the ravages of phthisis and other diseases endemic in the mines, and at entrenching the whites in all key positions. The mining companies were unwilling to recognize the miners' union. This issue came to a test in May–July, 1913, when a dispute over the dismissal of some white miners led to a general walkout by all white laborers on the Rand and even in Johannesburg. The government at first tried to remain neutral, but the critical situation that might develop if more than 200,000 native laborers got out of control compelled intervention. Because the Union as yet had no organized military force, imperial troops were brought in. A clash between soldiers and strikers resulted in the death of twenty-one and the wounding of forty-seven people, many of them innocent bystanders. Strikers threatened to shoot Botha and Smuts, who had come from Pretoria to bring peace. Peace was established on terms dictated by the strikers, which included recognition of their union. Smuts in particular felt deeply humiliated by a peace which some of the labor leaders considered a mere truce.

By January, 1914, the employees of the state-owned railroads had been organized, and they left their jobs to enforce demands presented by white coal miners in Natal. This walkout was followed by a general strike, and again a dangerous situation was created in Johannesburg. By issuing orders for military organization of their forces, the strike committee challenged the government. Forewarned by their experience six months earlier, Botha and Smuts struck swiftly. The Rand was placed under martial law, burghers were called out under the old commando regulations, and newly organized military defense units were mobilized; they had orders to shoot if strikers refused to heed warnings. Nine of their leaders were seized, rushed to Durban, and placed on a ship ready to sail for England. They were on the high seas before an attempt could be made to free them by writs of habeas corpus. The victory was complete, bloodless, and Pyrrhic. The illegal acts of the Botha government aroused bitter resentment in both South Africa and England. South African labor thereupon entered politics determined to get revenge on Smuts, whom it regarded as the chief culprit. Thus Hertzog found allies.

On the all-important color question the government generally held the Boer view — the sons of Ham shall serve. The labor regulations for the mines recognized the color bar, and a land act of 1913 restricted the right of natives to acquire land. This legislation was not sufficiently restrictive to please the Boers and too restrictive to suit the British. It outraged English humanitarians. Although the native and colored population of the Union lacked leaders of their own, not so the Indians. From being coolies under indenture bound to return to India after a limited period, thousands of Indians had become permanent residents. In Natal they were valued as laborers on tea and sugar plantations; they refused to be restricted, branching out as independent laborers and small traders. They underbid the whites and further tangled the skein of racial relations in South Africa. From Natal the Indians went into the Transvaal, where Kruger had legislated against them and the British colonial office had been their protector in the pre-war years. Milner had imposed more severe restrictions upon the Indians in the Transvaal than had Kruger; the Transvaal regime of Botha and Smuts went beyond Milner's.

The cause of the Indians was championed by one of their own men, Mohandas Karamchand Gandhi. The Transvaal in 1907 passed a law requiring all Asiatics to register and be fingerprinted; the Indians refused and appealed to London. When this was of no avail, at Gandhi's suggestion they offered passive resistance and went willingly to jail. Smuts, who led the fight for the government, was embarrassed. The jails became overcrowded; the imperial government, fearing the repercussion in India, urged repeal of the offensive law against Asiatics. But when this was done, another almost equally offensive took its place – Indians were forbidden to enter the Transvaal and those who were residents had to register. The laws of Natal were nearly as objectionable to them. With the Union, South Africa was prepared to offer a common front against the Asiatics. Again Smuts faced Gandhi. The situation in India was critical; hence the India government as well as the imperial government watched events in South Africa with misgivings.

For three years some of the best brains of South Africa, England, and India sought to find a compromise between the Indian demand for equality and the insistence on the part of South Africans that Asiatics be restricted and kept inferior to the Europeans. By 1914 various compromises had been reached. Specific references to Indians and Asiatics were omitted in immigration and other laws and the special tax on non-indentured Indians was repealed, but they were still limited with reference to landholding, trading licences, and traveling within the Union. Nor could they acquire the franchise except at the Cape. The indenturing of Indian coolies for Natal ceased in 1911; those then under indenture were to leave for India five years later. In the summer of 1914 Gandhi transferred his activities to the wider field of his native land.

The fateful year 1914 brought strife to South Africa. In the eighties commercial interests at the Cape had resented the establishment of a German colony in Southwest Africa, and Britain later had feared German intrigues with the Boer republics. The possibility of an Anglo-German war had been a factor in bringing about the formation of the Union, and for this reason the new government lost little time in providing South Africa with a military defense system. The commandos were abolished; in their stead the Defense Act of 1912 established the principle of universal liability for military service in the defense of the Union for all males of European descent between the ages of 17 and 60 and provided military training for youths between 17 and 25. The army was to be organized on British models along lines worked out by South African and imperial military authorities. The imperial troops were withdrawn from South Africa save for a small force at the naval base of Simonstown. The day before the war broke out between Britain and Germany Botha assured Asquith of South African cooperation in the impending conflict. Shortly afterward it was suggested that the Union should occupy the ports of Lüderitzbucht and Swakopmund in German South Africa and destroy her powerful wireless station at Windhoek. Botha agreed to do this, and the plan was sanctioned by the Union parliament, meeting in a brief special session early in September, 1914. This decision precipitated a civil war in South Africa which might have assumed dangerous proportions if it had not been for Botha's prestige and his resolute measures.

The roots of the South African rebellion of 1914 are found in the age-old hostility between Boers and British, the memories of the war of 1899–1902, the Boers' resentment of slights or fancied slights to their language and nationality, and Kruger's dream of establishing one great Afrikander republic. Ex-president Steyn of the Orange Free State, Generals Hertzog and de Wet, and a considerable number of backveld Boers were either jealous of Botha or disappointed with him as well as with the results of the union. They had no quarrel with Germany, whom they had once believed to be the friend of the Boers, and they objected to having the Union used by Britain for her own imperialistic purposes. The time seemed propitious for paying off old scores, for avenging the victims of the Anglo-Boer war. In Europe Germany was marching from victory to victory; Britain had not yet established an absolute control of the seas; the imperial troops were being removed from South Africa; the latter's own military defense force was commanded by an intransigent Boer, General Beyers; and the Germans had a considerable body of troops in Southwest Africa which could be counted upon if Britain's power on the subcontinent was challenged. The great barrier to the success of the rebels was General Botha. This strong and resolute man had taken an oath of allegiance which he would not break; he felt that Britain had kept her word to the Boers; he knew that the salvation of South Africa lay in the unity of the whites. The fomenters of discord must be struck down even though they were his old comrades in arms.

At a special session of the Union parliament convened on September 9, Botha proposed an attack upon German Southwest Africa; Hertzog opposed it, urging South African neutrality in the war. Botha's plan carried, and preparations for an expeditionary force went forward. Meanwhile German agents tried to stir up disaffection among the Boers in the western Transvaal. Herein they were aided by a Boer farmer, Nicholas van Rensburg, who prophesied that Germany would defeat Britain. Lieutenant-Colonel Solomon G. Maritz, commander of the military force on the border of the Union and German Southwest Africa, established treasonable contacts with the Germans shortly after the outbreak of the war in Europe. C. R. Beyers, commandant-general of the Union, resigned his commission as a protest against the projected attack upon the German colony, and both he and Botha strove hard to win over to their respective sides General J. H. de la Rey, who enjoyed great prestige in the western Transvaal. However, before the latter had committed himself, he was accidentally killed the evening of September 15 while traveling with Beyers to a gathering of young Boers at Potchefstroom. Botha's enemies accused the government of having murdered de la Rey. Despite the efforts of Botha and Smuts to keep things quiet, plans for a rebellion were in progress, with Maritz, Beyers, Major J. C. G. Kemp, and General Christian de Wet as leaders. Although the greatest number of rebels came from their province, the Orange Free State, General Hertzog and ex-President Steyn remained neutral.

Maritz led some of his troops into open rebellion on October 9, but was soon forced to seek refuge in German territory. Serious fighting between government forces and rebels began on October 29 but was of comparatively short duration. Kemp escaped to the Germans; Beyers fled, drowning in an attempt to swim across the Vaal River. Botha took the field in person against de Wet and shattered his forces. De Wet, the old master of escapes, found that conditions of guerrilla fighting had changed since the Boer War. He was captured early in December, and before New Year, 1915, the South African civil war was virtually ended. The government acted with wise moderation. The overwhelming majority of the rebels were granted amnesty; some were sentenced to fines and imprisonment; only one was executed.

The quelling of the rebellion enabled Botha to prosecute the war against the Germans with greater vigor. Here, too, he assumed personal command. Two columns attacked the Germans from the sea, a third advanced by land. After some sharp fighting the main German force surrendered on July 9, 1915, and the campaign was over save for small mopping-up operations. Shortly afterward Botha's political party, the South African, suffered reverses in the second general election of the Union, for many who had not dared attack him in the field stabbed him at the ballot box. His followers in the house of assembly were reduced to 54. Hertzog's Nationalists, now definitely in opposition to the government, mustered 27; the popular vote had been much closer – 95,000 to 77,000. The British party, the Unionist, led by Sir Thomas Smartt, held the balance of power. It supported Botha with the understanding that South Africa should do her bit for the empire.

An opportunity presented itself in East Africa. Britain could not spare military forces from home for the conquest of the German colony in this region, and the garrisons of the adjoining British colonies were inadequate for the task. Troops were gathered from India, the West Indies, and the various sections of British Africa. General Jan Smuts commanded this heterogeneous army from February, 1916, until January of the following year. The enemy proved elusive; the last remnant of his force did not surrender until November 25, 1918, two weeks after the end of hostilities in Europe. During the later guerrilla stages of this war another South African, General J. L. Van Deventer, commanded the British troops. South Africa made large contributions in both men and equipment to the campaign in Central and East Africa. The total number of white South Africans employed in this campaign has been given as 43,477, with 2762 casualties including 1611 deaths. Although the African sideshows absorbed a major portion of South Africa's war efforts, volunteers from the Union joined both English and Australian contingents in the early stages of the war; and in June, 1915, it was decided to send an infantry brigade to Europe. This force, complete with heavy artillery, signal, and field ambulance units, and consisting of nearly 7000 officers and men, left South Africa in August–October, 1915. After preliminary training in England it saw service first in Egypt against the Senussi on the western border, and later in France. Heavy casualties necessitated frequent replacements. It has been computed that South Africa raised 30,719 white troops of all ranks for service in Europe; her total for all fronts and the home establishment was 146,615, or approximately 20 per cent of her European adult male population. Another large contribution consisted of colored and native labor units totaling nearly 84,000 men, of whom 27,000 served in Europe.

By the end of the war Generals Botha and Smuts had won acclaim both within and outside the British empire as two of the truly great men of that generation. But the old saying, "A prophet hath no honour in his own country," held true in their case, for the Boers reviled them as traitors and renegades. With Smuts absent, first in East Africa and, after March, 1917, in Europe, Botha had to shoulder alone the heavy burdens of government, calumny, and vituperation. In 1917 Hertzog and his followers spoke openly of their desire to establish a South African republic and of their belief in the ultimate victory of Germany. Moreover, they held that their solution of the South African problem was in complete harmony with the doctrine of self-determination preached by President Wilson and Mr. David Lloyd George. The losses and sacrifices connected with the Union's participation in the war, the various war-time restrictions such as censorship, and above all the lower price fixed by the British government for the wool clip of 1917 as compared with the price prevailing in the previous year – all were used without stint by those who wished to arouse hostility against the British. Rumors of a second rebellion and the possibility of native disturbances were heard in 1917.

Botha and Smuts represented South Africa at the peace conference in Paris, 1919. They attracted much attention and the latter wielded great influence in the preparation of the Covenant of the League of Nations. The signing of the peace treaty by the German delegation reminded Botha of his own *via dolorosa* at Vereeniging seventeen years earlier. He and Smuts had deep misgivings concerning the effects of the treaty with Germany, and the fact that the former German colony in Southwest Africa was assigned to the Union as a mandate gave them little joy. Tired and disheartened, Botha returned home. The Nationalists, whose delegation had been given the cold shoulder by the peace conference, flung themselves at him; but his Lincoln-like plea for forbearance and united effort in healing the nation's wounds fell on deaf ears. On August 28, 1919, his weary soul found release, and South Africa lost her greatest son.

Deprived of the calm counsel and steadying influence of his friend, General Smuts took over the premiership. Parliament met, ratified the peace treaty, agreed to assume the administration of German Southwest Africa, and was dissolved shortly afterward. The elections of March, 1920, increased the strength of the Nationalists to 44; Smuts' South African party numbered 41, the Unionists 25, and the Laborites 21 in the new house of assembly. Smuts sought coalition with the Unionist and Labor parties, but the former was not willing to lose its identity as a British party and the latter had disliked him ever since he was attorney-general of the Transvaal. An appeal to Hertzog for a party truce met no encouragement. Hertzog had now adopted "South Africa first" (South Africa for the Afrikanders) as his slogan. With the support of three Independents and the Unionists Smuts carried on the government through the year 1920. Parliament was again dissolved on the last day of December, with election fixed for February, 1921. Before this took place the Unionists joined with the South Africans; the enlarged party secured 79 as against 45 Nationalists, 9 Laborites and 1 Independent in the new assembly.

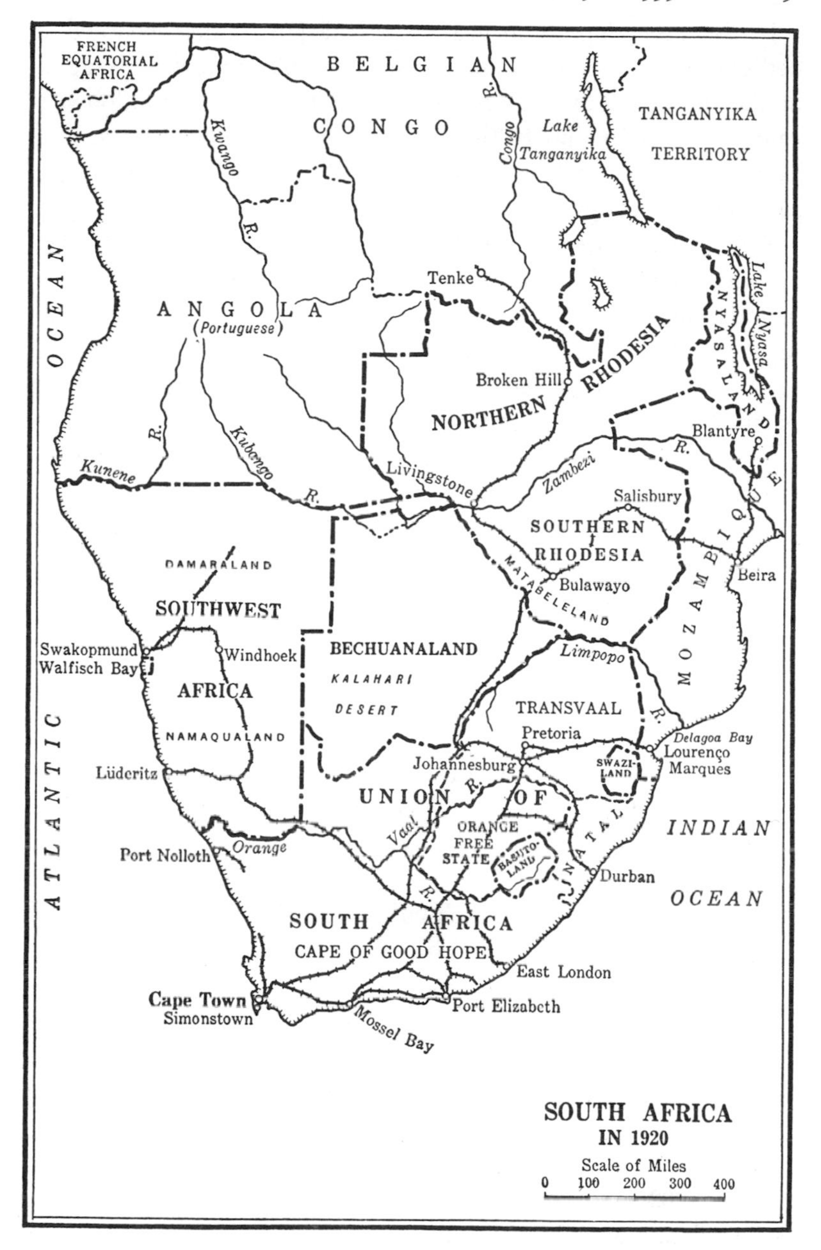
FRENCH EQUATORIAL AFRICA
BELGIAN
CONGO
Kwango
R.
Congo R.
Lake Tanganyika
TANGANYIKA TERRITORY
OCEAN
ANGOLA
(Portuguese)
Tenke
Broken Hill
NORTHERN RHODESIA
NYASALAND
Lake Nyasa
Blantyre
R.
Kunene
Kubango
R.
Livingstone
Zambezi
Salisbury
SOUTHERN RHODESIA
MATABELELAND
Bulawayo
Beira
MOZAMBIQUE
DAMARALAND
SOUTHWEST AFRICA
Swakopmund
Walfisch Bay
Windhoek
BECHUANALAND
KALAHARI DESERT
Limpopo
TRANSVAAL
Pretoria
Delagoa Bay
Lourenço Marques
NAMAQUALAND
Lüderitz
Johannesburg
SWAZILAND
UNION OF SOUTH AFRICA
Vaal R.
ORANGE FREE STATE
BASUTOLAND
NATAL
INDIAN OCEAN
ATLANTIC
Port Nolloth
Orange
Durban
CAPE OF GOOD HOPE
East London
Cape Town
Simonstown
Mossel Bay
Port Elizabeth
SOUTH AFRICA IN 1920
Scale of Miles
0 100 200 300 400

In the following three years General Jan Smuts occupied a pedestal outside his own country; at home his name was dragged in the mud and in 1924 he was flung from office and power. America, Europe, and British empire countries looked upon him as one of the great leaders of mankind. His opinions were solicited, his statements were quoted everywhere. He carried weight at the imperial conferences of 1921 and 1923. In 1921 he was asked to aid in bringing peace to Ireland, and direct negotiations between the Sinn Feiners and the British government resulted from his efforts; in 1923 he contributed materially to the settlement of the Ruhr question. But Smuts could not pacify South Africa. His failure at home may be attributed in part to the Boer distrust of the clever man, to Smuts' lack of the true politician's art of keeping friends and conciliating foes, and to his broad views concerning South African unity and the need for maintaining a British Commonwealth of Nations. The major reason for his failure, however, was the special post-war conditions in the Union — conditions prescribed by the general world situation as well by problems peculiar to South Africa. Dislocation of trade and industry, political and social unrest, unemployment and falling prices were among the aftermaths of the war of 1914–1918. South African soldiers found their jobs gone when they returned to civil life; the drop in gold prices which began in the twenties caused distress to the Union's key industry; natives in the labor corps returned from Europe with new ideas and demands; catchwords like "the dictatorship of the proletariat" made appeals to both whites and blacks. And among the Boers, whether in the labor unions on the Rand or in the backveld of the Orange Free State, there existed a deep, rankling hatred and distrust of Britain and the British, emotions kept alive and strengthened by the political agitation of General Hertzog and his Nationalists.

The South African natives were restive after the war. In 1920, 71,000 native workers in the mines on the Rand went on strike, demanding higher pay. At Port Elizabeth early in the same year a union of native laborers threatened to strike for increased wages; the president of the union was arrested, and six Europeans and sixty-eight natives were killed or wounded in a clash outside the jail. In old Kaffraria a native prophet, Enoch by name, announced that the millennium was at hand. Thousands of his followers encamped at a place called Bullhoek to await this happy event. They stayed for months, became a menace to the neighborhood, and defied orders to disperse. Finally, in April, 1921, the government resorted to force—"machine guns against assegais." The military lost one man while "nearly three hundred Kaffirs were killed and wounded." In 1922 a Hottentot rebellion in the mandated area of Southwest Africa was put down by the use of airplanes; rebel casualties were heavy. Although the Nationalists would doubtless have been equally if not more severe than Smuts in handling native disturbances, it gave them much satisfaction to denounce him as a butcher.

More serious than the trouble with the natives were the disorders among the whites on the Rand, January–March, 1922, which assumed the form of a revolution. The Rand area, stretching for a distance of about sixty miles with Johannesburg as the center, contains the great coal and gold mines of South Africa. At Pretoria thirty-five miles away are the shops for the government-owned railroads. As already mentioned, unskilled labor in the mines was done by natives, numbering in the twenties somewhat more than 200,000. In the early days many of the skilled miners were British, largely Cornish, but after the war Boers constituted perhaps three-fourths of the 22,000 whites normally employed at the mines. They were strongly unionized both for the purpose of getting better terms from the mine owners and in order to protect the color bar and the other devices designed to keep the natives in their humble position. Employees of the municipally owned public utilities of Johannesburg as well as of the state railroads and the railroad shops were also strongly organized and generally affiliated with the

Labor party led by Colonel F. H. P. Cresswell. Budgetary difficulties in the post-war years necessitated cuts in pay and reductions in staff which aroused resentment among government employees. A sense of grievance prevailed also among the white workers in the mines, many of whom could hardly be rated as skilled, for they were of course anxious to protect job and pay when falling prices on gold threatened both. Boers among them were infected with the anti-English virus, and since the government of Smuts was suspected of being pro-English this meant that a considerable section of the miners was anti-government. Moreover, memories of action taken against strikers in 1913–1914 made labor in general strongly anti-Smuts. Radical agitators, many of whom were English, found willing listeners when in 1921 they urged that labor, meaning thereby white labor, should seize the mines. The mine owners, represented by the Johannesburg chamber of mines, assumed an uncompromising attitude in labor disputes. Consequently labor began to prepare for armed conflict by organizing commandos, drilling, and securing arms.

In January, 1922, the entire Rand area was paralyzed by a general strike that affected both mines and public utilities. The situation assumed an ugly aspect with the hoisting of the red flag and much talk of a red republic. Organized labor in revolt apparently expected support from the Nationalist Boer farmers of the Orange Free State and the Transvaal, for the phantom of a possible labor-farmer alliance flickered in South Africa as elsewhere before those who hoped to organize society and government after a new model. Nationalists in the Union parliament, among whom Tielman Roos from the Transvaal was the most vehement, blamed the government for the troubles on the Rand. Smuts had no difficulty in assembling a burgher force for the purpose of putting down what appeared to be a revolution. He went to Johannesburg and took command. Guns, armored cars, and airplanes were used against the rioters; their Council of Action failed to strike quickly. After some fierce fighting and much bloodshed order was restored. The roll of dead and wounded included 292 police and soldiers, 157 rioters, 87 non-combatants, and 152 natives. The fact that snipers were shot without trial raised a great outcry among the Nationalists. Smuts was charged with failure to handle the strike in its early stages and with responsibility for the bloodshed; he was denounced as a man of blood.

To the north of the Transvaal lies the self-governing colony of Southern Rhodesia. Smuts hoped it would join the Union, but the proposal was turned down by the Rhodesians. Failure was written across his record as prime minister of South Africa. His prestige abroad, his reputation in the councils of the British empire counted for nought in the eyes of his own countrymen. Labor and Nationalists joined to bring him down. They succeeded. The returns for the general election of 1924 showed 63 Nationalists, 18 Laborites, 53 supporters of Smuts and 1 Independent. Aided by Labor, General Hertzog became the third prime minister of the Union of South Africa.

This change of regime supplies a convenient stopping place from which to survey the economic and social changes and policies in South Africa in the period 1902–1924. Few countries have experienced more kaleidoscopic changes within twenty-two years. Close on the reconstruction and reorganization necessitated by the Anglo-Boer war followed the establishment of responsible government in the Transvaal and the Orange River Colony, the formation of the Union, the Four Years' War, and the perplexing domestic and international problems of the post-war years.

Although there was little time for orderly progress in the fields of economic and social relations, some significant changes took place. Agriculture — the basic industry of South Africa — contended with many difficulties peculiar to the subcontinent. Among these drought and plant and animal diseases were of special significance. The droughts of 1903 and 1921 brought heavy losses to all South Africa. The fight against pests of various kinds as well as work to improve the quality and increase the quantity of the produce of the soil went on more successfully after the organization of the Union department of agriculture in 1911. The extent of its activities may be roughly gauged by the size of its budget which for the fiscal year 1919–1920 showed expenditures totaling £620,820. Considerable sums for agricultural education and laboratories and the work of governmental institutions were supplemented by those from voluntary organizations.

The success of these efforts is revealed by the fact that in the ten-year period 1910–1920 South Africa changed from an importing to an exporting country for beef, bacon, ham, and lard, that the production of cheese increased about 800 per cent and butter production nearly doubled. Excepting gold, wool continued to be the chief article of export. Its value of course fluctuated with the price on the world market. A record was set in 1919 when nearly £18,000,000 worth was exported, about two-fifths of which went to the United Kingdom. Among the minerals not subject to regulation of output, coal showed a gain in production of approximately 300 per cent between 1904 and 1920; the production of gold rose sharply from £12,621,781 in 1903 to £24,606,336 in 1906, an increase accounted for by the advent of Chinese coolies. In 1909 the output had passed the £30,000,000 mark and it continued to hover between this figure and a high of £39,489,522 in 1916. The production of diamonds became virtually a government monopoly after the Union gained control of German Southwest Africa. The output was regulated on a quota basis for the four leading mining areas — Southwest Africa, De Beers at Kimberley, the Premier near Pretoria, and Jagersfontein. Largely because of these regulations, 2,500,000 carats brought more than £14,000,000 in 1920, whereas 5,456,448 carats had a value of only £8,189,197 in 1910.

The trend of economic legislation in South Africa, 1910–1924, pointed toward self-sufficiency and state control. The Union brought railroads and harbors under one state department, and the South Africa Act stipulated that they should be "administered on business principles, due regard being had to agricultural and industrial development within the Union, and promotion, by means of cheap transport, of the settlement of an agricultural and industrial population in the inland portions of all provinces of the Union." Consequently the larger share of the increase in railroad mileage in 1910–1920 — about 2500 miles — went into branch lines, the construction of which was dictated by a combination of economic needs and political expediency. Freight rates were arranged to aid agriculture and develop trading centers in the interior. Similarly the tariff of the Union aimed to protect South African agriculture and industry against foreign competition although preferences were granted to goods of British empire origin. From the beginning the Union parliament passed numerous laws of special interest to farmers and pastoralists. Agricultural cooperation, education and experimentation, regulations devised to check or eradicate diseases of animals and plants, the fight against the locust, and plans to bring new land under cultivation by means of irrigation engaged the attention of the lawmakers. A great Mines and Works Act of 1911 placed the supervision of the mines under a government department, fixed hours of labor underground, provided regulations for the safety of the miners, and laid down rules governing inquiries into accidents. In general, however, the old mining laws were left in operation, especially those of the Transvaal which were of recent origin.

The race problems of South Africa have seriously complicated her efforts at social legislation. Since more than 50 per cent of the native laborers employed at the mines came from Portuguese East Africa, the Union government assumed special responsibility for their treatment. Apart from these regulations South Africa lagged behind Australasia in social legislation. Labor bureaus set up at the Cape in 1902 for the purpose of providing jobs for the unemployed were extended after the union to other sections of South Africa, but their activities were limited to the whites. Phthisis was the scourge of the mines and many of the Cornish miners employed on the Rand fell victim to it. An act of 1911 dealing specifically with miners' phthisis had the twofold purpose of combating it and providing care and compensation for the sufferers and their dependents. The decrease in the number of cases by two-thirds between 1913 and 1918 seems to indicate that the preventive efforts met with considerable success. Workmen's Wages Protection and Workmen's Compensation Acts were passed in 1914, but the war period produced fewer regulations of economic and social activities in South Africa than in Britain and the other dominions. Industrial disputes increased rapidly during the last years of the war — the number stood at two in 1915 and at sixty-six in 1920 — culminating in unrest among native laborers on the Rand in 1919 and the loss of 839,415 working days through strikes that year. The tendency of wages, especially those of the unskilled, to fall behind the cost of living was a factor in producing this unrest, although the influence of subversive propaganda and political maneuverings cannot be ignored. The government attempted to remedy grievances by establishing in 1918 a wages board for women and young persons and in 1919 an industrial advisory board to handle disputes between employers and employees. Rent, housing, and profiteering were dealt with in acts of 1920; but as already noted, agitation and unrest continued, making the early twenties an unhappy period in the history of South Africa.

The political unification brought with it a reorganization of higher education. Acts of 1916 created a University of South Africa, a federation of five colleges modeled after the University of London, and established the independent universities of Capetown and Stellenbosch. Later the Witwatersrand at Johannesburg was given the status of a university. While South African students continued to go abroad especially to England and Holland for advanced study, their own institutions were moving forward rapidly with broader curricula, better equipment, and well-trained faculties. Although hampered by the language problem, elementary and secondary education improved, but the improvements were in the main reserved for Europeans. The new constitutional arrangements brought little benefit to the Asiatic, colored, and native population. Their economic and social opportunities were restricted by color bars in industrial occupations and professions. More than ever before they were treated as "God's stepchildren."

A phenomenon in the intellectual history of South Africa shortly after 1910 was the emergence of Afrikaans as a literary language. Hitherto it had generally been treated with condescension as a Dutch dialect spoken by farmers; the two languages recognized by the constitution were English and Dutch. But the new generation of Boers considered themselves a national group, Afrikanders, and their language distinct from that of Holland. Afrikaans was spoken in parliament; books and newspapers were published in it, and the demand for its official recognition became a part of the Nationalist creed. This aim was achieved in 1925.

Interest in intra-imperial relations was stimulated by the war. In August, 1914, South Africa accepted the theory that she was at war when Britain was at war and shaped her actions accordingly, but both theory and actions displeased a large element in her population. Smuts alone among dominion statesmen was a member of the British war cabinet; he as well as Botha received marked attention from the British government. They stressed the voluntariness of the connection between South Africa and Britain, and declared emphatically against secession and a republic. The new title, the British Commonwealth of Nations, applied to Britain and the dominions gave them great satisfaction. South Africa like Canada gave no encouragement to plans for closer constitutional relations and offered stout opposition to the Indian demand for equal rights for all British subjects. The racial complexities within her own borders made South Africa an outspoken champion of white supremacy. She was pleased with the separate representation at the Paris peace conference and in the assembly of the League of Nations, and she desired diplomatic independence in the post-war years; but she was not eager for separate diplomatic representation at foreign capitals.

Absorbed with domestic problems, South Africa showed only a passing interest in the international complications of the years 1919–1924. Although the war had cost her approximately £38,000,000, she could not claim a share in the German reparations. The numerous conferences dealing with that issue caused little concern in South Africa. Although Smuts favored continuance of the Anglo-Japanese alliance, the solution of the problems of the Pacific adopted at the Washington conference in 1921 seemed satisfactory. The complications in the Near East made no impression in South Africa. She did not wish to support Greek pretensions in Asia Minor nor would she in October, 1922, pledge help to Britain in case of war with Turkey. The Union was not represented at the Lausanne conference, 1922–1923, and showed little interest in the result.

Nevertheless the relations of South Africa to Britain and the League of Nations were important issues in the political struggle between Generals Smuts and Hertzog. The former was satisfied with dominion status and the League; the latter described both as shams. A large number of his followers were republicans who expected that the advent of their leader to the prime ministership would result in a proclamation of independence. They were disappointed. Whether or not Hertzog prior to 1924 favored absolute independence for the Union is a moot question. He was never explicit on this issue. Nor did he have to declare himself in 1924, because his Labor allies who put him into office were not secessionists. Practical considerations suggested vagueness on the independence question. Better crops, the visit of the Prince of Wales to South Africa in 1925, and the definition of dominion status by the Balfour committee in the following year put Afrikanders in a better humor. Indeed, on returning home from the imperial conference of 1926, Hertzog declared himself completely satisfied with South Africa's position in the British Commonwealth of Nations. The question of status came up anew in 1927 when extreme Nationalists began clamoring for the old flag of the Transvaal, the "Vierkleur," to be the emblem of the Union. The flag controversy, which generated much heat, was settled with a compromise. South Africa was to have her own flag with a small Union Jack in the center, although the standard Union Jack might be flown side by side of the South African flag on some public buildings and on certain ceremonial occasions. Shortly afterward a commercial treaty with Germany placed that country on a footing of trade equality with Britain, to the indignation of those who favored close economic relations within the British Commonwealth.

South African politics in the twenties revolved around social and economic issues. The Nationalists continued their vendetta against Smuts, accusing him of selling out to the English. They were anxious to keep the natives within restricted areas and to limit them to unskilled labor. On the other hand the South African party under Smuts advocated more liberal treatment of the colored and native peoples, thereby provoking the accusation of favoring a "black policy." In the election of 1929 the slogan "South Africa a white man's land" figured prominently on posters and in the campaign literature of the Nationalists who also whipped up sentiment against Jews and mine owners. The returns gave them 78 and the South African party 61 votes in the new assembly. Coalition Labor dropped to 5, yet their aid gave the government a safe but small majority.

Shortly afterward the Union was in the trough of a worldwide depression. In 1931, when Britain went off the gold standard Smuts vainly urged that South Africa should do the same. Hertzog refused; it seemed absurd to him that the greatest gold-producing country in the world should abandon gold as the basis of its monetary system. South African exporters soon complained of losing their markets and were then subsidized by the government, a policy which in turn caused dissatisfaction among taxpayers. Clearly South Africa could not pursue an independent monetary policy without ruinous costs. Drought aggravated the economic difficulties and at the close of 1932 mutiny broke out among Hertzog's followers. Tielman Roos had abandoned politics on becoming judge on the appellate division of the supreme court. From the bench he watched with dismay Hertzog leading the country to ruin. The situation appeared so critical that shortly before Christmas, 1932, Roos resigned as judge and started a crusade to get the country "off gold." When Smuts had advocated this the Afrikanders had refused to listen; coming from Roos it seemed a new gospel and was welcomed by thousands. Almost overnight he became a person of first-rate importance. He made a special bid for the support of British South Africans by stressing the need for unity among the whites and offering his aid to Smuts for the purpose of overthrowing Hertzog. But Smuts knew that Roos' popularity was due to temporary conditions; furthermore, Roos was a sick man. If a South African union of hearts was to be a reality, Hertzog, the real leader of the Afrikanders, must be won over. And a union of hearts was Smuts' goal as it had been Botha's. With a magnanimity unusual in the annals of politics Smuts decided to bury the past; for the good of South Africa he offered to ally himself with Hertzog (provided the latter abandoned gold) and to serve as second in command in a reorganized government. After some hesitation and an initial rebuff the offer was accepted. Smuts became deputy prime minister and some of the other leaders of the South African party obtained posts in the government. South Africa went off the gold standard as did also the United States shortly afterward. Gold prices went up, new mines were opened, and South African production and profits reached new highs. The government took a heavy toll of the gold profit in the form of taxes; it wiped out its deficits; with the surplus it subsidized farmers and expanded its services. For the nonce the old animosities and rivalries seemed forgotten in a common enjoyment of unexampled prosperity.

Alas, the honeymoon was all too short. The past did not remain buried. The ghosts of earlier times—memories of wars, burned homesteads, concentration camps, children's graves — continued to haunt the veld. In the general election of May, 1933, Smuts was cheered where shortly before he had been reviled, and he reciprocated by supporting the most rabid among the old Nationalists, Dr. Malan. The result was that the combined forces of the two parties, the Nationalist and the South African, mustered 136 in the assembly whose membership had been increased to 150. Labor had practically disappeared, but there were six Independents and two Home Rulers. A new party, the United, replaced the two old ones and the Hertzog-Smuts government succeeded in passing far-reaching legislation affecting the natives. The details of this legislation will be discussed later; here we shall simply note that the old franchise law of the Cape was abrogated. Colored and natives lost their right to vote on equal terms with the whites; as a consolation prize they received the privilege of electing separately three Europeans to serve as their representatives in the assembly. Smuts was assailed for his desertion of the natives. Perhaps he was guilty; however, it should be remembered that neither he nor Botha ever believed in racial equality and that except for his presence in the government the new legislation might have been even more unfavorable to the natives. If he compromised on this issue so did Hertzog on the hotly debated question of a national anthem. In the early years of the Union it had been taken for granted that "God save the King" was the national anthem. But Afrikanders disliked it, and soon a hymn of their own, "Die Stem van Suid-Afrika" (The Voice of South Africa) gained wide popularity. This issue inflamed passions as had the flag controversy ten years earlier. The outcome — that South Africa should have *no* national anthem — suited none who really cared. Even before this issue was out of the way, the position of the protectorates — Basutoland, Bechuanaland, and Swaziland — came up for discussion. The South Africa Act of 1909 had provided for the possibility that they might at a future time be incorporated in the Union, and Hertzog maintained with some justice that it was impossible to solve the native question while the protectorates remained outside. In 1937 their annexation was demanded by the Union and the imperial government seemed inclined to grant the request. However, humanitarianism was not dead in England. Old sentiments flared up at what was deemed the injustice inflicted upon the South African natives by the repeal of the franchise law at the Cape. It was pointed out that the protectorates could not be transferred without the consent of their inhabitants; and since they preferred British to South African rule their position remained unchanged. Afrikanders were chagrined; they had a new grievance.

Before the discussions over the national anthem and the protectorates, extremists among Boers and British had broken away from the United party and gone into separate "caves." Dr. Malan gathered the most uncompromising of the Afrikanders into a new Nationalist party which soon mustered 21 votes in the assembly; those who felt that Smuts had sold out to Hertzog organized the Dominion party led by Colonel C. F. Stallard. The latter group was small, numbering only 5 in the assembly. The advent of Hitler to power in Germany stimulated Dr. Malan and his associates to greater activity. Though the Afrikanders have even less claim to racial purity than the Germans, it was convenient to use Nazi slogans against Jews, Asiatics, colored, and natives. Less religious than their forbears, the young Afrikanders were not repelled by the pagan aspects of Nazism; they readily adopted claims of racial superiority and willingly denounced the English and the Treaty of Versailles. Bitter words were exchanged on platforms and in the press. The Dominion party was alarmed at the inclusion of a rebel of 1914, General Kemp, in the government; Mr. Pirow, minister of defense, visited Germany as well as Britain in 1938 and was fêted by Hitler; speculation was rife as to the real object of this mission.

The growth of tension between British and Boers in South Africa kept pace with the rise of Anglo-German hostility in Europe. But in spite of all this the Hertzog-Smuts alliance held.

The elections of May, 1938, showed little diminution of the strength of the United party; it secured 111 members in the new assembly. The Nationalist members increased from 21 to 27, an increase that did not accurately measure their strength in the country; and the Dominion party rose from 5 to 8. As war became probable, South Africa began to improve her defenses and to argue the question of neutrality in case of an Anglo-German conflict. Dr. Malan and Colonel Stallard had no doubts. To the former South Africa was independent and could and should remain neutral, to the latter she was a member of the British Commonwealth of Nations with one indivisible crown. In the opinion of British South Africans, when Britain was at war South Africa was at war. Hertzog was believed to share Malan's views, and Smuts those of Stallard, but neither would commit himself before a crisis. The crisis came with Czechoslovakia in September, 1938, a quarrel of no concern to South Africa. Public sentiment favored neutrality, and it seems certain that the inner cabinet – Hertzog, Smuts, Pirow, and Havenga – agreed on this point. The Munich pact made a decision unnecessary. The peace proved of short duration, for on March 15, 1939, the Germans marched into Prague. The world rang with denunciations of this exhibition of contempt for a plighted word. The small nations evidently had no rights which the strong felt obligated to respect; Germany seemed launched on a quest for world dominion. In South Africa disputes waxed more bitter; the neutrality issue was suspected of being a cloak to hide pro-Nazi and anti-British sentiments. When the negotiations failed in Europe, South Africa was forced to choose.

During the last hectic days of August, 1939, Hertzog had been absent from Pretoria, but parliament had been called because the ten-year term of the senate expired September 5. Either its life must be prolonged by a special act or there had to be an election; the latter, however, was deemed undesirable. Consequently parliament met at Capetown September 2 amid great excitement. The senate bill passed – the war was the next and all-important topic for discussion. Hertzog demanded neutrality;

his cabinet divided 5 to 6. On September 4, he placed before the assembly a resolution favoring neutrality; he argued that South Africa's constitutional position made this possible and that her interests were not at stake in the war. The fact that in the course of his speech he defended Hitler's actions probably tipped the scales against neutrality. Smuts in a counter resolution declared in favor of severing relations with Germany and was sustained, 80 to 67. Hertzog then demanded dissolution of the house and new elections. When this was refused by Governor General Sir Patrick Duncan, he resigned and Smuts took his place. The neutrality issue split the United party as it had split Hertzog's cabinet. In the country the division followed racial lines in the main. Only a handful of Afrikanders rallied to the support of Smuts. As of old, Britons faced Boers in South Africa. The unity of hearts so earnestly desired by Botha and Smuts proved a phantom when the war drums began to beat.

Racialism in its narrower aspects — namely, the relations between British and Dutch South Africans — formed the basis for the politics of the Union during 1924–1939. As this period closes, the whites were again indulging in bitter factional fights. But more fundamental than the relations between Briton and Boer were those between Europeans and non-Europeans. Despite efforts to encourage emigration to South Africa after both the Anglo-Boer war and the war of 1914–1918, few left the British Isles for the subcontinent. Advertisements to attract people who had a capital of $25,000 proved unavailing, for not many of that class emigrate. To the jobless laborers of Europe South Africa offered no attraction. Indeed, about 10 per cent of her white population rate as "poor whites." The non-Europeans do most of the labor on the farms and at the mines. They are needed, exploited, and feared. The European population of the Union in 1936 was just short of two millions, while the non-Europeans numbered 7,536,915. For the fifteen years 1921–1936 the rate of increase for Europeans was 31.21, for non-Europeans 39.34 per cent. The black cloud over South Africa is hardly less threatening than it was in the time of Dingaan. The Europeans, conscious of this fact, have striven desperately to keep the natives segregated and in subjection. Attention has been called to acts barring non-Europeans from certain occupations and restricting their right to acquire land; South Africa was to be a white man's country. At the same time efforts have been made to let the natives develop along their own lines and take care of their own affairs by means of separate councils. These councils, first used in the Transkeian territory of the Cape province where the European population forms an insignificant minority, were later extended to other native reserves. Legislation of 1936 created a native representative council for the Union as a whole. Of its 22 members, 6 are officials, 4 are nominated by the governor general, and 12 are elected by the natives. The main functions of this council are advisory on all questions pertaining to native affairs. The non-European population at the Cape was deprived of the old franchise but received instead the right to elect 3 representatives to the Union house of assembly and 2 to the provincial council. Moreover, the Union was divided into four electoral areas which did not coincide with the provinces; each of these elects one senator to watch over the interests of the non-Europeans.

The Asiatics continued to be an embarrassment in some sections, especially in Natal where they outnumbered the whites. Negotiations with the government of India led to an agreement in 1927 whereby repatriation was to be aided and encouraged by both India and the Union. The latter also promised that its Indian subjects would be given educational and other facilities so that they would not "lag behind other sections of the people." This pious declaration has remained a dead letter, if the "other sections" referred to are taken to mean Europeans.

Excepting India, South African interests have not clashed with those of any other portion of the British empire; but, as already noted, the position of the Union within that empire caused much searching of hearts in South Africa and Britain.

Not content with the elevation in status secured by the declaration of 1926 and the Statute of Westminster of 1931, the Union in 1934 by special legislation emphasized its sovereignty and provided for a South African great seal for its state documents. In discussions during the abdication crisis of 1936 and after, the government of South Africa took pains to make it clear that the allegiance of South Africans to the king was to him as specifically king of the Union.

South Africa participated in the Ottawa conference of 1932 and accepted the agreements resulting therefrom. Consequently her trade treaty with Germany, which had given much umbrage in empire circles, was abrogated, although the good impression created by this was lost to some extent by the decision to subsidize an Italian steamship line. South Africa showed a strong inclination to be a "cat that walked by himself."

As might be expected, Hertzog was less interested in the League of Nations than was Smuts. Such agreements as the Geneva protocol, the Locarno pact, and the Kellogg pact aroused no enthusiasm at Pretoria; nor were Manchuria, Spain, and China of any concern to the average South African. On the other hand, the Italian conquest of Ethiopia caused a flurry of excitement. Some circles feared another partition of Africa. Smuts in particular was anxious to promulgate a Monroe doctrine for the continent south of the equator. He objected to any transfer of Portuguese territory or a restoration of the former German colonies. Of these, Southwest Africa was of course of special interest to the Union. Nearly a third of her 30,000 European inhabitants were Germans and fully 3000 of them had remained German citizens. Nazi agitators were active among them, a fact which Smuts and the British South Africans found more alarming than did Hertzog and the Afrikanders. Hertzog made it clear that though he wished to have Southwest Africa recognized as belonging to the Union, it should be done only with Germany's consent. He showed the same tendency to look to Germany as Kruger had; and like Kruger he wanted the Boers, the Afrikanders, who constituted about 55 per cent of the white population, to control the subcontinent.

On December 16, 1938 – Dingaan's Day – the cornerstone of a monument commemorating the Great Trek was laid at Pretoria. The Voortrekkers were lauded to the sky – they had left their old homesteads because they hated the English and because they wanted to live their own lives. A hundred years have wrought many changes in the outward circumstances of South Africa, but the old spirit of the Boers is still potent. Wealth, the amenities of civilization, self-government have not altered their determination to dominate the blacks and to live unhampered by the English. The world has changed, but they have not. As in Gladstone's day, South Africa is a great unsolved and perhaps unsolvable problem.

CHAPTER 32

THE COMMONWEALTH OF AUSTRALIA, 1901–1939

THE establishment of a federal government on January 1, 1901, marked the opening of a new epoch in the history of Australia. The six states of the new federation were united by limited constitutional ties designed to preserve their identity; but the Commonwealth of Australia soon became more important than the parts. The economic, social, imperial, and foreign problems which faced Australia at the opening of the present century made such a development inevitable. She grew into a nation, and her evolution toward nationhood is the guiding strand in her history. In tracing this history it will be necessary not only to follow the conventional topical arrangement of domestic, imperial, and foreign affairs, but to divide the period chronologically into the formative years, 1901–1914, the war and post-war era ending with the financial crisis of 1930, and the recent years.

The early years of the new federation were crowded and eventful. By having ten ministries and six elections in fourteen years Australia established something of a record for a British nation; labor became a dominant force in her politics; new social and economic legislation put her in the van among the democracies of the world; and her constitutional development showed an unmistakable trend toward strengthening the federal government at the expense of the states.

In 1901 Australia had no statesman who held a position equal to that of Sir John A. Macdonald at the inception of the Dominion of Canada. Edmund Barton of New South Wales was intrusted with the task of forming the first government of the Commonwealth of Australia. Elections were held shortly afterward, and the first parliament was inaugurated at Melbourne on May 9, 1901, by the Duke of York, later King George V. It was soon established that the government should be responsible to the house of representatives alone, and that deadlocks between it and the senate were to be broken by the dissolution of both houses. Barton had the requisite majority, but he was not a national leader. The chief political issue was protection vs. free trade. New South Wales had adhered to the latter, whereas Victoria had long had a protective tariff. Barton favored protection. However, the leadership in the fight on this question devolved upon his chief lieutenant and colleague in the government, Alfred Deakin of Victoria. George (later Sir George) Reid of New South Wales led the free traders. The Labor party, which was divided on the tariff issue, held the balance and used its strategic position very skillfully to build up strength in the country. Barton wearied of the political strife, resigned in September, 1903, and was appointed judge on the high court.

Deakin, who succeeded Barton as prime minister, preached protection unceasingly and marshaled his forces with great skill. Victoria was almost solidly behind him; the manufacturers of New South Wales were won over and so was labor. Since Australia exported foodstuffs her laborers did not, like those of England, fear the effect of protection upon the cost of food. On the contrary, Deakin and his followers could argue that a protective tariff system would bring positive benefits to labor by increasing the number of jobs and protecting the Australian standard of living. The federal tariff act of 1902 fixed duties on imports ranging from 8 to 25 per cent ad valorem. They were practically doubled by a new act passed by Deakin and his

Labor allies in 1908. Protection had won, and it became firmly intrenched in Australia in the prosperous years 1908–1914.

Labor tipped the scales for protection; it was indeed a dominant force in Australian politics during 1901–1914. The ground lost by the labor unions during the nineties was quickly recovered, with large additions, after the turn of the century. By 1914 the unions of Australia contained a larger percentage of the total population than did unions in any other country in the world. They formed the backbone of the Labor party, which, however, also had the support of a large middle-class element since its program was constructive and its policy dictated by national rather than class interests. Moreover, this party was well organized in the electoral districts and the states as well as nationally. Its political machine, unmatched in Australia, resembled that of political parties in the United States. Among the distinctive features of the Australian Labor party were the caucus of the state and federal parliaments and the powerful executive committees which functioned independently of the caucus. The Labor members of both houses of parliament constituted the caucus, a body that directed the party's work and policies and claimed the right to determine the composition of the ministry when Labor held office, and to settle disputes between the premier and his colleagues. The Labor party of Australia thus departed from the British government's theory that the ministry as a whole is responsible only to parliament. By 1913 the executive committee of the Labor party in New South Wales demanded authority over the parliamentary caucus; this meant that an outside influence might control legislation and government action.

Three Labor ministries held office between 1904 and 1913 without a safe majority in the house of representatives. But in 1914 elections following a double dissolution gave the Labor party majorities in both houses of the federal parliament. Moreover, at this time the party controlled five of the six state governments. In the decade between their assumption of office for the first time and their great victory, the Laborites were skillfully led first by J. C. Watson and then by Andrew Fisher. Laborites not only helped to bring about the triumph of protection but were largely responsible for the passage of the reform legislation which will be discussed later and which caused Australia to be placed beside New Zealand as a laboratory for state socialism.

But Labor did not climb to power without being challenged by the conservative element which sought to identify the Australian Labor party with Marxian socialism. In 1904 George H. Reid and Allan McLean attempted to establish an anti-Labor front, but their effort failed largely because they were identified with the dying cause of free trade. Deakin, who drove them from office, sought and obtained Labor support in gaining victory for protection and in passing important social legislation. In November, 1908, he had to give way to a Labor ministry, and it was his turn to unite the forces hostile to Labor, but he was not successful. Not until 1913 did a fusion party under the leadership of Joseph Cook offer a united opposition to the Labor party. Cook took office in June of that year with a majority of one in the house of representatives and without one in the senate. In the hope of bringing his government out of an extremely uncomfortable position he recommended double dissolution; the result was disastrous for both government and party.

These years of political confusion and ministerial instability were rich in constructive legislation. The Commonwealth franchise in the beginning was more democratic than that of the states; it is significant that no Australian party chose the name "Conservative." The parliament of the Commonwealth of course legislated for Australia as a whole, and this legislation early showed liberal and even leftist tendencies. One of the first laws dealt with immigration. Asiatics were excluded by an education test; Australia was to be kept "white." In 1903 a federal high court was established. The need for such a court was admitted by all, but the extent of its power later became a source of grave political and constitutional controversies. Included among the legislation which gave Australia a reputation for radicalism were woman suffrage, old age pensions, and the creation of a Commonwealth court of arbitration and conciliation. The last aroused violent disputes and became important both in shaping the economic and social policy of Australia and in influencing the development of the power of the federal government.

The court was established under the provision of the Australian constitution which gave the federal parliament authority to pass laws dealing with "conciliation and arbitration for the prevention and settlement of industrial disputes extending beyond the limits of any one State." Like the clause in the constitution of the United States which gave congress authority to regulate commerce "among the several States," the power of the Commonwealth to prevent and settle disputes transcending state boundaries was so flexible as to make almost nugatory the regulation of industries by the states. The pastoral industry knew no state boundaries, nor did shipping or labor unions. Standards set and principles fixed for interstate industries could not be withheld from those operating within narrower limits. Much depended, of course, upon the judges of the conciliation and arbitration court and the economic conditions of the time.

Henry Bourne Higgins, who in 1907 became president of the new court, was a friend of labor; the time was one of industrial expansion and rising prices. Shortly after his appointment Mr. Justice Higgins, in a famous case involving wages and conditions of work in a harvester factory, decided that laborers were entitled to remuneration sufficient to satisfy "the normal needs of the average employee, regarded as a human being living in a civilised community." Among these he included "frugal comforts," "provision for evil days," necessary leisure and recreation, and "security to marry and to rear a family of three children." The court fixed a basic wage which was considered sufficient to meet these needs. It thus rejected the nineteenth-century theory that labor was a commodity and proclaimed boldly that there was such a thing as a "just wage." Australians long accustomed to "rations" in the pastoral industry did not regard the minimum wage as so much of a novelty as did Europe and America in the early years of the present century. The decisions of the conciliation and arbitration court of Australia were classed as radical by Britain and other industrial countries.

The growth of Australian unionism and the sympathetic attitude of the arbitration court were aided by the expansion of primary and secondary industries, particularly in the years 1910–1913. An eight-year period of widespread droughts, which had reduced the number of sheep by about one-half, came to an end in 1902. The wool crop of 1902–1903 was valued at £13,670,000, that of 1907–1908 at £30,500,000; and it stood above the thirty-million mark again in 1910–1911 and 1913–1914. The governments of Australia borrowed for public works, especially railroads; five thousand miles were added to railroad mileage between 1901 and 1914. A commission of 1913 reported that since 1908 the number of factories had increased 21 per cent, that of factory workers 33 per cent, and the factory output 62 per cent.

Immigrants were flocking to Australia; however, she now began to frown upon those from southern Europe, especially the Italians. For the three years 1911–1913 the net gain by immigration was 207,816, the overwhelming majority of new arrivals coming from the United Kingdom. These newcomers were, of course, not interested in perpetuating the particularism of the states; they became Australians. The population of Australia grew from 3,750,000 in 1901 to nearly 5,000,000 in 1914. The census of 1911 showed that the percentage of British born persons, which included natives of Australia and the British Isles, had risen from 95 to 97 in the last decade. In 1911, despite the heavy immigration, 82.90 of every 100 white Australians were born in the Commonwealth. Australia was a white British nation.

When the colonies of Australia drew up their federal constitutions in the nineties they strove hard to provide safeguards for their own political identity, but many of these safeguards were circumvented or rendered nugatory by the march of events. The establishment of federal courts, the dependence of the states upon federal subsidies, the creation of federal territories, and the development of dominion status meant increased importance for the Commonwealth; the states became secondary to the larger whole.

The courts were important instruments of centralization. Labor learned to look to the Commonwealth court of conciliation and arbitration for aid and support. The decisions of this, in fact if not yet in theory, established precedence over those of the wage-regulating machinery of the states. An even greater extension of federal authority resulted from the creation of the Commonwealth high court, the apex of the Australian judiciary. In the early years it claimed an authority analogous to that established by Chief Justice Marshall and his successors for the supreme court of the United States. However, after 1907 this attitude was somewhat modified, for it was realized that the differences in origin and structure between the governments of Australia and the United States made it hazardous for the supreme court of the former to follow precedents set by that of the latter. Nevertheless, the high court of Australia held a strong position in the federal government.

The constitution of Australia delegated power over the customs tariff to the government of the Commonwealth. Expanding trade and the new tariff rates brought large sums into the federal treasury at a time when the state treasuries were in a deplorable condition, especially after the termination of the arrangement whereby the Commonwealth turned over to the states three-fourths of the revenue secured from customs and excise. Australians became accustomed to look to the federal government for economic and social benefits. As a preparation for a new financial agreement with the states, Deakin in 1909 proposed that the federal government should take over the debt of the states and guarantee to them forever an annual contribution of 25*s.* ($6) per head of the population. In a referendum the people approved the former and rejected the latter. The Fisher government in 1910 passed a Surplus Revenue Act which allocated to the states 25*s.* per head but for ten years only. The progressive parties now demanded that the fiscal power of the federal government be used to tax the large estates out of existence. Efforts in that direction were checked by the high court, but the right to levy a federal land tax as well as an income tax was admitted. Thus the Commonwealth gained in financial power and the states became dependent upon it for aid in a manner that made illusory their position as residuary legatee assigned to them by the constitution.

The prestige of the federal government was enhanced further by its control over Australian territorial possessions. In 1906 Norfolk Island and British Guinea were taken over by the Commonwealth; five years later Northern Australia was proclaimed a federal territory, and another one, Canberra, was created for the purpose of becoming the seat of the federal capital. Similar in effect was the solution found for problems in intra-imperial relations. Practical considerations made it desirable to have spokesmen for the Commonwealth represent all Australia at the colonial conference of 1902 and at the later imperial conferences. The office of high commissioner of Australia in London was established by the Commonwealth in 1909. The defense question called for federal action; hence an Australian council of defense was founded in 1905; this was followed by the creation of a military board. By an act of 1909 Australia adopted the principle of universal liability to military training. She created a citizen army based on the Swiss model, with training for all male youths beginning at the age of twelve and lasting, with brief annual training periods, until they reached twenty-six. In June, 1911, the military college of Australia opened its doors at Duntroon in the federal territory of Canberra. Australian statesmen, except Alfred Deakin, turned a deaf ear to proposals for imperial federation or an imperial customs union, but mindful of their country's exposed position they responded readily to suggestions for building a defense system which in time of war might fit in with that of the British empire. The defense forces of Australia were remodeled in 1912 along British lines, and Australian officers were sent to the dominion section of the imperial general staff in London. In 1907 Australia announced her readiness to build a fleet of her own; this was implemented in March, 1909, when the government ordered three destroyers which were to form the nucleus for this navy. By 1914 Australia had her own naval college at Geelong; she had taken over the imperial dockyard at Sydney; she had a fleet consisting of a battle cruiser, two light cruisers, and several destroyers and submarines; and her naval expenditures had reached £750,000 per annum. Although manned by Australians and maintained solely by the Commonwealth, this navy passed under the direction of the British admiralty when war broke out in August, 1914.

Australians were keenly aware of the interrelations between defense and the foreign policy. They had long tried to influence British imperial policy in the South Pacific and were deeply chagrined in 1885 when Germany seized northeastern New Guinea. They wished to proclaim a Monroe doctrine for Australia and therefore objected strongly to the Anglo-French agreement of 1906 concerning the New Hebrides because it had been concluded without consulting them. Australia raised the question of treaty-making at the imperial conference of 1907, and the British government promised to consult the dominions before signing treaties which might touch their special interests. Thus the Commonwealth of Australia showed a keen determination to assert its claims to nationhood. But Australia had a small population occupying a vast area; she was dependent upon the protection of the British navy; her fate was closely linked with that of the mother country. Moreover, her population was, as we have seen, overwhelmingly British in origin. Hence when the Four Years' War broke out she showed no hesitation in ranging herself with Britain and mobilizing all her resources for a vigorous prosecution of the struggle.

The outbreak of the war found Australia in the midst of a parliamentary election. A suggestion that it be halted failed to win support. This was, indeed, unnecessary since both the prime minister, Mr. Cook, and the leader of the opposition, Mr. Fisher, declared emphatically in favor of Australian participation in the war. The ships of the Australian navy were put under the supreme command of the British admiralty on August 3, and preparations went forward for sending an expeditionary force of 20,000 at an early date; but the presence of a strong German squadron in Far Eastern waters made postponement necessary. The first Australian contingent left Western Australia on November 1 escorted by one British, one Japanese, and two Australian warships. The report that a German cruiser, the *Emden,* was in the neighborhood caused much excitement; the light Australian cruiser, the *Sydney,* was detached from the convoy, and after a running fight the *Emden* was forced to run ashore at Cocos Island in the Indian Ocean.

The Australians landed in Egypt for intensive training, where they were joined by troops from New Zealand. The two contingents formed the famous Australian and New Zealand Army Corps, popularly known as the Anzacs, which saw heavy service in the ill-fated Gallipoli campaign of 1915. After the withdrawal from Gallipoli the bulk of the Australian forces went to France where under the command of Lieutenant-General Sir W. R. Birdwood they formed a part of the British army. In France the Australians saw much hard fighting, participating in some of the greatest battles of the war — the Somme in 1916, Messines Ridge, Ypres, and Passchendaele in 1917, Cambrai-St. Quentin in the spring of 1918, and the great Allied advance that forced the Germans to sue for peace in the autumn of that year. Smaller bodies of Australian troops aided in the defense of the Suez Canal and in the Palestinian campaign. Nearer home, Australian troops seized German New Guinea and the Bismarck Archipelago; and the battle cruiser *Australia* aided New Zealand troops in capturing German Samoa. Later both this vessel and the light cruisers *Sydney, Melbourne*, and *Brisbane* (the last-named was completed in England shortly after the outbreak of the war) saw service in the North Sea and the North Atlantic. All told, 420,000 Australians enlisted during the war; 330,000 of these went overseas. The Australian soldiers won fame as hard, reckless fighters; their casualty lists totaled about 320,000, of whom 60,000 were killed or died as the result of war service.

Australia never adopted conscription for overseas service. The debates on this issue became bitter in 1916 when enlistments fell off. Britain resorted to compulsory military service; should Australia lag behind? The Labor party split on the question; the prime minister, Andrew Fisher, opposed conscription, while a majority of his government, notably George Foster Pearce, minister of defense, and William Morris Hughes, the attorney general, favored it. When Fisher went to London as high commissioner in October, 1915, Mr. Hughes became premier. The following spring he, too, went to London, attended meetings of the British cabinet, and served as British delegate at an Allied economic conference in Paris. Shortly after his return to Australia he placed before his colleagues a military service referendum bill. The executive committee of his own party pronounced against it, and he was expelled from the New South Wales Political Labour League. But since the Labor party believed in using the referendum it could not reject Mr. Hughes' proposal to let the voters decide on conscription. After an incredibly bitter campaign the referendum was held on October 28, 1916. The vote was 1,087,557 for and 1,160,033 against — a hostile majority of only 72,500 in a total vote of nearly 2,250,000. The Labor party promptly expelled those of its old leaders who had urged conscription, among them the veteran, J. C. Watson, the first Labor premier of the Commonwealth, and W. G. Spence, organizer of the most powerful labor union, as well as Messrs. Hughes and Pearce. In February, 1917, Mr. Hughes, who was still prime minister, formed a national war cabinet composed of five Labor members and six members of the Liberal opposition.

A new party, the Nationalist, appealed for a mandate in a general election the following May. The government secured majorities in both houses but refused to introduce conscription without specific popular approval. This was sought in a new referendum on December 20, 1917. The result was an increase of 94,112 in the negative majority – conscription was dead. In the closing months of the war Australian recruiting fell off to a distressing degree.

Australia had her full share of the patriotic hysteria that afflicted the belligerents during the war. Legislation against enemy aliens was extended to include naturalized citizens of enemy origin and it might be applied even to natural-born citizens whose fathers or grandfathers had come from countries now at war with the British empire. Freedom of speech and of the press was curtailed; even the possession of proscribed literature was made an offense. Another effect of the war was the opportunity it gave Australia to satisfy territorial ambitions. As already noted, Australians had long advocated a Monroe doctrine and had objected strenuously to French and German colonial expansion in the South Pacific. The war gave Australia a chance to expel Germany from this area. She captured German New Guinea and adjoining islands in November, 1914, but she neglected to seize the German islands north of the equator, which were then occupied by Japan. At the peace conference, Premier Hughes stoutly opposed the Japanese plea for a statement affirming the principle of racial equality and demanded that the German colonies in the Pacific be divided between Australia and New Zealand. To his regret, those north of the equator were left in the hands of Japan; and Australia had to be content with a "C" mandate over German New Guinea and its dependencies.

The war transformed the British empire into a "Kriegsverein," and some of the Australian statesmen, Mr. Hughes in particular, almost outdid the British in making patriotic statements. Mr. Hughes' speeches on his visit to England in 1916 pleased the flag-waving section of the British press, and at the meetings of the Paris economic conference that year he supported proposals for an economic quarantine of the enemy countries after the war. Domestic problems kept him from attending the imperial conference of 1917 and the sittings of the imperial war cabinet that year, but in 1918 he was present at the meetings of both these bodies. When the war ended he protested against not having been consulted on the terms of the armistice. Mr. Hughes and Sir Joseph Cook, the minister of the navy, formed the Australian delegation to the Paris peace conference. By this time the prime minister was unpopular with a large section of the Australian public; furthermore, the Commonwealth ministers who stayed at home were less insistent than was Mr. Hughes upon separate representation of Australia at the peace conference and a recognition of the Australian Monroe doctrine. However, this did not check his activity in upholding his country's claims. At one time he created a sensation by implying that under certain circumstances Australia might "place herself in opposition to the opinion of the whole civilized world." Indeed the Welsh-born prime minister of Australia showed a certain spiritual affinity with the premier of France, M. Clemenceau, and was severely critical of the political idealism represented by President Wilson. Mr. Hughes was not sanguine about the prospects of the League of Nations; nor was he deeply interested in separate dominion membership in the League, the appointment of Australian diplomatic representatives at foreign capitals, or a clear definition of the international status of Australia.

Problems connected with foreign policy and intra-imperial relations caused little excitement in Australia after the war compared with that aroused by domestic issues. The question of reparations, the Geneva protocol, and the Locarno treaties were viewed languidly by Australians. Mr. Hughes responded to Lloyd George's appeal for support during the Chanak crisis in the autumn of 1922 by offering an Australian contingent; but Australia did not participate in the negotiations at Lausanne that settled the affairs of the Near East. As might be expected, she

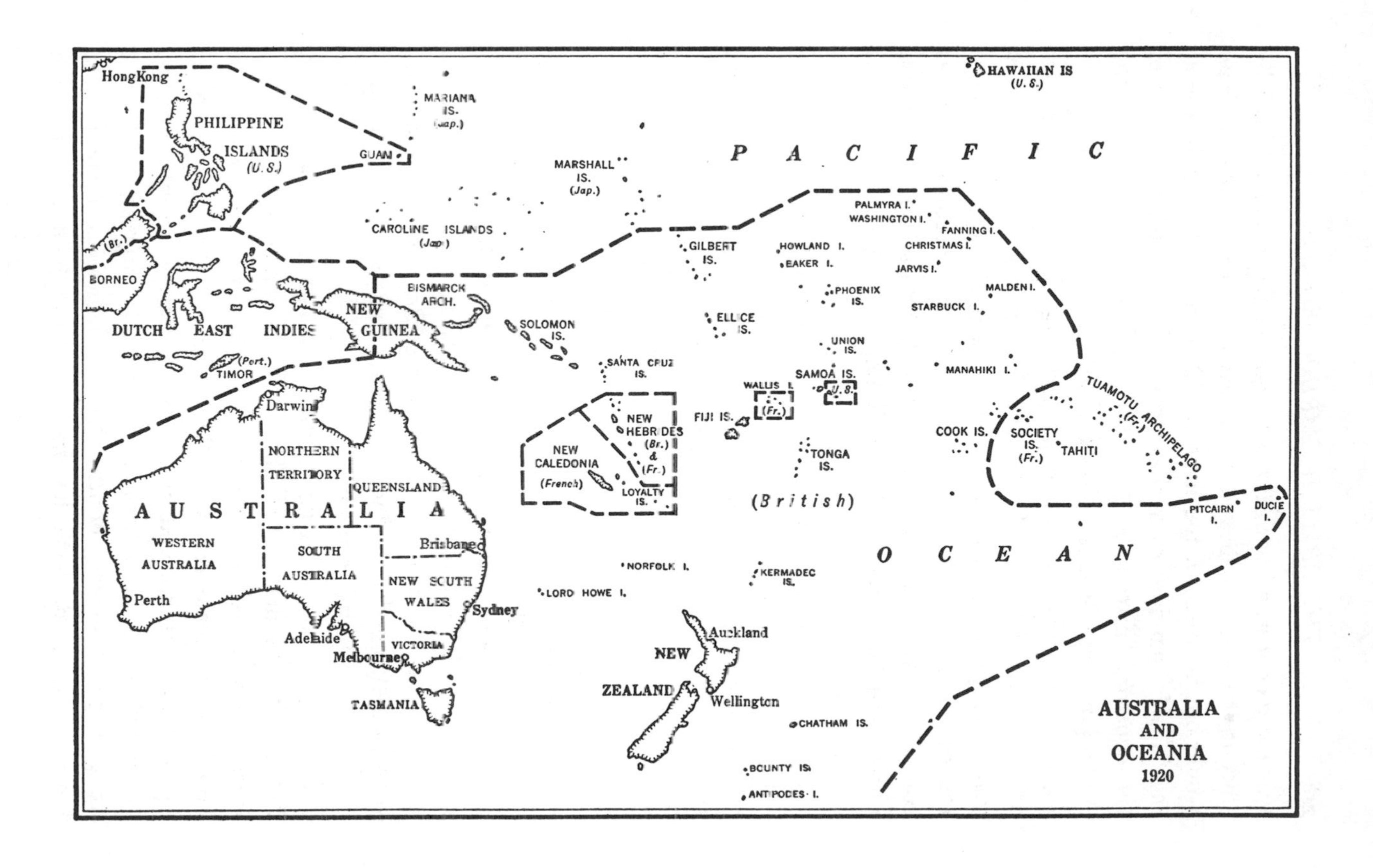
AUSTRALIA
AND
OCEANIA
1920
PACIFIC
OCEAN
(British)
Hong Kong
PHILIPPINE
ISLANDS
(U. S.)
GUAM
MARIANA
IS.
(Jap.)
MARSHALL
IS.
(Jap.)
CAROLINE ISLANDS
(Jap.)
HAWAIIAN IS
(U. S.)
BORNEO
(Br.)
DUTCH EAST INDIES
(Port.)
TIMOR
BISMARCK
ARCH.
NEW
GUINEA
SOLOMON
IS.
SANTA CRUZ
IS.
NEW
HEBRIDES
(Br.)
&
(Fr.)
NEW
CALEDONIA
(French)
LOYALTY
IS.
GILBERT
IS.
ELLICE
IS.
HOWLAND I.
BAKER I.
PHOENIX
IS.
UNION
IS.
WALLIS I.
(Fr.)
SAMOA IS.
(U. S.)
FIJI IS.
TONGA
IS.
PALMYRA I.
WASHINGTON I.
FANNING I.
CHRISTMAS I.
JARVIS I.
MALDEN I.
STARBUCK I.
MANAHIKI I.
COOK IS.
SOCIETY
IS.
(Fr.)
TAHITI
TUAMOTU ARCHIPELAGO
(Fr.)
PITCAIRN
I.
DUCIE
I.
AUSTRALIA
Darwin
NORTHERN
TERRITORY
QUEENSLAND
WESTERN
AUSTRALIA
SOUTH
AUSTRALIA
Brisbane
NEW SOUTH
WALES
Sydney
Perth
Adelaide
VICTORIA
Melbourne
TASMANIA
NORFOLK I.
LORD HOWE I.
KERMADEC
IS.
NEW
ZEALAND
Auckland
Wellington
CHATHAM IS.
BOUNTY IS.
ANTIPODES I.

was more concerned with the situation in the Pacific, especially since it was widely believed in the early twenties that this ocean would be the scene of the next world conflict. Although resenting Japan's mandate over the former German islands north of the equator, Australia in 1921 favored the continuance of the Anglo-Japanese alliance. She felt safe from encroachment by Japan and feared being drawn into a struggle between that power and the United States. With vital interests at stake, Australia gladly accepted the invitation to send delegates to the Washington conference of 1921. The arrangements resulting from this conference, aimed at preserving the *status quo* in the Pacific, pleased the Australians as did the limitations imposed upon naval armaments.

In harmony with the attitude shown at the peace conference, Australia was disposed to leave to Britain the general conduct of foreign affairs. However, she favored a definite procedure in the negotiation of treaties and supported proposals to that effect put forward at the imperial conferences of 1923 and 1926. Without regarding the question of status as of paramount importance, the Commonwealth of Australia insisted that her position be always on a par with that of Canada; she was determined to be regarded as a nation but as a *British* nation. Fully occupied at home, the Australians did not wish to be distracted by international problems; they hoped that the League of Nations would prove a success, supported proposals for disarmament, and showed their good faith by suspending their system of compulsory military training in 1929.

Mr. Hughes' National government cut across old party lines, but despite his undoubted ability the prime minister was not successful as a leader of the coalition; he alienated friends and failed to conciliate enemies. The official Labor party looked upon him as a traitor and made him the target of bitter attacks. Nevertheless, on his return to Australia in August, 1919, after an absence of sixteen months, he was hailed as a conquering hero. Landing at Perth he made a triumphant tour through

Western Australia, South Australia, and Victoria. New South Wales was less demonstrative, although the feeling was general that he had served Australia well while in Europe. But the period of popularity proved of short duration. The Commonwealth government had been invested with wide powers by the War Precautions Act and had used them freely in regulating trade and commerce. With the war over, clamor arose for the repeal of this act; but Mr. Hughes was in no hurry to relinquish the power which it gave his government. Dissension broke out within his own ranks. The old-style Liberals disliked state socialism; South Australia, Tasmania, and Western Australia asserted that their interests were sacrificed to those of the eastern states; and farmers and pastoralists grumbled because they believed that they were bearing a disproportionate share of the cost of the economic and social legislation.

Agrarian discontent had been in evidence before 1914; the war policies of Mr. Hughes hastened its growth. When the farmers began to organize for political action he poured scorn upon them. However, Nemesis soon caught up with him — the federal elections of December, 1919, returned 39 Nationalists, 26 Laborites, and 10 Farmers, and even this slim majority was obtained because of the existing system of preferential voting. On the first ballot the Nationalist party had polled 861,990, the Labor party 795,857, and the Farmers party 178,652 votes. Two constitutional amendments favored by Mr. Hughes and aimed at extending the legislative power of the Commonwealth over industry and commerce were rejected by the voters. The political current continued to run against the Nationalists. The party almost disappeared in South Australia in 1921, and the results of the federal elections of 1922 gave them only 29 votes in the house of representatives, a strength equaled by Labor. The Farmers, now called the Country party, with 14 members held the balance of power. This party could not support Labor and would not support Mr. Hughes. He was forced to resign in February, 1923, the last of the war-time premiers to give up office. A Nationalist-

Country party coalition came into being, with Mr. S. M. Bruce as prime minister and leader of the Nationalists. As his colleague in the government he had Dr. Earle Page, the chief of the Country party. Mr. Bruce was young and energetic, a war veteran, and an advocate of cooperation with the mother country. Dr. Page's party, although mustering only one-third of the coalition votes in the house of representatives, held five of the eleven posts in the government and could defeat any objectionable measure. The party refrained from riding the economy "hobby" it had used extensively in the early days, and was content with securing the passage of measures aiding the marketing of wool, wheat, and other agricultural products. The coalition remained in power throughout two elections, 1925 and 1928, but the waning twenties brought apprehension of hard times ahead. The Bruce–Page ministry sought to stave off disaster by tightening government control and reducing expenditures. This change of policy was displeasing to the electors, who in 1929 returned the Labor party to office and power after years of weakness caused by the 1916 schism.

Among the political events of the twenties were the transfer of the government to the new federal capital, Canberra, and the conclusion of a new debt agreement between the federal government and the states. The transfer came after a long battle involving state and federal interests, politics and art, charming dreams of a "World's City of Peace" and such stark realities as sewer disposal. The plans for Canberra were drawn by a landscape architect from Chicago, Mr. W. B. Griffin; they were elaborate and full of symbols. The capital was only a garden suburb in the wilderness when the parliament of Australia moved there in May, 1927; and five years later despite the large number of federal employees its population had not reached 6000.

The question of the financial relationship between the states and the Commonwealth presented problems as knotty as those of the federal capital. The states clung desperately to their vanishing powers in the face of mounting debts. Mr. Bruce, who had been a business man as well as federal treasurer before he became prime minister, was especially interested in finding a definitive solution of the financial problem. After prolonged negotiations and the rejection of several proposals, agreement was finally reached in 1927 on the basis that the Commonwealth would take over the existing state debts, to be extinguished in 58 years, and contribute to both the sinking fund and the annual interest charges. In return the states agreed to the creation of an Australian Loan Council to control all state borrowing, an arrangement which strengthened the constitutional position of the Commonwealth.

The war had hastened this process. The marketing of Australia's chief articles of export, wool and wheat, necessitated the creation of boards operating under federal auspices. Shipping difficulties forced the Commonwealth to establish strict control over coastal and overseas traffic and to buy a fleet of fifteen vessels that were operated by the federal government. An ambitious shipbuilding program was adopted in 1917 and contracts were let for 46 vessels to be built in Australia. This new industry raised the hope of permanent benefits for allied ones such as iron and steel.

Care of the ex-soldiers was of course a duty of the Commonwealth. For this purpose plans for land settlement were worked out, and loans up to £1000 were granted to each soldier-settler. By 1925, 34,995 soldiers had been placed on land at a total cost of £35,001,941. The federal government took over from the states the task of recruiting immigrants and transporting them to Australia, and cooperated with the British government under the terms of the Empire Settlement Act of 1922. Federal aid for roads and the creation of the Development and Migration Commission were but corollaries of the above-mentioned activities of the Commonwealth. Another step in the direction of unification was the change wrought in the position of the Commonwealth Bank. Established in 1911, this bank at first engaged in ordinary commercial banking activities while serving as the agent for the government in raising loans. But an act of 1924 gave it authority to issue notes and fix rates of discount; commercial banks were ordered to keep balances with the Commonwealth Bank, and the latter thus became "a central bank" for the continent.

The extension of the protective tariff system and the adoption of a policy of granting export bounties further enhanced the position of the Commonwealth government. The secondary industries of Australia had been assisted by the scarcity of goods and the high freight rates prevailing during the war. The cessation of hostilities in Europe brought a slump in the rates for freight and a decline in prices. To bolster her industries and protect her standard of living, the federal parliament in 1921 passed a new tariff act with higher customs duties on many articles. The old industries such as those manufacturing cloth, boots, and shoes and a host of new ones continued to demand aid and more aid, especially since the arbitration court insisted that a high wage scale must be maintained. This policy of "protection all around," however, was incomplete if it brought no benefit to the primary industries. Wool-growing and wheat-raising got along fairly well, but the dairy, sugar, and fruit industries faced heavy competition in the British market. These infants were the special responsibility of the Country party, which shared power with the Nationalists in 1923–1929. Aid to them took the form of prohibitive duties on imports, and export bounties. Money for the latter was obtained by levies on the goods produced, which meant, of course, that the consumers of Australia paid subsidies on the goods exported. Sugar offers a convenient illustration of how this system worked. In 1925–1926, the wholesale price of Australian sugar at home was £26 10*s.* per ton, while the price of exported sugar stood at £11 5*s.* 9*d.* The economic life of Australia thus entered a vicious circle with prices and cost of production mounting. Here, as elsewhere, "the more abundant life" demanded that someone should bear the burden of its cost.

Australia prospered during the twenties. Easy credit and heavy borrowing and spending by the federal and state governments supplied the basis for this prosperity. At the imperial conference of 1926 the premier of Australia, Mr. Bruce, declared that "men, money, and markets" constituted the primary needs of the British empire. Australia acted upon that principle. Her opportunities were advertised with the skill and conviction of the land speculator. British immigrants were aided, others from northwestern Europe were welcomed, a few from southern Europe were tolerated, but Asiatics were kept out. The census of 1921 showed a population of 5,435,734, of whom 207,571 were immigrants; the figures for 1933 were respectively 6,629,839 and 292,931 arrivals since 1921. Men were coming, and money was brought to Australia from London and New York. The war years, 1914–1919, added about £360,000,000 to Australia's public debt, two-thirds of which had been taken up at home. Between 1919 and 1928 Australian governments borrowed £388,000,000, but of this £223,000,000 came from overseas. A large portion of the new debt went into public works, harbors, irrigation, and railways. The great irrigation schemes for the Murrumbidgee and the Upper Murray proved disappointments. Millions were wasted. More millions were spent on the building of railroads, the mileage increasing about 5000 between 1915 and 1930. The new construction was financed by loans, and most of it, especially the transcontinental railroad linking Western Australia with South Australia, brought no cash return on the invested capital. In fact, the state-owned railroads became so many white elephants, with deficits conservatively estimated at £5,000,000 for the year 1928. During the boom period, 1922–1928, industrial production increased from £123,000,000 to £160,000,000; that of wheat from 109,000,000 to 159,700,000 bushels, and wool from £117,000,000 to £141,000,000. A comparison of 1928–1929 and 1922–1923 shows that the increased volume of trade boosted receipts from customs by nearly £7,000,000 annually. While the deposits in savings banks increased from £171,000,000 in 1923 to £225,000,000 six years later, the cash reserves of commercial banks declined in relation to deposits from an average of 25 per cent before 1914 to 15 per cent in 1929. Optimism was the keynote of Australian economic and political life and warnings of lean years to follow went unheeded.

From 1923 to 1928 the Bruce–Page coalition government rode on the crest of the wave of prosperity. The election of 1925 increased the number of their supporters in the house of representatives from 46 to 52; that of 1928, on the other hand, provided a setback for the ill-assorted Nationalist party which lost nine seats, thereby reducing the government's forces to 42 — a small majority in a house of 75. Soon the business barometer began falling rapidly. Somewhat belatedly the government urged precautions. Britain's return to the gold standard in 1925 tended to depress prices; wages were bound to follow. In Australia, however, wages were bolstered by the arbitration court whose sphere of action had increased to such an extent that it could invalidate state laws which threatened the established wage scale. Since its work often duplicated that of state wages boards and the employers in some of the states grumbled at the high wages, the Commonwealth government in 1929 took the bold step of proposing to the electors that the power of the federal arbitration court be severely restricted. This was interpreted as a threat to the Australian standard of living. Labor opposed the change and secured 46 seats as against 24 for the Bruce-Page coalition. The government resigned and the leader of the Labor party, Mr. J. H. Scullin, succeeded Mr. S. M. Bruce as prime minister of Australia.

The new government took office in October, 1929, at the time when the great stock market crash in the United States greatly speeded the recession of trade. At the end of the fiscal year 1928–1929 the accumulated deficits of the Commonwealth amounted to £5,000,000; those of the states were said to be £11,500,000, but they were probably much higher on account of the failure of several states to allow for depreciation of their railroads. In April, 1929, the Australian Loan Council failed to obtain a loan in London; Australian export figures, which had stood at £140,000,000, dropped to £97,000,000 the following year. Private industries suffered and unemployment increased. Facing declining revenues and rising demands for relief, the federal and state treasurers of Australia in 1930 sat by pools of "bottomless deficiency" fishing for their budgets.

The history of Australia since 1929 centers around the economic slump and recovery. Domestic politics, constitutional revisions, relations with the United Kingdom as well as with foreign countries, all have an economic background. Not until Japan became aggressive in Asia and Germany seemingly determined to acquire supremacy in Europe did Australia cease to be occupied primarily with internal affairs. In September, 1938, she began to think as imperially as she had in the decade before the outbreak of war in 1914. And when for the second time in the present century Britain was at war with Germany, the Commonwealth of Australia ranged itself without hesitation on the side of the mother country.

In the election of 1929 the leader of the Labor party, Mr. J. H. Scullin, denounced the program of the Nationalist government to curtail expenditures and restrict the power of the federal court of arbitration as a plot to set the clock back thirty years, thereby depriving the common man of the benefits secured since the establishment of the federation. The electorate supported Mr. Scullin, who assumed the task of leading Australia out of the depression. He realized immediately that the nationalization of industries proposed by his party eight years earlier could not be accomplished at this time, but he strove valiantly to stave off retrenchments and deflation which the rapid fall in the prices of Australian exports seemed to make inevitable. The Labor party was committed to the maintenance of the Australian wage scale and no curtailment of government expenditures; its radical wing clamored for socialization of industries and cheap money. On the other hand the banking interests of Australia and England, the economic experts invited from England to diagnose Australia's economic ills, and the conservative forces which controlled the federal senate and most of the state governments urged deflation. For the purpose of safeguarding the credit of Australia, the Commonwealth Bank took over all gold reserves; in December, 1929, the export of gold from Australia was forbidden; and six months later all balances kept in England were pooled with the stipulation that the interest on all government loans payable in London should be met before remittance was made on the now drastically reduced Australian imports. Early in 1930 the government passed a new tariff bill prohibiting the import of certain articles, rationing the purchase of others, and increasing by 50 per cent the duties on those in a third group. A sales tax was introduced, and the government hoped to stimulate export by promising the wheat farmers a price of four shillings per bushel and making arrangements for a wheat pool. But the bill aimed at implementing these plans was thrown out by the senate. A proposal for a wool pool was rejected by the wool growers and the wool brokers. The senate aided the bankers in defeating plans for the expansion of credit, and in June, 1930, the Loan Council decided to reduce loan expenditures 25 per cent. A premiers' conference of August, 1930, agreed to this.

The federal government now faced an impossible situation. Labor still opposed deflation; and in October, 1930, the electors of New South Wales supported Mr. J. T. Lang's program favoring restoration of wages and shorter hours. The slump in revenues and the loss of credit abroad compelled the government to reduce the budget and to increase sales and income taxes. A deficit could not be averted. The bankers demanded that all overdrafts or treasury bills of the governments of Australia should be treated as ordinary borrowing and be submitted to the Loan Council which favored deflation. In seeking a way to stave this off, the federal treasurer, Mr. Theodore, proposed to increase the note issue by £18,000,000, but the Commonwealth Bank and the senate thwarted this plan. Toward the close of 1930, Australian economists declared in favor of deflation. In the following January Australian exchange dropped to £130 5*s.* for one hundred English pounds, and the arbitration court ordered a 10 per cent reduction in the basic wage; deflation could not be averted. Despite old promises and strong opposition from the left-wingers, the federal government agreed to reduce expenditures by lowering wages and salaries 20 per cent, pensions 12½ per cent, and by means of conversion loans to cut the interest on government bonds 22½ per cent. This plan was accepted by the states. Interest on private debt was lowered in conformity with this general program, the Australian public showing real enthusiasm for it. Moreover, the fact that the depression hit Australia early proved an aid to recovery. For about eight months her cheap pound gave her definite advantages in the English market. Britain's abandonment of the gold standard in September, 1931, made a managed currency respectable; and the Australian pound was ultimately pegged to the sterling at the ratio of 125 to 100.

The recovery program of Australia was a success except for the government which adopted it. A large section of Labor could not forgive Mr. Scullin for surrendering to the deflationists; Mr. Lang organized a dissentient State Labor party. The conservatives considered Mr. Scullin weak and untrustworthy. Mr. J. A. Lyons, a Labor leader who stood second only to Mr. Scullin, gathered old Nationalists and conservative Laborites into a newly organized United Australia party which won 39 seats in the election of December, 1931. Mr. Lyons thus had a majority without the support of the 16 members of the Country party and the 2 anti-Labor independents. Labor, split in twain for the second time since 1915, could muster only 18 votes in the new house of representatives. In January, 1932, Mr. Lyons took office as prime minister with a strong conservative majority. But Mr. Lang was still premier of New South Wales, richest and most populous of the states of Australia. A year earlier he had submitted a recovery plan which included a proposal for non-payment of interest on Australian bonds held in Britain, and on April 1, 1931, New

South Wales defaulted. Capital fled the state and the State Savings Bank was forced to close. The Commonwealth government now took a hand and paid the interest on the debt of New South Wales. In May, 1932, Mr. Lang was accused of violating the federal debt agreement and removed from office by the governor. His successor, Mr. B. S. Stevens, won the ensuing as well as the subsequent elections of 1935 and 1938.

The defeat of Mr. Lang strengthened confidence in Australia's determination to meet her obligations to bondholders and to shun radical experiments. The federal government guided by Mr. Lyons favored non-interference with business. The Loan Council, the Tariff Board, the arbitration court, and the Commonwealth Bank were left to handle the problems of their respective spheres with help from appropriate experts. These agencies had been conservative in the crisis of 1930–1931 and remained so during the following years. By conversion of government loans held in London, an annual saving of £4,000,000 in interest was achieved, and by drastic reductions in imports Australia's unfavorable trade balance of £76,600,000 in 1929–1930 became a favorable balance of £16,400,000 for 1931–1932. Australia maintained her high tariff which, even with the reductions on goods of empire origin effected by the Ottawa agreements of 1932, afforded strong protection to her secondary industries. In contrast to the economic policy of the United States, Australia's policy sought to speed recovery by stimulating production in her primary industries. Fortunately, the world's demand for wool fell only slightly during the depression; her agricultural produce, especially chilled beef, lamb, and mutton, benefited by the Ottawa agreements. Although the industries of Australia cannot compare in efficiency with those of Canada and the United States, improvements were made during the depression. By means of a licensing system the Commonwealth tried to divert Australian imports to the countries which buy her goods. Her trade with the East, Japan in particular, grew in the thirties, and Australian industrialists made a definite bid for the market of

Holland's East Indian colonies. In 1935–1936 the Australian agricultural and pastoral industries supplied about 80 per cent of the export, with Britain taking more than one-half of the total. Next in importance to Britain as buyer of Australian goods was Japan, which purchased one-third of the goods sold to non-British countries, or 13.07 per cent of the total export.

The federal budget, balanced as early as 1931–1932, showed surpluses in 1932–1939. The states were less fortunate, partly because of the chronic deficits in railroad accounts. The Trans-Australian railroad, linking Adelaide with Perth, was an especially heavy drain on the treasuries concerned. However, political reasons made it difficult to abandon unprofitable lines; patriotic Australians were loth to give up their dream of a continent fully settled from sea to sea. The financial institutions of Australia survived the depression remarkably well; only two relatively small banks failed, in addition to the State Savings Bank of New South Wales. The Australian currency remained linked with that of Britain, and the Commonwealth Bank kept its reserve in English sterling instead of gold. Similarly, the banking interests of London remained closely connected with those of Australia. Financially the Commonwealth of Australia continued as a dependency of the mother country.

The conservative parties controlled the Commonwealth government during 1931–1939. The United Australia party lost its majority in the house of representatives in the election of 1934, but Mr. Lyons, receiving support from the Country party, continued in office until his death on April 7, 1939. After a brief interim with Sir Earle Page, leader of the Country party, in control, Mr. R. G. Menzies, a former attorney-general, was chosen as leader of both the United Australia party and the government. Page withdrew his support, but the threatening international situation enabled Mr. Menzies to carry on despite his lack of a clear majority. The Labor party suffered from internal dissensions in 1931–1936. Although the breach between the Lang and the Scullin wing of the party, now lead by Mr. Curtin, was healed in 1936, Labor secured only 29 seats in the election of 1937. The Communists tried vainly to win Australians to their creed. More success at one time crowned the effort of Major Douglas' Social Credit party, which in 1934 polled 171,000 votes in the federal election; this was halved three years later. Relief, credit, social security, defense were the dominant issues in the politics of Australia during the thirties. The demand for national insurance was particularly insistent, and the Lyons government strove ineffectually to solve this problem.

The depression strengthened the power of the federal government at the expense of the states. The relatively flourishing condition of the federal treasury brought insistent requests for aid, and a Commonwealth Grant Commission was created to handle these requests. Moreover, the four older federal agencies — the Loan Council, the Tariff Board, the arbitration court, and the Commonwealth Bank — virtually controlled the economic life of Australia. This process of centralization aroused misgiving especially on the part of the smaller states, Tasmania, South Australia, and Western Australia, who believed that their interests were being sacrificed. The last was particularly vocal in her complaints. A popular referendum of April, 1933, went nearly two to one in favor of secession, and a deputation was dispatched to London with a petition to the imperial parliament asking for the passage of an act which would enable the state to withdraw from the Commonwealth. The request was embarrassing to the home government inasmuch as the Balfour declaration of 1926 and subsequent legislation had recognized the Commonwealth of Australia as equal in status with the mother country. The petition was referred to a joint select committee of parliament, which, after lengthy deliberations and a careful study of the case as presented by both the state and the Commonwealth, reported in May, 1935, that no action could be taken except by request from the latter. Consequently the petition was not received. Meanwhile the Grant Commission had been investigating the effects of the tariff upon the smaller states. Its decision that they had valid grounds for their complaints led to an increased grant from the federal treasury which stilled for the moment Western Australia's clamor for secession.

Australia showed little concern over the question of status. British to the core, needing the protection of the British navy, and depending upon Britain for market and capital, the people of Australia were willing to let this issue rest. At the imperial conference of 1930, the prime minister of Australia, Mr. Scullin, said: "We are a free association of peoples; and to my mind there is nothing to be gained and perhaps a great deal to be lost by attempting to crystallize our relations too closely within the confines of any formal document." This declaration calls to mind the statement by Lord John Russell ninety years earlier that any definition of the relations between Britain and her colonies would say either too little or too much. But in 1930 the majority of dominion representatives thought otherwise, and the Statute of Westminster was the result. This act was passed by the parliament of Australia — she insisted upon equality with the other dominions. On the other hand she fell in readily with the suggestion that the governor general should be nominated formally by the dominion concerned. With the appointment in 1931 of Sir Isaac Isaacs as her chief executive, Australia led the other overseas dominions in having a native son chosen to that high office. She demanded to be consulted on problems of foreign policy, but was satisfied to leave the actual management of foreign affairs in the hands of the mother country. She did not request separate diplomatic representation and was not too well pleased with Canada's action in 1923 in negotiating the halibut treaty with the United States independently of the British ambassador at Washington. In conformity with their conception of "Unity in diversity," the Australians looked upon the crown as indivisible; consequently, when the United Kingdom was at war with Germany Australia too was at war.

The dominant forces shaping Australia's foreign policy were

the determination to ban Asiatic immigrants and the desire to maintain Britain as a first-class power. Australia realized that the former would be an empty dream without the latter. From Britain alone could she be sure of aid in case a foreign power attempted to seize some of her territory. During the twenties Australians were interested in the League of Nations, hoping that it would provide the necessary safeguards for peace. But the decade of the thirties was destined to be a stormy one in international relations, with wars in Asia, Africa, and Europe. In 1931 Japan invaded Manchuria; six years later she attacked China. The first was viewed tolerantly in Australia; the latter was severely condemned for humanitarian reasons. Even so, practical considerations led Australians to be neutral toward the Sino-Japanese war; Japan was a good customer and if blocked everywhere she might turn her attention to the continent of Australia. Italian colonial ambition created crises in 1935–1936. The Commonwealth joined Britain in imposing economic sanctions against Italy during the Abyssinian war, although not greatly interested in that struggle except in so far as it hamstrung the League of Nations. Australians refused to be alarmed by the cry that democracy was at stake in the civil war in Spain nor did they become agitated over the aggressive acts of Germany until the crisis of September, 1938. They realized that Britain lost prestige by the Munich agreement, and the occupation of Prague by the Germans in March, 1939, brought home to Australia that the new masters of Germany had no respect for the sanctity of treaties or the right of small nations. Both are important for Australia. She began to speed up the defense program adopted in December, 1838, which involved the expenditure of £60,000,000 on rearmament over a period of three years. Special efforts were made to build airplanes and munition factories with a view to making Australia second only to Britain among the British countries in these fields, a center supplying New Zealand, South Africa, and the British forces in the Far East and the South Pacific. The Commonwealth did not contribute to the cost of the Singapore base, but decided to fortify Port Darwin as a link in the chain of strong naval bases which includes, besides Singapore, Robben Island and Simonstown in South Africa, Trincomalee in Ceylon, and the island of Penang at the western entrance to the Straits of Malacca. Realizing her exposed position in case of trouble with Japan, Australia revived the interest in her navy and decided to build a battleship dock at Sydney. Upon entering the war in September, 1939, she planned to concentrate on the production of supplies, the building of aircraft, and the training of air personnel.

Australia has made great strides since the establishment of the federation. The population increased by three millions during 1901–1939, and determined efforts were made to insure its well-being. She became recognized as a pioneer in legislation; she provided her people with a decent standard of living, education for her young, and pensions for her old. The franchise was made universal and voting compulsory. Referenda were resorted to on amendments to the constitution and on other matters of special importance. Labor as organized both in unions and as a political party wielded much influence in shaping the political, social, and economic institutions of the Commonwealth. Although inequalities of wealth remained, the political power of the "squattocracy" became largely a matter of history. Democracy in Australia failed to fulfill all the hopes entertained for it by well-wishers at the opening of the century, but it proved capable of coping with the many complex and truly difficult problems which faced her people. History, geography, and the system of transportation helped to create a relatively large urban population. Two of her cities, Melbourne and Sydney, each has a population of more than a million, and one-half of her total population of 6,800,000 is concentrated in her capital cities. She has the concentration of labor important for industrial progress, and she hopes some day to rate as a great industrial nation. She is still a British nation, jealously guarding her racial purity not only against the races of the East but also against those of southern Europe. With the failure of a general League of Nations, she became more than ever convinced of the necessity of maintaining the British league of free nations and preserving the strength of the heart of that league, the United Kingdom.

CHAPTER 33

NEW ZEALAND, 1901–1939

THE thirty-eight years which intervened between the death of Queen Victoria and the outbreak of the Nazi War were for New Zealand a period of uneven growth, of interdependence with the outside world, and of economic and political changes. As a unitary state predominantly British she escaped racial and constitutional difficulties which beset her sister dominions, but she had her share of economic misfortunes. She participated whole-heartedly in the war of 1914–1918 and ranged herself without hesitation on the side of Britain in September, 1939, when war broke out afresh. A British nation bound closely to the mother country by racial, cultural, and economic ties, New Zealand was never troubled by the problem of status. She was proud of and satisfied with her position as a member of the British Commonwealth.

In the present century New Zealand has grown both by territorial annexations and by a large increase in her population. Early in their history New Zealanders opposed acquisition by foreign powers of the islands in the South Pacific; they urged British annexations, and like the Australians they favored a Monroe doctrine for Australasia; but their protests against the colonizing activities of France and Germany were without avail. Old desires were therefore gratified in June, 1901, when the Cook and other small islands were taken over by New Zealand and in 1919 when she secured the mandate over the German or western portion of Samoa. Since the opening of the present century the increased demand for fats has made whale hunting extremely profitable, and as its most important fields lie within the south polar region the icebound shores of Antarctica assumed international importance. New Zealand participated in the scramble for these frozen lands and by order in council of July 23, 1923, annexed the coasts of the Ross Sea and adjacent islands and territories.

These acquisitions appealed to the pride of New Zealand rather than increased her strength; the latter was achieved by the rapid growth of population and by economic and social progress. Between 1901 and 1936 her white population nearly doubled, increasing from 770,312 to 1,517,712, and the decline in the number of Maoris was checked. This interesting and gifted race has adapted itself to modern conditions of life and for more than seventy years has lived peacefully side by side with the European intruders. A considerable percentage of the increase in population was caused by immigration, but the larger share of it was due to natural causes. New Zealand has the enviable reputation of being the most healthful country in the world, a country which until the most recent years has maintained a high excess of births over deaths. The heaviest immigration occurred between 1901 and 1914 and in the quinquennium 1921–1925, arrivals exceeding departures in the latter period by 49,988. However, the sources of population increases have of late shown a tendency to dry up. In the five years 1931–1935 New Zealand suffered a net loss of 9918 by emigration; while this has since been reversed, legal restrictions have kept down the number of arrivals, and in recent years the birth rate has threatened to fall below the replacement level.

Population charts for the present century indicate that New Zealand has remained predominantly British; in other aspects many shifts have taken place. In 1901 the North Island overcame the population lead which the South Island had held since the early sixties. The change continued, the census of 1936 giving the North 62.95 and the South 37.05 per cent of the total population. The ratio of rural to urban dwellers changed even more drastically. A rural majority of 56.19 per cent in 1901 had by 1936 become a minority of 40.34 per cent; at the latter date nearly one-half of the people of New Zealand lived in cities of more than 10,000. Moreover, the chief cities of North Island, Auckland and Wellington, have grown more rapidly than those of the South, Christchurch and Dunedin. Trade and industry have tended to concentrate in the North, which is also a land of small farmers, whereas sheep-raising and wheat-growing predominate in the South. The alterations in the demographic chart of New Zealand will help to explain political changes as well as economic and social policies of the more recent period.

The relations between New Zealand and the mother country were altered outwardly on September 26, 1907, when her status rose from a colony to a dominion, which placed her on a par with Australia and Canada. Practically this elevation was of little consequence. New Zealand continued to exhibit strong attachment to Britain, to advocate imperial consolidation, to further the cause of imperial preferences, and to support imperial defense. The Liberal-Labor prime ministers, R. J. Seddon and Sir Joseph Ward, and their political opponent, W. F. Massey, agreed on all intra-imperial questions. At the colonial conference of 1902 Seddon supported Chamberlain's plans for tariff revision and imperial consolidation; at the conferences of 1907 and 1911 Ward proposed an imperial council; Massey, who became premier in 1912, was eager to have New Zealand participate in imperial defense; and in 1914 he showed no hesitation in throwing the whole strength of his country into the war on the side of Britain. In 1903 New Zealand granted tariff preferences to British goods; three years later preferential trade agreements were concluded with Canada and the South African customs union. In 1902 Seddon agreed to provide £40,000 per annum toward the cost of maintaining a naval squadron in the South Pacific; in 1908 Massey raised this to £100,000, and in 1909 he promised to present a battle cruiser to the royal navy. This ship, the *New Zealand,* rendered excellent service in the war of 1914–1918. Shortly before war broke out the Massey government began the founding of a New Zealand naval establishment. Nor was military defense neglected. An act of 1909 provided compulsory military training for the youths of New Zealand between the ages of 12 and 21 — limits later changed to 14 and 25. Thanks to her minister of defense, Sir James Allen, and her commander-in-chief, Major-General Sir A. J. Godley, the war found New Zealand ready with plans for raising, training, and equipping military forces of considerable strength.

On the eve of the outbreak of the war New Zealand promised to aid the mother country with all the military and naval resources at her disposal. She kept her word. The New Zealanders were enthusiastic for the cause of the empire. Ten days after war was declared a contingent was dispatched to capture German Samoa, a task soon accomplished; and on October 15–16, a force of 8500 officers and men embarked for service overseas. Before the war ended more than 100,000 New Zealanders, including 2200 Maoris, had left their home in the South Seas to fight in France, Gallipoli, and Palestine. The majority of them were volunteers, although conscription was introduced in May, 1916. The New Zealand casualty lists totaled about 58,000, of whom 17,000–18,000 were killed or died in service. In proportion to her population she provided more troops for active service than did any other overseas portion of the British empire.

During the war New Zealand was interested in discussions dealing with a possible constitutional reorganization of the empire but not eager for separate representation at the peace conference and on the assembly of the League of Nations or for an independent diplomatic service. The report of the Balfour committee of 1926, recognizing equality of status for all members of the British Commonwealth of Nations, was accepted by New Zealand as a boon solely because it helped to keep peace in the family by satisfying Canada and South Africa. She could see no real benefit accruing from the Statute of Westminster and did not deem it worth while to validate it by special legislation. In the abdication crisis of 1936 New Zealand cooperated wholeheartedly with the home government; and alone among the dominions she has continued to have her governor general appointed by the king upon the advice of the British government and to have him remain as the channel of communications with the government in England.

In the diplomatic crises of the post-war years New Zealand was content to leave the control of the empire's foreign relations in the hands of the British government. She had no direct interest in the affairs of the Levant; yet when Lloyd George in September, 1922, asked for aid in case of war with Turkey, she pledged support. And she accepted the decisions of the mother country on the Lausanne treaty, the Geneva protocol, and the pacts of Locarno and Paris. Lacking wide open spaces, New Zealand was less apprehensive than Australia over the plans of Japan, and she deprecated a provocative attitude on the part of Britain toward her former ally. From the beginning New Zealand supported the League of Nations and in the crises relating to China, Ethiopia, and Spain she was critical of Britain's failure to utilize the League machinery to its fullest extent.

New Zealand became politically independent of Britain but the economic relations remained unchanged; indeed perhaps they made her more of a colony than ever before. She was a land of primary industries, producing goods for which Britain was almost the only customer. Wool, frozen meat, butter, and cheese were her leading articles of export. Her dairy industry was the object of solicitous care on the part of successive governments. This industry was especially suited to the small farms which she sought to develop; furthermore, her farmers possessed the skill, education, and readiness to join in the cooperative enterprises that have proved essential for success in the mass production and marketing of dairy produce. Moreover, her position as a debtor country made it necessary for her to stimulate export, a need which increased with the additional debt burden, one of the legacies of the Four Years' War. Dairy produce offered the greatest possibility for expansion and the British market seemed limitless. Soon the New Zealand dairy farmers sold abroad about 60–70 per cent of their butter and cheese, bought principally by Britain, which indeed absorbed approximately 90 per cent of the country's total export. In return New Zealand purchased British manufactured goods — a neo-mercantilistic relationship developed between the two countries. There were complaints. In 1920 the importers of New Zealand accused British exporters of delaying to fill orders until prices had reached a high level, and New Zealanders alleged that goods made in Britain on which New Zealand granted tariff preference were inferior in quality to those manufactured in other countries. She objected to British quotas and was far from pleased with Britain's efforts to stimulate domestic production of dairy products. But these grievances were not serious and the tiffs resulting therefrom were no more alarming than those in any well-regulated family. However, in 1935 when Labor came into power in New Zealand efforts were made to develop her secondary industries, the new premier, Mr. Savage, taking pains to point out that only by such a policy could the country provide for and hope to increase her population.

The close commercial relationship between New Zealand and Britain and the former's relatively large export trade brought dependence on price fluctuations and monetary policies beyond her power of control. This was realized in 1920 when a sudden break in world prices of agricultural produce turned the trade balance against New Zealand, sent wages tumbling, and created great distress. New Zealand stood in a debtor relationship to Britain and while the percentage of her debt held abroad did not grow larger the increase in her total indebtedness caused her to contract heavier obligations in London. By 1938 this overseas debt amounted to about £160,000,000. The Colonial Stock Act of 1900 which enabled New Zealand to contract loans on favorable terms in the London money market also in a measure placed the regulation of her finances in foreign hands, a fact made even more evident when Britain in 1931 went off the gold standard and adopted special measures for safeguarding her capital assets and currency. After some hesitation New Zealand decided to peg her pound to the British at the ratio of 125 to 100 instead of the old one at par. This helped her exports but added difficulties in the way of meeting debt charges. Discussions on this point gave support to Mr. Savage's contention that New Zealand must foster economic self-sufficiency.

As this period opened, New Zealand was in the midst of far-reaching experiments in the fields of economic and social legislation; at its close she was similarly engaged. Between lies an era of economic and political adjustments and of fluctuations, some occasioned by economic and social experiments, others by war and post-war conditions.

As explained earlier, at the beginning of the nineties economic conditions brought about an alliance between the laborers and small farmers of New Zealand under the leadership first of John Ballance and, after his death, Richard John Seddon. The Liberal-Labor coalition achieved striking successes, and early in the present century New Zealand was considered a laboratory for economic and social experiments. Old age pensions, compulsory arbitration of labor disputes, purchase of land by the state to be leased on easy terms to small farmers, and state credit for agriculturists were among the measures then held to constitute state socialism. They brought tangible benefit to the voters who kept the Liberal-Labor government in power; the path of the reformers was smoothed by rising prices. Although Seddon was an able and resourceful leader, even before his death in 1906 a cleavage had appeared within his party. The farmers, having achieved their principal objectives, wished to settle down to quiet enjoyment of their gains, while labor remained restless. Hence Seddon's successor, Sir Joseph Ward, found it difficult to keep the team together; and in 1909 Labor broke away and formed a separate political party that attacked Ward's government.

The arbitration court became a cause of dissension. During the first ten years of its existence prices rose rapidly, and though employers grumbled against awards which usually favored employees, they were not seriously inconvenienced; labor was satisfied. By 1906 the work of the court had become standardized, the conciliation feature had all but disappeared, and its services were limited to the regulation of employment, wages, hours of labor, working conditions, and kindred topics. The upward trend in prices and wages was halted. In 1908 the court decided that disputes in agricultural and pastoral industries lay outside its purview; consequently the most numerous class of workers could get no real protection from it. About this time the character of New Zealand trade unionism began to change from a conservative craft union type to a revolutionary industrial unionism, and some of its leaders were ready to subscribe to the Marxian doctrine of the class struggle. Whereas in former years the employers had fought the court, from 1906 to 1913 the challenge came from labor. The miners especially were infected with the radical virus. In 1906 and 1907 workers struck against the court's awards; and despite efforts to revive its functions as an agency for conciliating disputes, industrial conflicts grew more numerous and more violent. Striking miners on the Waihi goldfield during May to November, 1912, received aid from several other unions; the contest was bitterly fought, ugly clashes occurring between strikers and police; the workers were defeated. In the following year a more widespread struggle between capital and labor, which began as a strike of the waterside workers in Wellington, was lost by the latter. Thwarted and discredited, the most radical of the trade union leaders lost their influence for the time being.

The end of the political alliance between Liberals and Laborites coupled with a widespread revulsion against the tactics used by the unions strengthened the conservatives. Reorganized politically by Mr. W. F. Massey, the conservatives took the name of the Reform party and pledged themselves to continue the constructive work of the old Liberal-Labor coalition. In spite of the division among the left-wingers, the Reform party in the election of December, 1911, secured only 37 of the 80 seats in the house of representatives. Ward continued in office until March following, and shortly afterward the Reform party assumed control with Massey as prime minister. Industrial strife as well as preparation for and the outbreak of the World War helped the Massey government to keep its precarious hold until the 1914 elections brought some comfort with a majority of one. In August, 1915, the Liberals and Reformers agreed to form a coalition government with Massey as premier and Ward as minister of finance, but the two leaders did not work harmoniously and upon their return from the peace conference in August, 1919, Ward resigned. The next election (two years overdue) took place the following December. Ward made a strenuous bid for the soldiers' vote by promising a large bonus, but the bait was not swallowed. Massey obtained a clear majority with 46 who took the whip of the Reform party.

Like the political, the industrial strife in New Zealand ceased in the early years of the war. More than 124,000 New Zealanders enlisted for military service, labor was in demand, and wages were high. Quiet lasted until November, 1916, when Labor began to oppose conscription for war or for national service. The miners, as usual the most truculent, objected to the principle of compulsion. Although bonuses were granted to labor, there was a strike of coal miners in 1917 and 1918 that caused real concern. In common with the other British nations, New Zealand made special efforts to provide bonuses and pensions for soldiers and their dependents. A boom followed the cessation of hostilities and everybody looked forward to a new era of peace and prosperity. Alas, disillusionment was near at hand.

Severe financial depression struck New Zealand at the end of 1920. For five export seasons the supplies department of the imperial government had bought New Zealand produce. With the exception of butter purchases, this arrangement came to an end in 1920. At the same time prices of agricultural products in the United States took a drastic slump. In 1919 the foreign trade of New Zealand showed a favorable balance of more than £23,000,000; in the following year the deficit was over £15,000,000 — a reversal blamed on the delay of British manufacturers in filling her orders until after the war was over. The dominion treasury immediately faced a critical situation. The war had added more than £80,000,000 to the public debt, which on March 31, 1921, stood at £197,561,247, or £162 1*s.* 7*d.* per head of the population. About one-half of this debt was held in London. Thus it came to pass that both exports and government revenues fell sharply in the face of mounting overseas debt charges and heavy outlays in connection with the settlement of soldiers on land. In June, 1921, a 6 per cent New Zealand loan of £5,000,000 was floated in London at 96; expenses were then cut drastically and taxes raised. The Massey government drew most of its political support from the small farmers of the North Island; therefore it made determined efforts to increase the export of agricultural produce, principally butter and cheese. The government's credit improved so rapidly that in 1922 London took a New Zealand loan of £5,000,000 at 5 per cent; but industrialists and farmers continued to suffer from the results of over-expansion and heavy borrowing in the years of plenty.

In the twenties the evil effects of faulty private finance were partly offset by increased government borrowing and expenditures for land settlements and public works. This was the old Vogel policy. The government borrowed, aided immigrants, and promoted settlement. Between 1919 and 1927 about £70,000,000 were added to the public debt, and more than 50,000 immigrants from Great Britain were brought in. The newcomers had been city dwellers and many were radicals in politics; hence swelled the urban population of New Zealand and voted the Labor ticket. The government was solicitous of agriculture, encouraged a change from leasehold to freehold tenure, and set up export boards which were expected to secure for the country's primary industries all benefits procurable from private ownership and initiative, public supervision of quality, and expert advice in marketing. Competition was keen in the world market, prices fluctuated, and the cost of production had to be kept down. In the depression years the arbitration court appeared to favor the employer. Labor complained of being exploited, demanded nationalization of industry, and urged social legislation. Not much was done in this field, although the Child Welfare Act of 1925, compulsory medical examination of school children, and school dental service indicated that the Reform party did not neglect vital health problems. New Zealand was proud of the fact that the infant mortality rate fell in the years 1908–1927 from 67.89 to 38.74 per thousand.

The Reform government pointed with pride to the rapid recovery after the slump of 1920, the growth in population, and the mounting exports; nevertheless, the voters were loath to give it full confidence. In the election of 1922 Massey lost his majority in the house of representatives; but since his party's principles were practically identical with those of the Liberal (renamed the United) party he held office till his death in 1925. His successor was Mr. J. G. Coates, a farmer and an ex-soldier, slow of speech but rapid in action, and not well known in 1925; perhaps for that reason he won a surprise victory in the election of that year. In New Zealand as in the world over the prosperity of the twenties was a fitful, unreal one; shots in the arm such as government aid and auto-suggestion in the form of stock market speculations failed to bring real health. After 1926 unemployment began to worry New Zealand. Growing uncertainty concerning the future brought the old Liberal-Labor leader, Sir

Joseph Ward, out of his retirement. He had been associated with Seddon in the prosperous days at the turn of the century; it was believed that the old pilot might find a safe course. In 1928 Sir Joseph undertook a whirlwind campaign. Accusing the government of timidity, he promised to bring back the good old days by a double dose of the old remedies – government aid to industry and easy credit. He proposed a huge development loan of £70,000,000, of which £60,000,000 should be used for agriculture. Because the promises of more and cheaper money were alluring, warnings by the minister of finance, Mr. W. Downie Stewart, went unheeded – Ward and his magic wand might lure prosperity from its hiding place. The good season of 1928–1929 strengthened the optimists and although Ward did not get a majority in the election of 1928 he secured sufficient support to be able to form a government with Labor aid. But the stars were against him. Shortly after he assumed office the stock market crashed in the United States, and no mumbling of the old formula that things were getting better and better could excoriate the evil spirits of depression. The false prosperity came to an end, New Zealand's export fell, the figures for unemployment rose. Ward strove manfully with ill luck and ill health, but the latter brought him down. In June, 1930, he handed the reins of government to Mr. G. W. Forbes.

By this time Labor was beginning to remove its support from the government. Its drastic remedies might bring the cure which the old ones could not effect. The Reform party now kept the government in office. As the Labor party grew more bitter in its criticism and more extravagant in its promises, the conservatives of New Zealand sought to form a united front against socialism. Efforts at fusion failed in May, 1931, but with an election approaching they succeeded in September, a Forbes-Coates coalition government being sworn in on September 22. The two parties were equally represented in the ministry and ultimately they combined to form the Nationalist party. The new united front won the election of December, 1931, but the task of recapturing prosperity was beyond its strength. Facing a deficit of £8,500,000, the minister of finance, Mr. W. Downie Stewart, proposed heroic measures — the increase of old and the imposition of new taxes, the slashing of wages, salaries, and pensions, the dismissal of government employees, and the discontinuance of public works for which he planned to substitute a dole. The latter was the cheaper method of caring for the unemployed but it ran counter to New Zealand tradition; furthermore, the recovery program exposed a wide front to the attacks of socialists. In 1935 when parliament was dissolved the Nationalists had 46 and the Laborites 24 votes in the house of representatives; when it met again after the elections Labor had 55 and the Nationalists 19, with 6 independents. The defeat of the government had been a rout. The leader of the Labor party, Mr. M. J. Savage, became the new premier.

The Labor government of New Zealand now launched policies as radical for the 1930's as those of Seddon had been for the 1890's. Energetically the Laborites proceeded to bring back the good old times. They used an inherited surplus to restore pensions and salaries, and they launched an ambitious and far-reaching program of reconstruction. Promoting employment took the place of fighting unemployment, and a fund for this purpose was created by a levy on industry; a new minimum wage law raised the lower limits in some brackets more than 50 per cent; the work week was reduced from 44 to 40 hours; a new wage scale was introduced also in agriculture; and a revived and strengthened arbitration court no longer regarded the agricultural and pastoral industries as outside the scope of its functions. The government resumed borrowing for public works and announced that the national income would be redistributed by an elaborate system of pensions for the aged, widows, invalids, war veterans and their dependents, and by increased family allowances. Though wage earners were the special object of the government's care, the farmers were not neglected. The export boards were abolished and their duties transferred to a department of marketing whose object was to stabilize and secure fair prices on farm produce in both domestic and foreign markets. Mortgage relief was of particular interest to the farming classes. Social security for all became an effective slogan for the government, and a large number of legislative measures bore testimony to its sincerity. The program of course aroused apprehension among the employing classes, including the farmers, but the growth of New Zealand's export (the figures for 1937 were £20,000,000 above those for 1935) was cited as proof of the success of the "new deal." Despite blistering attacks by the opposition headed by Mr. Adam Hamilton, the government lost only one seat in the election of 1938. Whether this was due to a wholesale indirect bribery of the electors by the measures mentioned above or to an honest conviction that the Laborites had found a path leading to "the more abundant life" will probably never be known. Encouraged by the mandate, the Savage government proceeded to introduce new legislation for the safeguarding of prosperity and social security in the country.

The radicals of New Zealand sponsored policies and expressed sentiments more nationalistic in character than those sponsored and expressed by their political opponents. Labor sought to foster the economic independence of the dominion and at times apparently doubted the value of membership in the British Commonwealth. Since agriculture could not absorb many more people, the Laborites turned their attention to the development of secondary industries. They pointed out the dangers lurking in New Zealand's dependence on the British market — a balanced economy was their goal. Consequently they encouraged the manufacture of goods which the dominion could produce cheaply and efficiently. Under the Industrial Efficiency Act of 1936 inquiries were made and agencies established for the building up of home industries in accordance with a "rationalised plan." Most of this work has not yet (1941) passed the embryonic stage; still it is worth noting that the number of employees in the so-called "true" manufacturing industries, which include those that must meet competition from imports, increased from 53,468 in 1934–1935 to 66,419 in 1936–1937. Although some of this increase may be attributed to a general upswing in industry, the balanced economy program has nevertheless made progress. Phases of this program included efforts for utilizing New Zealand's hydroelectric power to a larger extent and for domiciling the public debt.

With greater self-sufficiency as one of the aims of her government, New Zealand's relations with Britain as well as with the other dominions were subjected to scrutiny from various angles. It was pointed out that, except for the trade with Britain, the intra-Commonwealth trade was hardly sufficiently important to warrant the elaborate system of tariff preferences. Britain bought from New Zealand to about twice the value of what she sold to the dominion. Still New Zealand politicians showed a tendency to question the value of the imperial relationship; occasionally voices were heard expressing the belief that the dominion was exposed to danger because she was connected with Britain. However, this talk vanished like chaff in a storm when it appeared that Nazi Germany wanted to destroy the British empire. In 1926 Labor had condemned a proposed New Zealand contribution for the base at Singapore, yet in 1937 the Savage government informed the imperial authorities that it considered the base to be of the greatest importance. As the international situation became more threatening, New Zealand took steps to strengthen her defense forces, especially those of the air and the navy. A group of committees labeled the "Organisation for National Security" investigated defense problems in all their aspects and performed the function of a subcommittee of the Imperial Defence Committee. The Munich pact disappointed New Zealanders, for they hated to see the mother country suffer a diplomatic defeat. To them the declaration of war against Germany in September, 1939, came almost as a relief. Without hesitation New Zealand acted upon the theory that she was at war when Britain was at war. On September 5 her parliament confirmed the British declaration of war and approved plans for a special force to serve within or beyond the confines of the dominion. No longer was her connection with the mother country examined from the profit and loss point of view; the youngest of the British nations demonstrated the truth of Burke's prophecy that the silken bonds of love and affection would prove strong as steel in times of difficulty and danger.

CHAPTER 34

THE AWAKENING OF INDIA, 1905–1939

LORD Curzon was the last of the benevolent despots sent by Britain to govern India. Before his arrival Indians had become restive under and by reason of the English tutelage, and his seven years of efficient government inspired by western ideals increased their discontent. The nationalistic movement gained strength rapidly and the successors of Curzon as viceroys of India recognized that her people must be given a share in the government. Within the next thirty years India emerged from a servile status to one of power and influence, as was recognized by the India Government Act of 1935. Nor was her development confined to the field of government. Her industrial progress has in many ways been as significant as her constitutional advance, particularly in the manufacture of cotton goods. Her dependence upon the importation of cotton cloth decreased to such an extent that the cotton industry of Lancashire suffered severely — Nemesis overtook the industrial region of England which a hundred years ago ruined India's native cotton industry. The Indian metal industries have also grown remarkably since Curzon's day. Economically and socially as well as politically, India has taken long strides toward nationhood.

While much of this internal progress must be attributed to forces operating within India, the speed has been accelerated by external events, especially by the war of 1914–1918. The international situation as well as British imperial policies have acted and reacted upon the situation in India. Consequently, in tracing her history during the last thirty-five years it will be necessary to discuss the external affairs of India before we examine the course and nature of her economic, social, and political evolution. These topics will be treated in the order given, first for the years before and then for those after 1919.

India's external relations during 1905–1919 were of course linked closely with those of Britain and with the latter's foreign policy. Lord Curzon pursued a masterful and energetic Indian foreign policy, at times compelling the British statesmen at Westminster to follow his lead. After his recall in 1905 the home government recovered its old position as the directing force in shaping India's foreign relations. Concern for her safety continued in the twentieth century, as it had been in the nineteenth, to be a dominant factor in determining Britain's attitude toward rival powers and the character of her agreements with them. The Anglo-Russian Treaty of August, 1907, dealt exclusively with problems that concerned India; British opposition to the German plans for a Berlin-to-Bagdad railroad were motivated by fear that this railroad would endanger the safety of India; and the desire to protect her led to the scope of the Anglo-Japanese alliance being enlarged so as to include cooperation in her defense. Although the measures taken for their safety were applauded by Indians, some of them as well as other aspects of British foreign policy aroused suspicion among the Mohammedans of India. They had received special favors from the British, yet their allegiance was divided between Britain and Islam. As followers of Mohammed, they held in reverence the sultan of Turkey, the caliph of Islam, especially since Turkey was the only Mohammedan state of any consequence. The Indian Moslems had supported Britain's defense of Turkey against Russia. But in 1907 Britain concluded an agreement with Russia which implied friendship between these ancient rivals; in 1911 Britain watched while Italy despoiled Turkey of Tripoli and of islands in the Aegean; and during the Balkan wars of 1912–1913 British sympathy seemed to be on the side of the enemies of Turkey. Offended by the change in Britain's foreign policy, the leaders of Mohammedan India began to listen to the overtures from the Hindu National Congress, and by 1915 the Moslem League was actively cooperating with the Congress party.

Nevertheless, in August, 1914, a wave of loyalty to Britain swept over India, causing Indian princes and leaders of public opinion, like Mahatma Gandhi and Rabindranath Tagore, to vie with each other in expressing their attachment to the cause for which Britain fought. Princes came forward with gifts and placed their armies, the so-called imperial service troops, at the disposal of Britain; Gandhi offered to organize an ambulance corps; and in a poem, "The Boatman," Tagore gave utterance to his abhorrence of the German invasion of Belgium. The loyalty of India as a whole (the hostile demonstrations in Bengal were at first too insignificant to cause worry) proved a tremendous asset to Britain in 1914 and 1915. Even though the army in India was trained and organized only for guarding her frontier and keeping peace within her borders, not for modern European warfare, the 77,000 British and about 200,000 native soldiers of the Indian army formed a military reservoir upon which to draw in the critical early months of the war. The 530 officers of the Indian army on furlough in Britain when the war broke out were detained there; British troops were removed from India, their places being taken by British territorials. On August 25, 1914, a contingent of 16,000 British and 28,500 Indians left Bombay for France. Other contingents sent from India helped conquer the German Cameroons, German East Africa, and Kiaochau, the German stronghold in China; and guarded Egypt, Zanzibar, the Mombasa-Nairobi railroad in East Africa, and the oil fields and pipe line in southwestern Persia. The last effort developed into the Mesopotamian campaign, one of the most important of the military side-shows of the war.

Before the end of 1914 India had supplied more than 100,000 troops, exclusive of 35,000 recalled to Britain, for service outside her borders. The Indians were ultimately withdrawn from France, but their number was increased in other theaters of the war, especially in Mesopotamia and Palestine, so that her total contribution included 826,868 combatants, 445,592 non-combatants, 172,815 animals, and 3,691,836 tons of supplies and stores. The people of the Punjab, true to their fighting tradition, came forward in the largest number. This province with a population of 20,000,000 supplied about 500,000 recruits; the native state of Nepal, population 3,000,000, contributed 50,000; and Baluchistan and the North West Frontier Province furnished 30,000 volunteers. The Indian troops saw their heaviest fighting and suffered their greatest losses in the Mesopotamian campaign. Their casualty lists totaled 64,449 killed or dead and 69,214 wounded. Apart from these losses, India had little direct contact with the war. Her government could not pay for the cost of military operations beyond her borders but could make voluntary contributions which, all told, amounted to about £200,000,000. Moreover, the war necessitated careful guarding of the Persian and Afghan frontiers; the third Afghan war, 1919, had causal connections with the Four Years' War. Against the losses which India suffered in consequence of the war may be set several very tangible gains. Natives were granted high commissions in the army; her manufacturing industries were encouraged and made rapid progress in the war years; she secured the right to regulate her tariff; she was admitted to the imperial war conferences of 1917 and 1918; a large amount of self-government was conceded to her by the Government of India Act, 1919; and she was granted independent status as a member of the League of Nations. The war helped to crystallize Indian nationalistic agitation and advanced India on the path toward true nationhood. This development will be traced first in its economic and social and then in its political aspects to the end of the war.

We have already seen that a modern textile industry had been established and had made considerable progress in India by the end of the nineteenth century. This progress was stimulated early in the twentieth century by the Bureau of Commerce and Industry created by Lord Curzon, by the Indian Industrial Conference, an offshoot of the National Congress, and by Japan's success as an industrial nation. The Agricultural College founded at Pusa in 1905, and extensive new experiments in agriculture brought improvements to this basic industry, the area under crop rising from 242 to 272 million acres in the decade immediately preceding the outbreak of the war. But the progress in agriculture failed to keep pace with the needs of a population which grew by about 20,000,000 in the years 1901–1911. The population pressure supplied strong arguments for the building up of manufacturing industries, arguments powerfully reinforced by the needs connected with and arising from the Four Years' War. Scarcity of shipping and high freight rates made imported manufactured articles dear and scarce, and the disappearance of German goods coupled with the need for war material created new opportunities for industrial enterprise. The Indian Industrial Commission, dating from 1916, and the Indian Munitions Board of 1917 urged that the government of India take an active part in promoting manufacturing industries; her cotton manufacturers were aided by a new tariff which increased the rate on imported goods from 3½ to 7½ per cent, while leaving the excise on domestic manufactures unaltered.

The war years had a profound effect upon the domestic production and manufacture of cotton in India. The cotton-growing area was enlarged from 9,610,000 acres at the opening of the century to 23,070,000 in 1919, and yield per acre as well as quality was improved. During the war the import of English cotton cloth, measured by yardage, declined 70 per cent while the Indian production rose 20.8 per cent. Similar and perhaps even more startling progress was made by the iron and steel industries of India. In 1914 the Tata Iron and Steel Company,

Ltd., in operation since 1912, faced an uncertain future because of the stiff British, Belgian, and German competition. True, the government of India in 1912 had agreed to take for a period of ten years 20,000 tons of steel rails annually, but this was subject to the provision that the rails should be of the right quality and price. The war tipped the scales in favor of the Tata works. With foreign supplies practically cut off, the Tata expanded so that by 1919 the company had two blast furnaces, each making 350 tons of pig iron daily; its steel production had reached 17,000 tons per month; its rails had proved of good quality; and the company had secured control over iron and coal mines, limestone quarries, and magnesite deposits. The Tata had in fact become a vertical trust. An older organization, The Bengal Iron and Steel Company, Ltd., had been put on a really productive basis shortly before and grew rapidly during the war, and a large new Indian iron and steel company was founded in 1918. The need for domestic manufactures may be judged by the fact that the foreign import of iron and steel fell from 735,000 tons in 1913 to 152,000 tons in 1917. When the war ended, the domestic industrial interests had grown sufficiently strong and influential to be a factor in the economic and political life of India.

From the standpoint of the Indian Nationalists this growth was gratifying, while from that of British imperial interests it presented ominous aspects, especially since the decline in the import of British goods, particularly cotton, had been offset only in part by Indian manufactures. A new rival, Japan, more formidable than imperial Germany, had found the conditions created by the war favorable for the building up of an Indian market. In 1913–1914 England supplied 98.8 per cent and Japan 0.5 of one per cent of India's import of the cheaper grades of cotton goods, but by 1917–1918 the figures stood respectively at 64.3 and 35.5. While the statistics for the better grades of cotton goods were less unfavorable to Britain, the figures for India's whole foreign trade in 1913–1914 in comparison with

1917–1918, showed that the British share of Indian import had fallen from 63 to 54 per cent and that of Japan had risen from 2 to 12 per cent in the war years. Moreover, it was disclosed in 1919 that no British firm operating in India had financial backing or organization equal to that of the Japanese firm Mitsui Bussan Kaisha. The more extreme of the Indian Nationalists — their number grew during the war — favored Japan, an Asiatic power, as against Britain, the old exploiter and oppressor of India.

The great war promoted Indian industrialization but retarded the rate of her advance in education. Still, gains were scored. The total expenditures for education rose from 4 crores of rupees in 1901 to 7½ crores in 1911, and the number of pupils and students increased by one million between 1908 and 1912. Education continued to be under the control of the provinces and of private organizations, among which the missionary societies held the first place. The government of India, however, made grants from time to time; and in February, 1913, the department of education announced a new and ambitious program that foreshadowed greatly enlarged imperial contributions for educational purposes. This program was shelved during the war. For two years the government granted no aid to education; teachers and others connected with educational institutions were drawn into war service; and the missionary schools suffered from the curtailment of funds and workers. Significant advances were made in the field of higher education. The year 1917 saw the founding of a private university for women and the opening of universities at Benares, Mysore, and Patna. Since the University of Benares was Hindu and that at Mysore was a state institution, these universities represent distinct stages in the educational awakening of India.

This awakening was intimately associated with the nationalistic movement, whose origin and growth till the end of the Curzon regime have been discussed in an earlier chapter. Curzon taught Indians to think politically; some of his actions, the partition of Bengal in particular, evoked furious opposition. Japan's victories in the war with Russia, 1904–1905, stimulated the self-respect of the people of India and made them more resentful of overbearing treatment. The English were loth to grant even educated Indians the social equality which they held to be their due, and Indian immigrants were treated as members of an inferior race in the self-governing portions of the British empire. The virtual exclusion of Indians from Canada and Australasia was galling to their pride; in South Africa, where the British government had championed the cause of the Indians in the Transvaal before the outbreak of the Boer War, the grant of self-government to the new colonies and the formation of the Union resulted in the adoption of anti-Indian policies which Britain was unable to alter. Economic grievances growing out of colonization projects in the Punjab, complaints over land assessments, charges that Britain had drained and was draining India of her wealth, irritation with the excise levied on Indian cotton goods, and wild rumors connected with an outbreak of bubonic plague in northern India in 1906 were utilized by political agitators to foment hostility to Britain and the British. Vernacular newspapers were gradually finding their way into the villages and more classes were becoming interested in the nationalistic agitation. The assertions often made in England that Britain was being overshadowed by Germany and the United States diminished her prestige in India, and the Liberal victory in the British election of 1906 tended to accelerate a swing to the left in India. Even the moderates among Indian Nationalists soon presented demands that looked extravagant in the eyes not only of the ultra-conservative Anglo-Indians but also of English Liberals.

Gokhale, the outstanding leader of the Nationalists, kept their main body from presenting radical demands until his death in 1915. With him was associated Dadabhai Naoroji, the son of a Parsee priest, who lived in England for many years, served in the house of commons from 1892 to 1895, helped to organize the National Congress, and was its president three times. During the pre-war and war years, Tilak led the violent anti-British faction among the Hindus. A staunch defender of old Hindu customs such as child marriage, he represented the spirit of revolt of East against West. The moderates advocated reform by constitutional methods and hoped to achieve results by political evolution, while the extremists recommended terrorism and revolution. Tilak glorified the Maratha leader, Shivaji, who had assassinated a Mohammedan general, and openly asserted that political murder was not a crime. A wave of terroristic outrages swept sections of India in 1907–1912, culminating in an attempt upon the life of the viceroy, Lord Hardinge, in December, 1912. This was attributed to the teachings of Tilak, and in 1908 he was deported for a term of six years.

The violent anti-British agitation spread to Britain and the United States. On July 1, 1909, Sir W. Curzon Wyllie, an official connected with the India office, was murdered at the Imperial Institute in London. The assassin was a member of a radical Indian organization with headquarters in London. Lajpat Rai, historian and author of several books on India, was active and acquired considerable influence in the United States in the years 1910–1920. He was much interested in the humanitarian and educational as well as the political aspects of the Indian nationalist movement and strongly supported swadeshi, or the encouragement of native industries. Among the British sympathizers with the demands of the Indian Nationalists may be mentioned Sir Henry Cotton and Mrs. A. Besant. The former, a member of a family famous in the history of the Indian civil service, devoted the latter years of his life to championing the cause of India in the house of commons. The latter, a native of England and a well-known Theosophist, lived in India from 1890 till her death in 1933; she aided in founding the Hindu University at Benares, edited several radical newspapers, helped the extremists to capture the National Congress in 1916, and in the following year served as its president. In the war years new leaders appeared both among moderates and among extremists, but the discussion of their work belongs to a later period when they exerted their greatest influence.

Lord Minto, Lord Curzon's successor as viceroy of India, was a Conservative who had been governor general of Canada and had learned the need of compromise in politics. The change of government in England in December, 1905, brought John (afterward Lord) Morley to the India office. This distinguished scholar and statesman had long been classed as a radical, chiefly because of his early advocacy of home rule for Ireland. But age and new conditions had transformed him into a doctrinaire Liberal whose sympathy for those who rightly struggled to be free failed to include the people of India. The Conservative viceroy was in fact readier to make concessions than was his Liberal chief. They adopted for India a policy reminiscent of the treatment of Ireland by the Liberals — repression mixed with concessions. On the one hand those guilty of political crimes were severely dealt with and freedom of speech and of the press was curtailed; on the other Indians were given a greater share in the government of their country and the partition of Bengal was reversed. Constitutional changes of 1909 included the admission of two Indians to the India council in London and one to the executive council of the governor general, the enlargement of the legislative council for India and of those of the more important provinces, and a considerable increase in the number of elective members of these councils. The non-official members now outnumbered the official in the legislative councils of the larger provinces; in that of Bengal a majority was elected. But everywhere the franchise rested upon a narrow basis and recognized special interests. From the application of this principle arose the bitter controversy over the "communal" representation of the Mohammedans. The legislatures were given more freedom of discussion, and separate executive councils were established in the major provinces; but Morley emphatically disavowed any intention of extending to India the system of responsible government. She was to have representative government, not self-government.

Morley from the beginning had disapproved of the partition of Bengal. However, like his former chief, Gladstone, in the annexation of the Transvaal, Morley distinguished between the repudiation and the reversal of a policy. Hence at first he let well enough alone, but in the face of the mounting Indian discontent he decided finally to reverse the partition. This was announced at the coronation durbar of George V held at Delhi, June 12, 1911. Eastern Bengal was reunited with the old province, and Bengal was given a governor in council like Madras and Bombay. Bihar, Orissa, and Chota Nagpur were organized as a province with a lieutenant-governor, and Assam once more became a chief-commissionership. The governor generalship was separated from Bengal; the capital of India was moved from Calcutta to Delhi; and this city with the area immediately around it was set aside as a separate territory directly under the governor general.

These concessions failed, however, to satisfy the Indian Nationalists. The moderates among them now demanded the dominion type of self-government, and the radicals advocated separation. The grievances of Indians in Natal and Canada were discussed shortly before the outbreak of the war. A tentative settlement was secured in the case of the former; but Canada's refusal of admittance and her return to India of 373 immigrants, mostly Sikhs, in the summer of 1914 stirred up much hostile sentiment in the Punjab. The Sikhs who returned became active in spreading anti-British propaganda. The agitation grew in intensity after 1916, when the radicals secured control of the Indian National Congress. Investigations conducted in 1917 by a special sedition committee presided over by Judge Rowlatt disclosed a network of conspiracy against British rule in India that extended to Britain, France, and the United States, in addition to the multifarious activities of conspirators in India. Armed with wide powers obtained by war-time legislation, the government attempted to quell the rising storm, but it realized that suppression alone would not suffice. Moreover, the efforts made by millions of Indians and the loyalty shown by them deserved reward.

The opportunity for offering rewards came in 1917 when the study of the Mesopotamian disaster, the surrender of Kut in the preceding year, disclosed glaring defects in the administrative system of India. At the imperial war conference of 1917 India was represented by the Maharaja of Bikanir and Sir Satyendra Sinha. She was thus given a seat at the council table with the British dominions, and her grievances against their immigration laws were discussed. Of even greater significance was the declaration made by the new secretary of state for India, Edwin Montagu, in the house of commons on August 20, 1917, that the imperial government had decided to modify the constitution of India so as to increase the "association of Indians in every branch of the administration and the gradual development of self-governing institutions with a view to the progressive realization of responsible government in India as an integral part of the British Empire." Mr. Montagu stated, however, "that progress in this policy can only be achieved by successive stages," and that the British government "must be judges of the time and measure of each advance, and they must be guided by the cooperation received from those on whom new opportunities of service will be thus conferred, and by the extent to which it is found that confidence can be reposed in their sense of responsibility."

Meanwhile the Indian Congress party had in 1916 prepared a program for political reforms with home rule of the dominion type as the ultimate goal, and the British Round Table group under the leadership of Mr. Lionel Curtis had begun advocating dyarchy, or a dual government, for the provinces of India. This theory was discussed by Mr. Curtis in a work published in 1917; he also recommended the division of India into about twenty-four provinces, based at least in part upon racial and linguistic factors. These and other projects concerning the future government of India were before Mr. Montagu as he undertook the difficult task of implementing his historic announcement of August 20, 1917. As part of the preparation for this work he visited India in 1917–1918, making exhaustive inquiries on the spot and conferring with the new viceroy, Lord Chelmsford, and others conversant with Indian problems and conditions. The results of the study and inquiry were embodied in the great *Montagu-Chelmsford Report,* called officially *The Joint Report on Indian Constitutional Reforms,* 1918. This voluminous document contains an historical survey of the government of India, an analysis of its virtues and defects, and a plan for reform based on the principles of greater participation by Indians in the government of their country and the division of powers in the provinces into those transferred to the legislative councils and those reserved for the governors and their executive councils, a system labeled "dyarchy." Further studies of the issues raised in the report were made by two committees under the chairmanship of Lord Southborough, and the draft bill was subjected to close scrutiny by a joint committee of both houses of parliament. After this careful preparation the new government of India bill encountered little opposition, receiving royal assent December 23, 1919.

This great statute, the Government of India Act, 1919, provided a constitution for British India. As such it not only dealt with fundamental problems of government but also contained many specific regulations concerning administration. Although important concessions were made to the Indian demand for self-government, these concessions fell short of dominion status. The British parliament continued to be supreme in settling the most important questions concerning India, and the secretary of state was left with great influence in shaping her destiny. Moreover, her government remained centralized, and the governor general in council lost little actual power. The advances toward self-government were marked by the extension of the representative principle in the fields of central and provincial government and by the establishment of dyarchy in the major provinces. The act of 1919 granted to India a bicameral legislature. The upper house, the council of state, had 59 members; the lower house, the legislative assembly, had 143. In each, the majority was elected by a limited franchise, more restricted for the council than for the assembly. The members of the former were chosen for five and those of the latter for three years. The powers of the two bodies were coordinate, except as regards finance, where the assembly had more influence. Deadlocks between the houses were to be broken by joint sessions.

The constitution of 1919 enlarged the provincial legislative councils and stipulated that not less than 70 per cent of their members were to be elected. The powers which fell under the jurisdiction of the governments of the major provinces were divided into two categories, reserved and transferred. The boundary between them was the line between general and important subjects and those more local and of less immediate political significance. Thus the administration of justice was reserved, while agriculture, education, and local government were listed as transferred subjects. The reserved subjects were handled by the provincial governor assisted by a small executive council of two or four members of whom one or two were natives of India; in handling the transferred subjects he was advised by a ministry composed of the elected members of the legislative council. This ministry had to have the support of a majority of the council. The provincial franchise was restricted to a comparatively small body of people, and the electoral system recognized communal representation for Mohammedans, Sikhs, Europeans, Anglo-Indians, and Indian Christians wherever their number seemed to warrant it. The provincial legislative councils controlled appropriations, but both the governors and the governor general in council could interfere in financial and legislative matters, if the welfare of provinces seemed to demand it, by declaring a state of emergency. Such a declaration was, however, subject to scrutiny by the secretary of state. The smaller provinces and certain backward areas were placed under the direct control of the central government. The system of dyarchy was introduced at first in the provinces of Bengal, Bombay, Madras, Assam, Bihar and Orissa, the Central Provinces, the United Provinces, and the Punjab. To these were later added Burma, the North West Frontier Province, and Sind.

A grievance of long standing was removed in 1919 with the transference of the cost of the India office in London from India's budget to that of Britain. An exception was made in the case of services of direct benefit to India; these were gradually turned over to a new official, the high commissioner for India, the cost of his office, of course, being borne by that country. Amnesty was granted to political prisoners; and the arrangement whereby the working of the constitution should be studied after ten years by a special commission served as a pledge that the reforms were not to mark the end of concessions to Indian demands for autonomy. Indeed, the authors of the act of 1919 looked forward to the time when the provinces of India should be "self-governing under a central government." A step in this direction was the issuance of statutory rules distinguishing between central and provincial subjects. Nor were the native states ignored. They were drawn closer to British India by the establishment of a chamber of princes which was to meet annually with the viceroy for the purpose of discussing matters of common concern.

The new constitution for India encountered rough seas from the outset. Few, except its begetter, Mr. Lionel Curtis, had much faith in the double provincial executive, the dyarchy. The name conjured up the Roman governmental system founded by Augustus; it was a novelty used by people not vitally interested in proving its worth. The reforms embodied in the act and the supplementary rules fell short of what even the moderates among the Indian Nationalists expected; they were granted as concessions, not as rights restored; and they predicated the "training for self-government" that had been so obnoxious to British colonists in the mid-nineteenth century and was no less offensive to the proud intellectuals, standard bearers of an ancient culture, who voiced India's aspirations for self-government. Furthermore, a series of external circumstances militated against the success of the Montagu-Chelmsford reforms. In 1919–1920 all the world, including India, was confused and distraught by forces set in motion by the war; reason and moderation were at a discount. In 1918 the Rowlatt Committee reported on sedition in India. Its work brought fruit the following year in the form of laws gagging the press, legalizing trial without jury of persons accused of political offenses, and permitting political suspects to be imprisoned without due process of law. A war with Afghanistan in the spring of 1919 coincided with riots in the Punjab and other places. At Amritsar a mob murdered four Europeans and maltreated a lady missionary, leaving her for dead. Three days later, on April 13, General Dyer ordered soldiers to fire upon a large meeting held illegally in an enclosed space. They obeyed, took careful aim and kept on firing until their ammunition was exhausted. Conservatively estimated, the victims of the Amritsar massacre numbered 379 killed and 1208 wounded. General Dyer, his military superiors, the lieutenant-governor of the Punjab, and a strong body of opinion in England defended this act on the ground that "frightfulness" was necessary for the purpose of checking further and worse disorders. An investigating committee under the chairmanship of Lord Hunter condemned it, but not so unsparingly as the Indian members of that committee demanded. "The episode," says Professor A. B. Keith, "unhappily cast a dark shadow over the inception of the reforms and brought racial feeling out far more bitterly than at any time since the Mutiny." Nor was the anti-British feeling confined to the Hindus. The Mohammedans, aroused by Britain's anti-Turkish policy, the Anglo-Turkish war, the demands for the expulsion of the Turks from Constantinople, and the harsh terms imposed upon them in 1920 by the Treaty of Sèvres, joined forces with the Hindus against the British. The Mohammedans found capable leaders in the brothers Mohammad and Shaukat Ali, and the

Hindus were guided by the greatest of their modern leaders, Mohandas K. Gandhi.

This remarkable man combines the characteristics of a fearless, truth-loving, single-minded saint with those of a master politician. A student at University College, London, and a member of the English bar, Gandhi went to South Africa in 1893, was deeply impressed with the cruelty and wrongs inflicted by the Boers upon his countrymen, and acquired great skill in championing their cause. At an early age he adopted a pacifistic, humanitarian creed. He apparently also studied the pressure tactics employed by Irish nationalists and English suffragettes, and he improved upon them, adding touches of oriental refinement. In South Africa he began using the weapons of the boycott, civil disobedience, non-cooperation, and the closing of shops as a sign of public mourning, the so-called *hartal,* which he later employed so effectively in India. In him western culture is blended with oriental subtlety and religious mysticism. To an extraordinary degree Gandhi has succeeded in gaining a mastery over the minds of Indians and winning the sympathy of Europeans and especially of Americans. Some of this success is, however, due to a flair for publicity — Mohandas K. Gandhi works in the world, and his light is not hidden under a bushel.

When Gandhi came to South Africa, the British government was insisting upon civil rights for the Indians in the Transvaal. Hence he sided with the British in the Anglo-Boer war, but he was disappointed with the effects of the outcome of the war upon his countrymen. Nevertheless, he sympathized with and aided Britain during the World War, but again disillusionment followed, for the British government seemed bent on restoring pre-war conditions in India. The Rowlatt acts, the Amritsar massacre, and the reservations in the act of 1919 convinced him that India had been tricked. Soon he began mobilizing Indian opinion against the British. A non-Brahmin, Gandhi was not hampered by the restrictions which the caste system imposes upon Brahmins; he could work with the commercial and industrial classes as well as with the high-born Brahmins. And he was attractive to the Mohammedans. God and mammon who so often have worked for the British were now rallied against them. The effects of the opposition led or inspired by Gandhi upon the working of the new act were soon shown.

The first elections under the act of 1919 were held in October, 1920, "in an atmosphere . . . suffused by race enmities." The Congress party refused to participate, yet about one-third of the six million voters went to the polls. Ministries were formed in the provinces, but on account of racial, religious, and political divisions they were chosen from several groups. The new parliament for all India was opened at Delhi on February 9, 1921, by the Duke of Connaught, uncle of the king-emperor. In a message to the peoples of India, George V stressed the point that the new constitution signalized the beginning of home rule and offered India "ample opportunity for progress to the liberty which my other Dominions enjoy." In intra-imperial relations this statement was implemented by the signing of the peace treaties of 1919 and 1920 separately by representatives of India, by her independent representation in the assembly of the League of Nations and in subsidiaries of that organization, and by her participation in the imperial conferences on equal footing with the dominions. Moreover, the all-India legislature pursued a true Indian policy with reference to tariffs, defense, and other matters of vital importance; and provincial legislatures passed important legislation pertaining to health, education, and local government. But as already indicated, the Montagu-Chelmsford reform program was inaugurated under evil auspices. The Mohammedans were hostile and continued so until the new ruler of Turkey, Mustapha Kemal, in 1924 put the quietus on the Caliphate agitation in India by abolishing that institution. The boycott of British goods and the civil disobedience campaign started by Gandhi in 1919 caused much embarrassment to the government and also grief to its author when non-cooperators rioted violently during the visit of the Prince of Wales to India in November,

1921. Among the outrages was the murder of 21 police officers in February, 1922 – a crime strongly condemned by Gandhi, who nevertheless was sentenced to six years' imprisonment.

Meanwhile the political alliance between Mohammedans and Hindus was disintegrating. A fierce rebellion staged by a Mohammedan sect, the Moplahs, in southern India in August, 1921, led to the massacre or forcible conversion of several thousand Hindus. But the advantages that might have come to the government from these actions were largely lost when it leaked out that seventy out of one hundred Moplah prisoners had suffocated in a baggage car between Tirus and Coimbatore. This counterpart to the famous Black Hole of Calcutta did incalculable harm to the British position in India – harm intensified by the acquittal of the British sergeant generally held responsible for the tragedy.

With Gandhi in prison, a new home rule or "swaraj" party was formed under the leadership of C. R. Das and Pandit Motilal Nehru. This party captured the National Congress and decided to take part in the elections. The result was that the Congress party gained control of the legislatures in Bengal and the Central Provinces and formed a strong group in the legislative assembly for India. This formal participation of leading Nationalists in the political life of India sharpened the conflict between them and the representatives of Britain. The defects of the dual executive, the limitations on the powers of the legislative bodies over finance, and the opposition to the prerogatives of the governor general and of the governors produced bitter clashes. Nor did the representation of India at Imperial conferences help to bring peace and contentment. At those of 1921 and 1923 her delegates strove vainly for official recognition of the Indians' claim to equality of status with Europeans in the British dominions. The full rights of citizens were denied them, especially in South Africa. Not unnaturally, their political leaders inquired concerning the real benefits to be had from citizenship in the British empire. There were "scenes" in the Indian legislative assembly.

The swaraj party withdrew in 1925, by which time the period of constructive work under the dyarchy was over. In the meantime inquiries into the tariff, the civil service, and the possibility of further reforms led to the investigations by the Simon commission of 1927 and the so-called round table conferences. The trend of developments in India was a crystallization of the demand for immediate and complete dominion status; in England the course led in the same direction, although more slowly.

At the India office Mr. Montagu was in 1922 succeeded by Lord Peel, whose views were those of an enlightened Conservative. Of the later occupants of that post, Lord Olivier, secretary of state for India in the first Labor government, January to November, 1924, was most sympathetic, and Lord Birkenhead, 1924–1928, most cynical in viewing Indian problems. On the viceregal throne Lord Reading succeeded Chelmsford in 1921. His term was marked by sharp but relatively short conflicts and the constructive legislation mentioned above. Although a Liberal, Reading was less disposed to yield to the demands of the Nationalists than was Lord Irwin, later Lord Halifax, who arrived in India in 1926. Lord Irwin had been active among the younger Conservatives who in the early nineteen-twenties attempted something like a revival of the Disraelian Tory Democracy movement of the eighteen-forties, a movement inspired by a sense of duty and a desire to govern *for* the people. As a practicing Christian, the new viceroy sought to apply the doctrine of the brotherhood of man.

Lord Irwin entered upon his term of office as dyarchy was breaking down, as Hindus faced Moslem in bloody riots, and as disputes over commercial and currency policies stirred up much anti-British feeling in India. Indian industrialists injected new life into the nationalist agitation and found the boycott on English goods to their liking. The growing complexity of the Indian problems caused the British government to anticipate by two years the promised inquiry into the working of the Government of India Act. The Indian Statutory Commission, usually called the Simon Commission after its chairman, Sir John Simon, was appointed in November, 1927, and consisted of Britishers. The lack of Indian representation on it was immediately seized upon by nationalist leaders as an affront and a grievance. At the outset they were prepared to condemn the findings of the commission and they blocked its efforts to gain information by a widespread boycott. This was but one of the many obstacles hampering the efforts of the commissioners. The challenge to Indians to draft their own constitution issued by the secretary of state, Lord Birkenhead, with the implication that they were incapable of doing so, made them suspect a commission appointed by him. The appearance of a book, *Mother India*, by an American author, Katherine Mayo, containing strong condemnations of Indian social customs and praise for the English, was attributed by Indians to British machinations. In the wave of strikes and terroristic outrages that swept India in 1927–1928, the British saw sinister Russian influence and a possible prelude to a revolution. "Racial antipathy reached a stage at which nearly all social inter-course ceased." The reemergence of Gandhi upon the political scene spread the conflict without lessening its intensity. A draft constitution prepared by an Indian "All Parties Conference" envisaged a dominion status as defined by the report adopted by the imperial conference of 1926. The character of Indian economic nationalism was disclosed by the demand that Europeans be excluded from the coastal service of India. Furthermore, the successes scored by the British Labor party in the election of 1929 and the appearance of the second Macdonald government encouraged Indian extremists. Lord Irwin, impressed with the gravity of the situation, rushed to London for a conference with the new government. On October 31, 1929, he published, as an official statement, that he had been authorized to declare "that the natural issue of India's constitutional progress . . . is the attainment of Dominion Status," and he foreshadowed the calling of a round table conference between representatives of the British government and India to discuss the new constitution. These pronouncements had far-reaching effects. The work of the Statutory Commission was rendered nugatory, and Indian radicals resorted to riots, strikes, and boycotts for the purpose of wresting from the British the largest possible amount of self-government or even independence.

The report of the Statutory Commission, which appeared in May, 1930, ranks high as a state document, and contains a wealth of information concerning nearly all aspects of the life of India and balanced judgments on her problems. The commission recommended responsible government for the provinces where dyarchy existed, but not for the government of India. This restriction grew out of a realization of the divergences found in India – the divisions created by race, religion, and cultures; the complications presented by the question of defense; and an appreciation of the necessity of bringing the princes of India into the new constitutional arrangement which everyone expected. The commissioners had in mind the need for a federated India, although this topic was outside the range of their investigations. The views and recommendations presented in this report were, however, roundly condemned by Indian nationalist leaders, many of whom seemingly had made up their minds to do so before the report appeared. Despite their enthusiasm for things Indian, they wanted for their country a government cast in a western mold. Gandhi started a civil disobedience campaign, theoretically non-violent; but actually riots and mob violence became rampant over large areas and an attempt was made to assassinate Lord Irwin. Commercial boycott of English goods, supported by the industrial interests of India, added to the confusion; and in the Northwest a red-shirt movement led by a Mohammedan, Abdul Ghafur Khan, raised the bolshevik specter. Reluctantly Lord Irwin, whose generosity toward India had alarmed his own political party, the Conservative, in England, was forced to employ drastic measures for the preservation of order.

The policy of repression was nevertheless balanced by efforts at conciliation. The viceroy met Gandhi in private conferences, and between November, 1930, and December, 1932, three sessions of a round table conference were held in London. Two of them were attended by representatives of the three British political parties, but Labor was absent from the third. Care was exercised to have the conference represent various Indian interests and opinion; however, except for the second session, September 7 to December 1, 1931, when Gandhi attended, the National Congress refused to participate. Moreover, Gandhi regarded himself as speaking for all of India, an assumption neither pleasing to the minorities nor helpful in securing approval for the conference's final report. Gandhi's intransigence and the non-cooperative attitude of the National Congress constituted some of the gravest difficulties which beset the work of the round table conference. The first session was held while the Labor government was in office in Britain, a government expected to sympathize with Indian aspirations for self-government, although adherents of its ideology would naturally look with more favor upon the claims of the lower classes than upon the desiderata of the high-caste politicians who usually led the Congress. Before the second session, Labor had given way to the coalition Nationalist government with Macdonald continuing as prime minister. The financial crisis of August–September, 1931, with the abandonment of the gold standard, naturally influenced the attitude of British industrial and commercial interests toward the economic problems of India; they became less disposed to make sacrifices in her behalf. Between the second and third sessions Britain's tariff policy was revolutionized by the adoption of protection and a system of imperial preferences and by the Ottawa agreements. Even so, affairs in India, despite the opposition to the conference on the part of the Congress party, took turns which brought rays of hope. A Gandhi–Irwin agreement of March, 1931, put an end to civil disobedience; the commercial classes of India found the frequent boycotts and hartals ruinous to their interests; the lower classes began to realize that the independence program of the Congress might not benefit them; the violent outbursts of Hindu-Moslem strife caused moderate men to doubt the wisdom of demanding independence and to rally in support of law and order; and the princes of India commenced to show an unexpected spirit of cooperation. These factors aided the efforts of the new viceroy, Lord Willingdon, to end disorder.

The investigations conducted by the round table conference were supplemented by those of special committees; the results of these deliberations were embodied in proposals published as a White Paper in March, 1933. Following the precedent set in the case of the Montagu-Chelmsford reforms, these proposals were submitted to a joint select committee of the British parliament which accepted them, while calling attention to the need for safeguarding the existing pensions, the salaries of the police and the civil servants as well as other special interests. When the draft bill reached parliament the Conservatives were troubled by dissentients within their own ranks, prominent among whom was Mr. Winston Churchill; these standpatters opposed strongly all concessions which might weaken British supremacy in India. This Conservative opposition was responsible for the government's refusal to include in the new act any reference to dominion status as the ultimate goal for India. On December 20, 1935, the new Government of India Act completed its passage through parliament. The statute, which is so elaborate and complicated that only a brief summary can be attempted here, applies to all of India. Its most salient features are those dealing with a proposed all-India federation, the central and provincial machinery of government, and India's relations to Britain. These topics will be discussed in the order given.

Although the federal structure provided by the act bears some resemblance to those of Australia and Canada, it has many distinct characteristics due chiefly to the special conditions in the great Asiatic empire. The federated British dominions came into being as the result of actions by autonomous communities, equal in status and ready to delegate government functions to a new body politic created by themselves. The Government of India Act of 1935, on the other hand, originated largely in Britain, the creation of British not Indian brains; it changed the government of India from a unitary to a federal form, conferring new autonomy upon the political subdivisions thereof; and it made provisions for the inclusion of the native states in the new federation. For the provinces of British India this inclusion was automatic, but for the states it was to be voluntary. Consequently, the federal government for India could not be established until rulers who had the right to nominate one-half of the 104 members of the federal council allotted to the states and who govern at least 39,490,956 people decided to join the federation. In drafting the act great care was taken to insure that the surrender of powers by the native princes should be kept at a minimum. The amount surrendered differed between states, and it may be enlarged but it cannot be diminished after a state has joined the federation. The provinces of British India continued to be classified into governors' and chief commissioners' provinces. The former were granted a large amount of local autonomy while the latter were to remain under the control of the governor general. Since 1935 Sind has been separated from Bombay and Orissa from Bihar, but this gain in the number of governors' provinces was partly offset by the loss sustained when the connections between Burma and India were severed. At present (1941) British India is divided into eleven governors' and six chief commissioners' provinces and certain backward areas, which with the federal territory of Delhi are administered by the government of India. The number of provinces may, however, be changed by an Indian order in council.

At the head of the projected federal government of India stands the governor general, appointed as heretofore by the British government, normally for a term of five years. The situation created by the act of 1935, especially with reference to the native states, necessitated a careful definition of the duties and powers of the governor general as distinct from those of the viceroy, the representative of the king-emperor. Although these functions are now performed by one person, separate appointments are possible. The new federal government established dyarchy at the center. In certain matters, principally defense and external relations, the governor general of federated India is to be advised by three ministers appointed by and responsible to himself alone, while in others his ministers are to be selected in a manner similar to that employed in Britain and the dominions. These ministers are to be responsible to the federal parliament, though the extent of this responsibility is more limited than is the case in Canada or Australia.

The federal parliament is to be bicameral; a council of state consisting of 156 members from British India and ultimately 104 from the native states, and a house of assembly with 250 from the former and 125 from the latter. In both cases the figures given for the native states represent the maximum; the actual number will depend upon how many of them join the federation. Of the 156 legislative councilors for British India, 150 are to be chosen by direct election and 6 nominated by the governor general. Some of these councilors will be elected at large on a communal, that is to say, representation arranged by religion or caste, basis; others are allocated to the provinces in proportion to population. The legislative council will be permanent, with one-third retiring every year, whereas the members of the assembly are to be elected for five years. The 250 representatives of British India in the assembly are to be chosen by a complicated system of indirect election and in accordance with communal principles. Money bills are to originate in the assembly; otherwise the legislative powers of the two houses will be equal. Deadlocks between them may be broken by joint sessions. The powers reserved to the governor general and the restrictions which he may impose upon freedom of speech places the prospective federal parliament for India on a lower level than are those in the dominions and in the British colonies with responsible government — a fact which helps to explain Indian opposition to the new constitution.

Only a small group of Indian liberals greeted the act of 1935 with acclaim. Politically-minded Indians were, generally speaking, disappointed with it, and the princes of India failed to accept the federal plan. The Congress party objected to the large powers reserved by the act for the governors and the governor general, to the rigidity of the new constitution, to the absence of any reference in it to dominion status, to the separation of Burma from India, to the perpetuation of autocratic governments in the native states, and to the over-representation of those states in the federal parliament. The dyarchy at the center and the power to declare a state of emergency which automatically strengthens the executive at the expense of the legislative branch of the government of course limits the extent of Indian self-government. It is further restricted by the provision that the act can be amended only by the British parliament. These are limitations not imposed upon the dominions. Moreover, the silence concerning dominion status constituted a breach of promises contained in the preamble to the act of 1919 as well as in statements made by responsible British statesmen. The opposition to the separation of Burma rests upon less solid foundations and may be attributed to the imperial-mindedness of Indian political leaders. Neither historically nor racially has Burma been a part of India. The union was effected by Britain in the nineteenth century to suit the convenience of the British government. The ancient kingdom of Burma may well advance by a road of her own toward a self-governing status.

The Government of India Act of 1935 does not touch the internal administration of the native states which it proposes to federate with British India. Politically, economically, and socially, wide divergences exist between these states. The majority of them are tiny — some hardly larger than a fair-sized American farm — while others embrace extensive areas. Hyderabad, for instance, has an area of 82,698 square miles with a population

(1931 census) of 14,436,148. Some of them, notably Baroda, Cochin, Hyderabad, Mysore, and Travancore, have reached a high state of development and compare favorably with the most advanced sections of British India, but most of them are extremely backward. All, however, are anxious to preserve their identity and resentful of the agitation carried on and the unrest stirred up within their borders by the Congress party. The new constitution provided for elections in British India and made possible an extension of the franchise to about 6 million women and 28 or 29 million men who will choose the overwhelming majority of the provincial representatives in the All-India parliament; those from the states are to be selected by the rulers. A political alliance between them and the representatives of minority groups might easily prevent those elected by the majority of Indian voters from wielding their rightful influence. Congress leaders saw in the government devised for a federal India a scheme for perpetuating British dominance. In 1938 the National Congress rejected federation and went on record in favor of an independent India with a constitution of her own making. Meanwhile the princes became apprehensive of the possible results of joining the federation. They feared the effects of radical agitation and envisaged the possibility of exchanging the light yoke of British paramountcy for the heavy one of control by native politicians. Consequently, they have not yet (1941) agreed to federate with British India.

Other provisions of the Government of India Act of 1935 went into effect April 1, 1937. These deal primarily with the relations between India and Britain and with the new provincial governments. Aden and Burma have been separated from India and the latter given a constitution of a dyarchical character. In India the Congress party decided, after some hesitation, to participate in the provincial elections, with the result that before the end of 1938 it either wholly or by coalitions controlled all the governors' provinces except Bengal and the Punjab. The most important change in the relations between the governments of

India and Britain was the abolition of the India council in London. Moreover, the general effect of the constitution of 1935 tends to increase the importance of the crown in Anglo-Indian relations. Thus the evolution of those relations has shown the same trend as the constitutional development within the British Commonwealth of Nations.

The Congress ministries in control in governors' provinces attempted along several lines to put into effect parts of the National Congress program. They have pressed forward legislation prohibiting the manufacture and sale of intoxicating liquor and improving the position of agricultural tenants. At the instigation of the parliamentary subcommittee of the Congress, special efforts have been made to further the study of Hindi; but these have met strong opposition in southern India, particularly in Madras, where Dravidian dialects are spoken. Friction between the Mohammedans and the Congress party also hampered the activities of the latter. The Indian Mohammedans were much weakened as a political force in the late twenties and early thirties because of internal dissension; at one time it was split into three factions, the All-India Moslem Conference, the Caliphate Conference, and the All-India Moslem League. The first had the narrowest program and was outspokenly hostile to the Hindus; the second represented pan-Islamic aspirations which, in spite of the setback suffered by the abolition of the Caliphate, regained some of their earlier strength by reason of the advance of Arab states and the Arab-Jewish conflict in Palestine; the third adopted a middle-of-the-road policy and, though critical of Congress policies and methods, has at times cooperated with the Hindus. Reorganized in 1934 under the forceful leadership of M. A. Jinnah, the All-Moslem League has again become the spearhead of Mohammedan political influence in India.

Dissensions were not confined to the Mohammedans; the Congress party had its share. Left-wing groups led by the Pandit Jawaharlal Nehru and Subhas Bose showed strong leanings toward socialism and even communism. Neither creed appeals to the high-caste Hindus or to the Indian industrialists who have at times supported the anti-British campaigns of the Congress. The doctrines of the Nazis, spread sedulously by German oriental scholars, have made a certain appeal to Hindus and Mohammedans alike. The prolonged difficulties in the North West Frontier Province and more especially in Waziristan, where the building of military roads and the bombing of native villages have failed to bring peace, have been skillfully used by propagandists hostile to Britain. It is also well to keep in mind that although Indian political leaders have adopted tenets of English political thought, the latter contains many concepts wholly alien to the eastern mind, whereas the doctrines of the authoritarian states may find many contacts. The virility of Nazi Germany has been contrasted with an alleged British decadence. The spread of the cult of force has, however, made thoughtful Indians apprehensive of the future that may await them if Britain's power is destroyed. The actions of Italy in Ethiopia, Japan in China, and Germany in Czechoslovakia, Poland, Denmark, Norway, and the Low Countries have not endeared those states to Mohandas Gandhi. Caste is still too deeply embedded in the basic stratum of Indian life to make this people respond readily to the bolshevik program for establishing a dictatorship by the proletariat. Still the Anglo-German conflict of 1939 supplied the National Congress party with opportunities to demand fresh concessions.

Britain has made it clear that she has no intention of retiring from India in favor of Japan or a European power. Her great naval base at Singapore has been built to safeguard the Indian empire against attacks from Japan. In 1938 Britain agreed to increase the annual contribution toward the defense of India from £1,500,000 to £2,000,000, to advance upward of £5,000,000 for the mechanization and equipment of the Indian army, and to forego India's yearly grant of £100,000 for the maintenance of British warships in the Indian Ocean provided seagoing ships were added to her navy. The latter, a post-war development, is part of a general plan to strengthen the defense of the British empire by means of local navies. The Indian navy, however, remains under British control. On the other hand, the Indianization of the army took a step forward in 1932 with the opening of an Indian Military Academy at Dehra Dun in the United Provinces. This institution trains officers for all branches of the Indian army; the first batch of its graduates received commissions February 1, 1935.

Britain has thus begun to relax her grip on India's fighting services as well as on her political institutions. A similar change has taken place in the administrative system of India. Despite certain modifications, the famous India civil service in its higher brackets continued to be recruited almost exclusively from England until after the passage of the act of 1919. Since then the administration pertaining to the transferred subjects in the provincial governments has come more and more into Indian hands. General regulations of 1923 stipulated that 60 per cent of the superior posts in the engineering service, 50 per cent in the police, and 75 per cent in the forestry service should be held by natives. Acts of 1929 provided for the appointment of Indians as judges in the higher courts at home and as additional members of the judicial committee of the privy council for the hearing of appeals from India. This Indianization of the government of the Indian empire has caused English Tories to speak dejectedly of India as a "lost dominion."

The economic and to a lesser extent the social progress of India since 1919 has kept step with the constitutional. Gandhi has worked hard for the revival of village industries both as a means of developing Indian self-sufficiency and for the purpose of keeping villagers employed between the agricultural seasons. He even wanted to make skill in spinning a test for the franchise. On the other hand, the industrialization of India along modern capitalistic lines has moved forward steadily. The production of cotton piece goods increased on the average 5 per cent annually between 1920 and 1935; the annual production of pig iron rose from 300,000 tons to more than 1,500,000 and that of steel from

113,000 to 880,000 in the same period. The increment in the output of Indian paper mills during 1925–1930 amounted to about 10 per cent yearly. Even more startling has been the advance of India's cement industry. Of the 200,000 tons of cement used in India in 1920, more than half was imported; by 1935 the annual consumption had risen to 900,000 tons, of which only 43,000 came from the outside. On the basis of a comparison of 1930 with the average of the five years immediately preceding 1914, it has been computed that the leading manufacturing industries increased 62 per cent in the value of output and 80 per cent in the number of employees. The Indian census of 1931 lists 15,361,933 employed in industry, 7,913,797 in trade, and 102,-454,177 in agriculture. While the overwhelming majority of Indians work on the land, those in other occupations form a considerable percentage of the adult males gainfully employed. India's mineral output has increased about 182 per cent since 1914, and the development of hydroelectric power has aided the growth of her industries. Further stimuli have been supplied by research and subsidies provided by the government and by protective tariffs.

During the war of 1914–1918 India secured fiscal autonomy and was thus freed from the necessity of levying an excise on her internal manufactures to balance the duties on goods made in Britain. The Indian customs tariff falls into three categories, protective, revenue, and preferential, the last being reserved for Britain and the British nations. The duties on various types of cotton goods in 1937 were 25 per cent ad valorem on British and 50 per cent on non-British wares; on twist and yarn the rates were respectively 5 and 6 1/4 per cent. Despite the preference, Britain has found it difficult to compete successfully with Japan as far as the cheaper grades of cotton goods are concerned. Statistics of Anglo–Indian trade since 1913 make melancholy reading for British industrialists, especially those of Lancashire. The figures for exports to British India of goods produced or manufactured in the United Kingdom stood at £70,273,221 in 1913, but by 1937 they (Burma included) had fallen to £39,091,573. On the other hand statistics of imports from British India show a rise from £36,118,225 to £56,957,046. As in the earlier days of the East India Company, the balance favors India; Britain's profit, at least in part, will come from the entrepôt trade in Indian goods.

Agriculture continues to be of primary importance among the industries of India, more than three-fourths of her population being directly dependent upon it. In 1928 the Royal Commission on Agriculture of which Lord Linlithgow, the present (1941) governor general, was chairman, presented a series of recommendations for aid and stimulus to agriculture. As a result the Imperial Council of Agricultural Research was established in 1929, the post of agricultural adviser to the government created in 1935, and the Imperial Institute of Sugar Technology founded at Cawnpore in October, 1936. Cotton and sugar growing have benefited by the activities of these bodies, but progress in the scientific breeding of animals and the extermination of vermin has been handicapped by the various taboos on the taking of life embodied in the Hindu religion. Irrigation works have been pushed forward, especially in Sind where the great Lloyd Barrage has added extensive tracts to the area under cultivation. By 1933–1934, 29,888,000 acres, estimated at 12.8 per cent of the total cropped area of British India, were irrigated by government irrigation works. The productivity of Indian agriculture has increased greatly during the last thirty-five years; nevertheless, it threatens to be outstripped by the growth of the population. Between 1901 and 1911 the annual increase was more than two millions; in the next decade the influenza epidemic of 1918–1919 took such a heavy toll that the net gain for all India was only 3,786,048; but the census of 1931 showed an increase of 33,895,298 over 1921, and a total of 352,837,778, of whom 271,-526,933 belonged to British India and 81,310,845 to the states. Eleven per cent of the population was classified as urban and this has shown a slight tendency to rise; the rest was distributed among the more than half a million villages of rural India. The "spawning" of the peasantry presents the most serious economic and social problems for the government of the Indian empire.

The growth of Indian industries created a need for labor legislation. Agitation for such legislation began in England and, as previously noted, was not entirely altruistic. Much progress has been made within the last ten years. The Indian Trade Union Congress founded in 1920 split nine years later, partly over issues connected with labor strategy and the attitude to be assumed toward Russia. The four separate labor federations which existed in 1931 had little influence on labor legislation. More importance can be assigned to the Royal Commission on Indian Labor appointed in 1929. Its chairman, J. H. Whitley, had ten years earlier been chairman of a commission that had reported in favor of industrial councils in Britain, and he was known to be friendly to labor. In 1931 the Whitley labor commission for India presented an elaborate report covering a wide field and containing hundreds of recommendations dealing with labor disputes, hours of labor, workmen's compensation, etc. These recommendations guided the later labor legislation for India. Unfortunately, the world depression and the downward trend of prices made it difficult to improve the status of Indian labor. The Indian Factories Act of 1934, however, secured substantial benefits for labor; and it is interesting to note that statistics on Indian factory workers show that despite the considerable increase in the total number of employees, the number of children under 15 has decreased from 64,110 in 1918 to 12,062 in 1936. The limit of the hours of labor in India's so-called perennial factories has been fixed at 10 per day and 54 per week; that for the seasonal has been set at 11 and 60 respectively. An act of 1929 prohibited women from working underground in mines.

The reforms of 1919 placed public health and sanitation among the transferred subjects. Since then a number of provincial public health departments have come into existence. Although they are helped to some extent by the Indian Research Fund Association which has organized a special committee for nutritional research, the task is overwhelming. A large percentage of the population of India suffers from malnutrition; this, coupled with overcrowding in the urban centers in particular and disregard of elementary rules of hygiene, makes them easy prey to disease. Reports of the Simon commission disclosed that 70 per cent of the tenements in Bombay consisted of only one room, with an average of four persons per room, and that the situation in Karachi was even worse. For the five years 1931–1935 the Indian birth rate averaged 34.5 and the death rate 23.5 per thousand. While these are not much higher than similar rates in eastern European countries, the corresponding figures for New Zealand are 19.7 and 8.6. It has been computed, however, that since 1900 life expectancy in India has risen from 23 to 26½ years.

Since the high death rate in India is to a considerable extent attributable to the appalling mortality figures for infants and mothers — respectively 185 and 20 per thousand — improvements are expected to come from the rapid progress made in the work for elevating the status of Indian women and from the general advance in education. The women were given the franchise in the province of Madras in 1922, and despite Mohammedan and conservative Hindu opposition they had by 1929 secured the vote in seven of the provinces of India. As already indicated, the constitution of 1935 makes possible the enfranchisement of about six million Indian women. While this represents only slightly more than one-fifth of the total male voters, the advance since 1922 must be considered remarkable. The census of 1921 showed that more than 2,000,000 girls were married and about 100,000 were widows before the age of ten. To combat this evil, an act of 1927 fixed the legal age of marriage for girls at 14 and for boys at 18, but this reform aroused little enthusiasm among Indian Nationalists and has been hard to enforce in the face of old habits and traditions. Largely through the generosity of an English woman, Lady Thackeray, a special women's university has been established in Poona; the Lady Hardinge Medical College for Women in Delhi has done excellent work in training women for the medical profession; and the Seva Sadan Society founded by Mrs. Ramabai Ranade at Bombay early in the present century has rendered pioneer service in training nurses and midwives and promoting infant welfare. The Simon commission found about 400 women doctors in India, of whom 150 were working with the missionary societies. The Indian provincial authorities have, however, been reluctant to engage women in the public health service. In 1937 Madras stood alone in employing a woman as assistant director of public health with charge of the work in the maternity and child welfare field. In spite of the progress that has been made, the status of the Indian woman is still far below that of the man. Purdah or the seclusion of girls is still a common practice in northern India, and educational statistics of 1935–1936 for all of India show that there were 215,805 schools and colleges for males as against 38,390 for females and that only 17 per cent of the girls of school age were enrolled in primary classes.

Education in India has many obstacles to overcome, including those of poverty, social prejudices, divergent languages, and divisions based on caste, race, and religion. Still, it has moved forward. The number of Indian universities has risen from 4 in 1914 to 18 in 1938; and arts colleges, from 167 with 45,933 students in 1921–1922 to 261 with 94,479 students in 1935–1936. In the latter year the total enrollment in schools, exclusive of universities, was 11,968,411 males and 1,847,738 females, an increase of 200,000 over the figures for the previous year. The number of Indians going abroad has also increased greatly in recent years. In 1907, 780 Indians were enrolled in higher institutions of learning in Great Britain; by 1929–1930 this number had reached 1761, of whom 583 had entered the inns of court. The popularity of the study of law is probably explainable by the extension of self-government in India. The training for medicine, engineering, and agriculture has not proved attractive to Indians as compared with that of the general liberal arts college. The number registered in the arts colleges more than doubled in the years 1922–1936, while the attendance in the professional schools increased by only about one-third.

No account of social advances in India can omit a reference to the depressed classes. Members of these groups have benefited by the new educational opportunities, and they have found skillful leaders in their fight for social justice, prominent among them being Dr. B. R. Ambedkar and Rao Bahadur M. C. Rajah. During recent years Gandhi has devoted more of his time to social uplift. In December, 1936, the Maharaja of Travancore abolished untouchability for 2,000,000 of his 5,000,000 subjects; whether this can be accomplished for all India without the wholesale desertion of Hinduism appears doubtful. The census of 1931 shows that this creed kept its lead among the religions of India.

Except for the Afghan war of 1919, the interval of twenty years which separated the end of the Four Years' War and the outbreak of the Nazi War was for India a period of external tranquillity. Apprehensions of Russian designs on her were confined in the main to the effects of Bolshevism on the minds of her people. The fact that France was an ally of Britain throughout this period meant that no danger threatened from the direction of French Indo-China. With the advent of Hitlerism in Germany, however, a new enemy appeared to challenge British supremacy; furthermore, the economic competition with Japan has seriously affected British trade with India. In the frontier provinces of northwestern India troubles with the tribesmen have assumed a chronic character; and the government of India, having found aerial bombardment of villages an ineffective remedy, is falling back upon the means used to tranquillize the Highlands of Scotland two centuries ago, namely, highway-building and outside employment for the tribesmen. Since 1917, India has been represented at the imperial conferences, but this has brought her little in the way of tangible benefits. The dominions have virtually closed their doors against Indian immigrants and have been loth to bestow full civil and political rights upon those already domiciled within their borders. Nor have Indians fared much better in British crown colonies, Kenya in particular. This refusal of equality of status within the British empire has been used effectively by political agitators to advocate independence from Britain.

External peace was favorable to a closer study of the problems of India and the inauguration of the reforms detailed above. Commissions and committees investigated practically every aspect of the country's life and made available a vast amount of information concerning the problems of the Indian empire. Political changes advanced India on the road toward self-government; her industrial growth decreased her dependence upon foreign import; she secured fiscal autonomy; and though still lacking capital, private deposits in the banks of India rose from 954,000,000 rupees in 1913 to more than 2,300,000 rupees in 1933, which, allowing for a fall in the value of the rupee, amounted to an increase from 4*s.* 6*d.* to 10*s.* per person. Advance in education may in time diminish the number of different scripts used in writing and provide means for overcoming the obstacles to unity presented by the many languages, exclusive of dialects, found in India. Although political agitation has tended to break down the barriers of religion, they still remain and may be strengthened by communal political rivalry and new outbursts of religious fanaticism. Despite the advances made elsewhere by the forces of materialism in the realms of thought, economics, and politics, Indian religiosity is firm. Religion may bring either peace or the sword; an unbridgeable chasm separates the Hindus from the Moslems of India. To the Hindus, the impediments to unity presented by the caste system and especially by the position accorded the 60 millions belonging to the depressed classes are not as formidable as they appear to the outsider so long as faith in the transmigration of souls remains unshaken. Should this be undermined seriously and the untouchables begin to listen to the siren call of those who advocate a dictatorship by the proletariat, India may be convulsed by a social upheaval with the most tragic consequences. The lack of success which hitherto (1941) has crowned the effort to put into effect the federal arrangement provided by the India Constitution Act of 1935 bespeaks the strength of particularism within the native states of India. Efforts to overcome this force by amendments to the act may fail, because no system of representation devised by man's wit is likely to satisfy the divergent claims of the hundreds of states. But these obstructions may be destroyed either by revolutions from within or by pressure from without. Both are possible and may come at almost any moment — thrones may topple in India as they have elsewhere. The real cost of the transformation, whatever it may be, will fall on the patient, long-suffering peasant of India.

APPENDIX

PRIME MINISTERS AND FOREIGN SECRETARIES, 1815–1939

Prime Minister		*Foreign Secretary*	
1812–1827	Lord Liverpool	1812–1822 1822–1827	Lord Castlereagh George Canning
Apr.–Aug., 1827	George Canning		Lord Dudley
1827	Lord Goderich (later Lord Ripon)		Lord Dudley
1828–1830	Duke of Wellington		Lord Dudley Lord Aberdeen
1830–1834	Lord Grey		Lord Palmerston
July–Nov., 1834	Lord Melbourne		Lord Palmerston
1834–1835	Sir Robert Peel		Duke of Wellington
1835–1841	Lord Melbourne		Lord Palmerston
1841–1846	Sir Robert Peel		Lord Aberdeen
1846–1852	Lord John Russell	1846–Dec., 1851	Lord Palmerston Lord Granville
Feb.–Dec., 1852	Lord Derby		Lord Malmesbury
1852–1855	Lord Aberdeen	Dec., 1852– Feb., 1853	Lord John Russell Lord Clarendon

1855–1858	Lord Palmerston		Lord Clarendon
1858–1859	Lord Derby		Lord Malmesbury
1859–1865	Lord Palmerston		Lord John Russell (became Earl Russell, July, 1861)
1865–1866	Lord Russell		Lord Clarendon
1866–1868	Lord Derby		Lord Stanley (later 15th Earl of Derby)
Feb.–Dec., 1868	Benjamin Disraeli		Lord Stanley
1868–1874	W. E. Gladstone	Dec., 1868– June, 1870	Lord Clarendon Lord Granville
1874–1880	Benjamin Disraeli (became Earl of Beaconsfield, Aug., 1876)	Feb., 1874– Mar., 1878	Lord Derby (15th Earl of Derby) Lord Salisbury
1880–1885	W. E. Gladstone		Lord Granville
1885–1886	Lord Salisbury		Lord Salisbury
Feb.–Aug., 1886	W. E. Gladstone		Lord Rosebery
1886–1892	Lord Salisbury	Aug.–Dec., 1886	Lord Iddesleigh Lord Salisbury
1892–1894	W. E. Gladstone		Lord Rosebery
1894–1895	Lord Rosebery		Lord Kimberley
1895–1902	Lord Salisbury	June, 1895– Nov., 1900	Lord Salisbury Lord Lansdowne
1902–1905	Arthur J. Balfour		Lord Lansdowne
1905–1908	Sir Henry Campbell-Bannerman		Sir Edward Grey
1908–1916	H. H. Asquith		Sir Edward Grey
1916–1922	David Lloyd George	Dec., 1916– Oct., 1919	Arthur J. Balfour Lord Curzon

1922–1923	Andrew Bonar Law		Lord Curzon
1923–1924	Stanley Baldwin		Lord Curzon
Jan.–Nov., 1924	J. Ramsay Macdonald		J. Ramsay Macdonald
1924–1929	Stanley Baldwin		Austen Chamberlain
1929–1931	J. Ramsay Macdonald (Labor)		A. Henderson
1931–1935	J. Ramsay Macdonald (National)	Aug.–Oct., 1931	Lord Reading Sir John Simon
1935–1937	Stanley Baldwin	June–Dec., 1935	Sir Samuel Hoare Anthony Eden
1937–1940	Neville Chamberlain	May, 1937–Feb., 1938	Anthony Eden Lord Halifax

COLONIAL AND DOMINIONS SECRETARIES

Secretary for War and the Colonies, 1801–1854. Secretaryship for the Dominions Affairs established in July, 1925, held jointly with that of the Colonies until 1930.

1812–1827	Lord Bathurst
Apr.–Sept., 1827	Lord Goderich
Sept., 1827–May, 1828	William Huskisson
May, 1828–Nov., 1830	Sir G. Murray
1830–March, 1833	Lord Goderich
1833–June, 1834	E. G. Stanley (later Lord Stanley and 14th Earl of Derby)
June–Nov. 1834	T. S. Rice (later Lord Monteagle)

Dec., 1834–Apr., 1835	Lord Aberdeen
1835–Feb., 1839	Charles Grant (Lord Glenelg)
Feb.–Sept. 1839	Lord Normanby
1839–1841	Lord John Russell
1841–Dec., 1845	Lord Stanley
1845–July, 1846	W. E. Gladstone
1846–1852	Lord Grey
Feb.–Dec. 1852	Sir John Pakington
1852–June, 1854	Duke of Newcastle
June, 1854–Feb., 1855	Sir George Grey
Feb., 1855	Sidney Herbert (later Lord Herbert of Lea)
March–July, 1855	Lord John Russell
July–Oct., 1855	Sir William Molesworth
1855–1858	H. Labouchere
Feb.–June, 1858	Lord Stanley (15th Earl of Derby)
1858–1859	Sir E. Bulwer-Lytton
1859–Apr., 1861	Duke of Newcastle
1861–1866	Edward Cardwell
June, 1866–March, 1867	Lord Carnarvon
1867–1868	Duke of Buckingham

1868– July, 1870	Lord Granville
1870–1874	Lord Kimberley
1874– Jan., 1878	Lord Carnarvon
1878–1880	Sir Michael Hicks Beach
1880– Dec., 1882	Lord Kimberley
1882–1885	Lord Derby
1885– Feb., 1886	Colonel Stanley
Feb.–Aug., 1886	Lord Granville
1886– Jan., 1887	E. Stanhope
1887–1892	Sir H. Holland (created Lord Knutsford, 1888)
1892–1895	Lord Ripon
1895–1903	Joseph Chamberlain
1903–1905	Alfred Lyttelton
1905–1908	Lord Elgin
1908–1910	Lord Crewe
1910– May, 1915	L. Harcourt
1915– Dec., 1916	Andrew Bonar Law
1016–1018	W. H. Long (later Lord Long)
1919–1921	Lord Milner
Feb., 1921– Oct., 1922	Winston S. Churchill
1922–1924	Duke of Devonshire
Jan.–Nov., 1924	J. H. Thomas
1924–1929	L. C. M. S. Amery

1929–1931	Lord Passfield (formerly Sidney Webb)
Aug.–Oct., 1931	J. H. Thomas
1931–1935	Sir Philip Cunliffe-Lister
June–Nov., 1935	Malcolm Macdonald
1935– May, 1936	J. H. Thomas
1936–1938	W. G. A. Ormsby Gore
1938–1941	Malcolm Macdonald

DOMINION SECRETARIES

1930–1935	J. H. Thomas
1935–1938	Malcolm Macdonald
May–Oct., 1938	Lord Stanley
1938– Jan., 1939	Malcolm Macdonald
1939	Sir Thomas Inskip

PERMANENT UNDERSECRETARIES IN THE COLONIAL OFFICE

1825–1836	R. W. Hay
1836–1847	Sir James Stephen
1847–1859	Herman Merivale
1859–1871	Sir Frederic Rogers (later Lord Blachford)
1871–1892	Sir Robert W. Herbert
1892–1897	Sir Robert Meade
1897–1900	Sir Edward Wingfield
1900–1907	Sir Montagu Ommaney
1907–1911	Sir Francis Hopwood (later Lord Southborough)
1911–1916	Sir John Anderson
1916–1921	Sir George Fiddes

1921–1925	Sir James Masterton Smith
1925–1933	Brig. Gen. Sir Samuel H. Wilson
1933–	Sir John Loader Maffey

PERMANENT UNDERSECRETARIES FOR DOMINIONS AFFAIRS

1925–1930	Sir Charles T. Davis
1930–	Sir Edward J. Harding

INDIA

PRESIDENTS OF THE BOARD OF CONTROL, 1812–1858

1812–1816	Lord Buckinghamshire
1816–1821	George Canning
1821–1822	C. B. Bathurst
1822–1828	C. W. Winn
Jan.–Sept., 1828	Lord Melville
1828–1830	Lord Ellenborough
1830–1834	Charles Grant
Dec., 1834–April, 1835	Lord Ellenborough
1835–1841	Sir J. C. Hobhouse
Sept.–Oct., 1841	Lord Ellenborough
1841–1843	Lord Fitzgerald
1843–1846	Lord Ripon
1846–1852	Sir J. C. Hobhouse (Lord Broughton)
Jan.–Feb., 1852	Fox Maule (Lord Panmure)
1852–1855	Sir Charles Wood (later Lord Halifax)
1855–1858	R. V. Smith
Feb.–May, 1858	Lord Ellenborough
May–Aug., 1858	Lord Stanley

Secretaries of State for India, 1858–1939

1858–1859	Lord Stanley
1859–1866	Sir Charles Wood
Feb.–June, 1866	Lord de Grey (afterward Lord Ripon)
1866–1867	Lord Cranborne (Lord Salisbury)
1867–1868	Sir Stafford Northcote
1868–1874	Duke of Argyll
1874–1878	Lord Salisbury
1878–1880	Gathorne Hardy (later Lord Cranbrook)
1880–1882	Lord Hartington (later Duke of Devonshire)
1882–1885	Lord Kimberley
1885–1886	Lord Randolph Churchill
Feb.–Aug., 1886	Lord Kimberley
1886–1892	Lord Cross
1892–1894	Lord Kimberley
1894–1895	Sir H. H. Fowler
1895–1903	Lord George Hamilton
1903–1905	St. John Broderick (later Lord Midleton)
1905–1910	John Morley (Lord Morley)
1910–1915	Lord Crewe
1915–1917	Austen Chamberlain
1917–1922	E. S. Montagu
1922–1924	Lord Peel
Jan.–Nov., 1924	Lord Olivier
1924–1928	Lord Birkenhead
1928–1929	Lord Peel
1929–1931	Capt. W. Wedgwood Benn
1931–1935	Sir Samuel Hoare
1935–	Lord Zetland

Governors General and Viceroys of India 1813–1939

Until 1833 the title was governor general of Fort William in Bengal; the title viceroy was added in 1858 when the crown took over the administration of India.

1813–1823	Lord Moira (became Lord Hastings in 1818)
1823–1828	Lord Amherst
1828–1835	Lord William Bentinck
1835–1836	Sir Charles Metcalfe (later Lord Metcalfe)
1836–1842	Lord Auckland
1842–1844	Lord Ellenborough
1844–1848	Sir Henry Hardinge (made Lord Hardinge in 1846)
1848–1856	Lord Dalhousie
1856–1862	Lord Canning
1862–1863	Lord Elgin
1863–1868	Sir John Lawrence (Lord Lawrence)
1868–1872	Lord Mayo
1872–1876	Lord Northbrook
1876–1880	Lord Lytton
1880–1884	Lord Ripon
1884–1888	Lord Dufferin
1888–1893	Lord Lansdowne
1893–1898	Lord Elgin
1898–1905	Lord Curzon
1905–1910	Lord Minto
1910–1916	Lord Hardinge of Penhurst
1916–1921	Lord Chelmsford
1921–1926	Lord Reading
1926–1931	Lord Irwin (Lord Halifax)
1931–1936	Lord Willingdon
1936–	Lord Linlithgow

PRIME MINISTERS OF THE DOMINION OF CANADA, 1867–1939

1867–1873	Sir John A. Macdonald
1873–1878	Alexander Mackenzie
1878–1891	Sir John A. Macdonald
1891–1892	Sir John J. Abbot
1892–1894	Sir John S. D. Thompson
1894–1896	Sir Mackenzie Bowell
May–July, 1896	Sir Charles Tupper
1896–1911	Sir Wilfrid Laurier
1911–1920	Sir Robert L. Borden
1920–1921	Arthur Meighen
1921–1926	William Lyon Mackenzie King
June–Dec., 1926	Arthur Meighen
1926–1930	William Lyon Mackenzie King
1930–1935	Richard Bedford Bennett
1935–	William Lyon Mackenzie King

PRIME MINISTERS OF THE COMMONWEALTH OF AUSTRALIA, 1901–1939

1901–1903	Sir Edmund Barton
1903–1904	Alfred Deakin
Apr.–Aug., 1904	J. C. Watson
1904–1905	Sir George Reid and Allan McLean (joint ministry)
1905–1908	Alfred Deakin
1908–1909	Andrew Fisher
1909–1910	Alfred Deakin
1910–1913	Andrew Fisher

1913–1914	Sir Joseph Cook
1914–1916	Andrew Fisher
1916–1923	W. M. Hughes
1923–1929	S. M. Bruce
1929–1932	J. H. Scullin
1932–1939	J. A. Lyons
1939–	R. G. Menzies

PRIME MINISTERS OF THE UNION OF SOUTH AFRICA, 1910–1939

1910–1919	Louis Botha
1919–1924	Jan Smuts
1924–1939	J. B. M. Hertzog
1939–	Jan Smuts

BIBLIOGRAPHY

The history of the British empire, 1815–1939, touches a great variety of interests and a multitude of problems. The material for studying it is very rich; no attempt will be made to present a full bibliography, especially since *The Cambridge History of the British Empire* (see below under general histories) contains full and carefully organized lists of printed and unprinted sources, periodicals, pamphlets, monographs, and books for the study of British imperial history. The following is intended merely as a brief working bibliography for students interested in securing further knowledge of the subject; it covers only a fraction of the material used in the preparation of this book.

General Bibliographies and Guides

Adam, M. I., Ewing, J., and Munro, J. *Guide to the Principal Parliamentary Papers Relating to the Dominions, 1812–1911.* Edinburgh, 1913.

Lewin, E. *Subject Catalogue of the Library of the Royal Empire Society, formerly the Royal Colonial Institute.* 4 vols., London, 1930–1937. Vol. I deals with the empire as a whole and with Africa; Vol. II, Australia, New Zealand, the South Pacific, voyages and travels, the arctic and the antarctic; Vol. III, Canada, Newfoundland, the West Indies, and Colonial America; Vol. IV, the Mediterranean colonies, India, Burma, Ceylon, British Malaya, the East Indies, and the Far East.

Milne, A. T. *Writings on British History.* London, 1934–   , in progress. An annual bibliography with sections devoted to the dominions and dependencies.

Newton, A. P., editor. *A Select List of Books Relating to the History of the British Empire Overseas.* Third ed., London, 1929. Historical Association Leaflet No. 46.

Ragatz, L. J. *A Bibliography of Articles on Colonies Appearing in American Geographical and Kindred Journals through 1934.* 2 vols., London, 1935.

Ragatz, L. J. *Colonial Studies in the United States During the Twentieth Century.* Washington, 1934.

Descriptive Works: The Geography of the British Empire

Bowman, Isaiah. *The New World.* Fourth ed., New York, 1928. The portions of this popular work which deal with the British empire are very useful.

Demangeon, Albert. *The British Empire; a Study in Colonial Geography.* New York, 1925.

Domvile-Fife, C. W. *Encyclopaedia of the British Empire.* 3 vols., Bristol, 1924.

Fawcett, C. B. *A Political Geography of the British Empire.* New York, 1933. An admirable account of the various sections of the empire, with numerous maps.

Gunn, H., editor. *The British Empire. A Survey.* 12 vols., London, 1924.

Herbertson, A. J., and Thompson, R. L., editors. *Geography of the British Empire.* Third ed., revised by O. J. R. Howarth, Oxford, 1918.

Lucas, Sir Charles P. *Historical Geography of the British Empire.* 12 vols., Oxford, 1887–1923. This celebrated work contains excellent historical accounts of the various portions of the empire.

Tilby, A. Wyatt. *English People Overseas.* 6 vols., London, 1908–1914. Second ed. of Vols. I, II, 1910. Small handy volumes dealing with the different parts of the empire.

Whittlesey, Derwent. *The Earth and the State.* New York, 1939. This book has good descriptions of the British Empire, and excellent maps.

SELECTIONS FROM SOURCES

Bell, K. N., and Morrell, W. P., editors. *Select Documents on British Colonial Policy, 1830–1860.* Oxford, 1928. The documents are well chosen and the introduction is excellent.

Egerton, H. E., editor. *Federations and Unions Within the British Empire.* Second ed., Oxford, 1924.

Keith, A. B., editor. *Select Speeches and Documents on British Colonial Policy, 1763–1917.* London, 1917.

The Constitutions of All Countries. Vol. I, *The British Empire.* London, 1938.

GENERAL HISTORIES OF BRITAIN AND THE EMPIRE

The Cambridge History of the British Empire. Edited by J. Holland Rose, A. P. Newton, and E. A. Benians. 8 vols., Cambridge, 1929– . Each volume of this excellent and very comprehensive work contains admirable bibliographies. Vol. II, The Growth of the New Empire covers the period 1783–1870; Vol. III, in press, will continue the story of imperial policy and relations, with accounts of the dependencies. Separate volumes deal with the dominions and India. Vols. IV and V, India, appear also as Vols. V and VI in *The Cambridge History of India;* Vol. VI, British North America; Vol. VII, two parts, Australia and New Zealand; and Vol. VIII, South Africa.

Ensor, R. C. K. *England, 1870–1914.* Oxford, 1936. Last volume in the *Oxford History of England,* edited by G. N. Clark. Good for purely English affairs.

Hall, W. P. *Empire to Commonwealth, Thirty Years of British Imperial History.* New York, 1928. Covers last part of the 19th and early years of the 20th century.

Marriott, Sir J. A. R. *The Evolution of the British Empire and Commonwealth.* London, 1939. A sketch covering the entire history of the empire from the time of the Cabots to the present. Clearly written, conservative tone.

Muir, Ramsay. *A Short History of the British Commonwealth.* Vol. II, 1763–1919. Second ed., London, 1924.

Mullett, Charles F. *The British Empire.* New York, 1938. About half of this attractive work is devoted to imperial history, 1815–1914.

Newton, A. P. *A Hundred Years of the British Empire.* New York, 1940. The period covered is 1837–1939, and the book deals mainly with expansion and intra-imperial relations.

Newton, A. P., and Ewing, J. *The British Empire Since 1783: Its Political and Economic Development.* New ed., London, 1924.

Robinson, Howard. *Development of the British Empire.* New ed., Boston, 1936. The story begins with the founding of the earliest British colonies.

Williamson, J. A. *A Short History of British Expansion.* 2 vols., second ed., London, 1930. This covers the period from the founding of the old empire, and contains much material on imperial relations and imperial policy.

Woodward, E. L. *The Age of Reform, 1815–1870.* Oxford, 1938. The volume belongs to the Oxford history series (see above); it is confined mostly to England but has good chapters on foreign and imperial affairs.

Woodward, W. H. *A Short History of the Expansion of the British Empire.* Sixth ed., Cambridge, 1931.

Economic and Social Background for Imperial History: Emigration

Adamson, J. W. *English Education, 1789–1902.* London, 1930.

Bowley, A. L. *A Short Account of England's Foreign Trade in the Nineteenth Century, Its Economic and Social Results.* Rev. ed., New York, 1905.

Bowley, A. L. *The Change in the Distribution of the National Income, 1880–1913.* Oxford, 1920.

Buer, M. C. *Health, Wealth and Population in the Early Days of the Industrial Revolution.* London, 1926.

Carrothers, W. A. *Emigration from the British Isles, with Special Reference to the Development of the Overseas Dominions.* London, 1929.

Clapham, J. H. *An Economic History of Modern Britain.* 3 vols.,

Cambridge, 1926–1938. The most complete and authoritative work on this subject.

Cole, G. D. H., and Postgate, Raymond. *The British Common People, 1746–1938.* London, 1938. Rather dogmatic and with leftist tendencies, it nevertheless gives a fairly clear picture of economic and social conditions.

Coupland, R. *The British Anti-Slavery Movement.* London, 1933.

Cowan, H. I. *British Emigration to British North America, 1783–1837.* Toronto, 1928.

Fay, C. R. *Great Britain from Adam Smith to the Present Day.* London, 1928.

Fay, C. R. *Imperial Economy and Its Place in the Formation of Economic Doctrine, 1600–1932.* Oxford, 1934.

Fay, C. R. *Life and Labour in the Nineteenth Century.* Cambridge, 1922.

Hitchins, Fred H. *The Colonial Land and Emigration Commission.* Philadelphia, 1931. A careful study of the work of this important commission.

Hutchins, E. L., and Harrison, A. *A History of Factory Legislation.* Third ed., London, 1926.

Johnson, S. C. *History of Emigration from the United Kingdom to North America, 1763–1912.* London, 1913.

Johnston, Sir H. H. *History of the Colonization of Africa by Alien Races.* Cambridge, 1899.

Klingberg, Frank J. *The Anti-Slavery Movement in England.* New Haven, 1926.

Knowles, L. C. A. *The Industrial and Commercial Revolutions in England.* Fourth ed., revised. London, 1926.

Knowles, L. C. A. and C. M. *The Economic Development of the British Overseas Empire.* 3 vols., London, 1928–1936.

MacInnes, C. M. *An Introduction to the Economic History of the British Empire.* London, 1935.

Mathieson, W. L. *British Slavery and Its Abolition, 1823–1838.* London, 1926.

Mathieson, W. L. *Great Britain and the Slave Trade, 1839–1865.* London, 1929.

Mills, R. C. *The Colonization of Australia, 1829–1842.* London, 1915.

Olivier, Lord. *White Capital and Coloured Labour.* London, 1906.

Page, William, editor. *Commerce and Industry; a Historical Review of the Economic Conditions of the British Empire from the Peace of Paris in 1815 to the Declaration of War in 1914, Based on Parliamentary Debates.* 2 vols., London, 1919.

Redford, Arthur. *Labour Migration in England, 1800–1850.* London, 1926.

Redford, Arthur. *Manchester Merchants and Foreign Trade, 1794–1858.* Manchester, 1934.

Foreign Relations and the Expansion of Imperial Frontiers

Balfour, Lady Frances. *Life of Lord Aberdeen.* 2 vols., London, 1922.

Bell, H. C. F. *Lord Palmerston.* 2 vols., New York, 1936.

The Cambridge History of British Foreign Policy. Edited by Sir A. W. Ward and G. P. Gooch. 3 vols., Cambridge, 1922–1923. Covers the period 1783–1919.

Cecil, Lady Gwendolen. *Life of Lord Salisbury.* Vols. I–IV. London, 1921–1932. In progress.

Corbett, P. C. *The Settlement of Canadian-American Disputes.* New Haven, 1937.

Costin, W. C. *Great Britain and China, 1833–1860.* Oxford, 1937.

Coupland, R. *East Africa and Its Invaders.* Oxford, 1938.

Coupland, R. *Raffles, 1781–1826.* Second ed., Oxford, 1934. Biographical sketch of the man who secured Singapore for Britain.

Coupland, R. *The Exploitation of East Africa, 1856–1890.* London, 1939.

Crewe, Lord. *Lord Rosebery.* New York, 1931.

Cromer, Lord. *Modern Egypt.* London, 1908.

Fitzmaurice, Lord Edmond. *Lord Granville.* 2 vols., London, 1905.

Fox, Grace. *British Admirals and Chinese Pirates, 1832–1869.* London, 1940. A careful study of an interesting chapter in the history of British expansion.

Hallberg, C. W. *The Suez Canal, Its History and Diplomatic Importance.* New York, 1931.

Johnston, Sir H. H. *The Opening Up of Africa.* New York, 1911.

Johnston, Sir H. H. *The Story of My Life.* London, 1923. The autobiography of a man who played a prominent role in British expansion in Africa.

Knaplund, Paul. *Gladstone's Foreign Policy.* New York, 1935.

Knowles, Isabel M. *British Expansion in the Malay Peninsula, 1867–1884.* Unpublished Ph.D. Thesis at the University of Wisconsin Library.

Lloyd, Lord. *Egypt Since Cromer.* 2 vols., London, 1933–1934.

Lovell, R. I. *The Struggle for South Africa, 1875–1899.* New York, 1934.

Lucas, Sir Charles P. *The Partition and Colonization of Africa.* Oxford, 1922.

Lucas, Sir Charles P. *Religion, Colonising and Trade, the Driving Forces of the Old Empire.* London, 1930.

Lugard, Sir Frederick J. D. *The Rise of Our East African Empire.* Second ed., London, 1923.

Lyall, Sir Alfred C. *The Rise and Expansion of British Dominion in India.* Fifth ed., London, 1920.

Martin, K. L. P. *Missionaries and Annexations in the Pacific.* London, 1926.

Masterman, Sylvia. *The Origins of International Rivalry in Samoa, 1845–1884.* Stanford University, 1934.

Middleton, L. *The Rape of Africa.* New York, 1936.

Raphael, Lois A. C. *The Cape-to-Cairo Dream. A Study in British Imperialism.* New York, 1936.

Scholefield, G. H. *The Pacific, Its Past and Future, and the Policy of the Great Powers from the Eighteenth Century.* London, 1919.

Seton-Watson, R. W. *Britain in Europe, 1789–1914.* London, 1937.

Swettenham, Sir Frank. *British Malaya; an Account of the Ori-*

gin and Progress of British Influence in Malaya. New and revised ed., London, 1929.

Trevelyan, G. M. *Grey of Fallodon.* Boston, 1937.

Wellesley, Dorothy. *Sir George Goldie, Founder of Nigeria.* London, 1934.

Williams, M. W. *Anglo-American Isthmian Diplomacy.* Washington, 1916.

Williamson, J. A. *Builders of the Empire.* Oxford, 1925. Brief sketches of persons of importance in imperial history.

Imperial Policy and Constitutional Development

Adderley, C. B. (Lord Norton). *Review of the Colonial Policy of Lord John Russell's Administration and of Subsequent History.* London, 1869. A treatise by an active champion of colonial reform in the fifties and sixties.

Bodelsen, C. A. *Studies in Mid-Victorian Imperialism.* Copenhagen, 1924.

British Commonwealth Relations. Proceedings of the British Commonwealth Relations Conference at Toronto, Sept., 1933. Edited by A. J. Toynbee. London, 1934.

Buller, C. *Responsible Government for Colonies.* London, 1840. Edited by E. M. Wrong, Oxford, 1926. This celebrated pamphlet appeared first as a series of articles in the *Colonial Gazette.* Excellent in revealing the views of the colonial reformers but grossly unfair to the colonial office.

Cobb, Ethel. *Joseph Chamberlain as Colonial Secretary, 1895–1900.* Unpublished M.A. Thesis at the University of Wisconsin Library.

Currey, C. H. *British Colonial Policy, 1783–1915.* London, 1916. A brief sketch.

Dawson, R. M. *The Development of Dominion Status, 1900–1936.* London, 1937.

Dilke, Sir Charles W. *Problems of Greater Britain.* Fourth ed., revised. London, 1890.

Dilke, Sir Charles W., and Wilkinson, Spencer. *Imperial Defence.* London, 1892.

Egerton, H. E. *A Short History of British Colonial Policy.* Ninth ed., revised by A. P. Newton. London, 1932.

Egerton, H. E. *British Colonial Policy in the 20th Century.* London, 1922.

Egerton, H. E., editor. *Selected Speeches of Sir William Molesworth on Questions Relating to Colonial Policy.* London, 1903.

Elliott, W. Y. *The New British Empire.* New York, 1932.

Garnett, R. *Edward Gibbon Wakefield.* London, 1898. On the whole, the most satisfactory biography of this celebrated colonial reformer.

Garvin, J. L. *The Life of Joseph Chamberlain.* Vols. I–III. London, 1932–1934. In progress. Vol. III, which covers the period 1895–1900, is valuable for the history of the British empire.

Grey, Earl. *The Colonial Policy of Lord John Russell's Administration.* 2 vols., London, 1853. A very important work by a famous colonial secretary.

Hall, H. D. *The British Commonwealth of Nations.* London, 1920.

Hardinge, Sir Arthur H. *Life of Lord Carnarvon.* 3 vols., London, 1925.

Jebb, Richard. *The Empire in Eclipse.* London, 1926.

Jebb, Richard. *The Imperial Conference, a History and Study.* 2 vols., London, 1911.

Jebb, Richard. *Studies in Colonial Nationalism.* London, 1905.

Keith, A. B. *The Dominions as Sovereign States.* London, 1938. An analysis of existing conditions from a legal point of view.

Keith, A. B. *The Governments of the British Empire.* New York, 1935.

Keith, A. B. *Responsible Government in the Dominions.* 3 vols., Oxford, 1912. Second ed., 2 vols., Oxford, 1928. A detailed analysis of the development of self-government in Britain's overseas possessions.

Knaplund, Paul. *Gladstone and Britain's Imperial Policy.* London, 1927.

Lewis, Sir G. C. *An Essay on the Government of Dependencies.* London, 1841. Edited by C. P. Lucas, Oxford, 1891.

Lucas, Sir Charles, editor. *The Empire at War.* 5 vols., London, 1921–1926.

Lugard, Frederick J. D. Lord. *Representative Forms of Government and "Indirect Rule" in British Africa.* London, 1928.

Manning, Helen Taft. *The British Colonial Government After the American Revolution 1782–1820.* New Haven, 1933.

Merivale, Herman. *Lectures on Colonization and the Colonies.* London, 1861.

Morrell, W. P. *British Colonial Policy in the Age of Peel and Russell.* Oxford, 1930. The best analysis of the transition period 1840–1852.

Porritt, E. *The Fiscal and Diplomatic Freedom of the British Overseas Dominions.* New York, 1922.

Schuyler, R. L. *Parliament and the British Empire.* New York, 1929.

Stacey, C. P. *Canada and the British Army, 1846–1871. A Study in the Practice of Responsible Government.* London, 1936.

Stewart, Robert B. *Treaty Relations of the British Commonwealth of Nations.* New York, 1939. Traces the development since the Four Years' War.

Stokes, Robert. *New Imperial Ideas; a Plea for the Association of the Dominions in the Government of the Dependent Empire.* London, 1930.

Tyler, J. E. *The Struggle for Imperial Unity (1868–1895).* London, 1938.

Wakefield, E. G. *A Letter from Sydney.* London, 1829. New ed., 1929.

Wakefield, E. G. *A View of the Art of Colonisation.* London, 1849. New ed. by J. Collier. Oxford, 1914.

Zimmern, Alfred E. *The Third British Empire.* Oxford, 1934.

The Administration of the Empire

Fiddes, Sir George V. *The Dominions and Colonial Offices.* London, 1926.

Hall, Henry L. *The Colonial Office; a History.* London, 1937.

Henderson, G. C. *Life of Sir George Grey.* London, 1907. Biographical sketch of a famous governor who served in South Australia, New Zealand, and South Africa.

Knaplund, Paul. "Mr. Oversecretary Stephen." In *The Journal of Modern History,* Vol. I, No. 1.

Marindin, G. E. *Letters of Frederic, Lord Blachford.* London, 1896.

Morison, J. L. *The Eighth Earl of Elgin.* London, 1928. Elgin served in Jamaica, Canada, and India.

Smellie, K. B. *A Hundred Years of English Government.* New York, 1937. A brief sketch of changes and the reasons therefor.

Stephen, Caroline. *The First Sir James Stephen.* Gloucester, 1906. A privately printed memoir of the famous permanent undersecretary in the colonial office, written by his daughter.

Thompson, E. J. *The Life of Charles, Lord Metcalfe.* London, 1937. A good biography of an administrator who served in India, Jamaica, and Canada.

Worsfold, W. B. *Sir Bartle Frere.* London, 1913. The life of an important administrator who served in Africa and India.

The Dependent Empire (Except the West Indies)

Bell, N. *Heroes of South African Discovery.* London, 1884.

Burns, A. C. *History of Nigeria.* London, 1929.

Crooks, J. J. *A History of the Colony of Sierra Leone.* Dublin, 1903.

Dilley, Marjorie Ruth. *British Policy in the Kenya Colony.* New York, 1937. After a brief historical sketch the author presents a clear picture of the situation in this important colony.

Ellis, A. B. *West African Islands.* London, 1885.

George, C. *The Rise of West Africa.* London, 1904.

Goebel, J. *The Struggle for the Falkland Islands.* New Haven, 1927.

Gregory, J. W. *Foundations of British East Africa.* London, 1901.

Huxley, Elspeth J. *White Man's Country. Lord Delamere and the Making of Kenya.* 2 vols., London, 1935.

Johnston, Sir H. H. *Britain Across the Seas: Africa.* London, 1910.

Johnston, Sir H. H. *British Central Africa.* Second ed., London, 1898.

Lugard, Sir Frederick J. D. *The Dual Mandate in Tropical Africa.* London, 1922.

Lugard, Sir Frederick J. D. *The Story of the Uganda Protectorate.* London, 1900.

Macmillan, Sir Harold A. *The Anglo-Egyptian Sudan.* London, 1934.

Martin, E. C. *The British West Africa Settlement, 1750–1821.* London, 1927.

McPhee, A. *The Economic Revolution in British West Africa.* London, 1926.

Mills, Lennox A. *British Malaya, 1824–1867.* Singapore, 1925.

Mills, Lennox A. *Ceylon Under British Rule, 1795–1932.* London, 1933.

Niven, C. R. *A Short History of Nigeria.* London, 1937.

Orr, Captain C. W. J. *Cyprus Under British Rule.* London, 1918. Covers the period 1878–1914; treatment superficial.

Canada

Among the printed sources the most valuable are the reports of debates in the colonial, provincial, and Dominion parliaments, and the Sessional Papers. The publications of the Canadian Archives are also of great importance. The earlier ones deal chiefly with the history prior to 1815, but recent publications contain material pertaining to the history since that date. Of special value: *Documents Relating to the Constitutional History of Canada, 1819–1828,* edited by Arthur G. Doughty and Norah Story, Ottawa, 1935. *The Elgin-Grey Papers, 1846–1852,* edited by Sir Arthur G. Doughty, 4 vols., Ottawa, 1937. This is a selection from the voluminous private correspondence, now in the Dominion archives, between a famous Canadian governor general and an equally famous colonial secretary who was also the uncle of Lady Elgin.

Bell and Morrell. *Documents. Op. cit.*

Borden, Sir Robert Laird. *His Memoirs.* Edited by Henry Borden. 2 vols., New York, 1938.

Bovey, William. *Canadien, a Study of the French Canadians.* London, 1933.

Brady, Alexander. *Canada.* New York, 1932.

Buchan, John, editor. *British America.* In the Nations of Today Series. New York, 1923.

Burpee, Lawrence J. *An Historical Atlas of Canada.* New York, 1927.

Callahan, J. M. *American Foreign Policy in Canadian Relations.* New York, 1937.

The Cambridge History of the British Empire, Vol. VI.

The Canadian Almanac. The Copp Clark Company. Toronto.

The Canadian Annual Review of Public Affairs. Founded and edited, 1901–1922, by J. Castell Hopkins. The Annual Review Publishing Company, Toronto.

The Canadian Historical Review.

Cowan. *British Emigration. Op. cit.*

Dunham, Aileen. *Political Unrest in Upper Canada.* London, 1927. A careful study of the background for the disturbances in Upper Canada, 1837.

Grant, W. L., editor. *The Makers of Canada.* 12 vols., new ed., Oxford, 1926. Popular biographies of leading Canadians.

Howe, Joseph. *The Speeches and Public Letters of.* Edited by J. A. Chisholm. 2 vols., Halifax, Canada, 1909.

Innes, H. A. *The Cod Fisheries.* New Haven, 1940.

Keenleyside, H. L. *Canada and the United States.* New York, 1929.

Kennedy, W. P. M. *The Constitution of Canada. An Introduction to Its Development and Law.* Oxford, 1929.

Kennedy, W. P. M., editor. *Statutes, Treaties and Documents of the Canadian Constitution, 1713–1929.* Revised ed., Oxford, 1930. This is the most complete selection of its kind for Canadian history.

Lucas. *Historical Geography. Op. cit.*

Lucas, Sir Charles, editor. *Lord Durham's Report.* 3 vols., Oxford, 1912.

Macintosh, William A. *Prairie Settlement, the Geographical Setting.* Toronto, 1934.

Martin, Chester. *Empire and Commonwealth, a Study in British Colonial Government.* Oxford, 1929. An analysis of the evolution of the position of Canada with reference to Great Britain.

Pope, Sir Joseph. *Memoirs of Sir John Alexander Macdonald.* Revised ed., Toronto, 1930.

Shortt, Adam, and Doughty, Arthur G., editors. *Canada and Its Provinces.* 22 vols., Toronto, 1914–1917. A monumental work of the greatest value for students of Canadian history.

Siegfried, André. *Canada.* New York, 1932.

Siegfried, André. *The Race Question in Canada.* London, 1907. A shrewd appraisal of the most difficult among the internal problems of Canada.

Skelton, O. D. *Life and Letters of Sir Wilfrid Laurier.* 2 vols., Toronto, 1921.

Sydenham, Lord. *Letters from . . . to Lord John Russell, 1839–1841.* Edited by Paul Knaplund. London, 1931.

Trotter, R. G. *Canadian Federation, Its Origin and Achievement.* Toronto, 1924. An excellent concise survey.

Trotter, R. G. *Canadian History, a Syllabus and Guide to Reading.* Toronto, 1934.

Wallace, W. S., compiler. *The Dictionary of Canadian Biography.* Toronto, 1926.

Wallace, W. S., editor. *The Encyclopedia of Canada.* 6 vols., Toronto, 1935–1937.

Whitelaw, W. M. *The Maritimes and Canada Before Confederation.* Toronto, 1934.

Wittke, Carl F. *History of Canada.* Revised ed., New York, 1933. The most complete one-volume history of Canada.

Wrong, George M. *The Canadians: The Story of a People.* New York, 1938. A charmingly written survey of Canadian history by the dean among Canadian historians.

Wrong, George M., and Langton, H. H., editors. *The Chronicles of Canada.* 32 vols., Toronto, 1914–1916. Handy volumes devoted to lives of men and topics of significance in the history of Canada.

Newfoundland

Relatively little has been written on the history of Newfoundland since 1815. The best general accounts are those in the *Cambridge History of the British Empire,* Vol. VI, and *British*

North America. Op. cit. Innes' *The Cod Fisheries* contains much of value for students of the history of the island.

Birkenhead, Lord. *The Story of Newfoundland.* London, 1920. A convenient summary of essential historical facts.

Grenfell, Sir Wilfrid. *The Romance of Labrador.* New York, 1934. A picturesque account of this inhospitable land by a famous missionary.

McLintock, A. H. *The Establishment of Constitutional Government in Newfoundland, 1783–1832.* A Study of Retarded Colonisation. London, 1941.

Seitz, Don C. *The Great Island.* New York, 1926. A good journalistic description of conditions in the nineteen-twenties.

Smallwood, J. R. *The New Newfoundland.* New York, 1931. An optimistic account of the situation on the eve of the world depression.

The West Indies

Aspinall, Sir Algernon. *British West Indies: Their History, Resources and Progress.* London, 1912.

Aspinall, Sir Algernon. *A Wayfarer in the West Indies.* Third ed., London, 1934.

Burn, W. L. *Emancipation and Apprenticeship in the British West Indies.* London, 1937.

Caldecott, A. *The Church in the West Indies.* London, 1898.

Clementi, Sir C. *A Constitutional History of British Guiana.* London, 1937.

Cundall, F. *Bibliography of the West Indies, Excluding Jamaica.* Kingston, Jamaica, 1907.

Cundall, F. *Political and Social Disturbances in the West Indies.* Kingston, Jamaica, 1906.

Erickson, Edgar L. *The Indian Coolies in the British West Indies.* Unpublished Ph.D. Thesis at the University of Wisconsin Library.

Johnston, Sir H. H. *Pioneers of Tropical America.* London, 1914.

Lewis, M. G. *Journal of a West India Proprietor.* London, 1834.

Macmillan, W. M. *Warning from the West Indies.* London, 1936.

Mathieson, W. L. *The Sugar Colonies and Governor Eyre, 1849–1866.* London, 1936.

New York Public Library. *List of Works Relating to the West Indies.* New York, 1912.

Olivier, Lord. *Jamaica, the Blessed Isle.* London, 1936.

Penson, L. M. *Colonial Agents of the West Indies.* London, 1924.

Pringle, H. *The Fall of the Sugar Planters of Jamaica.* London, 1869.

Ragatz, L. J. *A Guide for the Study of British Caribbean History, 1763–1834.* Washington, 1932.

Ragatz, L. J. *The Fall of the Planter Class in the British Caribbean, 1763–1833.* New York, 1928. A careful study based upon source material.

West India Committee. *Catalogue of the Library of the West India Committee.* London, 1912.

Wrong, Hume. *Government of the West Indies.* Oxford, 1923.

South Africa

Barnouw, Adriaan. *Language and Race Problems in South Africa.* The Hague, 1934.

Bird, John, compiler. *The Annals of Natal, 1495 to 1845.* Pietermaritzburg, 1888.

Brookes, E. H. *The Colour Problems of South Africa.* London, 1934.

Brookes, E. H. *The History of Native Policy in South Africa from 1830 to the Present Day.* Capetown, 1924.

Bryce, James. *Impressions of South Africa.* London, 1899.

Buxton, Lord. *General Botha.* London, 1924.

The Cambridge History of the British Empire. Op. cit. Vol. VIII.

Colvin, Ian. *The Life of Jameson.* 2 vols., London, 1923. This is the standard biography of the leader of the famous "Raid" who afterward became prime minister of the Cape Colony.

Cory, Sir G. E. *The Rise of South Africa.* 5 vols., London, 1910–1930. A detailed account of South African history in the early part of the nineteenth century. Useful as a reference work.

De Kiewiet, C. W. *British Colonial Policy and the South African Republics, 1848–1872.* London, 1929.

De Kiewiet, C. W. *The Imperial Factor in South Africa.* Cambridge, 1937.

Du Plessis, J. *A History of Christian Missions in South Africa.* London, 1911.

Edwards, Isobel E. *The 1820 Settlers in South Africa.* London, 1934.

Evans, I. L. *Native Policy in Southern Africa.* Cambridge, 1934.

Eybers, G. W., editor. *Select Constitutional Documents Illustrating South African History, 1795–1910.* London, 1918. A very useful collection of source material.

Goodfellow, D. M. *A Modern Economic History of South Africa.* London, 1931.

Hattersley, A. F. *Portrait of a Colony; the Story of Natal.* Cambridge, 1940.

Hattersley, A. F., editor. *Later Annals of Natal.* London, 1938. Covers period, 1860–1900.

Hattersley, A. F., editor. *The Natalians; Further Annals of Natal.* Pietermaritzburg, 1940.

Headlam, C., editor. *The Milner Papers, 1897–1905.* 2 vols., London, 1931–1933. Of great value for the study of South African history.

Herrman, L. *The Jews in South Africa.* London, 1930.

Hofmeyr, J. H. *The Life of Jan Hendrik Hofmeyr.* London, 1913. The biography by a kinsman of the powerful leader of the Afrikander Bond.

Hofmeyr, J. H. *South Africa.* London, 1931. An excellent survey.

Hole, H. Marshall. *The Making of Rhodesia.* London, 1926.

Kennedy, W. P. M., and Schlosberg, H. J. *The Law and Custom of the South African Constitution.* Oxford, 1935.

Kruger, S. J. P. *The Memoirs of Paul Kruger.* 2 vols., London, 1902.

Lagden, Sir G. *The Basutos.* 2 vols., London, 1909.

Laurence, Sir Perceval. *The Life of John Xavier Merriman.* London, 1930.

Livingstone, D. *Missionary Travels and Researches in South Africa.* London, 1857.

Lovell, C. R. *General Hertzog and the South African Nationalist Party.* Unpublished M.A. Thesis at the University of Wisconsin Library.

Mackenzie, W. D. *John Mackenzie.* London, 1902. The biography of a famous South African missionary.

Macmillan, W. M. *Bantu, Boer, and Briton.* London, 1929.

Macmillan, W. M. *Africa Emergent: A Survey of Social, Political, and Economic Trends in British Africa.* London, 1938.

Macmillan, W. M. *The Cape Colour Question.* London, 1927.

Malherbe, E. G. *Education in South Africa, 1652–1922.* Cape Town, 1925.

Marais, J. S. *The Cape Coloured People, 1652–1937.* London, 1939.

Mendelsohn, Sidney. *South African Bibliography.* 2 vols., London, 1910.

Millin, Sarah Gertrude. *Rhodes.* London, 1933.

Millin, Sarah Gertrude. *The South Africans.* New ed., London, 1934. A vivid account of the people and the conditions on this subcontinent.

Moffat, J. S. *Lives of Robert and Mary Moffat.* London, 1885.

Molteno, A. P. *Life and Times of Sir J. C. Molteno.* 2 vols., London, 1900.

Newton, A. P., editor. *Select Documents Relating to the Unification of South Africa.* 2 vols., London, 1924.

Perham, M., and Curtis, L. *The Protectorates of South Africa.* London, 1935.

Schapera, I., editor. *Western Civilization and the Natives of South Africa; Studies in Culture Contacts.* London, 1934.

Smith, Sir Harry. *The Autobiography of.* London, 1903.

Theal, G. M. *History of South Africa Since 1795.* 5 vols., London, 1908–1910.

Uys, C. J. *The Era of Shepstone.* Lovedale, South Africa, 1933.

Van Der Poel, J. *Railway and Customs Policies in South Africa, 1885–1910.* London, 1933.

Walker, Eric A. *The Great Trek.* London, 1934. A careful and well-balanced account of this epoch-making event.

Walker, Eric A. *The Frontier Tradition in South Africa.* London, 1930.

Walker, Eric A. *Historical Atlas of South Africa.* London, 1922.

Walker, Eric A. *A History of South Africa.* Second ed., New

Morrell, W. P. *New Zealand.* London, 1935.

Morrell, W. P. *The Provincial System in New Zealand, 1852–1876.* London, 1932.

Murdock, Walter. *Alfred Deakin.* London, 1923.

Palmer, Nettie. *Henry Bourne Higgins.* London, 1931. The life of the famous judge of the Australian court of arbitration and conciliation.

Parkes, Sir Henry. *Fifty Years in the Making of Australia.* 2 vols., London, 1892.

Phillips, Marion. *A Colonial Autocracy; New South Wales Under Governor Macquarie, 1810–1821.* London, 1909.

Price, A. G. *The Foundation and Settlement of South Australia.* Adelaide, 1924.

Price, A. G. *The History and Problems of the Northern Territory of Australia.* Adelaide, 1930.

Quick, Sir John, and Garran, Sir R. R. *Annotated Constitution of the Australian Commonwealth.* Melbourne, 1901.

Reeves, W. P. *The Long White Cloud.* Third ed., London, 1924. An excellent description of New Zealand and its people.

Reeves, W. P. *State Experiments in Australia and New Zealand.* 2 vols., London, 1902.

Roberts, S. H. *History of Australian Land Settlement, 1788–1920.* Melbourne, 1924.

Rusden, G. W. *History of Australia.* 3 vols., London, 1883.

Scholefield, G. H. *Dictionary of New Zealand Biography.* 2 vols., Wellington, 1940. A valuable handbook for students of New Zealand history.

Scholefield, G. H. *New Zealand in Evolution.* London, 1909.

Scott, Ernest. *Short History of Australia.* Fifth ed., Oxford, 1927.

Shann, E. O. G. *An Economic History of Australia.* Cambridge, 1930.

Smith, A. N. *Thirty Years. The Commonwealth of Australia, 1901–1931.* Melbourne, 1934.

Sweetman, Edward. *Australian Constitutional Development.* Melbourne, 1925.

Taylor, T. Griffith. *The Australian Environment.* Melbourne, 1918.

Thwing, C. F. *Human Australasia: Studies of Society and Education in Australia and New Zealand.* New York, 1923.

Turner, H. G. *A History of the Colony of Victoria.* 2 vols., London, 1904.

Ullathorne, Bishop W. M. *Horrors of Transportation.* Dublin, 1838.

Watson, J. F., editor. *Historical Records of Australia.* Sydney, 1914– . In progress.

Willard, Myra. *History of the White Australian Policy.* Melbourne, 1923.

Wood, F. L. W. *The Constitutional Development of Australia.* London, 1933.

Wood, G. A. *The Discovery of Australia.* London, 1922.

India

Among printed *Parliamentary Papers* those relating to the renewal of the East India Company's charter are of great importance. For the renewal in 1813 see *Parliamentary Papers,* Vols. VI and VII, session 1812, and Vols. VIII–X, session of 1812–1813. For renewal in 1833, see *ibid.,* Vols. VIII–XII, session 1831–1832, and Vol. XXV, session 1833. For renewal in 1853, see *ibid.,* Vols. XXVII–XXXIII, session 1852–1853. Excellent material for the study of the economic history of India is found in *Report from the Select Committee appointed to examine into the matter contained in the petition of the East India Company complaining of the imposition of duties at present levied on East India produce; Parliamentary Papers,* Vol. VIII, session 1840.

Among recent reports on India the Montagu-Chelmsford report of 1918 (cd. 9109) and those of the Indian Statutory Commission, commonly known as the Simon Commission, published in 1930, are of special importance.

Andrews, C. F. *Mahatma Gandhi's Ideas, Including Selections from His Writings.* London, 1929.

Andrews, C. F., and Mukerji, Girija. *The Rise and Growth of the Congress in India.* London, 1938. Covers period 1885–1920.

Annual Lists and General Index of Parliamentary Papers Relating to the East Indies, 1801–1907. In *Parliamentary Papers, 1909,* LXIV, 89.

Anstey, Vera. *The Economic Development of India.* Third ed., London, 1936.

Appadorai, A. *Dyarchi in Practice.* London, 1937. An analysis of the working of the Government of India Act, 1919.

Baden-Powell, B. H. *Land Systems of British India.* 3 vols., London, 1892.

Balfour, Lady Betty. *History of Lord Lytton's Indian Administration.* London, 1899.

Brailsford, H. N. *Rebel India.* New York, 1931.

Buchanan, D. H. *The Development of Capitalistic Enterprise in India.* New York, 1934.

The Cambridge History of India. Edited by H. H. Dodwell. Vols. V and VI, 1497–1918. (Appear also as Vols. IV and V of *Cambridge History of the British Empire.*) 6 vols., Cambridge, 1922–1937. Each volume contains an excellent bibliography.

The Cambridge Shorter History of India. By J. Allan, Sir T. Wolseley Haig, and H. H. Dodwell. Edited by H. H. Dodwell. Cambridge, 1934. It is not a résumé of the larger *Cambridge History,* though based on the material found therein. About one-third of the *Shorter History* is given to the period after 1813. It is crowded with facts and has several good maps.

Chirol, Sir V. *India.* London, 1926.

Cotton, Sir Henry. *New India, or India in Transition.* New and rev. ed., London, 1904.

Cumming, Sir John, editor. *Political India 1832–1932, a Co-operative Survey of a Century.* London, 1932.

Curzon, Lord. *British Government in India; the Story of the Viceroys and Government Houses.* 2 vols., London, 1925.

Davies, C. C. *The Problem of the North-West Frontier, 1890–1908.* Cambridge, 1932.

Dodwell, H. H. *India.* 2 vols., London, 1936.

Dutt, Romesh. *India in the Victorian Age; an Economic History of the People.* London, 1904.

Fraser, Lovat. *India Under Curzon and After.* London, 1911.

Fraser, Lovat. *Iron and Steel in India; a Chapter from the Life of Jameshedji Tata.* Bombay, 1919.

Gandhi, Mahatma. *Young India, 1919–1922.* New York, 1924.

Gokhale, G. K. *Speeches of*. Second ed., Madras, 1916.
Holdich, Sir Thomas H. *The Gates of India, Being an Historical Narrative*. London, 1910.
Hunter, W. W. *The Indian Empire: Its People, History, and Products*. Second ed., London, 1886.
Hunter, W. W. *The India of the Queen*. London, 1903.
Ilbert, Sir Courtenay. *The Government of India*. Third ed., Oxford, 1915.
Ilbert, Sir Courtenay. *The New Constitution of India*. London, 1923.
Keith, A. B. *A Constitutional History of India, 1600–1935*. London, 1936.
Keith, A. B., editor. *Speeches and Documents on Indian Policy*. 2 vols., London, 1922.
Lee-Warner, Sir W. *The Life of the Marquis of Dalhousie*. 2 vols., London, 1904.
Lee-Warner, Sir W. *The Native States of India*. Second ed., revised. London, 1910.
Lee-Warner, Sir W. *The Protected Princes of India*. London, 1894.
Lyall, Sir Alfred C. *History of India*. London, 1907.
Lyall, Sir Alfred C. *The Rise and Expansion of the British Dominion in India*. Third and enlarged ed., London, 1905.
Marriott, Sir John A. R. *The English in India*. London, 1932.
Mayhew, Arthur. *The Education of India; a Study of British Educational Policy in India, 1835–1920*. London, 1926.
Minto, Lady. *India, Minto and Morley, 1905–1910*. London, 1934.
Montagu, Edwin S. *An Indian Diary*. Edited by Venetia Montagu. London, 1930.
Morison, J. L. *Lawrence of Lucknow, 1806–1857. Being the Life of Sir Henry Lawrence Retold from His Private and Public Papers*. London, 1934.
Muir, Ramsay, editor. *Making of British India, 1756–1858*. Manchester, 1915.
Mukerji, D. G. *Visit India with Me*. New York, 1929.
O'Dwyer, Sir M. F. *India as I Knew It, 1885–1925*. Second ed., London, 1925.

Panikkar, K. M. *The Evolution of British Policy Towards Indian States, 1774–1858.* Calcutta, 1929.

Panikkar, K. M. *Indian States and the Government of India.* London, 1932.

Prasad, Jagdish, *et al. Bibliography of Economic Books Relating to India.* Edited by H. Stanley Jevons. Allahabad, 1923.

Rai, Lajpat. *Young India.* New York, 1917.

Ray, Parimal. *India's Foreign Trade Since 1870.* London, 1934.

Roberts, Lord. *Forty-one Years in India.* London, 1898. The autobiography of a famous British soldier.

Roberts, P. E. *History of British India Under the Company and the Crown.* Second ed., Oxford, 1938. An excellent brief account.

Ronaldshay, Lord. *The Life of Lord Curzon.* 3 vols., London, 1927–1928.

Sen, D. K. *The Indian States, Their Status, Rights and Obligations.* London, 1930.

Seton, Sir Malcolm. *The India Office.* London, 1926.

Sitaramayya, B. P. *The History of the Indian National Congress, 1885–1935.* Madras, 1935.

Slater, Gilbert. *Southern India; Its Political and Economic Problems.* London, 1938.

Smith, Vincent A. *The Oxford Student's History of India.* Sixth ed., London, 1916.

Temple, Sir Richard. *Lord Lawrence.* London, 1889.

Temple, Sir Richard. *Men and Events of My Time in India.* London, 1882.

Thompson, E. J. *Reconstructing India.* New York, 1930.

Thompson, Edward, and Garratt, G. T. *Rise and Fulfilment of British Rule in India.* London, 1934. Comprehensive in scope and critical of many aspects of British rule.

Tilak, B. G. *His Writings and Speeches.* Madras, 1922.

Whitehead, Henry. *Indian Problems in Religion, Education, Politics.* London, 1924.

INDEX